THE JAPANESE COMMUNIST
MOVEMENT, 1920–1966

This volume is jointly sponsored by The RAND Corporation and The Center for Japanese and Korean Studies, University of California, Berkeley.

THE CENTER FOR JAPANESE AND KOREAN STUDIES of the
University of California is a unit of the
Institute of International Studies. It is the unifying organization
for faculty members and students interested in Japan and Korea,
bringing together scholars from many disciplines.
The Center's major aims are
the development and support of research and language study.
As part of this program the Center sponsors
a publication series of books concerned with Japan and Korea.
Manuscripts are considered from all campuses
of the University of California as well as
from any other individuals and institutions
doing research in these areas.

PUBLICATIONS OF THE CENTER FOR JAPANESE AND KOREAN STUDIES

Chong-Sik Lee
The Politics of Korean Nationalism. 1963

Sadako N. Ogata
Defiance in Manchuria: The Making of Japanese Foreign Policy, 1931–1932. 1964

R. P. Dore
Education in Tokugawa Japan. 1964

James T. Araki
The Ballad-Drama of Medieval Japan. 1964

Masakazu Iwata
Ōkubo Toshimichi: The Bismarck of Japan. 1964

Frank O. Miller
Minobe Tatsukichi: Interpreter of Constitutionalism in Japan. 1965.

Michael Cooper, S.J.
They Came to Japan: An Anthology of European Reports on Japan, 1543–1640. 1965.

George Devos and Hiroshi Wagatsuma
Japan's Invisible Race. 1966.

Ryutaro Komiya, ed.
Postwar Economic Growth in Japan. 1966

Translated from the Japanese by Robert S. Ozaki

ROBERT A. SCALAPINO

The Japanese Communist Movement, 1920-1966

UNIVERSITY OF CALIFORNIA PRESS
Berkeley and Los Angeles 1967

University of California Press
Berkeley and Los Angeles, California

Cambridge University Press
London, England

Printed in the United States of America

TO MY MOTHER AND FATHER

ACKNOWLEDGMENTS

I am greatly indebted to many individuals of widely varying ideological perspectives. To provide a full list would be impossible, but I would like to express my sincere appreciation to such political figures as Andō Jimbei, Arahata Kanson, Fukumoto Kazuo, Iwai Akira, Kasuga Shōjirō, Kazama Jōkichi, Nabeyama Sadachika, Naitō Tomochika, Nosaka Sanzō, Ōta Kaoru, Satō Noboru, Taniguchi Zentarō, Yamabe Kentarō, and Yamakawa Hitoshi. I am also very grateful to such scholars as Ishida Takeshi, Kōtani Etsuo, Maruyama Masao, Masumi Junnosuke, Oka Yoshitake, Ōkouchi Kazuo, Rōyama Musamichi, Seki Yoshihiko, Sumiya Mikio, Tsujii Kiyoaki, and Ukai Nobushige.

Hirotsu Kyōsuke, Chief of the First Department of the Public Safety Investigation Bureau, gave me invaluable assistance.

Several American scholars also aided me greatly by reading and criticizing an earlier version of this work, either in whole or in part. I am indebted to H. S. Dinerstein and P. F. Langer of The RAND Corporation; to G. J. Pauker, also of The RAND Corporation, with whom I worked closely in the preparation of the manuscript; and to Hans Baerwald, George Beckmann, Cyril Black, and Herbert Passin.

My research assistant, Mr. Ki-shik Han, performed many valuable services on my behalf, especially in the final stages of the work. Mr. Eiji Yutani worked with great skill to prepare the index. Mrs. Becky Goodman and Miss Lynda Spence were extraordinarily efficient and speedy in their editorial work on the manuscript.

Some of the individuals acknowledged above take violent exception to my ideological perspectives, and others, while sharing my general political views, would differ on matters of emphasis or interpretation. But persons in both categories saved me from errors and shared their views with me.

This study is a contribution to The RAND Corporation's continuing program of research undertaken for United States Air Force Project RAND.

CONTENTS

I. THE PREWAR LEGACY 1

II. MAKING COMMUNISM LOVABLE: THE INITIAL
TACTICS OF THE POSTWAR JAPANESE
COMMUNIST PARTY 48

III. THE SHIFT TO THE LEFT: GUERRILLA WARFARE,
JAPANESE STYLE 79

IV. THE RETURN TO LEGALISM AND THE ATTEMPT
TO CREATE A UNITED FRONT 97

V. JAPANESE COMMUNISM IN A DIVIDED COMMUNIST
WORLD—THE SWING TOWARD PEKING 136

VI. THE STRUGGLE ON TWO FRONTS 214

VII. THE CURRENT STATUS OF THE PARTY 292

VIII. PROSPECTS AND PROBLEMS 328

SOURCES 355

    1. Personal Interviews 355
    2. Documents and Monographs 355
    3. Articles 359
    4. Foreign Periodicals Cited or Mentioned 363
    5. Japanese Parties, Factions, and Government Agencies 365

INDEX 367

I

THE PREWAR LEGACY

Marxism was first introduced into Japan at the close of the nineteenth century by way of the most natural of all routes, the intellectual study society. On October 18, 1898, a small band of Westernized intellectuals held the first meeting of the Shakaishugi Kenkyūkai (The Association for the Study of Socialism) at the Tōkyō Unitarian Church. Although most of the founders considered themselves Christian Socialists, the association was open to any interested party. Needless to say, Marx was but one of many Western "socialists" whose works were studied and debated. He competed for attention with Henry George, Fourier, Blanc, and Lassalle, among others, and tended to receive much less attention than some of these men.[1]

The first phase of the socialist movement of the late Meiji period was marked by relative moderation and a strong support for parliamentarism. The dominant force was Christian humanism, which did much to set the tone of pacifism and internationalism that was so deeply embedded in early Japanese socialist thought. Five of the six men who met to launch the first socialist party of Japan in the spring

---

[1] For details on Shakaishugi Kenkyūkai meetings, see Rikugō Zasshi (*The Universe Magazine*), which was used as an organ by the new group. At the first meeting, Murai Tomoyoshi spoke on general principles of socialism and Takagi Masayoshi discussed appropriate readings on the socialist movement.

On November 20, at the second meeting, Katayama Sen lectured on the British landlord system and general socialist trends in Europe. In the discussion period, Charles Garst, an American missionary, proposed the Single Tax concept of Henry George as the best form of socialism for Japan.

Subsequently, each meeting was devoted to a prominent socialist writer. Midway in the series, Murai reported on Marx.

of 1901 were Christians. Only Kōtoku Denjirō came to socialism by a different path. The new party, the Shakai Minshutō (Social Democratic Party), was firmly committed to legalism. In its program were such themes as the widespread nationalization of the means of production and the equal distribution of land, goods, and basic political rights, but "anarchism" and violence were specifically denounced, and the pledge to adhere to parliamentary procedures was unequivocal.[2] Nevertheless, the party was banned within hours of its official formation, perhaps because it also demanded total abolition of armaments in Japan, the eradication of the peerage system, and the enactment of universal suffrage.

Once again, the true believers returned to the old formula of a study society. Starting with only six members, the Shakaishugi Kyōkai (Socialist Society) was organized. However, the socialist currents had become increasingly complex. Three, possibly four, major currents could be discerned: French revolutionary thought from the left-wing Jiyūtō (Liberal or Liberty Party) elements; German social democracy in its diverse forms; Christian humanism, still the most powerful force in many respects; and, if one looked closely, Japanese traditional thought with its strong anti-individualist, procommunal bent. This latter element, to be sure, should be considered less a main current and more a foundation on which contemporary currents could flow.

The struggle between the social democrats and the adherents of anarcho-syndicalism became the central battle of the period immediately after the Russo–Japanese war. In his rise to influence, Kōtoku, fresh from a trip to America and the stimulus derived from International Workers of the World (IWW) contacts, symbolized the leftward trend within Japan's tiny socialist movement. It was he who enunciated the theme that a true social revolution could not be achieved by universal suffrage and parliamentary policies. Socialism, he insisted, could only be brought about through the direct action of *organized workers*. Parliament would forever be the weapon of the propertied class, he argued, and it would always be bought, dissolved, or subverted in case of danger to this class.[3]

At the general convention of the minuscule Japan Socialist Party (Nihon Shakaitō) in mid-February 1907, the deep divisions within

---

[2] For the Manifesto of the Shakai Minshutō, see Rōdō Sekai (*Labor World*), May 20, 1901, a special issue published on the same day that the party was formally launched.

[3] For an enunciation of these themes, see Kōtoku's famous article, "Changes in My Ideas," *Heimin Shimbun* (*The Commoner News*), February 5, 1907, p. 1.

the movement were clearly displayed. A resolution sponsored by Kōtoku championing the cause of "direct action" was defeated by two votes (24 to 22), with a compromise resolution passing. The "moderates" who called for a full-fledged espousal of parliamentarism and a complete rejection of direct action received only two votes.[4]

The bitter cleavage between the social democrats and the anarchists continued, with the left gaining increasing influence and further isolating the tiny band of socialists from the mainstream of Japanese life. The culmination of this trend came with the Great Treason Case of 1910. The anarchists had finally moved from words to action, with a plot to assassinate the Emperor Meiji. Twelve Japanese radicals paid with their lives, including Kōtoku himself, although he had taken no active role in the plans. In a great pendulum-like swing, the Japanese socialist movement had veered to the left and, for the moment, ended. Its remnants consisted of a small group of isolated, persecuted men who had been forced into silence by an outraged community.

During World War I, only a few individuals, such as Arahata Kanson, Ōsugi Sakae, Sakai Toshihiko, and Yamakawa Hitoshi, sought to keep the socialist movement alive in Japan, through pathetic little journals and clandestine meetings. The tone was still strongly anarcho-syndicalist, reflective of earlier currents. The impact was negligible.[5] In this era Japan was enjoying unprecedented growth as a result of earlier preparations and wartime opportunities. With growth, however, also came vast socioeconomic changes and new forms of tension. It was during this period that Japan shifted from an essentially agrarian society to a predominantly industrial-commercial one. A greatly enlarged first-generation labor class was created, with the peasants serving as raw recruits. And a new intelligentsia, the product of intimate contact with avant-garde Westernism, was created.

In 1917 the Bolshevik Revolution provided a new source of stimulus

[4] *Ibid.,* February 16, 1907, pp. 1–2; February 19, pp. 1–2; February 20, p. 1

[5] For a time after the Kōtoku affair, the remaining Socialists scarcely dared to breathe, and any open political activities were impossible. Gradually, they started publishing small journals that contained articles impossible to censor. The authors became adept at double entendre, innuendo, and the other sophisticated methods of evading the censorship that were so common in the authoritarian societies of that era. Arahata began the monthly *Kindai Shisō (Modern Thought)* in October 1912; Sakai put out the first issue of *Hechima no Hana (Flower of the Gourd Squash)* in January 1914, and after nineteen issues, on September 1, 1915, this became *Shin Shakai (The New Society)*, the major organ of the radicals for several years. The radicals were by no means united in either ideological or personal terms. Arahata and Osugi were struggling to carry on the anarchist tradition. Sakai was already leaning toward Marxian socialism by 1916–1917.

for the Japanese left. Nosaka Sanzō, today an aging veteran of the Communist movement, can serve as an excellent example of the times.[6] Son of a prosperous merchant who had suffered financial reverses, Nosaka grew up in a totally bourgeois atmosphere and managed to attend Keiō, generally considered a "rich boy's school." There he became interested in the labor movement, largely through his professor, Horie Kiichi, and he decided to write his senior thesis on the Yūaikai (The Friendly Society), the moderate Japanese labor organization headed by Suzuki Bunji.

Nosaka began his youthful venture into labor and politics as a social reformer. To write his thesis, he contacted the Yūaikai head-quarters and soon was on close personal terms with the top leaders.[7] On his graduation from Keiō in 1915, he joined the Yūaikai publications and research staff and, subsequently, assumed the editorship for a brief period of *Rōdō Oyobi Sangyō (Labor and Industry)*, the union journal. Stimulated by world events and by the influx of new radical materials flowing into Japan from the West, young Nosaka gradually moved to the left. This development can be followed in the articles he wrote during this period.[8]

Initially, the radical stimuli consisted largely of traditional anarcho-syndicalist literature. Nosaka himself was later to write that he was greatly influenced by the numerous IWW publications imported from the United States and by Edward Bellamy's famous *Looking Backward*. His first significant contact with Marxism came in the 1918–1919

---

[6] For a recently published, "official" biography of Nosaka, see *Nosaka Sanzō no ayunda michi (The Road That Nosaka Sanzō Walked)*, edited by the Committee for the Publication of Materials on Nosaka Sanzō, Tōkyō, 1964. Also interesting is an earlier *Autobiography* prepared by Nosaka in 1946 (available in mimeographed form in English).

[7] Suzuki, who became very fond of Nosaka personally, remarked in his memoirs that when he first saw this young man dressed in striped kimono and "bird hunter's" hat pulled down in front, he wondered what kind of salesman was calling (Suzuki Bunji, *Rōdō undō ni-jū nen [Twenty Years in the Labor Movement]*, Tōkyō, 1931, pp. 85–86).

Nosaka's fashionable clothes, and the large dog that accompanied him, set him apart from the usual Japanese reformer, not to mention the worker. But he had another side. In personality, Nosaka was quiet, studious, and serious. An intro-vert, soft of speech and inconspicuous, he was a man who sat well in a library but seemed totally out of place at a demonstration.

[8] See, for example, "Love, Knowledge, and Power," *Rōdō Oyobi Sangyō*, No. 53, January 1916; an article on the Mazda Lamp Factory, *ibid.*, No. 82, June 1918; "No One Is Bad—If One Says 'Bad,' Then All Are Bad," *ibid.*, No. 86, October 1918; "Labor Aristocracy," *Shakai Kairyō (Social Reform)*, Vol. I, No. 2, June 1917; "The Path We Should Pursue," *ibid.*, Vol. I, No. 4, August 1917.

period when he read one of the two English-language copies of *The Communist Manifesto* that Koizumi Shinzō had brought back from the West. Until mid-1918, however, Nosaka remained a social reformer. Thereafter, he moved quickly toward the new theories of Marxism–Leninism, and when he departed for England in the summer of 1919, he was already a budding Communist. It was therefore not unexpected that he joined the British Communist Party when it was founded in 1920 and attended its first congress as a delegate from the London district.[9]

In many respects, Nosaka was typical of the young intellectuals who were moving into the labor movement during this period. These young men came to Yūaikai headquarters immediately after graduating from the universities of Waseda, Keiō, or Tōkyō. Sometimes they had had brief experience as journalists or government employees, but rarely had they done physical labor. Among them were such men as Hisatome Kōzō, Asō Hisashi, Tanabashi Kotora, Sakai Kamesaku, Takayama Yoshizō, and Furuichi Haruhiko.

Within a few years, these student cadres in the Yūaikai were sampling doctrines far to the left of those held by their senior mentors. This was an age of experiment and flux. Ideological positions were rarely pure or fixed. The root of Taisho radicalism lay in the vigorous new spirit of individualism that was emerging. The young avant-garde was seeking to liberate the "self" from the social organism, and once the "self" had been set free, the foundations for Western-style radicalism had been created.

The radical movement of this era, it must be emphasized, was still in the hands of a tiny band of men who had little or no connection with the main intellectual stream in Japan. The mainstream was dominated by theories of nationalism, democracy, and social reform. Within the radical movement itself, anarcho-syndicalism continued to be the foremost radical expression for some time after the Bolshevik Revolution. Tolstoi, Kropotkin, Bakunin, and Malatesta were all read

---

[9] Nosaka had announced his intention to study social problems in the West in the November 1918 issue of *Rōdō Oyobi Sangyō*. He actually sailed from Kobe on July 7, 1919, arriving in London on August 27. He immediately affiliated himself with some of the left-wing trade union leaders. From September 8 to 13, he attended the Glasgow Trade Union Congress, on which he reported at length in *Rōdō Oyobi Sangyō*, No. 100, December 1919, pp. 15–22. Nosaka's membership in the new British Communist Party brought him under the scrutiny of Scotland Yard, and he was finally given three days to leave England. After a period on the continent, he proceeded to Russia, attended the Far Eastern People's Conference, and returned to Japan in 1922, keeping his Communist Party membership a secret from Suzuki and the other moderate labor leaders.

more widely than Marx by the young radical intellectuals, and up to 1923 the anarcho-syndicalist currents were significant in the Japanese labor and socialist movements. In this period the Japanese Marxist movement itself was an overseas movement to a substantial extent. Its main adherents were overseas students or refugees, such as Katayama Sen. A brief sketch of some of these men and the influences that played on them can shed additional light on the origins of Japanese Communism.

Katayama left Japan on August 31, 1914, a broken, embittered man after serving nearly five months in prison as a result of his support of the Tokyo streetcar strike.[10] He was later to write in angry tones of the brutality and misery experienced in prison. Once released, Katayama found that his every move was under surveillance. Detectives lived on both sides of his house, he charged, and followed him wherever he went. To visit a friend meant placing that friend under suspicion. He had no way in which to earn a living. Thus, escape overseas became the only means of freedom.

At the outset life in America proved to be a series of frustrations for the middle-aged Socialist.[11] One friend reported visiting Katayama in San Francisco in a dirty, run-down flophouse used by day laborers. On an orange crate, which served as a table between two beds, lay his current reading material: an English edition of *Das Kapital* and two or three Japanese books. Katayama, however, was still taking the moderate line, arguing that socialism could be reached in Japan under the Meiji Constitution. Nevertheless, the Japanese consulate treated him as a dangerous public enemy, and his efforts to organize Japanese workers in the Bay Area failed, as did his personal ventures.

A new era for Katayama began, however, when an old socialist acquaintance, S. J. Rutgers, sent him funds to come to New York in the fall of 1916. Contact with Rutgers represented one of those quirks of fate that was to produce drastic changes in Katayama's last years. Rutgers, one of the earliest Marxist–Leninists, was in close touch with

---

[10] For Katayama's account of the strike, see his "A Japanese Victory," *International Socialist Review*, Vol. XII, No. 9, March 1912, pp. 581–582. See also "Letter from Japanese Comrade," *ibid.*, Vol. XIII, No. 8, February 1913, pp. 611–612.

[11] For Katayama's activities between 1914 and 1921, there are a number of sources, both in Japanese and English. In Japanese, the most useful are Watanabe Haruo, *Katayama Sen to tomo ni* (*Together with Katayama Sen*), Tōkyō, 1955; Kondō Eizō, *Comintern no misshi* (*Secret Messenger of the Comintern*), Tōkyō, 1949; and Oka Shigeki, "Katayama Sen and America," *Kaizō*, July 1951. In English, see the work of Hyman Kublin, *Asian Revolutionary: The Life of Sen Katayama*, Princeton, 1964.

a group of Russian revolutionaries living in exile in New York. Through him, Katayama became personally acquainted with Trotsky, Bukharin, and Madame Kollontai, among others. Under their influence, his Christianity totally disappeared and he became a Marxist–Leninist. With the advent of the Bolshevik Revolution, therefore, he could quickly move into a position of prominence in radical circles.

Within a short time Katayama was the leading Asian Communist of the world. His by-line appeared in many of the new Marxist journals, he worked closely with the left socialist movement, and he joined the independent Communist Party of America when it was established in September 1919. He also established an Association of Japanese Socialists in America, a small group that antedated the Japanese Communist Party by several years. Prior to going to the Soviet Union, moreover, Katayama helped to bring about a unification of the American Communist Party and undertook a Comintern mission to Mexico in an effort to stimulate organizational activities there. At the time of the Palmer raids, Katayama went into hiding in New Jersey and shortly, thereafter, in 1921, departed for Moscow to serve as chairman of the Far Eastern People's Congress, a conference of great importance to the Bolsheviks.

Katayama's small West 56th Street apartment had gradually become a salon, school, and workshop for an eager group of young Japanese radicals, and because one important aspect of the embryonic Japanese Communist movement began there, some note of the participants should be made. As usual, Katayama had very limited funds; he worked as a cook for an understanding American import-export merchant and occasionally sold popcorn in the summer on Coney Island. But he had debts, and he was trying to give his daughter ballet lessons. His entertainment consisted mainly of the theater—and politics. Eagerly, he greeted the young Japanese who made their way to his doorstep to talk socialism.

They came singly or in small groups. There was Watanabe Haruo, a would-be engineer and industrialist, who studied chemistry, industrial management, and socialism; Takahashi Kamekichi, who had had no formal education beyond primary school, but who was able to enter Waseda and graduate at the head of his class; and Taguchi Unzō, who had already lived a varied life in many countries and who, along with Yoshihara Tarō, attended the 3rd Congress of the Comintern.

Among the others were Maniwa Suekichi, an ex-sailor who had jumped ship to try the life of a cowboy in the western United States but, finding this much less romantic than he had supposed, drifted to

New York and into the socialist movement; Kondō Eizō, salesman, student, and amateur promoter of Japanese–American cultural relations, who was to be the first to bear the personal tidings of the new Communist movement back to Japan; Ishigaki Eitarō, a young artist with anarchist leanings, who labored with Katayama over the revision of the Socialist leader's autobiography; Suzuki Mosaburō, a young journalist, who was subsequently to have a long career as a left-wing Socialist leader; and Inomata Tsunao, bright young economist trained at Waseda and the University of Wisconsin, who later became a noted Waseda professor and leader in the Rōnō school of Japanese Marxism.

These were some of "Katayama's boys." There were casual contacts with many others, including Baron Ishimoto and his wife Shizue, who was later to marry Katō Kanjū. The inner circle around Katayama seems to have been composed of Taguchi, Watanabe, Maniwa, and Ishigaki. These and others provide an interesting composite picture of "the old man" during this period. Nearing sixty, but looking much younger, Katayama had sharp, penetrating eyes and a thin, rather wiry appearance, with closely cropped, graying hair. He was a practical revolutionist, not a theorist; his understanding of Marxism–Leninism remained always elementary. But he had a kind of peasant shrewdness, a feel for men and political situations, combined with a great dedication and fervor for the cause of socialism that could not fail to impress all of those with whom he came into contact. To his enemies, he was obstinate, unsophisticated, and stingy, but to his friends, he was serene, good natured, and of simple but sterling character.

Katayama's little apartment became the cluttered repository of the latest radical books and magazines. He himself was writing for, or editing, such magazines as *The Class Struggle* and, later, *The Revolutionary Age*. Some of these materials were mailed periodically to Sakai Toshihiko and other comrades in Japan; in exchange, the New York expatriates received Socialist literature from home telling of the rice riots and other exciting news that made them think that revolution was at hand even in Japan. The Association of Japanese Socialists in America quite naturally drew its key members from this circle of students and friends. The works of Marx, Engels, and Lenin served as major texts and the basis for lengthy discussions.

In early 1921, Katayama got word from Comintern authorities of the forthcoming conference for Asians, initially scheduled to be held in Irkutsk in the fall of that year. Delegates were requested. It was finally decided that three members of the League would go—Taguchi, Maniwa, and Watanabe. Katayama also invited two of his West Coast friends, and these five were joined by Suzuki Mosaburō, about whom Katayama had grave doubts. Since there was no Japanese Communist Party as yet, and the League was really nonexistent, most of these delegates carried papers identifying them as members of the Asian section of the American Communist Party.

Before the "First Congress of the Toilers of the Far East" finally opened in Moscow on January 21, 1922, these men were joined by seven other delegates who had come from Japan via Siberia. In the fall of 1921, a Comintern representative from Shanghai, Chang T'ai-lei, had visited Yamakawa and Sakai in Japan, requesting that delegates be selected. He assured them that the representatives could be anarcho-syndicalists, because, after visiting Russia, they would shift to Bolshevism. Thus, of the men selected, only two, Takase Kiyoshi, Sakai's son-in-law, and Tokuda Kyūichi, could be considered promising Communists. The rest were in the anarchist camp.

The Far Eastern Congress has been reported in detail elsewhere.[12] Deference was given Katayama who had already been appointed to the Comintern post, but the meetings were kept under complete Soviet supervision and control. Zinoviev and Safarov played the leading roles. The central themes were endlessly repeated over a period of nearly two weeks: the evil of imperialism as typified by Versailles and the Washington Conference; the importance—*and* the limitations—of nationalism for colonial regions; and the inevitable triumph of the Communist cause.

On the whole, the Japanese delegation was rather inconspicuous, perhaps because of the paucity of Communists in it and also because the main Congress themes were aimed more directly at the Koreans and Chinese. Nor were Chang T'ai-lei's optimistic boasts borne out. The Bolsheviks did not win over all of the Japanese anarchists. Anarchist–Communist quarreling marred the return journey of at least one Japanese group.

Meanwhile, many events had transpired in Japan. When Kondō Eizō returned home in the early summer of 1919, the Japanese labor and intellectual movements had already begun a pronounced shift to the left. Japanese socialism within these circles was on the rise. The

---

[12] Details are contained in Watanabe, *Katayama Sen*, p. 92; Kondō, pp. 168–169; Arahata, *Roshiya ni hairu* (*Entering Russia*), Tōkyō, 1924; and Suzuki Mosaburō, *Aru shakaishugisha no hansei* (*Half the Life of a Certain Socialist*), Tōkyō, 1958. For the official English language record, see *The First Congress of the Toilers of the Far East,* published by the Communist International, Petrograd, 1922.

predominant radical creed, however, was anarcho-syndicalism as we have noted, and the anarchists were not prepared to surrender without a struggle. Indeed, of the foremost Japanese radicals, only Sakai at this point could be considered close to the Marxist position.

It is difficult to say who precisely first introduced Leninism into Japanese intellectual circles. Certainly one of the first to place renewed emphasis on general Marxist writings was Takabatake Motoyuki, a young writer for Sakai's *Shin Shakai* (*The New Society*).[13] Many ideas came to Japan through translations of other languages. Thus because Ōsugi knew French, he could introduce French syndicalism. Takabatake knew German, and this opened the rich field of German Marxism to him. Using this literature, he raised some of the first searching questions about anarcho-syndicalist tactics.

By 1919, however, Takabatake had moved away from Sakai and organized his own state socialist group. But *Shin Shakai* continued on the course he had set. The May 1919 issue represented the first clear display of Marxist banners to be seen in Japan. "We are at the foot of the mountain," asserted the journal editor, "preparing to move forward. Everyone has been thrown into panic by the Russian, German, and Hungarian revolutions. And in Japan, a great Marxist fashion is coming."[14]

In the last sentence, there was some element of truth. The Russian Revolution and its guiding ideology, Marxism–Leninism, were now to have a rising influence on student, intellectual, and labor groups. The period from 1919 to 1921 witnessed the emergence of a multitude of societies, journals, and activities bearing the Marxist–Leninist imprint. One important segment of the "vanguard" consisted of students from the leading universities. As early as November 1918, students from Tōkyō University inaugurated the Shinjinkai (New Men's Association). Some idea of the group's ideological bent can be garnered from the program of its first anniversary meeting. All of the leading Japanese

---

[13] For Sakai's own recollections of this era, see Sakai Toshihiko, *Nihon shakaishugi undō shi* (*History of the Japanese Socialist Movement*), Tōkyō, 1954. In the February 1918 issue of *Shin Shakai*, Takabatake wrote what may be the first Japanese article introducing certain Leninist themes. The article was entitled "The Political Movement and the Economic Movement." Takabatake's basic thesis was that parliamentary policy was only one part of the political movement, never the whole of it, and that the political movement included all types, from Scheidemann to Lenin, just as the economic movement included those from Gompers to Haywood. He argued the unreasonableness of the thesis that an economic movement is invariably good, while a political one is decadent. In this article, Takabatake not only used the term "Bolshevism," but some of its ideas as well.

[14] Sakai, p. 35.

radicals were invited, and talks were delivered on Marx, Kropotkin, Lenin, Liebknecht, and Luxemburg.

Waseda University contributed several organizations. One portion of the radicals founded the Gyōminkai (Men of the Dawn Society), which, as we shall note, formed the nucleus of the first proto-Communist party in Japan. There was also the Bunka Dōmei (Cultural League) and the Kensetsusha Dōmei (League of Builders). Innumerable other radical societies sprang up among the students, with most of them emerging from one educational institution and a few cutting across institutional lines. Almost all of these societies published a newspaper or a journal disseminating the latest radical theories and activities from the West.

The mature intellectuals were also awakening to the new Western tides. The small radical group headed by Sakai and Yamakawa served as the vanguard in introducing "advanced socialism" to the larger intellectual community through their journals and newly organized societies.[15] They published a veritable flood of Socialist literature, much of it in the form of direct translation or lengthy paraphrasing of Western materials.[16] As quickly as materials were received from such sources as the League of Japanese Socialists in America, they were put into the Japanese stream. A few "theoretical" journals existed, such as Yamakawa's *Shakaishugi Kenkyū* (*Studies of Socialism*) and the *Shakai Mondai Kenkyū* (*Study of Social Problems*), edited by Kawakami Hajime, but there were many other outlets: labor journals, all-purpose socialist society organs, special pamphlets, and major publications such as *Kaihō* (*Emancipation*). Through these sources, Japanese readers could obtain the news and documents of world socialism only weeks, sometimes days, after the events.

It cannot be overemphasized, however, that this was a period of great flux and confusion for the Japanese radicals. To attempt any rigorous demarcation of ideological positions would be very misleading. Initially, many anarchists believed that the Russian Revolution was based on

---

[15] The old radical group, led by Sakai, had published *Shin Shakai* since 1915, and in January 1920 its name was changed to *Shin Shakai Hyōron* (*New Society Review*), which in turn gave way to *Shakaishugi* (*Socialism*) in September of the same year. The latter journal served as the organ for the Socialist League. But the radical group had separate study groups and journals. With the typical Japanese penchant for organization, even the tiniest element invariably formed a "society." Thus Sakai had his Friday Society, Yamakawa and his immediate followers had their Wednesday Society, and there were many others.

[16] A typical issue of *Shakaishugi*, for example, would contain news about the Chinese anarchists, the French radical union, and a translation of an article by William Z. Foster.

their principles. Certainly in these opening years there was a wide-spread belief in the possibility of a broad socialist-anarchist-Communist front. For these reasons among others, anarcho-syndicalism could continue to have a pronounced influence on such neo-Marxists as Yamakawa, although it would not have been easy in any case to shed the beliefs of two decades overnight.

To illustrate some of the above points, we can note the ties between Ōsugi, clearly the leading anarchist during this era, and the Comintern.[17] In June 1920, shortly after Ōsugi had finished a three-months prison term and when he was at a low ebb financially, even forced to suspend publication of his small newspaper, he was contacted by Yi Ch'un-suk, a young Korean, on behalf of the Shanghai Bureau. Yi and a Korean friend persuaded Ōsugi to go to Shanghai in the fall of 1920, where he met with Asian Communists connected with the Far Eastern Bureau—most of them Koreans, but including Ch'en Tu-hsiu and Gregory Voitinsky, the young Russian who headed the Bureau. Ōsugi accepted Bureau funds to reopen publication of Rōdō Undō (*The Labor Movement*) and, in exchange, added two Communists, Kondō and Takatsu Seidō, to his staff. Kondō has given us a graphic description of *Rōdō Undō* life during his time with the paper. The "editorial room" was Ōsugi's ten-mat living quarters, and space was so limited that conferences were held around Ōsugi's double bed. Personal relations among these men were characterized by great mutual respect, free thinking, and vigorous arguments. Ōsugi, despite the funds, did not cease being an anarchist, although he did not interfere with Kondō and Takatsu. Thus, at least one page of an anarchist journal featured Bolshevik wares.

Ōsugi had promised the Shanghai Bureau leaders to visit the Soviet Union, but the trip was postponed due to his health and never taken. Moreover, Ōsugi and the pure anarchists began to attack the Lenin government. By the fall of 1922, the attacks were increasing in vigor. Reports of the mistreatment of anarchists in the Soviet Union were now numerous, and the authoritarian nature of the Communist regime was denounced in stinging terms. Bolshevik theories of elitism and proletarian dictatorship came under heavy assault. "Workers will never be liberated," asserted one writer, "by relying on police power and a secret service force."

The Japanese anarchist-Communist struggle reached a climax in

---

[17] For details, see Ōsugi, *Nihon dasshutsu ki* (*Memoirs of Escape from Japan*), Tōkyō, 1923; and Kondō, pp. 106ff.

1923, but already the anarchists were slipping badly in strength and influence. The fundamental reasons for this can be easily summarized. Anarcho-syndicalism had failed as a revolutionary tactic, both in Japan and elsewhere, whereas Bolshevism had succeeded, at least in Russia. The failure of anarchism in Japan was particularly striking. In a depression period, when Japanese unions were conspicuously lacking in the capacity to struggle, caution and moderation would seem to have been the only guidelines that offered hope of success to the labor movement. But the anarcho-syndicalists ignored objective conditions. Theirs was the counsel of full-fledged assault, whenever and wherever a conflagration could be ignited. In the midst of weakness, they urged—and, in some cases, conducted—a campaign of violence. Sabotage, personal assaults, and quasi-revolts against governmental authority were launched, taking advantage of the legitimate grievances of the workers. Almost invariably, the result was defeat for the workers and destruction of the unions involved. Constant turmoil existed in anarchist-dominated unions, membership faded away, and the labor movement went into decline.

Observant socialists scanning the international horizon saw similar anarchist failures abroad, notably in Italy, where attempts to effectuate anarcho-syndicalism through the tactic of worker-factory seizure and control did not succeed. On the other hand, the rapid rise of communism within international labor circles did not pass unnoticed among Japanese radicals. Against the background of their recent failures, these radicals sensed a much needed element of realism—even moderation—in Communist tactics, particularly in the emphasis on mixed political-economic action and in the theory of the simultaneous use and abuse of parliamentarism. The sheer utopianism of the anarcho-syndicalist movement and its lack of realistic tactics was never illustrated so forcefully as during these years. In an era when the radical intellectual element in Japan was committed to revolution, communism rapidly succeeded anarchism as *the science of successful revolution.*

Finally, governmental severity against the anarchists played a considerable role in their demise. It was almost impossible for them to maintain any continuity of leadership or organization. Leaders were kept under constant surveillance and frequently arrested. Anarchist publications were rigorously censored and suppressed. Anarchist-dominated organizations were smashed by police almost as quickly as they developed. Only a small handful of true believers was likely to remain in so hazardous a movement.

Japanese anarchism did not go down without an intense struggle, however, as the events between 1921 and 1923 reveal.[18] By the spring of 1922, there were indications that Japanese intellectuals and labor groups were beginning to substitute militant political action for the policy of direct economic action advocated by the anarchists. Most of these indications related to activities on behalf of Soviet Russia. Such issues as recognition of the Soviet Union, the withdrawal of Japanese forces from Siberia, and the sending of relief supplies to the Russian people were increasingly advanced at political rallies. Moreover, demands for universal suffrage, expanded political freedom, and the organization of "proletarian parties" testified to the heightening interest in political action on the part of the new left.

The internal struggle between anarchists and Communists, however, was long and hard. In some areas, the anarchists even made temporary gains. The Sōdōmei (Japanese Federation of Labor) convention of October 1922, however, signaled the end of anarchist power in the Japanese labor movement.[19] Less than a year later, in September 1923, Japanese anarchism suffered a terrible blow with the murder of Ōsugi and his wife by the Secret Police in the aftermath of the Tōkyō earthquake. The anarchists, led by Ōsugi's followers, Mizunuma Kūma and Iwasa Sakutarō, continued to hold some labor strength and isolated intellectual support. After 1922, however, the anarchists never again threatened to ride the main current of the Japanese radical movement.[20]

By 1923 the new radical wave of communism had assumed significant proportions within labor and intellectual circles, although it still represented a tiny movement in comparison to the major Japanese political forces surrounding it. Kondō's memoirs, among other works, provide us with details concerning the origins of the Japanese Communist Party.[21] When Kondō left San Francisco for Japan in May 1919, he had two objectives: to foster closer Japanese–American cultural ties and to found a Japanese Communist party. His first action on returning to Japan was to visit government officials and other persons interested in Japanese–American relations, soliciting their aid for his projected

---

[18] The best primary source for studying the Japanese Anarchist movement during this period is *Rōdō Undō* (*Labor Movement*), Ōsugi's journal.

[19] See *Nihon rōdō nenkan* (*Japan Labor Yearbook*), 1923.

[20] The September 1, 1925 issue of *Rōdō Undō* contained a pathetic article entitled "Mourning for the Third Year of Ōsugi's Death." The author noted that it had been two years since Ōsugi was killed, and one year since Wada Kiichiro had shot himself. "Our camp is quite disorganized," he lamented, "and we cannot afford to indulge in sentimentalism. The time has come to test our spirits in action" (p. 1).

[21] See Kondō, pp. 62ff.

International Education League. Unable to obtain support, however, he gave up in disgust six months later and turned to the second objective, that of establishing a Communist party.

One might note in passing that the Russians, in their initial contacts with individual Asian radicals, had to gamble heavily on both character and ability. The Soviet tactic in Asia during this period was to approach promising radicals and provide them with funds for publication, organizational activities, and living expenses—as well as with ideological and political counseling. In comparison with other efforts, the amounts of money involved were not substantial; even the hard-pressed Soviet leaders could afford the losses sustained. The attrition rate, however, was substantial. As noted earlier, in Japan the Comintern had to work with men whose primary ideological commitment was anarcho-syndicalist, and relatively few of these men ever abandoned that commitment entirely. Some, like Ōsugi, remained ideologically pure. In other situations, the Soviet representatives found they were dealing with opportunists who either used the funds allotted them for personal purposes or gave up their new ideology when the monies ceased to flow.

The case of Kondō Eizō was perhaps a typical one. Kondō, like many of the postwar generation, had had "the short course" in socialism. The older generation of Japanese radicals had come to socialism through Christianity and its gospel of humanism, or after having become conversant with the radical egalitarianism so well displayed in French revolutionary thought and promulgated first in Meiji Japan in the course of the *jiyūminken undō* (civil rights movement). But the second-generation Japanese radicals started with Marx, sometimes with Lenin.

In his Socialist activities, Kondō ultimately became very intimate with Yamakawa. Sakai, he felt, had social-democratic tendencies; Arahata retained some anarcho-syndicalist leanings; Yamakawa was "most thorough." By early 1921, Kondō was meeting secretly with Yamakawa and Sakai, discussing plans for a Japanese branch of the 3rd International and drawing up a draft program, using as a model the British Communist Party Manifesto and Program.

This underground Communist group had its first formal beginnings in early 1921, when a Communist Committee was established with some seven individuals meeting in April at a place in Tōkyō near Ōmori station. Sakai served as Chairman, and Yamakawa presented a draft program. It was unanimously agreed that the group should constitute itself as a preparatory committee for a Japanese branch of the 3rd

International, and that Kondō should be sent as its representative to the Far Eastern Bureau in Shanghai. Kondō took an English translation of the committee prospectus and program, typed on thin paper and inserted into the binding of an English novel, on the trip; he carried "credentials" in the form of a small piece of silk on which were inscribed the names of committee members and which was sewn into the lining of his clothes.

Disguised as a Los Angeles import-export merchant, Kondō made his way to Shanghai, where he had lengthy conversations with Comintern representatives, mainly Koreans. They decided to drop their support of Ōsugi and shift to the new group. Yamakawa, acknowledged as the key intellectual in the group, was greatly desired as the Japanese representative to the 3rd Comintern Congress meetings, but since his health would not permit the journey, Kondō and another man were accepted. The sessions ended with Kondō submitting a budget that called for a monthly expenditure of 20,000 yen; he received 6,500 yen with a promise that Moscow would be consulted concerning the larger amount.

Kondō's return to Japan, however, resulted in a comedy of errors that turned into a fiasco for the new movement. On board ship, he had started a conversation with a Polish man who lived in Moscow; when the ship landed at Shimonoseki, Kondō sought to help the man by serving as his interpreter at the customs counter. Problems arose, and Kondō missed the express train to Tōkyō. He went to a restaurant near the railway station, expecting to catch the night express. The restaurant, however, happened to be near the prostitute quarters. Kondō had been away from Japanese food—and women—for some time, and he now had ample money. He got drunk, collected a girl, missed the night express, and in the process aroused the suspicions of the station police. In the middle of the night, he was awakened and searched. The money was discovered, and he was bundled off to jail. A master agent had come to a quick and sorry end.

With the help of an informer, the Shimonoseki police finally forced Kondō to tell them at least a portion of the truth. He admitted that the funds had come from the Comintern and that he had intended to organize a Communist party. According to his account, he did not involve Yamakawa, Sakai, or others in the scheme. However, a note from him to Sakai requesting help was intercepted, casting strong suspicion on the Tōkyō radicals.

Kondō was soon released and returned to Tōkyō where he urged fulfillment of the original plans. Quite naturally, the Tōkyō leaders were cautious since Japanese authorities knew some of the details. These

were men weary of being constantly arrested and hounded by plain-
clothesmen even when they were "free." Kondō's escapade, moreover,
had not increased their confidence in him or the venture. Nevertheless,
some of the money was used for its intended purposes. Sakai's publishing plant was reestablished, and on August 20 Kondō struck out in
another direction, meeting with some Waseda University radicals to
form the so-called Gyōmin Kyōsantō (Men of the Dawn Communist
Party).

Suddenly posters began to appear in Tōkyō with brief messages
urging the workers and peasants to arise.[22] In November, large-scale
army exercises were taking place in the Tōkyō area, and many soldiers
were housed in the city with private citizens. Through some source, the
Gyōmin group obtained lists of houses with military personnel and
early in the morning distributed antimilitary handbills containing such
messages as "Every day we hear the talk, 'Soldiers! A Japanese-
American war is near; you must die an heroic military death!' But the
time for your self-consciousness has come. Don't kill your brothers. Arise
and strike. Disobey the top officials!"[23]

Not surprisingly, Japanese authorities took a dim view of these activities and, after a rigorous investigation, arrested some forty persons including Kondō. The Gyōmin Kyōsantō was ended. Just before his
arrest, however, Kondō had dispatched one Shigeda Yōichi to Shanghai to report to the Bureau that his mission had been accomplished and
that a Japanese Communist party had been established. As usual, the
police were alert. Documents sent with Shigeda fell into their hands, and
they were also able to pick up a Comintern agent, B. Grey, when he
arrived by ship in Yokohama with funds for the movement and a notebook containing Kondō's name. Kondō suspected that Yoshihara Tarō
in Shanghai, who had had ties with the Bureau, was also serving as an
agent for the Japanese government, although this was never proven.[24]

[22] Yamakawa asserted that Kondō later told Sakai that the posters were his
receipts for Comintern money. (Interview with Yamakawa, October 12, 1957.)

[23] Kondō, pp. 157–158.

[24] According to the Japanese police, Grey, an Englishman born in Moscow
and married to a Russian, had moved back and forth between Australia and
Russia at an earlier period. His work for the Bolsheviks had started in 1920,
and he had become very prominent in the Far Eastern Bureau in Shanghai.
When Kondō's emissary Shigeda arrived with news of Communist activities,
Grey was dispatched to Japan to accompany him home. Grey carried seven thousand yen in cash and checks, and a notebook with the names of five Socialists.
Under questioning, Grey insisted that his object was to purchase medical instruments for a Shanghai chemical and medical company, but Kondō and others
seem to have told the full story, which Japanese authorities may already have
known through Yoshihara. See the account in *Japan Weekly Chronicle*, December 8, 1921, pp. 813–814.

By the spring of 1922, the underground Communist movement took new forms and involved new individuals. Kondō faded away. The main actors were now those who had returned from the Moscow meetings and the veteran Tōkyō radicals. Tokuda Kyūichi, whose subsequent career as a Japanese Communist Party leader was to be long and faithful, took the lead in reporting on Comintern desires. During the spring and early summer of 1922, he conferred with various individuals, and on July 15, 1922, a meeting was convened at which Tokuda reported on the Moscow Congress and the private sessions between elements of the Japanese delegation and Comintern officials.[25] The central theses learned in Moscow were outlined, as well as Comintern instructions on forming a branch party. July 15, 1922, is now regarded as the official date for the founding of the Japanese Communist Party.

In November of the same year, the standing committee of the party met and brought forth a program. Two men were dispatched to represent the Japanese branch at the 4th Congress of the Comintern. On February 4, 1923, a general meeting of the party was held at Ichigawa, in Chiba Prefecture, and active operations were set in motion.[26] Shortly thereafter, Arahata left for Moscow to report to the Plenum session of the Comintern Executive Committee.

Then came trouble for the Communists. In May 1923, clashes occurred at Waseda University over the issue of military training. In their investigations, the police found some incriminating documents, including a roster of the members of the Japanese Communist Party that was discovered in the quarters of Sano Manabu, a Waseda lec-

---

[25] Arahata, *Kanson jiden (Autobiography of Kanson)*, Tōkyō, 1960, p. 288. See also *Tokuda Kyūichi den (The Biography of Tokuda Kyūichi)*, edited by the staff of the *Rironsha*, Tōkyō, 1952, p. 92. The latter source suggests that the first meeting was held on July 5, followed by the first "convention" on July 15 in Shibuya, Tōkyō.

According to Watanabe, at the meeting of July 15th, provisional regulations and immediate tasks were determined, and seven members (Sakai, Yamakawa, Arahata, Yoshikawa Morikuni, Hashiura Tokio, Takatsu, and Tokuda) were selected as committee members, with Sakai as Chairman. Watanabe Haruo, *Nihon Marxshugi undō no reimei (The Dawn of the Japanese Marxist Movement)*, Tōkyō, 1957, p. 184.

[26] According to Tokuda, at the Ichigawa meeting the party regulations were revised and a new Central Committee was selected, with Arahata as Chairman. Yamakawa and Takatsu reportedly were not selected because they rejected the parliamentary struggle, opposing universal suffrage, thus continuing to reveal anarcho-syndicalist views. *Tokuda Kyūichi den*, p. 94. According to Kondō's account, however, he acted as Chairman, and the party rules and theses, mainly written by Yamakawa, were approved. Committee chairmen were selected, with Sakai being elected Chairman of the Executive Committee. Afterward, delegates relaxed, drank sake, and went back to Tōkyō separately. Kondō, pp. 180–181.

turer. Early on the morning of June 5, ten police cars spread out over Tōkyō and picked up almost every party member in the city; similar raids were conducted elsewhere. Except for those who were out of the country or managed to get out, all official party members were rounded up. The first Japanese Communist Party was wiped out.

Despite the short period of time involved, this opening era is worthy of study in depth if one is to understand the origins of the Japanese Communist movement. First, it is to be noted that this movement was the joint product of overseas and "domestic" elements, and, in both cases, the major role was played by intellectual-student types. Only five of the twenty-nine individuals convicted in connection with the first Communist Party Incident could be classified as workers. Clearly, at this stage the movement was predominantly an intellectual one, springing out of the innumerable study groups and the general radical ferment in Japanese university, literary, and journalist circles. Those actively involved in the Japanese Communist Party, it must be emphasized, were only a tiny group from within the radical camp, but a significantly larger number of Japanese intellectuals were finding emotional and intellectual stimulus in Marxism and hence were in some degree potential adherents or at least sympathizers.

Even within the small group of Communist Party members, ideological positions varied, and personal affiliations provided additional complexity. We have stressed the extensive anarcho-syndicalist background of some of the leading participants and the social democratic predilections of others. The development of "true Marxist–Leninists" would, of necessity, take time. In this early period, moreover, Soviet and Comintern authorities, however strongly motivated, could not know the details of the situation in Japan or the various personalities involved. A certain degree of freedom was thus possible, giving a measure of flexibility with respect to doctrine and practice.

Despite this fact, the evidence is overwhelming that the Japanese Communist Party, in its origins, was the creature of the Comintern and hence of the Soviet Union. On this point, the documentation could not be more complete: the Comintern funds dispensed from Shanghai were designated specifically for the purpose of establishing the party, and, as Tokuda and others made clear on their return, this action was taken at the request of the authorities in Moscow; the initial party program was drafted on the basis of detailed discussions with Soviet leaders in Moscow, and its main provisions most certainly had been "cleared" with them; all members of the party, moreover, recognized that they were a *branch* of an international movement having its headquarters in Moscow.

What was the ideology of the first Japanese Communist Party? *Zenei* (*Vanguard*), which began publication under Yamakawa and his wife on January 1, 1922, is an excellent source from which to ascertain the theoretical position of the party. *Zenei* became the Communist organ, and many young Marxists as well as the prominent party leaders wrote for it until March 1923 when publications ceased.[27] Yamakawa himself set the main tone, however, and fashioned the major doctrines. His old anarcho-syndicalist views were still clearly evident in the great hostility with which he regarded parliamentarism. At best, involvement in the parliamentary struggle could only be a tactic, and in the case of Japan, where capitalism had pursued an antiliberal, antidemocratic course, it was a dubious tactic.

Nevertheless, in his famous article, "A Change of Direction for the Proletarian Movement," published in the July-August 1922 issue of *Zenei*, Yamakawa struck hard at the vulnerability of Japanese anarcho-syndicalism and asserted the need for political action, both inside and outside of the Diet.[28] His main theme was "To the masses!," and his central arguments could be summarized as follows: Thus far, the Japanese proletarian movement had been a movement of a few pioneers, men who had been able to free themselves from bourgeois thought and hence were prepared to tutor the masses who were going to need time to acquire class consciousness and grasp socialist truth. But beyond this first step, socialist pioneers had been unable or unwilling to go. They were uninterested in any program that did not point toward the *immediate* abolition of the capitalist state. They preferred to bring together a handful of people and talk wildly about what would happen after the revolution, or to brawl aimlessly with the police and end up in jail, rather than to develop a sound set of political tactics and strategy. Thus, the masses had been alienated or made afraid. The most immediate task was to take up the urgent economic problems of the masses, combining realistic economic programs with meaningful political action and cultivating a practical, positive, and militant approach that accepted a stage-by-stage development of socialism.

There was nothing original in Yamakawa's heavily censored article. He had taken his themes directly from the 3rd Congress of the Comintern and other Communist theses. The message was put forcefully, how-

---

[27] *Zenei* was a monthly, and a number of young men such as Nishi Masao, Tadokoro Teruaki, and Ueda Shigeki helped Yamakawa and his wife with the publication. The journal was quite obviously Communist in nature and was subjected to very heavy censorship.
[28] *Ibid.*, pp. 16–25.

ever, and was well timed in light of the Japanese situation, particularly
as a frontal assault on the anarchists. It had a widespread impact, even
on moderates within the labor movement, many of whom hailed it as a
call to realism.

It is to be noted, of course, that the Japanese Communist movement
at this point paid relatively little attention to the peasants and made no
attempt to use Japanese nationalism. Nationalist symbols were almost
exclusively in the hands of the conservatives. The emphasis was on the
urban proletariat, and the arguments from the beginning related to the
nature and maturity of Japanese capitalism. In the main, the Communists of Japan were seeking to apply Marxism in its orthodox,
nineteenth-century sense to an advanced society. The critical questions,
as we shall see, became whether the revolution should be a one-stage
or a two-stage process, and whether capitalism in Japan was capable of
further advancing bourgeois liberalism.[29]

In August 1923, a few months after the mass arrests that ended the
first Japanese Communist Party, a small group of Japanese Communists
gathered in Vladivostok to discuss the future. It was decided to support
the rapid creation of a proletarian party that could bring together various labor and peasant union members and through which Communist
policies could be advanced. Arahata, one of the participants, returned
to Japan with this message, and shortly thereafter the Communists and
their sympathizers made strenuous efforts to develop a unified workers'
party.

At the same time, however, the primary issue was whether to attempt
a reorganization of the Japanese Communist Party itself. By the spring
of 1924, most of the former party members had been released from
prison. A substantial majority of them opposed party reestablishment
under prevailing conditions. This group, which acknowledged Yamakawa as its mentor, was known as the "natural development" faction
and argued that conditions in Japan were not ripe for the establishment
of a Communist party. First, it was necessary to prepare the mass foundations for that party by concentrating on the development of unions,
peasant associations, Marxian student organizations, and similar groups.
The existence of an illegal party, they believed, would hamper such
activities, isolating the vanguard from the masses and subjecting it to
useless persecution. In this stage, Communists should therefore work
through unions, intellectual societies, and a legal proletarian party,
seeking to create the conditions that would make a Communist party
possible at a later date.

---

[29] See Watanabe, *Nihon Marxshugi undō no reimei*, p. 112.

Consequently, at the so-called Morigasaki Conference on March 1924, Communist leaders decided to dissolve the party, leaving a small "caretaker" group to wind up business matters with the Comintern and others. The Japanese Communists were now prepared to pursue without distraction the task of molding the broader proletarian party and labor movements to fit their principles. This course of action, however, met with the violent disapproval of the Comintern authorities. To abandon "the only true party of the proletarian masses," even for tactical reasons, was completely unacceptable to the men in Moscow and Shanghai. Thus, when a small group of Communists went to the Shanghai Bureau in January 1925, they were severely rebuked by Voitinsky and ordered to reestablish the party as quickly as possible.[30] Under the direction of Voitinsky, the so-called January or Shanghai Thesis was prepared at this time.[31] This thesis sharply criticized previous Japanese Communist leadership for lacking a true understanding of Marxism-Leninism, for misunderstanding the basic principles of Communism and the Comintern, and for failing to provide a mass basis for the movement. From this point, Yamakawa and Sakai were treated as heretics by the Comintern.

It was impossible to reestablish the Japanese Communist Party immediately. The small group who returned from Shanghai first established a Bureau and began to assemble the faithful around it. Taking the January Thesis and the theses of the 4th Comintern Congress of 1923 as guides, the Bureau fixed its main policies as follows: The first duty of the Communists was to defeat the Akamatsu (Katsumaro) social reformists, the Abe (Isoo) Fabians, and all other Japanese "petit bourgeois" spokesmen in the struggle to guide and direct the proletarian party movement. Second, it was essential to create a proletarian party that had both *class* and *mass* as its basis. And, third, such groups as the Workers' Education Association, the Suiheisha (Levellers' Association), the Proletarian Youth League, and all left-wing unions should be brought under the direct leadership of the Communists. Democratic centralism was to be the basis of all organization, with factory and academic cells constituting the grass-roots units, and with fractions to be established in each worker and peasant union.

---

[30] According to Arahata, he went to Shanghai with Sano and Tokuda. Voitinsky scolded the group severely, and as one mark of his displeasure refused to give them funds for reorganization purposes, but instructed them to reestablish the party immediately. Interview with Arahata, August 23, 1957.

[31] For the January Thesis, see Yamamoto Katsunosuke and Arita Mitsuho, *Nihon kyōsanshugi undō shi* (*A History of the Japanese Communist Movement*), Tōkyō, 1950, pp. 71-72.

Meanwhile, in May 1925, the Profintern, in the presence of a Japanese representative, had discussed the Japanese labor movement and passed a resolution stating that the unity of Japanese labor was supremely important; consequently, the left should not leave the Sōdōmei, but should fight against "the right-wing deviationists" from within the organization. Profintern instructions, however, reached Japan too late. Before the message could be relayed, the small Japanese labor movement split in half after months of bitter wrangling. On May 25, 1925, the Nihon Rōdō Hyōgikai (Labor Union Council of Japan) was formally established, taking with it about one-half of the Sōdōmei membership, or approximately 15,000 workers.[32] The Hyōgikai, from its inception, was under very strong Communist influence and in essence served as the chief vehicle for the Japanese Communist movement between 1925 and 1928, when it was forcibly dissolved by the government. During these years, the struggle between the social democrats and the Communists for control of the Japanese labor movement was savage, notwithstanding the relatively small scale on which the battle could be waged.

The split in the labor movement was paralleled by a split in the movement to establish a proletarian party, as might have been expected. The details are exceedingly complicated, but essentially the basic issues were simple. Should the social democrats join in a united front with the Communists or not? Were the Communists seeking to impose their line on the new party, as they had on the Sōdōmei? Innumerable attempts were made to compromise or paper over various procedural and substantive differences, but the fundamental issues could not be resolved.

The Sōdōmei charged—with ample evidence—that the Communist line organizations, including the Hyōgikai, were seeking to control the new party and impregnate it with the Communist program. The old Communist tactic was to organize "district units" that could pose as party units once the national party had come into existence and take it over by purporting to represent a majority of the constituent party units. In the process, the Communists were painting Sōdōmei and other social democratic elements as traitors to the working class, corrupt bureaucrats, and opportunists. Such terms were scarcely conducive to

---

[32] See Taniguchi Zentarō, *Nihon Rōdō Kumiai Hyōgikai shi* (*A History of the Labor Union Council of Japan*), 2 vols., Tōkyō, 1948; this is a Communist account containing many specific details. See also Noda Ritsuta, *Hyōgikai tōsō shi* (*A History of the Hyōgikai Struggle*), Tōkyō, 1931, for a contemporary leftist account by a Hyōgikai leader.

comradeliness and cooperation. Thus, in the end, the social democrats rejected "the antirealist, extreme leftist, cliquish, plot-ridden, anti-ethical attitudes" of the Hyōgikai and its affiliates.[33]

As a result, in the 1925–1926 period, not one but four so-called proletarian parties made their appearance. The division of the Japanese socialist movement, a division that has never ceased to exist, was established in its essential forms at this point. The so-called right wing was represented by the Shakai Minshūtō (Social Mass Party), which became the political vehicle for the Sōdōmei and many of the moderate intellectuals such as Abe Isoo, Yoshino Sakuzō, and Horie Kiichi. The Nihon Nōmintō (Japan Farmers' Party), with its hopes riding on the rural areas, was also moderate to conservative in policies. The center position was represented by the Nihon Rōnōtō (Japan Labor-Farmer Party), which included such labor leaders and intellectuals as Asō Hisashi, Katō Kanjū, Kawakami Jōtarō, Suzuki Mosaburō, and many other non- or ex-Communists who generally considered themselves Marxists. A number of these men were subsequently sympathetic to, or affiliated with, the Rōnō Marxist group, which we shall discuss later. The left operated through the Rōdō Nōmintō (Labor-Farmer Party), a party containing both Communist and non-Communist elements but basically under Communist control.[34]

A careful study of the politically fragmented Japanese left of this era can be instructive with respect to postwar Japanese politics. The position of the moderates was one of strong support for parliamentarism, a stand on socioeconomic policies that was similar to that of the British Fabian Society, and complete opposition to any united front with the Communists. The center equivocated on certain basic issues: it supported parliamentarism-plus—that is, the use of *both* the Diet and the streets for purposes of mounting political action; generally, its leading members considered themselves Marxists or at least sympathetic to Marxism, and its socioeconomic policies reflected this fact; finally, the center favored a "broad united front," one that would include *both* the right and the left. It was ordinarily unwilling to join with one of these forces against the other, attempting to take a neutral position on many critical issues but criticizing both of its opponents for their "rigidity."

The left, as we shall soon note, took its tactical position firmly on behalf of a united front *with all progressive elements,* the latter phrase

---

[33] "Declaration Concerning the Withdrawal from the Labor–Farmer Party," *Rōdō Shimbun,* No. 186, November 1926, p. 3.

[34] The detailed programs and manifestos of the various "proletarian" parties can be found in *Nihon rōdō nenkan,* 1927.

representing a value-laden qualification that could be interpreted differently, depending on the occasion. It first attempted to secure this united front by working "from above," namely, by seeking a concord with the moderate leaders. When this failed, the left shifted to the "united front from below" tactic, appealing over the heads of the moderate leaders to their rank and file, and conducting intensive organizational efforts at the district level. On substantive issues, the legal left followed the leadership of the illegal Communist Party, which was now moving sharply to the left.

To appreciate this last trend, we must return to the Communist movement itself.[35] In August 1925, a Communist group was created as a preliminary step toward the formal reestablishment of the Japanese Communist Party. This was the same month, incidentally, that the meetings of the Preparatory Committee for a Proletarian Party got under way. Many leftists were simultaneously participating in legal and illegal activities in this era: above ground, they were fighting for the formation of a leftist-controlled proletarian party; underground, they were preparing for the organization of a new Communist party as the "only true party of the proletariat." All of this, of course, was very much in line with prevailing Comintern theses.

A new group of Communist leaders was now at the helm. Tokuda Kyūichi was made Chairman of the group, Sano Manabu, Chief of the Political Bureau, and Watanabe Masanosuke, Chief of the Organization Bureau. Arahata was given the responsibility for organizing the Kansai area. Once again, the party was essentially under intellectual leadership. Of these men, only Watanabe was a true worker, and this situation was reflected in the middle ranks of party membership as well.

By the fall of 1925, the Communists, while still very weak in an organizational sense, had a number of publications under their control or accessible to them: *Marxshugi* (*Marxism*), a theoretical journal; *Rōdō Shimbun* (*Labor News*), the Hyōgikai organ and a daily newspaper; and *Musansha Shimbun* (*Proletarian News*), which began publication in September 1925. The social democrats, on the other hand, were comparatively weak in this field, a source of genuine trouble for them.

The militance and commitment of the Communists, their superior

---

[35] For this section, I am greatly indebted to Fukumoto Kazuo who allowed me to have two lengthy interviews in his home in late September and early October 1957. Although our interpretations of many matters differ, I want to pay my respects to him as a gracious, generous host whose lively comments made important supplements to the documentary materials.

organizational and propaganda techniques, and the fact that they had a substantial fringe element of "progressives" who, although not Communists, provided varying degrees of protection, sympathy, and support all constituted sources of strength, real and potential. On the other hand, events of the past dictated that divisions within the left itself would present a growing problem for such groups as the Japanese Communists. By the end of 1926, the two currents that were running in such organizations as the Hyōgikai were "Yamakawaism" and "Fukumotoism." Progressively, the struggle became sharper, with Fukumotoism rapidly gaining power.

The rise of Fukumotoism was closely connected with the student movement of this period.[36] Student associations with a strong political commitment began to develop on a national scale in 1923. In August of that year, representatives of the Tōkyō University New Men's Society, now under Communist influence, visited higher schools throughout the country. As a result, the Kōtō Gakkō Remmei (Higher School Alliance) was organized in September. Two months later, this alliance merged with the New Men's Society and another student group, the Cultural League, to form the Zenkoku Gakusei Rengōkai (National Students' Federation). By the end of 1924, this association, renamed the Gakusei Shakai Kagaku Rengōkai (Student Social Science Federation), had 58 branches and some 1,500 members.

From this federation came a growing number of militant, dedicated young Communists. With a zeal unequaled in most other quarters, they infiltrated unions, parties, and "proletarian" associations. Because in most cases such organizations had a small membership and inexperienced leaders, they could be easily captured. And one could always establish a new group. By 1926 the student Marxists were a truly formidable force in the left-wing world of Japan. They dominated such publications as the *Proletarian News, Marxism,* and the *Labor-Farmer News (Rōnō Shimbun).* They were moving into control of the Labor-Farmer Party, and the Hyōgikai along with other left organizations had fallen under their influence.

A new figure now emerged to lead the student Marxists of this era. He was Fukumoto Kazuo, an intelligent, highly sensitive, egocentric young teacher who rose quickly from obscurity to dominate the Japanese Communist movement. In his own student days, Fukumoto had

---

[36] For an excellent summary of the student movement, see Watanabe, *Nihon Marxshugi undō no reimei,* pp. 116–119. See also *Sakei gakusei seito no shuki (The Notes of Leftist Students),* 3 vols., marked "Secret," and published by the Student Section of the Ministry of Education, Tōkyō, 1934–1935.

followed a typical pattern of development: beginning as a disciple of Yoshino and his theories of social democracy, he had gradually moved toward Marxism–Leninism. In the course of his peregrinations, he had been touched by a variety of influences—Bertrand Russell, G. D. H. Cole, Scott Nearing, Edwin Seligman, and Kawakami Hajime. He prided himself, however, on having turned quickly to original sources, the writings of Marx and Lenin. When he went to Europe in 1922, Fukumoto was already a budding Marxist.

His experiences and contacts in Europe strengthened his new position, and when he returned in 1924 to take up a teaching position in Yamaguchi Commercial Higher School, Fukumoto threw himself tirelessly into the study of Marxian literature. In such journals as *Marxishugi no hata no moto* (*Under the Banner of Marxism*) and *Marxism,* he began to set forth his views to the radical circle. His first contribution to the important journal *Marxism* was published in December 1924, and, from that time on, *Marxism* carried a Fukumoto article in almost every issue. Quickly, disciples began to gather.

In style of writing and thought, Fukumoto was Japogermanic. His articles carried all of the scholarly apparatus: extensive quotations from original sources, detailed textual criticisms, and lengthy, involved sentences. Drawing extensively on the writings of Marx and Lenin, and influenced by the work of contemporary European Marxists, Fukumoto made the need for a correct understanding of Marxist–Leninist fundamentals one of his central themes. This theme was not incompatible with the Comintern position that previous Japanese Communist leaders had failed to understand Marxian principles. Fukumoto, however, dared to take on the world. He criticized not only Yamakawa and the earlier political Marxists, but also Kawakami Hajime, the leading Japanese academic Marxist of this period. Indeed, the irrepressible individualism of Fukumoto even caused him to note some defects of Marx and Lenin, such as the fact that they could not go beyond an analysis of the social changes of their times. It is not surprising that young Japanese radicals swarmed to Fukumoto's banners.[37]

The first emphasis of Fukumotoism was on the importance of theory and the need to establish a correct theoretical base for any mass move-

---

[37] Fukumoto described his own path to Marxism as "via the routes of individualism, humanism, and antifeudalism." Interestingly, he asserted that Yamakawa, Sakai, and Arahata could not be called *Marxist* Communists, strictly speaking; they were rather *Bolshevist* Communists, with strong anarchist remnants. They followed the events of the Russian Revolution, asserted Fukumoto, but for the most part, they had neither read nor understood Marx. "Hence they ultimately turned to social democracy." Interview, October 1957.

ment. Arguing that in practice the earlier inadequacies of Japanese Marxism had stemmed from theoretical errors and misunderstandings, Fukumoto asserted that the first task of the labor-Socialist movement was to separate the correct Marxist elements and consolidate them. Initially, this required an emphasis on the theoretical struggle, because that struggle had to be won before the mass-action phase could be successfully undertaken.

Out of this argument came the theory of "separation and unity," a theory borrowed from Lenin. Fukumoto's position was that under the circumstances of the Japanese movement, it was essential for the correct Marxian group to separate themselves from the false Marxists and reformist elements, so that the movement could be purified and subsequently moved to greater unity on a sound theoretical basis. One of the reasons for the appeal of this doctrine, of course, was the fact that it rationalized the Hyōgikai split from the Sōdōmei as "a dialectical necessity" and also offered a comforting explanation for the failure of united front efforts.

By the end of 1926, the Fukumotoists were in solid control of the Communist movement in Japan and of such left organizations as the Hyōgikai.[38] They had also planted themselves at strategic points in the Labor-Farmer Party and were in a position to guide its policies. In truth, they dominated two parties, one legal and the other illegal. The Japanese Communist Party had been formally reestablished on December 4, 1926.[39] On the previous day, two young Tōkyō "business men" had arrived at an inn in Goshiki Hot Springs, Yamagata Prefecture, to make arrangements for a party to be attended by some twenty company employees. The "business men" were Fukumoto and Nakao Katsuō, ideological leader of the Hyōgikai. The "employees" who arrived the next day were fifteen additional comrades who had traveled from various places to reestablish the party.

The draft program for this second Communist party had been written by Sano Fumio, Watanabe Masanosuke, and Ichikawa Shōichi, but the doctrines were those of Fukumoto. At the meeting, his ideas were not seriously challenged. Many of the old leaders were not associated with this new venture, as we have noted; among that group, only Arahata took an active role. Power now lay with the young student and worker radicals, men theoretically "pure" and filled with the spirit of adventurism.

The ascendancy of Fukumotoism continued in 1927, and, indeed,

---

[38] Taniguchi, Vol. II, pp. 264–269.
[39] For details, see Yamamoto and Arita, pp. 76–81.

special study groups were created within student, union, and party
circles, using Fukumoto's writings as texts, so that "Marxian consciousness could be perfected." Some voices of disapproval, however, were to
be heard. Naturally, the Yamakawa faction objected vigorously, but
they had little standing at this point within "orthodox" Communist
circles. A more powerful source of opposition, however, was the old
Latvian revolutionary Jonson, who posed as Commercial Attaché in
the Tōkyō Russian Embassy, but who was in fact the primary contact
man for the Japanese Communists. Jonson was not a theorist but a
practical revolutionary, and undoubtedly for that reason he became
increasingly hostile to the "utopian, ultra-left" tendencies implicit in
Fukumoto's doctrines. Through Nabeyama Sadachika, who had formed
a close liaison with Fukumoto and who was subsequently sent to Moscow by the party, Bukharin was informed of the problem.[40]

It was finally decided to convene a Special Committee of the Comintern on "the Japan Problem." No members of the Yamakawa group
were invited, but most of the key leaders of the current party were
present, having left Japan in March 1927: Fukumoto, Sano Fumio,
Watanabe Masanosuke, Tokuda Kyūichi, Nakao Katsuō, and Kawai
Etsuzō. Nabeyama was already in Moscow, and when the sessions
started, he represented the anti-Fukumoto position, aided by a young
man studying in the Soviet Union, Takahashi Teiji. According to
Nabeyama, he was initially the only opponent of Fukumoto, although
men like Tokuda and Watanabe subsequently swung into line as the
Soviet position became clear.

The Moscow deliberations were lengthy, but finally on July 15, 1927,
an official thesis was issued.[41] The major contribution was that of
Bukharin, but some role was played by J. T. Murphy of Great Britain,
M. N. Roy of India, Béla Kun of Hungary, and a German representative. According to both Nabeyama and Fukumoto, Katayama participated only in a very minor way. The 1927 Thesis severely criticized
both the position of "Comrade Hoshi" (Yamakawa) and that of "Comrade Kuroki" (Fukumoto).[42] The doctrines of Yamakawa depreciated
the role of the Communist Party in the labor and revolutionary move-

---

[40] I am greatly indebted to Nabeyama Sadachika for his assistance in providing information on this period during a lengthy interview, August 21, 1957.

[41] The 1927 Thesis is published in full in Yamamoto and Arita, pp. 82–102.

[42] For the specific criticisms of Yamakawaism and Fukumotoism, see *ibid.*,
pp. 96–100. Fukumoto's later recollections and appraisal of his purge in Moscow
are most interesting and worthy of citation here: "The charge that I was a
disciple of Trotsky was complete nonsense. The basic issue was whether the
Japanese Communist Party could act or develop theoretically in any independent

ments. Yamakawa believed that a left-wing faction within the labor movement or a Labor-Farmer Party could be a substitute for a Communist party. But without a healthy, mass-based Communist party, revolutionary success was impossible. The struggle against the liquidationist attitude represented by the Yamakawaists was the first duty of the Japanese Communists.

To separate the Communist Party from the masses, however, was also an error, and Fukumoto's theory of unity through separation led to such an error, asserted the thesis. Fukumotoism was not Leninism, despite certain mechanical borrowings from Lenin. The practical effect of

---

sense, or whether it had to accept the line imposed by the Comintern and occupy a position of absolute obedience to Soviet leadership.

"Because I was not afraid to argue with people like Jonson and Bukharin, I was considered insubordinate. At that time, Stalin insisted that every Communist party be merely a branch of the Comintern which was, of course, controlled by him. He did not sit in on our sessions, but sent his secretary, who reported to him. I believed in the necessity of a full-fledged Communist Party at the national level. I was called an idealist, but who was the idealist in the end, Stalin or I?

"In order to understand developments at this time, you must also understand trends within the Chinese Communist movement. The Chinese Communists had accepted the organizational principle that it was necessary to clarify differences of opinion first in order to reach a common position. This was the doctrine which I espoused. Moreover, the CCP was then demanding some independence of thought and action, but the JCP had not yet demanded this. In effect, I was trying to recover the independence of the JCP from Comintern control.

"I admit that my theory of the necessity of a split before union, taken from Lenin's writings, was rather mechanical and clumsily worded, but I viewed the struggle against Yamakawaism as akin to Lenin's struggle against the Mensheviks. The 'split before unity' thesis, moreover, was not my invention. Even before I became a Bureau member, Sano Manabu had translated a piece by Engels dealing with this matter, and Aono Suekichi had done a poor translation of Lenin's *What Is To Be Done?* Moreover, the Hyōgikai–Sōdōmei split had occurred before I came into prominence in Communist circles and was the work of people like Nabeyama.

"While I had some doctrinal differences with Bukharin and had previously criticized some of his theories, when I first met him in Moscow, we got along well. Subsequently, however, Kawai of the Farmers' Union told him that I was speaking badly about him, and our relationship cooled. With Jonson, I continued to be on good personal terms. He invited me to his room in Moscow, introduced me to William Z. Foster of the United States, and promised to recommend that I be continued on the Central Committee." Interview, October 1957.

Undoubtedly, the above interpretation is self-serving and strongly influenced by some events after the fact. Fukumoto was speaking after the 20th CPSU Congress and at a time when the independence of the CCP was beginning to make itself manifest. Nevertheless, one cannot dismiss the above analysis. Fukumoto was not the type of person to wear another man's collar, and the issue of independence was involved both in his case and in that of Yamakawa.

Fukumoto's theories was to abandon all struggle to capture the workers on the right and the center, and to plunge the workers of the left into a class struggle for which they had not been prepared by tradition, experience, or organization. It was a basic error to split such organizations as the Sōdōmei and the Farmers' Union. The proper approach was to fight from within—to expose the reformist, opportunist leaders and to separate them from the masses. Not to understand that a broad proletarian mass organization was the only base for the Communist Party was a most dangerous error on the part of the young Japanese Communist movement.

Another of Fukumoto's mistakes, according to the 1927 Thesis, was the attempt to politicize mechanically the labor unions. He ignored the differences between parties and labor unions, seeking to make them identical. The Communist Party should operate as a faction within the Hyōgikai and direct it, the thesis pointed out, but the two organizations should not be confused. Moreover, Fukumoto's theories placed an excessive value on the intellectuals and represented a type of sectism. "A party based on people who 'think in correct Marxist terms' will essentially be a party of intellectuals. It will not be a mass struggle organization based on the proletariat. The small, illegal Communist Party of Japan should therefore unite and work through such mass organizations as the Labor-Farmer Party, the Unity League, and similar groups."

It is impossible to say precisely when the 1927 Thesis first became known in Japan. Certainly, it took some time for the details to reach there. The delegates themselves did not return until November. A digest of the Thesis was first published in the September issue of the *Bungei Sensen* (*Culture Front*). *Marxism* and *Proletarian News,* along with other organs controlled by the Fukumoto supporters, remained completely silent. Only in February 1928 was the full thesis published in *Shakai Shisō* (*Social Thought*), and the following month in *Marxism,* now under the control of a new group. A new Central Committee for the Japanese Communist Party had been named in Moscow. Fukumoto and Sano Fumio had been removed; Sano Manabu, Ichikawa Shōichi, Arahata Kanson, Watanabe Masanosuke, and Nabeyama Sadachika were appointed as new leaders.

On December 2, 1927, an enlarged Central Committee meeting of the party was convened in Ibaraki Prefecture. A report from the Moscow delegation was heard, and naturally the 1927 Thesis was approved. The party decided to place special emphasis on the creation of factory cells and through this medium come to the masses at last.

In that same month, the Yamakawa faction began publishing a monthly journal, *Rōnō* (*Labor-Farmer*), from whence subsequently they got their name, the *Rōnō* faction. Despite the repeated rebukes from Moscow, the *Rōnō* faction continued to struggle for Comintern–Russian support and blessing. Initially, *Rōnō* writers offered no criticism of the 1927 Thesis, nor indeed of any Soviet position. Russia remained "the Fatherland." The main enemies were the Fukumotoists and their successors, the men now running the journal *Marxism* and the Japanese Communist Party. Personal animosities combined with doctrinal differences to produce an unending series of bitter polemics.

Although the *Rōnō* faction sought Comintern blessing, it did not take positions in conformity with Comintern views. The *Rōnō* thesis was briefly as follows: Bourgeois power had been completely established in Japan, with the feudal elements assimilated into its ranks. The struggle between anachronistic feudal forces and the bourgeoisie was therefore not fundamental; the bourgeoisie had already triumphed. Consequently, the task of the proletariat was to form a strong antibourgeois front in alliance with the peasantry and seize power.

According to *Rōnō* theorists, the main objective should be the overthrow of imperialism and the establishment of a proletariat government, not the perfection of bourgeois democracy. At least for Japan, the concept of a two-stage revolution was a mistake. The thesis that the first need was to complete the bourgeois-democratic revolution and only then move to the second stage, the proletarian revolution, ignored the basic facts of modern Japan. Under Japanese historical conditions, the beginning of the revolution for bourgeois democracy was also and simultaneously the beginning of the proletarian revolution. To think at this point in terms of two stages was to court stagnation and defeat. There could be only one stage in the Japanese revolution, and the time had come for the proletarian class to strike for power.[43]

These concepts, quite naturally, were totally unacceptable to the Comintern, not only because they challenged Stalinism at certain crucial points, but also because they supported Trotsky's theories (although the *Rōnō* faction at no point made a conscious attempt to align itself with the Trotskyites). Nevertheless, at the very time when the Stalin–Trotsky struggle was at its climax, heresy of this type could not be permitted.

---

[43] For significant *Rōnō* articles setting forth these themes, see Yamakawa, "Toward a United Political Front!" *Rōnō*, Vol. I, No. 1, December 1927, pp. 3–48; Nezu Yūjirō, "The Essence of Reactionary Antagonism and Its Direction—A Refutation of Mr. Abe's Theory," *ibid.*, pp. 49–59; and Inomata Tsunao, "The General Strategy of the Japanese Proletarian Class," *ibid.*, pp. 118–125.

As time passed, the *Rōnō* group gradually abandoned its efforts to obtain Soviet support. Indeed, by 1930 *Rōnō* writers had begun to criticize various Comintern positions. Now, this group saw themselves as an independent Communist faction without international ties *and* not under international discipline.[44]

It is vital to appreciate the role that the *Rōnō* group played, together with elements of the center, in transmitting to postwar Japan a staunch Marxist stance, but one unconnected with the Communist Party. Some of the most important roots of the postwar Japan Socialist Party were cultivated in that soil. Over time, *Rōnō* national (not nationalist) communism became in fact left socialism. Merging with centrist forces, the *Rōnō* element, together with some new forces, came to represent the mainstream of the postwar Socialist ideology.

Shortly after the reorganization of the Japanese Communist Party and the emergence of the *Rōnō* group, the first Diet elections to be held under the new universal manhood suffrage law were conducted on February 20, 1928. As noted earlier, four legal proletarian parties had entered the lists, with left hopes riding on the Labor-Farmer Party, which at this point was firmly under Communist control. The Hyōgikai ran some of its key personnel under Labor-Farmer banners, including Yamamoto Kenzō and Sugiura Keiichi, two well-known Communist leaders. Left candidates openly used such slogans as "Establish a Worker-Peasant Government!" and "Long Live the Dictatorship of the Proletariat!" Young Communist firebrands passed out handbills containing such statements as "Overthrow the Emperor System." At rallies and demonstrations, the language was often violent, and there were frequent clashes with the police.

In the 1928 election, the electorate suddenly jumped from three million to thirteen million.[45] All of the proletarian parties had campaigned vigorously. When the results were tabulated, the Social Mass Party had elected four of its nineteen candidates and received 128,908 votes or 6,784 votes per candidate. The Japan Farmers' Party did not elect any of its ten candidates and polled 36,491 votes, or 3,649 votes per candidate. The centrist Japan Labor-Farmer Party elected one of its fourteen candidates and polled 93,400 votes or 6,671 votes per candidate. The Labor-Farmer Party elected two of its forty candidates and obtained a total of 188,141 votes or 4,703 per candidate. One local proletarian

---

[44] For example, see an article by Arahata, "The Profintern's Criticism of the Japanese Labor Movement," *Rōnō*, Vol. IV, No. 9, November 1930, pp. 2–12.

[45] *Nihon rōdō nenkan*, 1929, gives the detailed election statistics, and subsequent issues of that yearly provide the materials for subsequent elections.

party candidate was elected, making a total of eight successful candidates and a total vote of about 470,000. Compared to the 4,274,898 votes cast for official Rikken Seiyūkai (Friends of Constitutional Government Party) candidates and the 4,201,219 votes cast for official Minseitō (Democratic Party) candidates, this was pitifully small, only 4.95 percent of the total vote.

The left, in the form of the Labor-Farmer Party, actually polled the highest number of votes among the proletarian parties, but it had also run the largest number of candidates, and its vote record per candidate was not equal to that of the moderates or centrists. Nevertheless, it elected two men to the Diet, one of whom, Yamamoto Senji, was a Communist. Communist—and proto-Communist—gains were not purchased without a price, however. This election brought the Communists very close to the surface of Japanese political life for the first time. Enthusiastic young radicals campaigned vigorously for Labor-Farmer Party candidates; thousands of handbills were distributed that openly proclaimed the Communist line; and certain individuals made scarcely any effort to hide their affiliations.

The far left was soon to pay heavily for this bravado. The government augmented its security forces, collected evidence, and compiled lists, and on March 15, less than one month after the election, rounded up some 1,200 individuals. Approximately 500 were kept in jail and prosecuted. These included almost all of the top Communist leaders. In a follow-up action, on April 10, the Home Minister ordered the dissolution of the Hyōgikai, the Labor-Farmer Party, and the Proletarian Youth League as Communist-front organizations.

The only Japanese Communist leaders available to reorganize the party after the mass arrests of March 15, 1928, were those who had been abroad at the time. Sano Manabu, Watanabe Masanosuke, Ichikawa, Yamamoto Kenzō, and Namba Hideo had been in Moscow as representatives to the 6th Comintern General Congress. In the fall of 1928, these men returned to Japan, except for Sano who was stationed in Shanghai with the Far Eastern Bureau.

Beginning in this period, the Japanese Communist Party was forced to draw its "leadership" from the students returning from Moscow.[46] As the veterans were decimated in repeated dragnet operations, no other

---

[46] An additional important source for this period is Kazama Jōkichi, *Moskō kyōsandaigaku no omoide* (*Memories of the Moscow Communist University*), Tōkyō, 1949. In English, see A. Rodger Swearingen and Paul F. Langer, *Red Flag in Japan: International Communism in Action, 1919–1951*, Cambridge, Massachusetts, 1952.

source of guidance existed. In the period between 1924 and 1928, some forty Japanese youths had studied at the Far Eastern Workers' Communist University in Moscow. They were first sent to Shanghai in groups of two or three. After making contact with the Bureau, they were transported to Vladivostok. Here, they often stayed at the International Seamen's Club for a short time and then took the Siberian railway to Moscow. Their course generally lasted a year, sometimes longer. When finished, they received final instructions from Comintern officials, including Katayama or, at a later point, Yamamoto Kenzō and Nosaka.

Few of these young men survived long once they returned to Japan. Almost without exception, they were caught by police within a few months and given long prison sentences. But with a steady trickle of Moscow returnees, it was always possible to launch a new effort. Thus, under the guidance of Ichikawa and Maniwa, a Communist Bureau was once again established in Tōkyō in November 1928, with a Central Committee containing several young students. By December, *Akahata* (*Red Flag*), the party organ, was once more being published. Cell organizations were activated, and a successor to the old Hyōgikai was established.

Within leftist ranks during this period, one critical issue was legalism versus illegalism. The Comintern-affiliated Communists fiercely opposed the establishment of a legal party that would drain energy or support from the Communist Party. The *Rōnō* faction, on the other hand, with certain other leftist elements, championed the creation of a legal left party. On July 22, 1928, only three months after the dissolution of the Labor-Farmer Party, they formed the Musan Taishūtō (Proletarian Mass Party), with Suzuki Mosaburō as Secretary General. A bitter struggle ensued to get the old Labor-Farmer Party members to join. The *Rōnō* faction was estimated by government sources to encompass about three-tenths of the left. The new party claimed about 2,500 members and in its declaration asserted that it would fight in determined fashion against both extreme left-wing sectarianism and right-wing disruptionism.

At the same time, a portion of the old Labor-Farmer group not affiliated with the *Rōnō* faction was attempting to reactivate that party. Ōyama Ikuo, former head of the party, had declared that even if the government banned the party one hundred times, the struggle to reestablish it should continue. Together with Kawakami Hajime and Hososako Kanemitsu, Ōyama persevered, and on December 22, 1928, a three-day conference to inaugurate the party was opened. After the first two days, the government decided that the party was intended to duplicate the old Labor-Farmer Party and ordered the conference to disband.

A few days earlier, on December 20, the *Rōnō*-sponsored Proletarian Mass Party had joined with centrist and right forces to organize the Japan Mass Party, but this party split within six months. Meanwhile the Ōyama group continued in its efforts. On November 2, 1929, the legalist faction of the old Labor-Farmer group headed by Ōyama and Hososako established the Rōnōtō (Labor-Farmer Party). It is interesting that throughout this period the Ōyama group was subjected to violent attacks by the Comintern-affiliated Communists for deserting their old ally, the Communist Party. Once again, the line was left, and the Communists were busily attacking even those on the left who refused to accept the new emphasis on illegal activity.

A similar situation developed within the labor movement. The Comintern order to maintain at all times both the Communist Party and its revolutionary adjuncts had to be obeyed. After the March arrests, some radicals had been released due to lack of evidence. In late April a few of these sought to set up a successor to the old Hyōgikai, but the police quickly banned the new organization and arrested its leaders. Then the left decided to begin with the establishment of district councils, with industrial unions from each area participating, and to establish a national federation later. These activities, however, were carried out by a handful of men, almost all of them Communists, and only at the underground level. Police surveillance was now intensive, and it was impossible for the Communists to develop any type of large-scale movement.

On December 25, 1928, the underground successor to the Hyōgikai was officially launched. Some thirty men, representing twenty-four unions, established a thirty-three-man National Committee and approved a set of policies and slogans. The new organization was called Nihon Rōdō Kumiai Zenkoku Kyōgikai (National Council of Japanese Labor Unions) or Zenkyō in abbreviated form.[47] With few exceptions the Zenkyō leaders were young men, either in their twenties or early thirties. They were "intellectuals" or, more properly, quasi-intellectuals who had had some higher schooling. There were a few

---

[47] For a detailed survey of Zenkyō leaders, see *Shakai ūndō no jōkyō* (*Conditions of the Social Movement*), 1931, pp. 202–206. This top-secret report put out yearly by the Home Ministry beginning with the 1927–1928 issue, is an invaluable source for detailed information on the prewar Communist movement.

bona fide workers, such as Zenno Zenshirō and Hosoya Matsuta, but this type was rare.

Naturally, almost all of the Zenkyō leaders were also members of the Japanese Communist Party, and many of them had been student-disciples of Fukumoto. Frequently, they had entered the party or the Communist Youth League while they were still students and were then assigned the task of working on the union front. Usually their careers were short, like those of the students returning from Moscow. After a few months, or a year at most, they were uncovered by the police, arrested, and given lengthy prison sentences. Thus, the leadership turn-over within all branches of the Japanese Communist movement was exceedingly high. To maintain continuity was impossible.

The initial membership of Zenkyō was only about 5,500, and no more than half of this membership could be considered politically alert and committed to Zenkyō policies. Thus the Communists were reaching only the tiniest fraction of the Japanese workers, not to mention other elements of Japanese society. But Zenkyō, unlike the Hyōgikai, made no attempt to hide its Communist position. On January 30, 1929, *Rōdō Shimbun-Zenkyō (Labor News)*, the Zenkyō organ, asserted: "In order to liberate the working class from the pits of oppression, to sub-jugate capitalism, and to realize communism, our Council must be under the political leadership of the Japanese Communist Party which is the organizational unit of the most advanced element of the Japanese proletariat and must protect the class character of left-wing union-ism."[48] This same article spelled out very clearly Communist policy toward the other socialist groups: "It is our duty to struggle against the Social Mass Party which mouths revolutionary terms and sells the workers out to the capitalists, and against the middle-road socialism of the Japan Mass Party and the deceit of its class plots. We must learn from the valuable experiences of the Russian labor unions led by the Bolsheviks."

Zenkyō, which was the most active organization controlled by the Communists in this period, was progressively pushed further to the extreme, perhaps as much by the course of events as by the youthful fervor of its leaders. Moreover, although the Comintern and Profintern were always prepared to criticize "left-extremism" in the aftermath of a failure to attain mass status, the policies that these two organizations advocated for Japan could not avoid leading the Japanese Communists precisely in that direction.

---

[48] Editorial, "Open the Struggle in the Large Factories and Mines Based upon Action Principles,' *Rōdō Shimbun–Zenkyō,* No. 3, January 30, 1929, p. 1.

As we have noted, the current Communist position was that a legal political party would be useless and harmful. The Zenkyō view of its own function was still another example of the extremist, unreal attitude being taken by the Japanese Communists. At the grass-roots level, Zenkyō cells were to be created in various factories, interconnected by means of a factory representative system. The basic objective was to point toward national strikes, but "for the moment" Zenkyō should concentrate on fomenting trouble in key industries and major cities. In this manner, the struggle against imperialism could be "carried on to the heart of the enemy."

For an organization with a national membership of less than 6,000, fewer than half of whom were truly "loyal," talk of a national strike was foolish. But even small groups can create trouble. Sabotage, local strikes, and demonstrations were all attempted. For example, power plant assault units and car destruction units were organized in connection with a Tōkyō Transport Workers' strike. At one point, an assassination squad was created, a band that was supposed to operate against spies and betrayers. An effort was also made to organize a self-defense force.

One cannot ignore the parallels between the Japanese and the Chinese Communist movements during this period, despite the striking differences in the two societies. In both cases, an era of substantial gains had been followed by sharp reverses. The Chinese Communists had made inroads into the heart of the power structure out of all proportion to their true strength during the period of their alliance with the Kuomintang. With the death of Sun Yat-sen, however, the key to the united front had been lost, and suddenly the Communists were isolated, with both the right and the center turning against them. The Comintern and, more particularly, Stalin had to find an explanation for the Chinese fiasco that would exempt Stalin and the international Communist movement from blame. The technique the Communists resorted to has become standard and, indeed, is one that has always had great political utility no matter what the cause: by first lashing out at the "right-wing opportunists" and then striking at the "left-wing adventurers," Comintern authority usurped the *center*. It did not matter, of course (except to those involved), that that center was a constantly shifting one, defined by the Comintern alone. Nor was it relevant (again, except to those involved) that Comintern policy had created, indeed demanded, policies that led to "right and left mistakes," as these were subsequently defined. From an impersonal perspective, the Comintern managed to find indigenous scapegoats in the process of correcting its errors and redefining its policies in the light of the continuously shifting dictates of Soviet national interest and international experience.

Thus, in the case of China, Ch'en Tu-hsiu symbolized the "liquidationists," the rightist element that misunderstood the appropriate character for a united front and undervalued the importance of a Communist party possessing complete sovereignty and integrity. That role in Japan was assumed by Yamakawa and his followers. On the "left" came men like Ch'ü Ch'iu-pai and Li Li-san, both of whom thought they had correctly interpreted Comintern directives for vigor and militance, and whose primary guilt lay *in failure itself,* for which the Comintern could not possibly take responsibility. The Fukumotoists had to assume that role in Japan. Consequently, as the third decade of the twentieth century came to a close, the Communist movement in both China and Japan was in an unprecedented stage of retreat, confusion, and despair.

China, unlike Japan, however, provided certain physical and political conditions for "rest and recuperation." Thus, a man like Mao Tse-tung could retreat to the interior, take advantage of the great mountainous regions of Kiangsi, and build a base that depended more on grass-roots organization and power, and less on the latest Comintern directives. No such opportunity existed for the Japanese Communists. The Japanese Alps afforded neither the possibilities of defense in depth nor the vast areas in which to develop a science of guerrilla warfare. There was an enormous difference, moreover, in the nature of the "enemy." As we have noted, the Japanese government was not only stable in terms of having the overwhelming support of its people, but it also had a very high level of police and military efficiency. Thus, each successive wave of Communist leadership was wiped out long before it had managed to acquire the experience and acceptance that are so necessary if a movement is to be successful.

Although circumstances within China and Japan were greatly different for the Communists, the external pressures that influenced them, and the broad surge of Comintern policy, were similar. With limited knowledge of actual conditions in the Far East, Comintern authorities were establishing policy lines and demanding that the branches of their organization pursue these lines, whatever the cost. Comintern policies should not necessarily be characterized as wrong, but rather as involving certain clear paradoxes that could not be resolved: the paradox between the high premium on a united front and the constant emphasis on struggling for control of the proletarian movement, a struggle that tended to make the social democrats the most deadly enemies; the paradox between the emphasis on completing the "bour-geois democratic" stage of the revolution and the insistence on a militant, revolutionary ideology and program; the paradox between the emphasis on capturing and using the nationalist movement and the demand for absolute obedience to the directives of the Comintern. These and other paradoxes affected the entire Asian Communist movement, as did the basic pendulum-like swing within the Comintern from modera-tion toward radicalism, and back.

Thus, the tendency toward "left extremism" continued within Jap-anese Communist ranks after 1928.[49] In answer, the government tightened its surveillance and its repression. There were now spies in almost every branch of Communist Party operations. And one arrest could lead to another. When a prominent JCP member from Tōkyō was arrested on March 18, 1929, the Tōkyō district party organization chart was found in his home. A week later this lead brought about the arrest of Maniwa, top party leader, and with him the entire party roster was found. The roster was in code, but the key to the code was broken. The mass arrests of April 16 followed, in which practically every party member in Japan was picked up. On June 16, Sano Manabu was cap-tured in Shanghai, having been lured into a rendezvous without know-ing that the party code had been compromised.

Once again, the Communist Party of Japan had been wiped out. Among the top leaders, only Yamamoto Kenzō, ill in Moscow, remained outside prison. Thus, the party had to be restored by completely in-experienced and newly recruited youth. The succeeding period has been called the era of the armed Communist Party, a period of extreme leftism. In July 1929, the Communist Party Bureau was reestablished by Tanaka Seigen, Zennō Zenshirō, and Sano Hiroshi. Tanaka was made Chairman. District Committees were gradually set up in the lead-ing metropolitan areas, and in January 1930 a national meeting was held in Wakayama Prefecture.

Under the conditions of severe repression that now prevailed, many radicals favored party dissolution. As a result of amendments to the Peace Preservation Law, Communist leaders could be sentenced to death, and even for passing out Communist handbills the sentence was often seven years. Not to carry or send documents became basic, and at one point the code used for communicating with the Shanghai Bureau

---

[49] For an account of this period by a Communist leader, see Tanaka Seigen, "The Era of the Armed Communist Party, *Bungei Shunjū* (*Spring and Autumn Culture*), Vol. 28, No. 7, June 1950, pp. 188–203.

was carried in the muzzle of a pistol. Members talked of suicide rather than allowing themselves to be captured. It was truly an era of desperation. All the leaders carried pistols, furnished by foreign seamen who were Communists and were acting as couriers. Pitched battles with police were fought; arson, sabotage, and all forms of violence were used.

The conditions were also reflected in Zenkyō, as we have noted. In the April 1929 arrests, eighty-one top Zenkyō men were arrested and for a time the union was forced into almost complete inactivity. Reorganization took place, but the union was faced with internal dissension in its own top ranks by mid-1929. Ultimately, in mid-1930, the internal conflict was placed before the 5th Profintern meetings in Moscow, with both factions having representatives present. In its resolution on Japan, the Profintern was strongly critical of certain aspects of Zenkyō policy—its proclivity toward "ultra-leftism," and the lack of "democratic centralism" that had characterized the leaders' handling of the factional problem. At the same time, the minority faction was ordered to dissolve, an action that it took formally in November.

Internal factionalism was not the only problem faced by the Communists in this period. Toward the 1930 Diet election, the Communist Party and Zenkyō took a very radical position. The goal, announced Zenkyō's *Labor News,* was not to capture the Diet but to destroy it. Leaflets were distributed and speeches made "so that the workers would come to know the reactionary character of the Diet and the ideology of the Soviet Union." This flurry of activity naturally produced more arrests. The prevailing Communist theme now was "the united front from below," a theme in line with current Comintern instructions. Using the Profintern slogan "To the factories!," Zenkyō organizers sought to create cells in strategic plants, particularly munitions factories. Special attention was also given to Korean workers, and a Korean Committee was established within the union.

During this period, however, there were recurrent rumors of scandal within top Zenkyō and Communist echelons: the squandering of funds at houses of prostitution, and the "selling out" to management or the police. The personal indiscretions of some of the young leaders appeared to parallel their political immaturity. Meanwhile, bloodshed and the arrests continued. The Wakayama meeting of the party was followed by arrests in February. An organization was reestablished in July 1930, but before the month was over, the key leaders were in prison. Only one young man was left among the Central Committeemen, so thorough had been the dragnet. He eventually fled to Moscow to report the sad state of affairs to Yamamoto Kenzō and Nosaka. (Nosaka, released from prison for medical treatment, had tricked the police and managed to escape abroad, reaching Moscow in March 1931.)

Meanwhile, in December 1930, another young worker, Kazama Jōki-chi, arrived in Japan from Moscow with instructions to rebuild the party. Together with Matsumura Noboru, he managed to set up a party headquarters in August 1931, and immediately a new political thesis for the party was issued. The 1931 Draft Thesis sought to take account of the criticisms made against the 1927 Thesis at the 10th Comintern meetings of 1929, criticisms that were subsequently reiterated in private meetings between Japanese and Comintern Communists in Moscow. Bukharin, the primary author of the 1927 Thesis, had been purged. The Russian *eminence grise* of the Asian Communist movement had been liquidated, an event that made an attack on his earlier analyses of "the Japan problem" easier, indeed, essential.

In certain respects, the 1931 Draft Thesis was surprisingly close to the *Rōnō* position.[50] Viewing Japanese capitalism as relatively mature and possessing only minor feudal elements, the 1931 Thesis defined the character of "the coming revolution" in Japan as "a proletarian revolution which carries with it a wide range of tasks belonging to a bourgeois democratic revolution." If this was a compromise, it strongly suggested the possibility of a one-stage, hybrid revolution.

The stress on a worker-peasant alliance and a united front against imperialism under proletarian leadership was strong. The present goal was defined as the overthrow of the bourgeois-landlord coalition that took shelter under the Emperor system, and the establishment of a proletarian dictatorship.

The Comintern was strongly displeased with the 1931 Draft Thesis, despite the fact that Kazama and others believed that they were faithfully reproducing the Comintern views. The available evidence suggests that the Comintern itself, undergoing substantial changes during this period, had made a sudden shift on certain critical points. In any case, a new thesis was prepared in Moscow, with Nosaka playing some role in its preparation, and this draft was published in the spring of 1932.[51] The 1932 Thesis was to stand as the basic document for the Japanese Communist Party until 1946, and, even then, as we shall see, certain of its basic provisions were reiterated.

In the 1932 Thesis, the "Trotskyite error" of supporting a continuous,

---

[50] For the full 1931 Thesis, see Yamamoto and Arita, pp. 213ff.
[51] *Ibid.*, pp. 220–286.

one-stage revolution was strongly repudiated. The Japanese revolution had to be a two-stage process, with the first stage being the completion of the bourgeois-democratic revolution. Feudal remnants were still powerful, and these included an Emperor system that had to be crushed at all costs. The 1931 Draft, according to the 1932 Thesis, had placed insufficient emphasis on the role of the Emperor system as the dominant political force in Japan and also on the necessity for a thoroughgoing agrarian revolution. Throughout the new document, moreover, the language of militance predominated. Revolution required violence. Japanese imperialism could only be stopped by sacrifice and bloodshed.

Once again, in the fall of 1932, through an informer, the Japanese authorities were able to arrest almost all of the Communist Party members including Kazama, Konno Yojirō, and Iwata Yoshimichi. The fragments of the party were reassembled in January 1933 by another student sent from Moscow, Yamamoto Masami, but once again plans were rendered abortive by Yamamoto's arrest in May. Shortly thereafter, in the summer of 1933, two leading Japanese Communists, Sano Manabu and Nabeyama Sadachika, electrified the radical world by denouncing the Communist movement from their prison cells. The Sano-Nabeyama recantations, which were widely publicized, rested essentially on the charge that the international Communist movement was merely a vehicle for Russian national interests, and that the Japanese Communist Party had never been allowed to exercise any independence of judgment or freedom of action.

Both men proclaimed themselves still committed to the cause of socialism, but they announced that it would have to be a *Japanese* socialism, developed in accordance with the conditions prevailing in that society. A number of comrades followed Sano and Nabeyama in defecting from Communism, including Mitamura Shirō, Tanaka Seigen, and Kazama.

Now the nationalist tide was sweeping over Japan, and the swing was toward the right in all political circles. National socialism—expressed in many varieties—was the only form of socialism able to survive and grow in this era. Meanwhile, continuous arrests and serious internal friction reduced the Japanese Communists to a mere shadow. In late 1933, feuding within the tiny group reached a new height, with charges and countercharges concerning betrayals. Miyamoto Kenji, a Tōkyō University intellectual, served as Chairman of the Party Central Committee after the arrest of Noro Eitarō. He in turn was succeeded by Hakamada Satomi, a returned student. With Hakamada's arrest in early 1935, party activities practically ceased on an organized basis. Japanese

Communism, from this point until 1946, consisted mainly of secret thoughts nurtured in the minds of a few "true believers," most of whom were in prison.

How shall we summarize the prewar legacy that the Japanese Communist Party bequeathed to the postwar era? Perhaps the following factors stand out:

1. *A profound and continuous weakness that produced an unending series of frustrations and defeats.* The weaknesses of the prewar Japanese Communist Party stemmed from very basic causes. In the first place, the Japanese Communist movement was born too late for optimal results, given the evolution of its society. By the close of World War I, Japanese modernization was already well advanced. The nation-building process was nearly complete. Mass mobilization for various purposes of state had been accomplished. The transition from agrarian to industrial supremacy was currently taking place. Under a conservative elite, moreover, a number of traditional elements of Japanese society had been successfully adapted to the cause of modernity.

Thus, the Japanese Communist Party was not able to build on those great issues that inevitably penetrate to the very roots of late-developing societies in the first stages of "liberation" and modernization. The issues of nationalism, industrialization, science, and democracy had already been seized by others, notably an "enlightened," or at least modernized, conservative elite capable of keeping a firm rein on the processes and direction of change.

This fact is particularly clear with respect to nationalism. It is enormously significant that the Japanese Communists were unable to capture and use nationalism, but instead were forced to fight it because it was a deadly weapon in the hands of their opponents. Molded by the conservatives, Japanese nationalism had found its primary institutional-ideological expression in the Emperor system in this era. Japan, moreover, had been "liberated" from Western imperialism long before the Communists appeared on the scene, and nationalism was currently being used for expansionist purposes. Under certain circumstances, to be sure, Communists could have subscribed to the goal of "liberating Asia from Western imperialism," but not when the task lay with their bitter enemies, the Japanese military, and when the goal was also to smash communism.

This inability to utilize or combine with the nationalist movement naturally affected both the Communist ideological and programmatic positions. In one sense, the Japanese Communists were forced to be internationalists in the purest Marxist terms. Lacking any foundations in their own society, they had to think primarily in terms of the unfolding world revolution and place their supreme value in true proletarian solidarity. In practice, however, this had to be equated with Soviet national interests. Thus, the Japanese internationalists were involved in the paradox of having to become fervent Soviet nationalists.

Among the other factors contributing to the weakness of Japanese Communism, the power and efficiency of the Japanese state must certainly be underlined. The party, as we have repeatedly noted, had to operate under the gravest difficulties. In the first place, Japanese democracy in this era did not provide the political protection for the Communists that was available in certain Western societies. Civil liberties were limited by law, and despite liberal gains the authoritarian character of the state was still strong. Communism, by definition, was always an illegal activity in prewar Japan, and one subject to very heavy penalties.

State efficiency, moreover, was extraordinarily great when directed against radical movements. The centralized character of the Japanese state, its extensive public and secret police system, and the very nature of Japanese society made it possible for the authorities to wipe out the party time after time, as we have seen. Consequently, no continuity of leadership, no development of administrative experience, and no strong organizational fabric were possible.

Formal membership in the Japanese Communist Party never reached 1,000 in the prewar era. The party was always a tiny group of beleaguered individuals. It took great courage—and strong convictions—to remain a Communist in prewar Japan, and it involved in many cases a particular set of personal problems. One cannot always fathom the psychological motivations that may induce or compel an individual to participate in an extremist cause, but the compulsions that operate in totally alienated individuals are many and fierce. Many of these individuals are, in reality, substituting political action—often of the most daring type—for needed psychotherapy.

2. *Strong intellectual influence but increasing activist orientation in tune with the trend within the party toward extremism.* Throughout the prewar era, the role of intellectuals in the Japanese Communist Party was a vital one. The party, emerging in an era when the labor movement was still in its infancy, drew most of its leaders and many of its rank and file members from the ranks of students and mature intellectuals. Writers, artists, journalists, and academicians composed a significant portion of the party elite, and, even among Communist labor leaders, many in reality came from the intellectual class. In a number

of cases, however, the term "quasi-intellectual" would probably be more accurate. Generally, the Communist movement did not attract, or at least it did not hold, the top Japanese intelligentsia. Even when members of the intellectual inner circle were influenced by Marxism (and many were), they rarely became a part of the Japanese Communist Party. Communist intellectuals, with a few exceptions, were "second-rung" types, with the percentage of young students high.

Moreover, as the Japanese Communist Party came under the tighter control of the Soviet-dominated Comintern and diverged ever more from the trends of its own society, the academic Marxists withdrew. This left the more militant activist types in control, most of whom were young and inexperienced and often recent returnees from Soviet training, as we have noted. Continuity of leadership was impossible, and only a handful of veterans, most of whom were in prison, was in a position to claim authority at the conclusion of World War II.

3. *The adoption by the JCP, despite its total alienation from Japanese society, of certain structural characteristics of other Japanese social organizations, including the proclivities for factionalism.* The small leader-follower group so traditional to Japanese-style organization also played a significant role in the Japanese Communist movement. Rival leaders, each with his cluster of supporters, struggled for supremacy in battles that tested "loyalty," reciprocal obligations, and "superior-inferior ties," along with substantive policy differences. Sometimes, issues of loyalty were of equal or greater importance than issues of policy, a fact that frequently distressed outsiders such as the Comintern officials.

There was, however, a certain tendency for a division between the "intellectual" and the "pure labor" elements in the party, and periodically that division expressed itself in disputes over tactics or program. Regional factors also played a role in factional alignments. The rivalry between the Kantō area (Tōkyō and vicinity) and the Kansai area (Ōsaka-Kōbe-Kyōto) represented another source of Communist division. At no point in its prewar history was the Japanese Communist Party ever a tightly knit, monolithic organization dominated by one man. The Japanese oligarchic traditions penetrated even this citadel of iconoclasm, and always the party had its factions, feuds, and diversities.

4. *Continuous and extensive Soviet control over party leadership and basic policy, at least after 1924.* As we have seen, Comintern sources from the very beginning intervened repeatedly in the internal affairs of the Japanese Communist Party. Soviet funds and guidance created the party, and Soviet insistence, exercised through Voitinsky and

the Far Eastern Bureau, forced a reestablishment after the first major defeat. This pattern was to continue, as we have noted in detail, throughout the prewar era. Leaders were made and broken. Programs were drafted in accordance with current Comintern (Soviet) policies and altered as those policies changed.

As early as the mid-twenties, the Japanese Communist Party had had to face the charge that it was without any vestige of independence, an issue of critical importance to the Japanese left. The fact that as the prewar era was drawing to a close, individuals once prominent in the party were to echo that charge in the most devastating terms underlines the JCP problem. Japanese Communism, to be sure, represented one of the first movements to develop an "independent" or "national communism," strongly in evidence through the Yamakawa *Rōnō* group. But in this period, Moscow defined orthodoxy, and there was only *one* legitimate Communist Party, that dominated by the Soviet authorities. Consequently, most radicals could only accept foreign dictation for a certain period of time before rebelling. Echelon after echelon of young radicals moved into, or close to, the Japanese Communist Party only to march out in anger at some point, or be ousted because of a refusal to accept completely the latest party line.

This was the legacy that prewar communism bequeathed to the post-World War II era. It is now appropriate to explore how this legacy was continued or altered, and how it affected the initial efforts of the party after a war that had seen the Japanese conservative forces decisively defeated.

II

MAKING COMMUNISM LOVABLE: THE INITIAL TACTICS OF THE POSTWAR JAPANESE COMMUNIST PARTY

The reestablishment of the Japanese Communist Party began shortly after the Occupation era opened. On October 4, 1945, SCAP (Supreme Commander of the Allied Powers) ordered that all political prisoners be released. Six days later, a small band of Communists, some of whom had been imprisoned for nearly two decades, were freed. They began political activities immediately, with Tokuda Kyūichi and Shiga Yoshio playing leading roles.

In the first issue of *Akahata* (*Red Flag*) published after World War II, Tokuda, Shiga, and other released Communist prisoners issued an "Appeal to the People," dated October 10, 1945. In it the following themes were advanced:

1. Gratitude for the opening of the "democratic revolution" in Japan as a result of the Allied Occupation, and "enthusiastic support" for the peace policy of the United States, the United Kingdom, and the other Allied Powers.

2. A pledge to overthrow the Emperor system—described as a combination of the Emperor and his court, the military and the administrative bureaucrats, the nobility, the absentee landlords, and the monopoly capitalists—and to establish a People's Democracy.

3. Promises to eliminate militarism and police politics, to confiscate "parasitic" and idle land, distributing it to the peasants, to establish free

labor unions, to abolish the old security laws, to remove the military and bureaucratic cliques from power, and to set up a national assembly based on universal suffrage for all Japanese over eighteen years of age.

4. An attack on "phony liberals" and "pseudo-socialists" who had supported the Emperor system, declaring them unfit for leadership.

5. A call for the creation of a united front under *Japanese Communist Party leadership* of all those who shared the above objectives.[1]

Accompanying the appeal was an article[2] setting forth the new JCP line. It began with a vitriolic attack on the Socialist Party for its support of cooperatives and the Emperor system. In the extreme language so typical of their prewar approach to the Socialists, the Communists denounced the Socialist idea of cooperatives as a "scheme of state organization on behalf of monopoly capitalists," Fascist in character. They also alleged that the Socialists were dreaming of recasting the Emperor system so that it could have global implications, a dream not basically different from that of the old military clique. The Socialist Party, they charged, was really "the Social Emperor Party," and "the budding of Fascism" out of this group had to be noted. They stated that because the primary theme of the Socialists was the protection of the Emperor system, the Communists could not form a united front with them. At the same time, it would be wrong merely to exclude and ignore them. The party had to be subverted from within. Antileader, anticollaborator factions had to be built, factions that could then be united with the external masses.

Thus, the Japanese Communist Party started the postwar era with the paradox that was consistently to plague it. On the one hand, it was committed to a united front; on the other hand, it could not forbear a vicious assault on the very elements with which it was supposed to cooperate. The compromise, of course, was to seek a united front from below—a direct appeal to the masses over the heads of their leaders. Periodically, however, the JCP was forced to realize that without the cooperation of Socialist leaders, the chances for success were slim.

Naturally, the assault on the Liberal Party in the *Akahata* article was at least equally extreme. The Liberals were denounced as "unscrupulous reactionaries" and "lackeys of the monopoly capitalists." Again, the JCP urged a resolute struggle, although admitting that temporary unity with the Liberals against the military clique and the bureaucrats might be desirable.

---

[1] See *Akahata*, No. 1, October 20, 1945, p. 1. (Emphasis is the author's.)
[2] "On the New Line of Struggle—What the New Situation Demands of Us," *Akahata*, No. 1, October 20, 1945 p. 1.

In his speech at a welcome rally for released comrades on October 19, Tokuda also stressed the theme that the Emperor system had been responsible for the war. He asserted that the Emperor, the bureaucrats, the gigantic monopoly capitalists, and the hoodlums were busily engaged in seeking to escape punishment as war criminals and meanwhile were stealing the remaining food and daily necessities from the people. The militarists also were secretly hoarding weapons and continuing to drill, pretending that they were engaged in shrine worship. They regarded the Allied Powers as the enemy and were plotting a revenge war. Tokuda then made certain specific proposals: The Japanese people— including all Communists—should cooperate with the liberation army of the Allied Powers to overthrow the Emperor system and establish a People's Democracy. At once, moreover, the people should take over the control and management of food and other goods in storage; manage the industries now being sabotaged by the capitalists; distribute the land of the Emperor, absentee landlords, and the rich farmers to the poor peasants through farmers' committees composed of all farmers except the absentee landlords and rich farmers; and develop a popular front based on these principles. "If the Socialist Party cannot accept these proposals," asserted Tokuda, "it means that they are seeking political power by trying to deceive the Japanese people."[3]

The initial program of the Japanese Communist Party had been fashioned by early 1946. At first, the veteran Communists, out of touch with the world for many years, showed some uncertainties. Two initial meetings mirrored these uncertainties, a National Conference held on November 8, 1945, and the first postwar Party Congress, labeled the 4th Congress to indicate a continuity with the prewar era, held on December 1–2, 1945.

The essence of the program adopted at the 4th National Congress was as follows: A democratic revolution was sweeping over the world as a result of the defeat of Germany and Japan. At home, the main problems lay in the iniquities of the Emperor, the military clique, the bureaucrats, the *zaibatsu,* the landlords, and their chief agents. These evil forces were being resolutely opposed by the Allied Powers who were promoting a democratic revolution in Japan. Thus, the Japanese Communist Party should direct its primary attacks against the traditionalist forces, many of whom were trying to sabotage production. The immediate task of the workers was to manage industry so as to produce the vital necessities for the Japanese people and to render full support to the Allied Powers.

---

[3] For Tokuda's speech, see *Akahata,* November 7, 1945, p. 1.

Reactionaries were slandering the JCP, stating that it plotted a violent revolution under the auspices of the Soviet Union. In fact, the Communist Party was the only political force proposing measures for the stabilization of the people's livelihood. Were it not for the JCP, the Japanese government would violently suppress the masses in collaboration with the militarists and hoodlums.

The urgent task of the Japanese Communist Party was to develop a mass base, concentrating on the industrial worker. Thus, primary attention had to be focused on the labor unions, with the development of *one* massive industrial-type union as the first major Communist goal. Meanwhile, farmers' committees should be organized to deal with problems of food and village administration. These committees should include tenants, part-tenants, and owner-cultivators, thereby combining poor and middle-class farmers for the purposes of a popular front and the democratic revolution.

Women should not be organized separately, but as a part of workplace units, factory cells. Strong emphasis should be placed on youth activities since "to win youth is to win the future." The Communist Youth League should concentrate on recruiting youth above the age of fourteen and developing itself into a mass organization. Special attention should also be paid to the unemployed, and to the ex-soldiers, at home and abroad. Repatriation had not been solved because the Japanese government was "lazy and sly" and "not well trusted by the Allies." (Already, repatriation was a thorny problem for the Communists, as a result of Soviet policy.)

The present rationing system should be replaced with a democratic delivery system operated through farmers' committees and should be controlled by the people. The recovery of small and medium business had to be encouraged, with continuous efforts being made to prevent the reestablishment of the zaibatsu. "At present," stated the 4th Congress Report, "we do not advocate the nationalization of land." The farmers wanted land, and the properties of the absentee landlords and other parasites should be distributed to them. Urban housing should also be treated as a major problem, with military camps, factory dormitories, and big estates being "liberated" for use by the dispossessed.

Regarding constitutionalism, the Japanese Communist Party would oppose amendments by the Emperor and the bureaucrats "designed to preserve their privileges." A new Constitution should be enacted by a democratic Diet. It should provide for popular sovereignty; universal suffrage by all citizens over eighteen years of age; the establishment of a government responsible to the Diet; a fully elected Diet, accountable to the people; full political, economic, and social freedom for the people, with guarantees for popular livelihood and education; and the complete elimination of class and ethnic distinctions.

The 4th Congress Report admitted that some people had been bitter about the sharp attack on Socialist Party leaders in the first issue of *Akahata*, but it defended that attack on the grounds that, contrary to the situation in Europe, the Socialists of Japan had collaborated with militarism. Only the Communist Party of Japan had consistently fought against "the criminal war." Hence, the conditions of forming popular fronts in Europe and Japan could not be the same. It was essential in Japan to clarify the facts. *However,* the Communist Party should not be narrow-minded. A wide popular front had to be accepted if the democratic revolution were to be realized. For example, almost all political elements other than the Communists were opposed to the abolition of the Emperor system. Although a thorough completion of the democratic revolution was impossible without the overthrow of the Emperor system, the Communists should cooperate with groups that partially accepted the popular front program, even if they did not accept it entirely.[4]

The 4th Congress Report illustrated the strong, continuing influence of the 1932 Thesis and the JCP tactical line of the prewar era. It was natural that leaders who had been in prison for fifteen or eighteen years would tend to pick up where they had left off. The one issue that presented internal problems for the party was that of the tactics of the united front, especially the question of how to handle the Socialists and the thorny issue of the Emperor system. The initial, strongly "left" line was questioned by some party members.

Top party leaders, however, continued to be adamant on the subject of the Emperor in this early period. For example, Shiga, in a speech of early December 1945 before the People's assembly for the Prosecution of War Criminals, referred to the Emperor as the top war criminal, insisting that unless he and his associates were eliminated, Japanese democratization and the participation of Japan in international peace organizations would be impossible. Shiga also denounced as "fakery" the efforts to absolve the Emperor from responsibility for the war and to credit him with the surrender. He saw the Emperor system as likely to be revived in its old forms by the militarists if it were not totally dismantled.[5]

---

[4] For the 4th Congress Report, see *Akahata*, December 6, 1945, p. 1. For the earlier National Conference resolutions, see *ibid.*, November 22, 1945, p. 1.

[5] For Shiga's speech, see *Akahata*, December 19, 1945, p. 1.

By early 1946, however, the Japanese Communist Party had established its major themes more confidently. On January 10, Nosaka had returned to Japan after fourteen years in exile, the last five having been spent in Yenan. The very timing of the 5th Party Congress, held in February, indicates the significance of his return. Armed with the latest concepts from Moscow and Yenan, Nosaka quickly assumed a leading role in policy formation.

On January 14, 1946, Nosaka and the Central Committee on the party issued a joint statement in which a new tone and certain new emphases were to be discerned, reflective of influences from Yenan.[6] All parties were "in perfect agreement" that the Emperor system had to be overthrown if world peace were to be achieved and the Japanese nation were to be reconstructed. The abolition of the Emperor system, however, referred to the destruction of an institution. The question of the maintenance of the Imperial family was a separate matter, to be determined by the will of the nation.

According to the statement, the Communist Party, unlike those elements interested only in their own status and privileges, was deeply concerned about mass welfare, evidence of its deep love for the nation. To accomplish common objectives, all true democrats should join together, forming a united front based on a program mutually acceptable to every one of the participants. Such a front did not require a complete uniformity of views, however. Each party should be allowed to develop its own position freely, without external dictation. Compromises could be effected for united front purposes when necessary. Mutual criticisms of the positions of other parties, of course, were also permissible if they were based on a true fraternal spirit.

Clearly, a strong new wind was now blowing, despite the fact that the substantive changes of policy were not major ones. The era of making the JCP "lovable" and of attuning it to patriotism—to a new nationalism—had begun. Both of these developments were closely connected with the stimulus provided by the Chinese Communist example. Chinese influence on the Japanese Communist Party, in certain respects, can be dated from January 1946.

What was the basic Japanese Communist Party program at this time? In this period, as in subsequent ones, critical issues for Japanese Communism could be subsumed under three major questions. First, what attitude should be taken toward the American Occupation and U.S. policies? Second, what form should the Japanese revolution take—

---

[6] For the joint statement, see *Akahata,* January 22, 1946, p. 1.

what should be its stages and goals? Finally, what were the appropriate tactics for revolution? These three questions contain the fundamental issues that have occupied the Japanese Communist Party during the past twenty years. Let us begin by noting the positions taken at the outset of the postwar era, by the time of the 5th Party Congress.

The first and perhaps the most fundamental decision was to regard the American Occupation as a liberation force and to seek cooperation with it. That position was taken at the very outset. In their opening statements, the released Communists welcomed the Americans as liberators, depicted the future in hopeful terms, and pledged full support for Occupation objectives. The Tokuda and Nosaka reports to the 5th Party Congress reiterated these positions.[7] The Allied Powers, Nosaka asserted, had not come to colonize Japan, nor would they stay long in the country. They had promised that when Japan became a truly peaceful and democratic society, they would depart. Moreover, the four countries jointly administering Japan were all democratic nations.

Both the Tokuda and Nosaka reports had important nuances. The strong emphasis on "joint occupation," a condition not existing in fact, was an attempt to uphold the Soviet role and support certain restraints on SCAP power. Nor was the analysis of the United States wholly favorable. Seeking to prove that world capitalism and imperialism had been greatly weakened by the war, Nosaka asserted that whereas there had been six imperialist nations before the war, only two remained at present, and one of these, Great Britain, had been severely reduced in power. Only America represented a stronghold of capitalism.

There can be no doubt, however, of the main thrust of these reports or of the official JCP policy regarding the Occupation. In tactical terms, SCAP was a part of the "progressive" bourgeoisie that had the historic function of completing the bourgeois-democratic revolution in Japan. Indeed, it might be argued from the events that were transpiring that SCAP represented the first and only powerful "progressive" bourgeois force in Japanese history. The weakness of the democratic elements in prewar Japan and the extensive "feudal remnants" involved in Japanese capitalism had been a source of constant frustration to the Communists.

---

[7] The April 1–15, 1946 issue of *Zenei* was devoted exclusively to the party leaders' speeches and reports at the 5th Party Congress, held February 24–26, and all references to them are taken from that source. The general report, delivered by Tokuda, appears on pages 2–13. The report on the Party Declaration by Nosaka, and the Declaration itself, are printed on pages 14–21, with a separate brief statement on the united front by Nosaka on pages 21–22. Other speeches include those of Shiga, Miyamoto Kenji, Hakamada Satomi, and Itō Ritsu.

A united front with such elements had been impossible. Only with the "petite bourgeoisie"—the intellectuals—had any rapport been achieved. Now, however, as the Communists saw it, a true bourgeois force, albeit a foreign one, had come into power. *Under its aegis, the first major stage of the democratic revolution could be rapidly advanced.*

There were a few JCP members who found this thesis difficult to accept. The sustained threat from fascist or militarist quarters in the prewar era had not prevented Japanese Communists from viewing the Western "capitalist" societies, including the United States, as "imperialist forces." It was not easy to reorient one's thinking at this point, even for tactical purposes. Japanese radicalism of every type, moreover, harbored some anti-Western sentiment; and the Communist movement was no exception. Thus, when the new position on the United States was first outlined, some reservations and unhappiness were expressed. In an effort to meet such criticisms, both Tokuda and Nosaka, in their reports to the 5th Party Congress, stressed what they hoped would be the enhanced role of the Allied Council. The involvement of the Soviet Union, China, and Great Britain in Occupation decisions, asserted Tokuda, would permit the introduction of "world democratic policies."

The great majority of JCP members, however, had no difficulty in following the new line. Practical considerations powerfully buttressed (and, indeed, guided) ideological ones. The international situation was still reasonably favorable. The Soviet Union and the United States had been wartime allies, and whereas certain clouds had already appeared on the horizon, the atmosphere created at Cairo and Yalta had not completely disappeared. The united front of the international "democratic forces" still appeared to be a viable idea. Even the Chinese Communists were indicating a willingness to accept American mediation in the tangled Chinese political situation. On the domestic front, the Japanese Communists had been liberated in a very literal sense by American forces, and SCAP for the foreseeable future would determine the fate of the Japanese Communist Party, as well as that of all other political groups in Japan. To attack the Occupation would represent an act of political suicide. And for what? Currently, SCAP was dedicated to two primary objectives: punishment and reform—the destruction of Japanese militarism and the democratization of Japanese society. The Japanese Communists had absolutely no difficulties in supporting those objectives, as far as they went.

Connected with the issue of the American Occupation was the question of what type of revolution the Japanese Communist Party should seek. Here, the official party position drew heavily on prewar ideology.

Taking their stand with the two-stage revolution, party spokesmen firmly asserted that the immediate task was the completion of the bourgeois-democratic revolution. Nosaka opened his report to the 5th Congress with a discussion of this matter. Prior to the Thesis of 1932, he started, Japan had been defined as a mature capitalist state in the same category as Great Britain and the United States. As a result, the call had been for a proletarian revolution. The purpose of the 1932 Thesis, said Nosaka, was to crush this Trotskyite error. The correct position was that Japan was a highly developed capitalist state with many feudal remnants. Consequently, it was necessary to complete the bourgeois-democratic revolution before proceeding to socialism.

This portion of the 1932 Thesis was staunchly upheld by a majority of the postwar Communist leaders. The immediate tasks before the party were thus defined largely in "bourgeois-democratic" terms: elimination of the Emperor system; land reform; basic improvements in the conditions of the workers; and full civil liberties guaranteed by a democratic Constitution. It was made clear, however, that the party had an obligation to prepare the way for the transition to socialism even while pursuing bourgeois-democratic goals.

Having defined the character of the revolution, Japanese Communist Party leaders turned next to the question of tactics. On this point, a new position was taken, that of espousing "peaceful revolution." Once again, Nosaka's report to the 5th Party Congress is revealing. Admitting that the 1932 Thesis had advocated the tactics of violence as the necessary and proper revolutionary technique, Nosaka insisted that the new situation with which the party found itself demanded new tactics. What was the new situation? World capitalism and imperialism had been greatly weakened, whereas socialist strength was rising. Military and police power at home had been crushed. The conservatives could be brought down by political activity, since their sources of support, including the monopoly capitalists, had been undermined. Japan now had freedom, and the "progressive" forces, including the Communist Party, could speak freely. Conditions in Japan were thus vastly different from those in the age of Lenin.

Even Lenin, however, had asserted that power could be won by peaceful means, stated Nosaka. The main point to emphasize was that peaceful revolution did not mean mere parliamentarism, he insisted. The Communist Party would naturally contest for political office. But it would also be a revolutionary party, fighting militantly against its enemies, operating through mass organizations, using a variety of techniques to educate and lead the people.

The basic tactic of the "peaceful revolution" was that of the united front. It was essential to unify the workers, peasants, and "progressive" bourgeoisie under the leadership of the working class and its vanguard party, the Communist Party. Expressed in political terms, this meant a union between the Communist and Socialist parties. Nosaka confidently predicted that the right-wing Socialists would probably become a bourgeois party, while the left wing would join the Communists.

This initial policy of the Japanese Communist Party, first spelled out in detail in early 1946, remained the basic Communist policy until 1950, although some adjustments were made at the time of the 6th Party Congress in December 1947.[8] That Congress, which opened on December 21, faced a very different world—and an equally different Japan—from that which had existed two years earlier. The international "united front" had been completely broken. Relations between the United States and the Soviet Union had steadily deteriorated. In the Far East, conflict over policies toward Korea and Japan had become intense, matching the grave problems in Europe. In September 1947, less than three months prior to the 6th Congress, Andrei Zhdanov had delivered his famous "two camps" speech, signaling a major Soviet policy change.[9] Clearly, the Zhdanov speech would have to be translated into global Communist policy, and now a new international organization, the Cominform, existed to coordinate and enforce policy decisions within the Communist world.

The Chinese Communists, scenting victory, had begun a hard-line policy toward the United States, leveling their guns not only at the Kuomintang but also at America. Thus Sino–Soviet pressures on behalf of Communist militancy throughout the world were mounting. The cold war had begun, and no Communist party would be allowed to forget that fact.

In Japan the situation was also substantially changed. The era of punishment and reform was drawing to a close, and SCAP emphasis was

---

[8] The April 1948 issue of *Zenei* was devoted to the speeches of Tokuda, Nosaka, and other JCP leaders at the 6th Party Congress, and all references to those speeches are taken from that source.

[9] Zhdanov's report, delivered at the founding meeting of the Cominform in Poland at the end of September 1947, was published in *For a Lasting Peace, For a People's Democracy!*, November 10, 1947, pp. 2–4, under the title "The International Situation." On October 19, 1947, incidentally, *Akahata* carried a Japanese translation of a *Pravda* editorial stressing the independence and sovereignty of each Communist party. According to the editorial, the dissolution of the Comintern had placed the responsibility of carrying the fight against imperialism and the right-wing social democrats in the hands of each individual Communist party.

now on reconstruction and stabilization. The political trend had been to the left, and indeed a Socialist-Democratic coalition government, headed by Socialist Katayama Tetsu, had just come to power. But as we shall note later, the Communist Party had suffered several notable failures and was far from its projected goals. Moreover, there were already indications that the political orientation of SCAP would be increasingly conservative. SCAP reforms had encompassed a wide range of problems and had truly changed the sociopolitical outlook for the Japanese nation. Many reforms had been radical, and their general thrust had been of assistance to the left, although they had robbed that left of certain issues. Now, however, with the emphasis on reconstruction, SCAP was likely to turn toward the conservatives, particularly because there was no long-range basis for an alliance between SCAP and the Japanese "progressives," especially the more radical segment.

Not all of these facts were clear at the end of 1947, but most of the trends indicated above had been established. Why then did the program adopted in December 1947 by the Japanese Communist Party not take fuller account of them? Obviously, the Japanese Communists faced a serious dilemma. SCAP remained the only political-military force of consequence in Japan. To break sharply with the Occupation, or even to criticize it in serious fashion, was to court destruction. The party had profited greatly from its legal status, despite its various failures and party leaders had no desire to return to the underground to which they had been confined for twenty-three long years. The tactics of peaceful revolution, moreover, had paid dividends. In every sense, the party was far stronger than it had been at any time in its history, and most leaders were optimistic about the future.

Thus, the 6th Congress program represented no basic shift in tactics or policies. Clearly, SCAP was now regarded with suspicion, even hostility, but there was no attempt to deal openly with the problem of "American imperialism." Communist speakers contented themselves with rather vague references to ties between domestic reactionaries and certain international forces, and to the means for attaining and enforcing the complete independence of Japan. Various disparaging remarks were also made about the SCAP reform program. On the whole, however, the Japanese Communist Party treated the American issue with the greatest caution. An attack was being mounted, but it was still veiled.[10]

---

[10] Typical of the handling of SCAP was Miyamoto's assertion that certain points, such as "the economic recovery of the people and *the complete independence of Japan*," along with "the defense of world peace and the elimination of war agitators," had to be reemphasized in the light of the events of the past two years. "On the Amendment of the Action Program, *Zenei*, April 1, 1948, pp. 21–22 (emphasis supplied).

The previous positions of the party on the nature of the revolution and the appropriate revolutionary tactics were staunchly defended. Nosaka, in his report to the 6th Party Congress, admitted that these positions had met with internal criticism. Indeed, he proceeded to outline two "erroneous" theories. One viewpoint, he announced, was that the democratic revolution had already been completed in Japan, and that the Communist revolution must therefore be a socialist or proletarian revolution. Another opinion was that the changes of the last two years had not really had much influence in eradicating feudalism, and that the 1932 Thesis was therefore fully applicable.

The first position, held by Comrade Nakanishi Kō and others, if adopted would result in failure, Nosaka insisted. It would force the party to attack all capitalist forces within Japanese society and to rely solely on the workers and poor peasants. The middle-class and rich peasants, along with all segments of the bourgeoisie, would drop out of the Communist camp. The Communist Party would be split and weakened, while the enemy camp would become strong. The basic question was a tactical one: "When and how do we defeat our various enemies?" At this stage, Nosaka argued, it was imperative for the Japanese Communist Party to appeal broadly to the whole of the peasantry, to the medium and small businessmen, to the petite bourgeoisie, and to all of those who would fight for national independence.

The Japanese Communist Party, he asserted, should be a party of one million, firmly rooted in mass support. When the peace treaty was finally concluded, he argued, major political changes would occur. The critical issue would then become who would head the masses and who could enforce the Potsdam Treaty and the complete independence of Japan.

In defense of the current tactical and strategic lines of the party, Nosaka offered the following analysis of the domestic situation: Japan's democratic revolution had been produced essentially from outside and above, although the support of the Japanese masses should not be ignored nor the role of any given foreign power overly stressed. Revolution was incomplete and inadequate in a number of respects. Militarism, feudalism, and the old Emperor system had suffered heavy blows, but three important forces in Japanese society remained a serious threat: the Emperor-oriented bureaucracy, the exploitative rural elite, and the monopoly capitalists. If these forces were to gain in strength and further develop their international ties, they might be able to defeat the democratic revolutions. Hence, the elimination of the old forces around the bureaucracy was the first task of the revolution at this point. It was particularly important to break the power of the rural gentry and the urban monopoly capitalists. By undertaking this task, the party would be completing the bourgeois-democratic revolution *and* carrying out the transitional tasks of the socialist revolution.[11]

In the light of international developments, the issue of "peaceful revolution" undoubtedly caused deep concern among party leaders. Nosaka's defense of this tactic was firm, but his choice of words indicated some shift in interpretation and emphasis. Certain individuals, he asserted, regarded peaceful revolution as a new form of revolution, not conceived by Lenin and Stalin. This was false. Peaceful revolution implied *the possibility* of the peaceful development of revolution, not a new form of revolution. It was no more than a tactic that might change as the objective and subjective conditions changed. But at this point, it was the appropriate tactic for the Japanese Communist Party.

As one reviews the documents and events surrounding the 6th JCP Congress, several points become clear. First, while holding to the basic positions enunciated earlier, party leaders were engaged in a modest but meaningful shift toward the "left" in response to the global and domestic changes of recent months. Party policy, however, still failed to reflect the sharply militant tactics being advanced by Moscow. It is also apparent that factional groups within the Japanese Communist Party, always existent, were now beginning to focus on the gap between Yoyogi[12] and the Kremlin. Nevertheless, the Mainstream leaders continued the same basic policies for another two years, until a public attack from Cominform headquarters forced major changes.

On January 6, 1950, the Cominform organ, *For a Lasting Peace, For*

---

[11] Tokuda's report supplemented and reenforced the Nosaka themes. Spending most of his time on an analysis of the internal situation, Tokuda argued that the SCAP-sponsored democratic reforms were in many cases superficial and inadequate. The zaibatsu were already in the process of regrouping, in close cooperation with the government. Demobilized military officers were maintaining secret societies and plotting a return to power. The abolition of the Emperor system was essential if fascism were not to be resurrected. Meanwhile, capitalism had proven to be completely inadequate to meet the financial crisis. As a stopgap measure, foreign capital was being introduced, with the support of the Japanese government and Japanese monopoly capitalism. The Communist Party must oppose this trend, fighting for "popular control" of finance and industry. The government was also sabotaging the land reform program in an effort to aid the landlords, according to Tokuda. The primary struggle, however, should be directed against the monopoly capitalists, not the rural gentry. It was the former class, together with the government, that represented the key to the problem.

[12] The term *Yoyogi"* has been commonly applied to the Japanese Communist Party in the postwar era, since party headquarters are located in the Yoyogi district of Tōkyō.

a People's Democracy!, published an anonymous article entitled "Concerning the Situation in Japan."[13] The article contained a stinging criticism of Nosaka and his views. The Japanese Communist leader was accused of trying to prove that all of the necessary conditions were present in Japan for effecting a peaceful transition to socialism, even with the Occupation present, and of further arguing that this approach represented "the naturalization of Marxism–Leninism on Japanese soil."[14]

Nosaka was also strongly criticized for his argument that American Occupation forces were playing a progressive role, helping in the furtherance of Japan's development toward socialism by peaceful means. This doctrine, asserted the anonymous author, "misleads the Japanese people and helps the foreign imperialists to turn Japan into a colonial appendage of foreign imperialism, into a new center of war in the East."[15]

Toward the conclusion of the article, the attack became truly savage:

All this "naturalization" of Marxism–Leninism is nothing more than a Japanese variation of the anti-Marxist and anti-Socialist "theory" of the peaceful growing over of reaction to democracy, of imperialism into Socialism, a "theory" which was exposed long ago and which is alien to the working class. Nosaka's "theory" is the theory of embellishing the imperialist occupation of Japan, the theory of boosting American imperialism, and consequently a theory of deception of the popular masses in Japan.

As we see, Nosaka's "theory" has nothing whatever in common with Marxism–Leninism. Actually Nosaka's "theory" is an anti-democratic, anti-Socialist theory. It serves only the imperialist occupiers in Japan and the enemies of the independence of Japan. Consequently, the Nosaka "theory" is, simultaneously, an antipatriotic, anti-Japanese theory.[16]

The Cominform blast struck the Japanese Communist Party like a bombshell. There is no indication that party leaders had an intimation that a public attack against one of their group was being contemplated. Indeed, when the first word of the article reached Japan and a party spokesman was queried, he made the mistake of asserting: "The United Press and other reports on Comrade Nosaka are clearly an act of enemy provocation aimed at throwing into disorder the solidarity of the

---

[13] The article, signed "Observer," appeared on page 3 of the Cominform organ.

[14] *Ibid.*

[15] *Ibid.*

[16] *Ibid.*

party."[17] This view could not be held long, but it is interesting to note the immediate concern over party unity. Debate over the soft line being pursued by Tokuda and Nosaka had been growing in party circles. Any external interference could easily set off internecine warfare.

The full story of the dramatic events that surrounded the Cominform criticism may never be known. For example, was there prior communication between the anti-Mainstream elements and Soviet or Cominform sources? Did the Russians make any attempt to produce a policy change by appealing directly to Nosaka or Tokuda before the January 6th article?[18] Although answers to such questions are not available, the main developments of this period can be traced with reasonable certainty.

The Mainstream Japanese Communist Party leaders, deeply shocked by the public character of this attack and its high-handedness, were initially determined to offer some resistance. After a few days of silence, an official statement was issued that could scarcely have pleased Soviet circles. After some rather perfunctory praise of the Cominform and an admission that Nosaka's theory was inadequate, the party statement went on to defend its recent actions and ended with a sharp criticism— even rejection—of portions of the Cominform article.[19] The shortcomings of the Nosaka thesis had been discovered and remedied, it asserted,

---

[17] For this initial reaction, see the JCP Central Committee statement of January 8, 1950, published in *Akahata* the following day and republished by the Japanese Communist Party in the 3-volume *Nihon Kyōsantō gojūnen mondai shiryō shū (A Collection of Documents Concerning the Japanese Communist Party Incident of 1960)*, Vol. I, p. 3. This work is a very good documentary source for this period. For an excellent English-language study of this general period, see Toshio G. Tsukahira, *The Postwar Evolution of Communist Strategy in Japan,* Center for International Studies, M. I. T., Cambridge, Massachusetts, September 1954. Tsukahira's study covers the period October 1945–July 1952.

[18] Thus far, the only "inside" information concerning the Cominform attack has been supplied by the Russians. In their letter to the Central Committee of the Japanese Communist Party of April 18, 1964, the CPSU Central Committee made the following statement: "We informed the delegation of the Communist Party of Japan that the publication in the *Informburo* paper on 6 January, 1950, of the 'Commentator' article, 'On the Situation in Japan,' was effected on the personal initiative of Stalin and that the Central Committee of the CPSU not only disapproves of such methods of criticizing the fraternal parties but, as is well known, the 20th Congress of the CPSU strongly criticized Stalin's personality cult, which caused deviations from Leninist norms in mutual relations among the fraternal parties." Text of the 18 April 1964 Letter of the CPSU Central Committee, as translated in *Translations of International Communist Developments* (hereafter cited as *TICD*) 636, Joint Publications Research Service (hereafter cited as *JPRS*) 26,058, p. 30.

[19] *Nihon Kyōsantō gojūnen mondai shiryō shū,* Vol. I, pp. 4–5.

and the party was now developing in a healthy fashion. Naturally, under the special conditions prevailing in Japan (the American Occupation), it was not always possible to spell out objectives and tactics in frank language. But if foreign comrades criticized the party without understanding these conditions, they did serious harm both to the Japanese people and the party. Moreover, since the errors had been corrected, the argument advanced in the article that errors had been piling up for the last four years "gives the masses a very erroneous impression." Finally, the party flatly rejected the last four paragraphs of the article, those containing the most violent criticism of Nosaka. The statement ended defiantly with the assertion: "Comrade Nosaka is a most courageous proletarian patriot who has the confidence of the masses."[20]

At the same time, the Mainstream moved quickly to smash its most vulnerable opponents within the party. Nakanishi Kō was ousted on January 10 on charges of defying party leaders, frequently violating party regulations, and recently resorting to "schismatic activities." Nakanishi himself insisted that Mainstream leaders were "corrupt and bureaucratic," and that he had been ousted only because he strongly endorsed the Cominform position. Two days later, his brother, Nakanishi Atsushi, Miyahara Toshio, and Satō Noboru were also ousted, charged with distributing literature containing "antiparty" and "schismatic" views.

In the heat of battle during the days that followed, words like "Titoist" and "Trotskyite" were repeatedly used by the warring factions. The anti-Mainstream faction, which came to be known first as the Kansai, and subsequently as the International faction, gathered under the leadership of Shiga and Miyamoto.[21] This group vigorously attacked the Tokuda–Nosaka leadership with charges of "bureaucratism" and erroneous policies, demanding that the Cominform criticism be accepted as fully correct. Otherwise, the group argued, the party would surely tread the path of Titoism. Mainstream leaders fought back, alleging that Trotskyite policies of "ultra-left adventurism" would destroy the party and denying in heated fashion that theirs was a Titoist position.

It is difficult to know how far the Tokuda–Nosaka group might have carried their defiance of the Cominform had not the Chinese comrades joined the Soviets in interfering in the internal affairs of the

---

[20] *Ibid.*, Vol. I, p. 5.

[21] For the first attack on the Tokuda–Nosaka group, see Shiga's article of January 15, 1950, which was not published in *Akahata* until April 26. *Nihon Kyōsantō gojūnen mondai shiryō shū*, Vol. I, pp. 5–8.

Japanese Communist Party. On January 17, only hours before an important JCP Central Committee meeting which had been called to make a final determination of the party position, the Chinese Communist official organ, *Jen-min Jih-pao* (*People's Daily*), published an editorial supporting the main themes of the Cominform article.[22] The editorial charged that Nosaka had been guilty of "serious mistakes of principle," and that his view that the Japanese Communist Party could use a bourgeois parliament to gain state power by peaceful means under the conditions prevailing in Japan was false. The language of the Peking editorial was more restrained, less ruthless than that of the Cominform article, but the viewpoint was essentially the same.

Probably this editorial came as a great disappointment to the Mainstream leaders. It is possible that they had hoped for some aid from Peking. Relations between Nosaka and Mao Tse-tung were supposedly close. Moreover, there were rumors of a developing strain in Sino–Soviet relations. Amidst much fanfare, Mao had made his first trip to Moscow in December 1949, presumably to obtain Soviet assistance and protection. His stay, however, stretched far beyond the time normally required to reach such agreements. Stories of hard bargaining and rising disappointment circulated in certain quarters. Were the Russians treating the hero of China in the same high-handed fashion as they had treated Nosaka?

Not until the main crisis over the Nosaka criticism had passed did it become publicly known that Russia and China had negotiated, among other things, a mutual defense agreement directed primarily against Japan and her allies, signed on February 14, 1950. Under the circumstances, the Chinese Communists would surely choose to join their Russian allies in condemning any theory or tactic that suggested cooperation with the American Occupation forces. Had the Japanese comrades studied closely the speech of Liu Shao-ch'i several months earlier, moreover, they might have anticipated Peking's action on January 17.

In the late fall of 1949, Liu had made a vitally important speech before the Peking Conference of Trade Unions of Asia and Oceania, in which he outlined a program of action for the Communist parties of Asia.[23] Liu's major themes were in complete conformity with the Zhdanov line, but the speech made it unmistakably clear that the

[22] *Jen-min Jih-pao,* January 17, 1950, p. 1; reproduced in *Nihon Kyōsantō gojūnen mondai shiryō shū,* Vol. I, pp. 9–11.

[23] "Speech by Liu Shao-ch'i at the Conference on Trade Unions of Asia and Oceania," *For a Lasting Peace, For a People's Democracy!,* December 30, 1949, p. 2. The quotations used here are taken from that translation. This speech was also published in *Pravda,* January 4, 1950.

Chinese regarded their revolution as a model for the rest of Asia and that they expected to play a leading role in guiding the revolutionary movement of this area. The speech, widely circulated throughout the Communist world, is sufficiently important to cite at some length.

Liu began by stressing the fact that imperialist forces had fastened a colonial or semicolonial system upon Asia, and that such a system was critical to the survival of imperialism. Hence, the peoples of the colonial world, together with the workers of the imperialist states, had to unite and fight the common enemy. It was essential for colonial and semicolonial people to conduct an armed struggle to win their independence. Already, wars of national liberation were spreading: Vietnam had liberated 90 percent of its territory; the struggle was developing well in Burma and Indonesia; guerrilla warfare was in progress in Malaya and the Philippines; and an armed struggle for emancipation had also started in India. Liu said, "In Japan, a progressive labor movement and a progressive people's movement against the conversion of Japan into a colony of American imperialism are developing."

Those promoting "national liberation wars" in Asia were acting "entirely correctly," according to Liu, and should be given full support. Moreover, "the path taken by the Chinese people to defeat imperialism and its lackeys and to establish the People's Republic of China is the path that should be taken by the peoples of the various colonial and semicolonial countries in their fight for national independence and people's democracy."

Liu then proceeded to outline that path in four points:

1. The working class must unite with all other classes, parties and groups, organizations and individuals who are willing to oppose the oppression of imperialism and its lackeys, to form a broad, nation-wide united front and be ready to wage a resolute struggle against imperialism and its lackeys.
2. This nation-wide united front must be led by the working class which opposes imperialism most resolutely, most courageously and most unselfishly and by its political party, the Communist party, both of which must become the center of this front. It cannot be led by the wavering and compromising national bourgeoisie or the petty bourgeoisie and their political parties.
3. In order to enable the working class and its political party, the Communist party, to become the center for uniting all the national, anti-imperialist forces and successfully to lead the national united front to victory, it is necessary to build up through patient struggle a Communist party equipped with the theory of Marxism–Leninism, a party mastering strategy and tactics, a party practicing self-criticism and strict discipline and which is closely linked with the masses.

4. It is necessary to set up wherever and whenever possible a people's liberation army led by the Communist party, an army which is powerful and skillful in fighting enemies, as well as strong points for the operations of these armies and also to coordinate the mass struggles in the enemy controlled areas with the armed struggle. Moreover, armed struggle is the main form of struggle in the national liberation struggle in many colonies and semicolonies.

This was the main path followed by the Chinese people, Liu asserted, and it could also be the main path followed by other colonial and semicolonial peoples, although he added the proviso "where similar conditions prevail." He made it emphatically clear, moreover, that an armed struggle was essential—anyone attempting to take an easier path "would be committing a mistake." Naturally, armed struggle should be combined with other forms of struggle. In the countryside, links with the peasants should be established and popular revolutionary armies created; in the towns and districts controlled by the enemy, all forms of legal and illegal struggle should be developed.

The evidence is strong that in the 1949–1950 period, Soviet and Chinese Communist views on the tactics and strategy of revolution in Asia were identical. Both the CPSU and the CCP were currently pursuing a "left" line, one that emphasized the creation of united fronts, the seizure of united front leadership by the Communist Party, and the overthrow of imperialist or "reactionary" regimes by force, using the techniques of guerrilla warfare and "national liberation" movements. In this period, there appears to have been no difference in Russian and Chinese evaluations of tactical and strategic requirements for Communist success in Asia and no divergencies in the "suggestions" given Asian Communist parties.

Indeed, there is some indication that the Soviet Union, burdened with its own problems of reconstruction and the task of supervising East Europe, had either promoted, or acquiesced in, the idea of a special Chinese sphere of influence in the Far Eastern Communist movement. If some differences in national interests had already made their appearance, there were as yet no tactical or ideological differences to preclude such an arrangement. Thus, Liu's thesis, echoing as it did all of the basic Soviet themes, probably met with Russian approval despite its clear call for an emulation of Chinese, not Bolshevik, revolutionary practices.[24]

---

[24] See Tsukahira, pp. 46–49; and John H. Kautsky, *Moscow and the Communist Party of India*, New York, 1956, pp. 86–117. My differences in interpretation with the latter work are substantial on some points.

The meeting of the enlarged Central Committee of the Japanese Communist Party opened on January 19 to make a final determination of the party's attitude toward Sino–Soviet criticism. A fiery debate ensued, with Shiga, Miyamoto, and various other members of the Kansai faction pressing the attack against the Mainstream leaders. They insisted that Tokuda, Itō Ritsu, and Shida Shigeo should join Nosaka in making full self-criticisms, and that the party should accept the international line without equivocation. Given the solidarity between the Soviet and Chinese parties, the Mainstream had no choice except to capitulate. Nosaka issued an apologetic self-criticism making all of the necessary concessions. The Party Central Committee passed a resolution "unanimously" agreeing with the "positive contribution" of the criticisms.[25]

The Mainstream group, however, did not yield control of the party, nor did it allow further official condemnation of its leaders. Even Nosaka was praised as a man who was "fighting now for the national independence of Japan." The Politburo continued to have five Mainstream leaders (Tokuda, Nosaka, Shida, Itō, and Konno Yojirō) and only three members of the opposition (Shiga, Miyamoto, and Hasegawa Hiroshi). In retrospect, it can be said that the Mainstream faction, confronted with massive external intervention against its policies, capitulated on the basic issues, but managed to preserve its leadership intact. Considering the severity of the attack on Nosaka, his survival is almost without precedent in the history of the international Communist movement.

The shift dictated in JCP policy, however, indicated that a stormy era lay ahead. Before exploring it, let us assess the results attained by the Japanese Communist Party in the period when "peaceful revolution" was its guide and being "lovable" its motto. One measurement of strength, of course, was party membership. On this score, party leaders could be reasonably satisfied. As noted earlier, in its twenty-three years of illegal existence prior to 1945, party membership never reached 1,000. The following official party figures for the period 1945–1950 indicate fairly rapid growth:

December 1945—	1,180
February 1946—	7,500
December 1947—	70,000
April 1950—	108,693
(unofficial estimate—	150,000)

[25] For the resolution, see *Nihon Kyōsantō gojūnen mondai shiryō shū,* Vol. I, p. 16. Nosaka's self-criticism appears on pp. 18–22.

By 1950 the Japanese Communist Party had a formal membership equal to that of any party in Japan, including the Liberal Party. Communist cells had been organized throughout the country, with special emphasis on the Kantō (Tōkyō) and Kinki (Ōsaka-Kōbe-Kyōto) areas. Factory and university cells predominated, and there were very few meaningful rural cells; but given the fact that the party had existed legally for less than five years, there was reason for optimism among the party faithful.

More critical to an assessment of growth than formal party membership is party strength within various mass organizations. If the Japanese Communist Party were to achieve its goal of being a mass-based party, and if the united front tactic were to be successful, it was essential to infiltrate and capture the key organizations. Naturally, the Communists focused most sharply on the trade unions. At no time in the prewar era had more than 7 percent of all industrial workers been unionized, but under SCAP protection and guidance the trade union movement skyrocketed in the first two years of the Occupation. By the end of 1947, union membership totaled over 6,000,000, with approximately 50 percent of all industrial and mining workers organized.[26]

Within a year after the American Occupation commenced, two major federations had emerged. The first, Sōdōmei (General Federation of Labor), was controlled by veteran Socialists and had strong prewar roots. The second, Sanbetsu (Congress of Industrial Unions), was under Communist control.[27] Sanbetsu was organized in August 1946, with a membership of about 1,500,000. From the beginning, its top officers were predominantly Communists, and it represented the major Communist bid to dominate the Japanese trade union movement. Sanbetsu unions occupied a strategically important position because a preponderance of the civil service and government enterprise unions were members of this federation, including the key communications and transportation unions. Thus a large number of white-collar workers came under Sanbetsu jurisdiction.

Sanbetsu scored a number of initial successes both in organizational

---

[26] For English-language studies of the postwar labor movement, see Solomon B. Levine, *Industrial Relations in Postwar Japan,* Urbana, Illinois, 1958; and Robert A. Scalapino, "Japan," in Walter Galenson (ed.), *Labor and Economic Development,* New York, 1959. In Japanese, see Yamazaki Gorō, *Nihon rōdō undō shi (A History of the Japanese Labor Movement),* Tōkyō, 1957.

[27] A recent study of Communist influence in the Japanese labor movement has been completed by A. Rodger Swearingen, entitled *Communist Strategy in Japan, 1945–1960,* the RAND Corporation, RM–4348–PR (AD 462101), April 1965.

activities and in its political-economic tactics. By the end of 1946, it was clearly the dominant federation. Under its aegis, plans were drafted for a massive general strike, which would involve the cooperation of all unions and effect the complete paralysis of the Japanese state. The strike was scheduled for February 1, 1947. However, problems of maintaining unity between Communist and non-Communist elements grew progressively more serious. In a dramatic last-minute act, moreover, SCAP intervened to prevent the strike from taking place, citing its responsibility for the general welfare and safety of the Japanese people.

The abortive general strike of February 1, 1947, marked the high tide of Communist influence in the labor movement. In its aftermath, criticism against the Japanese Communist Party mounted, with the charge that the Communists were completely willing to sacrifice the Japanese working class to their own special interests, advancing in dictatorial fashion a policy that was so unrealistic as to be disastrous to the trade union movement. Even within Communist ranks, some significant defections took place at this point.

Thus, the poststrike efforts of the Communists to establish a single All-Japan Federation of Labor failed. This represented their great bid for a united front in the labor field over which they could exercise hegemony. By the beginning of 1948, moreover, a so-called democratization movement aimed at reducing Communist influence or control had begun within some major unions. Ultimately, amidst much travail, the Minrōren (Democratic Labor League) was formed, and by the spring of 1949 the league had made substantial inroads against Communist enclaves of power. In this same period, mounting pressures against Communist labor leadership also came from industry and government, including SCAP. Key Communist leaders were dismissed, and restrictions imposed on the union activities of government employees also contributed to Communist problems. Thus, Sanbetsu was plagued with a series of secessions and a general membership decline. By the end of 1949, its union affiliates numbered less than one-half of those who had belonged during the peak period, and its total membership was only 400,000.[28]

The inability of the Japanese Communist Party to seize and retain control of the Japanese labor movement was undoubtedly its most serious failure in the initial period. Without substantial labor support, the party could not hope for a mass base. This failure was not due to a lack of promises. Communist Party programs regularly contained a

---

[28] See Labor Ministry, *Rōdō undō shi shiryō—1949* (*Documents on the History of the Labor Movement—1949*), p. 422.

lengthy list of benefits to which all workers were entitled and for which the Japanese Communist Party pledged a struggle. Invariably, the Communists outbid Socialist rivals in the specific socioeconomic proposals that they advanced for the working class. In fact, however, the Communists minimized the importance of concrete economic gains in devising their labor tactics and struck hard for broad political objectives, particularly those advancing the fortunes of their own party. The mobilization of the workers for such objectives became increasingly difficult, especially after a few costly failures. The conspiratorial character of Communist operations within the labor movement, moreover, alienated an important segment of middle- and upper-echelon leadership among the out-group, abetting intensive factional rivalry.

The reorientation of SCAP labor policy at the beginning of 1949 also contributed to Communist failure. Whereas the Communists had once been defined by SCAP in neutral or even friendly terms, after the abortive general strike they were categorized as opponents or enemies. There definitely were pro-Communist elements in the initial SCAP task force, and a larger number of politically naive or—to be more kind— inexperienced individuals. Some of these never changed; others were educated in the course of their experiences. However, the more important factor was that the *context* in which they worked shifted from one of "reform" to one of "reconstruction." Thus, in a variety of ways, SCAP—often acting through the Japanese government—now operated to reduce Communist power. In addition, the gradual stabilization of the Japanese economy contributed in its own way to the Communist decline. Initially, labor had won its victories easily, benefiting from SCAP aid, management confusion, and rampant inflation. With stabilization, however, and with the stiffening of both government and management, the cost of victory rose. Purely political strikes became less attractive, and Communist Party manipulation of the labor movement more damaging. The trend was toward economic unionism.

If their failure to capture the labor movement was a source of great disappointment, the Japanese Communists found themselves totally frustrated in their efforts to develop a mass base in the countryside. Taking a lesson from their Chinese comrades, they had hoped to make land reform the cardinal issue. Indeed, this was logical. In prewar Japan, the pure tenant class accounted for nearly one-third of all farm families, and more than 50 percent of all cultivated land was cultivated by tenants. Although large-scale land holdings were rare, absentee landlordism was a serious problem.

Suddenly, however, the Communists found the issue of land reform taken away from them by SCAP.[29] The SCAP land reform program was both radical and successful, and as a result the Communists were never able to get any leverage in rural Japan for operational purposes. Each JCP program contained broad statements that the power of the rural gentry in the villages had to be eliminated, and specific pledges to redistribute forest and pasture land. But the Communist call for "land reform" had a hollow ring in the light of events. To the traditional conservatism of the Japanese peasantry had been added a new quotient of satisfaction in the course of socioeconomic change, and this combination provided an impenetrable wall against Communist infiltration. A few Communist or proto-Communist peasant associations were formed and a few cells in rural areas flourished, but the general effort of the Communists to secure a broad rural base was a total failure.

As this first period ended, the Communists could probably claim that their greatest success lay in penetrating student-intellectual circles. There were many reasons why the Communists had certain advantages with respect to these groups.[30] The role of the intellectual in Japan has been essentially that of the social critic, and Marxism was an excellent weapon of social criticism. In terms of recent history, moreover, the Communists had been "right" and the overwhelming majority of intellectuals "wrong." A guilt complex concerning support of the Emperor system and the war was fairly widespread. When to these factors were added the multiple frustrations and stimuli of the early postwar era, the attraction of Communism can be understood. In student-intellectual circles, moreover, the Communist form of organization was particularly effective; a small number of individuals working purposefully and with dedication could manipulate or influence a much larger group.

Communist influence within the Japanese student movement came to be exercised primarily through Zengakuren (National Federation of Student Self-Government Associations). Zengakuren was organized in September 1948 by Communist leaders, and throughout this period it was under complete Communist control. Every major university and college student government was represented in the association, which could claim to speak on behalf of all "organized students." Meanwhile,

[29] For a thorough study of land reform, see R. P. Dore, *Land Reform in Japan*, London, 1959.

[30] Two articles outlining some of the factors pertinent to this problem are the penetrating study by Herbert Passin, "The Sources of Protest in Japan," *The American Political Science Review*, Vol. LVI, June 1962, pp. 391–403; and Robert A. Scalapino, "The Left Wing in Japan," *Survey*, No. 43, August 1962, pp. 102–111.

a large variety of "cultural," literary, and special purpose associations designed to attract Japanese intellectuals were set up under Communist auspices, or with extensive Communist participation. Many of these associations had their own organs, so that Marxist literature flowed forth in unprecedented quantities. Typical of the Communist-connected special purpose groups was the Society for the Defense of Peace, organized in April 1949 in conjunction with the First World Conference for the Defense of Peace, held in Paris and Prague. As the international Communist "Peace Movement" became a major tactic, this society and others played their assigned roles.

On one other front, the Communists enjoyed a substantial measure of success, namely, with the Korean minority. Some 600,000 Koreans remained in Japan after the repatriations of the immediate postwar period had been completed. Most of these Koreans lived in the major metropolitan centers, particularly Ōsaka, in deplorable economic and social conditions. Victims of discrimination, often lacking in skills, and consequently with a high level of unemployment, the Koreans were a logical source from which to recruit Communists. Even in the prewar era, Koreans had formed a significant percentage of Japanese Communist members and sympathizers. A Communist regime in Pyongyang was now prepared to cultivate the Koreans resident in Japan, turning their poverty, frustration, and bitterness to political advantage. Funds and personnel were committed to that purpose. Korean language schools quickly moved "left," and Communist propaganda flourished in the Korean community. The South Korean government, concentrating on the domestic political struggle, offered little competition. Korean schools came under Communist control, as did the major Korean association, the General Federation of Koreans in Japan.

At the end of this initial period, the Japanese Communist Party had a hard core of support numbering about 1,000,000. This hard core could be counted on to aid the party in many ways—strikes, demonstrations, and, above all, votes. Note the following House of Representatives election results from 1946 to 1949: [31]

	Total JCP Vote	Percent of Total Vote	Number of Candidates Elected	Percent of Total Candidates Elected
10 Apr. 1946	2,135,757[a]	3.8	5	1.1
25 Apr. 1947	1,002,903	3.7	4	0.8
23 Jan. 1949	2,984,780	9.7	35	7.5

[a]Plural voting system in effect.

[31] For additional election statistics and analyses see Chapter VII.

The major Communist gains in the 1949 House of Representatives election, although extremely gratifying to the party, reflected an abnormal situation. A period of coalition government involving the Socialists and the moderate conservatives had ended in failure, indeed, in a welter of scandal and mutual recrimination. Not only did the Socialist Party have to bear some responsibility for this situation before the electorate, but it was also faced with an open right-left split within its own ranks. Hence, the Communists received a much higher percentage of the vote than was normal. Unfortunately for them, this victory came at a point when they had already lost their dominant position in the labor movement. If they were to hold and advance their electoral gains, they would have to recapture that position and hope that the Socialists remained weak, discredited, and divided.

One key to regaining power lay with the success or failure of Communist united front tactics. The attempt to establish a united front in this period had two prominent aspects, namely, the quest for a working relationship with SCAP and the continuous effort to effect an alliance with some or all of the Socialists. Both ventures ended in failure. The favorable relationship with SCAP lasted only about one year. The alliance with the Socialists never really came into existence.

It has sometimes been asserted that pro-Communist elements within the initial American Occupation force were primarily responsible for the friendly treatment accorded the Communists at the outset of the postwar era. Although there were some pro-Communist elements in SCAP the main reasons for the favorable treatment given the Communists lie elsewhere. In this period, SCAP was primarily concerned with purging all militarist and ultra-nationalist elements and sparking a massive reform program. The Communists were almost alone in having a clean record with respect to militarism (even the Socialists were, in a number of cases, "impure"). Moreover, the Communists initially gave unstinting support to SCAP reforms, whereas the conservatives engaged in a variety of holding or delaying actions.

Neither the Japanese Communists nor the leading SCAP officials, however, had any illusions about the true nature of this relationship. To the Communists it was primarily a question of how to work with a powerful bourgeois force to consummate quickly the bourgeois-democratic revolution, but still keep their own power and position independent and intact, and be ready to assume leadership at the appropriate time. To SCAP, it was essentially a question of utilizing all available elements that supported the broad SCAP objectives, rewarding cooperation and punishing obstructionism. By early 1947 the atmosphere governing Communist–SCAP relations had already changed. If it took an additional three years and massive foreign intervention before the Japanese Communist Party fully altered its tactics and policies toward the Occupation, that was primarily because the party wanted to continue enjoying the many benefits of legality and unlimited freedom.

The failure to establish an indigenous united front was perhaps more serious for the Japanese Communists in the long run. On the surface, the chances for such a front between Communists and Socialists seemed relatively good in the early Occupation era. Many Japanese Socialists were Marxists; some claimed to be Marxist–Leninists. Moreover, even the right-wing Socialists were anxious to disassociate themselves completely from the legacy of Japanese conservatism. They wanted almost desperately to be identified with the "progressive" forces of the new era. And certainly, Japanese society, in the midst of defeat and chaos, was ready for very basic changes, changes that would rip out some of the very roots of that society. Why, then, was a united front of all "progressive" forces never consummated? In part, the reasons are uniquely Japanese: the omnipresence of personal factionalism in Japanese politics, and the supreme difficulty involved in effecting any lasting, broadly gauged political coalition. But these "Japanese" factors were powerfully abetted by the obstacles implicit in Communist tactics: the open admission that the united front was a method of ultimately attaining absolute power for "the only true party of the proletariat"; the simultaneous cultivation of, and assault on, Socialist rivals; the conspiratorial method of organization and political operation of the Communists within any larger unit.

Ironically, *because* many of the Japanese Socialists were Marxists, and because not a few of them were ex-Communists, they discerned these tactics readily and proved very difficult to snare. There were, finally, very few if any reasons why coalition with the Communists would benefit the Socialists. Despite its postwar growth, the Japanese Communist Party was still too weak, too readily identified with the Soviet Union at a time when the Russians were an anathema, and too unpopular with the broad masses of the Japanese people to be, on balance, an asset to the Socialists. Thus, the Japanese Communist Party was able to secure Socialist cooperation on some specific issues and for certain periods of time, but every effort to establish a permanent liaison, whether at the party level or through mass organizations, failed. Only with a very small fraction, such as the Labor-Farmer Party, a far-left socialist group, was something approximating a united front achieved.

In sum, the tactic of "peaceful revolution" had proven less successful than JCP leaders had hoped. The Japanese Communist Party, in spite of gains, remained basically separated from the masses, unable to develop any issue that would bring it into a position of power with urban labor or the rural peasantry. Nationalism, whatever its potentials for the future, was not a promising issue for the Japanese Communist Party during this period. The party had chosen to attack with vigor all of the traditional nationalist symbols, including the Emperor system. Circumstances were not yet ripe to mount an offensive against "American imperialism," although that was clearly the goal as this period came to a close. SCAP had "stolen" the issue of land reform, and in spite of desperate attempts the party had been unable to find leverage for significant rural operations. The issue of workers' livelihood—the problems of housing, employment, and wages—were serious and provided the Communists with some advantages. Communist tactical errors, however, together with a reorientation of SCAP policy, dissipated these advantages. After a very promising start, Communist leaders saw the labor movement gravitate away from them. And the united front with all "progressives" never materialized. The overwhelming majority of Japanese socialists—right and left—continued to view the Communists as opponents, not allies.

It would be misleading to equate the situation confronting the Japanese Communist Party after World War II with that faced by such Communist parties as those of France or Italy. For more than two decades, the Japanese Communist Party had been not only illegal, but popularly identified with everything that was foreign to Japanese culture and behavior. No segment of the Japanese citizenry could easily identify with this party, and it had no prewar base on which to build. At the end of 1949, that situation had not really changed. Measured in statistical terms, the Japanese Communist Party continued to be a minor party, polling about 3 percent of the national vote on a regular basis, and no more than 10 percent under the most favorable conditions.

Despite the somewhat disappointing results of the initial period, however, could it be argued that the party would have made more rapid progress by following a different tactic? The answer is almost certainly negative. "Peaceful revolution" was the tactic best calculated to blur the old and strongly unfavorable image of the party. It was also the only tactic that would permit the party to operate with a substantial degree of freedom, enabling it to present its case to the masses. After 1945 there were few risks in being a Communist in Japan. It is not surprising that party membership increased a hundredfold. and that the party could at least note with satisfaction its important gains within labor, student-intellectual, and minority circles. In "qualitative" terms, at least, the party had made significant strides under the banners of "peaceful revolution."

History was to repeat itself, however. As in the period after 1924, the Japanese Communist Party once again found itself subjected to foreign discipline after an initial period of relative autonomy. For the first four years of the postwar era, the Japanese Communist movement operated without direct foreign guidance or interference. Many factors contributed to this situation. In the early postwar years, all political elements in Japan were relatively isolated from international contacts. Travel was restricted, and the focus, of necessity, was on the chaotic and rapidly changing domestic scene. A sizable Russian Mission was, of course, established in Tōkyō in early 1946, and toward the latter part of this first period, at least, there were undoubtedly frequent contacts between certain Communist leaders and Soviet representatives.

At the outset, however, it is doubtful whether the Russians had a strong, coherent policy for the Japanese Communist Party that required any special supervision or enforcement. The Japanese Communists, moreover, were well aware of the political risks involved in being closely identified with the Soviet Union. Indeed, in these years Russia became even more unpopular with the Japanese people than it had been in the past, as a result of Soviet callousness toward Japanese prisoners, espousal of an extremely severe reparations program, and occupation of territories considered by the Japanese to be theirs. Repeatedly, Tokuda and others denied that the party had direct ties with the Soviet Union and in party meetings argued that such ties would be very damaging. The concept of being an independent party was carefully nurtured, and to many elements within the party, no doubt, it had a strong appeal.

Direct ties, however, were not essential for the purpose of knowing and following the international Communist line. Radio and a large variety of publications provided Japanese party leaders with a detailed account of events and trends. And as we have noted, if the Japanese Communist Party did not satisfy Soviet leaders, it at least made a general effort to stay abreast of changes in Soviet policy. On a more moderate scale, it moved "left" after mid-1947 in conjunction with the strong "left" trend emanating from Moscow. These were the last years of Stalinism, however, and it was not easy to satisfy the Soviet leaders. In the aftermath of a costly war, the Soviet Union was not in a mood to be generous toward enemies—or even allies. The rigid internal authoritarianism characteristic of the Stalinist regime, moreover, naturally affected relations with other Communist parties as well as those with foreign states. The purge of Earl Browder and the break with Tito were but two indications of how ruthless the Soviet leaders could be when they felt challenged, and how determined they were to enforce conformity within world commusim on their terms. The frontal assault on Nosaka in January 1950 was thus part of a much larger pattern, entirely consistent with Soviet attitudes and actions elsewhere.

For a brief period, as we have noted, the Mainstream Japanese Communist Party leaders contemplated defiance. The lines of that defiance were significant in the light of things past and future: Nosaka's call for the "Japanization" of Marxism–Leninism represented an attempt to adapt Marxist theories creatively to the needs and special conditions of Japanese society. Nor was his approach static; in the aftermath of changes in the international and Japanese fronts, it had been altered. The Cominform attack, however, was filled with dogmatic assertions based on a complete ignorance of Japanese conditions. It was certain to damage the party both internally and before the masses.

The great issues of a decade later were even now being raised in embryonic form: the right of each Communist party to be independent and to formulate its tactics and policies in accordance with its own circumstances; the importance of mutual consultation and the avoidance of "big-power chauvinism" in intraparty relations; and the vital issue of the appropriate Communist tactics for revolutionary victory in the mid-twentieth century.

Insofar as the international Communist movement was concerned, the Soviet Union represented the only source of final authority, the only legitimizing agency. The Yugoslavs were heretics, standing alone and being subjected to unprecedented abuse. The Chinese, representing the only other Communist party having many of the prerequisites for independent authority, had barely emerged on the world scene as rulers of a huge nation. Their presence had already been felt, however, and Liu's speech, cited earlier, suggested that the Chinese Communists expected to play a major revolutionary role in the non-Western world. As mentioned, there is no reason to believe that the Russians were explicitly or consciously opposed to this idea. On the contrary, the Chinese may well have been encouraged to undertake this assignment by their Soviet comrades. But one must distinguish the conscious from the subconscious, the immediate and "real" from the future and potential. The implications of an independent role for Communist China in the Communist world could not long be hidden from a Soviet leadership so accustomed to its prerogatives and so suspicious of competitors. And the first test, for obvious reasons, was likely to come in Asia.

Only months after the establishment of the People's Republic in

Peking, the Chinese played their first significant role in Communist international affairs. Their intervention in support of Cominform criticism of the Japanese Communist Party at the height of the 1950 crisis probably proved decisive insofar as the Mainstream leaders were concerned. It may be doubted, of course, whether Japanese Communist Party defiance could have been sustained, even if the Chinese comrades had remained silent. The position of Nosaka and the Japanese Communist Party was not that of Tito and the Yugoslav Communists. The Japanese Communist Party had no independent power base, no massive popular support, and no tradition of an independent existence. In short, it had none of the qualities necessary for self-sufficiency. In any case, Chinese intervention was significant in another sense. While straightforward in their condemnation of the "mistaken tactics" of the Japanese Communist Party, the Chinese managed to avoid the bone-crushing, humiliating language of the Cominform attack, showing a sensitivity and cultural understanding that were notably absent from Soviet diplomacy. Could the Chinese sustain such moderation in inter-party relations, and if so, what rewards would it bring?

III

THE SHIFT TO THE LEFT: GUERRILLA WARFARE, JAPANESE STYLE

Some Japanese Communists have described the period after the Cominform criticism of January 1950 as "the first Chinese era," a period when the Japanese Communist Party gravitated increasingly closer to their Chinese comrades, both with respect to policies and in personal relations. Two other conditions marked this period: bitter factionalism within the party and active Russian–Chinese involvement in the internal affairs of the Japanese Communists. Let us briefly explore each of these factors, beginning with the Japanese Communist Party struggle to establish a new program.

At the famous Central Committee Plenum of January 19, 1950, Tokuda, as Secretary-General of the party, presented a report that pointed to the path of the future.[1] His analysis of the general world situation followed Soviet themes almost verbatim: The revolutionary forces were everywhere becoming stronger, while the capitalist world was lapsing into confusion and decay. Tokuda placed particular emphasis on the rising crescendo of revolutionary battle in Asia. The forces of socialism and democracy had made significant gains in Vietnam, Burma, and Malaya through struggles for national liberation. And, he asserted, the Chinese revolutionary victory had major implications for the Far East and the world.

---

[1] Tokuda Kyūichi, "Report to the 18th Enlarged Central Committee Plenum, *Nihon Kyōsantō gojūnen modai shiryō shu,* Vol. I, pp. 11–16.

In his analysis of the Japanese internal situation, Tokuda again drew heavily on China for purpose of comparison. The Yoshida government, he proclaimed, represented "a government of national betrayal." Its intentions were to reestablish monarchist imperialism and to serve as the agent of monopoly capitalism. "This testifies to the treacherous character of the government and shows that the fate of the Kuomintang government in China awaits the Yoshida cabinet."

The parallelism was pushed further. What difference, asked Tokuda, is there between Japan today and the old Shanghai? In both cases, international monopoly capitalism took command, "making the people docile slaves of foreign capital and its agents." There followed a lengthy exposé of zaibatsu-foreign capitalist iniquities, and the assertion that national capitalists were being ruined along with the owners of small and medium enterprise, making all of these segments of the bourgeoisie available for a democratic national front, a front that would have as its primary objectives peace and the complete independence of Japan. The workers, who were becoming more militant, would lead that front, and the peasants, now victims of "unbelievable plunder," would fill its ranks. Only a handful of traitors would resist the call to liberation.

Tokuda's survey of the Socialist Party was not in total conformity with this optimistic analysis. As he had done so frequently before, the Communist leader proceeded first to denounce right and center elements of the Socialist Party with such epithets as "betrayers of the people," and to warn that their activities had to be watched and their character exposed. Having dismissed fully 80 percent of the Socialist leaders with such statements, Tokuda still insisted, however, that it would be possible to cooperate "to a certain extent" with the Socialists. But the thrust of his remarks was to emphasize a "democratic national front from below," through direct contact with the masses and a championing of the key issues of "peace and independence."

The Tokuda report represented a close approximation of historic Chinese Communist tactics. That it also had the full support of the Soviet Union is indicated by the fact that the Cominform organ (*For a Lasting Peace, For a People's Democracy!*) carried the full text on April 14, 1950. Various other Japanese Communist Party policy statements—some brief, some lengthy—were drafted in the months that followed. The most important document was a policy paper prepared by Tokuda in May 1950. This paper served as the basis for the "New Program," a document prepared after numerous discussions in Moscow and Peking. This New Program, also known as the 1951 Thesis, was

intended to remedy recent errors and replace past directives. It was the
first fundamental change since the old Thesis of 1932. Supposedly, it
was drafted at a JCP Central Committee Plenum held August 19–21,
1951, and was adopted at the 5th National Party Conference held
October 16–17. As we have noted above, however, its main themes
had been spelled out earlier, in the period from May 1950 to February
1951. Recent evidence indicates that the 1951 Thesis was in reality
drafted by Tokuda after extensive contact both with Russian and
Chinese leaders.[2]

The 1951 Thesis has been accurately described by former Japanese
Communist Party members as an amalgam of late Stalinism and mature
Maoism.[3] It is interesting to compare it with the 1946 program on the
three basic issues discussed earlier: attitude toward the American Oc-
cupation, character of the revolution, and revolutionary tactics. A
startling contrast is revealed. The 1951 Thesis, far from regarding the
Americans as liberators, began with a condemnation of the United
States as extreme as the Japanese vocabulary would permit.[4] American
imperialists had brought the Japanese people "only chains and slavery."
They controlled every aspect of Japanese life and now sought to involve
Japan in a new aggressive war as their junior partner. The Yoshida
government was a perfect running dog of American imperialism, serving as its "moral-political pillar."

---

[2] Once again, the Russians have supplied us with some interesting information. Note the following statement in their April 18, 1964 letter: "One of the
main questions about which the delegation of the Communist party of Japan
complained was that the CPSU had allegedly 'imposed' upon your party the
1951 Program and 'ultra-left-wing and adventuristic tactics' during the Korean
War. The delegation of the CPSU had to restore the truth on the basis of the
available archive documents and show the full insolvency of such fabrications.

"As for the program, 'Immediate Demands of the Communist Party of Japan,'
the delegation of the CPSU drew the attention of your comrades to the fact that
its draft was completed by Stalin at the request and with the direct participation
of the leaders of the Communist party of Japan—Comrades Tokuda, Nosaka, and
others—and is known to have been met with full approval by your Party. Separately from the draft program the Japanese comrades drew up a document on
the tactics of the Communist party of Japan, and no one from the CPSU had
anything to do with its compilation." 18 April 1964 Letter from the CPSU CC
to the JCP CC, *TICD* 636, *JPRS* 26,058, pp. 29–30.

[3] Interviews with Naitō Tomochika, dissident Communist and Editor of
Atarashii Rosen (*The New Line*), Tōkyō, November 27, 1963; and Kasuga
Shōjirō, leader of dissident Communist group, Tōkyō, November 26, 1963.

[4] For the English-language text of the 1951 Thesis, see "Immediate Demands
of Communist Party of Japan—New Programme," *For a Lasting Peace, For a
People's Democracy!*, November 23, 1951, p. 3.

Thus, the revolution that lay immediately ahead was for the purpose of establishing a "national-liberation democratic government." Such a government had to be based on an alliance of workers and peasants, aided by handicraftsmen, small traders, small and medium businessmen —indeed, all the "progressive" forces in Japan who wanted to see the nation free and independent. Only with the overthrow of the reactionary Yoshida government and the establishment of a new national-liberation democratic government could the Occupation be finally ended. The 1951 Thesis no longer used the term "bourgeois-democratic revolution," preferring such terms as "national-liberation democratic revolution" and "new national-liberation democratic government" to convey the idea of a combined nationalist-"democratic" upsurge of the type that had just occurred in China and that would create a Japanese People's Republic.

"Peaceful revolution," moreover, was a tactic of the past. The New Program stated specifically: "It would be a serious mistake to think that a new national-liberation democratic government will arise of its own volition, without difficulties, in a peaceful way, that the 'liberal'-reactionary Yoshida government will relinquish its post voluntarily, without struggle, and make way for a new democratic government. Such an assumption would be altogether erroneous. . . . No, the peaceful way of liberation and democratic transformation of Japan is the new way of deception." Once again, the contrast with the 1946 program was striking.

In early 1952 Tokuda, in analyzing the New Program, shed further light on Japanese Communist Party goals.[5] He began by asserting that the program recently enacted by the party was rapidly becoming the program of the entire Japanese people, a statement that could scarcely have been further from the truth. Much of his analysis was devoted to a defense of the concept of a national-liberation democratic revolution involving a broad united front. Although Tokuda made it clear that the model for Japan was China, he was careful to cite at length from a report presented by Stalin to CPSU leaders on August 1, 1927. In this report, Stalin sought to differentiate the role of the bourgeoisie in various revolutionary situations. In imperialist countries, the bourgeoisie was reactionary, according to Stalin, and had to be fought as an enemy. In colonial or dependent countries, however, "the national bourgeoisie, at a certain stage and for a certain period, may support the revolutionary movement of its country against imperialism, and the national element, as an element in the struggle for emancipation, is a

---

[5] "On the 30th Anniversary of Founding the JCP," *For a Lasting Peace, For a People's Democracy!*, July 4, 1952.

revolutionary factor." Said Tokuda, "This is the theoretical basis of the New Program of our party."

Naturally, the Tokuda statement contained a full-scale attack on the United States and its role in Japan. "It is now absolutely indisputable," he asserted, "that Japan has been turned into a country completely dependent on America." At the same time, the facts showed that American imperialism was basically a "paper tiger," unable to prevent revolutionary victories in China and various parts of Southeast Asia. The implication was clear: by following militant tactics, the party could also achieve victory in Japan. But Tokuda (and other Mainstream leaders) also evidenced concern about ultra-leftist adventurism—policies that isolated the party from the masses. The objective, of course, was *successful* militancy.

Tokuda outlined a new slogan for the party: "Under the Banner of Peace and Democracy." Under Cominform (Moscow) guidance, *peace* had now become a prime tactic, a promising method of getting close to the masses. International communism was shrewdly playing on both ends of the tactical spectrum. Its attempt to create and then to capture the peace movement, like its efforts to seize the nationalist movement, represented a drive to play on the most deeply felt emotions of the masses, and thereby to forward the party's mass base. Peace was an excellent contrapuntal theme, moreover, to the militant revolutionary tactics now being advocated for victory. In this strongly "leftist" era for the Communists, how were peace and violence to be linked? The Communist answer was simple: one had to struggle for peace against imperialist depredations; one had to fight to establish the sociopolitical conditions ("People's Democratic Republics") that alone would make permanent peace possible.

The stage was being set—quite unconsciously—for a later battle within the international Communist movement over the relationship of peace and peaceful coexistence to the questions of revolutionary tactics and the struggle against imperialism. At this point, however, there was no debate. Peace was a tactic, not a policy. As such, it was proving to be quite successful, and it had the unanimous support of Communists everywhere. Tokuda, incidentally, proudly announced that 6,000,000 signatures on the Stockholm Peace Petition had been obtained in Japan, and he featured the peace movement as one of the most promising routes to mass support. Indeed, the peace tactic had a special meaning for Japan, a nation so ravaged by war that the very word "peace" had a deep emotional appeal.

What themes in "Democracy" did Tokuda choose to stress? Significantly, he began with the call for agrarian reform, revealing once again the powerful pull of the Chinese revolutionary model. Denouncing the SCAP land program as a "bogus reform," Tokuda urged that attention be given first to the abolition of "feudal relations in the countryside." Furthermore, the mountainous and forested areas not affected by land reform should be divided among the peasants. The Japanese Communists were constantly impressed by the tactical importance of devising an agrarian program, but one has only to read these words of Tokuda and the themes carried in other Communist documents of this period to realize the difficulties that the Communists faced in matching SCAP performance in the agrarian field. They could only engage in gross exaggeration and promise additional fringe benefits—but Japanese farmers, now enjoying unprecedented prosperity, were not likely to be impressed. Nonetheless, with the Chinese model before them, the Japanese comrades had to try. Toward the other social groups—the workers, the intellectuals, and the national bourgeoisie—the usual, now somewhat prosaic, appeals were made.

The New Program of 1951 epitomized the "left" era that had been thrust on the Japanese Communist Party both by the CPSU in this, the waning Stalinist period, and by the Chinese Communist Party which was in full bloom following its smashing victory. Particularly impressive is the degree to which the new Japanese Communist Party thesis adopted not only the tactics and programs of Maoism, but its vocabulary as well. Clearly, a new era was dawning for the Japanese Communist Party leaders, an era when the primary guidance would come from Peking.

Implementation of the New Program was in the hands of those who remained in Japan after many of the top leaders had fled to China. Some exploration of internal party trends is now essential. Long before the 1951 Thesis was drafted, of course, the drift to the left had begun for the JCP, with the International faction often taking the lead. Indeed, the Japanese government accused the Commuinsts of fomenting sabotage and violence in connection with labor disputes in 1949. A series of celebrated cases, mainly connected with the railroads, erupted in that year. Shortly after the January 1950 Central Committee meeting, the party began to prepare for its possible suppression and for the illegal activities that were a concomitant of militancy. Attacks on the American Occupation became less veiled, and several incidents involving violence occurred in May. On June 6, SCAP retaliated. The political purge of twenty-four members of the JCP Central Committee was ordered, and the following day an additional seventeen Communists were purged, including the key personnel working on the party newspaper *Akahata*.[6]

The party reacted quickly. A Central Directorate was established to take the place of the old Central Committee and Politburo. Shiino Etsurō, a Mainstream man, took the Chairmanship. Meanwhile, leading figures of the party disappeared, one after another. Preparations had been well made for underground activities, and few individuals wanted by the police were actually apprehended. The underground railway had its terminus at Peking. From this point, the JCP was an iceberg, with only a small portion of its activities on the surface—and with only a limited number of decisions made in Japan.

The 1951–1952 period marked the height of militancy. There is no question that many of the actions later condemned as "ultra-leftist adventurism" were unauthorized by headquarters officials. Young extremists, some of whom were affiliated with the International faction, seemed determined to prove their mettle—and their allegiance to international orders—by whatever means. As we shall note later, the situation within the party was chaotic as a result of SCAP–Japanese government policies and the deep factional split. Many party members and groups acted in an autonomous fashion. Nevertheless, official party pronouncements during this period all gave fundamental support to extremist activities.

For example, in the illegal JCP journal, *Naigai Hyōron* (*Internal-External Review*), two articles, entitled "The New Task of Communists and Patriots—Struggle Against Power with Power" (No. 4, October 12, 1950) and "Why Has Armed Revolution Not Become the Issue of Our Party?" (No. 5, January 24, 1951), set the tone for the new era.[7]

---

[6] For a detailed account of the Red purges, see Yaginuma Masaji, *Nihon Kyōsantō undō shi* (*A History of the Japanese Communist Party Movement*), Tōkyō, 1953, pp. 173–180. For other general studies of postwar JCP history, see Koyama Hirotake, *Sengo Nihon Kyōsantō shi* (*A History of the Postwar Japanese Communist Party*), Tōkyō, 1958) Murakami Kanji, *Nihon Kyōsantō* (*The Japanese Communist Party*), Tōkyō, 1956; Nikkan Rōdō Tsūshinsha (ed.), *Sengo Nihon Kyōsanshugi undō shi* (*A History of the Communist Movement in Postwar Japan*), Tōkyō, 1955; Ōi Hirosuke, *Sayoku Tennōsei* (*The Left Wing Emperor System*), Tōkyō, 1956; and Tagawa Kazuo, *Nihon Kyōsantō shi* (*A History of the Japanese Communist Party*), Tōkyō, 1960.

[7] For a summary of these articles, see Shinoda Tatsuji, *Nihon Kyōsantō Senryaku senjutsu shi* (*The History of the Tactics and Strategy of the Japanese Communist Party*), Tōkyō, 1952, p. 197. According to Shinoda, "With these articles, the Japanese Communist Party adopted the strategy of armed struggle, which became the main political line of the JCP at the 4th National Party Conference held on February 25–27, 1951."

With these articles, the JCP indicated its complete support for the strategy of armed struggle. That line, moreover, was "officially" ratified by the 4th National Party Conference held February 25–27, 1951.[8]

At the 4th Party Conference, discussions centered on the question of developing military and paramilitary units within the party. The idea was to begin with "self-defense units" and move toward the development of full-scale guerrilla forces and a Japanese Red Army. The main theme of the conference was that the people had to engage in an armed struggle to smash the "violent oppression organs pitted against them and force American troops out of Japan." Accordingly, it would be necessary to amend party regulations so that the party took on the discipline and structure of a military organization. Only in this way could illegal activities be strengthened and full preparations for armed struggle be completed.

Taking its signals from earlier pronouncements, both foreign and domestic, the Japanese Communist Party had moved "left" without waiting for the final New Program of October 1951.[9] And what was accomplished? By the end of 1952 the party could look back on a number of terrorist acts carried out by individuals or small groups. This was the Molotov cocktail era, when ardent young men bombed police stations, sabotaged factories, assaulted law enforcement officers, and conducted various other acts of violence. And while these fire-bottle struggles were taking place in metropolitan areas, the party undertook an even more ambitious program for the countryside. Seeking to imitate their Chinese comrades, party leaders encouraged the creation of "activist units" in selected mountain villages, areas with a potential for

---

[8] For a full record of the official resolutions of this conference and the following one, see *Nihon Kyōsantō daiyon-kai daigo-kai zenkoku kyōgikai kettei shū* (*The Collected Resolutions of the 4th and 5th National Conferences of the Japanese Communist Party*), Shinyō-sa, 1952. An English translation of the resolution on "the struggle against factionalists" is carried in *For A Lasting Peace, For a People's Democracy!*, August 10, 1951, p. 2.

The general report and the resolutions of the 4th National Conference emphasized the absolute necessity of an armed struggle against oppressive forces and withdrawal of the American army. Such a struggle was called a prerequisite of the revolution, and the open call for the creation of self-defense corps and guerrilla forces was made. Organizational proposals were tailored to the new militant line. In preparation for conflict, the party was to be shaped in military fashion, with a premium on discipline and security.

The resolution on factionalism was a necessity, since the party remained deeply split, as we shall note. The anti-Mainstream faction violently opposed the convening of this conference, regarding it as a power play by their opponents.

[9] As noted earlier, the 1951 Program was formally approved by the 5th National Party Conference, held on October 16–17, 1951. Endorsement came immediately from both Moscow and Peking.

defense that could be developed into guerrilla bases. These were to be Japan's Yenan.

The uniform result of these activities was catastrophic failure. Japan circa 1950–1952 was not China circa 1935–1949—in terrain, in socio-political conditions, or in international involvements. Most of the young terrorists, if they did not manage to escape to China, were captured and sentenced to lengthy prison terms. The party rapidly became a symbol for extremism, and all except the most firmly committed fell away. Party membership dropped precipitously. Election results spelled disaster. All of the sacrifices were being made to no avail. Not a single act undertaken by the Communists during this period had any political significance except to make the task of those fighting communism easier; not a single "guerrilla base" lasted more than the briefest period. In truth, most illegal units had been penetrated by government agents, and many Communist plots were known in advance, some possibly fomented by undercover men to trap militants.

By 1953 many Japanese Communists had begun to doubt that armed struggle represented a promising tactic for the Japanese Communist party. The search began for modifications, if not basic alterations, in tactics and strategy. It was in this period that some party leaders first became interested in the program of the Communist-controlled Italian Federation of Labor and thus prepared themselves for the Togliatti "structural reform" theory that was first spelled out in detail in 1956.[10] Even the Mainstream leaders, most of whom were in exile, now realized that the 1951 Thesis had produced only failure. No basic change could be effected, however, unless it had international support. No element within the party was prepared to undertake an independent course of action after the jolting events of 1950, and particularly not the Mainstream group which was now working closely with the Chinese.

Thus international developments in the 1953–1955 period, particularly those involving the world Communist movement, were of critical importance. In these troubled, transitional times for the Japanese Communist Party, two leading actors suddenly departed from the stage: Tokuda died in Peking in November 1953 (although his death was not made known publicly until much later), and Stalin succumbed in the Kremlin in March 1953. The death of Stalin in particular affected the situation. It signaled the beginning of a period of intense maneuvering

---

[10] According to Kasuga Shōjirō, an interest in Italian theories began as early as 1953, although formal writings on structural reform were to come considerably later. Interview, November 26, 1963, Tōkyō.

and great uncertainty in Soviet domestic politics that did not abate until 1957.

It would be difficult to exaggerate the effect of this situation on the international Communist movement. A Soviet Union that had for so long been a supreme symbol of authority, power, and monolithic unity for the Communist world now stood as a specter, uncertain and disunited. Russian leaders who had been praised extravagantly by all Communists for their virtue, wisdom, and dedication to the cause were suddenly attacked savagely by those closest to them. Beria, Malenkov, Molotov, and Kaganovich—even Bulganin—were to precede Stalin into obloquy and oblivion, as embarrassment mounted throughout the Communist world.

In these years China gradually acquired some of the symbolism formerly held by Russia, especially for Asian Communists. The opening years of the Peking regime had been notably successful in terms of both domestic and foreign policies. The big gamble—Korea—had paid off. The Chinese had avoided an all-out war with the United States and had preserved the existence of North Korea. The end of the Korean War, incidentally, lessened the immediate necessity for disruptive activities against American forces in Japan. The hot war, at least, had ended. In 1955, moreover, the Chinese Communists launched a major diplomatic offensive at Bandung, with primary emphasis on peaceful coexistence and other symbols of moderation. Chou En-lai's campaign to make the CCP lovable on an international scale bore a surprising resemblance to Nosaka's earlier efforts on the Japanese domestic front.

This was the setting in which the Japanese Communist Party held its 6th National Party Conference, July 27–30, 1955.[11] The primary

---

[11] Documents concerning the 6th National Party Conference are published in the July 30, 1955 issue of *Akahata* and the September 1955 issue of *Zenei* (pp. 8–36).

The 6th National Conference analysis of internal conditions represented no departure from previously established lines. The main themes were as follows: The partial treaty of San Francisco and the purely formal end of the Occupation had not truly restored Japanese independence. American imperialism continued to control industry, agriculture, trade, and finance in Japan, exploiting the Japanese people. Moreover, the United States had built more than 700 military bases, airfields, and other military installations, making Japan the most important beachhead for their aggressive designs on Asia. Nevertheless, the aggression in Korea by American imperialism had failed, and the Americans, realizing that their forces were inadequate to dominate the Far East, had cultivated the slogan, "Let Asians fight Asians." In line with this goal, they were seeking to rearm Japan and to induce the Japanese, along with their other puppets like Syngman Rhee and Chiang Kai-shek, to join in a Pacific Military Alliance.

purpose of this conference was to end party strife. A revised program was indispensable to accomplish this, and it was also essential if the catastrophic failures of the recent past were to be remedied. Nevertheless, the resolution proposed and adopted by the conference did not repudiate the 1951 Thesis. Indeed, it asserted that all events since the adoption of the New Program and all party experiences had proven that the thesis was "entirely correct." The resolution, however, stressed three "errors" demanding correction: Despite promises made at the 5th Party Conference, party leaders had not fully supported measures to end the split; many "sincere comrades" had been left in unfortunate circumstances. Moreover, the party had been guilty of serious tactical blunders, of pursuing "ultra-leftist adventurism." As a result, the resolution pointed out, party authority among the masses had been damaged, and the construction of a national liberation democratic united front had been made more difficult. Since 1953, to be sure, the party had gradually overcome its errors in these respects. In January 1955, for example, party leaders had resolved to abandon ultra-leftism and to give up the theory that revolution was imminent in Japan. Meanwhile, however, much damage had been done. Finally, the party had failed to strengthen its ties with the masses. Often it had been guilty of making high-handed and unrealistic demands on the masses, thus alienating them and isolating itself.

In conclusion, the 6th Conference Resolution pledged that the party would seek national unification on the basis of "the struggle for independence and peace." The basic principles enunciated in 1951 were

---

The reactionary Yoshida and Hatoyama governments had played the role of spiritual and political supporters of the American forces. However, their days were numbered. The Yoshida Cabinet had been overthrown (1) partly because of opposition to its antinational and reactionary policies, its total support for American interests, and (2) partly because of the inner contradictions arising within Japanese reactionary circles as a result of the growing economic problems caused by pro-American policies. Everywhere in Japan the movement for peace and independence was developing. As a result, the party was again gaining strength among the urban workers and farmers, enforcing its ties with the masses.

In its evaluation of the international situation, also, the 6th Conference played on familiar themes: The confrontation between the international war forces headed by the United States and the peace forces headed by the Soviet Union and the People's Republic of China continued to be the main element in world politics. But while the solidarity of the Socialist states was steadily being strengthened, and global support for the Socialist peace-loving policies growing, inner contradictions within the imperialist camp were deepening and opposition to imperialist war forces by the masses of the world was becoming more intense. Political developments within Japan, including the defeat of the Yoshida faction in recent elections, were indications of this trend.

thus retained—*but* the tactics of the party were substantially altered.

Despite the element of ambivalence displayed, the 6th Party Conference marked the official end of the "left" swing and represented a considerable victory for the old International faction, which now stood on the "right." Members of that faction were readmitted to the party, and their leaders improved their power position. Indeed, the International faction had gained ground even earlier. In the absence of the Mainstream leaders, and as a result of repeated failures on the part of their deputies, the International faction had gradually assumed positions of importance after 1952. Now they were prepared to go on the offensive. To understand the complex factional picture of the Japanese Communist Party during this period, we must return briefly to the period around 1950.

The postwar Japanese Communist movement, like all political movements in Japan, always had factional divisions. Immediately after World War II, the broadest division was between groups sometimes known as the Fuchū and Kuramae factions. The Fuchū faction derived its name from Fuchū Penitentiary, where its members—Shiga, Miyamoto, Hasegawa Hiroshi, Itō Ritsu, Hakamada Satomi, and various others—had been imprisoned for many years. The Kuramae faction was composed of those Communists who had followed "legal tactics" and remained free. Its ranks were made up largely of intellectuals—Kamiyama Shigeo, Nakanishi Kō, Hosokawa Karoku, and Horie Yūichi, among others. The faction chose the name Kuramae because its members had first sought to establish a Communist organization after the surrender in Kuramae Industrial Hall, in the Shinjuku district of Tōkyō.

These two factions changed composition and ultimately disintegrated in the first years after the Occupation and were replaced by the so-called Chūō and Kansai factions. The Chūō or Central faction represented the dominant group in the party: Tokuda, Nosaka, Itō Ritsu, Shida Shigeo, Hakamada Satomi, and many others. The Kansai faction, taking its name from the Ōsaka region where its strength was centered, included Shiga, Miyamoto, Hasegawa, Kasuga Shōjirō, and Takenaka Tsunesaburo. The development of the cleavage between these two factions occurred about 1947 and was connected with friction among "the big three" in the party during the initial period—Tokuda, Shiga, and Nosaka.

The factional divisions within the party, both during this early period and later, were in considerable part the product of power struggles and personal rivalries. Naturally, however, it was necessary to justify divisions or defend them in policy and ideological terms. Undoubtedly, policy differences played an independent role in some cases. Whatever the situation, however, these internal rivalries were greatly exacerbated by external interference in party affairs. When the Cominform first challenged the Central (Mainstream) leaders, it was inevitable that their opponents would rush to take advantage of these circumstances. As noted earlier, the debate between Mainstream and anti-Mainstream forces within the Japanese Communist Party was bitter and protracted in the weeks that followed the Cominform attack of January 6, 1950.

Shiga presented the Central Executive Committee of the party with a written document that included a very sharp attack on party leadership. He called for an immediate struggle against those who were "distorting the truth within the party," and for a forthright recognition of the "complete Titoization of our party at the present time." He also attacked the unwillingness of the Politburo to conduct frank self-criticism, the excessive bureaucratism of party leaders, and the lack of sufficient emphasis on the international role of the Soviet Union.

The document, so clearly aimed at securing Soviet support for the minority faction, struck the party like a bombshell. Before presenting it to the enlarged Central Committee Plenum on January 18, 1950, Shiga moderated some of the language, but it remained a challenging condemnation. Moreover, after the January meetings had been concluded, the document in its unexpurgated version was circulated widely throughout the party, presumably by International faction supporters. Consequently, on April 15, the Mainstream struck back. *Akahata,* the party organ firmly under control of the Mainstream, sharply attacked Shiga and Miyamoto as "Trotskyites" who were heading a movement, "identical with the attack of the ruling class," to overthrow Tokuda and Nosaka.

The use of such terms as "Titoist" and "Trotskyite" was, of course, significant. In the final analysis, the struggle for power within the Japanese Communist Party was very likely to be determined by the reaction of Soviet and Chinese leaders. By mid-April, there were signs that these leaders had rallied behind the Mainstream. It is extremely interesting that precisely one day before the *Akahata* attack on the Shiga group, the Cominform organ published the complete Tokuda report to the January 19th meeting of the JCP Central Committee.

Shiga, threatened with expulsion, was forced to apologize for some of his actions and attitudes in late April. On May 1, in connection with presenting Tokuda's new proposals for party action, the party asserted through its spokesman Itō Ritsu that all "deviationism" had ceased. At this point, incidentally, relations between Tokuda and Itō were very close, despite the suspicions harbored against Itō by certain party members. Itō's announcement proved to be very premature. Personal relations were now inflamed, and disagreements on tactics were also serious. The struggle for power continued. The purges of early June found the Japanese Communist Party badly split, with International faction elements disregarding headquarters instructions in many cases and advancing their own policies.

Headed by Shiino, the eight-man Party Directorate that replaced the purged Central Committee on June 7, 1950, was composed entirely of Mainstream representatives. Immediately a drastic purge within the party got underway. Hundreds of International faction supporters were ousted from party posts and, in many cases, excluded from party membership. In retaliation, Mainstream opponents published numerous pamphlets and other forms of polemic literature denouncing Yoyogi. A state of intermittent civil war continued for some four years.[12]

---

[12] The foregoing account of factional disputes is drawn from my interviews with Satō Noboru, Kasuga Shōjirō, Andō Jimbei, Naitō Tomochika, and Yamabe Kentarō in Tōkyō, November 26-28, 1963, and from the following published sources: Koyama Hirotake, *Sengo Nihon Kyōsantō shi* and *Sengo no Nihon Kyōsantō* (*The Postwar Japanese Communist Party*), Tōkyō, 1962; Shinoda, *Nihon Kyōsantō senryaku senjutsu shi; Tokushin Geppō* (*The Monthly Report of the Public Safety Investigation Bureau*), April 1951; and Yaginuma, *Nihon Kyōsantō undō shi.*

The lines of policy division within the Japanese Communist Party, confused as they were by personal factors, became enormously complex in the period after the Cominform criticism. Both factions moved "left," but the International faction initially took up the more militant stand, stressing illegal activities, insisting that the main issues were the elimination of American power from the world scene and the strengthening of ties with the Soviet Union, China, and other Communist forces to achieve a true unity of the world's proletariat. They forecast the advent of World War III within two or three years and argued that a second front should be established in Japan immediately to aid the North Korean army. Accordingly, they sought to establish cells in strategic locations, such as in important factories, and they planned various sabotage operations. They were sharply critical of Mainstream "right wing opportunists," who in their eyes were content with local power struggles based on such issues as wage increases and similar matters of little consequence.

The Mainstream, utilizing the slogan "Build a National Liberation United Front!" after the onset of the Korean War, continued to emphasize the creation of mass organizations and sought to cover illegal activities under the veil of legal action. It attacked the extremism of the Internationalists, charging that their policies constituted Trotskyist provocation of the enemy and represented a form of "left infantilism." The Mainstream argued that legal and illegal activities had to be blended in such a fashion as not to frighten or antagonize the masses.

Later, the International faction shifted its position and sought to divorce itself from the extremist programs of 1951-1952. By the time of the 6th National

Meanwhile, most Mainstream leaders and nearly one hundred younger cadres had fled into exile in Peking. An efficient "underground railway" had been established. Leaders facing detention or young terrorists wanted for acts of violence suddenly disappeared, and Japanese police were unable to locate them. Their whereabouts remained a secret, although it was suspected that at least some were in China. Beginning in 1955 and continuing until 1958, these men reappeared, and it was established that almost all had spent the intervening years in Peking. The younger cadres had received intensive training in such centers as the Marx–Lenin Institute of Peking. Older leaders had worked closely with their Chinese comrades. As we shall emphasize throughout this study, it would be difficult to exaggerate how much this exile influenced the subsequent orientation of the Japanese Communist Party.

The death of Tokuda in late 1953 precipitated an even more complicated situation within the Japanese Communist Party. Shiino had been purged by the Japanese government in September 1951 and succeeded by Komatsu Yūichirō. On the surface, however, the two primary leaders were Shida Shigeo and Itō Ritsu. Following Tokuda's death, a new struggle for power took place, with these two—both Mainstream in origin—playing the key roles. Ultimately, Shida emerged victorious, and Itō was ousted from the party on charges of being a spy and informer. He subsequently disappeared in what remains one of the great mysteries of Japanese left-wing politics.[13]

Meanwhile, the Internationalists, benefiting from the absence of the key Mainstream leaders and the struggle within Mainstream ranks, were gradually strengthening their position within the party. Moreover, as noted earlier, they had begun to shift their policies. Starting as strong

---

Conference in 1955 it was seeking to get Mainstream leaders to join in "thorough self-criticism" concerning the ultra-left program.

The International faction, not a large element in the party, had its chief centers of strength in the Chūgoku region, and in the prefectures of Nagasaki, Fukuoka, and Fukushima. Intense struggles took place at the local and prefectural levels throughout the period 1950–1955 in the course of efforts by both factions to recruit or hold supporters. In many areas, the party was in total chaos. Significant numbers of International faction partisans were formally ousted from the party by the dominant Mainstream faction, and they, in turn, tried to set up separate cells and communication facilities.

[13] For the formal declaration on the purge of Itō, see *Akahata*, September 21, 1953, p. 1, and *Zenei*, September 1955, pp. 38–39. In the most savage language, Itō was accused of selling out the party to foreign and domestic reactionaries, and his case was compared to that of Lavrenti Beria. Did he meet the same fate? Itō disappeared without a trace, and rumors persist, without any evidence, that he was liquidated at party orders.

advocates of militancy, responsible for many of the "ultra-leftist adventurist" activities of the 1950–1952 period, the International faction
leaders became increasingly disillusioned with the 1951 Draft Thesis.
It is to be reiterated that they did not participate in the 4th Party Conference held in February 1951, nor did they regard this conference and
the 5th Party Conference, held in October, as legitimate. As far as the
anti-Mainstream group was concerned, the 1951 Thesis had never been
officially approved by the Japanese Communist Party. By 1953, trends
at home and abroad had begun to benefit them. The tide was running
against the "leftist" policies for which Shida was now the prime symbol.

Thus, at the 6th Party Conference in 1955 the old International
faction leaders pressed hard for a "full self-criticism" on the part of
Shida and other Mainstream leaders. Their hope, of course, was to
effect a coup d'etat and capture control of the central party organization. They were thwarted, however—apparently by the activities of
Miyamoto Kenji, erstwhile International faction leader. Miyamoto, who
had been in close contact with Mainstream leaders and with the
Chinese, came forth in the role of compromiser, rather than supporter
of the International faction cause. Although the 6th Party Conference
represented a substantial gain for the Internationalists, the Mainstream
retained control of the organization—and the policies—of the party.
The party split was formally mended, and International faction members were readmitted and given a larger role in party affairs. Mainstream leaders did engage in some self-criticism, as we have noted, but
they did not relinquish the reins of power. Moreover, key Mainstream
leaders such as Nosaka, Shida, and Konno reemerged into the open,
prepared to assume leadership, thereby complicating the plans of the
Internationalists.

The factional struggle within the Japanese Communist Party was thus
far from ended. Both the Russians and the Chinese, moreover, were
now deeply involved. The 1950 Cominform criticism itself had produced the first deep fissure in the postwar Japanese Communist Party.
Had the Mainstream persisted in its resistance to that criticism, it is
likely that Soviet support would have been thrown to the Shiga-
Miyamoto group. The Mainstream bowed to the militant line, however, and the Russians likely discovered that the International faction
was a small minority, controlling scarcely more than 10 percent of the
party. The Chinese, with their better knowledge of JCP affairs and
personalities, quite possibly urged support for the chastened Mainstream
leaders.

In any case, both the Russian and Chinese parties threw their support to Tokuda and his followers. They indicated that support first by printing Tokuda's speeches and reports in prominent party organs. The 1951 Thesis was officially endorsed by the Cominform journal on November 23, by *Pravda* on the following day, and by Peking Radio one week later, on December 1. This is scarcely surprising because, as we noted earlier, the indications are strong that the thesis was compiled in its final form only after lengthy consultations in Moscow and Peking.

Coupled with support for the Mainstream leaders were Sino–Soviet exhortations for unity within Japanese Communist ranks. No better example of the Chinese approach to the Japanese Communist Party during this period can be cited than the Peking *People's Daily* editorial of September 3, 1950.[14] Due to a lack of experience, claimed the editorial, the Japanese Communist Party had committed certain errors, but these had been corrected after January, and a proper general line for the party had been defined. Certain JCP members had doubted or rejected the correct Central Committee line, Peking asserted, and had advanced certain incorrect leftist slogans; these members had also demanded that the party enter into agreements with them and take certain unnecessary organizational measures. Such an attitude was wrong, according to the editorial. The dissidents should unite with the majority.

This was strong language, and without doubt it was directed against the International faction. At the same time, Peking indicated some concern about the cavalier attitude of certain Mainstream leaders and the serious dangers of continuing disunity. It was important, asserted the editorial, for the majority to adopt a careful attitude toward comrades who held divergent opinions. They should be heard with patience, and differences of opinion allowed if the comrades would accept party discipline. A distinction must be made between loyal comrades and spies who had infiltrated the party. The editorial concluded with the view that unity was vital, and that this represented "our sincere proposal to the Japanese comrades" for attaining unity.

In Tokyo, Shiino Etsurō immediately expressed his appreciation for the advice of the Chinese comrades and called on all members to heed it. As we have seen, however, unity remained illusive, and the CCP was forced to continue its efforts as peacemaker. There is good reason to believe that the proposals advanced at the 6th National Party Conference in mid-1955 reflected Chinese views, and resulted in part at least from lengthy sessions with Chinese comrades, despite later denials.

---

[14] For a Japanese translation of this editorial, see *Nihon Kyōsantō gojūnen mondai shiryō shū*, Vol. II, p. 125–129.

Essentially, those proposals represented a compromise, with the object of reunifying the party. The Mainstream leaders would engage in some self-criticism, and party tactics—but not the basic program—would be altered. The old International faction members would be invited to rejoin the party, and some positions would be given to them. Perhaps, as some ex-Communists now believe, there was another aspect to the Chinese formula for peace—namely, a plan to make Miyamoto Kenji Secretary-General of the party.[15] In any case, Miyamoto shifted his position in this period, deserting the International faction and becoming a leading figure in the new Mainstream coalition.

By mid-1955, the Chinese Communists were thus deeply involved in the internal affairs of the Japanese Communist Party. In the midst of a major crisis for that party, they had served as hosts—and tutors— to more than one hundred first- and second-generation Japanese Communist leaders. For five years or more these individuals had worked, studied, and lived with their Chinese comrades, thereby establishing ties of the greatest intimacy. When this factor was added to the influence of the Chinese revolutionary model, which had been steadily growing since the victory of 1949, the Chinese Communist Party was able to exercise an influence over Japanese Communism second to none. There is, of course, no indication that Soviet leaders objected to these Chinese advances. Indeed it is entirely possible that in Soviet opinion Japan represented a legitimate Chinese "sphere of influence."

The extent of Chinese authority can perhaps be suggested by the report of a participant in a discussion of high Japanese Communist officials in 1955. According to Kasuga Shōjirō, when the issue of self-criticism of "ultra-leftist adventurism" was being debated, Nosaka cautioned that extensive self-criticism regarding militant tactics would be unwise because it would have an adverse impact on the Chinese comrades. Nosaka then proceeded to mention the names of several Chinese leaders, asserting that they had promised to provide any form of aid that the Japanese Communist Party might need, including military equipment when and if it were required.[16]

Thus, even before the CPSU 20th Party Congress and the first rumblings of dispute between the Soviet and Chinese parties, the leaders of Peking had established a position of substantial influence with the majority faction of the Japanese Communist Party.

---

[15] This view was expressed by Kasuga in his November 26, 1963 interview with me.

[16] Interview with Kasuga, November 26, 1963.

IV

THE RETURN TO LEGALISM
AND THE ATTEMPT TO CREATE
A UNITED FRONT

Once again, in the period after 1955, trends in the international Communist movement played a major role in determining events within the Japanese Communist Party. Briefly, let us review the crucial happenings of the 1956–1957 period. In 1956, Khrushchev and his supporters consolidated and advanced their position within the Soviet Union, and, in certain respects, the 20th Party Congress of the CPSU held in February of that year sealed the Khrushchevian victory. In his continuing struggle for power, the Soviet leader had increasingly emphasized two themes: substantial improvements in living standards for the Russian people and an end to terrorism. These themes were developed extensively in the 20th Party Congress, climaxed by the famous secret speech denouncing Stalin.

De-Stalinization had almost immediate repercussions, especially in East Europe. In June the workers' riots occurred in Poznan, and soon Poland was seething with unrest. The resurrection of Wladyslaw Gomulka, previously ousted as a Titoist, and the refusal of the Polish Central Committee to reelect Soviet Marshal Konstantin Rokossovski marked a major challenge to Russian authority. Within a few months the famous Hungarian uprising occurred, and the Russians, after a period of indecision, decided to intervene directly with Soviet troops. Hungarian resistance was crushed in November, but the Russians were placed on the political defensive throughout the world. East Europe was now vibrating with unrest and anti-Russian sentiment.

These developments enabled the Chinese Communists to play a significant role in Europe as well as in Asia. We now know that the Chinese counseled the Russians to allow the Polish Communists somewhat greater freedom of action, but urged Soviet intervention against the Nagy regime in Hungary.[1] Chinese involvement in the complex events of this era may well have been the determining factor in some Soviet decisions, since it is clear that Soviet leaders themselves were divided and uncertain. Meanwhile, the Chinese undertook their own "liberalization" experiment, quite probably with the unrest in East Europe in mind. On February 27, 1957, Mao Tse-tung delivered his famous "Let One Hundred Flowers Bloom" speech, outlining the inevitability of contradictions even in a Socialist society, and the importance of resolving "nonfundamental" contradictions in a peaceful manner. For a few months an extraordinary freedom of criticism prevailed in China, until the volume and intensity of that criticism forced the Chinese leaders to retreat. A most severe campaign against "Rightists" followed, during which thousands were forced to undergo thought reform. This campaign was at its height in the summer and early fall of 1957.[2]

Meanwhile, Khrushchev was also moving against domestic opponents. On June 29, 1957, Molotov, Malenkov, and Kaganovich were removed from the Politburo and Central Committee of the CPSU, and Shepilov was removed from the Central Committee. On October 26 Marshal Zhukov was ousted as Minister of Defense and Commander of the Army while he was on an official visit to Yugoslavia. Thus both the Soviet and Chinese "Mainstream" were in a relatively strong position by the time of the International Conference of Communist Parties, which was convened in November to commemorate the 40th anniversary of the Russian Revolution, and from which emanated the famous Moscow Declaration of 1957.

This conference witnessed the first significant escalation of the dispute between Russia and China. Previously, problems had been dis-

---

[1] For the Chinese account of their role during the troubles in East Europe, see *The Origin and Development of the Differences Between the Leadership of the CPSU and Ourselves,* Comment on the Open Letter of the Central Committee of the CPSU by the editorial departments of *Jen-min Jih-pao* and *Hong-ch'i,* September 6, 1963, English pamphlet edition, pp. 17–18.

[2] Mao's speech was carried by *Jen-min Jih-pao* on June 19, 1957; it was published in English, under the title *On the Correct Handling of Contradictions Among the People,* by the New Century Publishers, New York, July 1957. For other accounts, see Dennis J. Doolin, *Communist China—The Politics of Student Opposition,* Hoover Institution Studies, Stanford, 1964; Roderick MacFarquhar, *The Hundred Flowers Campaign and the Chinese Intellectuals,* New York, 1960; and articles in the *China Quarterly,* No. 12, October–December 1962.

cussed privately, and there is no evidence that third parties were aware of any difficulties. Now, however, disagreements were aired before the chief representatives of other Communist parties. The Chinese came to the conference disturbed by the attack on Stalin, particularly by the fact that it had come without warning and seemed to be primarily connected with Khrushchev's bid for personal power rather than the welfare of the international Communist movement. While the Chinese publicly supported the 20th Party Congress of 1956, including the position taken on Stalin, they also attempted to delimit carefully Stalin's errors and highlight his contributions. At the conference itself, the Chinese took the lead in insisting that *both* revolutionary and peaceful methods should be available in the course of the transition from capitalism to socialism. They criticized the draft resolution as placing exclusive emphasis on peaceful revolution. While the final declaration took some account of their views, the Chinese were later to proclaim that they had been dissatisfied and had signed only to preserve the unity of the Communist world.[3]

All of these events were pregnant with implications for the Japanese Communist Party. As has been noted, a shift in JCP policy had begun some months before the 20th CPSU Congress. Indeed, as early as January 1, 1955, certain changes had been signaled by an *Akahata* editorial entitled "Party Unity and Solidarity with All Democratic Forces," and by Watanabe Mitsuru's article, "Meeting the Year 1955," in the January 1955 issue of *Zenei*. These articles, reflecting the increasing influence of the anti-Mainstream forces within the party, called for a departure from "ultra-leftist adventurism" considerably in advance of the 6th Party Conference.

At the time of the 6th Party Conference in mid-1955, a number of JCP leaders suddenly appeared in the open after a long period of exile and underground activities. These included Nosaka, Shida Shigeo, and Konno Yojirō who came forth in public for the first time since 1950. Their appearances were shrewdly timed and handled to achieve maximum press coverage and public sympathy. Nevertheless, pressure within the party against the old Mainstream continued to be heavy, as we have noted, and a number of anti-Mainstream elements obtained significant party posts.

The 1955 Conference, indeed, marks the beginning of a fundamental realignment of forces within the JCP, with the old factional designa-

---

[3] For the official Chinese version of their role in the 1957 Moscow meeting, see *The Origin and Development of the Differences Between the Leadership of the CPSU and Ourselves*, pp. 18–24.

tions such as the International faction gradually losing their meaning. The star of Miyamoto Kenji and his so-called "neutral" or "centrist" group was now on the rise.[4]

The new program of the 20th Congress of the CPSU had almost immediate repercussions on the Japanese Communist Party, as it did on all other Communist parties. The first response came in a JCP Plenum resolution of March 24, 1956, lavishing praise on the Soviet Congress—but with no reference to the issue of Stalin. Incidentally, after his ouster, Kamiyama was to charge that the party's concern for the cult of personality problem "ended with a criticism of Tokuda."[5]

Nevertheless, at its 7th Plenary meeting in June 1956, the Central Committee of the Japanese Communist Party agreed to consider a new program for peaceful, parliamentary revolution because, according to the resolution, the 1951 Thesis did not fit the changed situation. On the surface, at least, this represented a triumph for the old International faction. Internal controversy increased within the party, however, and the 7th Party Congress was not convened for more than a year, finally meeting from July 21 to August 1, 1958, in Tōkyō.[6]

Prior to the congress, several significant internal developments occurred in the party. Shida, erstwhile leader of the Mainstream faction, faded away, sidelined by the new leaders because he, of all figures, had come to symbolize the era of left adventurism. No doubt, the hope was that his absence would prevent the International faction from insisting on a thorough review and criticism of the old extremist policies. Miyamoto, now leading the Mainstream, drafted a new program. Hakamada also seems to have played a significant role.[7] It was this program that was presented to the 7th Party Congress.

---

[4] It is interesting a note the assessment of the JCP 6th Party Conference by Kamiyama Shigeo after his ouster from the party. According to Kamiyama, "the nationalist tendencies" that had been prevailing within the party appeared to be partly overcome. In fact, however, the new program had "a strong Stalinist influence." Furthermore, the compromises that had been effected resulted in the gradual disintegration of the old factions, and the realignment of new forces. Kamiyama Shigeo, *Nikkyō shidōbu ni atau—kokusai kyōsanshugi no sōrosen o mamotte* (*An Open Letter to the Japanese Communist Party Leaders—In Defense of the General Line of International Communism*), Vol. I, Tōkyō, August 30, 1964, p. 117.

[5] *Ibid.*

[6] The official documents and reports pertaining to the 7th Party Congress are printed in the September 1958 special issue of *Zenei*. These include the Political Report to the Central Committee delivered by Nosaka and other reports by Shiga, Miyamoto, and Hakamada.

[7] Again, the later account by Kamiyama of internal events in the party is interesting. *Akahata* first published the new program on September 30, 1957. Prior to this, on July 22, Hakamada had emerged from his long period of

The 1957 program had a very strong Chinese flavor. Even its title— *Tōshō* (Party Program)—was an innovation borrowed from Chinese Communist practice. Discussion on the draft lasted for many days, and in the end a final decision was postponed in order to avoid an open party split. The anti-Mainstream group, shorn of some of its old members but still controlling nearly one-third of the congress votes, fought to amend the proposal with respect to several critical points.

Once again the three basic issues that had been vital to the party since 1945 were hotly debated. The Mainstream position on the United States continued to be hard. The draft defined Japan as a semicolonial nation and stipulated that the United States should be regarded as the primary enemy, since the fate of its Japanese lackeys would be determined by American success or failure. The anti-Mainstream position was that the primary enemy was Japanese monopoly capitalism. If the capitalists were defeated, the United States would be compelled to retreat. In these two rival positions, one sees the conflict between nationalist priorities and priorities for the class struggle, the classical Marxist position. In them also are reflected the mounting differences between the People's Republic of China and the Soviet Union.

With respect to the nature of the revolution, the Mainstream defined it as "a people's democratic revolution for national liberation and democracy." It continued to insist that the emphasis should be on a broad united front encompassing national bourgeois elements as well as workers and peasants, but a front led by the working class. The opposition argued that "the democratic bourgeois revolution" in Japan had been completed and that the coming revolution *had to be socialist in content and form.* Again, this separation of views mirrored the differing experiences and interpretations of China and Russia in considerable degree.[8]

---

hiding and appeared openly at party headquarters. Kamiyama asserts that his influence was substantial in connection with the draft program. Of course, both Miyamoto and Hakamada had been in close contact with their Chinese comrades.

However, the anti-Mainstream faction, according to Kamiyama, was able to force certain changes both in the draft program and in the Political Report, first published in *Akahata* on November 7. These changes were never supported in good faith by the Mainstream faction, he charges, and were accepted merely for tactical reasons.

On November 27, 1957, the Moscow Declaration was made public. Immediately, Kamiyama and a few others insisted that the Japanese Communist Party take formal action in support of this declaration. This move was initially opposed by Miyamoto and Hakamada, according to Kamiyama (Vol. I, p. 118).

[8] It is also to be noted that the differing interpretations of "the coming revolution" harked back to the prewar debates between the *Rōnō* faction and their Comintern Communist opponents, a factor of no small significance.

Finally, the draft anticipated violent resistance from "the reactionary forces" in power and insisted that whether forceful or peaceful means should be employed depended on the action of the enemy. The anti-Mainstream group, on the other hand, argued that a peaceful transition to socialism by means of the peace movement and the parliamentary struggle was possible. On this point, the two factions took positions remarkably close to those debated in Moscow a few months earlier, positions faithfully reflecting the Soviet and Chinese views. By this time the old International faction, and particularly the Kasuga group within that faction, had begun to espouse the structural reform theories outlined by Togliatti, arguing that the Japanese and Italian situations had much in common and that the tactics being followed by the Italian Communist movement, properly Japanized, could be extremely effective.

While structural reform was given a variety of philosophic expressions, its most basic essentials can be set forth simply.[9] Modern capitalism, according to the structural reformists, had undergone substantial alterations in the course of its evolution. The old dependence on colonies had disappeared, and the exclusive control over all facets of the capitalist system by a small elite had been changed. At present, capitalism was characterized by mass ownership of stock, the separation of ownership from management, and the prominence of long-range planning in big enterprise. The public policy and social welfare aspects of capitalism, moreover, had been greatly strengthened.

Under these circumstances, a new approach to the drive for socialism was possible and essential. Simple parliamentary reformism on the one hand, and sole dependence on war or revolution on the other, were mistaken tactics. Rather, it was necessary for the working class to combine two struggles. First, this class had to abet and accelerate capitalist reform. This meant increased worker participation in management; support for profit-sharing, cooperative, and nationalization programs; and a struggle for ever broader welfare provisions. Quantitative reforms could ultimately lead to a qualitative change in the power structure, particularly if they were coupled with a second fight: the struggle to gain control through parliamentary means of the political decision-making process itself. The working class had to so influence and control basic national policies that these policies would gradually shift

---

[9] For detailed expositions of structural reform doctrine from a variety of viewpoints, see Sakisaka Itsurō, *Shakaishugi kakumei ron* (*Theories of Socialist Revolution*), Tōkyō, 1961; and Sakisaka (ed.), *Kozo kaikaku ron* (*Theories of Structural Reform*), Tōkyō, 1961. The latter work includes a symposium presenting different views on structural reform.

from supporting the interests of monopoly capitalism to supporting the interests of the whole people.

Structural reform, thus, did not end with the concept of individual reforms. Rather, it focused on the ultimate goal of socialism and represented a new formulation of the thesis that parliamentarism and the mass struggle had to be combined in some fashion to achieve Socialist victory. The most immediate tasks in a broad sense within Japan were to establish a neutralist state and to concentrate on the fight against Japanese monopoly capitalism (rather than emphasize American imperialism). To attack Japanese monopoly capitalism by combining the political and economic struggle against it would make possible a peaceful democratic route to socialism.

Since nearly one-third of the delegates to the 7th Party Congress were opposed to the original draft, a temporary action program was adopted pending further discussion. That program omitted or obscured the truly controversial issues and repeated standard party positions: the struggle for world peace and peaceful coexistence among nations with different social systems; normalization of diplomatic relations with all countries; opposition to American imperialism and to the reactionary forces in Japan, to military bases and to U.S. control of Okinawa and Ogasawara; a fight against the subversion of democratic rights in Japan and for the improvement of the people's livelihood; guarantees for the workers; opposition to the confiscation of farms by the U.S. Army; liberation of the forests and pasture lands of the big landowners for the poor peasants; and opposition to the financial and economic policies of the U.S. imperialists and monopoly capitalists.[10] The party also pledged its full support at this time for the Moscow Declaration of 1957.

Thirty-one members were elected to the Central Committee, together with six candidate members. The International faction made gains, with such men as Naitō Tomochika, Yamada Rokuzaemon, and Nishikawa Yoshihiko replacing Nishizawa Ryūji, Hasegawa Hiroshi, Matsumoto Saneki, Konno Yojirō, and Takenaka Tsunesaburō. As noted earlier, however, the Mainstream, augmented by Miyamoto and some other ex-International faction men, held firm control of the Central Committee

---

[10] The following themes summarize the basic points of disagreement between the two JCP factions: What was the main enemy—U.S. imperialism (Mainstream) or Japanese monopoly capitalism (anti-Mainstream)? What should be the nature of the coming revolution—a people's democratic revolution for national liberation and democracy (Mainstream) or a Socialist revolution (anti-Mainstream)? What means were required for a successful revolution—both peaceful means and violence (Mainstream) or a peaceful transition via the peace movement and the parliamentary struggle (anti-Mainstream)?

and, more importantly, of the Presidium or Executive Council.[11] Miyamoto himself had attained the post of Secretary General. Seen in retrospect, the old International faction was close to the zenith of its power and influence. The exiles were now flowing back from China in increasing numbers, taking over top- and middle-echelon positions within the party. Between sixty and ninety individuals returned during this period, almost all of them young militants affiliated with the Mainstream. This group proved decisive in the power struggle for control of the Japanese Communist Party.

That struggle, which dominated the party in the years prior to the 8th Party Congress of July 1961, was increasingly affected by the widening rift between Russia and China. Once again, a brief review of key developments in the international scene will be helpful. We now know that the year 1959 marked a new and much more serious phase in the rising tensions between Moscow and Peking.[12] Suddenly, a number of concrete issues inflamed relations between the two governments and parties. In June 1959 the Russians "tore up" the military agreement of October 1957, refusing to furnish the Chinese with an atomic bomb sample or technical data concerning its manufacture. The Sino–Indian border controversy, now involving bloodshed, also produced grave tensions. An official Soviet statement released by Tass in September was correctly interpreted by the Chinese as indicating some sympathy for the Indian position. Even more infuriating to Peking was the trend toward Russo–American rapprochement, and the fact that Khrushchev, returning home from Washington by way of Peking, saw fit to lecture the Chinese leaders on such issues as peaceful revolution, the communes, and proper relations with the United States.

The Chinese struck back in the spring of 1960 with the publication of "Long Live Leninism!" in the April issue of *Hong Ch'i* (*Red Flag*). This article constituted a direct challenge to Khrushchev's views on a wide range of subjects, although the Yugoslav "revisionists" were

---

[11] According to Kamiyama, after the 7th Congress the Executive Council, operating secretly and "without authorization," systematically limited the role and powers of the Central Committee, where the anti-Mainstream faction had its only effective representation (Vol. I, pp. 118, 128).

[12] Voluminous materials, both of a documentary and an interpretative nature, now exist on the Sino–Soviet dispute. For varying approaches and extensive bibliographies, see William E. Griffith, *The Sino–Soviet Rift*, Cambridge, Massachusetts, 1964; Richard Lowenthal, *World Communism—The Disintegration of a Secular Faith*, New York, 1964; Klaus Mehnert, *Peking and Moscow*, New York, 1963; G. F. Hudson, R. Lowenthal, and R. MacFarquhar, *The Sino–Soviet Dispute*, London and New York, 1961; and Donald S. Zagoria, *The Sino–Soviet Conflict*, Princeton, 1962.

made the public target. The CPSU retaliated at Bucharest in late June. On the eve of the Bucharest meeting, the CPSU distributed a "Letter of Information," dated June 21, to all participating parties. This letter, which had been sent to the Chinese Communist Party, represented a trenchant criticism of CCP policies and actions. At the meeting itself, moreover, Khrushchev personally launched a bitter attack on the Chinese, charging them with desiring to unleash World War III, being "purely nationalist" with respect to the Indian border conflict, and employing "Trotskyite ways" against the Soviet Union. Various East European parties joined in the attack, although many representatives, stunned by events of which they had no prior notice, remained silent.

The Chinese defended themselves vigorously and then insisted that the future of the international Communist movement would never be decided "by the baton of any individual." The CCP spokesman also asserted that "our party believes in and obeys the truth of Marxism–Leninism and Marxism–Leninism alone, and will never submit to erroneous views which run counter to Marxism–Leninism." The Bucharest crisis reverberated throughout the Communist world. It also caused drastic changes in official relations between China and Russia. Furious with the Chinese, Soviet leaders in July suddenly recalled all Soviet technicians and experts working in China, closed down certain publications devoted to Sino–Soviet friendship, and took other drastic actions in an effort to put maximum pressure on Peking.

Against this background, the November 1960 Meeting of the Eighty-one Communist Parties was held in Moscow. The atmosphere was tense; not surprisingly, the meeting was marked by many heated debates. Earlier, in September, a top-level Chinese delegation had come to Moscow to discuss differences, but no agreement was reached. Thus, the controversy was projected into the Drafting Committee of Twenty-six Parties and into the full sessions of the conference. Every party was drawn into the dispute, directly or indirectly. The issues, of course, were not new: peaceful coexistence versus militancy; international economic integration of socialist societies versus national self-sufficiency; the danger of factionalism and a refusal to accept majority decisions versus the importance of decision-making on the basis of consultation, consensus, and unanimity; and the question of whether "dogmatism" or "revisionism" represented the supreme danger to the international Communist movement.

The resolution as finally adopted—the so-called Moscow Statement—represented a compromise which left neither the Russians nor the Chinese entirely happy, but which had a sufficient number of ambiguous or alternative sections to allow considerable freedom of interpretation. All parties signed the statement, but no basic questions had been resolved, no true unity existed. At the close of 1960, the situation within the international Communist movement was charged with tension and bitterness.

Inevitably, the Japanese Communist Party was deeply affected by these events. The divisions already existing in that party were both deepened and solidified by the Sino–Soviet cleavage. It is difficult to determine precisely when JCP leaders first learned of the trouble between Moscow and Peking. Certainly, there were intimations from an earlier period. In the autumn of 1957, for example, an editorial on the JCP in the Chinese Communist *People's Daily* caused the International faction to suspect sharp differences of opinion between the Chinese and Russians.[13] Increasingly, moreover, members of that faction recognized that their debate with the Mainstream largely paralleled certain questions being discussed in international circles. Thus, even in the 1957–1958 period, some Japanese Communist leaders of the International faction knew or suspected trouble. It is likely that the Mainstream leaders were much better informed, because their contacts with Peking were extremely close. Some evidence suggests, indeed, that at first Mainstream leaders kept information concerning the dispute to themselves, and that, when questioned by the opposition, they denied that the trouble existed or was serious, claiming support for their position from *both* the CPSU and the CCP.[14]

After Bucharest, however, International faction leaders were fully aware of the serious nature of the problem.[15] Consequently, in the summer of 1960, Kasuga Shōjirō, now leader of the so-called structural reform group, urged that the party have a high-level discussion of the dispute in order to clarify its official position prior to sending JCP rep-

---

[13] Naitō Tomochika told me that the *Jen-min Jih-pao* editorial alerted him and other anti-Mainstream adherents to the fact that disagreements between the Soviet Union and China existed. Indeed, he dated his consciousness of real differences from this point. Interview, November 27, 1963.

[14] According to Naitō, when the anti-Mainstream forces confronted Miyamoto and Hakamada with the evidence that trouble existed between the Soviet Union and China, the Mainstream leaders denied that such was the case and insisted that their position had full support from both the CPSU and the CCP.

[15] There is wide agreement among such men as Satō, Naitō, and Kasuga that the serious character of the Sino–Soviet cleavage first became known within top party echelons in the summer of 1960, after the Bucharest Conference. First accounts of the problem may have been given to Hakamada and other Mainstream leaders by Liu Shao-ch'i at an earlier date (Satō), but after Bucharest, the problem could no longer be kept from the inner circle of party leaders, whatever their factional identification.

resentatives to Peking for the October celebrations. A Japanese delegation led by Miyamoto and Hakamada was scheduled to go first to Peking for National Day celebrations, and then to Moscow to attend the Soviet anniversary celebration and the International Conference of Eighty-one Parties that was to follow. Mainstream leaders rejected Kasuga's proposal, but a compromise was arranged. Miyamoto would return to Japan with a report after the anniversary celebration; then the party could develop its position on basic issues and instruct Hakamada before the international conference.[16]

This plan was carried out. Thus the first official discussion of the Sino–Soviet dispute took place within the JCP Central Committee in November 1960.[17] Central Committee members were strictly enjoined not to discuss this matter outside the committee, even with other members of the party. The Miyamoto report, in essence, seems to have been a studied attempt to hew to a neutralist line between Moscow and Peking, but with some positions being taken that accorded with current Chinese emphasis. Miyamoto argued that it was unrealistic to eliminate force as a revolutionary tactic as long as imperialism continued to exist, and that it was essential for Japan to participate wholeheartedly in an anti-imperialist front. He also emphasized the thesis that while Japan was a highly developed society in economic terms, it was also a semi-colonial nation under American domination, consequently, the Japanese Communist Party could not follow the same tactics as those being pursued by the Communist parties of Western Europe. He further argued that it was not necessary for the Japanese Communist Party to take a position on the struggle between the Soviet Union and China. Rather, the party should determine its stand on concrete issues, solicit the friendship of all Communist parties, and serve wherever possible as a mediating influence.

It is interesting to study the Mainstream tactics of this period. The primary attempt was to depreciate Sino–Soviet differences and to insist that Mainstream policies had broad international support. For example, according to a participant in the Central Committee meeting, Miyamoto asserted that the evaluation of Japan as a semicolonial nation basically different in character from the societies of Western Europe had actually been advanced by the Canadian and East German parties, and that if it were altered or eliminated, many parties would object. But if available information is correct, the Mainstream leaders were moving in directions certain to disconcert Moscow greatly. Miyamoto,

---

[16] This account, given me by Kasuga, is corroborated by Naito and Satō.
[17] From Kasuga's account.

for example, reportedly praised Enver Hoxha and the Albanian Workers Party in the course of the discussion.[18]

Mainstream views prevailed in the November 1960 Central Committee meeting and formed the basis for the JCP position at the Moscow Conference of Eighty-one Parties later that month. It would be incorrect to say that the Japanese Communist Party openly supported the Chinese at the Moscow Conference. Their position was rather an eclectic one, with the primary emphasis on trying to unify the Soviet and Chinese parties, a role which they shared with the parties of North Korea and North Vietnam.[19] This was an era when the Communist parties of Asia were striving desperately to establish a neutral position from which they could serve as mediators and thus avoid the serious internal repercussions of commitment.

Nevertheless, the events of this conference tended to identify the Japanese Communist Party increasingly with the Chinese. The Japanese delegation participated in the committee discussing the revolution in non-Western countries, and the views expressed by this group, which were incorporated into the final statement, were reportedly influenced strongly by Miyamoto, Hakamada, and the Chinese delegates. Russian

---

[18] "What impressed me most during the course of Miyamoto's report was his praise of Hoxha." Kasuga interview, November 26, 1963.

Kamiyama recounts earlier issues that bore overtones of the Sino–Soviet dispute and related it to the Japanese Communist Party. For example, at the 4th Plenum meeting of January 10–12, 1959, a vigorous discussion centered on whether Japan should aim at "independence" first and foremost, achieving "neutrality" later (a position supposedly having Chinese support), or seek to attain "independence" *through* neutrality (a position in line with Soviet thought). The original proposal was based on the former position, but in the course of debate the latter position was essentially adopted. However, Kamiyama remarks, in the course of drafting the actual resolution, and particularly in implementing it, a "roll-back" took place, reflective of the strength of the Mainstream faction.

Kamiyama also asserts that at the 5th Plenum, March 20–21, 1959, Miyamoto reported on his trip to the Soviet Union, China, and North Korea, and that thereafter "peace" disappeared as the featured theme, and "independence" took its place. Incidentally, it was rumored at this time that Mao Tse-tung himself had apologized for his party's role in the events of 1950–1051, events that produced the internal JCP split and the 1951 Thesis. Throughout this period, according to Kamiyama, the issue of "independence" was central to internal party debates, suggesting the power of the Chinese line that each Communist party should be free, independent, and sovereign, and should not submit to "the baton" of the Soviet party (Kamiyama, Vol. I, pp. 107–147).

[19] According to Kamiyama, Hakamada bragged at length about the JCP role in inducing compromise, a role shared with such men as Ho Chi Minh (*ibid.*).

attitudes, moreover, appeared overbearing and crude to Mainstream leaders. Miyamoto is said to have related an incident where various foreign Communists were being queried on an issue under dispute between the Chinese and Russians. When the Japanese delegate was polled, he replied, "No comment." At this point, Suslov reportedly stood up, banged the table, and said, "That is no way for a Communist to respond!" Miyamoto is said to have cited this as an example of "big-power chauvinism."[20]

During this entire period, relations between the Mainstream and its opponents within the Japanese Communist Party were growing steadily worse. As noted earlier, the Kasuga faction had strongly opposed the draft program presented at the 7th Party Congress, advancing ideas that were basically similar to those presented by Togliatti in June 1956 and developed earlier within the Italian labor and Communist movements. The anti-Mainstream group had drawn its primary strength from within the Tōkyō, Ōsaka, and Hyōgo Prefecture party organizations and from the student leaders of Zengakuren. Its principal ideological leaders were drawn from the old International faction, although, as we have noted, two key figures in that faction, Miyamoto and Hakamada, had now joined the Mainstream and were top party leaders. After the inconclusive 7th Party Congress, the Mainstream, led by Miyamoto, Hakamada, and Nosaka, made the Kasuga structural reform group its central target. They insisted that the party had to wage an all-out struggle against structural reform theories, doctrines being advanced by "social democrats and revisionists who were distorting Marxism–Leninism."

By the spring of 1961, the Mainstream felt secure enough to seek a showdown. The 16th Plenary session of the JCP Central Committee held in April 1961 adopted a draft program fundamentally identical to the program presented to the 7th Party Congress. However, the strength of the anti-Mainstream group was even greater than it had been before the 7th Congress, when only two members of the Central Committee had opposed the Mainstream. Now, eight members voted against the draft, and two abstained. A solid majority supported the program, however, against protests that full opportunity had not been given for discussion and debate. Within a few weeks, on the eve of the 8th Party Congress, Kasuga withdrew from the party, together with six other Central Committee members and candidate members.

Kasuga's statement of defection vigorously outlined a series of griev-

[20] Kasuga interview, November 26, 1963.

ances.[21] Once again Kasuga insisted on the primacy of *the class struggle* and the importance of relating Japan to *the universal fight* between socialism and capitalism. The Miyamoto draft, he asserted, stressed only the "anti-American, patriotic struggle," ignoring the fact that Japan was itself an imperialist nation in which the economic and political power of the old war criminals and reactionaries was rapidly being rebuilt. Japan was aligned with, but not necessarily subordinate to, American imperialism. To place extensive emphasis on the themes of subordination and semicolonialism was to challenge the correct thesis that the Japanese struggle should be an organic part of the world struggle for peaceful coexistence and total disarmament, via Japanese neutralization. Furthermore, argued Kasuga, the Miyamoto draft failed to appreciate the fact that Japanese monopoly capitalism had developed rapidly after the war, reaching the stage where its contradictions could only be solved by a fundamental socialist transformation of Japanese society. In Kasuga's opinion, to speak of a people's democratic revolution, minimizing or ignoring the imperative need for an immediate socialist revolution, was to misunderstand the socioeconomic evolution of Japanese society.

His second major category of grievances related to the destruction of of intraparty democracy and the violation of party regulations. Kasuga charged that anyone who dared to criticize the Executive Council was threatened with being purged as a liberal, revisionist, or antiparty element. "No matter what kind of mistake headquarters may make," he said, "party members are forced to say that it is fundamentally correct." The past dogmatic and autocratic behavior of party leaders which caused the collapse of the party after 1950 had never been thoroughly criticized or corrected, he asserted. Moreover, Mainstream opponents had been gravely restricted in expressing their views. Although organs existed for the purpose of presenting different points of view, the Executive Council had progressively denied access to such organs and sought to prohibit public discussion of Council policies. Violations of party regulations, he said, would make the 8th Party Congress an abnormal, unrepresentative gathering. Under its present leadership the Japanese Communist Party had become *a tool of the cadres,* above the masses and contemptuous of them. When would Leninist principles of organization be reestablished?

---

[21] Kasuga's statement of defection, bearing the title "The Japanese Way to Socialism," appeared in several publications. An amended, longer version, entitled "On Behalf of the Japanese Road Toward Socialism," is given in *Atarashii Jidai* (*The New Age*), No. 1, November 1961, pp. 76–80.

Rather than continue as a party faction, Kasuga said that he and his group elected to leave the Japanese Communist Party because they doubted that it could become "the genuine vanguard of a mass party," and they set this as their objective. The Kasuga group defection had certain clear implications in terms of the storm now raging on the international Communist scene. The Kasuga line was, in essence, the Soviet line. Kasuga and his followers argued that the main assault should be made against Japanese capitalism, and that American imperialism should be regarded as an important, but secondary, force. Moreover, they insisted that the Japanese struggle be seen as part of the global struggle of socialism against capitalism, not as a special Afro–Asian national-democratic revolution. These were two themes that fitted closely with current Soviet policies and desires. And when Kasuga charged Japanese Mainstream leaders with being dogmatic and undemocratic, when he demanded that Leninist principles of organization be restored, he was playing on the very de-Stalinization themes that were being advanced by Moscow. Whereas, before the 20th CPSU Party Congress, Tokuda had been widely criticized as being paternalistic and dogmatic, now he and current Mainstream leaders were accused of being undemocratic and Stalinistic.

At one point, Kasuga touched quite openly on the question of JCP-international Communist relations. Speaking of the undemocratic tendencies of Mainstream cadres, he asserted that they had confined discussions of the draft program to a very small group, seeking meanwhile to put the program into actual effect and "pretending to have the full support of foreign Communist parties." The dissident leader, moreover, made a strong effort to utilize the Moscow Statement on behalf of his cause, maintaining that the genius of the statement must be applied to the nature, tasks, and forms of the Japanese revolution. The Miyamoto draft, which in many respects stood in contradiction to the basic themes of the statement, should be corrected, and party organization and methods of operation adjusted to conform with it.

Thus, by the spring of 1961, the struggle within the Japanese Communist Party was developing a closer relationship with the titanic battle now preoccupying the Soviet Union and China. The issues, analogies, and even the epithets were becoming increasingly identified with the Sino–Soviet cleavage. Where this did not happen naturally, it could be induced. It is true that the Mainstream leaders of the Japanese Communist Party tried desperately to secure *full* international support for their positions, and to this end they sought to avoid identification with Peking. Indeed, for as long as possible, they stoutly refused to acknowledge that any cleavage between Russia and China existed, taking this line inside as well as outside the party. And, after being forced to admit that serious troubles within the international Communist movement existed, the Mainstream leaders attempted to restrict discussion of the problem to the greatest possible extent, even within the party, and to preserve an air of neutrality.

Despite these efforts, however, the Mainstream could not conceal for long the fact that its basic tactics and policies were in many respects derivative from the Stalinist era and were almost identical to those being pursued or advocated by Peking. In many cases, these represented the very tactics and policies under sharp assault by Khrushchev. Naturally it was in the interests of all anti-Mainstream groups to highlight these facts. If possible, these opponents had to secure Soviet support, and the most promising method of accomplishing this was to pin the label "pro-Peking" squarely on the Mainstream leaders. Consequently, Kasuga was following sound tactics in alleging that the Mainstream had abandoned the Moscow Statement (Soviet version) and had continued to pursue "ultra-leftist adventurist" policies, misusing the peace movement, misunderstanding the tactic of peaceful coexistence, and removing Japan from the world revolutionary stream. It was also appropriate to denounce the Mainstream leaders as Stalinists, as men guilty of violating Leninist principles of party organization and democracy. The Mainstream could only answer by charging men like Kasuga with pursuing "revisionist, social democratic doctrines," comparing them with those "dangerous enemies of Marxism–Leninism," the Titoists.

In this fashion, the Japanese Communist Party was drawn ever closer to the whirlpool. It was under these circumstances that the 8th Party Congress opened on July 25, 1961. There was no serious debate over the new party program. The Kasuga group was officially "ousted" from the party. With the departure of this faction, the anti-Mainstream forces were greatly weakened; Shiga and a few others remained, but they were in no position to challenge the Mainstream which now represented or controlled fully 90 percent of the party. Thus the old 1951 Thesis was formally replaced at last.

The 8th Congress Program did not differ greatly from the Miyamoto draft presented to the 7th Congress three years earlier.[22] Once again it is instructive to explore the party position on the three basic issues that had been crucial during the postwar era. Dealing with "the American problem," the program defined Japan as a highly developed capitalist

---

[22] The September and October 1961 issues of *Zenei* are devoted entirely to the reports, resolutions, and speeches of the 8th Party Congress.

country, but one still virtually dependent on the United States. Why was it appropriate to define Japan as a semicolony? According to the 1961 Program, this was accurate because Okinawa and the Ogasawara Islands remained under U.S. military occupation; over two hundred military bases with extraterritorial privileges were being operated by American military forces in Japan; and the subservience of the Japanese government to American political and economic policies was "overwhelmingly great."

The Japanese revolution thus had to be a people's democratic revolution with its initial objective the destruction of two enemies: U.S. imperialism and Japanese monopoly capitalism. The former enemy, however, was first in importance and in strength. The program sought to distinguish between its revolution and the Chinese model: The Japanese revolution "must be considered a new revolution in the sense that it is not an anti-imperialist, antifeudalist revolution like the Chinese revolution, but it is an anti-imperialist, antimonopoly capitalist revolution." The central concept of a two-stage *but* uninterrupted revolution was retained. This revolution, moreover, would be carried out by a multiclass, "national democratic united front," led by the Japanese Communist Party. In all significant respects, the Mainstream leaders were now defining the Japanese revolution in Chinese terms.

What were the proper revolutionary tactics? The Communist-led united front should seek to capture as many parliamentary seats as possible. If a majority of seats could be won, then parliament would be transformed from a tool of reaction to an instrument of the people. To commit the party to electoral contests, however, did not imply sanction for a "parliamentary, peaceful revolution." It merely meant that the parliamentary system should be used to further the course of the revolution. If the party emphasized only peaceful revolution, stated the program, the revolution might be defeated; but if the party advocated militant tactics, then its enemies might be provided with an excuse for persecuting it. Hence the question of peaceful or violent revolution hinged on the tactics of the party's enemies. However, it was not conceivable that "the present regime would give up state power to the people willingly." Clearly this was the hard line on revolutionary tactics.

The basic slogan of the 8th Party Congress had been "Struggle for Peace, Independence, Democracy, and the Improvement of the People's Livelihood!" It was not accidental that "peace" and "independence" were placed at the forefront of Communist goals. The development of a massive united front based on the successful exploitation of these issues had long been at the very heart of JCP tactics. After the 8th Party

Congress, therefore, the party faced two central challenges: Utilizing the peace issue, could it develop and lead a genuine and lasting united front, extending deeply into the Japanese masses? And could it handle the growing cleavage between the Soviet Union and China so as to minimize the damage to the Japanese Communist Party? These are the two critical and interrelated problems with which we now deal.

The Japanese Communists had good reason to hope that the strong desires of the Japanese people for peace could be exploited politically. The massive struggle over the revised Mutual Security Treaty in 1960 had represented the most significant united front in Japanese history.[23] An unprecedented number of Japanese participated in the political events of May and June 1960. They signed petitions, engaged in street demonstrations and work stoppages, and attended meetings. At its height, the so-called anti-Ampō movement against renewal of the Mutual Security Treaty probably had enlisted several millions of Japanese in some form of involvement. Initially, the movement was largely in the hands of professionals, those elements of the left that had traditionally been engaged in such activities—Sōhyō (General Council of Trade Unions), the Japanese Socialist Party, Zengakuren, and the Japanese Communist Party, among others. However, through a combination of circumstances, particularly those related to the tactics of the Kishi government, participation suddenly broadened. At its climax, the anti-Ampō movement had attracted a huge number of normally apolitical groups and individuals, and even some conservatives. A mounting nationalist sentiment, deep factional rivalries within the Liberal-Democratic Party, and concern over an issue such as "the tyranny of the majority" each played a role in broadening the united front.[24]

---

[23] For fuller details and a variety of views on this movement, see George R. Packard, III, *Protest in Tokyo, The Security Crisis of 1960*, Princeton, 1966; Robert A. Scalapino and Junnosuke Masumi, *Parties and Politics in Contemporary Japan*, Berkeley, California, 1962; "Japan Today," a 42-page supplement to *The New Leader*, November 28, 1960, with an introduction by I. I. Morris and articles by Kiyoshi Nasu, Kosaku Tamura, Kikuo Nakamura, Kazuo Kuroda, and Sadachika Nabeyama; "Japanese Intellectuals Discuss American–Japanese Relations," *Far Eastern Survey*, Vol. 29, No. 10, October 1960, with an introduction by Robert A. Scalapino and articles by Kanichi Fukuda, Mokoto Saitō, Yoshikazu Sakamoto, and Takeshi Ishida; Edwin O. Reischauer, "The Broken Dialogue with Japan," *Foreign Affairs*, Vol. 39, No. 1, October 1960, p. 11; and David Wurfel, "The Violent and the Voiceless in Japanese Politics," *Contemporary Japan*, Vol. 29, November 1960, pp. 663–694.

[24] The Japanese press certainly abetted the movement by its general cirticism of the Kishi government. Press attacks were particularly hostile as a result of the "May 19 Incident," when Kishi forces in the Diet voted to extend the session beyond midnight and passed the revised treaty in the absence of the

It would be a mistake to exaggerate the success of the antitreaty struggle. Participation was largely confined to people of the great urban centers, especially Tōkyō. Attempts to enlist rural support were generally unrewarding. The resignation of the Kishi government, moreover, took much of the steam out of the movement, and it was not possible for the Japanese left to make the treaty issue a telling one in the November 1960 elections. It is equally important to note that the Japanese Communist Party did not play a commanding role in the organization—or in the tactics—of the movement. Indeed, the primary Communist objective of making the focus of the movement a struggle against American imperialism, not the Kishi government, failed. In general, the Mainstream faction of Zengakuren and the Socialist Party–Sōhyō forces were far more important elements in the movement than were the JCP and its auxiliaries.[25]

The public opinion polls also indicated the surprising fact that the Japanese left, including the Communist Party, did not gain strength as a result of the movement. The *Asahi Shimbun* poll, for example, showed that less than 1 percent of the Japanese voters supported the Communist Party in January 1960, and only 1 percent supported that party in May, a period close to the height of the incident.[26] In short, while the struggle against the revised Mutual Security Treaty did represent in many respects the most successful mass movement in Japanese political history, political gains for the Japanese left in general, and the JCP in particular, proved to be much more limited than might have been ex-

---

Socialists (who had boycotted the session) and some conservatives. After this, the movement "to defend democracy" and "against the tyranny of the majority" blossomed, becoming the most prominent aspect of the crisis. There can be no doubt that the mass media, particularly the leading newspapers, helped to focus attention on these issues and did much to sway Japanese public opinion against the Kishi government.

[25] The JCP faction within Zengakuren was responsible for the airport demonstration against James Hagerty, President Eisenhower's press secretary, and for some other anti-American incidents. The most amazing aspect of the entire antitreaty movement, however, was the almost total absence of personal anti-Americanism and the very limited animosity toward the United States in general. Americans were able to mingle freely among the demonstrating crowds, and at no point did the Communists succeed in creating a truly anti-American flavor.

[26] See Scalapino and Masumi, p. 148. Interestingly, the Socialist Party dropped from 36 percent support in February 1959, to 31 percent in January 1960, and to 30 percent in May 1960. The Liberal Democrats garnered 48 percent both in February 1959 and January 1960, but dropped to 40 percent in May 1960. In short, none of the national parties benefited from the crisis, with the exception of the Democratic Socialists who rose from 4 percent in January 1960 to 8 percent in May 1960, still a rather negligible figure.

pected. The majority of the Japanese people, whatever their sentiments about the Security Treaty and the tactics of the Kishi government, continued to resist any permanent identification with the Socialist or Communist parties.

Nevertheless, the antitreaty movement of 1960 proved conclusively that under certain conditions a fusion of Japanese nationalism and Japanese fear of involvement in war, together with support for "democracy," could become the base for a powerful political movement. How to continue or to rebuild such a movement, and how to capture its leadership were thus matters of primary concern to the Japanese Communists during this period.

The Communist strategy was essentially simple. First, the Communists had to capture control of the leading peace organization by securing representation in it for numerous Communist-controlled groups and by operating on the basis of "democratic-centralist" principles. Then the Communists had to express their own policies through this organization, make no basic concessions to the opposition, and at the same time fight to retain the united front character of the organization. If a united front *from above* failed, then it was necessary to pursue the tactic of a united front *from below*, by a direct appeal "to the masses."

These policies, of course, were not new. They had been a part of the Communist tactical arsenal—both in Japan and elsewhere—since the Leninist era. Now, however, they were to receive a new test with the peace movement as a focal point. If they succeeded, Japanese Communist Party leaders hoped eventually to build their own National Liberation Movement, Japanese style.

The issue of "peace" was multifaceted. After the enactment of the revised Mutual Security Treaty, a number of issues were developed by elements of the Japanese left, including the Communists: opposition to the berthing of U.S. atomic-powered submarines in Japanese ports and to the stationing of F-105D jet planes on Japanese bases, the struggle against the creation of NEATO (Northeast Asian Treaty Organization) or against any normalization of relations between Japan and the Republic of Korea; and restoration of Okinawa to Japanese administrative control and the abolition of American bases there. The most promising issue of this period, however, appeared to be that of opposing the manufacture or testing of atomic weapons, an issue that went to the heart of the East–West confrontation. Given the unique history of Japan's experience with the bomb, this was a most logical point on which to focus.

Available for these purposes was Gensuikyō (The Japanese Council

Against Atomic and Hydrogen Bombs), a critical united front organization. The antibomb movement first emerged in 1954 as an apolitical movement, but it was soon taken over by the leading "progressive" forces and converted into a vehicle for such groups as Sōhyō, the Japanese Socialist Party, Zengakuren, the Japanese Communist Party, and the numerous front organizations of these primary associations.[27] In its early years, Gensuikyō had no difficulty in maintaining a united front based on the concepts of total disarmament and an absolute prohibition against the use of nuclear weapons. Beginning in the late 1950's, however, the Gensuikyō left wing (essentially the Communists) had already begun to seek a broadening of the movement to include the struggle against American imperialism and support for national liberation movements. By this means, the Japanese Communist Party progressively brought Gensuikyō into conformity with its policies.[28]

---

[27] The primary Communist-front organization was the Japan Peace Committee. This association grew out of the old Society for the Defense of Peace, which was founded in April 1949 by JCP members and "progressive" intellectuals in response to the appeal of the first World Peace Conference held in Paris and Prague. Affiliated with the Communist-sponsored World Peace Council, the Japan Peace Committee had faithfully echoed the international Communist line and actively participated in all united front organizations of the left dedicated to "peace."

In this period, it was headed by Hirano Yoshitaro, Communist-line intellectual and Director of the Peking-oriented Institute of Chinese Studies. Yasui Kaoru, Gensuikyō Chairman and Lenin Peace Prize winner, served as adviser, and Uchino Takechiyo, Chief of the United Front Bureau of the JCP, acted as Director of the Board. The organization claimed some 43 prefectural and city-level branches, 270 district-level branches, and 847 workshop groups. It reportedly had a membership of 17,000 in 1963, of whom 6,000 were JCP members, with the party being in absolute control of the entire operation. Hirano and several other leaders including Yasui were regularly sent as representatives to the World Peace Council meetings.

[28] The Gensuikyō had its direct antecedents in 1954, when a group of some fifty political, educational, and religious leaders met to discuss the establishment of an organization that would focus on the problem of nuclear weapons. It was determined that the organization should be nonpolitical, and to this end, no parties or political factions should become unit members, nor should any specific country be made the object of the movement. Rather, various bipartisan or nonpartisan organizations dedicated to peace should become constituent members, and a general appeal should be made to all nations for a universal ban on atomic and hydrogen bombs. The movement should be directed centrally toward the humanistic goal of safeguarding the lives and happiness of mankind.

The first "World Congress for a Ban on Atomic and Hydrogen Bombs" opened on August 6, 1955, in Hiroshima. Actually, local officials in Hiroshima had begun to comemorate that date with a peace rally earlier. The Conference of Asian Nations held in New Delhi in April 1955, moreover, had resolved to observe August 6 as peace commemoration day. At the first con-

The 6th Gensuikyō Conference held in Tōkyō in 1960 illustrated beautifully the high level of success which the Communists had attained by that time in their basic objective. The 1960 World Conference adopted an "Appeal" underlining the thesis that the banning of atomic and hydrogen bombs could be accomplished only by a resolute struggle against world imperialism "headed by the United States." It contained numerous other political stands identical to current Communist positions. A number of more moderate elements had abandoned Gensuikyō by this time. Zen Nihon Rōdō Kumiai Kaigi (Zenrō) (General Federation of Japanese Trade Unions) and the Democratic Socialist Party, for example, had left the organization to form their own group, the Kakkin Kaigi (Congress for the Prohibition of Nuclear Weapons). As long as Sōhyō and the Japanese Socialist Party cooperated, however, Gensuikyō remained a formidable united front.

The Gensuikyō Constitution provided for a typically Leninist form of organization, operating on the basis of "democratic centralism." A board of directors, nominally the supreme policy-making body, was chosen from the member organizations and prefectural branches. This board in turn selected some eighty standing directors who formed the executive organ; and a smaller number of directors chosen by this organ

---

ference, some 2,000 Japanese delegates and 54 foreign delegates participated. A wide spectrum of political opinion was represented, and this first meeting even secured official blessing. Premier Hatoyama sent a message wishing the conference success, as did former Premier Higashikuni, the man who had presided over the surrender of Japan in 1945.

In the aftermath of this first conference, Gensuikyō was formally established, with its initial objectives those of pushing forward the signature collection campaign, seeking relief funds for atomic bomb victims, opposing U.S. military bases in Japan, and soliciting broad international support. The movement took on an increasingly political, partisan flavor, and the left established a firm control. Even by the time of the 2nd World Conference, held in Tōkyō and Nagasaki in August 1956, such issues as Okinawa and American bases in Japan were prominently advanced. By the time of the 4th Conference in 1958, the resolutions approved included those praising the Soviet Union for its unilateral suspension of nuclear tests; condemning "the plot" to bring nuclear weapons into Japan and Okinawa and to create a Northeast Asian Treaty Organization; demanding the normalization of relations with the People's Republic of China and the severance of ties between Japan, South Korea and Taiwan; and denouncing U.S. and British military policies in the Middle East as a threat to world peace. The Chinese government at this point presented Gensuikyō with 7.5 million yen for its relief fund.

The 5th World Conference, held in Hiroshima in 1959, was even more highly politicized. To the basic theme of outlawing nuclear weapons were now firmly attached the struggles against the rearming of Japan and against the renewal of the U.S.–Japan Mutual Security Treaty. Conservative Japanese groups, with few exceptions, were no longer affiliated with Gensuikyō, and foreign representation came overwhelmingly from Communist or Communist-affiliated groups.

were designated as the Executive Committee of Standing Directors, the truly critical group in the decision-making process.

Major storms within Gensuikyō first developed in 1961. At the 7th World Conference a significant cleavage developed between Communist forces on the one hand and Socialist and allied forces on the other. The main issue was whether the struggle against American imperialism and closely related issues, such as the problems of military bases and military alliances, should be made matters of central concern to Gensuikyō. The battle lines were drawn with increasing clarity as organizations taking a Socialist Party line, such as Sōhyō and other groups of an even more moderate position, decided to resist the mounting Communist thrust. Just before the opening of the conference, an agreement was reached that the meetings would focus on four goals: total disarmament, a nuclear test ban, denuclearization, and the relief of atomic victims. From the beginning of the conference, however, the Communists challenged this agenda. With foreign delegates from Asia (notably Peking) and Africa serving as the spearhead, the Communists insisted that "the enemies of peace" had to be clearly defined, and that the struggles against colonialism and imperialism (particularly American imperialism) must be incorporated into the Gensuikyō program. The basis goals, according to the Communists, should also include effective campaigns against American military bases and the American–Japanese military alliance.

Forces representing the Socialist Party and its policies of "positive neutrality" argued that to include these issues would be tactically unsound, since it would antagonize all moderates and make a broadly based movement impossible. They further asserted that there were other organizations especially created for such activities. A bitter struggle ensued throughout the conference, with the Sōhyō–Socialist forces ultimately suffering defeat. The 7th Conference resolutions covered the major political issues noted above and took positions on them indistinguishable from the international Communist line. But a price was paid by the Communists for this victory. At the close of the conference, Sōhyō, the National Federation of Regional Women's Organizations, the Japanese Council of Youth Organizations, and the Japanese Socialist Party issued a strongly worded protest, demanding that Gensuikyō thoroughly reform itself. Making it clear that they intended to reject Communist control, these groups asserted, "We have no confidence in the present Gensuikyō."[29] In other statements, Sōhyō and Socialist leaders blamed foreign delegates and organizations for much of the

---

[29] The statement issued by the four organizations, dated August 14, 1961, is reproduced in *Sōhyō News*, No. 193, September 10, 1961, pp. 17–18.

trouble. Foreign delegates, they announced, "had little understanding of the Japanese people's fight against atomic and hydrogen bombs."[30] The 7th World Conference, they observed, was under the strong influence of the World Peace Council. These and other statements indicated that the Japanese Socialists were well aware of the degree to which Gensuikyō had become an instrument of the international Communist movement.[31]

A new crisis developed when the Soviets decided to resume nuclear tests. This decision, announced on August 31, 1961, was activated the following day. Immediately, Japanese Socialist and Communist forces were thrown into turmoil. In one sense, Soviet actions proved enormously embarrassing to the Japanese Communist Party and other pro-Soviet groups. Only a few weeks earlier, at the 7th Gensuikyō Conference, the chief Soviet delegate, Y. M. Zhukov, had boldly asserted that the first power to resume nuclear testing had to be considered an enemy of peace. Consequently, with full Soviet approval, the following statement had been inserted into the formal conference resolution: "Today, the government which first resumes nuclear testing is to be censured as the enemy of peace and of mankind." It is not surprising that the Japanese Communist leaders, while loyally supporting the Russians, were privately furious with Soviet leaders for this blunder.[32]

---

[30] *Ibid.*, p. 15.

[31] As might have been expected, *Jen-min Jih-pao* in its editorial of August 17, 1961, hailed the 7th World Conference as a brilliant success, asserting that it had dealt resolute blows to the imperialist forces of war headed by the United States. The conference had given full support to the national liberation movements in the Asian, African, and Latin American countries, the editorial maintained, and had thereby fought for peace in the correct manner.

As noted earlier, this period coincided with a lull in the Sino–Soviet dispute. Consequently, Soviet and East European delegates to the conference worked harmoniously with the Peking bloc, and no problems within such groups as the World Peace Council were presented.

[32] Much later the Japanese Communist Party was to complain bitterly about this episode in its letter of August 26, 1964, to the CPSU. In that letter it asserted: "At the Seventh World Conference against Atomic and Hydrogen Bombs in August 1961, the Soviet Union's delegation asserted that 'The first to resume nuclear testing is the enemy of peace.' At this time, our delegate checked with the chief of the Soviet delegation, Mr. Y. M. Zhukov, to make sure whether they really meant to make such an assertion. The reason was that obviously, depending on changes in circumstances, the Soviet Union might be forced to resume nuclear testing first, and, supposing that such a situation occurred, the Soviet Union should not be called 'the enemy of peace.' Comrade Zhukov, however, insisted that it was not possible that the Soviet Union should resume nuclear testing first. As a result, the famous words, 'Today, the government which first resumes nuclear testing is to be censured as the enemy of peace and mankind,' were inserted in the resolution. . . ." (For an

The critical issue for the Japanese left was now posed very graphically: should nuclear tests from whatever source be condemned, or should a distinction be made between tests conducted by "U.S. imperialism" and those undertaken by "peace-loving states," such as the U.S.S.R.? This issue related directly to the basic incompatibility between Communist and Socialist "neutralism." The JCP had long preached neutralism and peaceful coexistence, but it defined these terms in a very special manner. A neutralist policy, according to the Communists, was that of disengagement from the military alliance with America, a struggle against imperialism in all of its forms, and the establishment of peaceful and friendly relations with all nations, irrespective of their social systems.[33] But this final goal did not include the United States, since America was the leader of the imperialist world and the struggle against the United States was an inextricable part of the national liberation struggle. In sum, JCP "neutralism" was no more than a temporary tactic advanced on the Japanese scene to achieve the dismantling of the American–Japanese alliance, a first step toward the final goal of alliance with all Marxist–Leninist states.

The Japanese Socialists, championing a concept of "positive neutralism," conceived of themselves as a genuine third force standing between the Communist and capitalist worlds, playing a positive role in realizing peaceful coexistence between the two systems, but committed to neither. This is Socialist theory. In reality, Sōhyō and the Japan Socialist Party on a number of occasions have taken positions clearly more favorable to the Communist bloc than to the democratic bloc, particularly the United States. Indeed, a strong anti-American current has operated within the Socialist Party for many years. In part, this is a result of the continuing influence of Marxism on the Japanese Socialist movement. In part, it is the product of international political conditions, and especially of the close connection between American policies and those of the Japanese conservatives. But such an issue as that of nuclear tests was certain to strain relations between the Socialists and Communists, relations that had been deteriorating because of other factors.

Both Sōhyō and the Japan Socialist Party immediately delivered protests to the Soviet Union, declaring that Soviet actions had truly

---

English translation of this letter, see *TICD* 653, *JPRS* 26,892. The above quotation is from pp. 84–85.) If any evidence were needed as to international Communist control over the issues, and even over the wording of Gensuikyō resolutions, this information presented by the JCP should be sufficient.

[33] See *Akahata,* May 6, 1962, p. 1.

shocked the people of Japan.[34] Naturally, the JCP rallied to the support of the Russians along with other Communist parties of the world. The split within Gensuikyō widened, and by the spring of 1962 there was no indication that the cleavage could be healed. Later that spring, the Kennedy announcement that the United States would conduct nuclear tests in the Pacific further exacerbated the internal conflict and set off large-scale Gensuikyō-sponsored protest meetings. For example, at the Gensuikyō rally of April 13 in Tōkyō, proceedings were disrupted by Zengakuren Mainstream students (the anti-JCP faction) shouting slogans against Soviet testing. The Communists continued to insist that Soviet tests had been resumed to forestall the danger of nuclear war arising out of the Berlin crisis and that all antitest propaganda was in fact a support for reactionary forces. But these arguments failed to appeal to Socialist circles, and indeed, many Socialists were inclined to blame the Russians for triggering the American decision to reopen tests.

The Japanese Communists realized that their central tactic of building a united front via the peace movement was now in jeopardy. Efforts were made to prevent further slippage by mobilizing as many existing joint struggle associations as possible. Thus, the National Council in Opposition to the Security Treaty and for the Safeguarding of Peace and Democracy, an offspring of the central united front organization formed during the antitreaty struggle in 1960, was instructed to call rallies and demonstrations on the occasion of the second anniversary of the revised treaty.[35] The National People's Council for the Settlement

---

[34] Sōhyō's initial protest to the Soviet Union, directed to the All–Soviet Trade Unions Central Council, was couched in conciliatory language. In a cable dated September 1, 1961, Ōta Kaoru expressed Sōhyō appreciation for the past efforts of the Soviet workers and people to attain a relaxation of international tension and peaceful coexistence. The cable continued, however, by expressing Sōhyō regrets that the Soviet government had decided to resume tests, warning that the Japanese people would react very adversely and requesting that the decision be reversed immediately. The Socialist Party organ, *Shakai Shimpo (Socialist News)*, took a similar position, voicing the opinion that nuclear testing could not be justified under any circumstances.

In its September 1 issue, *Akahata* approved the Soviet tests as "an appropriate measure to defend world peace," and immediately attacked the Sōhyō–Socialist position, claiming that it stemmed from basic errors of ideology and policy. The Socialists viewed the United States and the Soviet Union as two war forces of exactly the same nature, asserted *Akahata*, so naturally they could not understand correctly the need for the Soviet tests.

[35] This association is actually the successor to an earlier group active in the actual struggle, the product of a reorganization in March 1961. It has undertaken drives "in the defense of the Constitution," on behalf of "democracy and neutralization," against the revised Security Treaty, in opposition to Japan–South Korean talks, and against visits by U.S. nuclear-powered sub-

of the Okinawan Problem was also activated.[36] These organizations, however, could be effective only if harmony existed between Communists, Socialists, and other groups having a common purpose. After the summer of 1961, no such harmony existed.

Consequently, when the 8th World Conference sponsored by Gensuikyō opened in Tōkyō on August 1, 1962, united front activities were at a low ebb. This conference, moreover, resulted in an open and bitter break that extended throughout the Japanese left. Even before the conference began, a new complication had emerged. Just eight days before the opening session, the Soviet Union had announced that it would again resume nuclear tests because of the recent American tests. Immediately, Japanese Socialist and Communist elements took radically different positions on the Soviet announcement.[37] From the very beginning of the 8th Conference, it was apparent that the Socialist–Communist split could not be bridged. It was equally clear that the Chinese Communists in particular were playing a very powerful role,

---

marines to Japan. It is composed of thirteen basic groups, mainly Socialist and Communist in their political orientation. The JCP has played an important role in this association, particularly since another organization, the National Council in Opposition to Military Bases, has been the primary Socialist vehicle. Communist influence in this latter organization is also apparent, however, especially at the local level.

[36] This group, first established in 1955, has also been a joint struggle organization composed of Sōhyō, Socialist, and Communist Party representatives. Both in this association and in the National Movement for the Return of Okinawa, the JCP has been very influential, making full use of the voting power of such front organizations as the Democratic Youth League, the Japan Peace Committee, and the New Japan Women's Society.

[37] Within hours after the Soviet Government announced its decision to renew testing on July 22, protests were issued by Sōhyō and the Socialist Party. On this occasion, the tone was considerably sharper than that of the previous autumn. Even the Gensuikyō Executive Committee, by a majority vote, voiced a protest. Yasui Kaoru, Gensuikyō Chairman, issued a statement asserting that the Soviet decision was not unexpected in view of the continuation of American testing but that "we had hoped that the Soviet Union, responding to the voice of world public opinion, would not resort to this step." Ten Gensuikyō representatives and Chairman Yasui handed a note of protest to the Soviet Embassy in Tōkyō.

Not unexpectedly, the JCP strongly opposed this action and within forty-eight hours of the Soviet announcement sought to justify the Soviet decision. In an editorial published on July 23, Akahata laboriously argued that the Soviet Union, much against its will, had been forced into this position for security reasons and that the only solution was an unconditional nuclear test ban treaty signed by all countries possessing nuclear weapons. It cited Khrushchev's oft-repeated statement that he would sign such a treaty without waiting for agreement on general and complete disarmament (*Akahata,* July 23, 1962, p. 1).

serving as the real leaders of the international and domestic Communist forces in Japan.[38]

Two critical issues confronted Gensuikyō: Should *all* nuclear tests be opposed, or only those made by the "imperialists"? Should the question of nuclear weapons take precedence or could such issues as American imperialism and national liberation also be incorporated? Disorder prevailed from the very beginning. Some 150 Zengakuren Mainstream students attempted to force their way into the meetings to denounce the support for Soviet nuclear tests, and the police had to be summoned. (As a result of the April Incident, the Zengakuren had been formally expelled from Gensuikyō on May 16.) The Japanese Communist Party, moreover, had made it clear on the eve of the conference that no compromise could be expected from them on the critical issues, and had thus alerted the Socialists to the necessity for an all-out struggle.[39]

The Communist position received major support from the foreign delegations, a majority of which appeared to be in the Peking camp.[40]

---

[38] At the very outset, the Chinese delegation opposed the plan to hear three special reports from other international organizations, including the World Congress for General Disarmament and Peace which had recently met in Moscow. It soon became apparent that the Chinese felt that the Moscow Congress had made two mistakes: one in not being able to clarify the enemy of peace and the other in treating the struggle against colonialism too lightly. The Chinese delegation did not want this congress to set a pattern for the Gensuikyō Conference. Sino–Soviet differences were thus introduced at the beginning of the 8th Conference. These issues, along with the question of renewed Soviet nuclear tests, were to dominate the sessions.

[39] Just before the conference, Uchino Takechiyo, JCP United Front Bureau head, had written: "We are a little worried by the Socialist contention that all nuclear tests, irrespective of their source, be opposed." This "indiscriminate" opposition could only help the U.S. Government and the Ikeda administration, he asserted, blocking an ultimate test ban. Moreover, Socialist insistence that all emphasis should be placed on disarmament, not on the national liberation movement or American imperialism, was wrong, he insisted. These were intimately connected questions. Finally, the thesis that such wider issues would divide participants, causing the moderates to withdraw, was in Uchino's view "unreasonable." Gensuikyō, he argued, should be open both to those who were simply opposed to atomic weapons and to those who wished to struggle against American imperialism and Japanese monopolistic capitalism. *Akahata*, July 27, 1962, p. 1.

[40] A number of the foreign representatives, permanent residents of Peking and trotted out for such purposes as this, were essentially bogus. The "Sudanese delegate," Ahmed Mohammed Khier, was a more or less permanent Peking exile who had minimal contacts with his homeland (where the Communist movement was actually associated with Moscow, not Peking). Rewi Alley, supposedly representing the Peace Liaison Committee of the Asian and Pacific Regions, had long lived and served in China, and was completely identified with the Chinese cause. There were a number of similar cases, and later, as we shall note, the Russians strongly challenged the Chinese on this matter.

The head of the Chinese delegation, Pa Chin, reviewed the whole catalogue of American crimes in his opening speech, making it clear that American imperialism had to be condemned as the common enemy of the Chinese and Japanese people, and that the national liberation movements had to be supported by all peace-loving people. The Soviet delegation, composed of seven members headed by M. B. Mitin, came late, arriving on August 3. It acted in a more subdued fashion than the Chinese, and Khrushchev's message to the conference was a model of restraint, stressing the need to prevent nuclear war and repeating the standing offer of the U.S.S.R. to sign a test ban agreement, provided no foreign inspection system were involved. The message did not contain any sharp attack on the United States. On the more critical issues, however, all Communist delegates stood together.

The keynote report presented to the conference was the product of heated debates within Gensuikyō and had been finally approved on July 23 at an Enlarged Standing Director's meeting. In general, it was in conformity with Sōhyō–Socialist views that Gensuikyō action should be restricted to the original purpose of the association. This keynote report became the focal point of Communist attack, and a frontal collision between Socialists and Communists occurred in the committees charged with drafting Gensuikyō resolutions. No agreement on the fundamental issues could be reached. Final drafting was undertaken by a subcommittee composed of ten Japanese and ten overseas delegates, a representation very unsatisfactory to the Socialists, who recognized the heavily Communist cast of the foreign contingents.

While the draft resolutions were being debated, news reached the conference that the Soviet Union had set off a massive atmospheric nuclear explosion in Siberia. This August 5 explosion showed extraordinarily bad timing on the part of the Russians. Japanese mass media naturally devoted full attention to the event, and condemnation poured in from many quarters. Immediately, Sōhyō and its allies pressed for a motion demanding that cables be sent to both the American and Soviet governments protesting their nuclear tests. Naturally, the Communists resisted this move. After an emergency Executive Committee meeting, the Japanese Socialist Party decided to withdraw its representatives from official positions within Gensuikyō (without quitting the organization altogether), because "there was very little chance" that the protest against Soviet tests would be approved.

On August 6, the 8th World Conference ended in chaos. The Socialists sought to present their urgent motion to the general session, but Chairman Yasui attempted to ignore them, passing on to the next item of business. Earlier attempts at compromise had failed. Socialist Party Youth League members then rushed to the platform, and a tussle with Democratic Youth League (Communist) members took place. All Socialist representatives walked out in protest before the end of the session, and total confusion reigned. No formal action had been taken on the resolutions.[41]

The 8th Gensuikyō Conference provided little evidence of a Sino–Soviet cleavage. The Russians and the Chinese appeared to be standing close together at this point, implying that earlier storms had abated. The Chinese statements, of course, bristled with anti-American themes and demands that the revolutionary cause be given full support. The Chinese clearly wanted to go beyond the pronouncements of the recent Moscow Peace Meeting. Scheduled to be delivered on August 6, the speech of M. B. Mitin, chief Soviet delegate, could not be given because of the chaos that enveloped the conference. It was transmitted via the mass media, however, and was not out of line with the CCP-JCP position. Praising the "brilliant heroic traditions" of Japanese pacifism, Mitin attacked specific Americans, such as Edward Teller and Sidney Hook. He also charged that the true enemies of peace and of the masses were the U.S. imperialists and the bellicose elements of the monopolistic munitions industries of the U.S. and other Western nations. Significantly, he proclaimed that the 8th Conference resolutions were in line with the views of the World Congress for General Disarmament and Peace, held in Moscow the previous month.

The difference between the Soviet and Chinese positions as expressed in this conference was one of degree, not of kind. Russian pronouncements were somewhat more qualified, less shrill. This fact was certainly not unimportant. It signified that basic tactical differences between the

---

[41] On August 6, eleven organizations representing the Socialist element within Gensuikyō issued a joint statement criticizing the 8th World Conference and pledging continued efforts to advance the struggle against nuclear weapons by improving the movement. Earlier, the Socialists had urged a meeting of Japanese delegates only, a proposal rejected by the Communists. Various compromises had also been proposed whereby a showdown on the conference floor would be avoided, but none had been acceptable to all parties. The Communists, of course, claimed that the so-called Tōkyō Declaration of the 8th World Conference had been adopted "by acclamation." It was widely circulated by the JCP as a repudiation of Socialist "positive neutralism," emphasizing as it did the evils of American imperialism, the importance of the national liberation movement, and the interrelated character of the struggle against imperialism and for peace—key Communist themes.

two Communist states continued to exist.[42] The Chinese Communists, moreover, gave every evidence of being much closer to their Japanese comrades. Together with their carefully chosen Afro–Asian bloc, they were the real leaders of the conference. The Russians almost appeared to be outsiders. Symbolic of the Chinese commitment to Gensuikyō was their additional gift to Yasui for Japanese atomic bomb victims, a sum of 7,500,000 yen.

Immediately after the Tōkyō meetings, Hiroshima and Nagasaki became the scenes of further quarrels and struggles, with the non-Communists in control on these occasions.[43] Under Socialist–Sōhyō direction, the Hiroshima meeting approved an appeal calling on both the U.S.S.R and the U.S. to cease nuclear tests, in spite of vigorous Communist protests. A similar appeal was read at Nagasaki on August 9.[44] At approximately the same time, incidentally, word reached Japan

---

[42] The Russians were later to accuse the Chinese of dogmatic tactics with respect to the 8th Gensuikyō Conference, tactics that "were chiefly responsible for its failure."

[43] It is intriguing to note that while the Communists had only a fraction of the support held by the Socialists—whether in reference to the general public, the labor movement, the student-intellectual community, or the peace movement—they nevertheless managed to dominate Gensuikyō and to keep the Socialists in a minority position. Why?

The answer lies largely in organizational techniques and the discipline characteristic of the Communists when confronted with an outside force. Since the Communists used "democratic centralism" as their basic principle and a system of representation via branches and "all interested organizations," both their strength and that of competitors depended upon how many branches and front organizations each was able to establish and control. Once a sufficient number of fronts had been created by the JCP, then it was simply necessary to make certain that through the established controls, a majority of party members and front types voted the straight party ticket, especially with respect to key appointments. Thus, Gensuikyō could only be captured by the Socialists if they were willing to engage in a lengthy struggle for branch control and also compete with the Communists in the technique of establishing front organizations. Increasingly allied with Peking, at this point, the JCP had great advantages in obtaining the support of foreign delegates, especially from Africa and Asia, most of whom had had close contact with the Chinese and were already strongly committed to the Chinese line.

[44] The Hiroshima Conference Against Atomic and Hydrogen Bombs was held on August 6 and attended by 2,600 Japanese and 17 foreign delegates. When the Chinese delegates were prevented from speaking against "the appeal," they walked out in company with Soviet and Korean delegates. The local JCP protested vigorously, delcaring that the Hiroshima appeal was null and void because the Chinese had been precluded from speaking and foreign delegates had been denied participation in the drafting committee meetings.

On August 9, the Nagasaki Conference was held with over 4,000 participants, including foreign delegates. The appeal opposing all tests was read but not put to a vote.

that Zengakuren delegates en route to the Leningrad International Youth League Congress had been arrested for conducting a protest in Moscow's Red Square against Soviet resumption of testing. Apparently for the first time since the Bolshevik Revolution, Red Square had been the scene of an open protest against Russian governmental policy, albeit one conducted by foreigners.[45]

The Communists had scored a partial victory at the 8th Gensuikyō Conference, but at the cost of cracking the united front wide open. Immediately after the conference, Communist and Socialist spokesmen engaged in sharp attacks on each other. Hakamada Satomi, one of the top three JCP leaders, sent an open letter to Socialist leader Eda Saburō, who had headed the Socialist delegation, protesting "the outrageous actions" of the Socialists. The Socialist Party and Sōhyō representatives in turn announced that Gensuikyō would have to be completely reorganized if it were to remain viable.

The sharpest repercussions of the growing Socialist–Communist split were felt in the labor and youth movements. Let us look first at the situation within Sōhyō, sketching the essential background. From the mid-fifties, the Ōta–Iwai line (left Socialist) had predominated within Sōhyō. Ōta Kaoru had regularly been reelected President and Iwai

---

[45] Zengakuren Chairman, Nemoto Hiroshi, leader of the Mainstream faction, later made a report on his Soviet trip in mid-September. He asserted that while en route to the Youth Congress, the Zengakuren representatives learned via Swedish radio that the Russians were resuming tests. Based on their June decision to oppose all tests, the Zengakuren leaders decided to conduct a protest in Red Square on August 6. Using a crude hand-printed press which they had with them, they printed some handbills and made a banner. They had marched about 100 feet and distributed approximately 100 handbills when police whistles blew and Russians swarmed around them, shouting "Fascists!" They were taken behind the Lenin mausoleum to be interrogated for two hours by the police, after which they were released.

At the Leningrad Conference, the Zengakuren group continued to turn out leaflets, much to the horror of the Russians. According to Nemoto, the Russians finally got a West African to accuse Zengakuren of acting illegally, as a printing press could not be permitted in private hands in the Soviet Union. When the Japanese answered by saying that "then there is no freedom of expression in Russia," the issue was dropped. The Chinese Communist representatives stoutly defended the Soviet tests and attacked Zengakuren. Nemoto made a speech on the third day of the conference attacking both China and Russia. He was very critical of Soviet conditions, charging that the government had no relations whatsoever with the common people; that people were kept ignorant of government actions until after they were determined; that the Soviet students were merely representatives of the bureaucracy, which maintained strict controls, and that these students told the Japanese that if they wanted to become socialists, they should try to see only the good things about the Soviet Union.

Akira Secretary General by approximately a two-thirds majority. The Ōta–Iwai line, veering somewhat toward the moderate side by 1960, was supported by nearly three-fourths of the Sōhyō delegates at the general conventions. By the early sixties, Ōta and Iwai appeared to have firmly consolidated their power, carefully maintaining an ideological position "slightly left of the Socialist center," between the Kawakami faction on the right, and the Heiwa Dōshikai (Comrades for Peace) group on the left.[46] The anti-Mainstream forces within Sōhyō, representing mainly Communist and proto-Communist elements, had slipped below their traditional "one-third" position in terms of strength.

Nevertheless, the Communist faction within Sōhyō was large enough and strategically enough placed to be a matter of continuing concern to Sōhyō leaders. Where did the key Communist strength lie in the 1962–1964 period?[47] That strength fell into two basic categories: those unions that were dominated by the Communists, or were under their strong influence, and that were part of the anti-Mainstream group within Sōhyō; and those Mainstream unions that had a significant Communist minority faction.

Let us note first the most important unions in the former category, beginning with the government unions. The Ministry of Construction Workers, with a membership of 27,000, represented a typical example of a federation under strong Communist influence. Nine of the eleven central headquarters officials were JCP members, although the total number of party members in the federation probably did not exceed 450, with some 90 of these in positions of local union leadership. Nevertheless, the federation, affiliated with the World Federation of Trade Unions (WFTU), was an important anti-Mainstream element, following the JCP line and maintaining a close relationship with Soviet and Chinese organizations.[48] A number of other government unions had

---

[46] Ōta, in an interview with me in Tōkyō on November 28, 1963, described his political position as "a little bit left—about midway between the Heiwa Dōshikai and Kawakami positions."

[47] This survey of Communist strength within Sōhyō relies heavily on materials published by the Public Safety Investigation Bureau (Kōan Chōsachō). *Nihon Kyōsantō gaikaku dantai ichiran* (*A Survey of Organizations Around the Communist Party*), Tōkyō, 1962, has been particularly valuable, and all of the specific data used here, unless otherwise noted, have been taken from that source.

[48] This federation, along with the All-Japan Free Labor Unions and the National Federation of Auto Transport Workers, served as primary representative of the WFTU in Japan, and its Chairman, Honjō Sumio, was a member of the WFTU Executive Committee. The Construction Workers issued joint communiqués with the Soviet Trade Unions in February 1962 and March 1963, and with the Chinese in December 1962.

similar political commitments and ties. The National Tax Commission Workers, the National Ministry of Justice Workers, the National Customs Workers, the National Electric Workers, the Port Construction Workers, the Ministry of Labor Workers, the Ministry of Commerce and Industry Workers, and the Ministry of Transportation Workers were all anti-Mainstream unions under Communist control or affected by extensive Communist influence.[49]

Among the nongovernmental unions, several powerful federations fell into the same category. The All-Japan Free Labor Unions, a federation with its nucleus in the Tōkyō construction industry and a membership of 216,000, was under direct Communist control. Fourteen out of fifteen of the central headquarters officials were JCP members, and an esti-

---

[49] The National Tax Commission Workers, with some 8,000 members in 1962, had followed the JCP line since 1958, but this produced a split with more than 12,000 members setting up a rival union. Twelve of the eighteen headquarters officials of the federation were Communists, with about 350 JCP members in the organization.

The Ministry of Justice Workers, comprising 17,000 members, supported the JCP on all major issues, despite some ciriticisms from within the organization. Nine of the thirteen headquarters officials and approximately seventy-two of the local union officials were JCP members. Party members in the union numbered about 350.

The National Customs workers, with a total membership of 5,400, also belonged to the anti-Mainstream forces. Its headquarters were dominated by JCP members, and five of the eight locals were under Communist Party control. About 200 JCP members were in the federation.

The National Electrical Workers, with a membership of 2,800, had followed the JCP line since its establishment, with nearly all of its twenty-six locals under Communist control, five of the eight headquarters officials members of the party, and some 100 party members in the organization.

The Port Construction Workers had a membership of 4,600 and was in a similar position, with five of its eight headquarters officials party members, and some 200 JCP members in the federation. The Ministry of Labor Workers, numbering 16,000, also had a majority of headquarters officials in the JCP or strongly sympathetic toward it, and some 250 party members in the organization. The Ministry of Commerce and Industry Workers, numbering 10,000, and the Ministry of Transportation Workers, numbering 2,400, were in similar positions.

It is to be noted that without exception these unions had a relatively small membership and consequently could not truly challenge the Sōhyō Mainstream in numerical terms, although the system of representation at Sōhyō General Conventions gave them a stronger position than their actual size would have warranted. It is also important to note that the technique of Communist control in the unions was to apply the principles of "democratic centralism," seizing control of the federation headquarters. In no case did the Communist Party members constitute a majority of union members, and in most cases JCP members were only a small fraction, maintaining their control through skillful organizational techniques and a continuous commitment to political participation on an intensive basis.

mated 15,000 party members were union members, some 100 of them serving as party cadres. Once again, this union had the closest ties with the WFTU and the key international Communist labor figures. Another important anti-Mainstream federation was the National Metal Workers Labor Unions, with a total membership of 202,000. Some 15,000 JCP members belonged to these unions. Three party members served on the Executive Committee, and some forty party cadres were union members. Other nongovernmental unions with strong Communist influence included the National Pulp Industry Workers, the National Federation of Auto Transport Workers, the National Federation of Printers and Publication Workers, the All-Japan Harbor and Bay Construction Workers, and the Japan Newspaper Workers.[50]

Among the Mainstream federations having important Communist factions, the National Railway Workers Union was an excellent example. Within that federation was the so-called Kakudō faction, the "Revolutionary Comrades Association." This faction, directly controlled by the JCP, had a membership of approximately 70,000, with its main centers of strength in Niigata, Aomori, and Hakodate. The Japan Teachers Union, with a membership of 600,000, was a Communist–Socialist battleground for years. Although the Communists had the upper hand for a considerable time, they finally lost their control. Nevertheless, the Communist faction remained important, with some 7,000 JCP members, including 300 party cadres, and with party members holding some 180 local official posts. Other Mainstream federations having substantial Communist factions included the All-Japan Local Government Workers, the National Electric and Communications Workers, and the Japan Coal Miners.[51]

---

[50] The Pulp Workers, numbering 58,000, had only some 200 JCP members in their organization, but the chairman of their Executive Committee and various other headquarters officials were implementing the party line. The Auto Transport Workers, with 39,000 members, had approximately 500 JCP members in the union, but Communists constituted a majority of the forty-four-man Executive Committee, and the union was strongly attached to the WFTU. The Printers, numbering 20,000, had some 400 JCP members, including several party men on the Executive Committee. The Harbor and Bay Construction Workers, with 18,000 members, had some 300 party members, including sizable JCP committees in Yokohama and Kōbe. The Newspaper Workers, with 30,000 members, had about 500 JCP members in the organization.

In all of these federations, however, considerable friction existed between non-Communist and Communist factions, and in some cases the situation was precarious for the Communists.

[51] The local Government Workers, with a membership of 67,400, had approximately 5,000 JCP members, including 140 cadres. Some 300 party members held local union Offices, and the JCP was particularly strong in Kyōto,

Almost without exception, the major labor federations were under the primary control of non-Communists after 1960, and the trend during recent years has clearly been against the Communists in most cases. Nevertheless, the Communist faction within Sōhyō remained sizable enough, especially in certain government unions, to create problems. After the 8th Gensuikyō Conference, the JCP launched a direct attack on Sōhyō and its leaders. An *Akahata* editorial proclaimed: "It is a grave mistake to force four million Sōhyō workers to accept the diplomatic policies of the Socialist Party which are based on 'positive neutrality.' " This was not a new line for the Communists, of course, since they had long urged "free choice" for Sōhyō members rather than a union commitment to the Socialist cause. Now, however, the clash between Socialist and Communist factions within Sōhyō grew much sharper, as clearly indicated during the 19th National Sōhyō Convention held in Tōkyō in late August 1962. The Ōta–Iwai line continued to represent a cautious attempt to find a centrist position and avoid identification with either "right" or "left." Ōta and other Mainstream leaders, however, had expressed their opposition to JCP tactics at the Gensuikyō Conference in unmistakable terms, and both the JCP and foreign Communist delegates to the Sōhyō Convention responded with critical remarks.[52]

Thus in the aftermath of the 8th Gensuikyō Conference, JCP plans for a broad united front with Sōhyō on the issues of peace, independence, and democracy had been completely disrupted. Bitter infighting was taking place. Communists and Socialists were more deeply divided both in the labor movement and in party relations than had been the case for some years.

These trends were also mirrored in the student movement. Zengakuren, the National Federation of Student Self-Government Associations, had first been organized in September 1948 under the leadership of the JCP. Established for the purposes of "defending peace and democracy" and improving student livelihood, it had been affiliated with the

---

Osaka, Fukuoka, Saitama, Iwate, Niigata, Shizuoka, Okayama, Sendai, and Matsuyama. The National Electric and Communications Workers, with a membership of 189,000, had an anti-Mainstream faction—the United Front faction—representing the Communists. Some 2,500 party members were in the organization, including 50 cadres. The Coal Miners, with 120,000 members, had about 1,800 party members, including 55 cadres, and with two party members on the union Executive Committee.

[52] The JCP Central Committee issued a statement sharply protesting the opening speeches of Ōta and Eda, accusing them of "employing sophistry and slanders" to abuse the Japanese Communist Party. The Chinese and Soviet

Communist-controlled International Student League. After approximately one decade of Communist domination, however, Zengakuren came into the hands of an anti-JCP group in June 1958. The new Mainstream, somewhat erroneously denoted as Trotskyites, took a radical Marxist position, denouncing all Communist states for their excessively statist, bureaucratic character, and reflecting in some measure the earlier currents of anarcho-syndicalism so prevalent in Japanese radical circles before the Bolshevik Revolution. At this point, Zengakuren became deeply factionalized. The dominant Revolutionary Marxist faction (the Japan Marxist Student Alliance) controlled the Zengakuren Executive Committee. Two significant factions opposed it: the JCP faction (the Democratic Youth League); and the Structural Reform group plus certain other minor factions basically committed to the Socialist Party.

The trend after 1960 showed a sizable decrease in Zengakuren strength and, at the same time, a substantial increase of JCP power within the organization.[53] By 1962, however, Zengakuren had become so frag-

delegates also criticized the Sōhyō position. After the convention, *Akahata* attacked Sōhyō for "abandoning the position of the working class" in order to support the petite bourgeoisie.

Kamiyama, incidentally, was later to charge that the JCP Mainstream approach to the Socialists, by becoming progressively more rigid and reverting to "the old Comintern line," made inevitable the failure of united front efforts during this period (Vol. I, pp. 117–143).

[53] At the end of 1963, one Zengakuren leader analyzed that organization's composition as follows: four main factions existed, with the JCP (Yoyogi) faction controlling 40 percent of the organizational strength; the Marxshugi Gakusei Dōmei (Marxist Student League) Mainstream, 30 percent; the Structural Reform faction (Kasuga group and some Socialists), 20 percent; and other elements, 10 percent. He further asserted that the organization was in a chaotic condition, with its powers having greatly decreased and its headquarters officials having limited control. Interview with Andō Jimbei, Zengakuren founder and leader of the Structural Reform group, Tōkyō, November 26, 1963.

Andō's report is confirmed by other sources. By 1962, Zengakuren Executive Committee control scarcely extended beyond certain parts of Hokkaidō, Tōkyō, and Kyūshū. The Central Executive Committee, consisting of twenty-seven members, was headed by Nemoto Hiroshi and composed exclusively of Marxist Student League members. Under the Executive Committee were four regional student federations and nine metropolitan and prefectural student federations, totaling 270 separate college and university student governments, supposedly representing some 300,000 students.

Within Zengakuren, no more than 1,500 students were actually JCP members, but approximately 6,000 students belonged to the Democratic Youth League, the JCP youth front organization. In October 1962, however, the JCP organized the Heimin Gakuren (Student Federation Against the Security Treaty and for the Defense of Peace and Democracy) with the objective of taking over Zengakuren. This organization has grown rapidly and quickly established mented that any coordinated action on its part was almost impossible. Thus, in the youth movement, as in the labor movement, prospects for a united front were exceedingly dim. This was also true in the much less significant peasant movement and within intellectual circles.[54] Within every socioeconomic group and at every level of Japanese society, the Communists had thoroughly isolated themselves, despite a plethora of seemingly effective issues for united front purposes.

---

itself throughout Japan. It encompasses some 72 universities having a total student body membership of 130,000 students.

The most significant Communist Party youth organization, however, remains the Nihon Minshu Seinen Dōmei (Japan Democratic Youth League), organized May 5, 1951. With some 93,500 members, of whom 27,000 are JCP members, and approximately 5,000 cells and 380 district committees, the Democratic Youth League has been invaluable to the JCP in connection with election campaigns, demonstrations and rallies, and general propaganda work. It retains a permanent representative in Budapest as a member of the World Democratic Youth League Secretariat and sends representatives to most of the international Communist youth conferences.

[54] The official organ of JCP rural activities is the Central Federated Council of Rural Labor Unions, with approximately 14,000 members. This organization was founded in June 1962 by the JCP to serve as the nucleus and training center for party peasant activities. Larger in membership, however, is the Buraku Liberation League, with 74,000 members. This association was first organized as the National Committee for Buraku Liberation in February 1946, inheriting the traditions of the prewar Suiheisha (Levellers' Association), which had been dedicated to emancipating the outcast community. All of the headquarters officials have been either Communists or left Socialists, and four of the seven Central Executive Committee posts have been held by Communists. In particular, the local organizations in Kyōto, Ōsaka, and Okayama have been controlled by the JCP. The All-Japan Federation of Peasants' Cooperatives, numbering 250,000 members, also has some Communist participants. Approximately six of the forty headquarters officials are JCP members, and a number of local officials of the federation also belong to the party. As of 1963, some 360 of the 80,000 members of the local land commissions and 201 of the 210,000 Farmer Coop officials were JCP members. Clearly, the JCP has not been able to make much headway within these two critical agrarian bodies.

In the intellectual and professional world, there have been a large number of Communist controlled or influenced groups, but most of them have been small in membership and short-lived. Shortly after World War II, the Japan Democratic Culture League was formed under JCP auspices in an effort to establish unity and integrate cultural-intellectual associations. Its activities, however, were characterized by intensive factionalism and frequent cleavages. Moreover, the appeal of the JCP to the Japanese intellectual community was seriously weakened by such events as the Hungarian uprising and also by the general influence of the international Communist movement on the JCP throughout the postwar period.

There is no question that support for the JCP within cultural and intellectual circles had declined in recent years. As of September 1963, there were reportedly 271 Communist Party members teaching in national universities, 150 in private universities, and 85 in prefectural universities—a total of 506 Communist Party professors. In regional terms, 159 of these were in Kinki, 121 in Kantō, 75 in Chūō, 47 in Hokkaidō, 36 in Kyūshū, 28 in Shikoku, 22 in Tōhoku, and 18 in Chūgoku. Osaka City University, with 57 JCP members on its staff, had the largest number, followed by Hōsei (28), Ritsumeikan (26), Hokkaido (24), Nagoya (22), Hokkaidō Science and Arts College (15), Kyōto (15), Kōbe (12), Tōkyō (11), Aichi (10), Miyazaki (10), and Tōkyō Technical College (10). Eleven Communist Party members and an additional 41 pro-Communists have been elected to the Japan Academy of Arts and Sciences.

In one other area the Communists have been reasonably active in organizational terms, namely, in the field of women's associations. The New Japan Women's Society, founded under the aegis of the JCP on October 19, 1962, was formed from a group of leftist women's organizations, with a total membership of approximately 50,000. Through firm control of the headquarters, the society is virtually an adjunct of the JCP, although a variety of ideological and political elements are represented at lower levels. The larger Federation of Japanese Women's Organizations, numbering some 250,000 members and affiliated with the International Democratic Women's League, is also under Communist control. Four of the six key officials are members of the JCP. Several smaller Communist or proto-Communist women's associations exist in addition to these primary organizations.

V

JAPANESE COMMUNISM IN
A DIVIDED COMMUNIST WORLD—
THE SWING TOWARD PEKING

As the Japanese Communist Party was being pushed into greater isolation, what was its internal situation and what were its relations with the international Communist movement? Let us return briefly to the mid-1961 period immediately after the 8th Party Congress. As we have noted, the JCP was overwhelmingly dominated by the Mainstream faction, now led by Miyamoto, Hakamada, and Nosaka. The old anti-Mainstream group centered mainly around Shiga Yoshio, Suzuki Ichizō, and Kamiyama Shigeo. It certainly represented no more than 10 percent of the party, although a number of older intellectuals tended to be sympathetic to this group and its pro-Soviet position.

The first great test for the JCP in the international scene, as for other Communist parties, came during the 22nd Congress of the Communist Party of the Soviet Union, which opened in Moscow in late October 1961. Khrushchev's public attack on Albania and Chou En-lai's sharp retort, followed by his abrupt departure from Moscow before the end of the congress, represented a significant escalation of the Sino–Soviet conflict. With the split now brought into the open world arena, every Communist party was under greatly increased pressure to declare its allegiance.

Against this pressure, the Japanese Communist Party stood firm. In his speech before the Soviet Congress on October 23, Nosaka, Chairman of the Japanese delegation, refused to criticize the Albanian leaders.[1] He restricted his remarks to a recital of JCP gains in which the success of recent united front tactics was claimed, growth in party strength was heralded, and the party role in the labor and youth movements was featured.[2] Nosaka also bitterly attacked "the handful of antiparty elements" who had left the party and were seeking to undermine it. Concerning the crisis within the international Communist movement, Nosaka confined himself to urging unity on the basis of the 1957 and 1960 Moscow agreements.

Subsequently, we have been told that high Russian sources, gravely concerned about the JCP position, sought to obtain reliable information about possible divisions within the party.[3] For their part, the Japanese Communist leaders were also deeply worried by the escalation of the conflict within the international Communist movement. With respect to the Mainstream leaders, this worry was not primarily due to uncertainty or ambivalence over tactics, policies, and allegiances. As we have seen, a strong trend with respect to these matters had been established earlier, and a reversal of that trend was most improbable. Rather, the concern of the JCP leaders was over the effect that the widening international cleavage would have on the strength and unity of the Communist Party in Japan. If the JCP were forced into an open declaration of support for the Peking line, the party would be further divided, and the Kasuga–Naitō forces, in addition to gaining new recruits, might garner open Soviet support.

Consequently, the Mainstream leaders decided to pursue a tactic of neutralism in the immediate aftermath of the 22nd CPSU Congress. This tactic, in its essence, involved the following rules: Publicly, the gravity of the Sino–Soviet dispute would be depreciated, and every effort would be made to discourage discussion of the dispute both inside and outside the party. It would be asserted that those who "exaggerated" the problems within the international Communist movement were doing so for reactionary, antiparty purposes. No derogatory comments about the Soviet or Chinese parties and leaders would be issued

---

[1] The full text of Nosaka's speech was carried by Radio Moscow.

[2] "The Democratic Youth League has increased in membership more than thirty times in the past three years," he said.

[3] In the letter of August 26, 1964, the JCP Central Committee's response to the April 18, 1964 letter of the CPSU Central Committee, it was charged that during the 22nd CPSU Congress, a "functionary" of the Soviet Central Committee tried to get information from the Moscow *Akahata* correspondent about JCP factionalism, urging him not to report this request to party leaders. He disobeyed instructions, and when JCP leaders heard his story, they supposedly lodged a serious protest with Soviet party leaders. See the August 26 letter in *TICD* 653, *JPRS* 26,892, pp. 30-31.

publicly, and roughly equal billing would be given both parties, with praise meted out wherever feasible. Party organs would make the most minimal comments possible on such issues as Albania and other divisive questions, cloaking whatever statements they were forced to issue in highly obscure and extremely cautious language. At the same time, however, the party would pledge to publish "various Communist points of view" for the information of its readers, providing translations of Chinese, Soviet, and other materials in party journals; a very strong stand would be taken publicly on behalf of the Moscow Declaration of 1957 and Statement of 1960, but no attempt would be made to define precisely how they were to be interpreted in the light of current issues. All disputes over these agreements would be handled in accordance with the procedures outlined in the documents, namely, through *private* consultations and bilateral conferences. Privately, every effort would be made in concert with other Asian Communist parties to contain the dispute and to bring the CPSU and the CCP into serious bilateral discussions. In the face of assaults from various quarters over its pro-Peking position, the JCP would vigorously assert its position of "independence and autonomy," insisting that the allegation of its subservience to Peking was a calumny and that it would determine its own position on all issues from the standpoint of correct Marxism–Leninism.

This neutralist tactic was put into effect immediately. The Japanese delegation returned to Tōkyō on the evening of November 6, 1961, not remaining in Moscow to celebrate the anniversary of the Soviet Revolution, scheduled for the following day.[4] Nosaka made a speech on the occasion of the celebration in Tōkyō, however.[5] In it, he was laudatory of the new CPSU program, stressing the fact that it had been adopted by the entire party and nation through a series of meetings and discussions. Nosaka also placed the CPSU ahead of all other parties in pushing forward the construction of communism. Emphasizing the coming triumph of socialism and the downfall of the capitalist camp, he paid tribute to productive increases within the So-

---

[4] Nosaka, anticipating questions on this point, asserted in his prepared speech of November 8 that although the delegation naturally wanted to attend the Moscow celebrations of the 44th anniversary of the October Revolution, they had decided before leaving Tōkyō to return immediately so that they could participate in the ceremonies at home. In reality, of course, this action prevented identification with Khrushchev and the Soviet cause, and appears to have been a policy agreed on by those Asian Communist parties in a position similar to that of the JCP.

[5] For the full text of Nosaka's speech, see *Akahata*, November 22, 1961, pp. 2, 5.

cialist world and to national liberation movements, particularly that of Cuba. He gave only brief attention to the problem of disunity within world communism, which he defined as a problem "involving Albania." He insisted that the unity of the world Communist parties, "linked by the blood of Marxism–Leninism," was unbreakable, regardless of any imperialist machinations that might be undertaken. Of course, he admitted, internal contradictions and differences might develop, but these could be settled in accordance with the Moscow agreements of 1957 and 1960.

Nosaka thus dismissed in a few sentences what was in fact a burning issue within the JCP and went on to discuss at length Soviet achievements under Khrushchev—the great increases in industrial productivity, the "bold" experiment in developing virgin lands, and the major improvements in Soviet working conditions and living standards. Interestingly enough, Nosaka spoke of the fact that the Soviet Union was in a transitional stage with respect to the proletarian dictatorship, since direct popular participation in government was increasing in the absence of exploiting classes.[6]

Nosaka's speech revealed the deep concern felt by Mainstream leaders over the use to which the Kasuga group had put recent Soviet pronouncements and policies. The Japanese Communist leader went to some pains to deny that the changes in basic CPSU statutes were in the direction claimed by the Kasuga group. Democratic centralism was still the guiding principle, and Kozlov's defense of this system was quoted at length in an effort to counter the Kasuga faction's charges of antidemocratic tactics on the part of the JCP headquarters group.

The November 8 speech also contained a lengthy defense of Soviet resumption of nuclear testing, and Nosaka ended by asserting that Kishi's and Ikeda's grandchildren would live under communism, a clear paraphrase of Khrushchev's oft-quoted assertion to the Western world.

Certainly there was no indication in this speech of the gravity of the Sino–Soviet split or of the anxieties which, in reality, the JCP felt. One could not easily have guessed, listening to Nosaka's words, that the Mainstream leaders were burning with resentment over certain Russian actions and attitudes, and were deeply suspicious of Khrush-

---

[6] As is well known, the charge that the CPSU under Khrushchev was abandoning the proletarian dictatorship in favor of a national people's state and thereby distorting Marxism–Leninism was later to become a favorite theme of the CCP. In this and other respects, Nosaka's speech was much more favorable to the Russians than was any Chinese statement of this period.

chev. Nosaka's speech was an excellent example of the application of conscious neutralism.[7]

On November 7, *Akahata* had carried a congratulatory telegram sent by the Central Committee of the JCP to the CPSU Central Committee, on the occasion of the 44th anniversary of the Bolshevik Revolution.[8] Then, for nearly two months, party officials maintained a conspicuous silence in the face of mounting indications of a major split within world Communist ranks. Finally, on December 29, an *Akahata* editorial cautiously set forth some JCP views.[9] The editorial emphasized the urgent need for unity within the world Communist movement. It admitted that "the beginnings of an open dispute" were seriously affecting the relations between several Communist states and were also having some influence on "the democratic movement" in Japan. The solution to this problem lay in the strict application of the Moscow agreements, which provided clear-cut standards for mutual relations among Socialist countries and fraternal parties.[10] The internal problems of the party and their relationship to the international crisis were discussed at length.

---

[7] It is interesting to compare this speech with those given by Kim Il-sŏng and D. N. Aidit at approximately the same time. Kim's report on the 22nd CPSU Congress was also cautious and "neutral" in its general tone, but somewhat less guarded. Aidit's speeches and informal remarks contained reasonably frank criticisms of Khrushchev's actions. For example, in an interview with the author in December 1961, Aidit asserted that the open attack on Albania was a mistake, that Stalin had made a great contribution to the development of Asian Marxism, and that Yugoslavia was following a revisionist path and could not possibly be recognized as a true Marxist–Leninist state. Publicly, the Workers' Party of North Vietnam seemed to be taking the position closest to that of the JCP. Ho Chi Minh failed to mention either Albania or de-Stalinization in his report on the 22nd CPSU Congress and maintained a position of public silence on all aspects of the controversy except to reiterate the necessity of settling disputes peacefully in accordance with the provisions of the Moscow agreements. For a brief analysis of these and other positions, see Robert A. Scalapino, "Moscow, Peking, and the Communist Parties of Asia," *Foreign Affairs,* Vol. 41, January 1963, pp. 323–343.

[8] Akahata, November 7, 1961, p. 1. There is no evidence that the JCP sent a similar telegram to Albania on the following day to commemorate Albanian Red Army Day, as did North Korea and North Vietnam. In this, as in other respects, JCP neutralism seemed more cautious, hence more favorable to the CPSU, than that of the other Asian Communists. This caution, however, was due mainly to the fact that the JCP had to determine its public stance with due regard to the charges of the Communist dissidents and the "bourgeois" press, problems that did not concern Kim, Ho, or even Aidit in the same degree. The evidence indicates that Miyamoto in particular championed the cautious neutralist line, a fact that was to have continuing significance.

[9] "For the Unity of the International Communist Movement and for the Struggle Against Two Enemies," *Akahata,* December 29, 1961, p. 1.

[10] *Ibid.*

Members of the Kasuga group, the editorial charged, were seeking to use—or misuse—the split in an effort to justify their antiparty, anti-revolutionary actions. They were misinterpreting the Moscow agreements as supporting capitulation to American imperialism, and they were slandering the JCP by accusing it of undemocratic organizational principles and partisanship (following the Peking line) in the international scene.

Since both the bourgeois mass media and the Kasuga faction were publishing various documents to distort trends in the international Communist movement and to slander the JCP, the editorial announced that the JCP itself would soon undertake the publication of relevant literature so that party members and sympathizers could "study the problems more comprehensively."[11] Thus a new tactic was launched, one that was intended to preserve the fiction of JCP "neutrality" while enabling the party to present the anti-Soviet position as fully as it wished.[12] This tactic, an ingenious one certain to antagonize Soviet leaders, was ultimately challenged by them in a bitter exchange.

The December 29th editorial ended with the thesis that the JCP had struggled since 1955 to overcome the harmful effects of ultra-leftist adventurism and "paternalist" leadership, fighting against opportunisms of both the left and right such as Trotskyism, revisionism, and dogmatism. It had adopted a program (the 8th Party Congress Program) which represented "a creative adaptation of Marxism–Leninism to the concrete and historical conditions of Japan," and, no matter what incidents occurred, the party would defend Marxism–Leninism and proletarian internationalism.

Thus as 1961 came to a close, the Japanese Communist Party was still seeking to pursue a neutralist policy in public toward the Sino–Soviet dispute, which was now in a more advanced stage as a result of Khrushchev's open attack on Albania. Indeed, in certain important re-

---

[11] *Ibid.*

[12] In my interview with him on January 16, 1962, Nosaka referred to this decision while talking about the Albanian question. I had asked him why Yugoslavia was treated as an enemy while Albania was not so considered. His answer was: "Yugoslavia is called an enemy because all parties agree on this position. In the case of Albania, matters have not reached that state. My next statement will be made as a leader of the JCP. I discovered the problem of Albania for the first time when I attended the CPSU Congress in Moscow. Since then, our party had been studying the problem, and the JCP is planning to issue the views of all parties concerned, including the Albania Workers' Party. Thirty parties, it will be recalled, did not express any view on the Albanian problem. All Communists would like to consider this matter an internal one."

spects, the JCP had taken a more cautious attitude than any Communist party in Asia. Unlike the other Communist parties, the JCP had not sent, or at least made public, a congratulatory telegram to the Albanians on the anniversary of their liberation from Fascism. Nor had the JCP made any statement that could be construed as a direct criticism of Khrushchev's open attack on Albania. On the question of de-Stalinization, the Japanese Communist leaders had also maintained a discreet silence, although Nosaka had privately indicated a divergence from the latest Khrushchev tactics.[13] In general, however, the Mainstream leaders had made an extreme effort to avoid antagonizing the Soviet Union or taking an open stand that would lend support to those who were alleging that the JCP was already in the Peking camp. As we have noted, Khrushchev, while not mentioned often, was praised for certain accomplishments, and there was extensive comment of the most laudatory type concerning progress in the Soviet Union. No prominent or disproportionate praise of China was carried in party organs or delivered in party speeches. Indeed, China was mentioned very little during this period.

The JCP had finally been forced to admit that the Sino–Soviet rift was serious and was having some effect on the situation in Japan. But even in its December 29th editorial, the party set forth its position in an extremely cautious, almost oblique fashion. Only general—and unexceptionable—themes were advanced: the importance of settling disputes through mutual consultation in accordance with the Moscow agreements; the need to uphold Marxism–Leninism and proletarian

---

[13] In my interview with Nosaka on January 16, 1962, his comments on de-Stalinization were particularly interesting. I inquired, "What is your position on Stalin and the current de-Stalinization campaign?" Nosaka responded: "As far as de-Stalinization is concerned, my party and I recognize two facts: first, his achievements, especially in the war against Germany and in the establishment of socialism; second, the fact that there is a dark side also, especially in the later years. There were some Stalinists in our party. I take the same view as Khrushchev." But at a later point in our conversation, he stated that he wished to amend his earlier remarks, saying, "I take almost the same view as Khrushchev. My agreement, however, refers only to the point that both Khrushchev and I recognize merits and faults in Stalin, but at present Khrushchev seems to place more emphasis than I upon Stalin's faults in his later years."

When I asked why it was necessary to carry the de-Stalinization campaign further in the 22nd CPSU Congress, Nosaka replied, "The problem of Stalin came to the front at the very end of the 20th CPSU Congress. Consequently, it was not discussed sufficiently. Perhaps Khrushchev did not have enough facts at that time. Khrushchev has been very severe on Stalin to show the Russian people that his party will never make the same mistakes. However, it was not necessary to attack Molotov in the way in which he did."

internationalism; and the importance of struggling against Trotskyism, revisionism, and dogmatism.

The careful observer, however, could not fail to discern certain basic trends within the Mainstream during this period. In part, this was revealed in the *nonactions* of the party: the refusal to criticize Albania, the failure of the party delegation to stay in Moscow for the October Revolution anniversary celebrations, the absence of any criticisms of Chinese actions and attitudes toward the CPSU, and the unchanging attitude toward Yugoslavia. These negative positions, moreover, were coupled with some strongly suggestive affirmative positions: the continuous emphasis on *the independence and equality* of each Communist party;[14] the repeated insistence that American imperialism was the foremost enemy of the Japanese and all progressive peoples; the demand for strict adherence to the principles of the Moscow agreements in the solution of disputes; and the assertion that—no matter what happened—the JCP would stand firmly on Marxism–Leninism and proletarian internationalism. These positions, negative and positive, were clear enough signals to the initiated. Nevertheless, in some degree, the policy of neutralism achieved the desired effect by leaving considerable uncertainty concerning the JCP position in the minds of outside observers and by forestalling more serious conflicts within party ranks.

There is good reason to believe that during this period the Mainstream leaders were in close touch not only with Peking, but also with the other Communist parties of Asia. Indeed, the outlines of a common strategy are very apparent, with the Indonesian, Vietnamese, Korean, and Japanese Communist parties playing the leading roles. It is in this era that the first signs of an Asian bloc—some degree of policy coordination, particularly among the Indonesian, Vietnamese, Korean, and Japanese parties—appear. The vital significance of this development will subsequently be noted.

It was clear, however, that the JCP tactic of public neutralism and

---

[14] When I raised the question of the Sino–Soviet dispute and the position of the JCP with Nosaka, it is significant that his first comment was, "There are two Moscow declarations, one of 1957 and one of 1960. First, let us look at the background. In the Comintern era, before 1943, the CPSU was always the center of the international Communist movement, but now the situation is changed. Those two Moscow declarations assert that every Communist party in every country is equal. When one Communist delegation proposed that the Soviet party be the leader, Khrushchev himself rejected this proposal—I believe this happened in 1957. We Communists are thus planning to solve our problems on the basis of equality." Interview with Nosaka, January 16, 1962.

private leaning—open aloofness from the dispute and secret pressure
for a negotiated settlement—could not long be sustained, especially if
the controversy between Russia and China became more intense. Consequently, in Japanese Mainstream circles, an anxiety amounting to
desperation developed over the question of containing the conflict.

In early 1962, it appeared as if the cumulative and joint pressures
on the two Communist giants for a settlement were having their effect.
A lull in the international storm developed and lasted throughout the
spring and summer. The JCP, of course, had been among those parties
urging cessation of public attacks by Russia and China, and bilateral
discussions. While there was a noticeable reluctance on the part of both
parties to undertake full-fledged negotiations, the tensions created over
the previous eighteen months eased somewhat. Open polemics ceased,
and the tortuous examination of how to knit together different con-
ceptions of national interests and have to mend the deep wounds of
personal confrontation began.

THE COMMUNIST DISSIDENTS

Meanwhile, the Japanese Communist Party was having its own internal problems. On October 9, 1961, the Kasuga group had formed a
Preparatory Commission for a Socialist Reform Movement, with Kasuga
and Naitō as its leading figures. This group wanted to prepare for the
establishment of a "unified mass party that could construct a peaceful
democratic road to socialism in Japan." Commonly known as the Socialist Renovation group, the Kasuga–Naitō faction repeatedly attacked the JCP (which it labeled "the Yoyogi group") on three main
counts. First, in its analysis of the present age and the status of Japan,
the party had deviated from Marxism–Leninism and the principles of
proletarian internationalism. Second, the leadership had established a
strongly bureaucratic, Stalinist-type control, silencing all opposition and
making renovation from within the party hopeless. And finally, the
party had become a mere tool of Peking, parroting the Chinese line in
such a fashion as to make clear its lack of independence.[15]

In positive terms, the Communist dissidents, in company with an increasing number of Socialists, subscribed to the theories of structural
reform that had been imported from the Italian left, as we noted earlier. Despite the considerable body of theory that they shared, however,
the dissidents were unable to remain united. Kasuga and a small num-

---

[15] See *Atarashii Rosen* (*The New Line*), May 21, 1962, p. 1, for a general
outline of the group's position on the JCP.

ber of followers objected to some aspects of the proposed Socialist Renovation program and left the organization in the spring of 1962.[16] The
Kasuga group established its own unit, the Unified Socialist League,
on May 3, 1962, and began publishing a monthly journal, *Kōzō
Kaikaku* (*Structural Reform*). The League took a position on the JCP
identical to that of the Socialist Renovation group, attacking its ideological-policy views, charging its leadership with antidemocratic practices, and critizing JCP subservience to Peking. Like the Socialist
Renovation group, moreover, the League upheld the Soviet position and
took every opportunity to show how the JCP was diverging from the
CPSU.

Obviously, if the dissident groups were to succeed, they had to have
Soviet approval and support. It was thus in their interest to widen the
breach between the JCP and the CPSU. And in this respect, they had
certain special advantages. Men like Kasuga, who had been high in
JCP circles until early 1961, were in a position to reveal much inside
information, some of it extremely damaging to the Mainstream claims
of neutrality.[17] It is not surprising that JCP leaders were seriously
alarmed by these groups.

In sheer numbers, of course, neither of the dissident Communist
groups seemed formidable. The Socialist Renovation movement had a
membership of approximately 1,200 and circulated about 4,000 copies
of its organ, *Atarashii Rosen* (*The New Line*). Many of its supporters
were students, and financial resources were meager. Local committees
of its youth unit, the Communist Youth League, were established in
Kyōtō, Saitama, Ōsaka, Hiroshima, Fukuoka, and Ibaraki. The Unified Socialist League numbered 600, and its monthly organ, *Structural
Reform,* had a circulation of about 2,200. Again, a fairly high percentage of members were students, and its Socialist Student Front, led by
one of the founders of Zengakuren, Andō Jimbei, operated mainly in
the Kansai area in cooperation with the Communist Youth League.
Together, these two organizations composed the Structural Reform
group within Zengakuren. Both groups were heavily populated by ex-
JCP students who had either resigned or been expelled from the party.

Thus, by early 1962 the Japanese Communist movement was extensively fragmented. In addition to the "party renegades," the party itself

---

[16] For an explanation of Kasuga's objections to the Socialist Renovation
prospectus, see his article, "Organizational Problems of the Socialist Renovation Movement," *Atarashii Jidai* (*The New Age*), February 1962.

[17] All of the members of the Kasuga–Naitō group wrote articles of an
exposé nature, and the group organs carried a number of stories indicating
the nature of the internal splits within the JCP.

continued to have a small but troublesome anti-Mainstream group. The same basic groupings within the party existed as had been present at the time of the 8th Party Congress. The Mainstream, comprising some 90 percent or more of the party leadership, was made up of two major factions. Hakamada Satomi led one group, a faction containing many pro-China elements. A veteran Communist and one of the few with a genuine "proletarian" background, Hakamada had now become one of the top party leaders. Nosaka, commonly associated with Hakamada, but regarded above faction by some, was now frequently referred to as *Tennō Heika* (the Emperor) because he held a prestigious position as Party Chairman but wielded very little real power. Miyamoto Kenji, once an important leader in the old International faction as will be recalled, now held the post of Secretary General and headed the so-called Neutral faction. His policies and his role were critical to the party during this period. The pro-Soviet faction, led by Shiga Yoshio, Suzuki Ichizō, and Kamiyama Shigeo comprised less than 10 percent of the current leadership of the party, but the fact that a number of older intellectuals in or near the party were inclined in its direction gave it some additional significance. Those Japanese intellectuals long committed to Marxism–Leninism and emotionally identified with Soviet traditions proved resistant in a number of cases to the Chinese tides now sweeping over the party.

To understand the real power structure of the Japanese Communist Party, however, it is essential to appreciate the rising significance of a new generation of postwar Communists, most of whom had been trained in China and who were now occupying key party positions. Like the Young Officers of the militarist era with whom they were often compared, these men pressured their seniors for a militant program, concentrated on organizational and propaganda activities at the grass-roots level, and many of them displayed a commitment to the Chinese revolutionary model in a variety of ways.

Who were they? Among the most important figures were Doki Tsuyoshi, Chief Editor of *Akahata;* Ishida Seiichi, Assistant Editor; Anzai Kuraji, Chief of the Personnel Section of the party; and Fujii Keiji, Chief of the Finance Section. These men and others like them constituted the new power center within the Japanese Communist Party.[18] All of them were China-returnees. They controlled vital as-

[18] For details on JCP personnel, organization, and the structure of front groups, see Kōan Chōsachō (Public Safety Investigation Bureau), *Nihon Kyōsantō no genjō* (*Current Conditions of the Japanese Communist Party*), Tōkyō, July 1, 1962. I am also indebted to former members of the party who confirmed and added details concerning key party figures.

pects of party work, and some observers went so far as to say that the senior party officials were essentially puppets in their hands. Obviously, the powerful influence of the Chinese Communist Party on the internal affairs of the JCP was intimately related to this group. And there was evidence that a key figure among the Young Officers was a younger man named Hayashi Inoue who served as Editor of *Sekai Seiji Shiryō* (*Documents on World Politics*). It was this JCP journal that was entrusted with publishing Communist documents from all quarters of the world for the guidance of party members on such questions as Albania. Thus, this China-lobby leader held one of the most sensitive and vital posts in the party, a post critical to JCP-CPSU relations.

THE EXPANDING CRISIS IN THE COMMUNIST WORLD AND THE JCP

The uneasy truce established between the Soviet Union and China in early 1962 lasted throughout the summer. As we have seen, the Russians and Chinese stood firmly together at the time of the 8th Gensuikyō Conference in August, despite important shadings of difference and influence. In the fall of 1962, however, a new series of crises developed. The eyes of the world were suddenly focused on the attempts at Soviet–Yugoslav rapprochement, the Indian border dispute, and the serious Cuban crisis. Once again the Japanese Communist Party was put under severe strain. After a brief sketch of the immediate background, we shall examine these events and their relationship to the Communist movement in Japan.

Throughout the spring of 1962, the Japanese Communist Party gave every public indication of maintaining, and even strengthening, its neutralist stance. By the end of February, *Akahata* Assistant Editor Ishida was again prepared to deny that the Sino–Soviet dispute was serious and to blame anti-Communist forces for making an issue of it. Party organs took various opportunities to praise both the CPSU and the CCP for their policies, and particularly for their contributions to world peace. Nosaka's seventieth birthday at the end of March brought messages from the entire Communist world. The Chinese and Russians— and the Albanians—seemed to vie with each other in praising the veteran Japanese Communist. The messages from Mao and from the Soviet leaders were strongly eulogistic. Enver Hoxha, the Albanian dictator, unable to restrain himself from continuing his polemical fight against the Khrushchevites, praised those "true Marxist–Leninists" who were fighting resolutely against American imperialism. Nevertheless,

Nosaka and his party seemed to be riding the narrows without dashing against either shore. Indeed, Pravda published an article by the JCP Chairman, one devoted mainly to attacks on the Ikeda government and the Kasuga antiparty faction.

During this period, the neutralist policy of the JCP was given essential support by the fact that a further deterioration of intra-Communist relations had been prevented and hopes for an international settlement were brighter. Thus the JCP neutralist policy seemed both appropriate and beneficial. It remained, however, a precarious neutralism. At no point did the Mainstream leaders abandon or weaken those policies that put them at variance with current Soviet positions, as evidenced by the JCP views on the American and Albanian "problems."

With respect to the United States, the Japanese Communist leaders stood firmly by the position that American imperialism was the primary enemy and should be treated as such Nosaka and others repeatedly expressed the view that the influence of "corrupt American culture" must be eradicated from Japan, and that the struggle for Japanese independence from American imperialism must receive first priority by those people fighting for peace. Shortly after the 1962 Moscow Congress for General Disarmament and Peace, *Akahata* asserted that the Japanese Communist Party had always insisted that the peace movement must state clearly *who is the enemy,* a point which openly divided the Russians and Chinese at that congress.[19]

Meanwhile, as promised, the JCP Central Committee had ordered a special issue of *Sekai Seiji Shiryō* in January 1962 devoted to the Albanian question. In this issue, the Soviet position was amply presented, but Albanian views, including Hoxha's vehement attacks on Khrushchev and CPSU policies, were also given full coverage. Naturally, So-

---

[19] Uchino Takechiyo, member of the Central Committee and chief of the United Front Department, wrote an article entitled "Attending the 'World Congress for Peace and Disarmament,'" which appeared in the July 27 and 28, 1962 issues of *Akahata.* He asserted that while the congress had a generally positive significance, the principal message was "a necessary concession and an unavoidable compromise in favor of the advanced units and experienced nations. Consequently, in the case of Japan, it would not be appropriate to remain at the stage of this 'message.'"

In their letter of 18 April 1964, the CPSU Central Committee cited this article as one example of the "all-out support" being given the Chinese by Japanese delegations to international conferences (*TICD* 636, *JPRS* 26,058, p. 47). The JCP Central Committee answered in their letter of 26 August 1964 (*TICD* 653, *JPRS* 26,892, pp. 105–109).

viet leaders were made aware of this fact, with the Kasuga group, among others, sounding the tocsin.[20]

Then came September. President Brezhnev's visit to Yugoslavia followed by Tito's vacation in the Soviet Union represented a serious attempt to improve Soviet–Yugoslav relations and rehabilitate Tito as a true Communist. The reaction of Peking was strongly negative. No amount of rationalization, asserted CCP spokesmen, could obscure the fact that the Yugoslav party had made no basic changes in policies —the very policies condemned by all Communist parties as revisionist at the 1960 Moscow meetings. Indeed, the Yugoslav retreat to capitalism was proceeding at an accelerated pace, according to Peking.

What was the attitude of the Japanese Communist Party? On September 17, 1962, precisely one week before the Brezhnev trip, *Akahata* carried an interview with Takahara Shinichi, head of the party's Propaganda, Education, and Culture Section. Speaking of events at the 8th Gensuikyō Conference, Takahara asserted that the Yugoslav delegation had acted as "the ringleaders of the revisionists of the world."[21] It was clear that the JCP had no intention of rehabilitating Tito, and that was to remain the party's consistent position.

In early October, the party Central Committee held its 4th Plenum meeting since the 8th Party Congress, and *Akahata* subsequently spoke of "heated discussions," indicating that some struggle continued within the party.[22] The language of the 4th Plenum Resolution, however, together with its specific recommendations, paralleled the Chinese line which had been advanced much earlier. In late October, the Indian and Cuban incidents provided new evidence of JCP views. The

---

[20] Almost every issue of *Atarashii Rosen,* the dissident organ, carried some account of the anti-Soviet activities of Mainstream leaders.

[21] *Akahata,* September 17, 1962, p. 2. The party also reproduced the *Jen-min Jih-pao* editorial of September 17, which attacked Yugoslavia violently. The editorial, entitled "We Will See How the Modern Revisionists Have Degenerated," was published in *Akahata* on September 20 in its entirety.

[22] For an account of the 4th Plenary meeting and the resolutions passed, see *Akahata,* October 13, 1962, pp. 1–2. As an interesting footnote to intraparty affairs at this time, Kamiyama gives the following account. He reports that during this period he was ill. The doctors who examined him at the hospital submitted a report to the party Secretariat suggesting that he be sent to the Soviet Union or Western Europe for treatment. On October 15, in the course of an Executive Council meeting, Miyamoto and Hakamada told him to go to China for treatment (no doubt suspecting a plot), whereupon Kamiyama decided to stay home! See Kamiyama, *Nikkyō shidōbu ni atau— Kokusai Kyōsanshugi no sōrosen o mamotte,* Vol. I, Tōkyō, August 30, 1964, p. 131.

Chinese military action against India got under way on October 20, and on the morning of October 23 President Kennedy proclaimed a naval blockade of Cuba and alerted all U.S. military forces following the revelation that Soviet missiles were on the island.

With respect to the Indian border dispute, the Japanese Communist Party sided wholly—and belligerently—with the Chinese, in contrast to the decided coolness with which the CPSU viewed Peking's actions. As is well known, the Chinese were later to accuse the Russians of having begun their campaign of hostility against China in September 1959 with an entirely unwarranted statement of support for India, and of having maintained this position by continuing to give economic and military aid to the "reactionary bourgeois government" of Nehru, despite the fact that it was rapidly becoming "a tool of American imperialism."[23] On October 31, 1962, *Akahata* published an editorial entitled "The Sino–Indian Border Problem Must Be Settled by Means of Negotiation."[24] In this editorial, the Chinese themes were unequivocally and energetically pressed; the American imperialists, who had driven the world to the edge of nuclear war, were now assisting the big bourgeoisie of India, agitating the border issue in order to weaken the world peace camp. While admitting that the border dispute was complicated and that both China and India had made contributions to world peace in the past, *Akahata* exonerated the Chinese from any blame for the present crisis. (It was "natural" for the Chinese to deny a border fixed by British imperialists, and "the problem was raised" when the People's Government had been forced to suppress a rebellion of Tibetan reactionaries.) The Indians had aggravated the situation by rejecting repeated Chinese peace proposals.

In this same issue of *Akahata*, moreover, a detailed summary of the

---

[23] See *The Origin and Development of the Differences Between the Leadership of the CPSU and Ourselves*, p. 26. Said the CCP, "On the eve of Khrushchev's visit to the United States, ignoring China's repeated objections, the leadership of the CPSU rushed out the Tass statement of September 9 on the Sino–Indian border incident, siding with the Indian reactionaries. In this way, the leadership of the CPSU brought the differences between China and the Soviet Union right into the open before the whole world." And in the same article, "The leadership of the CPSU has become increasingly anxious to collude with the Indian reactionaries and has been bent on forming a reactionary alliance with Nehru against socialist China. . . . Two-thirds of Soviet economic aid to India has been given since the Indian reactionaries provoked the Sino–Indian border conflict. Even after large-scale armed conflict on the Sino–Indian border began in the autumn of 1962, the leadership of the CPSU has continued to extend military aid to the Indian reactionaries" (*ibid.*, p. 48).

[24] *Akahata*, October 31, 1962, p. 1.

Jen-min Jih-pao editorial of October 27, "More on the Philosophy of Nehru," was presented. This was a scathing attack on Nehru and the Indian government, comparing them to Chiang Kai-shek and the Kuomintang.[25] Again, on November 8, commenting on Premier Ikeda's letter of support to Nehru, *Akahata,* repeated its full-fledged support of China and of China's attack on the Nehru government.[26]

The position of the JCP with respect to Cuba was also made clear in the final months of 1962. At the outset, during the period when a confrontation seemed probable, *Akahata* and other Communist organs presented a vigorous defense of the Soviet position. In an *Akahata* editorial of October 25, the first reactions were set forth:[27] the United States was provoking war in its demands for missile removal and its threats of a Cuban blockade. Blockade would be an illegal, pirate action, and it had to be resisted. American aggression against Cuba had to be prevented by the united action of Japanese progressive groups, supporting the peace-loving forces of the world. Thus, the demand that all U.S. aggressive action against Cuba cease and that Kennedy's statement be rescinded should be coupled with the insistence that Okinawa be returned to Japan, U.S. military bases be evacuated, Japanese–R.O.K. talks be suspended, and the Mutual Security Treaty be abolished. The editorial was careful to note that the position of the Soviet government was fundamentally the same as that of the JCP Central Committee.

Within hours, Khrushchev acceded to the American demands for the evacuation of missiles. *Akahata* carried the briefest account of this event with no editorial comment.[28] JCP sources then remained silent for several days, but on November 1 *Akahata* launched a broad-scale attack on U.S. policies regarding Cuba, with some final remarks that clearly indicated JCP apprehensions concerning Soviet policies: "The

---

[25] *Ibid.,* p. 2.

[26] "The important thing," asserted *Akahata,*" is that the peace-loving countries and people are denouncing the Indian government for its attitudes, whereas imperialist countries are sympathizing with India, and strengthening their military aid to that country. Public opinion in Burma, Pakistan, Nepal, Bhutan, and other countries is denouncing Indian expansionism. Thus India is becoming more and more isolated in the world, and losing standing in its international position." "On Premier Ikeda's Letter to Premier Nehru," *Akahata,* November 8, 1962, p. 1.

[27] "Emergency Action Against the War Provocation Policy of American Imperialism," *Akahata,* October 25, 1962, p. 1.

[28] On October 27, *Akahata* carried the brief item that Premier Khrushchev had agreed to the proposal transmitted by U.N. Secretary U Thant. No details concerning the proposal were given, and the remainder of the article was devoted to an attack on President Kennedy for the rigidity of his position.

situation regarding Cuba does not allow any opportunism. Although Kennedy pledged the upholding of Cuban independence and sovereignty, the U.S. government is still flying its planes over Cuba and still continuing its blockade. Imperialists will never retreat by themselves. To heighten our alertness and strengthen the common struggle and solidarity of the people against American imperialism which is the common enemy of the world, is the surest way for the defense of world peace."[29]

A few days later, *Akahata* was to warn again that American aggression against Cuba continued and that it was "a very dangerous matter" inasmuch as reactionaries were now asserting that the policy of threatening war had been successful and that "a hard-line policy against socialist countries would work."[30] The editorial gave full endorsement to the five demands of Castro.[31]

The *Akahata* editorial of November 7 celebrating the 45th anniversary of the October Revolution was the clearest indication to date of JCP dissatisfaction with Khrushchev's foreign policies and ideological positions. In striking contrast to the 1961 statement, this editorial contained no direct mention of contemporary Soviet leaders or policies at all. Prominently featured, instead, was the Chinese revolution, "which has dealt a fatal blow to the power of the imperialist position in Asia, and greatly changed the world balance in favor of the socialist side." Cuba was also featured, and the Cuban crisis was coupled with a recitation of other imperialist crimes—all of which proved the validity of the Moscow Statement regarding the threat of war and the central position of American imperialism in fomenting war. Events clearly showed, asserted *Akahata*, "how mistaken and dangerous is the opinion of antiparty revisionists and right-wing social democrats who insist that the character of war has changed fundamentally due to the emergence of nuclear weapons, that one cannot make the distinction between just and unjust wars, and that the problem of man versus nuclear weapons has become the fundamental problem of the modern world."[32]

---

[29] "Under No Circumstances Can Burglar Actions be Justified," *Akahata* editorial, November 1, 1962, p. 1.

[30] "The Aggressive Action of U.S. Imperialism against Cuba Is Still Continuing," *Akahata* editorial, November 3, 1962, p. 1.

[31] These five demands were: the suspension of the economic blockade; the ceasing of all subversive activities against the Cuban government; the suspension of all "pirate attacks" from the United States and Puerto Rico; the suspension of aerial invasion by American planes over Cuban territory; and the return to Cuba of the U.S. military base at Guantánamo.

[32] "On the Occasion of the 45th Anniversary of the October Socialist Revolution," *Akahata* November 7, 1962, p. 1.

As 1962 came to a close, the neutralist policy of the JCP was in a state of considerable disarray. Clearly, it was no longer easy to maintain that the divisions within the Communist world, and particularly those between the CPSU and the CCP, were unimportant or figments of a bourgeois imagination. Nor was it possible for the JCP to mete out roughly equal amounts of praise to the Soviet and Chinese parties; indeed, it was not even possible to give equal billing or even equal attention to the views of each if the JCP were not to be caught in a gigantic paradox. Events had forced the party to reveal its position on the immediate issues, and this position—even the terminology used to express it—had indicated an ever stronger affinity for the Chinese position. This fact could not be hidden, and it grew more significant as the great crisis within the Communist world deepened once again.

Nevertheless, there were still very good reasons why the JCP Mainstream leaders tried almost desperately to avoid open alignment with Peking against Moscow. If at all possible, the pro-Soviet faction had to be kept within the party and the external Communist dissidents had to be prevented from acquiring Soviet blessing. That the Soviet Communist Party might openly support and give international recognition to some group or party other than the JCP was too grave a risk to be ignored. Any direct attacks on Khrushchev and the CPSU might well create that situation. In this sense, the JCP was in a different position than those parties with which it shared common views—such as the Korean Workers' Party.[33]

The new tactical line of the Japanese Communist Party was to assert its position on the substantive issues (neutralism does not mean that we are neutral on issues of principle), while avoiding direct criticism of the Soviet party or direct identification with the Chinese party. The *Akahata* editorial of December 4, 1962, is an example of this approach.[34] Written to commemorate the second anniversary of the Moscow Statement, the editorial emphasized the importance of supporting the revolutionary elements within Marxism–Leninism. Most of the familiar themes were present: imperialism would not leave the world

---

[33] By this period, Kim Il-sŏng appeared to have absolute control over the Korean Workers' Party, having eliminated his opponents through a long series of purges. Thus, the threat of serious factionalism was negligible. For a revealing statement of the North Korean position at this point, see "Let Us Defend the Unity of the Socialist Camp and Strengthen the Solidarity of the International Communist Movement," *Rodong Shinmun*, January 30, 1963. Its support of the Chinese line was strong and unequivocal.

[34] "Let Us Maintain the Revolutionary Position of Marxism-Leninism on the Second Anniversary of the Moscow Manifesto," *Akahata*, December 4, 1962, p. 1.

stage quietly, and it was essential to unite in the struggle against American imperialism; the most important aspect of the Moscow Statement was its forthright condemnation of modern revisionism as manifested chiefly by Yugoslavia, and modern revisionism remained the primary danger to the international Communist movement. The editorial, however, also spoke of the great development of the socialist countries, "headed by the U.S.S.R. and the People's Republic of China." Moreover, it noted certain dogmatic and sectarian qualities within the JCP that had weakened united front activities and needed correction.

At first, the JCP remained completely silent while the Chinese, Albanians, and North Koreans were criticized during the European Communist Party Congresses, held between November 1962 and January 1963, and also when the aggrieved parties—even the Koreans—answered back. For weeks the JCP merely translated and printed various polemics from both sides, defending itself at the same time against charges that it had moved into the Peking camp. In a significant editorial of January 24, 1963, for example, *Akahata* writers asserted:

They [the Kasuga–Naitō groups] are attacking us saying that our party's stand regarding the dispute is ambiguous, or that the line of our party is following that of some fraternal party, or that there is a factional struggle within the party leadership regarding this problem. All of these stories are groundless. If our party has not gotten involved in these disputes, it is because our party has been abiding by the Moscow Statement, and any public arguments about these matters will not help in the settlement of the problem. We are merely hoping for the suspension of public disputes between fraternal parties and the settlement of the dispute by an international conference.[35]

These sentiments were reiterated in the Resolution of the 5th Plenum meeting of the JCP Central Committee, issued on February 15 after a three-day meeting. The 5th Plenum Resolution was an extremely interesting illustration of the new line.[36] Proper homage was paid to the CPSU, which was described as the vanguard of the international Communist movement and a party that had "consistently supported" the national liberation struggles.[37] The unity of the Soviet and Chinese

---

[35] "The Manoeuvres of the Reactionary Forces and Anti-Party Revisionists around the International Communist Movement," *Akahata*, January 24, 1963, p. 1.

[36] The Resolution of the 5th Plenum of the Central Committee was published in *Akahata*, February 19, 1963, p. 2.

[37] Kamiyama was to claim that he and Nakano Shigeharu "forced" the Plenum to insert this point.

parties, moreover, was labeled as a matter of "decisive importance," since there could not be any genuine solidarity of the international movement or the people of the world without solidarity between the CPSU and the CCP. The call for an international meeting aimed at resolving differences of opinion, as advanced by the Chinese, Korean, Vietnamese, and Indonesian parties, was supported. The resolution criticized the attacks on "a certain party" at recent Communist Party Congresses—but urged that all public polemics cease, no matter what the justification. Again, it proclaimed modern revisionism as the principal danger to the international Communist movement, citing the antiparty activities of the domestic revisionists at length.

The 5th Plenum Resolution proved to be the last serious effort on the part of the Japanese Communist party to maintain a neutralist stance for nearly three years.[38] In part, a change was now forced because the Soviet leaders had grown weary of what they regarded as the duplicity of the Mainstream faction and were determined to force a showdown. On February 22, 1963, just one week after the 5th Plenum Resolution had been adopted, the Central Committee of the CPSU sent a confidential letter to the JCP, suggesting that bilateral talks be held to prevent further deterioration of CPSU-JCP relations.[39] The JCP answer, dispatched on March 6, agreed in principle to such a meeting, but indicated that party leaders could not come immediately because of the forthcoming elections. In fact, the JCP leaders did not wish to meet with Soviet leaders until after the Russians had met with the Chinese, in the hope that the cleavage could be resolved, or at least moderated.

THE STRUGGLE TO REKNIT THE UNITED FRONT

Thus, relations between the Yoyogi leaders and Moscow remained cool during the spring of 1963. JCP organs carried full information concerning the preparations for the Moscow talks between Soviet and Chinese party leaders. They also reported extensively the statements and speeches from Peking on a wide range of subjects. The party, however, did not take any new positions relating to the dispute. Its energies were devoted mainly to the local elections, in which it made a strong

---

[38] The key individual in the maintenance of this policy appears to have been Miyamoto, leader of the so-called "neutralist" or independent faction. It is probably significant that Miyamoto was in ill health during the 1962–1963 period and frequently was forced to miss party meetings.

[39] This fact was first made public in the 18 April 1964 Letter from the CPSU CC to the JCP CC, *TICD* 636, *JPRS* 26,058, p. 23.

and partially successful attempt to achieve a united front with left Socialists in certain contests for governor and major. At its 6th Plenum
meeting in May, the Central Committee proclaimed that it had scored
a 10 percent increase in votes in those places where it had run party
candidates, winning 22 seats in city and prefectural assemblies, and 699
seats in town and village councils.[40]

Once again, the party had sought to use the "peace and independence" issue as its key theme. It had featured its opposition to the berthing of U.S. atomic-powered submarines, Japan-R.O.K. talks, American
control of Okinawa, and the continuance of American military bases
in Japan. The JCP was also using these issues in its effort to rebuild
those united front organizations that had been shattered by the events
of mid-1962 and their aftermath. Let us turn to the united front activities, concentrating again on "the peace movement."

The Socialist Party and Sōhyō had sponsored a two-day "Mass Rally
Against A and H Bombs and for Peace" in Hiroshima, December 3-4,
1962. The primary purpose of this rally had been to establish the peace
movement on the basis of principles laid down by the non-Communist
left. Iwai, Secretary General of Sōhyō, had expressed the problem
frankly from a Sōhyō standpoint when he asserted that recent Gensuikyō
conferences had been controlled by "minority militants," and that conference resolutions consequently bore little relation to the actual desires
of the Japanese people. He called for the development of new principles so that the Gensuikyō charter could be revitalized and the Japanese antibomb movement rebuilt.[41]

At the beginning of 1963, negotiations for the reorganization of the
Gensuikyō began. Discussions and debates were heated and prolonged.
Finally, on February 21, the Gensuikyō Executive Board unanimously
approved a compromise statement on the basis of which it was agreed
to hold a jointly sponsored National Rally on March 1 to commemorate the Bikini Incident and to convene the 9th World Conference
in August. The statement represented a major Socialist victory. The
first point proclaimed "opposition to nuclear tests by any country"
and support for "the immediate conclusion by nuclear powers of
an agreement to ban nuclear tests."[42] However, on February 28, a
furious debate developed within Gensuikyō over the issue of opposition

---

[40] For a report on the 6th Plenum meeting, see *Akahata*, May 20, 1963,
pp. 2–3.

[41] Iwai's speech is reported in *Sōhyō News*, No 214, January 10, 1963, pp.
1–2.

[42] *Ibid.*, No. 216, March 10, 1963, pp. 6–8.

to nuclear tests by *any* country, the Communists having been given instructions in the meantime to fight on this point. The meeting ended
with the resignation of the directors en masse; once again, Gensuikyō
had been shattered by Communist intransigency. Now, Sōhyō and other
Socialist Party-affiliated organizations began to discuss the reorganization of the association on the basis of five principles: opposition to
nuclear tests by any country and efforts to obtain an immediate nuclear
test ban agreement; opposition to the nuclearization of Japan; support
for the creation of a nuclear-free zone in the Pacific and Asian region
and opposition to nuclear bases anywhere in the world; opposition to
the berthing of atomic submarines in Japanese ports; increased social
security for atomic victims and legislation to strengthen their relief. The
position of Sōhyō was that support of these principles was essential for
an effective anti-A bomb movement, and that it would cooperate only
with organizations so pledged.

Once again, extensive efforts were made to reconstruct the united
front between Socialists and Communists through the rehabilitation of
Gensuikyō. Finally, after many arduous debates and extraordinary Socialist firmness, the Gensuikyō Executive Board once more accepted
the February 21 statement at a meeting on June 21.[43] On the surface,
it appeared that the Communists, determined to achieve a united front,
had made a major concession. However, a closer reading of the agreement indicated that any concession might be temporary, depending on
who could gain control of Gensuikyō organizations at the grass-roots
level. It was agreed that future decisions would be made by a majority
vote when there were differences of opinion, and it was further stipulated that all members of the board would resign and a new board be
selected so as to bring "a fresh viewpoint" to the association. Everything hinged, therefore, on which political faction could gain majority
power by the time of the summer conferences. The Communists were
evidently confident that with hard work they could capture a majority
of the local Gensuikyō delegations, a confidence that proved to be warranted.

Until the very eve of the 9th Gensuikyō Conference, it appeared that
the precarious unity established in June would hold, at least until the
opening session had taken place. However, when Sōhyō and the Socialist leaders discovered that the Communists had successfully mobilized
a majority of delegates and were prepared to outvote the Socialists on
such crucial issues as the total test ban question, they decided to shun

---

[43] *Ibid.,* No. 221, July 10, 1963, pp. 7–9.

the meetings.[44] Thus, the 9th World Conference opened in Hiroshima on August 5 as an almost purely Communist performance.

THE SINO–SOVIET STRUGGLE TRANSFERRED TO JAPAN

The 9th Gensuikyō Conference took place at a critical juncture in international politics, shortly after a series of events that were having the most profound repercussions within and outside the Communist world. The Moscow talks between top representatives of the CPSU and CCP had ended in complete failure, and the Chinese Communists, in a lengthy philippic, had made an open bid for global leadership of the Communist movement, setting forth a "revolutionary Marxist–Leninist" program and proclaiming Khrushchev and the Soviet party unfit for the vanguard position.[45] The conflict had been escalated to a point where compromise seemed utterly impossible, and where all veils were being shed, with opponents being named, crimes being catalogued in detail, and a struggle to the death being proclaimed. Just ten days before the 9th Gensuikyō Conference opened, moreover, the limited test ban treaty had been signed by the United States, the Soviet Union, and Great Britain. This treaty, representing the first concrete evidence of a possible Soviet–American rapprochement, had been bitterly denounced by Peking almost immediately after it was announced. As the Chinese used the treaty to illustrate Khrushchev's revisionist and capitulationist tendencies, so the Russians used it to demonstrate the Chinese commitment to nuclear war. Quickly, the treaty became a litmus-paper test for Communists throughout the world, a test which they could not escape.

Understandably, therefore, the Hiroshima Conference became a

---

[44] The Sōhyō position was fully set forth in its journal, *Sōhyō News.* It argued that the 9th World Conference had theoretically failed to open, because all Sōhyō and Socialist Party representatives had withdrawn. Hence the meeting was merely one of the Communist Party and its satellite, the Democratic Youth League. The substantive issue, of course, was the question of opposing *all* nuclear tests, but, as noted above, the Communists had captured a sufficient number of delegates to control the convention, and when this was discovered it was the decisive factor. See *ibid.,* No. 223, September 25, 1963, pp. 3–6.

[45] "A Proposal Concerning the General Line of the International Communist Movement," Text of the 14 June 1963 Letter of the Central Committee of the Communist Party of China in Reply to the Letter of the Central Committee of the Communist Party of the Soviet Union of 30 March 1963, republished in pamphlet form by the Foreign Languages Press, Peking, 1963.

deadly struggle among the Communists themselves, with some exceedingly bizarre events taking place. Over 10,000 Japanese delegates were present, together with some 70 foreign delegates supposedly representing 20 countries. Because of the Socialist attitude toward the conference, the great bulk of these were Communists or Communist-front types. At the very outset, however, trouble developed. Georgi A. Zhukov, head of the Soviet delegation, held a conference on August 4 with Socialist Party leaders who were boycotting the conference and stressed the significance of the test ban treaty. The Soviet delegation, moreover, questioned once again the credentials of many overseas "representatives," especially those individuals who were fugitives living in Peking and had no legitimate claim to represent anyone—except the Chinese. Questions were raised as to whether an international session should be held and whether foreign delegates should be full-fledged participants.

The Chinese position on the critical issues had already been made clear in the message of greeting sent by Kuo Mo-jo, well-known Communist intellectual. Kuo called the test ban treaty "an utter fraud to fool the people of the world—a design to prepare war under the cover of 'peace.' " He charged that the treaty was an attempt to preserve the monopoly of power possessed by the present nuclear states, and a method of helping the United States achieve complete nuclear superiority, conduct nuclear blackmail, and prepare for nuclear war. Kuo hoped that the conference would make "positive contributions" to the "just, patriotic, anti-U.S. struggle of the Japanese people."

The opening session of the 9th World Conference was held in the Hiroshima Peace Park, with Hirano Yoshitarō, Chairman of the Japanese Peace Committee and veteran Communist front man, presiding. The first incident occurred when Chao Pu-chu, head of the Chinese delegation, began to speak. Suddenly, members of the Soviet delegation, together with delegates from India, Czechoslovakia, Hungary, Yugoslavia, and some other pro-Soviet groups, arose, marched to the monument in memory of atomic bomb victims, and remained there, heads bowed, backs turned away from the podium, throughout Chao's speech. As might have been expected, Chao delivered a blistering attack on the Moscow Treaty: "It is an utter fraud designed to pull the wool over the eyes of the people of the world." He added that the people must be aroused so that they would not fall into the trap.

The session of August 6 produced even more excitement. Amid scenes of unprecedented bitterness, Chinese and Soviet speakers, together with their various factions, poured out attacks on each other. Chinese delegate Chu Tzu-chi was given the major assignment. As a leader of the Chinese Peace Committee, he had been a delegate to the 1962 Moscow Peace Congress, and now he proceeded to denounce it as a "disgrace," because of its utter failure to name the enemy of peace, truly oppose imperialism, or render support to national liberation movements. Chu insisted that the conference rectify these mistakes by calling for the elimination of all nuclear weapons, by fighting against American imperialism and exposing the United States as the true enemy of peace, by supporting those who were engaged in patriotic, anti-American struggles, by extending relief to the victims of atomic bombs, and by giving complete support to the national liberation struggles of the Asian and African peoples.[46]

When Zhukov mounted the rostrum, he quickly launched a stinging attack on the Chinese position. There were madmen, he asserted, who were opposed to the test ban treaty, some of whom were present in the hall. " 'Conduct nuclear weapons tests! Contaminate the seas! Create deformed people!,' they say." Zhukov continued in this vein, charging that the Chinese were saying that the Soviet Union was afraid of imperialists, but that Soviet deeds spoke louder than Chinese words. Had the Chinese forgotten all of the assistance they had received from the Soviet Union? he asked dramatically.

When the Soviet delegate finished, Chu asked for the opportunity to make a rebuttal. Speaking rapidly and in a furious tone of voice, he declared that China had not been helped by the Russians but had carried out its revolution alone. He then left the rostrum but quickly returned to shout, "The Soviet Union is incapable, and always will be, of achieving a single one of the things that China has achieved." Zhukov, in a rage, retorted that the Soviet Union had been treating China with too much respect and that he had no intention of answering such slander.

Such was the level—and the intensity—of the debate. Naturally, full publicity was given these events throughout Japan, a fact that did nothing to aid the reputation of Gensuikyō or enhance the prestige of the Communist movement. On August 7, after an all-night session of the drafting committee, an "Appeal for International Common Action" was approved by the conference. Despite the fact that it was finally supported by the Soviet delegation, the appeal represented a Russian defeat. There was no mention of the test ban treaty, and all of Chu's

---

[46] For the Chinese version of events and the key themes from Chinese speeches, see the *Peking Review*, No. 33, August 16, 1963, pp. 28–33.

proposals had been incorporated into the resolution in one form or another. The Chinese simply had the votes.[47]

THE JCP SHIFT FROM NEUTRALISM

The events surrounding the 9th World Conference were extremely painful for the Mainstream leaders of the Japanese Communist Party and produced a major shift in JCP tactics. The policy of neutralism, established and maintained with such difficulty after October 1961, could no longer be sustained. In reality, of course, relations between the JCP and the CPSU had been cool and distant for many months, as noted earlier.[48]

From the documents, it is apparent that the Mainstream JCP leaders maneuvered desperately to avoid a confrontation with the Soviet Union. The caution—and anguish—with which they approached the Moscow Treaty was beautifully illustrated by an *Akahata* editorial of July 29, published just four days after the treaty had been signed and just a few days before the opening of the conference.[49] The editorial stated that among the Japanese people, who had suffered so much from atomic weapons, the news of the treaty had produced "an outcry of joy as well as a voice of caution." The problem lay in the double-faced nature of American imperialism. While talking about peace, Kennedy had pursued a policy of placing nuclear weapons everywhere in the world, including Japan. He had asserted, moreover, that the treaty would not affect American security adversely. Thus, if vigilance were to be relaxed, or if the struggle against American imperialism were to be halted as a result of the treaty, the editorial pointed out, it would be a serious mistake: "The nuclear test ban treaty can have a positive meaning only if it leads to the conclusion of a total nuclear ban and total disarmament. But now that U.S. imperialism is utilizing this treaty to conceal

---

[47] The English text of the 9th World Conference Resolution, entitled "Appeal for International Common Action," is printed in *ibid.*, pp. 32–33.

[48] By this point, the CPSU had written a second letter (dated July 13, 1963) in an effort to arrange a bilateral conference between the two parties. Many grievances had grown worse in the Soviet mind, and new ones had developed. For example, the JCP organs were now printing Chinese materials immediately, such as the June 14 letter, but delaying important CPSU documents. The July 14 CPSU answer to the Chinese letter was not published until September 27, according to the Russians, and then "in impermissibly abridged form with crude distortions of the content." See the 18 April 1964 Letter from the CPSU CC to the JCP CC, *TICD* 636, *JPRS* 26,058, p. 23.

[49] "On the Partial Nuclear Test Ban Treaty," *Akahata* editorial, July 29, 1963, p. 1.

its further development of nuclear weapons and nuclear armament, we must strengthen our struggle, demanding that nuclear power be used for peaceful purposes alone."

While the thrust of this editorial was clearly negative, it did not appear to commit the Japanese Communist Party unequivocally to a stance of opposition. One Russian commentator at least was able to read the JCP position as one of support for the treaty. On August 3, however, after what must have been a period of intensive Chinese pressure and internal party debate, the JCP Central Committee issued an official statement leaving no doubt as to its position.[50] To regard the Moscow Treaty as the first step toward a total ban on nuclear weapons, asserted the Committee, was in fact to sanction the nuclear war preparations of the American imperialists while restraining the hands of people (Chinese?) who were struggling for peace and independence against U.S. imperialism. "This in itself is to invite the danger of nuclear war."

The Central Committee, admittedly worried about the unity of the forthcoming conference, presented its formula for handling the problems. Neither the issue of opposing nuclear tests by *any* country nor the issue of the partial test ban treaty should be presented for a discussion and vote. Rather, the conference should focus on those matters on which there was total agreement: the banning of American atomic-powered submarines and F-105D jets from Japan; opposition to the nuclear arming of Japan, to American military bases in Japan, and to the continued American control of Okinawa; the establishment of an international agreement providing for a total ban on nuclear weapons; the creation of a nonnuclear zone in Asia and the Pacific; and the provision for the relief of atomic bomb victims.

The effort to obscure the various divisions within international communism in this manner failed, as we have noted. There now ensued a furious power struggle, involving both Russians and Chinese, and affecting every element of the Japanese left wing. As early as the fall of 1962, the Soviet Union had begun to cultivate Sōhyō and Socialist Party leaders in earnest, seeing in them a possible alternative to reliance on the Japanese Communist Party. Thus, Zhukov's "frank talk" with JSP leaders on August 4, the day after the JCP Central Committee report, was significant. Evidently, Soviet contacts were also made with representatives of the Kasuga–Naitō group, notably Maeno Ryō and Katsube

---

[50] *Akahata,* August 4, 1963, p. 1.

Gen.[51] Now, the Russians were seeking actively to create their own united front in Japan, hoping to isolate the Mainstream JCP leaders.

The struggle extended into the Japanese Communist Party itself. Immediately after the Hiroshima Conference, Zhukov called on the JCP Central Committee. A JCP account states that he discussed the Moscow Treaty with Nosaka and accepted the idea that since the two parties had different positions on this matter, it should be discussed in the forthcoming bilateral talks.[52] The Russians, however, did not wait for these talks before challenging the JCP position. Zhukov, writing about the Hiroshima Conference in the August 25 issue of *Pravda,* openly criticized the Japanese Communists in the following terms: "It is to be noted that some JCP members attempted to ignore the positive characteristics of the partial test ban treaty at the behest of the CPR delegation."[53]

At approximately the same time, Russian authorities were urging members of the Japan–Soviet Union Society then touring Russia to sign a joint communiqué supporting the treaty. If JCP sources may be trusted, Soviet pressure on this delegation and a youth group that followed was intense. Reportedly, the Russians warned their visitors that unless support to the treaty was given, a split in the society and in the Japanese Communist Party itself was inevitable.[54] The Japan–Soviet Union Society was, of course, a critical battleground, since its historic mission had been to serve as a transmission belt for Soviet cultural and political materials both within and outside the Japanese Communist movement. Composed of party and nonparty members, it was the most logical stronghold of Soviet influence. Thus the Russians made a determined effort in the months that followed August 1963 to retain some control over it.

They failed. Just as the Mainstream JCP leaders were busily remov-

---

[51] At least, so the Japanese Communist Party Mainstream leaders charged. According to them, "The Soviet delegation encouraged the maneuverings of certain of the right-wing Social Democrats who insisted on such things as making this Congress not a World Congress but a Japanese Congress, and from the outset were busy concocting schemes of this sort, and also carried out clandestine meetings with anti-party revisionists such as Ryō Maeno and Gen Katsube, who had been expelled from our party and had come to constitute one wing of divisive scheming." 26 August 1964 Letter of the JCP CC in Reply to the Letter of the CPSU CC of 18 April 1964, TICD 653, *JPRS* 26,892, pp. 19–20.

[52] *Ibid.*, p. 20.

[53] See "A Reply to Zhukov's Open Charges," *Akahata,* July 15, 1964, p. 2.

[54] 26 August 1964 Letter, p. 22.

ing all pro-Soviet elements from key party posts, similarly, they began to crack down on the activities of front organizations like the Japan–Soviet Union Society. Labeling this society "the last stronghold of anti-party elements," they ordered policy alterations and personnel changes.[55] Beginning in the fall of 1963, moreover, JCP headquarters took a number of actions aimed at restricting or prohibiting the dissemination of Russian propaganda in Japan. These actions affected every outlet over which the party had any influence or control.

Naturally, the Russians became aware of the Mainstream drive to stop their propaganda. They could scarcely fail to feel its impact, and, in any case, informants within the party provided them with concrete information concerning developments. At a later point, they were thus able to confront JCP leaders with specific charges. Did not party head-quarters issue a directive dated January 27, 1964, to the effect that the dissemination of all Soviet propaganda materials should cease and em-phasis be given to materials from the People's Republic of China?[56] Later, on June 6, 1964, did not the Science Book Agency, a JCP outlet, give orders to all branches to make only a minimal amount of Soviet literature available for sale and to destroy the rest?[57]

The Russians fought back in the only manner left open to them. Using their Tōkyō Embassy as an outlet and obtaining mailing lists from friends in and out of the party, they started mailing materials directly to prefectural party branches and cells, front organizations, and individual members, seeking to work below the top leadership level. Nor did they stop with materials. Using Soviet personnel stationed in Japan, they launched a grass-roots campaign for support.

Some specific information is available from JCP sources. According to them, Comrade Chekhonin, "a special correspondent of *Izvestiia*" stationed in Japan, "sought to incite our party members to struggle against the Central Committee" on the issue of the Moscow Treaty.[58] Beginning in October 1963, moreover, Soviet Embassy staff members frequently attended and spoke at public and private meetings organized by "anti-party elements" and held in universities and various other places. A number of invitations to visit the Soviet Union were given to leftists not under JCP discipline, both as groups and as individuals. The Soviet drive to create its own united front gathered momentum,

---

[55] 18 April 1964 Letter, p. 27.

[56] *Ibid.*

[57] 11 July 1964 Letter of the CPSU Central Committee, *TICD* 636, *JPRS* 26,058, p. 54.

[58] 18 April 1964 Letter, p. 22.

with increasing attention being given to Socialists as well as to pro-Russian Communists.[59]

Meanwhile, Peking was by no means inactive. The Chinese Communists were also busily propagating their views at the grass-roots level, sending an unprecedented amount of literature into Japan, some of it disseminated through Japanese Communist Party outlets (with the very considerable profits going into party coffers), some of it distributed directly via mailing lists compiled from various sources. And the Chinese were making even greater use of the "cultural mission" technique than their Soviet opponents. Scores of groups and individuals were being invited to Peking for cost-free tours and exchanges of views. As we have noted, in the case of Sōhyō at least, the Chinese deliberately ignored headquarters, reaching down into the ranks for promising or committed individuals. They, quite as much as the Russians, could bypass organizational leadership when it was desirable. Nor were the Chinese contacts limited to the left. Pursuing the strategy of cultivating anyone who might be of service either in securing the recognition of Peking or in weakening American–Japanese ties, the Chinese invited a number of conservatives for talks and visits. The Chinese united front efforts were thus on an even wider scale than those of the Soviet Union.

Rarely, if ever, had the Japanese left been so fragmented and so frantically engaged in internal combat as it was by late 1963. And rarely had external forces impinged so directly on the Japanese left in almost all of its branches. In this setting, the Japanese Communist Party was now forced to define its position more sharply. The 7th Plenum meeting of the Central Committee, held between October 15 and 18, provided the first major opportunity. The 7th Plenum Resolution, entitled "The Present Situation and the Party's Tasks Centering Around the General Elections," represented a significant policy statement. With respect to the forthcoming House of Representatives election, the party put forward its "five great policies," mere restatements of long-held positions.[60] In the analysis of the international situation and the relation of the Japanese Communist Party to it, however, a new tone—and certain new themes—were present. The resolution began with a familiar recital of imperialist decay and socialist triumph, making clear the ultimate victory of communism. However, disunity within the international Communist movement, "due to ideological disparity on issues of principle," was jeopardizing this victory, particularly since "American imperialism was pursuing its aggressive policies in sly fashion," using a

---

[59] 26 August 1964 Letter, p. 19.

[60] For the 7th Plenum Resolution, see *Akahata,* October 22, 1963, pp. 2–3.

disguise of peace and liberty to take advantage of Communist disunity. A case in point was the Moscow Treaty which the party could not support, since it provided no basis for restraining the nuclear war policies of the United States.

In the final section of the resolution, moreover, the party spoke with an unprecedented sternness, clearly focusing on Moscow. The ideological dispute within world communism was becoming increasingly severe and affecting Japan in a variety of ways. The obligation of the Japanese Communist Party was to stand on a position of independence and autonomy, based on the revolutionary principles of Marxism–Leninism, proletarian internationalism, and the Moscow agreements. The Japanese Communist Party would not interfere in the internal affairs of other fraternal parties, and it was incumbent on them not to interfere in JCP internal affairs. The struggle against modern revisionism was more important than ever under present circumstances, and it was also vital to oppose modern dogmatism, which now manifested itself in the mechanical pursuit of another fraternal party's line rather than creatively adapting Marxism–Leninism to the special circumstances of one's own society. (This latter theme could, of course, be used against comrades other than the Russians as later events were to illustrate.) It would be a mistake, finally, to underestimate the power of the American imperialists and the Japanese reactionaries—but it would be an even greater mistake to overestimate their power and fall into tactics of passiveness and retreat.

These statements left no doubt whatsoever about the position of the Japanese Communist Party. There was still no criticism of the Soviet party or Khrushchev by name, but the JCP had now begun to define its position on most of the critical issues in such a fashion as to remove any ambiguity that might have existed earlier.

The 7th Plenum Resolution, moreover, contained certain omissions or "corrections" of the 5th Plenum Resolution (February 1963) that were extremely significant and, by later party admission, very deliberate.[61] The 5th Plenum Resolution had stipulated that all open polemics should cease, even if this required that certain attacks go unanswered. The 7th Plenum Resolution, at least by implication, supported answers to such attacks on the score that any other position would violate the principle of the independence and equality of each party. The historic concept of the Soviet Union as "the universally recognized

---

[61] See the Report of the Japanese Communist Party Central Committee to the 9th Party Congress, November 25, 1964, presented by Secretary-General Miyamoto, *TICD* 691, *JPRS* 28,456, pp. 210–211.

vanguard of the international Communist movement," ritualistically included in almost all basic party documents, was omitted from the 7th Plenum Resolution, since it "has been wrongly used to justify blind subservience to the CPSU."[62] Similarly, the 5th Plenum assertion that the CPSU "consistently supports" the national liberation struggle "had the danger of being used in justifying unconditionally the policy of the CPSU," and was consequently "corrected."[63] Finally, the 5th Plenum statement that the unity of the Soviet Union and China was essential to the progress of world communism was dropped.

With these changes, the Japanese Communist Party was in a position to charge Soviet leaders with the crimes of modern revisionism, "splittism," and interference in the internal affairs of fraternal parties. A major shift in JCP tactics had occurred since the spring of 1963, a shift intimately connected with various events of the summer. Two other party pronouncements issued approximately one month later further confirmed and amplified the new JCP line. On November 10, an editorial entitled "For the Unity and Advance of the International Communist Movement" was published in *Akahata,* and in that same issue answers to questions concerning the Sino–Soviet dispute were presented.[64]

In these documents, a further step was taken to escalate the conflict with the CPSU. Specific criticisms were now directed at various actions of the Soviet party and its leadership, particularly the practice of open criticisms of fraternal parties starting at Bucharest in 1960 and continuing through the recent European Party Congresses. The practice of treating the Titoists as a fraternal party was also condemned. And now the Mainstream leaders, while still avoiding the use of names, began to use the phrase "some fraternal parties" when speaking of Russian "errors," a formula long employed by the Chinese.

For the first time, moreover, the party defined "independence." The term did not signify taking the role of a "neutral, mediatory spectator" or taking "a passive attitude toward the truth," the *Akahata* editorial maintained. Every Communist had to distinguish between right and wrong, truth and falsity. Each party, as an independent and equal entity, had the responsibility for the revolutionary movement in its own country. It had to formulate its own policies, successfully integrating the actual situation with the principles of Marxism–Leninism. The

---

[62] *Ibid.,* p. 211.

[63] *Ibid.*

[64] For a translation of the editorial, see *TICD* 539, *JPRS* 22,197, pp. 80–86; for a translation of the article, "How Does the Japanese Communist Party Think of the So-called 'International Ideological Conflict'?" see *TICD* 538, *JPRS* 22,194, pp. 20–31.

correct unity of proletarian internationalism and patriotism, proclaimed the *Akahata* editorial, was a new and important duty. Obviously, the JCP was trying to raise the nationalist quotient in its ideological-policy appeal, both as a defensive measure against its historic dependence on the Soviet Union, now apparently shifting to the Chinese, and as a method of taking the offensive against those dissidents who were "mechanically following another fraternal party [the CPSU]." Once again, in strident tones, the party asserted that it would submit to no coercion and take no orders from any fraternal party. A stand was also taken against any international Communist conference that was "hurriedly convened" and took decisions by majority vote. Such a conference, said *Akahata,* would irreparably damage Communist unity and could only serve the cause of splittism.

In discussing the Sino–Soviet dispute, the *Akahata* writers first made it clear that the quarrel was mislabeled, because many parties were participating in the conflict, not merely the Soviet Union and China. The primary issue was the question of how to oppose "American imperialism and all the reactionaries of the world." Could the struggle against the United States be won by means of diplomatic negotiations with the American government, or did it require a fight on the part of the people of the world? On these and similar issues, the Japanese Communist Party took an independent position, based on Marxist–Leninist principles. It was thus totally false to accuse the party of belonging to either a "Soviet" or a "Chinese" clique.

Taken together, these statements of October and November 1963 constituted a new party line, one supported by all except a small number of party leaders.[65] The line was to be put to its ultimate test in the spring of 1964, when Japanese and Soviet delegates confronted each other in a showdown conference. As noted earlier, the Russian leaders had been requesting such a meeting since February 1963, and the Japanese had repeatedly sought postponement. The second Soviet letter urging talks had been dispatched to Tōkyō on October 12, 1963, with the Japanese responding on October 22. Once again, the Japanese found excuses for delaying any meeting. The November elections and the postponement of the 9th Party Congress made it advisable to wait. Neither Nosaka nor Miyamoto could come to the Soviet Union, but if the Russians wanted to send a delegation to Japan, it would be wel-

---

[65] For an analysis of inter-party factionalism during this period, see Fukuda Katsuichi, "The Trend of the Japanese Communist Party with Respect to the Sino–Soviet Dispute," Kōan Jōhō (*The Report of the Public Safety Investigation Bureau*), July 1964.

comed. Asserting their "independence and autonomy" in this manner, the Japanese maneuvered for time. At this point, however, the Russians became more insistent. In a third letter of November 26, the Soviet leaders approved in principle the idea of sending a CPSU delegation to Japan but doubted whether the Japanese government would authorize visas for such a group. Once again, a speedy meeting was urged. Finally, in a letter dated January 10, 1964, the Japanese Central Committee informed the Russians that they were considering the possibility of sending a delegation, and shortly thereafter the Hakamada mission set out for Moscow.

The Soviet–Japanese party talks took place between March 2 and March 11, and produced no agreement. Indeed, as the talks were coming to a close, the intransigence of the Mainstream JCP leaders was beautifully symbolized by the publication in *Akahata* on March 10 of a lengthy anonymous article entitled "Kennedy and U.S. Imperialism," a scathing if indirect assault on every aspect of recent Soviet policy.[66] When the meetings ended, the Japanese delegation resolutely refused to sign a Soviet-prepared joint communiqué, insisting that any action that suggested Soviet–Japanese agreement would mislead party members and that a true statement would benefit the enemy by revealing basic differences between fraternal parties. Thus, the meetings remained a secret, and the Japanese group began a leisurely trip home on March 13, visiting China, North Korea, and North Vietnam, and arriving in Tōkyō on April 30.[67]

The CPSU leaders, meanwhile, had not been idle and resigned to their fate. If JCP reports are to be credited, the Russians had strengthened their ties with the Shiga faction within the party even as the Moscow talks were proceeding. On April 18, moreover, the CPSU Central Committee dispatched a lengthy letter to the Central Committee of the Japanese Communist Party, outlining in detail its challenges to the Mainstream leaders. The April 18 letter can only be read as a full-fledged assault on JCP Mainstream practices and policies. It contained no hint of compromise, no suggestion of reconciliation.

NEW SPLITS IN THE JAPANESE COMMUNIST PARTY

On May 15, the long-awaited vote on the partial nuclear test ban treaty was taken in the Japanese House of Representatives, with Anastas

---

[66] This article was reprinted in English in pamphlet form by the Foreign Languages Press, Peking, 1964, and when it is cited hereafter, this edition will be used.

[67] Report to the 9th Party Congress, *TICD* 691, *JPRS* 28,456, p. 208.

I. Mikoyan, Soviet First Deputy Premier currently on a visit to Japan, sitting in the visitors' gallery. In opposition to his four Communist colleagues, Shiga Yoshio cast a white ballot, voting for the treaty. In a press conference after the vote, Shiga dramatically defended his actions. An enlarged JCP Presidium meeting was called into session at 8 o'clock that evening, and Shiga was heard. For twenty-four hours, there was no official party statement, but on May 17, *Akahata* carried on its front page a Central Committee announcement that Shiga's conduct was "antiparty" because he had not consulted any of the party organs before his vote, had held a press interview and distributed literature without permission, and had expressed views running counter to official party policies. Subsequently, it was announced that Shiga's activities as a JCP member of the Diet were being suspended.

Secretary-General Miyamoto, who, with his wife and children, had been "recuperating" in south China since mid-February, hastily returned home, and a Central Committee meeting was convened on May 21. After ten hours of debate, the Central Committee voted to expel Shiga and Suzuki Ichizō, House of Councillors member and second leader of the pro-Soviet faction, from the party. The vote was fifty-three to three, with one abstention, an indication of the ironclad control now possessed by the Mainstream faction over top party leadership. The three negative votes were cast by Shiga, Suzuki, and Nakano Shigeharu, writer and intellectual. Kamiyama Shigeo abstained. While the pro-Soviet group was revealed to have negligible support at the Central Committee level, the ouster of Shiga and Suzuki was more damaging to the party than the small vote on their behalf might indicate. The Japanese Communist Party had too few Diet members to oust them with abandon, and Shiga in particular had a significant electoral following in Ōsaka. Both of these men, it might be noted, were currently members of the nine-man Executive Council of the Central Committee, the highest authority within the party, and their removal left Nosaka as the only Diet member in that group. Moreover, the Shiga–Suzuki group had a definite appeal to many of the Communist intellectuals who, although not strongly represented in top party posts, were important.[68]

In the press conference announcing the expulsions, Miyamoto denounced Shiga and Suzuki for "treacherous, factional activities" aimed

---

[68] For an earlier article by a JCP leader on the problem of "antiparty" intellectuals, see Takahara Shinichi, "Concerning the Party Literati Who Signed Anti-Party Statements Last Year," *Akahata,* November 23, 1962, p. 5 (*TICD* 341, *JPRS* 17,111, pp. 1–16).

at creating a split in the party. Shiga responded by stating that he had taken the only course that could save the party. He insisted that the Moscow Treaty was the first step in realizing the dreams of the Japanese people, and that he remained a Communist irrespective of the Central Committee decision, which he could not accept.

The action of May 21 was a spectacular finale to a drama that had been in progress for many months. As mentioned earlier, the removal of individuals suspected of pro-Soviet views from positions of influence had been intensified in the fall of 1963 and further accelerated in January and February 1964. Among the persons removed were Hoshino Tsutomu, Assistant Managing Editor of *Akahata,* Uchino Takechiyo, head of the United Front Bureau, and Kanda Asano, Director of the Women's Bureau (whose husband, Horie Muraichi, was Director of the Japan–Soviet Union Society). Some forty lower-echelon posts had also been shifted to Mainstream elements, a number of whom were regarded as representatives of the "China lobby."

THE OPEN BREAK BETWEEN
MOSCOW AND THE JCP MAINSTREAM

The ouster of Shiga and Suzuki led directly to a further escalation of the struggle between the CPSU and the Mainstream JCP leaders. The Soviet Union was quick to publicize and praise the actions of the two men. Soviet organs such as *Pravda* and Radio Moscow began to treat the Shiga faction as the upholders of true Marxism–Leninism in Japan, repeatedly providing space and time for the views of Shiga and his friends, and criticizing their opponents.[69] Bolstered by this support and by the defection of additional party members, Shiga announced the formation of the "Voice of Japan Comrades Society" on June 30, a move suggesting that a rival Communist party might be in the offing. Immediately, *Akahata* Editor Doki denounced the new society as "blindly subservient to the party of a certain foreign country," a charge repeated by Nosaka and Miyamoto a few days later.

This was the context in which the Soviet leaders suddenly made public their letter of April 18 addressed to the JCP Central Committee, together with a new letter dated July 11, which updated some of the

---

[69] For some details, see "Why Kamiyama and Nakano were Expelled from the Japanese CP," *Akahata,* October 1964, p. 2 (*TICD* 665, *JPRS* 27,224, pp. 61–78); and "The Nature of the Criticism of the 'Draft Report' by the Voice of Japan," *Akahata,* November 18, 1964, p. 5 (*TICD* 679, *JPRS* 27,830, pp. 27–52).

charges against the JCP and complained bitterly about the refusal of the Japanese party to respond to the first letter. Outraged by the fact that these two documents had been released by the CPSU to help the Shiga faction, the JCP Mainstream leaders quickly replied in a letter of July 15, promising to provide a detailed answer to the April 18 letter later. That answer was finally completed and sent on August 26. It was published in *Akahata* on September 2.

After these documents had been made public, it was much easier to see clearly the full dimensions of the spreading conflict between the Soviet and Japanese Communist parties. Two fundamental areas of strife were revealed by the letters. One related to the norms governing interparty relations. The other pertained to appropriate Communist tactics and strategy in connection with the contemporary revolutionary struggle in the world—and in Japan.

INTERPARTY RELATIONS

The CPSU Central Committee had a series of charges to make against their Japanese comrades concerning interparty relations. The April 18 letter to the JCP Central Committee claimed that the Soviet Communist Party had always rendered full support to the Communist Party of Japan, and, before their complete seduction by Peking, JCP leaders had been properly appreciative of that fact:

You know that fraternal friendly relations based on profound trust, mutual understanding and respect existed for decades between our parties. They were built on the principal basis of Marxism–Leninism. One can boldly state that nothing has ever spoiled the fraternal relations between our parties.

Soviet Communists know well and highly appreciate the fact that in the cruel conditions of police terror and persecutions the Communist party of Japan has held high the banner of Marxism–Leninism and proletarian internationalism and has consistently struggled for the cardinal interests of the Japanese people and for the victory of the great cause of Communism. The relations of fraternal friendship and cooperation between our parties found their further development in the postwar period. No small number of meetings were held between the representatives of our parties, at which we discussed questions of interest to both parties in a businesslike and comradely atmosphere, with full mutual understanding. Abiding by the principles of proletarian internationalism, the CPSU always treated attentively the views and wishes of the Japanese comrades and rendered all-round support to the Communist party of Japan. In turn, we valued the fraternal assistance which the Japanese Communists gave our party and people in the struggle to strengthen the world's first Socialist state and in the construction of Socialism and Communism in the USSR. . . .

The Central Committee of the CPSU also knew that Japanese Communists have always treasured friendship with the CPSU. In particular, this found its reflection in the resolution of the 5th Plenum meeting of the Central Committee of the Communist party of Japan in February 1963, which said: "From the moment of its inception it has been the tradition of our party to defend the Soviet Union and the construction of socialism it is conducting, proceeding from the deep respect for the CPSU and strong solidarity with it to come out against any encroachments on the part of the enemy and to fight for this to the end. This struggle and determination of our party will never undergo any changes now or in the future."[70]

Under Chinese influence, however, the Japanese Communist Party had begun to cater to nationalist and chauvinist sentiments, the CPSU stated, and had departed from the agreed line of the international Communist movement. It had openly and repeatedly attacked the CPSU, using the sly method of "presenting the facts concerning the present dispute" to its members. Employing this ruse, Mainstream leaders had reprinted every slander and falsehood uttered against the CPSU and its leaders, from whatever source:

The leading comrades from your party try to explain the publication of such material by saying that they allegedly want "to give the Communists a chance of getting an objective picture of the differences." We think, however, that this is not so. The Central Committee of the CPSU sees, of course, that there is not a single gram of truth in these materials and, what is more, they cannot be regarded as documents related to the polemics within the framework of Marxism–Leninism. This means that the leaders of the Communist party of Japan had some other motives when they allowed the stream of slander against the CPSU and other Marxist–Leninist parties to overflow the pages of the Japanese Communist press.

The fact that the press of the Communist party of Japan systematically keeps silent about the statements of the CPSU on questions of the international Communist movement shows that objectivity is out of the question. In those rare cases in which the documents of the CPSU were published, this was done with great delay and in extremely abridged form and quite often in intentionally distorted form.[71]

---

[70] April 18 Letter, pp. 21–22. In the light of later developments, particularly the tactical changes made at the time of the 7th Plenum, the Japanese Communist Mainstream leaders undoubtedly found this Soviet use of the 5th Plenum resolution both embarrassing and infuriating.

[71] *Ibid.,* pp. 25–26.

No source was too obscure or too disreputable, the CPSU charged, if it provided new grist for the anti-Soviet mill; thus, the Chinese and Albanians were featured, but representation was also given to minority factions in such Communist movements as those of Brazil, Ceylon, and Belgium. JCP organs, particularly *Sekai Seiji Shiryō* and *Akahata,* made it a practice to distort and limit Soviet views, while giving full coverage to Russia's enemies.

More recently, indeed, the CPSU letter continued, the Japanese Communist Party, at the bidding of Peking, had launched a drive to root out all Soviet literature from Japan and to purge the party of all members favorable to Soviet positions. Current JCP leaders seemed determined to eradicate everyone who challenged their slavish adherence to Peking. Thus, systematically, they had removed "true Marxist–Leninists" in such organizations as the Japan-Soviet Union Society from positions of authority within the party and, in a number of cases, had ousted them from the party completely:

The mouthpiece of the Tōkyō City committee of the Communist party of Japan, the magazine *Toso Dzeho,* alleged, on 20 December 1936, that "at present the Japan–Soviet Union Society is the last stronghold of anti-party elements." The members of the Central Committee of the Communist party of Japan know well that the Japan–Soviet Union Society has lately actually stopped the dissemination of Soviet publications, photographs, and other materials sent in from the Soviet Union. . . .
The matter has gone so far that some comrades from the Communist party of Japan are now striving to use the Japan–Soviet Union Society for disseminating Chinese materials of an anti-Soviet character.[72]

The CPSU April 18 letter charged that at the meetings between JCP and CPSU delegations held in Moscow in March, JCP leaders had ignored fundamental issues and directed all their efforts toward accusing the Soviets of interference in the affairs of their party:

One of the main questions about which the delegation of the Communist party of Japan complained was that the CPSU had allegedly "imposed" upon your party the 1951 Program and "ultra-left wing and adventuristic tactics" during the Korean War. The delegation of the CPSU had to restore the truth on the basis of the available archive documents and show the full insolvency of such fabrications. Our delegation showed that the CPSU had nothing to do with the "ultra-left wing, adventuristic" tactics of the Communist party of Japan during the Korean War, as Comrade Hakamada characterized them. These tactics were to a large measure a dogmatic copy of the experience of the Com-

---

[72] *Ibid.,* p. 27.

munist party of China (preparation for guerrilla warfare in the mountain areas, creation of "support bases," etc.) and they troubled, in effect, the leadership of the CPSU.[73]

The CPSU further charged that JCP hostility toward the Soviet Union had been carried into the international Communist movement. For many months, JCP representatives to various international meetings had echoed the Chinese line, giving either active or passive support to Peking's disruptive actions and false policies: "It is common knowledge that the Japanese comrades have recently been rendering all-out support to the Chinese delegations in their actions designed to split authoritative international democratic organizations, the World Peace Council, the World Federation of Trade Unions, the Women's International Democratic Federation, and others."[74]

In sum, the CPSU letter pointed out, the JCP Mainstream leaders had declared war on the Soviet party, despite the lengthy historic friendship between the two parties and the valiant efforts of the Soviet party to strive for unity and harmony. This war was a dictate of the Chinese, indicating that the Japanese Communist Party had subordinated the interests and desires of the Japanese masses to the authority of the Chinese Communist Party.

The JCP Mainstream leaders naturally had a full rejoinder to these charges. Indeed, they said, the delegation headed by Hakamada *had* insisted at the Moscow meetings in March that the first issue to be settled was the gross and unpardonable interference of the Soviet Union in the internal affairs of the Japanese Communist Party.[75] Unless that

---

[73] Ibid., pp. 29–30. In this same section of their letter, the Soviets blamed Stalin personally for the Cominform attack of January 6, 1950, and for his participation in the 1951 Draft Program with Tokuda, Nosaka, and others. It is interesting to note that while the JCP later took exception to the Soviet interpretation of the 1950–1951 events, the Mainstream leaders resolutely refused to discuss this era. No doubt this was partly because of the reluctance to criticize Stalinism, and thereby feed the Soviet side of this particular argument with the Chinese (the Russians obviously took delight in recounting *Stalin's interference* in the internal affairs of the JCP, and *the JCP request for aid*). The main reluctance, however, undoubtedly stemmed from the fact that Miyamoto, current Secretary General of the party, had been in the anti-Mainstream faction, as was also true of several other JCP leaders.

[74] Ibid., p. 47. This point, revealed first by the Russians in their April 18 letter, was not denied by the Japanese.

[75] In its July 15 letter, the JCP asserted that after the two-party talks, there was ample proof that "it was precisely you who launched the most brazen and unpardonable direct intervention against our party. This shows that our delegation was entirely justified in attaching special importance during the Moscow talks to this question of your interference with our party." See the July 15 letter as carried in the Peking Review, July 31, 1964, p. 22.

intervention ceased, they had then warned, a permanent breach would inevitably ensue. The heart of the problem, in the opinion of the JCP leaders, was simply the fact that the Soviet party was guilty of "big-nation chauvinism" in its dealings with all other Communist parties of the world. Long accustomed to absolute authority in the international Communist movement, it could not adjust to the post-Cominform era when every party had been declared independent and equal. Thus, it continued to insist that every party must follow its baton, that all policies must be in accord with its views. When any party declined to accept Soviet policy, that party was subjected to unending pressures and interference, as well as being slandered as a puppet of some foreign party. As a result, every Communist party was being forced to fight for its independence and autonomy against Soviet attempts at big-power domination. The tone of the August 26 letter from the JCP to the CPSU was vitriolic on these points:

In your letter of 18 April you say that relations between the two parties of Japan and the Soviet Union have deteriorated because our party's leadership "has separated itself from the several earlier resolutions of the party and is situated on a new course." . . . This insistence of yours that the blame for the deterioration in the relations of our two parties rests on the side of our party is completely removed from the truth. To state the conclusion first, the cause for the worsened relations between the JCP and the CPSU lies in that (1) you have unilaterally started the public polemics within the international Communist movement and wanted our party to follow your line unreservedly in the polemics; (2) you have become so impatient of our rejection of your unjustifiable demand and our upholding of independent views that you have repeatedly attacked our party by name, interfered in our internal affairs, and made trouble with us. . . .

You are asking other fraternal parties to follow unreservedly your road of violation of the Moscow Statement, and this is the approach of big-nation chauvinism which is incompatible with the principle of solidarity in the international Communist movement. Your position is that any disagreement with the stand and views of the CPSU leaders does not contain a single grain of truth and runs counter to the Moscow Statement.

What kind of thinking is this? This is out-and-out subjectivism and self-conceit. The chief cause for the disunity in the international Communist movement and the socialist camp today is precisely your self-conceit and the flagrant intervention with and attacks on the fraternal parties unleashed brazenly by you from this self-conceit.[76]

---

[76] August 26 Letter, pp. 5, 12.

The Japanese Communist leaders had cited numerous concrete cases to "prove" this basic theme at the March meetings: Beginning with his attacks on the Albanians and the Chinese in 1960, Khrushchev and his followers had repeatedly violated the standards of proper conduct among comrades and then insisted that others support them in their improper actions. As early as the June 1960 Bucharest meeting, great pressure had been put on the Japanese Communist Party to join Khrushchev's fratricidal war against Albania and China. This pressure had been increased at the time of the November 1960 Moscow Conference and again during the 22nd CPSU Congress of October–November 1961. It had reached a new peak in the course of the European Party Congresses held between October 1962 and January 1963. On all of these occasions, the Japanese Communist Party had resisted Soviet pressure, insisting on taking an independent position, seeking to mediate various disputes, and standing firmly by the principles outlined in the Moscow agreements of 1957 and 1960. Unable to coerce the JCP into acceptance of their domination, the Soviet leaders had finally used the same anti-Marxist tactics on the Japanese party that it had used against other independent parties.

The open assault on the JCP had begun with Zhukov's *Pravda* article of August 1963, as the JCP delegation had pointed out in the March meeting in Moscow. This article was in complete violation of the method stipulated for handling interparty disputes by the Moscow Statement. Direct Soviet interference in the internal affairs of the JCP, moreover, had steadily mounted, culminating in the all-out support being given the Shiga faction and other "anti-party renegades." The JCP August 26 letter reviewed this problem of interference:

The facts which our party's delegation presented as a problem—those of a series of cases of interference in our party beginning with Comrade Zhukov's open attack on our party and the destructive activities against our party of Soviet Embassy staff members and special correspondents—represent a matter of principle wherein the standards prescribed in the Moscow Statement relative to relations among fraternal parties are being trodden upon. We may point out further your subsequent conspicuous and unpardonable activities in blatantly supporting Shiga Yoshio and Suzuki Ichizō who openly conduct anti-party activities in violation of the Leninist organizational principle. Can it be said that this is not a matter of principle or not in crude violation of the principles guiding relations among the fraternal parties? When our party delegation had talks with you in Moscow, you secretly entered into closer contact with Shiga and others with whom you had formed contacts some time ago, and positively backed their anti-party activities. This proves that it was altogether necessary and appropriate for our party's delegation to call special attention to the question of your interference in our party affairs.[77]

JCP charges continued as follows: The Russians had not hesitated to use informants and spies in an effort to disrupt the Japanese Communist Party. They had supported a wide range of right-wing social democrats, as well as those revisionists who had been ousted from the party. For example, they were giving open support to the peace movement currently sponsored by the Socialist Party and Sōhyō, even though that movement was quite frankly directed against the Communists. And while complaining about the manner in which the Japanese Communist Party presented Soviet views to its members, the Soviet leaders would not even allow the Russian people to read points of view other than the official CPSU line, with rare exceptions. Almost all literature published by the Japanese Communist Party, for example, had been prevented from circulating in the Soviet Union in recent months. In essence, the Communist Party of the Soviet Union sought to dictate to the Japanese Communist Party what its members should read and think, just as it sought to order party leaders with respect to basic policies. And when the Japanese Communist Party, true to the principles of Marxism–Leninism, fought to protect its equality and independence, it was subjected to unending abuse and active Soviet attempts to overthrow the duly elected leadership.

Responding to the Soviet charges of its subordination to the Chinese Communist Party, the JCP stated:

In your letter you branded our party as a follower of the Chinese Communist party practically on all questions. When you want to accuse or attack a fraternal party which does not agree with your views, you do so almost invariably with the allegation that it has followed blindly the line of the Chinese Communist party. This invariable allegation and approach are utterly wrong. . . . Your way of demanding of all the fraternal parties that they unconditionally follow your own line, and if they refuse to do so, concluding that those fraternal parties are followers of the Chinese Communist party is contrary to both fact and reason and constitutes a matter of "classifying" the entire lot of the fraternal parties of the world into followers of the CPSU and followers of the Chinese Communist party. When all is said and done, this is quite the same as having slanders spread by anti-Communist hacks against the international Communist movement.

Our party does not follow any other party unreservedly or obey it blindly, but determines its approach to all matters, including the polemics within the in-

---

[77] *Ibid.*, p. 27.

ternational Communist movement, independently and in accordance with Marxist–Leninist principles. However, this independent stand has nothing in common with the ambiguous stand of the so-called doctrine of compromise, neutralism, or eclecticism. We are loyal to the principles and truth of Marxism–Leninism, and we will certainly criticize those who violate them, and distinguish right from wrong. This is the stand which all Communists should adopt.[78]

COMMUNIST TACTICS AND STRATEGY

The more far-reaching arguments between the two parties, however, pertained to proper Communist revolutionary tactics. Here, the Soviet case against the Japanese Communist Party, as given in the CPSU April 18 letter, can be stated as follows. First, the Japanese comrades had failed to appreciate the historic role of the socialist system in the struggle against imperialism. Intent on belittling the importance of the Soviet Union, the Japanese mentioned the role of the socialist system only in passing, insisting that the main contradictions of the modern era lay in the conflict between the national liberation movement and imperialism. The correct Marxist–Leninist position, however, was not to oppose the national liberation movement to the world system of socialism, but to work for the unity of these two forces in the joint struggle against imperialism. The stronger the Soviet Union and all other socialist countries, the more successful would be the liberation movement and the more attractive would be the socialist revolution to the people of the capitalist world. To stress only the national liberation movement was in effect to pit the backward world against the advanced world, ignoring the contributions which could be made to the revolution by both the socialist countries and the workers of the capitalist nations.

Defending its role in supporting national liberation movements, the CPSU gave the following analysis in its April 18 letter to the JCP:

The historical significance of the existence and struggle of the socialist system lies precisely in the fact that its role in rendering assistance to the national liberation movements and in preventing the export of counterrevolution by the imperialist powers grows yearly and becomes more and more efficient and effective. No matter in what area of the world the threat of imperialist aggression arises—in the Caribbean Sea, in East Africa, or in the area of Cyprus—the Soviet government takes timely measures to stop imperialist aggression and to support resolutely the struggle of the liberated peoples.

---

[78] *Ibid.*, pp. 32–33.

This means that the stronger the Soviet Union and all the socialist countries are, the more successful is the development of the world liberation movement and the more opportunities these countries get to render assistance to the peoples fighting against imperialism and colonialism. This means that the bigger the successes of the socialist countries in their economic, political, and cultural development, the bigger is the attractive force of the example of socialism for all the working people.

Of course, it is obvious to every Communist that between imperialism and colonialism, on the one hand, and the national liberation movement on the other, there are implacable contradictions which weaken and undermine imperialism, and that the anti-imperialist liberation struggle of the peoples of these continents is of exceptional significance for the final defeat of capitalism. But it is no less obvious that the disintegration of the colonial system of imperialism and the unprecedented upsurge of the national liberation movement are inalienably connected with the growth of the forces of the socialist camp and the revolutionary workers movement. That is precisely why a number of countries of Asia, Africa, and Latin America become "weak, vunerable links" in the chain of imperialism.

The correct Marxist–Leninist position is not to oppose the national liberation movement to the world system of socialism, but to work on the strengthening of the unity and cooperation in the joint struggle against imperialism. The ultimate victory over imperialism can be achieved only through the joint efforts of the world socialist system, the international workers movement, and the national liberation struggle of the peoples. Therefore, one is surprised by the insistent attempts of some of your representatives to belittle at any cost and contrary to objective facts the historic role of the socialist system and to oppose it to the national liberation movement. We see by the example of the leaders of the Chinese Communist party that such concepts are advanced to substantiate far-reaching plans aimed at separating the national liberation movement from the world system of socialism and the international workers movement and its subordination to hegemonistic plans and strivings. We would not like to think that the leadership of the Communist party of Japan intends to assist the implementation of such plans, having nothing in common with Marxism–Leninism or with the interests of the world revolutionary movement.[79]

In addition, the CPSU asserted that the position of the JCP on questions of war, peace, and revolution showed an inability on the part of the Mainstream leaders to understand the basic principles of modern Communist strategy. In specific terms, opposition to the Moscow Treaty was based on a failure to appreciate the nature of modern warfare and the current balance of world power. Nuclear war could not be seri-

---

[79] April 18 Letter, pp. 32–34.

ously contemplated by responsible leaders. Such a war, to be sure, was always possible as long as imperialism existed. No one argued that imperialism had changed in its basic nature. However, the profound shift in the global balance of power had greatly reduced the risks of total war. The imperialists had lost their military superiority and hence the basis for conducting a policy resting on "positions of strength." The power of the Soviet Union was now too formidable to be challenged, and from this position the question of nuclear tests appeared in a different light.

Therefore, according to the CPSU letter, the Moscow Treaty did not represent grave military risks for socialism as charged by the Chinese and their allies:

The continuation of these tests could only whip up the nuclear arms race. At the same time, the prohibition of tests did not weaken the defensive potential of the socialist community, because the Soviet Union's nuclear might is not based on the types of nuclear weapons which are perfected by means of underground tests, but rather on weapons in which the Soviet Union wields superiority.

There can be no doubt that the Moscow Treaty binds the hands of all the imperialist world, including the West German revanchists and Japanese imperialists in their desire to possess nuclear weapons.[80]

Although only a first step, the Moscow Treaty did signify a great gain for peace, with major political advantages for the socialist world. By forcing the imperialist powers to accept this treaty, the Soviet Union had won the gratitude of all the peace-loving people of the world. Could one ignore the fact that more than 100 nations had become signatories, including all of the leading neutralist states?

At the Moscow meetings in March, the CPSU letter pointed out, the JCP delegation had claimed that the treaty did not meet the aspiration of the popular masses and had nothing in common with their struggle because with the exception of eight socialist states, all signatories were capitalist:

Thus, scores of other countries which have gained national independence in the struggle against the imperialists and colonialists, such as Algeria, Ghana, Mali, the UAR and other signatories of the Moscow Treaty, were included unconditionally at one stroke in the camp of capitalism.

The press of the Communist party of Japan goes far out of its way to exaggerate the fact that five socialist states have not signed the Moscow Treaty.

---

[80] *Ibid.*, p. 38.

But, this in no way means that each of these states is against the treaty. We regard with respect and understanding, for instance, the special circumstances under which the treaty could not be signed by the government of Cuba, which nonetheless acclaimed the discontinuance of nuclear tests in the three environments as a victory of the peace-loving forces.[81]

Naturally, the Japanese people were overjoyed by the treaty, since no people had suffered more than they from atomic weapons, the CPSU letter continued. The Japanese Communist Party complained that it had been forced into a difficult political position because of the treaty, with the reactionaries using the treaty as a test of faith in peace. But why did the JCP not take the issue away from the reactionaries by supporting the treaty?

We were most surprised by the statements of representatives of the Central Committee of the Communist party of Japan that the Moscow Treaty allegedly does not meet the interests of the Japanese people. And, this is being said on behalf of people who were the first victims of atomic air raids!
It is common knowledge that the Japanese people, who have experienced on three occasions the horrible consequences of nuclear blasts, have always actively demanded the discontinuance of nuclear tests. . . . It is not without reason that news about the conclusion of this treaty was received with great approval in Japan. . . .
Our Japanese comrades! Take a more sober look at things. For it is the leaders of the Communist party of Japan who themselves are isolating their party by stubbornly attacking the Moscow Treaty and thus making it easier for the right-wing forces to struggle against it. . . . Would not the political situation in Japan be more profitable for the progressive forces if the Communist party of Japan, continuing the line of struggle for the ending of nuclear tests, did not oppose the Moscow Treaty but showed the facts as they are: the Japanese people have forced the Ikeda government to sign the treaty and are firmly continuing, together with all the peoples, the struggle for the final prohibition of tests, for the prohibition and destruction of nuclear weapons, and for disarmament.[82]

It was tragic that the Japanese Communist Party was willing to isolate itself from the Japanese masses by joining Peking in being prepared to sacrifice millions of lives for special egotistical goals:

---

[81] *Ibid.*, p. 36.
[82] *Ibid.*, pp. 37, 39.

Worthy of profound regret is the fact that there are leaders of Communist parties and socialist states—we have in mind leaders of the CCP and CPR —who do not care at all about the danger to the health and life of millions of people and who are ready to sacrifice all this for the purpose of achieving their special egoistic goals. They resort to all kinds of refined arguments to conceal the very substance of the treaty and slur it. Unfortunately, their ranks were joined by the members of the delegation of the Communist party of Japan at the Moscow talks. They presented the case as though the question of radioactive fallout caused by nuclear tests was inconsequential. But, the peoples, including the Japanese people, will not believe that sinister radioactive fallout caused by nuclear weapons tests is of no substantial significance.[83]

In broader terms, the Japanese Communist Party, according to the CPSU, had begun to renounce the policy of peaceful coexistence between states of different social systems, although it still paid lip service to this doctrine: "Is the opposition of the leadership of the Communist party of Japan to the Moscow Treaty fortuitous? No, it is not fortuitous. It was motivated by the general turn of the leaders of the Communist party of Japan toward renunciation of the struggle for the policy of peaceful coexistence of states with different social systems."[84]

The CPSU charged that the Japanese Mainstream leaders had followed the Chinese in accepting the thesis that war was inevitable, and that the people were impotent in the face of this inevitability. Thus, the critical issue was posed. Should Communists pursue an adventurist policy, pushing revolution by means of war and insisting that communism can prevail only in the context of a global nuclear holocaust? Or should Communists apply the principles of peaceful coexistence, so that socialism can achieve victory through economic and political competition, and through the increasing appeal of the Socialist system to the peoples of the world? In the words of the CPSU letter:

Should we set course toward a military clash between the two systems and establish Socialism with the aid of arms or should we orientate toward another prospect: to fight to curb the bellicose forces of imperialism, prevent world war, apply the principles of peaceful coexistence between states with different social systems and strive for socialist victories in economic competition, thus strengthening the attractive forces of Socialism, creating favorable conditions for unfolding the revolutionary struggle and facilitating

---

[83] *Ibid.*, pp. 37–38.
[84] *Ibid.*, p. 40.

in every way the revolutionary struggle of the working people in the capitalist countries and the liberation struggle of the people?[85]

It was false to equate peaceful coexistence with appeasement or to assert that the Soviet Union was prepared to give up the struggle against American imperialism. Nor was it legitimate to claim that the Russians had failed to give full support to national liberation movements. Deeds spoke louder than words. All of the bravado of Peking had not frightened the imperialists. But Soviet power had deterred aggression in Cuba, in Asia, and throughout the world. Throughout the emerging world, moreover, the Soviet Union had given great support to the liberation movements:

Who is forced to bear the brunt of the expenditures on nuclear weapons so that the entire socialist camp can reliably oppose imperialism's nuclear might? The whole world knows that this mission is being fulfilled by the USSR. Or, do the Japanese comrades think that the creation of a nuclear potential capable of holding back the belligerent maniacs should not be regarded as a struggle against imperialism? Who had the main task of containing the aggression of American imperialism in the period of the "Caribbean crisis"?

Some people measure the acuteness of the struggle against American imperialism by the amount of "strong" words addressed to them. But, insults do not affect the imperialists; what affects them is real strength and firmness. The Soviet Union does not limit itself to demonstrations when imperialists commit acts of aggression, but renders effective aid to the victims of attack and forces the imperialists to retreat.

It is useful to recall in this connection what a serious blow at American imperialism was the warning made by N. S. Khrushchev in 1958 that "an attack on the CPR, which is our great friend, ally, and a neighbor of our country, is an attack on the Soviet Union." As is known, the American aggressors were forced to give up their intentions in the area of the Taiwan Strait.[86]

However, the thesis that the struggle must be directed solely at the isolation and extermination of American imperialism was a lopsided policy, according to the CPSU. It was wrong, for example, to underestimate the importance of the monopolistic Japanese bourgeoisie who were promoting an imperialistic policy both inside and outside the country. It was also folly to ignore the West German, British, and French imperialists.

---

[85] *Ibid.,* pp. 44–45.
[86] *Ibid.,* pp. 40–41.

Some people think that the struggle of the Communist parties and of all progressive forces must be directed not at the isolation of the imperialist forces of war and reaction, no matter in what country they raise their head, but exclusively at the isolation of American imperialism. We believe this to be a lopsided policy. Mobilizing the masses to struggle against American imperialism as the main enemy and the international gendarme, the CPSU considers it erroneous to ignore the aggressive policy of the imperialists of other countries: West Germany, Japan, Britain, and France. Who does not know that it is precisely Japanese imperialism that is the main ally of American imperialism in the Far East and in Southeast Asia? That is why we treasure the heroic struggle of the Japanese people against American imperialism. However, it would be wrong to lose sight of and underestimate the significance of the struggle against the monopolistic Japanese bourgeoisie which is now promoting an imperialist policy inside and outside the country.[87]

In the CPSU's final analysis, the Japanese Communist Party, in line with the CCP, was determined to move the world toward nuclear war, brazenly oblivious of the costs of such a war and the impact of their policies upon the people of the world. In fact, the changed balance of world power in favor of the socialist camp made peaceful coexistence the only logical policy, and one that assured socialist victory. Such a policy did not depend on any change in the nature of imperialism. Rather, it rested on the inability of the imperialists to pursue war profitably and their incapacity to match socialist productive gains. Only a small minority of Chinese-bloc parties within the world Communist movement failed to appreciate this fact and were seeking to overturn the main themes enunciated in the Moscow Declaration of 1957 and the Moscow Statement of 1960.

The CPSU letter quoted some of the criticisms of Kikunami, JCP delegate to the Warsaw World Peace Council, regarding Soviet-backed peace policies, and then asserted:

What follows from these somewhat disguised statements by the Japanese representative? It follows that the policy of peaceful coexistence between states no longer suits the Japanese comrades. . . . Something else is noteworthy: the comrades from the Communist party of Japan obviously wanted to discredit the policy of peaceful coexistence by setting against it all other forms of struggle for the liberation of the peoples including the struggle for social progress, that is, for socialism. Nor is this a new trick; from Chinese sources we hear daily discussions that the policy of peaceful

---

[87] *Ibid.,* p. 42.

coexistence allegedly "runs counter" to revolution, that it allegedly spells "replacement" of the class and national liberation struggle and "renunciation" of the revolution.

V. I. Lenin taught us that "the socialists have always denounced war between peoples as barbarous and atrocious." But what does it mean in this case to oppose the policy of peaceful coexistence? What does the statement of Comrade Kikunami and his friends mean in this light? This means to come out for war, for another world war and hence thermonuclear war between states with different social systems. There is no third way.[88]

In their August 26 reply, the Japanese Mainstream leaders had much to say about these accusations. It was false for the CPSU to accuse the Japanese Communist Party of underestimating the importance of the socialist world in the struggle against imperialism, or of failing to appreciate the significance of uniting socialism with the national liberation movement. The Soviet leaders, however, were guilty of simplifying the global conflict to one of a struggle merely between the socialist and capitalist systems, and then making Russian productivity the key to that contest:

In actuality, your letter argues to the effect that the growth of the revolutionary influential power of the socialist camp in the process of world revolution mainly depends on overcoming capitalism in the aspect of material productivity. . . .

At the talks between our two parties, too, you particularly emphasized the importance of overcoming capitalism in the field of material productivity and you insisted over and over that the higher the level of economic development of the socialist nations becomes, the greater the appeal of the example of socialism will be. . . .

From time to time, you use the phrase "socialist world system" as synonymous with the Soviet Union (or the Soviet Union and the socialist countries which are aligned with it), and the other socialist countries are treated as though playing nothing but a secondary role in this world system. It must be said that this shows that it is you who belittle the unity and solidarity that are the source of invincible power in the socialist system and that constitute important main factors in the political, economic and military superiority of that system as a whole, who are giving assistance to the imperialists in their seeking to take advantage of the lack of solidarity in the socialist camp, and who are in fact falling into the actual position of being unable to guarantee that the socialist world system will fulfill its historic role. . . .

---

[88] *Ibid.,* pp. 45, 46.

We make the appraisal that the world system of socialism, the international worker class, the forces opposed to imperialism and the forces that are struggling for a socialist revolution in society constitute the "prime force determining the main content, direction and character of the development of world history in the present-day era," and that the entire body of these forces is striking new blows at imperialism and all the while turning the socialist world system into a decisive main factor for the development of human society and, in the ultimate sense, prescribing a "course of development for world history" which will lead to the destruction of imperialism and the victory of socialism in the whole world. . . . Thus it is your viewpoint which simplifies the primary conflict of the modern period to a mere struggle between the socialist system and the capitalist system, that amounts to a mistaken viewpoint which does not agree with the propositions given in the Moscow Statement but belittles the historic role of the struggle of the worker classes and peoples in the capitalist countries and the national liberation movements in the colonies and dependencies.[89]

Russian spokesmen, the JCP leaders charged, consistently undervalued the importance of the liberation struggles in Asia, Africa, and Latin America. The Soviets were afflicted with Europo-centrism. And one of the expressions of Europo-centrism was the thesis that only the economically advanced states in which the working class was numerically strong should assume leadership in the world revolution. The JCP argued that the struggles of the people of Asia, Africa, and Latin America against imperialism were becoming "the main battleground" of the struggle against imperialism; that the Soviets were implying that only the working class in the Soviet Union and other Socialist countries in Europe could be leaders of the revolution:

The history of the world revolutionary movement in the past few decades shows that even the workers in the developed capitalist countries cannot be the "leaders" of world revolution or even of the revolution in their own countries if they are under the sway of a revisionist and opportunist policy. On the other hand, if the leadership of a genuine Marxist–Leninist party is established in a certain country among the working people led by the working class, it not only can effect a democratic and socialist revolution in its own country but also can contribute greatly to the whole world revolution as a most revolutionary unit in the international working class, even if that country is economically backward and its working class only accounts for a small proportion of its total population.
If you forget this historic lesson and formally and abstractly entertain the idea that only the countries which are economically advanced and where

---

[89] August 26 Letter, pp. 38, 40, 41–42.

the basic masses of the working class are concentrated should assume "right of leadership" of the world revolution, then it should be pointed out that this idea is one of Europe-centrism which is alien to the Marxist–Leninist view.[90]

Soviet economism—the reliance on rising productivity—ignored the political dimension in revolution, according to the JCP argument. Was it Chinese productivity that had made possible the great Chinese revolution? Could not the masses of the non-Western world be given guidance by the revolutionary overthrow of exploiting classes, irrespective of the status of Russian development? So-called backward societies had demonstrated that they too could conduct massive social revolutions and, in the process, greatly change the balance of world power. Noting that "the appeal of the example of socialism" was found not only in rising productivity and material living standards, the JCP writers asserted:

The "power of example" consists, above all, of the whole of such things as the great revolutionary experience of having overthrown the exploiting classes through the socialist revolution and, through the power of the people, of setting up a new society free of exploitation; the tremendous revolutionary spirit of the people who have crushed imperialist and reactionary interference, aggression and counterrevolution, and [who] protect the work of the revolution; the proletariat internationalism wherein the worker classes which have seized power have aided and supported the revolutionary peoples of the world; the world role as a bastion of world peace standing in the forefront of the fight against the forces of imperialist aggression; the correct political line guided by Marxist–Leninist ideology; the political, military, economic, and cultural results which have been built up by the dictatorship of the proletariat with the support of the people; the economic superiority of the socialist system revealed in the rapid development of national economics; and the like. . . . If one fails to grasp this fundamental point and falls into the view of economism in summing up the socialist "power of actual examples" as purely or mainly consisting of productive power for material wealth brought about by socialism, . . . then the significance and role of the socialist camp in the course of world revolution will in fact be minimized, lopsidedly assessed or underestimated.[91]

Speaking in specific terms, however, what had the Socialist system— defined by the Russians as the Soviet Union and its allies—contributed to the struggle against world imperialism? In the recent tests, the JCP

[90] *Ibid.*, pp. 49–50.
[91] *Ibid.*, pp. 38–39.

pointed out, Russian policy had been marked by weakness and failure. In the Cuban crisis of October 1962, for example, the Khrushchev government had capitulated to American demands for missile withdrawal and international inspection of Cuba, without even consulting the Cuban government. Its surrender to American threats, combined with its cavalier attitude toward the sovereign rights of the Castro government, could only bring joy to imperialist hearts:

The way in which you, at the time of the so-called "Cuban crisis" in October 1962, without even any necessary consultation with the Cuban government beforehand, acceded to the demand for "international inspection" put forward by the American government and, for the purpose of compromising with American imperialism, sought to make a sacrifice of the sovereignty of the Cuban nation and the Cuban people was a representative instance of this mistaken tendency [of underrating national liberation struggles in order to compromise with imperialism].[92]

Similarly, the attempt to rehabilitate the Communist League of Yugoslavia was a move to split the Socialist world, in defiance of the Moscow agreements. Contrary to Russian claims, the Titoists remained archrevisionists, false Marxists who sought to undermine international Communist solidarity.[93]

Finally, in signing the partial test ban treaty, the Soviet Union had completely reversed its previous position and handed the imperialists a major victory, the JCP August 26 letter charged. The Russian argument that this treaty represented no military risk to the Socialist world was specious. Kennedy himself had noted with satisfaction that the treaty did not in any way adversely affect American military efforts. In truth, the treaty granted the imperialists the opportunity to continue with their nuclear war preparations, and thus it was a step in the direction of supporting war, not peace. In essence, the treaty was another sign of the big-nation chauvinism characterizing Soviet policy, the willing-

---

[92] *Ibid.*, pp. 45–46.

[93] The JCP writers remarked that "the Moscow Statement lays upon all Marxist–Leninist Parties the obligation to fight positively in order to expose the leaders of the Yugoslavian revisionists" and to defend the international movement against their "anti-Leftist thinking" (*ibid.*, p. 43). Interestingly, no mention is made of the Sino–Indian border dispute in the JCP Central Committee letters, although the party leaders clearly regarded Soviet support of the "big bourgeois" government of Nehru as further evidence of the lack of true comradely feelings on the part of the Khrushchev government and of its implacable hostility toward China. Probably this subject was avoided so that it could not be used by the Russians as another proof of the complete support given by the JCP to Chinese causes.

ness to plot with the Americans in making nuclear arms the exclusive property of a few Western states. Khrushchev and his followers were quite prepared to aid the United States in its attempt to contain China and prevent the Chinese people from acquiring nuclear weapons with which to defend themselves and the cause of world peace. Soviet apologists for the Moscow Treaty had advanced two basic arguments in favor of it, the JCP letter noted, but both could be refuted:

The first assertion assumes that the treaty is the natural first step leading to the complete prohibition of nuclear tests and banning of nuclear weapons. This represents an attempt to justify the treaty *unconditionally*. The second assertion assumes that even though partial banning of nuclear tests was not the correct method to solve the question of nuclear tests in the past, it has gained new significance with the recent changes in the international situation and has turned into something deserving support. This represents an attempt to justify the treaty *on the ground of the changes in the situation and in the correlation of forces*. That these two assertions are entirely different in nature and in their viewpoints and even contradict each other is clear even in terms of rudimentary logic. . . .

No matter what chicanery you try to work out you simply cannot conceal the fact of history that you reversed yourselves from advocating the approval of the legalization of underground testing in 1963. . . . The more you obstinately insist that the central matter of the nuclear test ban question lies in the prevention of radioactive contamination, the more you land yourselves in the position where you yourselves have no recourse but to criticize the action of the Soviet government in first resuming testing in the fall of 1961, after an approximately two years' period of voluntary cessation, as one in which it disregarded the danger which radioactive fallout meant for mankind and pursued the "special egoistic objectives" of the Soviet Union. . . .

You think that you can heap any dirty abuse on the efforts made by the socialist countries other than your own [China] to develop and possess defensive nuclear weapons in the face of the threats of the American imperialist policies of nuclear war preparations and nuclear blackmail. What you insist upon is nothing but an absurdity based upon complete self-flattery, according to which the nuclear weapons possessed by the Soviet Union are for the purpose of peace but the nuclear weapons possessed by countries of the same socialism, yet different countries, are just something that proliferates the danger of injury due to radioactivity and of nuclear war. In the final analysis this can only lead to the conclusion that the only reliable guarantee to prevent a nuclear war is to preserve the system of nuclear monopoly with the United States and the Soviet Union as the axis and maintain the present American–Soviet compromise on this basis. This can only obstruct the efforts of the socialist countries other than the Soviet Union to strengthen their defenses, aid and abet the ambition of American imperialism to keep nuclear weapons forever, and facilitate its nuclear blackmail.[94]

Perhaps opposition to this treaty would cost the Japanese Communist Party some temporary losses, the JCP admitted. The Japanese people, however, would ultimately come to see that the strengthening of the Socialist forces was the only real hope for peace, since the struggle for peace was inextricably connected with the fight against imperialism. And Lenin had warned against the type of opportunists who were willing to sacrifice principle for short-range gains. Defending the JCP position, the letter stated:

Our party has not in the past, and will not in the future, become a tool of American imperialism or provide help for this sort of deception [the Moscow Treaty]. Even if it should ever be that our party appears isolated from "public opinion" that is formed of the cult of worship of the Partial Nuclear Test Ban Treaty, to one wing of which you adhere (to borrow your expression—even if there should ever be a matter of our "suffering loss"), our party would by no means have any fear. The founder of your party, Lenin, always severely condemned persons who, on account of their immediate interests or their computing of gains versus losses, hesitated to speak the truth to the people or sold out the basic interests of the laborer classes and the working people.[95]

In their rebuttal and counterattack, the Japanese Mainstream leaders quickly advanced to the central questions of war and peaceful coexistence. The essence of their argument can be summarized as follows: The charge that those who opposed Soviet views on these matters were warmongers intent on a nuclear war was a vicious slander. Neither the Chinese leaders nor the Japanese Communist Party favored nuclear war. Both the Chinese and Japanese parties had supported the concept of peaceful coexistence with states of differing social systems; indeed, the CCP had pioneered in the establishment of this concept.

However, the doctrine of peaceful coexistence should not be distorted in such a fashion as to make it a basis for the support and embellishment of American imperialism. Unless U.S. imperialism were treated as the central enemy of peace and all people of the world, Socialist victory would be in doubt. Despite this fact, Soviet leaders had recently pursued policies of opportunism and revisionism, seeking to avoid a struggle with the United States at any cost. Khrushchev had substituted appease-

---

[94] *Ibid.,* pp. 51, 56–57, 57–58.
[95] *Ibid.,* p. 70.

ment via diplomacy for struggle via popular mobilization. To justify these policies, modern revisionists were busily erecting false theories, such as the theory of the polarization of American imperialism into two wings. According to this theory, there were "good" imperialists and "bad" imperialists. The fallen Kennedy belonged to the former category according to the revisionists, and was a man of good will and peaceful intentions.[96]

The efforts to praise Kennedy were both stupid and dangerous. Far from being peace-loving, the Kennedy administration was more militarist, adventurous, and ferocious than the Eisenhower administration. Rather than supporting peaceful coexistence, Kennedy aimed at an imperialist hegemony, a "Holy Alliance" headed by the United States for the purpose of enslaving the peoples of the world. And critical to American plans was the creation of a détente between the United States and the Soviet Union. American leaders saw Asia as one of the key areas to future world control. Consequently, they were concentrating their political and military attention on this theater, with the primary objective of containing China and stifling the national liberation struggles of the

---

[96] The views of the Mainstream leaders on the subject had been strongly expressed in "Kennedy and U.S. Imperialism," an anonymous article published in *Akahata,* March 10, 1964: "Some say that raising the banner of 'freedom' and 'progress,' the 'young and courageous President' struggled against the strong opposition of the die-hard cold war warriors and the extreme Right of the 'free camp.' On the diplomatic front, these same people say that while reorganizing and strengthening U.S. military power to maintain an 'equilibrium' and in order to cope with a 'crisis of the destruction of mankind' as had been demonstrated in the 'Cuban crisis,' he resolved courageously to seek 'peaceful coexistence' between the United States and the Soviet Union and finally concluded the partial nuclear test-ban treaty which became the 'historic first step.' On domestic policies he raised the Negro question, that stigma of American democracy, and bravely made the challenge for ending racial discrimination." "Kennedy and U.S. Imperialism," Foreign Languages Press reprint, Peking, 1964, pp. 1–2.

Indeed, "some people within the forces of peace and democracy have also joined the chorus in praise and embellishment of Kennedy and are already producing certain ideological and practical influences which cannot be overlooked. . . . Kennedy was none other than the top leader of U.S. imperialism, which is bellicose and reactionary by nature. Therefore, if one embellishes Kennedy's policies, one cannot avoid embellishing U.S. imperialism. . . ." (*Ibid.,* pp. 3, 5.) "Fundamentally speaking, the nature of the Kennedy Administration and its policies were not determined by the personality of Kennedy as an individual, but by the characteristics of the 'new stage of the general crisis of capitalism" and those of the present international situation. It follows that the Johnson Administration, which succeeded the Kennedy Administration, will now follow the main direction of the latter's policies." (*Ibid.,* p. 68.) In fact, the Johnson Administration's policies, reflecting "the deepening of the crisis of imperialism" will be "even more fraudulent and more reactionary." (*Ibid.,* p. 69.)

Asian peoples. The Moscow Treaty, representing the first major step in the American–Soviet détente was a major victory for U.S. imperialism.[97]

Equally important to the Americans, however, was the use of nuclear blackmail to frighten the people of the world into capitulation before American demands. In this respect, moreover, Soviet policies were perfectly designed in the interests of American imperialism. The Khruschevites, frightened out of their wits by American threats of nuclear war, had given up all struggles and had even advanced from capitulation to the positive embellishment of imperialism. To defend this outrageous betrayal of the proletariat, the Russians had purposely exaggerated the horrors of war, denounced their opponents as madmen, and thus split the socialist movement.[98]

---

[97] "The measures for a certain 'detente' with the Soviet Union which U.S. imperialism had rapidly adopted since the summer of 1963, such as the conclusion of the partial nuclear test-ban treaty, the installation of the U.S.–U.S.S.R. direct 'hot line.' the call for U.S.-U.S.S.R. cooperation in space exploration, export of wheat to the Soviet Union, reduction of some items in the military budget, etc., do not mean a real relaxation in any sense; essentially, they are turning into a new factor which is aggravating the tension. These measures are connected with the extremely dangerous scheme of U.S. imperialism." (*Ibid.*, p. 61.)

This new scheme, according to the JCP writers, was to "contain China" in Asia, and with this policy as the core, step up U.S. aggressive policies in Asia. "The United States now regards Asia as the key area where it is executing its policies of aggression and war, not because Asia is an 'exception' lagging behind the world trend for 'relaxation of tension,' as the modern revisionists allege, nor because the Communist parties in Asia have adopted 'adventurist tactics' and provoked imperialism, as the impermissible slanders the modern revisionists have fabricated. But it is because precisely in this area the U.S. imperialist policies of war and aggression, suppression and reaction have continuously suffered their most serious setbacks as a result of the vigorous growth of the national liberation struggles and the rising prestige and influence of the new socialist countries—China, Vietnam and Korea." (*Ibid.*, p. 64.)

[98] According to JCP writers, "the 'polarization theory' is nothing but an apology for imperialism, made by the opportunists who are scared out of their wits by nuclear blackmail and want to avoid fighting imperialism. . . . At present the policy of nuclear blackmail, which aims at dividing the anti-imperialist forces and wringing concessions and demanding submission to imperialism through the threat of the 'destruction of mankind,' is exactly one of the main props of the global policy of U.S. imperialism. The slightest submission to its nuclear blackmail will encourage its policies of war and aggression, like pouring oil over a fire." (*Ibid.*, pp. 13–15.)

Quoting Lenin on the "fallacy of imperialist economism fabricated out of the 'depression' produced by the 'horror of war,'" the writers finally asserted "the modern revisionists, frightened by imperialist nuclear blackmail, have given up all struggles and gone down from capitulation to imperialism to embellishment of it." (*Ibid.*, p. 15.)

The Mainstream leaders saw American imperialism as the most ferocious, most dangerous enemy in the world. It was essential that it be
isolated and destroyed. All efforts to divert attention from this task by
emphasizing the importance of German, French, or Japanese imperialism were attempts to undermine the struggle against the primary
enemy. Every other imperialist group, including the Japanese monopoly
capitalists, was clearly subordinate to and dependent on American
power. The drive to shift the focus from American imperialism to "all"
imperialism, the desire to avoid a struggle with the United States, the
slighting of the national liberation movement, and the assertions that
the enemy of peace is not imperialism but "war" and "nuclear weapons," represented what Lenin called "European chauvinism." It was
a manifestation in even more corrupt form of the Kautskyist theses
which Lenin denounced and destroyed.[99]

In sum, the revolutionary momentum must be maintained, the JCP
leaders emphasized. There must be no capitulation before American

---

[99] "A theory which may be called the 'theory of directing the main
blows at German and French imperialism' has been derived from the modern
revisionist theory of the embellishment of Kennedy, and these two theories are
interconnected." (*Ibid.*, p. 22.) This is "a revisionist theory to which Marxist–
Leninists absolutely cannot subscribe." (*Ibid.*, p. 23.) "U.S. imperialism, 'the
chief imperialist country of today,' is the common enemy, the most ferocious,
and the number one enemy of the peoples of the socialist countries. . . . It is
indisputable that the important common tasks for the peoples of the world
is to isolate and deliver blows at U.S. imperialism." (*Ibid.*, p. 26.)
    The United States had three props in connection with its basic strategy:
First was its military apparatus (and the Kennedy administration had been
"in essence a militarist, reactionary regime, more adventurous, more war-
like and more ferocious then the Eisenhower Administration"). (*Ibid.*, p. 48.)
The second prop was its antisocialist program, and, in pursuance of this, the
United States sought to avoid a total clash with the Soviet Union. "If
the modern revisionists do not perceive this imperialist plot to split the socialist
system, they are politically stupid. If they perceive it and still ignore it instead
of exposing it, they are in effect helping U.S. imperialism to destroy socialism."
(*Ibid.*, p. 54.)
    The third prop was to spread new colonialism and suppress movements for
national independence. And in this connection, Kennedy himself had believed
that the main battleground was not Europe, where a stalemate had been
achieved, but Asia, Africa, and Latin America. For these areas, consequently,
American imperialism was prepared to wage a fierce struggle. Thus, those
modern revisionists who had accepted Kennedy's "lip-service to peace as a real
change of policy" and sought to "beautify the Kennedy line" were traitors
to the Socialist cause. "As Lenin said about the Kautskyites, they have
'turned Marxism into a most hideous and stupid counterrevolutionary theory,
into the filthiest clericalism.' But their sycophantic eulogies of U.S. imperialism
will be defeated by reality, by the everyday activity of U.S. imperialism and
the world people's struggle against this activity—and their defeat is certain." (*Ibid.*, p. 57.)

nuclear blackmail. Peaceful coexistence could only be realized by smashing the reactionary plans of U.S. imperialism. It must not be made into a vehicle whereby concessions were made to America. Thus, the entire thrust of Soviet policy under Khrushchev was misdirected. The Communist Party of the Soviet Union had ceased being the vanguard of the world proletariat and had become the leader of the modern revisionists.

BASIC ISSUES OF SINO–SOVIET CONFLICT

To appreciate the full implications of this confrontation between the Japanese Communist Party and the Communist Party of the Soviet Union, one must understand the three basic issues underlying the great dispute within the Communist world.[100] First, a conflict raged over the problems of organization, decision-making, and leadership in the international Communist movement. The shift from monolithism to polycentrism, the transition from the era when communism had only one state, one army, and one source of authority to the era when the power structure had become infinitely more complex inevitably produced vast new problems.

Neither Marx nor Lenin could have foreseen that mid-twentieth century communism would come to represent the fulfillment, not the denial, of nationalism. Indeed, the Communist movement in the emerging world only succeeded where it was able to capture and use nationalism, or where it could rely heavily on external sources of support. The rise of new Communist *nation-states*—more precisely, the use of communism for nation-building purposes—created a whole new range of problems. In many cases, the Communist and nationalist movements peaked at the same time; an ideological commitment to proletarian internationalism conflicted with a deep emotional commitment to land, folk, and state. Concepts such as sovereignty, equality, and territorial integrity competed with those of universality, uniformity, and the brotherhood of the proletarian class.

Concretely, the questions related to the structure of the international Communist movement were: What form of organization was appropriate? What type of decision-making process was operative? How should one define the scope and authority of leadership? Clearly, the Comintern–Cominform era was ended. The old Soviet empire began to

---

[100] The section which follows borrows heavily from my article, "The Sino–Soviet Conflict in Perspective," *The Annals of the American Academy of Political and Social Science,* Vol. 351, January 1964, pp. 1–14.

disintegrate in a fashion not greatly different from that of the British and French empires. A rising nationalist surge within the Communist world challenged Soviet domination and control. The Moscow conferences emerged as the new form of international Communist organization. In these conferences, the principles of the sovereign independence and equality of each party were legally established. Helpfully, the Russians themselves were induced to declare that the image of the Soviet party as the vanguard, the primary leader of international communism, was outmoded. More importantly, the principle of decision-making on the basis of consensus was established. *Within* a given party, the principle of democratic centralism would continue. Each party would be constructed out of a hierarchical tier of units developed by the familiar Leninist system. Legitimacy would derive from the masses, with a series of elections producing a structure in which all power rested at the top. Decisions would be made on the basis of full discussion and debate, decision by a majority vote and the complete acceptance by the minority of the majority position. *Among* parties, however, the principles were to be those of absolute sovereignty and equality, with no summit authority or hierarchical structure. Decisions would be made on the basis of full discussion and debate, compromise, consensus, and unanimity. Thus was a *liberum veto* built into the new supranational Communist organization. No party could be bound to any decision without its consent.

The Moscow Declaration of 1957 and the Moscow Statement of 1960 were both issued as *unanimous* decisions of the parties assembled. This unanimity, however, could be purchased only with great difficulty. Moreover, it was less the product of fundamental ideological or policy compromises than of the deliberate obfuscation of certain basic issues. Read closely, the Moscow documents are revealed as magnificent examples of how to provide some ammunition within the same paper for basically different views and how to blur certain important problems by a careful choice of words. The critical question became: Which section of the declaration or statement should be emphasized, and how should a particular passage or phrase be interpreted?

Unanimity is a dubious principle on which to rest a complex organization. Moreover, the concept of the equality of each Communist party was incompatible both with Russian instincts on such matters and with historic Soviet practices in the international Communist movement. A radical departure from the past would not come quickly or easily. The Soviet Union continued to rely heavily on "big-nation practices," despite its verbal acceptance of the new order. It rationalized the use of its power on the score that it continued to bear primary responsibilities for supporting and defending the Communist world in economic, political, and military terms. Gradually, moreover, it moved in the direction of defending the principle of majoritarianism. Soviet spokesmen denounced the thesis that "a small minority" should be able to inhibit and defy "the overwhelming majority," imposing its heretical views on the mainstream of the international movement.

The Chinese and their allies, striking the natural pose of the minority, placed great emphasis on the absolute equality and autonomy of each party. As we have noted, they insisted that no decisions in the international arena could be binding on a party against its will, and thus they posed a new doctrine for the international Communist movement, that of the sanctity of individual party sovereignty—a doctrine that conflicted with the concept of proletarian internationalism, both in theory and in practice. As the controversy grew wider and deeper, the Chinese grew more belligerent. Relying on Lenin's own historical struggle, they boldly asserted that any quantitative distinction between minority and majority was invalid because today's minority would be tomorrow's majority since *truth* lay with them.

Such a struggle could only end in a crisis over the nature of leadership. This was the logical culmination, indeed, of most struggles in communism, whether they took place within a single party or at the international level. The seemingly inevitable gravitation toward one-man rule or single-party domination was related partly to the organizational structure of the Communist movement, to the application of "democratic centralism" and the consequent pyramidal orientation of authority. But even more importantly, it was related to the very nature of Marxist–Leninist ideology. A movement that was now pluralistic in terms of its centers of power and cultural bases was still monolithic in terms of its ideological roots. In this paradox lay the Communist dilemma. Communists now talked incessantly about the importance of adapting Marxism–Leninism *creatively* to the particular circumstances and needs of their respective societies. But how was the line to be drawn between creativity and heresy?

In defining and defending their national interests within the framework of Marxian ideology, the Soviet and Chinese leaders were inevitably forced to fight for the right to determine Marxist orthodoxy. Marxism–Leninism, in the final analysis, represented a single truth, and all challenges to that truth were deviations. To support deviation was to be guilty of heresy, and no heretic could be tolerated. Whether in Asian or Western terms, the ethical-religious implications of this situation are clear. The issue became who had the moral right to rule. In tones echoing their Confucian past, the Chinese and their supporters proclaimed that the Soviet dynasty had lost the mandate of heaven, and they asserted the historic right of revolution. No one could overthrow a monarch (a true Marxist–Leninist), but anyone could destroy a tyrant (one who had abandoned Marxism–Leninism). Russian leaders had proven themselves unfit to guide the international Communist movement, having forsaken correct precepts and espoused modern revisionism in its most vicious form.

The situation could also be translated into Western religious experience. Like Luther, the Chinese—sickened by the corruption and decay that had eaten into the mother church, and unconsciously expressing the new nationalist challenge to an old internationalist movement—had nailed their pronunciamento on the door of the Communist cathedral. That pronunciamento, issued on June 15, 1963, was both implicitly and explicitly a bid for supreme leadership, just as it was a demand for a new set of policies. It symbolized the fact that the Chinese were prepared to abandon the tactics of reform within the movement for those of revolution and a fundamental reestablishment of *truth*. They were now prepared to go beyond the theses that there be no vanguard party, that decisions be reached on the basis of unanimity, and that procedures be fully "democratic" so as to ensure minority rights. They were now prepared to say, in a fashion far more radical than Luther, that the Pope was anti-Christ, and that only with his destruction could the honor and nobility of the sacred cause be reestablished.

It was curious to see the Communists turn the full array of their techniques against each other, techniques normally reserved for such opponents as social democrats. Once the decision to revolt had been reached, the Chinese vied with their Soviet opponents in employing every method to undermine and destroy the enemy: funds, propaganda, subversion and, above all, an emphasis on organizational work. A major effort was made to build new types of competitive united fronts that cut across Communist and non-Communist elements and to create disciplined, efficient inner centers of control.

The second basic issue was one closely connected with the first: namely, what was the obligation of one comrade to another, of an advanced and powerful Communist society to the emerging Communist world? A story, possibly apocryphal, illustrates the typical Russian position on this issue. Khrushchev supposedly remarked on one occasion that "some people" believed that communism meant that all individuals sat around the same table and shared the same food, looking very equal

—"and very *hungry!*" That was not his idea of communism, he reportedly asserted, adding that the Soviet Union had made great sacrifices in progressing toward communism; other societies, starting at a later point in time, would have to do likewise.

After World War II, the Soviet Union was faced with multiple claims on its limited resources. With vastly lower productivity and living standards than the United States, Russia was called on to bear similar burdens. To achieve and maintain military parity with America was —and perhaps had to be—a primary task. Politically, it was also essential to take increasing account of Soviet consumer demands, demands that pressed incessantly beyond productive capacities. The greatly expanded Communist world demanded special types of aid, even when some of its resources were susceptible to exploitation. Finally, if peaceful coexistence were to be pursued to the fullest extent, a well-developed program of economic aid and technical assistance had to be extended to the crucial neutralist non-Western societies. It is not surprising that, for the Russians, top priority went to the first two of these claims, namely, the military and economic growth of the Soviet Union. Such a priority could be rationalized by the assertion that Russian strength, both in military and economic terms, was absolutely indispensable to the security and growth of communism everywhere. Did not the Soviet Union serve as the umbrella, defending all Communist movements? Was it not Soviet strength that in the final analysis provided the only true deterrent against a nuclear war launched by Western imperialism? Would not Soviet prosperity, occurring in the *first* Socialist society, produce a universal yearning for a Socialist revolution?

Despite these arguments, and the hard facts that underlay them, Russia did not neglect its "fraternal obligations," at least as it interpreted these. By Chinese admission, Soviet aid to the People's Republic in the decade that followed 1949 had made "a striking contribution" to their economic development. Russia had helped to build 166 core projects during the first Five Year Plan, 125 core projects during the second plan. Soviet aid had come in many forms other than money and equipment. In the period up to 1960, some 10,800 Russian experts had served in China, some 6,000 or 7,000 Chinese students had been receiving a higher education in the Soviet Union, and a vast quantity of Russian factory blueprints, scientific discoveries, and industrial patents were given to the Chinese.

Despite the extent of this aid, the Chinese were profoundly dissatisfied for two reasons. In the first place, neither the terms nor the amount of the aid were as generous as they had hoped. Soviet money and equip-

ment were granted in the form of loans to be repaid with interest on a
short- or medium-term basis. A considerable amount of the aid, moreover, had to be military in character, expended in the Korean War—a
war from which only Russia profited, at least initially. Russian gifts in
any form were few. In comparison with Chinese need, even the loans
seemed small and there were the usual complaints about the quality
of Russian material, as well as its cost.

A far more important grievance, however, related to Soviet attitudes
and policies in connection with aid. The Chinese bluntly charged the
Russians with the pursuit of nationalist—indeed, imperialist—policies
in their relations with fraternal parties and states: In the first place,
Soviet experts and political leaders alike took a haughty, bureaucratic
attitude toward their Chinese comrades, an attitude totally unbefitting
fraternal brothers. They drove harsh economic bargains that were sometimes less advantageous than economic agreements with a capitalist
state would have been. More serious, the Soviet leaders used economic
aid and technical assistance as a weapon, a form of blackmail in order
to obtain their political desires. Their withdrawal of nearly 1,500 Soviet
technicians in the summer of 1960, the tearing up of hundreds of agreements, and the virtual severance of economic relations represented an
effort to bring China to its knees, to force it to capitulate to false Soviet
policies.

That effort had failed, but the Soviet government and party continued to attempt in every manner to interfere in the internal affairs of
the Chinese Communist Party. Notorious examples of this were the
efforts to subvert certain high officials, to ridicule the Mainstream
leaders of Peking, and to undermine the prestige of the party, both
with the Chinese people and throughout the world. And were not these
actions, both on the economic and political fronts, akin to classical imperialism? Had not the big-nation chauvinism practiced by the Soviet
leaders completely betrayed proletarian internationalism, the proper attitude between comrades?

The refusal to provide the People's Republic with all-out assistance
in connection with its nuclear weapons program in 1959, and the conclusion of the partial nuclear test ban treaty five years later were cli-
mactic examples of the betrayal of comrades for a narrow and false
concept of self-interest. These actions, together with the continued support to India, made it clear that Khrushchev and his followers had no
desire to distinguish between fraternal brothers and the motley crew of
bourgeois reactionaries that threatened the Communist world. Blindly
pursuing their own immediate national interests, the Russians seemed

intent on developing a big-power alliance with American imperialism, an alliance that would seek world domination and that bore no relation to the true Marxist–Leninist principles of building through one's own efforts.

The Soviet response to these charges was naturally violent—and broadly gauged: At great sacrifice, the Soviet people had given massive aid to the People's Republic of China. Yet important Russian advice had often been ignored, resulting in misuse of machinery, needless waste on a large scale, and serious setbacks in China's economic development. For example, against Soviet advice the Maoists had plunged into the ultra-radical commune program, with ensuing disaster. In seeking to "walk on two legs," to accelerate simultaneously both the agrarian and the industrial revolutions, the Chinese leaders were defying all modern economic laws with predictable results. Similarly, in advancing the thesis that men, not weapons, were the true determinants of modern war, the Maoists were once again revealing the strong element of primitivism that characterized so much of their ideology and their policies. Yet, with an inordinate stubbornness born out of a fierce pride and a deeply ingrained antiforeignism, they resisted all suggestions on these matters and, in doing so, cost both themselves and the Russian people huge losses. In terms of sheer principle, moreover, Chinese nationalism and racism had obliterated any true adherence to proletarian internationalism.

Denying all charges of internal interference, the Russians moved onto the offensive: Who had ceaselessly denigrated the top Soviet leaders and sought to circulate propaganda against them even within the Soviet Union? Who had secretly supported the antiparty group headed by Molotov? From a Russian point of view, the Chinese had attempted at every opportunity to undermine the confidence of the Soviet people in their own government and its policies. They had encouraged and on many occasions given active support to factional operations within the Communist movement directed against the Soviet Union and the CPSU throughout the world. Had not the Chinese leaders even directed their students who were guests in the Soviet Union to play a subversive role?

Russian spokesmen repeatedly denounced these actions not merely as the antithesis of a true comradely mode of conduct, but as conduct that would not even be tolerated by capitalist states in their relations with each other. Nor did the Soviets admit the charges of using aid to blackmail fraternal governments. Why should Soviet resources be used, indirectly, to support the Hoxha regime, a proclaimed enemy of the Soviet Union? If Peking wished to conduct a lavish program of aid to various states, moreover, with one of its primary purposes to undermind Russian prestige and rebuff Russian policy, why should the Soviet Union help finance it? When a party turned away from true Marxism–Leninism, it was entirely proper to admonish it and, if the condition persisted, to adjust one's policies accordingly. The Chinese leaders had now announced that each Communist state should be built largely through its own efforts in order to maintain its independence and integrity. This was a policy aimed at undermining organizations like the Council for Mutual Economic Aid (COMECON) and all elements of true internationalism within the Communist movement. However, let the Chinese live by that rule and cease slandering the Soviet Union.

Unquestionably, the two great issues discussed above were extremely important, but the third issue lay at the very roots of the crisis. Put simply, it was the question of the appropriate tactics and strategy for Communist victory against "imperialism" and "capitalism" in this, the latter part of the twentieth century. On the surface at least, there appeared to be an important measure of agreement on this matter. All Communists proclaimed themselves in favor of peaceful coexistence between states of different social systems. On the other hand, all Communists firmly announced their support of national liberation wars, since there could be no peaceful coexistence between slaves and masters.

Despite these "agreements," however, the gulf between the Soviet Union and China over tactics and strategy was enormous. In essence, the Soviet Union was committed to nation-to-nation competition with the United States, prepared to gamble on the continued growth of its economic and military power relative to that of its opponent. The Soviet leaders firmly believed that within a few decades, Russian productivity would surpass that of America. This would be translated both into greater power and greater appeal. As Socialist capacities grew and capitalist capacities declined, a profound shift in the world balance of power would take place; indeed, that process had been under way since World War II.

Victory could and would come through this evolutionary process, via the technique of peaceful coexistence. This did not mean an abandonment of the class struggle, nor a policy of softness toward imperialism. Peaceful coexistence signified an all-out competition involving every economic and political weapon, including a commitment to national liberation struggles, as we have noted. Nuclear war, however, could be avoided, and human survival itself depended on policies devoted to that end. Modern weapons had profoundly altered the nature and significance of global war. Such a war could not serve the cause of socialism, and any tactics or strategy based on the inevitability of war were both irresponsible and erroneous. Nuclear war could be prevented, not because imperialism had changed its nature, but primarily because the modern imperialists did not dare to attack their Socialist opponents whose power had grown so greatly. It was also true that within the imperialist camp itself there were moderates, men of peace who, recognizing the horrors of nuclear war, played a creative and important role in retraining the extremists.

Those who argued in effect that the policies of peaceful coexistence constituted capitulation to imperialism, as did the Chinese leaders, were madmen who did not understand the nature of nuclear war. They still lived in a primitive age when guerrillas, swarming out of the hills, could fight effectively with small arms, and they were not able to comprehend phenomena that lay beyond their historic experiences. Thus, they seemed oblivious to the risks of nuclear war, particularly since it was the Soviet Union, not they, who would be centrally involved. A major paradox could not be overlooked. While advocating ultra-leftist, adventurist policies for world communism, the Chinese leaders pursued a cautious policy for themselves, carefully avoiding a direct confrontation with imperialist power while accusing others of cowardice and appeasement.

Mao's oft-repeated maxim that American imperialism was a paper tiger was foolish and dangerous if caused to serve as the base for an operative policy. That paper tiger had nuclear teeth. To challenge the United States in an overt, massive fashion, leaving no room for retreat, could lead to war, despite the fact that this was both irrational and unnecessary for Communist victory. In sum, the Chinese attitude toward peace, war, and peaceful coexistence was reflective of the type of dogmatism and immaturity that characterized Chinese "Marxism," a product of the excessive nationalist, chauvinist, and primitivist sentiments that burdened the Chinese movement. Such were the Soviet taunts.

The Chinese, quite naturally, held radically different views. Unable to think realistically about nation-to-nation competition with the United States, they envisaged such competition in the form of unfolding the world revolution. Like the Bolsheviks when they presided over a weak and backward Russia, the Chinese leaders saw the extension of revolution as the most effective method of challenging imperialist power. Such a tactic would cause the dispersal of American resources, the dissipation of American power in fruitless attempts to contain national liberation struggles, and the rise of the proletariat everywhere. The United States was like a man with ten fingers on ten fleas. Release even one of those fleas and he would lose all of them in seeking to recapture that one.

It would be criminal, argued the Chinese, to lose the revolutionary momentum abroad in the world today. Why should victory be postponed, with the global proletariat forced to await the perfection of socialism in the Soviet Union? The Russians, victims of a nationalist urge to achieve indisputable big-power status and domination of world communism, had deliberately chosen tactics and strategy attuned to their self-interests, but which were in complete violation of the interests of the international Communist movement and contrary to the most basic principles of Marxism–Leninism.

Exaggerating the risks and costs of war, the Russians were seeking to abandon *the revolutionary principles* of Marxism and to turn it into a doctrine supporting accommodation with imperialism. Terrified themselves, they were seeking to frighten all revolutionaries and were allowing the nuclear blackmail of the American imperialists to succeed. The Chinese leaders did not wish war and had constantly supported the concept of peaceful coexistence with states having a different social system. However, reliance on peaceful methods alone in order to accomplish revolutionary purposes was contrary to Marxism–Leninism. Imperialism would not retreat voluntarily from the world stage. To appease American imperialism, to abandon the revolutionary struggle on behalf of sole reliance on diplomatic negotiations with the United States, and to enter into bilateral, big-power alliances with that nation directed against the revolution itself were acts of betrayal to the sacred cause of Marxism–Leninism. Peaceful coexistence did not mean a willingness to coexist with imperialism, and American imperialism was the most ferocious, most powerful, and most dangerous enemy of the peoples of the world. Thus, the struggle for peaceful coexistence was inseparable from the struggle against American imperialism.

Were the Russians guilty of the above crimes? From the Chinese viewpoint, the record in recent years indicated clearly that Khrushchev and his associates had abandoned the revolutionary struggle on behalf of the proletariat of the world and had engaged in an elaborate program of collaboration with world capitalism and imperialism. Having first taken the adventurist policy of placing missiles in Cuba, Khrushchev had capitulated to American threats and had been prepared to leave the Cuban revolutionaries to the tender mercies of the Americans, allowing their sovereignty to be violated without their consent. Throughout the Asian, African, and Latin American world, the Russians were counseling caution and accommodation. Their "don't-rock-the-boat" philosophy and the meager aid that they provided were forms of sabotage against the revolutionary aspirations of the masses. Whether in the Congo or in Vietnam, Russian policy amounted to a timid, defeatist program that could only end in capitulation.

The culminating betrayal had come with the limited nuclear test ban treaty. This treaty represented an attempt to freeze China out of the nuclear club and preserve the present major power monopoly. It was a typical example of Soviet big-power diplomacy, Russian Western-centrism, and the abandonment of Leninist principles. The revolutionary cause so carelessly abandoned by the Russians now had to be advanced by others.

These three issues underlying every aspect of the Sino–Soviet dispute naturally produced subsidiary issues. As the conflict intensified, Russia and China became involved in attempts to subvert minority peoples living near the Sino–Soviet borders or in such areas as Outer Mongolia. Serious issues of an overt nationalist character thus emerged, issues involving both people and boundaries. Broader ideological questions were also raised in an effort to prove that one party or the other was totally abandoning Marxism. The Chinese advanced the thesis that the Soviet leaders, in giving up the dictatorship of the proletariat for "a state of the whole people," were in reality preparing the way for the restoration of capitalism, a policy in line with many of their economic and political policies at home and with their attempted rehabilitation of Yugoslavia. The Russians in turn denounced "Maoism" as a spurious deviation from Marxism–Leninism, reflective primarily of the combination of primitivism and Greater Han chauvinism that had characterized the Chinese revolution.

At its roots, the Sino–Soviet dispute was between two national-Communist states that shared a general ideology but had major differences in cultural tradition, timing of revolution, stage of development, and degree of power. The result was a fundamental clash of national interests, as interpreted by the respective elites of the two nations. Cultural differences produced certain significant distinctions in political behavior that exacerbated a conflict issuing from other sources. In all of the traits that constitute political styles—sense of propriety, method of handling opponents, even use of words—Russian and Chinese custom varied greatly. Moreover, the quotient of ethnocentrism in both nations was exceedingly high. These were two continental-mass societies, with a long history of isolation and self-sufficiency, a history underwriting a deep suspicion of foreigners and a strong sense of cultural uniqueness. Indeed, it is the supreme paradox of the late twentieth century that global power is held by continental-mass societies which preach cosmopolitanism but often practice exclusivism.

For both societies—and particularly for China—Marxism, turned on its head, became an instrument for the completion of the nation-building process. Nationalism not only survived communism; to a major degree, it triumphed over it. The stage was thus set for a true conflict of national interests on the part of two ascending states, developing approximately a half-century apart. The different timing of the two revolutions affected policies and attitudes in a great variety of ways. For example, the Soviet Union was now governed by second- or third-generation revolutionaries, men who had generally ascended through the bureaucracy. In general, these men were *functionaires,* leaders who in the course of careers in party or government had acquired the administrative skills and technical training important to the operation of a state in which the basic political forms had long been established. In very general terms, these men were technicians—more pragmatic than ideological, more administrative than political, and more establishment-minded than revolutionary. Few of them possessed charisma. China, on the other hand, was governed by first-generation revolutionaries in whom burned an inner fire. These men were true ideologues, supremely political, and dedicated to the fulfillment of revolutionary goals irrespective of obstacles and costs. Veteran guerrillas, these were men who had spent thirty years in the hills and on their bellies in the rice fields, fighting, talking, and dreaming revolution. Until the end of their lives, they would think and act largely in military terms. They too had acquired an important element of pragmatism —otherwise, they would not have survived, let alone triumphed. But pragmatism was not the most pronounced characteristic of this group, except in sheer tactical terms. These were true believers, first-generation revolutionaries not prepared to give up their purity lightly. They could not appreciate "Communists" who appeared to be disinterested in theory and revolution alike.

The timing of these two revolutions, together with the developmental conditions characterizing the two societies in the sixth decade of the twentieth century, also produced major differences in status and power. These differences, in turn, affected values, policies, and goals. The Soviet Union, one of the two superpowers of the mid-twentieth century world, acquired some degree of responsibility to match its power and an increased stake in the status quo. China, on the other hand, remained profoundly dissatisfied with its status and rate of growth, as well as with the world around it, and hence was determined to create radical changes in the shortest possible period of time. Internal weakness and noninvolvement in international decision-making processes combined to produce a high level of frustration, anger, and irresponsibility.

Differences in power and status also resulted in very rational differences in policy. It was logical for the Soviet Union to emphasize nation-to-nation competition with the United States and to stress peaceful coexistence as it defined that term. Given their general position, however, the Chinese leaders could most easily defend the concept of unfolding the world revolution as the most effective method of competition with America—an approach which dispersed and dissipated American power, despite the relative weakness of the Chinese People's Republic. Indeed, the Chinese were persuaded that their formula for internal victory was entirely serviceable on the international scene: a united front of proletariat (Socialist countries not under false leadership), peasants (the Asian–African–Latin American world), and national bourgeoisie (such advanced states as could be pried loose from American alliance), against the compradors and big bourgeoisie (the United States) and antiparty renegades (the Soviet Union).

These were the basic issues of the Sino–Soviet dispute and the fundamental conditions that underlay them. The escalation of that dispute can be charted in terms of five stages, each marked by distinctive characteristics. The first stage, covering the period 1956–1957, was characterized by private bilateral discussions between Russian and Chinese leaders, with each trying to persuade the other of the merits of and reasons for their respective views. These discussions and communications, mainly oral in nature, were couched in restrained language and were shared with a very small number of comrades from other parties. At this point, the controversy was strictly on a party-to-party basis and was confined to the most trusted comrades. Even within the top echelons of most parties, there was no knowledge of any problem.

The second stage, dating from the fall of 1957, represented the beginning of formal disputation, carried on through regular party channels. Quickly, the debate was transmitted into the mainstream of the international Communist movement, and the leadership of every party was acquainted with the most critical issues. This stage culminated in the savage interparty and interpersonal arguments that took place in Bucharest and Moscow in 1960. Already, the dispute had produced or exacerbated factionalism, both among and within parties. Moreover, the Soviet Union had commenced punitive actions against Albania and China in a desperate effort to stop their defiance of Soviet policy. Attempts to subvert opposition parties by supporting "antiparty" factions were also being made on both sides. Thus, the controversy now involved state-to-state relations. The language used in the controversy was also becoming more extreme, although no direct attacks were being made in written form.

The public assault by Khrushchev on Albania in October 1961 inaugurated the third stage, marking the formal entry of the dispute into the public arena. In this period, as in the preceding one, Albania and Yugoslavia were used to symbolize China and Russia, respectively, and through them, the full range of issues and the bitterness attending them were progressively explored and revealed to the world. Publicly, Communist leaders still denied that the controversy was of major importance. There could be no real doubt, however, either within or outside the Communist movement, as to the serious nature of the cleavage. Communist parties everywhere were now forced to take positions on many of the burning issues, although a few parties, notably in Asia, sought to establish a neutralist position. Most parties elsewhere lined up behind Moscow on the critical points. A noticeable weakening of discipline developed, however. Moscow was now paying a heavy price for the dispute, with Peking involved in intensive propaganda efforts throughout the world, but directed especially toward the non-Western areas. State-to-state relations between the Soviet Union and China deteriorated sharply, with each side accusing the other of subversive activities, uncomradely treatment, and repeated interference in internal affairs.

A fourth stage developed in the fall of 1962, after a temporary lull. The crises over India, Cuba, and Yugoslavia were centrally involved. The use of Albania and Yugoslavia as stand-ins for the major targets was gradually abandoned, and the targets themselves—still garbed in anonymity—were brought forward. The Chinese tactic was to use terms like "some people" and "some parties." Over time, other terms were employed by both sides: modern revisionists, neo-Trotskyites, Kautsky renegades, ultra-left adventurists, and dogmatists. Finally, the Soviet Union, furious at Chinese criticisms of Russian policy, promoted open attacks on the CCP at the various party congresses of Eastern Europe in late 1962 and early 1963. Chinese authorities quickly responded by issuing a running series of lengthy articles surveying in comprehensive fashion their position and excoriating their opponents. The dispute was now deeply affecting all Communist parties, forcing them to take positions and producing splits in a number of parties. Neutralism was no longer a viable tactic. Attempts to bring about some reconciliation failed. China garnered support from most Asian parties and sought to make the Asia–Africa–Latin America region a center of Chinese strength. But Moscow held firmly to its influence in most of the official party organizations outside the Far East. At the same time, however, internal factionalism developed everywhere, and the old domination of the Soviet Union over external parties was, almost without exception, drastically reduced.

The famous June 14 letter from Peking and the abortive Moscow meeting of July 1963 that followed opened the fifth stage of the Sino–Soviet dispute. Now, the two opponents attacked each other openly by name and in the most vehement terms. The Chinese demanded nothing less than the total repudiation of Khrushchev and the removal of the CPSU from its vanguard position. In *de facto* terms, they issued a call for the establishment of a rival international movement, one dominated by "the revolutionary principles of Marxism–Leninism." A furious battle for parties took place, with Moscow retaining the lead, but with Peking scoring certain tactical victories. The new note of independence continued to be sounded among parties basically supporting Soviet positions, with indications that the nature of power relations within the Communist world had been fundamentally and irretrievably altered. Meanwhile, state-to-state relations between Russia and China continued to deteriorate and reached a point where trade was negligible, border incidents were frequent, and only formal relations were maintained.

Against this broad background, the position and the problems of the Japanese Communist Party can be seen more clearly. As we have noted, on each of the fundamental substantive issues at stake, the JCP position was nearly identical to that of the Chinese Communist Party. Like the Chinese, Japanese Mainstream leaders insisted that minority rights within the international Communist movement be safeguarded via the principle of absolute equality and full autonomy for each party, with all decisions being made on the basis of consultation, consensus, and unanimity. They too came to denounce Soviet practices as dictatorial, characterized by big-nation chauvinism, and completely anti-Marxist. They too came to couple Khrushchev and the CPSU with leadership of the modern revisionist movement, and hence unfit for vanguard status or international leadership.

In the end, the bitterness of the Japanese Mainstream leaders over Soviet treatment was scarcely less than that of their Chinese comrades. As we have seen, Russian leaders were accused of having engaged in totally uncomradely behavior toward the fraternal party in Japan. According to JCP documents, they had consorted with class enemies, had sought to bully and blackmail the Japanese Communist Party, had pursued capricious, changing policies without consulting or even informing fraternal parties, and had repeatedly interfered in JCP internal affairs.

Finally, on the critical issue of appropriate Communist tactics and strategy, the Japanese Mainstream followed precisely the Chinese line. The Soviet Union was condemned for its basic support of the status quo and its disinclination to challenge American imperialism. The JCP, like the CCP, insisted that the United States had to be forced into a retreat from Asia and the world in general by a program of unremitting pressure, even at the risk of war. National liberation movements had to be given all-out support. The Communist camp *as a whole* had to continue the development of its nuclear capacity. Peaceful coexistence had to be subordinated to the struggle against American imperialism. In place of reliance on diplomatic negotiations and the development of Russian power for victory, true Communists would put their faith in the upsurge of revolution throughout the world and give it their full support.

The rising conflict between the Japanese Communist Party and the Communist Party of the Soviet Union followed in general the five stages marking the Sino–Soviet dispute. Initially, as we have noted, most JCP leaders had only a vague notion of trouble, although a privileged few were probably briefed by the Chinese as early as 1956. It was not until the spring of 1960, however, that the existence of the conflict, and its broad dimensions, came to be known to all of the top party leaders. Even then, party officials were discouraged from discussing the matter, and every attempt was made to keep the details from the party rank and file. The official line was that the dispute was essentially a figment of bourgeois imagination. In reality, of course, the top party leaders now knew that the quarrel could become serious, and they also knew that a basic cleavage would gravely damage the JCP.

With the inauguration of stage three, signaled by the events of the 22nd CPSU Congress in 1961, the JCP adopted the tactic of neutralism, hoping to prevent a party split and determinedly playing for time, meanwhile applying pressure for an international settlement. This basic policy remained in effect until the summer of 1963, although not without increasing difficulties. It thus survived in some measure the escalation of the Sino–Soviet dispute into stage four. Meanwhile, however, Mainstream control of the JCP organization was tightened, with minority elements departing, being ousted, or demoted in authority. With the advent of stage five, however, neutralism had to be abandoned. In the aftermath of the Moscow Treaty and the 9th Gensuikyō Conference of August 1963, the Japanese Communist Party was forced to break openly with the CPSU and engage in bitter conflict. The new tactical line was "independence and autonomy," and full support was given to the positions taken by the Chinese Communists. Relations between the JCP and the CPSU were frigid and minimal by the summer of 1964. The Soviet party was giving major support to the Voice of Japan group as the legitimate Marxist–Leninist element and attempting to set up a united front among other various leftist forces, excluding the JCP.

What fundamental reasons explain the increasing influence of the Chinese Communist Party on the JCP between 1950 and 1965? Three factors stand out. First, the geographic and cultural proximity of China was one factor of major importance. Communications were facilitated in every sense. Interviews clearly reveal that most Japanese Communists felt they could *understand* their Chinese comrades, whereas the Russians frequently seemed bureaucratic, high-handed, foreign, and aloof. The cultural relations between Japanese and Chinese, to be sure, have never been simple or unambiguous. Traditionally, as is well known, the Chinese regarded Japan as merely one of many barbarian countries on their peripheries, qualified only to pay tribute to a superior civilization. Despite all of their modern travails, moreover, the Chinese never abandoned entirely the attitudes of paternalism and superiority so characteristic of their traditional position. Indeed, such attitudes have undoubtedly contributed to events after 1965 which we shall shortly explore. At the same time, however, the Chinese Communist leaders, when it suits their purpose, have frequently shown themselves capable of a level of subtlety, graciousness, and intimate understanding with respect to their Asian comrades that the Russians have rarely, if ever, been able to reach.

Understandably, the Japanese have had mixed feelings about China, in broad, historic terms. At times they have deeply resented Chinese condescension and attempts to place Japan under Chinese influence. In the modern era, moreover, certain new stereotypes were developed; for example, the image of the Chinese as a decadent people who would never be able to govern themselves. Despite these aspects of the historical record, Japanese of many different political persuasions have often found it possible to interact meaningfully with the Chinese—to understand and appreciate their thought patterns and political responses. Interpersonal relations between Japanese and Russians have rarely been marked by true warmth and intimacy, even in the Communist movement. A different relationship developed between Peking and many of the Japanese comrades.

Connected with this first factor has been a second, namely, Chinese aid and assistance to the Japanese Communist Party. As we have seen, the ascendancy of the Chinese over the Russians with respect to the Japanese Communist movement began in 1950. At that point, scores of young Japanese Communists, along with a majority of their senior leaders, took refuge in China. There they received political training and funds for subsistence and a number of them developed lasting personal ties. These were significant years in terms of the future. And in the succeeding period, Chinese assistance to the Japanese Communist Party continued, some of it in the form of direct financial aid. There is no question that the JCP budget was augmented until recently as a result of Chinese funds. Proceeds from the sale of Chinese publications in Japan, contributions from Japanese trading companies doing business with China, and direct grants both to the party and to front organizations, as well as to individuals, have been of major importance, as we shall later note. Soviet aid during this period was not comparable in any sense.

Finally, and most importantly, the Japanese Communists, in company with a number of other Asian comrades, found themselves increasingly opposed both to Soviet policies and to Soviet methods of operation. Khrushchevism came to symbolize an accommodation to the status quo on the one hand, and a crude, authoritarian attitude toward the Communist world on the other. In reaction and greatly stimulated by Peking, an Asian Communist bloc began to emerge in this period. At first, this bloc—as symbolized by North Korea, North Vietnam, the PKI, and the JCP—was dedicated to "neutralism" and a desperate effort to mend the Sino–Soviet breach. As these efforts failed, the bloc gravitated away from Moscow, taking positions that approximated those of Peking and taking them openly. The JCP evolution was thus part of a larger trend, a fact that must be underlined.

Peking during this period symbolized to other Asian Communists success, power, and commitment. It combined a formidable presence in Asia with dynamic, militant policies that offered hope to other Asian Communists—in and out of power. For example, the thesis that Japan was a quasi-colony dominated by American imperialism and that the struggle against the United States took precedence over all other issues naturally appealed to many Japanese Communists, playing as it did to nationalism and to those xenophobic, racial sentiments which, together with an engrained sense of inferiority, have long formed a part of Japanese political culture. In sum, the elements of nationalism, Asianism, and militancy explicit in Chinese doctrines, the fervent anti-Westernism and the racial overtones served as a powerful magnet, especially to younger Japanese Communists.

Implicit in this situation, however, were several major paradoxes. Unlike all other Asian states, Japan was an advanced industrial society. Until the Japanese Communists could come to grips with this central fact, any significant gains would be impossible. Thus, other than their nationalist, Asianist elements, did Chinese Communist tactics and doctrine have much to offer to the Japanese comrades? Maoism both in concept and in practice was attuned to a vast, sprawling, backward peasant society. Its essential primitivism bore no relation to the nature of contemporary Japan. Neither its political nor its military principles fitted the stage of development, socioeconomic structure, topography, and communications grid of Japan. These facts made doctrines like "structural reform" much more logical for Japanese Marxists. Whatever their basic weaknesses, such doctrines bore infinitely greater relation to the nature and proclivities of Japanese society than Maoism did.

Beyond this paradox lay another. The rebellion against the Soviet Union, undertaken so reluctantly, had found its ultimate expression in the demand for "independence and autonomy." Historically, as we have noted, the Japanese Communists had had a long record of total subservience to the Kremlin. Thus, the trauma of the break must have been intense. In one sense, therefore, it was natural to seek a substitute for Moscow in Peking, especially since the JCP was fundamentally so weak. The extraordinary degree of nationalism characterizing Chinese Communism at this point, however, was certain to make this difficult. Moreover, if the Chinese Communists could transmit any value to their Japanese comrades, it was likely to be nationalism and Asianism, as noted above. And this was in line with the general polycentric tendencies within the Communist world. Thus, it was conceivable that the JCP might wish to come closer to "independence and autonomy" than at any time in their previous history.

As 1964 came to a close, the JCP faced two major challenges: Could the party retain close ties with Peking and still successfully establish an image as an independent, autonomous party, thereby getting into a position to make more effective use of Japanese nationalism? In addition, could successful united front operations be launched at home, parleying the thin JCP ranks into the leadership of a mass movement?

VI

THE STRUGGLE ON TWO FRONTS

On November 25, 1964, the Japanese Communist Party finally opened the 9th Party Congress, previously scheduled for 1963 but postponed because of the international crisis in which the party found itself.[1] Once again, the party spoke officially on such critical issues as its attitude toward the United States, the proper stages of the revolutionary movement, and the appropriate tactics to be used. On each of these issues, the basic positions adopted earlier were reiterated. The 9th Party Program was essentially a repetition of the program adopted by the 8th Party Congress in 1961. American imperialism remained the central enemy, with Japanese monopoly capitalism as its subordinate ally. Against these two opponents, the JCP pledged an unremitting war. With respect to revolutionary objectives, the first goal was to establish a people's democracy, formed out of a worker-peasant alliance, with elements of the petty and national bourgeoisie participating. This alliance was to be led by "the vanguard party" and was to permit the ultimate attainment of a socialist state. With respect to tactics, parliamentarism was to be combined with mass struggles outside the Diet. There was to be no exclusive reliance on peaceful tactics; force had to be met by force.

The 9th Congress analysis of the world situation stressed the themes of the Moscow Statement of 1960 and those of the 8th Party Congress, with certain special emphases. The socialist world was showing marked progress, and national liberation movements were everywhere advanc-

---

[1] As noted earlier, the full text of the Central Committee Report to the 9th Party Congress is translated in *TICD* 691, *JPRS* 28,456, pp. 1–298.

ing, but the aggressive character of imperialism had not changed. Indeed, American policy in Vietnam indicated how dangerous the United States could be. In the midst of this threat, modern revisionism had become serious, threatening to split the international Communist movement in a drastic fashion.

In providing details concerning these trends, the Japanese Communist Party revealed its view of the world and of Japan proper. Everywhere within the "capitalist world," the Central Committee saw rising contradictions and insuperable crises. The United States was in the process of "the deepest decay and decadency," although one had to avoid the revisionist error of viewing American imperialism lightly. Conditions in Japan were "ruinous", the Japanese people were being crushed by a variety of problems. The unprecedented prosperity in the West and in Japan did not deter the party from coming up with the same old prophecies of doom and gloom, balancing these not too adroitly against a thesis that imperialism remained a powerful, menacing force.

Little space was devoted to chronicling the advances of the socialist world, partly because the JCP Central Committee did not wish to omit the Soviet Union on the one hand, or to lend any support to Khrushchev on the other. Such an omission, however, was also in line with basic JCP theory about primary and secondary arenas for confrontation. With respect to national liberation movements, the account was voluminous. South Vietnam, Laos, South Korea, Indonesia, North Kalimantan, and Cambodia were all placed in the category of societies where a strong people's liberation movement had developed. In surveying recent trends, the JCP took heart at the military and political defeats of the United States in South Vietnam, the failure of the Indian–Yugoslav "plot" to thrust proimperialism and anti-Chinaism into the 2nd Non–Aligned Conference in Cairo; and the growing isolation of the Indian government, coupled with the "solidarity" of the Asian–African–Latin American peoples.

Much attention was devoted to the Chinese nuclear test of October 16, 1964, which was acclaimed as a breaking of the nuclear monopoly and the striking of a blow for peace, as well as a demonstration of scientific prowess in Asia. The removal of Khrushchev was hailed as a "setback" for the international revisionist movement. In short, the most encouraging developments lay in the gains of the revolutionary movement in the non-Western world and the multiple blows suffered by "liberal-bourgeois" and "revisionist" elements. This analysis, of course, sustained the thesis that the primary arena for confrontation between communism and its enemies lay in the emerging world, and that national liberation movements, together with the rising contradictions within the capitalist world, represented the basic ingredients of socialist victory.

In a detailed treatment of internal conditions in Japan, the Central Committee Report to the 9th Congress pressed the old charge that Japanese reactionaries were pursuing a policy of reviving imperialism and militarism. Ties with American monopoly capital, moreover, were being strengthened. These trends, while creating an illusion of prosperity, were in reality causing "greater humiliation and suffering" for the Japanese people of all classes.[2] And despite its revival and consolidation, Japanese monoply capitalism remained subordinate to American imperialism. An American–Japanese ruling class was pursuing antinational, antipopular policies centering on the revival of imperialism.[3] Such an analysis was close to the historic Chinese Communist model, involving the concepts of the quasi-colonial state and the comprador class under foreign imperialist control.

The answer to these machinations was a revitalized united front, and to this objective the 9th Congress Central Committee Report devoted extensive attention. In the lengthy discussion of such a front, its composition and its purposes, the JCP begrudgingly revealed some of its most basic problems. With whom to combine? The Liberal Democratic Party was scarcely structured to be an ally, since it was "centered upon monopoly capital."[4] The Democratic Socialist Party was "a right-wing socialist democratic party," openly supporting the Japanese–American ruling class and its policies, playing the role of a detachment

---

[2] *Ibid.*, p. 15.

[3] *Ibid.*, pp. 15–16. According to the report, recent developments had raised the position of Japanese monopoly capitalism in relation to American imperialism, but even now the former was subordinate to the latter. Why?

"First, Japan's military and diplomatic subordination to United States imperialism remains as strong as before. The United States has many military bases and troops stationed in Japan, is continuing the occupation of Okinawa and the Bonin Islands, and has chained Japan to the American imperialist policy of Asian aggression and nuclear warfare. When the reinforced Self-Defense Forces shoulder part of the United States Army's burdens, due to the system of joint United States–Japanese military operations, they are as a body included under the United States Pacific Command. In actual fact, its nucleus is molded by American hands. The diplomatic policy of Japanese monopoly capital is [developed] on the basis of American approval, and although it has a few characteristics of its own in diplomacy with Europe and close relations between China and Japan, its basic lines follow United States imperialist world policy, especially in being bound deeply to the policies of 'isolation of China' and Asian aggression."

[4] *Ibid.*, p. 26.

of the Liberal Democrats.[5] The Socialist Party, although the chief Socialist group in Japan, was "one more social prop for the petty bourgeoisie of various hues in the urban and rural areas." It had a certain positive aspect, but, "as a middle-of-the-road political party," it could not "escape being unthorough and vacillating" and could not "overcome its anti-Communist sectarianism."[6] Thus did the Central Committee deal with its potential ally, once again revealing the propensity of the Communists for simultaneously attacking and wooing the Socialists.

The newly established Kōmeitō (Party for Justice and Fairness), the political arm of Sōka Gakkai (Value Creation Society), was characterized as another centrist party with some progressive slogans relating to peace and democracy, but often aligned with the Liberal Democrats and was sectarian in outlook. From the JCP Central Committee analysis, it was clear that no other party was to be trusted, nor could any other party undertake the historic class role of the Japanese Communist Party. The report analyzed the problem of the united front and blamed its failure on "a rightist tendency in the leadership of the Democratic Socialist Party and Dōmei Kaigi [Japanese Confederation of Labor], and also within the Socialist Party and Sōhyō, abetted by the interference of the international forces of modern revisionism."[7]

The Central Committee admitted its "serious mistake" in opposing the April 17 strike of the past spring and, in analyzing this problem, revealed the possibility of a new tactical stance that could have far-reaching repercussions. The Communist movement currently faced a dual danger, that of both right and left opportunism, and, in this instance, the party had been guilty of both deviations, although the primary mistake had been of a leftist character. To insist in a mechan-

---

[5] *Ibid.*

[6] The key sentences of the section on the Japan Socialists in the Central Committee Report to the 9th Congress were as follows: "The Socialist party is the chief socialistic party in Japan, and is an arm of Sōhyō and other labor union federations. It gains its right to leadership by socialist democratism. It is under the influence of the properly large portion of union laborers. The Socialist party is one more social prop for the petty bourgeoisie of various hues, of the urban and rural areas. Finally, it presents a positive policy which reflects the demands of the petty bourgeoisie and the farmers against oppression and robbery by Japanese–American monopoly capital. But, as a middle-of-the-road political party, it cannot escape being unthorough and vacillating and cannot overcome its anti-Communist sectarianism. Especially, one portion of the anti-Communist right wing of the Social Democrats is heading down the road of fractionalism and opportunism within the forces of democracy and is bound to foreign and domestic contemporary revisionism" (p. 31).

[7] *Ibid.,* pp. 40–41.

istic fashion that American imperialism *always* be the central target
could disrupt every united front effort. It was important not to underestimate the possibilities of united action with the Sōhyō–JSP forces
nor to underestimate the importance of struggling against domestic
monopoly capitalism.[8]

At the same time, the united front movement, essential though it
was, could not deter the party from making clear "the true nature of
revisionism" and "the petty bourgeois socialism" of Sōhyō and the
JSP. The workers had to be armed with true Marxism–Leninism.[9]
Thus, the national-democratic united front had to be established *on
Communist terms with Communist leadership*. The masses must have
"scientific socialism" and nothing else, and all rival doctrines had to
be fought.[10]

In reviewing the previous three years' efforts to create a united front
on the Mutual Security Treaty and various peace issues, the Central
Committee underlined all of these themes. It admitted no mistakes,
no shortcomings, blaming all the failures on "the negative attitude" of
the Socialist Party and other social democratic forces. With the single
exception of the decision concerning the April 17 strike, the JCP had
been correct.

For the future, it would be necessary to have "prompting from above
and a united action from below."[11] The party had to avoid sectarianism and should not disregard the necessity for unity from above based
on compromise between parties and the leaders of the mass organizations. But at the same time, the development of the party's own independent movement, mass-based action, and the initiation of a united
front from below were critical.[12]

Once again, the historic dilemma of the Japanese Communist movement was set forth in stark fashion. How to use and abuse the social
democrats as the same time? How to get them into a united front
while simultaneously attacking them, seeking to undermine their policies and subvert their members? How to condemn the Japan Socialist
Party for splittism, while at the same time insisting on the full independence and autonomy of the Japanese Communist Party within any
front movement?

The only answer presented to these dilemmas was to borrow a fa-

[8] *Ibid.*, pp. 47–52. For more details on this issue, see pp. 229–253.
[9] *Ibid.*, pp. 76–77.
[10] *Ibid.*, pp. 79–80.
[11] *Ibid.*, p. 88.
[12] *Ibid.*, pp. 125–127.

mous phrase from the Chinese Communist vocabulary and to proclaim that the basis of the party's work had to be *the mass line*. Such a phrase, to be sure, echoed the distant longings of the Japanese Communist Party. At its very beginning, it will be recalled, the party had thrilled to Yamakawa's call, "To the masses!" The party's long record of slighting policies attuned to that cry did not diminish its appeal. But the Chinese had made the mass line work. Their victory was a triumph more of organization than of ideology. Born in the age of the mass man, the Chinese Communists had found methods of mobilizing men to do their bidding, whether voluntarily or under various forms of coercion. Could the JCP, now so strongly under Chinese influence, find a similar path? Could it shift from being primarily concerned with ideology to a focus on tactics and, more particularly, on organization as a key to revolutionary victory?

These questions raised the issue of how to reach the masses. In its socioeconomic analysis of Japanese society, the Central Committee naturally began with the working class, which it described as 53 percent of the employed population. In Communist eyes, the labor movement had many serious weaknesses. It had been under the social democrats for a long time, organized labor having been forced to support the Socialist Party. Freedom to join any party was essential, as was "class education" for the workers.[13] Sōhyō had to be criticized because its policy against American imperialism was "constantly negative," linked to its social democratic policies.[14]

Regarding the farmers and fishermen, the party admitted that its success had been very minimal despite recent efforts. Party influence in the fishing villages was negligible because "the power of the bosses was still great," but in these areas the struggle against military bases and similar issues "could be important."[15] Gains had been made in rural party cells and unions; such units had been established in more than one-half of the prefectures since 1961. The electoral gains in rural Nagano and Kochi were closely related to organizational successes. The tactic was to put primary stress on farm laborers and poor farmers, uniting these with the middle-class farmer, and pulling the rich farmer to their side.[16] Thus, thirty years later, the JCP Central Committee was seeking to find the road outlined by Mao in Honan and sketched still earlier by Lenin as he dreamed of the inexhaustible supply of peas-

---

[13] *Ibid.*, p. 131.
[14] *Ibid.*, pp. 133–134.
[15] *Ibid.*, pp. 148–149.
[16] *Ibid.*, p. 145.

ants that might be drafted for the revolutionary cause. But the rural Japan of 1964 bore little relation to the Honan of 1927, even assuming that the Maoist formula had scored significant successes prior to the Anti-Japanese War, an assumption not fully warranted. The agrarian element of the Japanese population was steadily declining, and, within this group, those engaged purely in agriculture were at this point no more than one-third of the total. Nothing revealed the inherent dogmatism of the Japanese Communist Party and its continued inability to break away from the mechanical adoption of foreign ideas more than its policy toward the peasants.

The intellectuals presented a problem causing serious concern. According to the Central Committee report, their "petty bourgeois instincts" had come strongly to the fore, causing them to join the deviationist movement or recant Marxism in some equally drastic fashion. Other special groups also deserved attention. With respect to women, the JCP had a formidable opponent in the Sōka Gakkai. Indeed, that militant religious association had penetrated the urban community as a whole, especially its poorer elements, and this challenge had to be met. Not surprisingly, the report placed a strong emphasis on the organization and indoctrination of the outcast communities. With respect to youth, substantial gains had been made. The Democratic Youth League had greatly increased its membership and Zengakuren was once again moving into the JCP orbit. Indeed, the party report and independent information suggested that the JCP was scoring its only successes with youth, a result of the hard organizational efforts of the JCP "Young Officers" and the funds at their disposal.

How should the broad principles of the party and its basic tactics be translated into a concrete program? A lengthy section of the 9th Congress Report outlined the four banners, six tasks, and ten common needs.[17] Once again, the approach—indeed, the precise vocabulary— suggested the strong influence which Peking had had upon the party. The term "banner," for example, had been extensively used by the Chinese Communists. It conjured up a vision of ancient Chinese or Mongol horsemen riding to the attack at least as much as it did an image of proletariats marching toward the seat of power.

None of the specific policies advanced in the Central Committee Report to the 9th Congress were new. The four banners were those of "the national democratic revolution against imperialism and monopoly capital; of the national democratic united front; of the building of a

---

[17] *Ibid.,* pp. 52–71.

strong powerful JCP; and of opposing imperialism headed by the U.S. and striving for an international united front for national liberation and peace."

The six immediate tasks were the following. First, it was necessary to strive for Japan's independence, security, and neutralization. This related centrally to the questions of Okinawa and the Bonins, the revised Mutual Security Treaty, the berthing of U.S. atomic-powered submarines, and the presence of American military forces in Japan. Pointedly, attention was called to the fact that the Mutual Security Treaty could be revised in 1970, although an attempt might be made merely to extend it automatically. That year was obviously the target date for a massive new united front effort.

The second task was to defend Asian and world peace and strive for the peaceful coexistence of countries with different social systems. When the Central Committee had finished spelling out the implications of this task, however, peaceful coexistence took on a strongly bellicose coloration. At home, the party had to conduct "an energetic struggle" against the policy of anti-Communism and aggression, block talks between Japan and the Republic of Korea, and demand normalization of relations with the Communist states. Abroad, the party had to align itself with the forces of "world peace and democracy," demanding a total nuclear ban, complete disarmament, and a struggle against American imperialism.

The third task was to support "the oppressed nations and peoples of the world" in their struggle against imperialism. The South Vietnamese people, in particular, deserved full support in their fight "against the barbarous aggression by imperialist America." It was also essential to demand the withdrawal of American forces from all parts of Asia and thwart the conspiracy of a Northeast Asian military alliance.

The fourth task was to oppose the attempt of the American–Japanese ruling classes to revive militarism, and to defend and expand the democracy won by the Japanese people since World War II. All "reactionary amendments" to the Constitution had to be adamantly fought, and compliance with its democratic provisions, such as Article 9, had to be demanded.

The fifth task was "to oppose the exploitation and plundering by U.S. and Japanese monopoly capital; to defend the Japanese people's livelihood; to strive for an independent and peaceful development of the Japanese economy and life, promoting security and a higher standard of living." To accomplish these goals, drastic wage increases and general improvements in working conditions were necessary; American control over the Japanese economy had to be broken and the militarization of that economy reversed; and the people's control had to be established through state ownership.

Finally, it was essential to fight against "the ideological and cultural aggression of U.S. imperialism in Japan." Intensive propaganda was required to counteract the "anti-democratic and anti-people" schemes of the American–Japanese reactionaries. "Correct Marxism–Leninism" had to be popularized, and the insidious activities of the rightist social democrats and the anti-party revisionists had to be counteracted. A revolutionary democratic culture, based on the national and revolutionary traditions of Japan, had to be built.

Each of these six tasks focused directly or indirectly on "American imperialism," leaving no doubt as to the central target of the Japanese Communist Party. The "ten common needs" merely reiterated the themes set forth above, outlining in very specific form the policies needed to achieve short- and long-range party objectives.

Toward the end of the report, the Central Committee dealt with the critical problems of "anti-party revisionism" and the split in the international Communist movement.[18] First, the objectives of the Japanese "renegades" were outlined: the destruction of the Japanese Communist Party, the creation of an anti-Communist united front, and the espousal of so-called creative Marxism, doctrines involving "freedom for Japanese imperialism, anti-Marxist 'structural reform,' transition by peaceful means only, the peace movement solely for peaceful purposes, the beautification of American imperialism, the plural vanguard theory, and polycentrism in Marxism."[19]

The true character of the revisionists as "splittists and opportunists" had been revealed by the activities of men like Shiga Yoshio and Suzuki Ichizō. They had betrayed their party "by being subservient to a certain foreign power which has been attempting to disrupt the battle line of our party." Their Society of Comrades for the Voice of Japan was an attempt to compete with the JCP, but, despite its support from the foreign revisionist movement, it would fail. The sudden dismissal of Khruschev was a great blow to them, because "it ruined their subservience to the leadership of the CPSU, their worship for Khrushchev, and it rendered their theory incoherent."[20]

The excoriation of the antiparty revisionists led naturally into a discussion of the international Communist movement and its troubles.

---

[18] *Ibid.*, pp. 186–236.
[19] *Ibid.*, pp. 186–198.
[20] *Ibid.*, p. 192.

While the 9th Congress Report added little to earlier analyses by the JCP, the clarity and comprehensiveness of coverage warrant some attention on our part. Never were the critical issues as seen by the Japanese Communist Party Mainstream so succinctly and trenchantly set forth.

The basic cause of the present disunity, the report pointed out, lay in the trend toward modern revisionism and in the fact that a certain fraternal party had unilaterally violated the rules governing relations among Communist parties. The historic responsibility for the great split had to be borne by a few Communist leaders, particularly the leaders of the CPSU, who first openly attacked another fraternal party in violation of the principles enunciated in the Moscow Statement. Subsequent anti-Marxist actions by the CPSU, extending into state-to-state relations, exacerbated the conflict. These actions included breaking diplomatic relations with socialist Albania, unilaterally abrogating various agreements with socialist China, and adding the reactionary Indian government while it was engaged in a conflict with China. Another important cause of the cleavage was the partial nuclear test ban treaty, "an unprincipled concession to American imperialism."

What produced modern revisionism? The report stated: "The bourgeois elements which still linger in socialist states and the controlling bourgeois influence in advanced capitalist states are the internal sources of modern revisionism, while submission to pressure from the policy of war and aggression, centering on the nuclear threat of American imperialism, is the source externally, and modern revisionism is gradually developing its own theoretical system."[21]

The submission to pressure from imperialism was plainly manifest in the revisionist theories on war, peace, and imperialism, the report charged. The modern revisionists were advocating a theory of the total annihilation of mankind by nuclear war, claiming that Marxist–Leninist theories on war were obsolete as a result of nuclear missiles. This, in turn, led to a theory beautifying American imperialism and to the insistence that the mainstream of American imperialism had sincerely adopted a policy of peaceful coexistence in the face of the fundamental changes in the global balance of power and in the nature of war. Such concepts produced the opportunistic thesis that glorified peaceful coexistence between the two superpowers, America and Russia, and insisted that the protection of that relationship had become the primary duty of the people of the world. Thus, disarmament had become an affair of the big powers, and cooperation with imperialism in the devel-

---

[21] *Ibid.*, p. 220.

opment of backward nations was being openly advocated by the revisionists, as was the creation of a pro-imperialist peace movement, isolated from the anti-imperialist struggle.

According to the report, the modern revisionists were also intent on profoundly changing the Marxist doctrine of revolution. They were promoting a new economism, seeking to make the chief driving force of world revolution that of "communist construction" under a system of peaceful coexistence and subordinating the various peoples' revolutionary movements and national liberation struggles to it. The revisionists were advancing doctrines of structural reform, insisting that a transition to socialism was possible without the revolutionary overthrow of monopoly capitalism. They were willing to rely exclusively on parliamentarism and peaceful transition, ignoring the danger of suppression by the reactionary forces. These policies led to the belittlement of the armed struggle for liberation, reducing the struggle against colonialism to the achievement of political independence and economic development. Indeed, the revisionists even claimed that noncapitalist development and Socialist construction were possible under the leadership of the national bourgeoisie, if Socialist states gave assistance. Thus, they promoted right-wing united fronts that resulted in the subordination of the working class and the Communist Party to social democratic forces or the national bourgeoisie.

Finally, the report pointed out, modern revisionism had led to a major deviation from Marxist–Leninist thought with respect to the character and role of the Communist Party. The revisionists advocated a type of bourgeois liberalism that would dissolve democratic centralism, the guiding organizational principle of communism, and develop petty bourgeois debating societies. Under the revisionists' aegis, the leadership role of the Marxist–Leninist vanguard was being destroyed, and a plural vanguard was being created in its place, denoted as the "parties of the working class" or "socialist parties." This was a negation of the historic role of the only true Marxist–Leninist party as the sole vanguard party.

All of these revisionist doctrines were linked with a type of economism and a special theory of Socialist construction and "proletarian internationalism" fashioned to suit the big-power chauvinism of the Soviet Union. The Russian leaders, dominated by their own self-interests, were seeking to use all Marxist–Leninist parties as tools, forcing them into blind subservience.

The removal of Khrushchev was fortunate, the Central Committee believed. It had produced some change of atmosphere which might be helpful. And by revealing the bankruptcy of modern revisionism, it had strengthened genuine Marxism–Leninism and had caused increasing internal divisions in world revisionist circles. However, there was no reason for great optimism concerning the immediate eradication of the errors of the past. The mere criticism of Khrushchev by the new CPSU leaders did not mean that they had produced a definite course for the fundamental solution of various problems. As yet there was no indication of any basic changes in CPSU policy. Unless and until such changes took place, the struggle against modern revisionism would continue.[22] Furthermore, the proposal for an urgent international conference put forward by certain parties under the leadership of the CPSU had to be rejected. Such a conference would be an act of dangerous splittism that might well destroy all hope for the unity and solidarity of the international Communist movement. Until bilateral discussions could resolve some of the problems, the Communist parties of the world should avoid any showdown meetings.[23]

In the course of outlining the views expressed above, the JCP Central Committee reviewed briefly the history of its recent relations with the CPSU and the international movement in general. Most of the details have been set forth earlier. Two points are of special interest, however. In the 9th Congress Report, the JCP dated the deterioration of relations with the CPSU as beginning in October 1961, "when the CPSU headed by Khrushchev began to interfere in the internal affairs of the Japanese Communist party by demanding our party's uncritical, blind obedience to the CPSU." From that point on, conditions grew steadily worse, culminating in the disastrous Moscow conference of March 1964. According to the report, that conference failed because the CPSU showed absolutely no sincerity, preferring to slander and condemn the JCP. Shortly thereafter, in "an unprecedentedly vulgar action," the CPSU began to openly assist and encourage the Shiga group, which started its antiparty activities in mid-May.[24]

A second point of interest was the emphasis that the report placed on the Japanese Communist Party's contacts with other Asian Communist parties, especially the Communist Party of Indonesia (PKI). The report noted that joint JCP-PKI statements were issued on May 23, 1962, June 26, 1963, and September 7, 1964, in connection with various fraternal visits.[25] It might also have noted that many of the concepts

---

[22] *Ibid.*, pp. 232–234.
[23] *Ibid.*, pp. 228–229.
[24] *Ibid.*, pp. 217–218.
[25] *Ibid.*, pp. 208–209.

advanced by the JCP, particularly those relating to the party's attitude toward the Sino–Soviet dispute, had earlier been advanced by D. N. Aidit or other Indonesian Communist leaders. As suggested previously, the evidence is strong that in the midst of the Communist global crisis, significant regional cooperation among the Asian Communist parties had developed, with frequent exchanges of views and the development of some joint tactics and policies. Thus, Japanese Communist Party programs, while strongly influenced by the Chinese model at this point (as, indeed, were the programs of other Asian Communist parties), were also the product in part of collective decisions involving party leaders in Djakarta, Hanoi, and Pyongyang. Among these parties, moreover, the massive and seemingly successful Communist Party of Indonesia appeared to be the most influential with Japanese comrades during this period.

Presenting the 9th Congress Report of November 1964, Secretary General Miyamoto announced that the Japanese Communist Party had "more than 100,000 party members, nearly 200,000 *Akahata* daily subscribers, and 600,000 *Akahata* Sunday edition subscribers."[26] He further stated that the total volume of party publications had doubled since the 8th Party Congress of 1961, and that there had been a notable expansion in the membership of such front organizations as the Democratic Youth League, the New Japan Women's Society, the Japan Peace Commission, the Society To Protect Life and Health, and various international friendship associations.

Party leaders claimed to be particularly pleased with gains in local elections. A much larger number of Communist Party candidates had been run in recent elections, with sizable increases in total popular vote. In local elections, the 9th Congress Report claimed a 78 percent increase in the number of votes for JCP candidates, with the vote rising from 990,000 to 1,760,000, as the number of JCP candidates increased from 818 to 1,096. In the general elections, too, recent increases in the number of candidates and votes had occurred. The party noted a gain of 43 percent in votes in the most recent election, with the party obtaining 1,650,000 votes as compared with 1,150,000 in the 1960 elections.[27]

In stating its goals for the future, the Central Committee announced an intensive two-year party developmental program aimed at increasing party membership by one and one-half to two times the current strength and at effecting similar increases in the number of *Akahata* subscribers. To accomplish these gains, the party outlined four steps: the creation

[26] *Ibid.*, p. 243.
[27] *Ibid.*, p. 244.

of firm ideological and political foundations; the preservation of party traditions; an emphasis on organizational activities, and reform of the guidance work of the party.

As in the past, the party leaders called for efforts to acquire mass support by emphasizing day-to-day needs and by concentrating particularly on the worker-peasant masses and the intellectuals. "Instead of leaving problems of the labor union movement to the labor unions," proclaimed the 9th Congress Report, "all organs of the party must learn the real situation in this sector, develop their guidance in a meaningful fashion, take part in union activities, and make efforts to organize the toiling masses on a class basis." Party organizational activities in such basic industries as chemicals, transportation, and communications were signaled as being of special importance.

Similarly, the 9th Congress Report called for a major effort in rural Japan. If the basis for a national democratic united front were to be attained, it was essential to strengthen the party in the rural areas. A much larger number of farm and fishing village cells had to be established, taking advantage of the gap between rural and urban incomes and the unrest over encroachments on farm land. It was also important to emphasize cells in educational institutions among teachers and students. Intellectual party members, asserted the report, had a special meaning in a highly developed capitalist society like Japan. They could be pillars of strength in the anti-imperialist and antimonopoly movements.

The strongest emphasis of the 9th Congress Report, however, was on expanding and improving the cadre system.[28] In many respects, the report heralded *a turn toward organization.* Establishing its two-year goal as one cadre for every ten party members, the Central Committee announced that the selection, education, and placement of cadres were crucial tasks for the immediate future. Thus, a training school had been established, with three points being stressed in its program: party construction, the struggle of the masses, and united front operations. In this fashion, party cadres would be equipped to handle various assignments. Some would guide the party in its ideological and political development. Others would be placed in the mass movement, playing a critical role in front organizations, labor unions, peasant associations, and similar groups. Some would be fed into the political stream, running as Diet and prefectural assembly candidates, and serving in such offices when successful.

---

[28] *Ibid.,* pp. 290–293.

The party announced its intention to emphasize electoral activities, especially at the local and prefectural levels. Such activities, to be sure, would in no way interfere with various extraparliamentary commitments, nor would they bind the party to pursue solely parliamentary tactics. However, any increase in electoral activities would heighten the dangers of capitulation to "bourgeois parliamentarism," as had happened in the cases of Shiga and Suzuki. Hence, it was important to have well-trained cadres as candidates, men who were steeled against temptation.

Cadres were also important to the defense of party organization. According to the Central Committee, "the reactionaries" were seeking in every possible manner to destroy the party, with the government using one spy to each cell, tapping telephones, making secret recordings, taking pictures, and stealing documents. The party, therefore, had to have well-formulated security measures and trusted officials. Party meeting places had to be carefully examined beforehand to guard against hidden microphones and other devices. Members had to be scrutinized carefully, and it might even be necessary to search the bodies of members, including cadres, if there was any suspicion that spies had infiltrated a given cell or organization. Secret documents had to be guarded at all costs.

Naturally, the report did not mention more sinister methods of defense, such as the liquidation of traitors, or the development of armed "self-defense" units. The disastrous experience of the party with such units in the period of "ultra-leftist adventurism" had left permanent scars. There has been evidence, however, that reprisals against "party traitors" in Japan can take a variety of forms, including violent ones. In any case, the extensive emphasis on cadres and the new organizational activities again reflected the heavy influence of the Chinese Communists, who had pioneered in this field.

In essence, the 9th Congress reiterated the themes first enunciated by the 8th Congress in 1961, but foreshadowed as early as 1955, at the time of the 6th National Conference. The new Mainstream, led by Miyamoto and Hakamada, was gradually consolidating its position, depending upon a working coalition between so-called "neutral" and "pro-China" elements within the party. The party program itself reflected this fact, representing an attempt to balance certain conflicting pressures. The "left adventurist" policies of the 1950–1955 era had been sharply condemned, but in its basic program, the party still leaned to the "left." On the international front, it was clearly seeking a new image, one epitomized by the phrase "independence and autonomy."

Its most positive thrust in that direction had been the open break with the Soviet Union and the establishment of close liaison with other Asian Communist parties. At the same time, however, party tactics and policies were so strongly reflective of Chinese influence and the stance of the party was so one-sidedly anti-Soviet that the image of independence was impossible to achieve.[29]

On the domestic front also, a dilemma existed. The party was firmly committed to the tactic of united front politics, realizing the importance of augmenting the slender resources of the JCP with the substantial strength of Sōhyō and the Japan Socialist Party. Yet the strongly "left" orientation of the party and the high level of rigidity that characterized its attitudes on such crucial issues as peace and independence obstructed all efforts in that direction. Once again, as had happened so often in the past, the JCP felt forced to denounce in extreme terms all of the groups whom it wished to woo. And now, there was an added complication of major proportions, the Sino–Soviet split. That cleavage, as we shall note, gradually affected *all* elements of the Japanese left in a profound manner, thus making internal unity even more difficult.

Indeed, it is appropriate at this point to turn to relations between Sōhyō and the Socialists on the one hand, and the Japanese Communist Party on the other. As 1964 opened, relations between the Communists and Sōhyō were bad. As has already been suggested, moreover, a further deterioration took place in April, as a result of a bitter incident that occurred shortly after the ill-fated Moscow conference between the CPSU and the JCP. Sōhyō leaders had called for a half-day general strike by public employees on April 17 as a part of the spring offensive for higher wages. Unexpectedly, on April 8, the JCP announced its opposition to the strike, publicizing this fact in *Akahata*

---

[29] It is interesting to note, however, that at the 9th Party Congress, Yamaguchi Prefecture delegates sharply attacked Mainstream policies as being insufficiently militant and resolute, raising issues that identified them solidly with the Peking line. Party leaders had Oka Masayoshi and Okamoto Hiroyuki answer these charges with countercharges against the "anti-center" conduct of the Yamaguchi representatives and a staunch defense of the current party line.

In the election of the new Central Committee, moreover, while almost all members were reelected including those who had undertaken self-criticism in connection with the April 17th issue, the Miyamoto control was strengthened, with such Miyamoto supporters as Ueda Koichiro and Fuha Tetsuzō newly elected, and Oka, Okamoto, Nishizawa Tomio, and Yonehara Akira advanced in rank.

For a subsequent analysis of these and other developments, see Hirotsu Kyōsuke, "The Japanese Communist Party at a Turning Point," *Toki no Kadai* (*Topics of the Time*), August 1966, pp. 6–12.

the following day. Immediately, Communist Party trade union members, following party discipline, began to distribute handbills denouncing the strike. Some contained violent language, claiming that the strike had been "carefully plotted" by "splitters" and "Trotskyites" within Sōhyō.[30]

On April 11, Sōhyō issued a statement, in the name of Secretary General Iwai, attacking the Communist action as an attempt to split the labor movement. The statement urged the workers to disregard Communist instructions and to continue the wage struggle until the goals were attained. The strike, however, was finally postponed. Later, on May 13, Sōhyō officials held an emergency meeting and labeled the Communist Party action "an act of treachery" which had ignored the wishes of the workers, paving the way for government and "monopolistic capitalist" oppression on the one hand, and for external political interference with union administration on the other.[31]

Sōhyō did not confine its activities to words. In early July the powerful Railway Workers Union punished 148 workers (JCP members) for violating union discipline in connection with the April 17 strike. Thirty-one of these men were expelled.

At the time of its 26th National Convention, Sōhyō was preparing a massive assault on the Communists when an unexpected development occurred. On July 19, one day before the Sōhyō Convention opened, *Akahata* published a statement admitting that its position on the April 17 strike had been an error. Suddenly, the fault lay not with "splitters" and "Trotskyites" but with those who did not recognize the important role economic action should take in the struggle against American imperialism. In this fashion, the JCP leaders admitted that the basic reason for Communist opposition to the strike had stemmed from the fact that it lacked sufficient political content; more specifically, that it was not oriented around the anti-America campaign which had become the touchstone for all party activities.

Kasuga Shōichi, speaking to the Sōhyō Convention, reiterated these points. The Communist-dominated unions, moreover, withdrew the amendments they had prepared for the draft program and adopted a "low posture" attitude throughout the convention. JCP leaders had obviously realized that their April 8 decision threatened to lead to widespread expulsions of Communists from Sōhyō and a full-fledged campaign against the JCP. Unprepared for such a struggle and certain to lose heavily, the party decided to retreat in an effort to save its position.

---

[30] *Sōhyō News*, No. 232, May 25, 1964, p. 7.
[31] *Ibid.*, p. 8.

As a result of the Communist recantation, the 26th Sōhyō Convention was marked by relative calm. With only the most minimal opposition, Ōta was reelected Chairman for a seventh term, and Iwai reelected Secretary General for a tenth term. However, Sōhyō leaders were not mollified by the reversal of Communist policy. Supported by Kasuga's speech and the *Akahata* statement, they continued to attack the JCP. It was following an ultra-nationalist line, they charged, and forcing all movements and organizations to emphasize the struggle against American imperialism. It was attempting to subvert and subordinate trade unionism to its own political ends.

United front prospects were not enhanced by developments within the peace movement during this period. Clearly, the peace movement offered the best hope to the Communists in the long run, because it was precisely there that the Sōhyō–Socialist forces were prepared to go farthest in the direction of unity. Despite all the events of the past, for example, Sōhyō and the Socialist Party were willing to conduct a joint service on the morning of March 1 at the grave of Kuboyama Aiichi, the Japanese fisherman who had died as a result of radiation from the Bikini nuclear test. March 1 had been designated Bikini Day by the peace movement leaders to commemorate the anniversary of that event. The JCP, however, insisted that any memorial service must be conducted with Gensuikyō as the sponsoring organization. Since the Socialists no longer participated in Gensuikyō, this was unacceptable to them, and separate memorial services were held.

Meanwhile, preparations for a new Sōhyō–Socialist Party peace movement continued. In late March representatives of Hiroshima, Nagasaki, and Shizuoka prefectures (the three so-called victim prefectures) met to discuss basic principles and organizational plans for summer rallies. A public statement issued April 7 outlined policies and plans, and the Liaison Committee of the Three Atomic-Victim Prefectures met in Tōkyō April 24. Some 112 persons were present, representing 6 organizations and 36 prefectures.[32] Under the guidance of Sōhyō and the Socialist Party, the Liaison Committee decided to call the rallies by the jaw-breaking title "The Hiroshima and Nagasaki Rallies To Call for a Nuclear Ban, Relief of Atomic Victims, Nuclear Armament Prevention and Total Disarmament."

In connection with these activities, both Sōhyō and the Socialist Party issued statements outlining their views on the peace movement.[33]

---

[32] *Ibid.*, p. 5.
[33] For a lengthy Sōhyō statement and various related documents, see *ibid.*, No. 234, July 10, 1964, pp. 1–30.

They charged that Gensuikyō was now administered solely by the Communists, with a handful of officials—all under JCP control—running the organization. Although the Socialists stated that they favored the unity of "all progressive forces," they also pointed out that cooperation was impossible as long as the JCP continued to slander its opponents with "vile words," even while it called for unity. The wording of the JSP position left some room for doubt as to basic Socialist intent. To what extent was this wording a tactical device to shift the onus of disunity to the Communists? To what extent did it indicate a lack of fundamental opposition to united front activities—providing Communist tactics were altered?

The Socialists, to be sure, set forth certain policy differences between themselves and the Communists that seemed to preclude any meaningful united front. No peace movement was acceptable, they asserted, which took orders from a given political party. Nor could a "one-sided view" of the problems of nuclear weapons and disarmament be tolerated. "Positive neutrality" had to be the basis for the peace movement, and the Socialists could join forces only with those willing to uphold this principle. Thus, the main lines of division between Socialists and Communists had not changed at this point.

"Positive neutrality," however, did not keep the Sōhyō–Socialist Party group from seeking the support and participation of Soviet bloc representatives, and this was to become an increasingly vital element of Socialist policy. It will be recalled that since the summer of 1963 close contacts had been maintained between the Russians and those seeking to launch a new peace movement. Congratulatory messages had been exchanged, and various contacts initiated. During 1964 these ties continued to develop. As the split between the CPSU and the JCP widened and became an open issue, the Russians moved toward a new tactic in Japan: greater cooperation with as many of the anti-JCP elements of the Japanese "left" as possible, a tactic well attuned to Sōhyō–Socialist susceptibilities at that point.

In June 1964, the Chief of the Sōhyō Political Bureau, Yasutsune Ryōichi, who had just returned from a tour of the Soviet Union and Europe, reported that the Soviet Peace Committee and other Soviet bloc organizations were prepared to help the new peace movement. A few weeks later, an important Socialist Party delegation headed by Secretary General Narita Tomomi spent two weeks in Russia, between June 29 and July 14. During that time, intensive discussions concerning the Hiroshima-Nagasaki Antibomb Conference took place, and final preparations for Soviet participation were made.

The Russian leaders had settled on the following strategy: they and their allies would go to Japan prepared to participate in both the Gensuikyō Conference and the Hiroshima–Nagasaki Conference, posing as a force dedicated to the reunification of the Japanese peace movement. In reality, of course, the Russians must have known that the Chinese would not countenance such a maneuver, and that the Soviet Union was scarcely in the proper position to serve as mediator in this particular situation. The tactical line was a good one, however, since it put the blame for splitting the peace movement on the Chinese and their JCP allies.

The 10th World Conference sponsored by Gensuikyō opened first, being held in Tōkyō from July 30 to August 2.[34] Conference officials reported that some 200 foreign delegates were present, representing more than 50 countries and 9 international organizations. The Japanese Communist Party and its allies had accomplished some very effective publicity and propaganda work, claiming to have given out 1,250,000 peace badges and some 450,000 pamphlets. In addition, they had established many new Gensuikyō local branches in preparation for the conference. Once again, Communist organizational work was quite extraordinary.

The issue of Soviet participation was handled quickly and decisively. G. A. Zhukov and his delegation had arrived, announcing that by taking part in both peace conferences, the Russians hoped to aid in the reunification of the Japanese peace movement. The Gensuikyō directors responded by voting that "supporters of other peace movements" could not be elected to leading posts of the international session. Unable to tolerate this open rebuke, the Russians and all other pro-Soviet delegations withdrew from the Tōkyō conference, leaving it completely under the control of the CCP–JCP bloc. Zhukov, in a press interview, stated that Gensuikyō had steadily lost prestige and was now faced with a serious crisis. Gensuikyō spokesmen retorted that the Soviet delegation had done everything possible to disrupt the conference. Moreover, it was charged that the Soviets were 130,000 yen in arrears in their contributions to the 9th World Conference of the previous year, although they had paid 3,300,000 yen to the "right-wing social democratic sponsors of a schismatic meeting."[35]

---

[34] Communist coverage of the 10th World Conference is presented in *Peking Review*, No. 32, August 7, 1964, pp. 16–21. This includes Chou En-lai's message of greetings and portions of Liu Ning-i's speech of July 31. For Socialist Party coverage, see *Shakai Shimpō (Socialist News)*.

[35] *Peking Review*, No. 32, August 7, 1964, p. 19.

Thus, a Chinese–JCP coalition totally dominated the 10th World Conference. Both Mao and Chou had sent messages of congratulations prior to the opening of the sessions, emphasizing the heroic struggle of the Japanese people against American imperialism and the importance of maintaining the correct line against modern revisionism and all activities on the part of splittists.[36] Liu Ning-i, head of the Chinese delegation, in his speech of July 31, blasted the "completely erroneous line" of the World Council of Peace, asserting that this Soviet-bloc organization had been afraid to condemn the U.S. imperialist policies of war and aggression and had constantly praised and beautified American imperialism.[37] These and other familiar Chinese themes were woven into the appeal which was issued at the conclusion of the conference. That appeal noted that some people, "while paying lip service to 'a unified peace movement,' have acted erroneously by putting on a par the 10th World Conference, which inherits the historical traditions of the movement and upholds the 9th World Conference resolutions, and the schismatic meetings which negate the conference."[38] The appeal further stated: "They [the modern revisionists] try to impose their preconceived political line on others so as to retard the movement and reduce it into one completely harmless to imperialism and colonialism. It is of paramount importance to crush these intrigues."[39]

The specific policies spelled out in the appeal were identical with earlier positions. There were demands to end American "aggression" in Indochina, ban Polaris submarines from Japan, establish a denuclearized zone in the Asian–Pacific area, prevent the militarization of Japan, dismantle missile bases on Okinawa, oppose reactionary Japanese constitutional revision, halt the talks between Japan and the Republic of Korea, and restore diplomatic relations between Japan and China. The key theme was that American policies constituted the gravest threat to world peace and represented the source of another world war.

A few days later, on August 3, the Hiroshima-Nagasaki Conference opened its first session.[40] The broad principles governing the conference had previously been approved by the Liaison Committee on June 23, when a keynote report by Moritaki Ichirō had been adopted. Moritaki's report asserted that the new peace movement was to rest on humanism, would not be "influenced by any particular country's in-

---

[36] *Ibid.*, p. 19.
[37] *Ibid.*, pp. 20–21.
[38] For the appeal, see *ibid.*, pp. 19–20.
[39] *Ibid.*, p. 20.
[40] For details, see *Sōhyō News*, No. 236, October 10, 1964, pp. 4–8.

terest or narrow-minded factional maneouvering," but would be based on a truly "non-partisan and impartial spirit." While openly attacking the JCP for an impatient, factional, nationalist approach that had caused it to force the Chinese position on everyone, the Moritaki report used strongly militant language of its own in attacking American policies, reflecting both the leftist traditions and the present trends within the Japanese Socialist Party.

The Moritaki report did assert that the new movement would not regard any particular nation or government "as our predetermined enemy or friend. Therefore, we do not discriminate against any nation or government; instead, based upon the right of the individual to live, we will do whatever little we can in pushing the movement forward, if it will serve for the banning of A and H bombs, and we will oppose any threat, however small, if it means expansion of the danger from A and H bombs."[41] This was a statement giving voice to the "positive neutrality" which the Socialists insisted was the heart of their foreign policy creed. The issue, of course, was what did such "neutrality" mean when translated into specific policies and actions?

The Hiroshima International Conference, sponsored by the Socialists, was attended by 108 delegates, supposedly representing 45 countries of Asia, Africa, and Europe, and 11 international organizations. A pro-Soviet complexion was clearly discernible within the foreign contingent. An additional 96 Japanese delegates attended this international session. Attacks on the 10th Gensuikyō World Conference were featured, with such pro-Soviet delegations as those from Mongolia, Czechoslovakia, and Bulgaria, as well as the Soviet Union itself, taking part. At times, it appeared that the Sino–Soviet dispute had been transferred into the center of the Japanese left-wing movement, with the Russians suddenly developing new allies and a new platform from which to operate.

In certain respects, as has been suggested, the resolutions of the two rival conferences in 1964 paralleled each other closely. The Hiroshima International Conference fiercely denounced "the aggressive interference of the U.S. imperialists" in Vietnam and Laos, as well as their "provocative actions" in Cuba and in other newly independent countries. It was also asserted that the struggle for peace and against nuclear weapons was indissolubly linked with the struggle for national independence. The people of the world would never yield to armed intervention for the purpose of suppressing the struggle for national

---

[41] For the Moritaki report, see *ibid.*, No. 234, July 10, 1964, pp. 6–25.

independence, nor to threats of the possible use of nuclear weapons.

Specific resolutions were passed urging relief for A and H bomb victims, protesting the sanctions being applied to Cuba, supporting total disarmament, and opposing Polaris submarine bases in Japan, the Mutual Security Treaty, American retention of Okinawa, and the nuclearization of Japan. In all of these respects, there was no discernible difference between the Tōkyō and Hiroshima resolutions except for the more severe language used on occasion by the Peking-oriented group.

At Hiroshima, however, unanimous support was given to the Moscow Treaty, with the hope that an immediate ban on underground tests could be obtained. Opposition was stated to the transmission of nuclear weapons by any nuclear power to any other country, and to the preparations for nuclear armament by any country. The Hiroshima resolutions, moreover, omitted any broadside attack on American imperialism as the "foremost enemy of world peace, the primary target of all peace-loving peoples," as in the case of the Gensuikyō resolution. Its attacks on the United States, while trenchant, were confined to specific actions such as Vietnam, Laos, and Cuba. There were other differences, some of them subtle—such as the strong oppsition expressed in Hiroshima to the continuance of French nuclear tests and the praise extended to the six nonaligned Afro–Asian countries for their efforts to mediate the Sino–Indian dispute. But the differences as well as the similarities suggested that the Socialist-sponsored conference had taken on a distinct Soviet hue in terms of policy, in contradistinction to the Peking orientation of the Gensuikyō Conference. Were there going to be *two* united fronts within the Japanese left-wing movement, both strongly interacting with a foreign force?

On the final day of the Hiroshima sessions, August 7, the purely Japanese Conference opened. With some 30,000 Japanese participating, this conference passed the "Hiroshima Appeal," which took precisely the same line as the International Conference resolutions, including a paragraph praising the Moscow Treaty as having "given us a bright perspective for our future movement, [and] as a step forward toward total disarmament through the complete stoppage of nuclear testing."[42]

In the months that followed, the new peace movement continued to function, and a Working Committee to push its work forward was established. On September 23, the anniversary of the death of Kuboyama, the committee met in Yaizu City, Shizuoka, his home, and agreed on the future course of the movement.[43] The Gensuikyō Conference

---

[42] *Ibid.*, No. 236, p. 6.
[43] *Ibid.*, No. 237, October 25, 1964, pp. 4–7.

was criticized as an attempt to substitute an anti-America movement for an anti-A and H bomb movement. Under the direct orders of "a certain political party," the anti-America movement opposed American nuclear tests only, thus forsaking Japan's "traditional stand on behalf of peace." The ten resolutions passed at the time, however, included the standard positions, which in sum opposed all aspects of American–Japanese military cooperation and most elements of American policy in Asia. It was also agreed to send delegations to two international conferences: the Conference for International Cooperation and Disarmament in Sydney and the World Conference for Peace and International Cooperation in New Delhi.

When China exploded an atomic device on October 16, Iwai of Sōhyō, along with other leaders of the Hiroshima movement, issued a statement deploring the test, asserting "We are of the opinion that nuclear tests by one country will lead to an endless nuclear testing competition in the world. . . . Will this test not encourage the Japanese and West German militarists?"[44] In some respects, nevertheless, the Iwai statement was exceptionally mild: "We are not indifferent to the fact that China has to develop nuclear weapons to 'defend its country in the course of seeking to contain U.S. imperialist policies toward China.' But it is impossible for us to understand that such a situation constitutes ample justification for China's testing."

While criticizing Peking in cautious language, Sōhyō and the Socialist Party continued to fight on the opposite front with much greater vigor. On the eve of the arrival of a U.S. nuclear-powered submarine in Sasebo on November 12, Sōhyō ordered all unions to hold stop-work meetings, with its statement declaring in part: "Uniting with all forces within and outside the trade union movement, we will do everything we can to crush the reactionary policies of the Cabinet, and prevent submarines from entering our ports."[45] It continued by asserting, "We will persist in fighting against the war policy of the governments of the U.S.A. and Japan by any possible means including a general strike to be organized on the basis of a broad national protest movement." Such statements were much more militant in vocabulary and content than those directed at China a month earlier.

The trends with respect to united front activities and the peace movement which had taken shape by 1964 were continued during the following year. Sōhyō and the Japan Socialist Party continued to take an increasingly anti-American position on almost every critical issue

---

[44] *Ibid.,* No. 238, November 10, 1964, p. 1.
[45] *Ibid.,* No. 239, November 25, 1964, p. 1.

and also to pursue a close relationship with the Soviet Union. Even more complex divisions were beginning to evidence themselves in leftist circles, however, reflective of the Sino–Soviet split, as we shall soon note. Meanwhile, certain limited "united front" activities were initiated with the Japanese Communist Party for the first time since 1960, although actions were cautious and there were indications of a deep division of opinion concerning this tactic within Socialist ranks.

The sequence of events that affected the Sōhyō and Socialist Party political positions deserves analysis. On April 10, 1964, prior to the 1964 peace conferences, a Soviet All-Union Central Council of Trade Unions delegation arrived in Japan at the invitation of Sōhyō. Ten days later, both parties signed a joint declaration indicating friendship and a wide range of agreement. The Soviet delegates pledged full support for "the militant actions of Japanese workers in the defense of their vital rights and interests, for the improvement of their economic living conditions, against the scattering of nuclear weapons, for the stoppage of all nuclear tests and universal and complete disarmament, for the withdrawal of American military bases in Japanese territory and for world peace."[46]

Sōhyō participants responded with the assertion that "Japanese workers and trade unions express the greatest praise to the Soviet people for their great success in constructing a Communist society and note with gratitude the powerful support of the U.S.S.R. for the victory of the suppressed peoples in their movements for national freedom and for the struggles on behalf of social progress and world peace."

It should be noted, of course, that some Sōhyō officials had long been anxious to balance such activities with international Communist forces by establishing additional ties with the American labor movement. From the beginning of the Kennedy administration, various Sōhyō officials had made it clear that they would welcome an expansion of contacts. Only in this fashion could the image—and possible meaning—of "positive neutrality" be enhanced. Some contacts between Sōhyō and the AFL–CIO were developed, but these were generally at a low- and middle-echelon level or on an informal basis. Serious political ideological problems blocked a meeting between top officials of the two movements, particularly since American ties were primarily with the Japanese moderate unions outside Sōhyō. Nevertheless, when an American labor group headed by George Meany, AFL President, visited Japan to attend the inauguration of the new moderate federa-

---

[46] *Ibid.*, No. 231, May 10, 1964, pp. 1–3.

tion, Dōmei Kaigi (Japanese Confederation of Labor), a meeting of top officials was arranged. On November 14, 1964, Chairman Ōta, Secretary General Iwai, and a delegation of Sōhyō officials called on Meany and his colleagues at their quarters in the Imperial Hotel.

Sōhyō treatment of this meeting in their own journals was guarded but mild, and an attempt was made to convey a note of hope. Jay Lovestone, director of AFL–CIO international affairs, was quoted as having said that the meetings had been "quite instructive," and the official Sōhyō position was that "an exchange of views" should be continued.[47] Sōhyō also took a moderate approach publicly toward the new All-Japan Federation of Labor, expressing the hope for ultimate labor unity in Japan. The desire for some political balance—both internationally and domestically—was clearly present, provided it could be accomplished without paying any substantial political price. But politics within Sōhyō and within Japan, together with international trends, continued to keep both Sōhyō and the Japanese Socialist Party moving to the "left."

The Sōhyō position was beautifully outlined in an exchange of letters with Lovestone that followed the November meeting. On January 6, 1965, Lovestone had addressed a letter to Iwai raising a number of "questions which puzzle many American trade unionists."[48] Most of the questions had to do with Sōhyō's attitude toward communism both at home and abroad. The joint declaration with the Soviet unionists was described as a "pro-Communist resolution which was strictly in the service of Soviet imperialism." It was asserted that Sōhyō had moved away from the International Confederation of Free Trade Unions (ICFTU) and very close to the Communist-led World Federation of Trade Unions (WFTU). "In reality," asserted Lovestone, "there is no ideological or political neutrality on your part towards the WFTU. You have been supporting actively the basic positions of the WFTU in regard to the international situation. In doing so, you are not 'promoting world peace,' but in effect, aiding and abetting the Communist drive for world domination."[49]

Lovestone also charged that Sōhyō had shown a "consistently unfriendly attitude" at the top leadership levels toward the United States, and that this attitude was "in striking contrast to your consistent friendship for the dictatorship countries, particularly the totalitarian Soviet regime." Lovestone ended with a strong defense of U.S.–Japan

---

[47] *Ibid.*, No. 239, November 25, 1964, p. 2.
[48] *Ibid.*, No. 243, February 25, 1965, pp. 3–8.
[49] *Ibid.*, p. 5.

treaty relations, and an invitation to Iwai to visit the United States again, together with Ōta.

Lovestone was answered first by Suzuki Seiichi, Assistant Director of the International Bureau; subsequently, a letter was sent to Meany by Ōta. The former letter was dated March 1, 1965; the latter, April 3.[50] Suzuki challenged Lovestone on matters of both fact and interpretation. The most important themes in the Suzuki letter can be summarized as follows: to expel Communists from Sōhyō would be undemocratic and would help to revive fascism, a menace now rising in Japan. Sōhyō's praise of Soviet socialism was merely an acknowledgment of Soviet accomplishments and an attempt to emphasize the good points of Russia: "As the same human beings living on this planet, there is nothing to gain from leveling criticism at other countries regarding the way of life of their own choosing." A rebuttal to Lovestone's defense of American policy in Japan centered mainly on Okinawa. "To Communist China," insisted Suzuki, "Okinawa is what the missile base in Cuba meant to the United States."

The Ōta letter was a more elaborate defense of the Sōhyō line. It did not contain any startlingly new themes. Ōta insisted that a union could not make a particular philosophy or belief a qualification for membership.[51] Nevertheless, he asserted, "Sōhyō is today fighting against the Communist Party of Japan, in the first place because, as Secretary General Iwai has rightly pointed out, they are attempting to place the activities of our union under the control of their political party. As has been previously stated in the materials we presented to your delegation when they visited Japan, the history of the foundation of Sōhyō is closely connected with the fight against the domination of the Japanese trade unions by the Communist Party."[52] Ōta then recounted the April 17 Incident of the previous year.

The Sōhyō president's defense of the Soviet–Japanese joint commu-

---

[50] The Suzuki letter is carried in *ibid.*, pp. 8–12; the Ōta letter in *ibid.*, No. 246, April 10, 1965, pp. 1–12.

[51] Said Ōta, "A trade union is not a political party, we feel, and we consequently allow any workingman to join our union to consolidate the unity of the working class. The Japanese trade unions exist on the basis of the guarantees of the fundamental human rights by the Japanese Constitution, and therefore we cannot discriminate against certain workingmen for their personal beliefs or for their economic, political, or social relations. In addition, we cannot violate the freedom of thought and conscience of trade union members, and their freedom of religion must be guaranteed. We believe that this is the case in all free and democratic countries." *Ibid.*, pp. 5–6.

[52] *Ibid.*, p. 6.

niqué reveals much about Sōhyō theoretical perspectives and international views:

Mr. Lovestone criticized us for adopting this resolution which he says serves Soviet imperialism, and for hailing and encouraging the great success of Soviet dictatorship, etc.

Our feeling is, however, along with that of most of the Japanese working class, that in a country such as Japan, which suffers from a poverty of natural resources, a Socialist system offers the best possibilities for enrichment of the working man's life. Even though the positions and policies may be different, the objective of Dōmei and Chūritsu Rōren parallel ours on this point. Regardless of the historical development in the past, I believe we can say, at least, that there does not exist in the Soviet Union today the capitalist exploitation which exists or has existed in other countries, and that the Soviet Union is making progress in achieving for their workingmen peace, happiness and freedom. It is these efforts of the Soviet workingman that we praise, and it is in this sense that we wish to achieve, although through more democratic methods, the same benefits of an improved living standard, the advance of peace and freedom, and a greater political voice for the workingman.

The meaning of the statement that both organizations had "the same opinions" on the international trade union movement is that both organizations feel that working people in every country should broaden their contacts with each other in order to secure a peaceful world and a high standard of living for everyone.

With regard to the emancipation from the tyranny of the Tsar of Russia through revolution, the Soviet people declare that under the conditions prevailing at the time, it was the only way possible. Present-day Japan of course is not under the despotism of a Tsar, and further we have a Constitution which guarantees peace and democracy. We believe, therefore, that we will be able to realize the transition to socialism in Japan through peaceful and democratic means with the assistance of a majority of the Japanese people, and we intend to realize it in this manner.[53]

Ōta denied having always supported the position of the Soviet Union, citing the Hungarian Revolution as an example. He quickly added that Sōhyō had protested to the British government when Suez was attacked, and now it was protesting to the United States because the Vietnam War threatened to escalate into another world war. It may be unavoidable, asserted Ōta, for trade unions under capitalism to pursue their own national interests, but a strong effort should

---

[53] *Ibid.*, pp. 7–8.

be made to overcome such narrow nationalistic thinking, so as to secure world peace and better living conditions for the workingmen.[54]

According to Ōta, Sōhyō's neutral position with respect to the international labor federations stemmed from the ICFTU resolution of
July 1951, which supported the speedy conclusion of a unilateral peace
treaty with Japan (one excluding the Communist bloc countries that
were refusing to accept the terms set forth).

Ōta vigorously attacked the American military bases in Japan as being
primarily for the national interests of the United States and not related to the needs or desires of the Japanese people. He ended with a
curious theme, one that paralleled the type of approach frequently used
by the Communists in overtures to the "proletariat" of "capitalist"
countries:

We are strongly opposed to war, and the problem therefore that bothers us
most is that the policies pursued by the American Government in Asia do
not benefit the Asian people. However, we clearly distinguish between our
opposition to the policies of the American Government and our friendship
for the AFL-CIO. We know that the AFL-CIO is also in opposition to war.
We do not think that you and your Government completely agree with each
other in this respect. For this reason, since our fight against the Security
Treaty we have desired to exchange views with the trade union members of
your country.[55]

Under the circumstances, Ōta's final sentence, "We hope our relations will be promoted through these exchanges," almost had the ring
of the "Greetings to fraternal comrades" that concluded some of the
Sino–Soviet polemical exchanges.

Prior to the Suzuki and Ōta letters, the United States had commenced the bombing of North Vietnam, in retaliation for increased
Viet Cong terrorism and stepped-up northern involvement in the south.
Immediately, Ōta had dispatched the following cable to the Hanoi
trade union federation, which had earlier feted Sōhyō delegates:

VIETNAM FEDERATION OF TRADE UNIONS HANOI SOHYO
CANNOT BUT FEEL UNBEARABLE ANGER OVER BOMBING RAIDS

---

[54] *Ibid.*, p. 9. Ōta's position on the Russian unions was somewhat different.
He quoted selected passages from the International Labor Organization (ILO)
Report of 1960 to the effect that the Soviet trade union situation could
only be understood if the differences between the conditions of private capitalism
and those of the Soviet State were considered. When the means of production
were the property of the people, then the position of the workers changed
radically, he stated. *Ibid.*, p. 8.

[55] *Ibid.*, p. 12.

THAT HAVE RECENTLY BEEN COMMITTED ON YOUR HONORABLE
COUNTRY BY U.S. RECKLESS FORCES STOP WE EXPRESS OUR
RESOLVE TO FIGHT ON SIDE OF COURAGEOUS PEOPLE OF
VIETNAM IN THEIR RIGHTEOUS STRUGGLE FOR VIETNAM'S
COMPLETE NATIONAL INDEPENDENCE AND FOR PEACE IN ASIA
AND WORLD
        OTA PRESIDENT SOHYO[56]

Even before the escalation of the Vietnam War, however, Sōhyō
and the Japan Socialist Party had taken the first steps toward recon-
structing a united front on an issue-by-issue basis. On February 1,
1965, the Socialist–Sōhyō Committee against U.S. Nuclear Submarine
Visits agreed with its Communist counterpart to establish a "liaison
conference" so as to coordinate actions. The JCP was overjoyed and
proclaimed this step "a valuable advance toward the development of
united action on the part of the Japanese people."[57]

"Unified action is possible," proclaimed the *Akahata* editorial, "if
we work strenuously on the basis of both principles and moderation."
Once again, the JCP was pursuing a soft line—without abandoning
"principles," of course. The immediate issues on which a united front
could be built were the U.S. nuclear submarine visits, the Japan–Korea
treaty, and the Vietnam War. By developing and refining united front
tactics on these issues, the stage could be set for the critical struggle
that lay ahead: the 1970 struggle against continuance of the U.S.–Japan
Mutual Security Treaty. Increasingly, the Japanese Communist organs
talked about the urgent necessity for rebuilding the anti-Ampo movement in an even stronger form.

At the JCP Central Committee Plenum of March 23–24, 1965, the
united front issue was prominent in the discussions: "Although the
Socialists have many ambiguities and a lack of thoroughness in their
political line, we must emphasize the identities that exist in terms of
immediate, concrete objectives and strive to realize a unified, democratic strength."[58]

---

[56] *Ibid.*, No. 243, February 25, 1965, p. 1.

[57] *Akahata,* February 3, 1965, editorial, p. 1.

[58] *Ibid.,* March 26, 1965, p. 1. This Plenum was devoted primarily to
establishing the party line for the House of Councillors elections. The
Plenum resolution proclaimed that the major differences "between the Japanese people and the Japanese and American reactionaries" were to be found
in five points: first, the attitude toward American imperialism—whether one
would fight in determined fashion against war and aggression ("the reactionary
suppression and exploitation" of American imperialism) or follow it; second,
whether the American and Japanese "monopolists" would be allowed to in-

Just three weeks earlier, at the Sōhyō 27th Special Convention, a resolution pertaining to foreign policies had been passed which once again objected violently to American and Japanese government policies in Asia: the entry of nuclear-powered American submarines into Sasebo Port could lead to the "nuclearization" of Japan. Already Japan was being used as a major base for the Vietnam War: "We strongly oppose the policy of the Sato Government which sides with the aggressive actions of America in Vietnam. Needless to say, the only key for a fundamental solution of disputes in Indochina is an approval of the Vietnamese people's right to self-determination and an immediate withdrawal of foreign troops from Vietnam."[59]

The treaty with Korea, according to the resolution, was in response to American pressures and had as its aim the creation of a Northeast Asian Treaty Organization. The willingness of "Japanese monopoly capitalists" to prop up the Pak government violated the ardent wishes of the Korean people who wanted "the peaceful unification of their "motherland."

The resolution ended by calling on the workers to "rise up in unity to prevent the call of U.S. nuclear submarines, to smash the Japan-

---

tensify the economic difficulties of the people or whether the people would win livelihood improvements and "an independent, peaceful development"; third, whether the betraying, reactionary policies of the Liberal Democratic Party government would be continued or whether the independence, peace, and neutrality of Japan would be won; fourth, whether the Constitution would be undermined and reactionary policies strengthened, with the resurrection of militarism and imperialism, or whether democracy and popular rights would be safeguarded; finally, whether the Liberal Democratic government would be maintained or whether it would be replaced by a "democratic, coalition government" pledged to fight against any deterioration of the Constitution and against the Mutual Security Treaty.

The JCP attitude toward the other parties as revealed in this Plenum resolution was as follows: The Democratic Socialist Party talked of opposition to Liberal Democratic policies, but in practice they approved of the Japan–Korea talks, were hostile to China, and thus openly supported the American and Japanese reactionary group's policies of war and aggression. The Komeitō stood "in a most contradictory position" with respect to policies and action. They opposed Constitutional change and the berthing of U.S. nuclear submarines, and favored the restoration of Japan–China relations. But they approved of the Mutual Security Treaty, the Self-Defense Corps, and a Japan–Korean Treaty, "thereby collaborating with U.S. and Japanese ruling groups." Furthermore, even when their policies coincided with those of the JCP, they refused to join the popular struggle, "thereby helping the position of the Liberal Democratic Party." The Socialist Party must be considered "an important political force" for united action despite its weaknesses. *Ibid.*, p. 1.

[59] "Resolution for Defense of Peace, Independence, Democracy of Japan in the Tense National and International Situation" (dated March 4, 1965), *Sōhyō News*, No. 244, March 10, 1965, p. 9.

South Korea talks, to take Okinawa back to our administration, to stop the adverse revision of the Constitution and to entirely abrogate the Security Treaty with the U.S.A."[60]

Three months later, a one-day united front protest was finally conducted, with Ōta and other Socialist leaders speaking from the same platform as JCP representatives. The rallies, billed as a Day of Nationwide Protest Action against U.S. Aggression in Vietnam, were held on June 9. The pledge was made to collect forty million signatures against the Vietnam War, and some 30,000 marchers paraded before the U.S. Embassy until late in the evening.

On the surface at least, trends should have been very encouraging to the Communists. Could not the progression from a liaison conference to a one-day united front operation be continued and developed into a full-fledged, permanent organization? A major article in *Akahata* on June 22 indicated that the Communists were far from satisfied with developments up to date.[61] The main thrust of this article, as we shall note later, was an attack on the CPSU. In the course of the argument, however, the anonymous authors made the following points. Japan stood at the crossroads between two routes. One led to subservience under American imperialism and the revival of Japanese militarism, a route that would destroy the people. The other was the route of "independence, democracy, peace, neutralism, and the improvement of livelihood."

The struggle that lay ahead urgently demanded the unity of all "democratic people." Such issues as Vietnam, the Japan–Korea Treaty, the recession, reactionary amendments to the Constitution, and the resurrection of militarism could only be met through a united front approach. Thus far, united front activities had been far from satisfactory, and a thoroughly integrated national-level operation such as the joint struggle organization that conducted the campaign against the Mutual Security Treaty had not materialized. The *Akahata* writers blamed the problem essentially on the Soviet Union, particularly on Soviet interference in the Japanese peace movement, actions abetting and intensifying splits among Japanese "progressives."

What were the current trends in the peace movement? On February 1, 1965, the Sōhyō–Socialist group had finally inaugurated the Japan Congress Against A and H bombs (Gensuikin) in Tōkyō. Moritaki

[60] *Ibid.*, p. 10.
[61] "On the Intervention and the Subversive Activities of the CPSU Leadership and Organization in the Democratic Movement of Our Nation and People," *Akahata*, June 22, 1965, p. 1 (reprinted in *Zenei*, August 1965, pp. 15–31).

Ichirō, one of the leading sponsors of the new organization, keynoted the criticism of the old Gensuikyō: "The confusion in the movement against A and H bombs started when we forgot our original intention, and the movement was divided."[62] Sōhyō authorities spelled out the implications of this statement: Gensuikyō had become the tool of a particular political party in advancing its political activities. Democratic forces had been trying hard for more than three years to correct the mistakes of Gensuikyō, but to no avail. Now political organizations, youth groups, labor unions, and religious organizations, together with some 247 delegates from local organizations, had formed a new group "to end the confused situation." It was announced that greetings had been received from the World Council of Peace, the U.S. National Committee for a Sane Nuclear Policy, and the Soviet Committee for Defending Peace.

The Gensuikin program centered on opposition to "the manufacture, stockpiling, testing, use, and expansion of nuclear weapons by any of the countries of the world." The new organization pledged itself to strive for a complete ban on all such weapons, and took the position that complete disarmament was possible under the principle of peaceful coexistence among states having different social systems. "Therefore, our movement will never be partial to any particular countries or blocs, but will cooperate widely with the friends of peace the world over.[63]

The final paragraph of the Gensuikin Manifesto is particularly interesting: "In connection with the relations between this movement and other movements, if there are points in common, close cooperation must be sought among them from the standpoint of a firm opposition to atomic and hydrogen bombs and for complete disarmament. Joint actions are organized in full respect for the opinions of participating organizations so that they act on the basis of mutual agreement."[64]

Clearly, the Sōhyō–Socialist group had not ruled out united front "peace" activities with the Communists. On the other hand, fairly detailed rules for any new game were likely to be imposed, rules designed to protect Socialist positions. Socialist leaders, moreover, were not taking an identical position on the issue of the united front. Sasaki Kōzō, Chairman of the Socialist Party and leader of the Mainstream faction, asserted in late June that the Socialist Party was willing to consider a

---

[62] For details of the inaugural meeting, see *Sōhyō News,* No. 242, February 10, 1965, pp. 5–8.

[63] *Ibid.,* p. 7.

[64] *Ibid.,* p. 8.

joint struggle with all "democratic forces," including the Japanese Communist Party, to block ratification of the Japan–Korea Treaty. However, Eda Saburō, Chief of the Socialist Organization Bureau and Sasaki's rival, had expressed reservations about any official tie with the JCP, and that was also the view of Wada Hiroo, Vice-Chairman of the party.

Indeed, the strong swing to the "left" on the part of Sōhyō and Socialist Party leaders was now beginning to evoke a reaction from moderate elements. Within the Socialist Party, the Eda, Wada, and Kawakami factions of the party were applying pressure on various issues, not only against any united front that would include the Communists, but also for a return to "positive neutralism," and an abandonment of strongly "pro-Soviet" or "pro-Chinese" stances. At this point, the moderate voice was a minority one, however, and the leftward swing continued under the guidance of leaders like Sasaki.

Even the left was cautious about united action with the Communists, especially the Sōhyō leaders. Ōta had insisted that any joint struggle should be carried out only after a consensus had been reached among the Socialist Party, Sōhyō, and the neutral labor federation, Chūritsu Rōren (Federation of Independent Unions). Iwai had asserted that while a united front was needed, the JCP still had to atone for its actions in connection with the April 17 Incident of 1964.

Thus, in a press interview of July 2, 1965, Miyamoto, Secretary General of the JCP, expressed the same type of concern that had earlier been set forth in *Akahata*.[65] The Sasaki position was essentially a positive one, he asserted, but there was some doubt as to whether it would be effected by the Socialist Party and Sōhyō, given the internal opposition. One-day joint struggles like that of June 9 were fine as far as they went, but there was a major need for the resumption of a joint struggle organization of the anti-Ampo type. Indeed, the Socialist Party leaders had promised this to the Japanese masses, and they should fulfill their pledge. Developments were still moving too slowly to please JCP leaders, although they were pleased by the position of Sasaki himself.

The rival peace conferences of July–August 1965 did not advance the cause of a Socialist–Communist united front. The Gensuikyō 11th World Congress opened in Tōkyō on July 27.[66] Some 171 foreign dele-

---

[65] For the press interview, see *Zenei*, September 1965.

[66] For a Communist version of the 11th Gensuikyō World Congress, see Yonehara Akira, "Let Us Widely Propagate the Significance of Victory in the 11th Gensuikyō World Conference," first published in *Akahata*, August

gates, supposedly representing 50 nations and 9 international organizations, were present. At the meeting on August 2 in Tōkyō, some 30,000 to 45,000 Japanese were present, and at the Hiroshima meeting on August 5, 14,000 were reportedly involved, with 18,000 in attendance at Nagasaki on August 8. No Soviet representatives attended these meetings. This time, the JCP and its cohorts were armed against Soviet bloc tactics. The Russian-dominated World Council of Peace and the Soviet Peace Committee had continued to play on the theme of unity for the Japanese peace movement, making positive statements about both the Gensuikin and the Gensuikyō movements, although expressing concern for the "errors" of the latter. These two organizations were invited by Gensuikyō authorities to the 11th World Conference *on the proviso* that they not attend any other Japanese peace conference, and that they agree to support the 10th World Congress resolutions. There ensued a long silence from the Russians, and no delegates were sent— a situation duplicated by the Soviet bloc countries.[67]

Thus, there were no problems. The resolutions adopted followed the Peking line completely: the primary emphasis was on the supreme danger of American imperialism and the need for a resolute struggle for peace; support for nuclear testing by China; an attack on modern revisionism; unmeasured criticism of American policies in Asia, the Japan–Korea Treaty, and Japanese governmental policies. The Japanese Communist Party sent sixteen official delegates headed by Yonehara Akira, and they played a major role. The Chinese delegation numbered

---

21, 1965 (reprinted in *Zenei*, October 1965). Said Yonehara, "In spite of the fact that the Satō government refused permission for the [North] Vietnam and [North] Korean representatives to enter Japan and despite the maneuvers of the international splittists," the number of foreign delegates was unprecedented and more than 70,000 Japanese took part. The conference, asserted Yonehara, focused on three great objectives: the prevention of nuclear war, the complete prohibition of nuclear weapons, and relief to nuclear bomb sufferers. It sought to fulfill these objectives by emphasizing the struggle against the American imperialists' campaign of war and agression. "One more important factor was that this conference successfully crushed the machinations of the internal and external splittist forces who were seeking to destroy it, lifting high the traditional flag of Gensuikyō which had always opposed splittism and fought to preserve solidarity."

[67] Said Yonehara, "The Secretariat of the World Council of Peace and the Soviet Peace Committee have been promoting the splittists in the movement and sending ambiguous messages that seem to support our conference as well as the splittist conference, still hoping for unity and solidarity. Our conference this time unanimously rejected this message. Thus, the wide body of participants realized the conspiracy in which the internal and external splittists had been engaged since the 8th World Congress and resolved to isolate the splittists from the peoples of the world, strengthening our solidarity." *Ibid.*

twenty-three and was led by Liu Ning-i, whose major speech stressed the absolute necessity of struggling to the end against American imperialism and fighting at the same time against "splittism" and the modern revisionist errors.

Almost simultaneously with the Gensuikyō Conference, Gensuikin launched its "World Conference Against A and H Bombs Held in Commemoration of the Twentieth Anniversary of the Hiroshima–Nagasaki Bombings."[68] Delegates selected from local organizations met in Hiroshima on August 6 and in Nagasaki on August 9, with the sponsors claiming attendances of more than 10,000. The International Conference was held in Tōkyō, August 11–13. A fifty-man Japanese delegation was matched by thirty-four overseas delegates representing eleven countries and two international organizations. Six of the eleven countries were Bulgaria, Czechoslovakia, Hungary, Yugoslavia, Mongolia, and the U.S.S.R., indicating clearly where the Soviet bloc and Yugoslavia were casting their lot.

The Russians, to be sure, had felt it necessary to avoid top-level representation. They could thus play out their tactic of support for unification and dodge criticism from within the Communist camp that they were giving total support to a Socialist-dominated organization. Soviet leaders "solved" this problem by not sending Russian representatives from the Soviet Peace Committee or the World Council of Peace, dispatching instead a five-man delegation headed by Soviet Red Cross official, G. Alexandrov. This group first attended the Sōhyō 28th National Convention where Alexandrov presented President Ōta with the Lenin Peace Prize.[69]

---

[68] For a brief account of the Gensuikin Conferences, see *Sōhyō News*, No. 252, October 25, 1965, pp. 8–11. Also see "A Report on the Anti-Bomb World Conferences and Their Characteristics," *Kōan Jōhō*, No. 143, August 1965.

[69] In response, Ōta stated: "I don't think the Lenin Peace Prize was given to me personally. The struggle of Sōhyō for peace—the struggle of the Japanese working class for peace and against war—is thus appreciated by the people of the world. Keeping this in my mind, I pledge you brothers to persistently carry on, hand in hand with the fighters for peace in our country and the world, my fight against the Vietnam War, against the national trend for war and against the monopolies." *Sōhyō News*, No. 252, October 25, 1965, p. 8. The 28th Sōhyō Convention itself deserves brief attention for several reasons. The political trend continued to move "left" as a result of the Vietnam War. Sōhyō leaders made the antiwar struggle an item of first priority, and the phrase "American imperialism," which had disappeared from Sōhyō official pronouncements in 1962, was reinserted into the main policy statement.

This did not prevent the Chinese delegate, Tang Tseung, from sharply criticizing Sōhyō's protest against Chinese nuclear testing. Much to the em-

The Gensuikin conferences focused on "an immediate peaceful solution" of the Vietnam War. The bombing of North Vietnam should
cease, and ensuing negotiations should involve the withdrawal of all
foreign troops from South Vietnam and a settlement of the political
issues by the Vietnamese people themselves.[70] Complete disarmament,
denuclearization, and support for all atomic bomb victims were also
demanded. Gensuikyō was denounced for its support of nuclear weapon
propagation as a means of opposing American imperialism, a position
that Socialist spokesmen insisted was contrary to the wishes of the Japanese people.

Thus, the issues of the test ban treaty and nuclear proliferation
continued to split the left-sponsored Japanese peace movement. Two
loosely-knit coalitions were tending to harden. Gensuikyō represented
the Mainstream Japanese Communist Party, Peking and its international allies. Gensuikin spoke for the Sōhyō–Socialist group; various
youth, religious, and civic organizations—some connected with the
Socialists, others separate; the dissident, pro-Soviet Japanese Communists; and—at least unofficially—the Soviet bloc.

At the close of 1965, the Sōhyō–Socialist position on united front
activities with the Communists continued to be hotly debated. The
predominant attitude within Socialist ranks was one of cautious and
limited approval, with the provision that the rule of mutual agreement
be strictly followed. However, a number of Sōhyō–Socialist leaders remained opposed to joint Socialist–Communist action, and almost all
except the extreme left within these organizations favored slow, deliberate steps. Thus, the concepts of one-day joint actions, liaison conferences, and simultaneous but separate demonstrations continued to
be regarded with greatest favor, and the rebuilding of a full-fledged

---

barrassment of the Sōhyō leaders, Tang read a message openly attacking
their position. Moreover, when Ōto commented afterward that while he understood the Chinese view, Sōhyō would not change its line, Tang became
indignant and left the convention, returning to China earlier than was scheduled. The Chinese delegations had also departed from the conference hall
at an earlier point, when the Soviet representatives were greeted. Furthermore,
they had demanded that their hotel rooms be changed because they had
been placed next to the rooms reserved for the Soviet delegates!

In the midst of troubles of this nature, the Sōhyō leaders were also confronted with sharp "left-right" pressures on such issues as the united
front, support for the Socialist Party, and the peace problem. The Ōta–Iwai
line prevailed: exclusive support for the Japan Socialist Party; no present
joint struggle with the JCP but the maintenance of a "flexible attitude" on
this question; and the dispatch of a peace mission abroad, but a continuation
of the struggle at home against American "aggression" in Vietnam.

[70] *Ibid.*, p. 9.

united front organization remained in the talk stage.[71] With the vital target date of 1970 fast approaching, this situation was clearly frustrating to the Japanese Communist Party, which was now seeking to woo the Socialists with a relatively soft line.[72]

At this point, however, as suggested earlier, politics within the Sōhyō–Socialist camp had become exceedingly complex, with forces external to Japan deeply involved. The overall trend continued to be sharply left. Identification with the Vietnamese Communists in particular was commonplace, with intimate ties also being formed with the Communists of North Korea. There was a strong tendency to regard Asian Communists—if they were outside Japan—as "liberators" and legitimate allies. On the other hand, opposition to both American and Japanese government policy in the Far East had reached the most extreme levels. Within Socialist ranks generally, nationalism and Pan-Asianism had rarely if ever taken on such overtly pro-Communist and anti-American forms.

One result had been the emergence of a strong "pro-China" group within the Japan Socialist Party itself, primarily involving the Mainstream Sasaki faction. Naturally, the Chinese Communists sought to expand this beachhead. At an earlier point, of course, they had pur-

---

[71] On October 6–7, 1965, Sōhyō held its 29th Special Convention, and once again the united front issue was at the forefront of discussion. It was agreed to develop one-day joint struggles with the Communists during October to block Japan–Korea Treaty ratification, and strengthen joint struggle activities in November by appointing liaison personnel to meet with JCP representatives. Yonehara, who delivered the Japanese Communist Party's greetings to the convention, approved the proposal for expanded one-day struggles, but urged the immediate reestablishment of an Ampo joint struggle organization.

Just prior to this convention, the JCP had held its 3rd central Committee Plenum, from September 29 to October 4. The Plenum resolution expressed concern over the relative "stagnation" of united front efforts and urged the immediate drive for an organization that could cope with the crisis of 1970.

[72] Miyamoto's frustrations were well expressed in his press interview of July 2, 1965. For all practical purposes, he asserted, there were no disagreements among the Socialist Party, Sōhyō, and the Japanese Communist Party on the vital necessity for abolishing the Mutual Security Treaty, crushing the Japan–Korea talks, opposing American aggression in Vietnam, forcing U.S. imperialism out of Asia, halting Constitutional deterioration, and strengthening Afro–Asian solidarity. On all of these matters, fundamentally, they agreed. Moreover, all parties had pledged themselves to democratic solidarity and development of a large-scale mass struggle that would surpass the anti-Ampo movement. But significant elements of doubt and indecision within the Socialist forces still existed, and if the "progressives" did not soon fulfill their promises, they would "lose the confidence of the masses." *Zenei*, September 1965.

sued a similar path, in the era of Asanuma Inejirō.[73] Then, a period of coolness had ensued as Peking came to doubt the power of the Socialists—and also their good will. Now, redoubled efforts to woo the Socialists were being made. In the fall of 1965, for example, nearly two hundred youth were invited to China, many of them drawn from the ranks of Socialist Party young people. And this was but one example among many of the efforts currently being made by Peking to influence assorted elements of the left—youth, labor, and the intelligentsia. Clearly, the Chinese Communists hoped to have their supporters within *all* branches of the Japanese socialist movement, not merely within the Japanese Communist Party.

As we have seen, however, a majority of the Sōhyō–Socialist group found united front operations with the dissident Japanese Communists, the Soviet bloc, and third party elements like Komeitō easier and more appealing at this point than close ties with the JCP and Peking. Indeed, the JCP had suffered heavy losses in the labor movement as a result of the April 17, 1964 fiasco. Moreover, alignment with, or affinity to, the Soviet bloc provided some psychological and political satisfaction to Japanese left Socialists, despite the culture gap that existed. Such alignment permitted the retention of Marxist doctrines, orthodox or revised. It allowed further experimentation with "structural reform," for example, and with other doctrines which the hard line JCP-Peking position currently defined as heresy. Moreover, a tie of this type paradoxically gave many left Socialists a sense of *nonalignment* between two major forces, Washington and Peking. It was sometimes convenient to posit the "moderation" of Moscow against the "extremism" of the United States and China. In the new triangular encroachment of Russia, China, and America upon Japanese politics, the ideological-psychological proclivities of many left Socialists were such as to make the Soviet Union an appealing "centrist" force. An urge to oppose America, of course, could easily be combined with the quest for centrism. Japanese Socialists were well aware of the fact that the Soviet Union—not China—was the primary global counterforce to the United States.

---

[73] In March 1959, in the course of a visit to China, Asanuma, then Secretary-General of the Socialist Party, had asserted that the United States (later corrected to read U.S. imperialism) "is the common enemy of the Japanese and Chinese peoples." This statement had been repeated by Suzuki Mosaburō in the course of a visit to Peking in January 1962, causing a major storm within the party. Sasaki, however, in 1965 was prepared to go even further, insisting that U.S. imperialism was the enemy of all of the people of the world. See George R. Packard, III, *Protest in Tokyo, The Security Crisis of 1960*, Princeton, 1966, p. 85, notes 6 and 7.

Moscow was naturally anxious to take advantage of this situation. Using its network of international front organizations such as the World Federation of Trade Unions, the World Council of Peace, and the World Federation of Democratic Youth, it sought maximum contact with the entire spectrum of the Japanese left outside the JCP. At this point, delegations of Japanese were streaming to Russia in unprecedented numbers, and Soviet visitors to Japan were also increasing. In these respects, the East European Communists could also be of major service.

Thus the Japanese left was being wooed—and undercut—from all sides. Naturally, the Soviet bid for Socialist Party and dissident Communist support infuriated the Yoyogi leaders. This was clearly revealed in the June 22, 1965 article in *Akahata* noted briefly earlier.

In this major article (which was promptly reprinted by Peking), the JCP leaders accused the CPSU leaders of deliberatly seeking to split the Japanese Communist movement and of intervening repeatedly in internal Japanese affairs. Soviet aid to Gensuikin, to the "antiparty" Shiga–Kamiyama–Kasuga group, and to other "renegades" was recited at length. The new Soviet leaders, charged the *Akahata* writers, were continuing to follow the old Khrushchev line of seeking to impose opportunism, the cult of American imperialism, and the modern revisionist line on the international Communist movement. Indeed, despite pledges to the contrary, the new Russian leaders had actually intensified their intervention into internal Japanese affairs in various ways. Support for the partial test ban treaty had been demanded in "big-nation chauvinistic" fashion, and this had been the primary cause for a split in the Japanese "democratic" movement, a split for which the Russians would have to take full responsibility. In fact, the Soviet technique was "split and rule," charged *Akahata*. Both with respect to the peace movement and with respect to Communist Party affairs, the Russians were determined to impose by fiat their false revisionist views. Thus, they used Gensuikin as a tool to smash Gensuikyō, they attempted to undermine the true leaders of the Japan–Soviet Friendship Society, replacing them with toadies of the Moscow line; and they assisted the subversive activities of Shiga, Suzuki, Kamiyama, and Nakano against the Japanese Communist Party.[74]

The *Akahata* article presented the "facts" to substantiate these charges. First, with respect to the peace movement, the leaders of the Soviet Peace Committee, headed by G. A. Zhukov, had long been in secret contact with the Gensuikin leaders. Yoshikawa Yūichi, who had

---

[74] *Akahata,* June 22, 1965, p. 1.

been expelled from the Japan Peace Council, was contacted by the Russians when they were in Japan in 1964, *Akahata* asserted. He and his group were encouraged in their "splittist" activities and were subsequently brought to Moscow, where they were given concrete assistance so that Gensuikin could be launched. Meanwhile, certain Japanese representatives to the World Council of Peace were ousted, and the Russians talked about replacing them with Gensuikin adherents. Indeed, the Secretariat of the Council had invited Gensuikin representatives to the Helsinki meetings scheduled for July 1965. "The ruse that this is an action of the World Council of Peace, and not the Soviet Peace Committee, will not fool anyone," stated the *Akahata* writers.

In 1964, after the Soviet line of attending two conferences had been completely exposed and debunked, trumpeted *Akahata,* not only did the Russians fail to correct their errors, but they attended the "splittist" conference. Now, the JCP organ charged, in advance of the 11th Gensuikyō World Congress, they were intensifying their disruptionist tactics.

Second, according to *Akahata,* Russian activities in connection with the Japan–Soviet Friendship Society were "scandalous illustrations" of interference. "Splittist" organizations had been founded with Soviet connivance merely because the Japan–Soviet Friendship Society "refused to accept the pressure of CPSU leaders on such issues as the test ban treaty and modern revisionism." (If the idea of an Anti-Soviet Japan–Soviet Society struck even the JCP as faintly ludicrous, no hint of the grim humor involved has been given.)

It was claimed that at a meeting of the Japan–Soviet Society in April 1964, E. V. Ivanov, Vice-Chairman of the Federation of Soviet Friendship and Cultural Exchange Organizations, had instructed Sōhyō leaders to oppose the society because of the line it had adopted. Furthermore, the *Akahata* writers asserted, in July a Soviet trade representative in Japan, Gubanov, had told the president of a Japanese business firm trading with the Russians to reform the society or withdraw, and, in the same month, Zhukov had demanded "thorough reform." Thus, in October 1964 Matsumoto Shichirō, Chairman of the society, began his "splittist" activities. Following his return from Moscow, he launched a movement for the "constitutional improvement" of the society.

In the same month, *Akahata* stated, a Socialist delegation invited to Moscow was told that the JCP was using funds from the Japan–Soviet Institute and the Japan–Soviet Travel Agency to engage in anti-Soviet propaganda, and that JCP members of the society should be removed or it should be abandoned. When Matsumoto's scheme for "constitutional improvement" failed, two new organizations were founded by pro-Soviet cliques, the Japan–Soviet Liaison Society and a second Japan–Soviet Friendship Society. The Soviet Embassy in Tōkyō directed both of these activities, it was claimed.

Finally, *Akahata* pointed out, Russian leaders had been guilty of aiding the subversive activities of Shiga and company, thereby violating the norms of relations among fraternal parties as prescribed in the Moscow agreements of 1957 and 1960. The CPSU had given direct support to the candidacy of Kamiyama Shigeo in the 1965 House of Councillors election when he sought to hinder the election of Nosaka. In various parts of the Soviet Union, the circulation of *Akahata* was prohibited, but the *Voice of Japan,* the Shiga organ, was circulated in its place. Shiga, moreover, was given extensive publicity in Soviet journals. He and Suzuki were invited by the Soviet Embassy in Tokyo to the celebration of the 20th anniversary of victory over Hitler on May 8, 1965. And when the organ of the Soviet Peace Committee, *For Peace,* published the names of Japanese organizations supporting the Helsinki Peace Conference, it listed the "Japanese Communist Party (Voice of Japan)" along with Sōhyō and the Japan Socialist Party. "Not only did the Soviet Peace Committee bestow the glorious name of the Japanese Communist Party on the antiparty group of Shiga in this authoritative journal," but "they listed our party as the "Japan Communist Party (Yoyogi)" in the same fashion as the American and Japanese reactionaries and the antiparty group would call us."

The actions of the Communist Party of the Soviet Union, proclaimed *Akahata,* were of inestimable benefit to the American and Japanese reactionaries. To attack the JCP and allied "democratic forces" in Japan—"a country which is most important fortress of American imperialism"—represented a direct attack on the entire international progressive movement and a source of support to the American policies of war.[75]

With arguments and words such as these, Japanese Communist Party leaders continued throughout 1965 to heap abuse on Soviet tactics and policies. Indeed, at this point, no Communist Party of Asia outside of Peking itself was more bitter in its open attacks upon the Soviet Union. Typical was the editorial in *Akahata* on November 7, commemorating the 48th anniversary of the October Revolution.[76] During the periods led by Lenin and Stalin, proclaimed *Akahata,* the Soviet Party and people had strongly championed aid to people's revolutionary

[75] *Ibid.,* p. 1.
[76] *Ibid.,* November 7, 1965, p. 1.

movements and the liberation struggles of all countries. They had resolutely opposed the imperialists' policies of war and aggression, setting a glorious example of proletarian internationalism. Under Khrushchev, however, revisionism had triumphed, the road of the October Revolution had been betrayed, and the Soviet Party had completely abandoned the path of Marxism–Leninism.

Although history had already passed rigorous judgment upon Khrushchev, asserted *Akahata,* the current Soviet leaders have been unable to understand the significance of this fact. They have continued to launch attacks upon the JCP and intervene in its internal affairs, practicing revisionism, big-power chauvinism, and splittism. However, according to *Akahata,* the JCP had fought revisionism to a finish and triumphed over it. The party had also waged a vigorous struggle against dogmatism, the slavish adherence to, or mechanical adoption of, a foreign party's program. Cited as examples of *both* sins were the Shiga–Kamiyama groups, who were described as "tools of the Soviet Party."

Unless the point about dogmatism could be interpreted as a veiled threat to others (and it was not precisely a new theme), there was nothing in this editorial to suggest that the Japanese Communist Party was contemplating any change in its international policies. Two little-noticed developments, however, occurred during this period that were to relate to the future. In September 1965, a small group calling itself the Japanese Communist Party (Liberation Front) had been organized in Kyōto with the old Shida (Shigeo) faction as its nucleus. Behind this action lay an intriguing chain of events. Shida, it will be recalled, had led the JCP for a time during the turbulent "leftist" era between 1950 and 1955. He had gone into eclipse after 1955 when the party abandoned "leftist adventurism" and the Miyamoto–Hakamada–Nosaka triumvirate assumed power. For a number of years, Shida and such comrades as Shiino Etsurō, Yoshida Shirō, and Goda Hideichi had occupied themselves with local cell activities, brooding over developments and keeping in touch with each other.[77]

The crisis within the JCP over the April 17, 1964 strike issue evidently provided the Shida group with an opportunity to raise the level of their activities; it is likely that they had long been looking for a convenient issue. At about the same time that the Mainstream JCP leaders had ordered a retreat from the "dogmatic error" of opposing

---

[77] Shiino had been chairman of the temporary JCP Central Committee, Yoshida had served as head of the Hokkaido party organization, and Goda had been Chief of the Labor Bureau of the party. For background on the Liberation Front, see *Kōan Jōhō,* No. 153, June 1966.

that strike, a small Ōsaka group centering around Yoshida Shirō began publication of a journal, *Leninshugi* (*Leninism*), in the name of the "Marxist–Leninist Study Society." In Hokkaidō, moreover, another group emerged calling itself the Japanese Communist Party (Leninist Faction). Some months later, in February 1965, an Ehime Prefectural group announced the formation of a Japanese Communist Party Reconstruction Committee, and it too began a publication, *Marxshugi–Leninshugi* (*Marxism–Leninism*). These were the groups that convened in September 1965 with assorted individuals from other regions to launch the Japanese Communist Party (Liberation Front).

The new group took its basic positions from the 1951 Program, demanding that the Party turn back from the revisionist course it had pursued since 1955 and rededicate itself to militant Marxism–Leninism. Primary efforts should be directed toward the forceful overthrow of the Satō government and the establishment of a "national liberation democratic united front" in its place. Using "land reform" as a war cry and guerrilla warfare as a technique, Communists should strike for power. The "two-enemies" thesis of the Yoyogi faction, insisted Liberation Front spokesmen, obscured the fact that American power in Japan could only operate through the Satō government. To concentrate primarily upon "American imperialism," therefore, was to retard the liberation struggle. Similarly, to become preoccupied with parliamentary tactics and delude oneself concerning the possibilities of a peaceful transition to socialism was to betray Leninism and lose the revolution.

In essence, the Liberation Front program was a return to the 1951 Thesis, promoted by some of the very men who had played such a prominent role in that era. Implicit in this program was all-out support of current Chinese Communist themes, combined with vehement attacks upon the Miyamoto–Hakamada Mainstream leadership. The present united front tactics of the JCP were criticized as "a complete betrayal" of the working class, conducted by "right-wing opportunistic leaders." Party attitudes toward the Sino–Soviet cleavage were condemned on the score that the JCP had first sought to ignore the dispute and then had adopted a so-called "neutral" attitude, printing various articles on both major sides. Such a policy represented "an extremely irresponsible stand which abandons leadership." By refusing to stand clearly on the side of Marxism–Leninism, the Japanese Communist Party (Yoyogi) had fallen into a narrow, nationalist position. The central issues were whether or not a Communist Party recognized violent revolution and proletarian dictatorship as indispensable elements of Marxism–Leninism. No party, hiding under the guise of independence and autonomy, could avoid coming to grips with these issues.[78]

Throughout the fall of 1965 and the spring of 1966, the Liberation Front faction continued its attacks upon the Yoyogi leaders via hand-bills, leaflets, and its regular publication, *Heiwa to Dokuritsu* (*Peace and Independence*). Every new development in the international scene became grist for its mill. Thus, the abortive coup of September 30 in Indonesia, which was to affect all elements of the Japanese left so profoundly, was cited by the LF group as *prime facie* evidence that peaceful, parliamentary tactics were doomed to failure.

In this fashion, the fragmentation of the left continued to mount in Japan, one of the high prices which the Japanese Communists had to pay for the mounting crisis in the Communist world. Now, the party was confronted by two different types of dissidents. The Shiga–Kamiyama faction, together with the followers of Kasuga Shōjirō and Naitō, was ceaselessly attacking the party for its close adherence to the Peking line and the old-fashioned rigidity implicit in its tactics and policies. To these dissidents, the JCP (Yoyogi) remained Stalinist, bureaucratic, and stagnant. The Liberation Front faction, in contradistinction, was condemning the Mainstream leaders for their revisionist tendencies and their refusal to stand squarely with others in the defense of "true Marxism–Leninism." Could this situation be turned into a tactical advantage, a political gain? With minor factions championing Soviet and Chinese lines, could the theme of "independence and autonomy" provide the party with that desirable "centrist" position from which to smash its opponents, right and left?

A second interesting series of events occurred in December 1965 in the form of three editorials by the Korean, Japanese, and Chinese Communists. On December 6, *Rodong Shinmun,* the official organ of the Korean Workers' Party, published an editorial entitled "Unite all Revolutionary Forces and Wage a More Powerful Anti-Imperialist Struggle!"[79] The North Korean Communists, like the Communists of North Vietnam and Japan, had moved from "neutralism" to a bitterly anti-Soviet position in 1963–1964, openly condemning Soviet leadership and Soviet policies, and taking a position on all major substantive issues that accorded with the position of Peking.

The December 6th editorial indicated no shift from the hard line

---

[78] For additional information on Liberation Front theories and policies (and a spirited refutation), see Shimotsukasa Junkichi, "The Essence and Absurdity of the Anti-Party Dogmatists," *Zenei,* July 1966, pp. 56–70.

[79] For an English translation, see *The People's Korea,* No. 249, December 15, 1965, pp. 1–2.

with respect to the United States, and no softening of opposition to "modern revisionism." To fight against American imperialism, proclaimed the newspaper, "is the all-important, pressing revolutionary task facing all parties and all Communists." No one could talk about the victory of the revolutionary cause or world peace, it insisted, apart from the struggle against the United States. The assault upon "modern revisionism," moreover, was as harsh as possible. "Modern revisionism which emasculates the revolutionary essence of Marxism–Leninism and paralyses the revolutionary struggle of the people remains still today the main danger to the international Communist movement.

"The harm of modern revisionism is found, above all, in its capitulation to U.S. imperialism. The modern revisionists, scared by the nuclear blackmail policy, spread illusions about imperialism and preach unprincipled compromise with it, paralysing the revolutionary fighting spirit of the masses, and dampening and weakening the anti-imperialist revolutionary struggle of the people."

Clearly, these thrusts were directed at the Soviet Union, although it was not specifically named. The latter part of the editorial, however, was devoted exclusively to another theme: the imperative need for "socialist" unity and solidarity, especially in view of the vital stakes for the Communist world involved in Vietnam. Unity, the editorial proclaimed, "is unthinkable apart from the anti-imperialist struggle, but all possible strength must be pooled to support the Vietnamese people."

On the surface perhaps there was little that was new in this editorial. All of the major themes had long been in circulation. Read carefully, however, the editorial contained some significant nuances. While staking out a position of *no retreat* from an "antirevisionist" line, the North Koreans, deeply concerned about trends in the Vietnamese war, had established two additional criteria for judging "correct" Marxist–Leninists: was concrete aid being advanced to the Vietnamese Communists to the maximum extent possible, and were supreme efforts being made to unify the Communist camp so as to prevent "American imperialism" from winning a victory in Vietnam?

On December 7, one day later, *Akahata* published an editorial, "Let Us Fight Against Modern Revisionism and Strengthen the International Struggle Against American Imperialism."[80] The similarity of basic themes with the *Rodong Shinmun* editorial and the timing of publication were too close to have been coincidental. Coordination of some type must have taken place. *Akahata,* to be sure, was even more vehe-

---

[80] *Akahata,* December 7, 1965, p. 1.

ment in its attack upon "modern revisionism" than the Korean comrades, and the Soviet leaders were repeatedly specified by name. They were charged with having "spread the cult of Kennedy and Johnson," advancing the cause of American–Soviet cooperation, and avoiding the anti-imperialist struggle by distorting in an opportunistic fashion the policies of peaceful coexistence. The leaders of the Soviet party, insisted *Akahata,* had in no sense abandoned their revisionist line or returned to the Moscow statements of 1957 and 1960. They had not corrected their basic errors, including those of "beautifying Johnson" and engaging in illicit intervention against the Japanese Communist Party. However, events had forced them to pay more homage to the principles of united action against American imperialism in connection with Vietnam.

Despite the fact the Soviet leaders were pursuing dual-faced tactics and not fully matching words with action in connection with a united struggle, it would be wrong, asserted *Akahata,* to ignore or reject all efforts for a united front merely on these grounds. The JCP, it proclaimed, had been urging unity since 1964, and it would continue to do so. On the one hand, there must be a struggle on two fronts—against revisionism which was the primary threat, but also against splittism and doctrinarism, forces woven into the antiparty revisionist movement. On the other hand, it was essential to pursue every possibility of united action within the international Communist and democratic world. To struggle on behalf of a correct Marxist–Leninist line and to fight for unity were the dual tasks confronting all Communists.

On December 30, the Chinese Communists set forth once again their position on these vital matters, in an editorial entitled "The Leaders of the CPSU Are Betrayers of the Declaration and the Statement," published in the *People's Daily.*[81] After castigating the current Soviet leaders in the most violent terms as traitors and renegades, the editorial came to the vital question:

The new leaders of the CPSU are shouting themselves hoarse for "united action." Above all, they are clamouring for "united action" on the question of Vietnam. But it is precisely on this question, which is the focus of the present international struggle, that their anti-revolutionary position is revealed in its most concentrated form. Far from believing that the Vietnamese people can win in a people's war against U.S. imperialist aggression, they are afraid that this will bring them "troubles" and hamper their collaboration with U.S. im-

---

[81] For an English translation, see *Peking Review,* No. 1, January 1, 1966, pp. 9–12. Emphasis in the following quotation supplied.

perialism. . . . *The slogan of "united action" has now become a poisoned weapon in the hands of the Khrushchev revisionists for sowing dissension. In coordination with U.S. imperialism, they are vainly trying to use this slogan to undermine the fighting friendship between the Chinese and Vietnamese peoples and the Vietnamese people's unity against U.S. aggression.* The Vietnamese people are waging a victorious struggle against U.S. imperialism and for national salvation. *It is the duty of the Marxist–Leninists and revolutionary people to give their staunch support to the just revolutionary struggle of the Vietnamese people and firmly expose the plot of "united action" hatched by the new leaders of the CPSU.*

In this fashion, the Chinese leaders emphatically and totally rejected the united front proposal. Indeed, in the concluding section of the editorial, the words used to attack the idea suggested that the Chinese regarded anyone who advanced such a concept as either a fool or a knave. To combine in any manner whatsoever with the Soviet revisionists, asserted the editorial, would be to betray Marxism–Leninism, enter the service of U.S. imperialism, undermine the Vietnam revolution, accept subordinate status to a "patriarchal father Party," and prepare for the restoration of capitalism at home. "As a serious Marxist–Leninist Party, the Communist Party of China can only give the categorical answer that we will do none of these things either now or in the future." The Korean and Japanese Communists now had their answer.

Events of the next twelve months, both on the international front and within Japanese leftist circles, were to highlight the significance of the two developments noted above. Let us begin with certain key trends on the domestic scene. The Japanese Socialist Party held its 27th Party Congress on January 19–22, 1966, amidst conditions of deep division and heated debate. As has been emphasized, the party had been moving sharply to the left under the guidance of the Mainstream Sasaki faction. Once again, the Socialists were cooperating with the Communists on issues of mutual concern, using the tactic of one-day joint struggles and liaison committees for purposes of coordinating action. Both approaches had been used in the unsuccessful struggle against ratification of the treaty between Japan and South Korea, and they continued to operate with respect to such issues as Okinawa, the visitation of U.S. nuclear-powered submarines, "reactionary" amendments to the Constitution, Vietnam, and the proposal for an electoral change to single-member districts. With respect to foreign policies, the Socialist Party under the Sasaki–Narita leadership had retained the theme "positive neutrality," but in actuality its position had become scarcely distinguishable from that of the Communists on many issues, and every recent action of the Japanese government had been opposed in the most vehement terms.

The principal statements of resolutions of the 27th Party Congress underwrote the "left" swing, although a substantial internal challenge was mounted, as we shall see. The Mainstream positions were militantly anti-American, strongly pro-Communist and exuded a doctrinaire Marxism. The Sasaki analysis of the Vietnam War can serve as one example: "We must interpret the struggle of the Vietnamese people as the focus of struggles against newly appearing imperialists and colonialists who are striving to protect their own regime during the transitional process from capitalism to socialism."[82] The American imperialists, he went on to assert, were planning to invade Laos and Cambodia, and thus the war would ultimately develop into an American–Chinese clash. (These themes and, indeed, some of the very terminology employed echoed the Chinese line.)

The resolution on Vietnam was basically in line with Sasaki's views. It asserted that a peaceful solution would be reached only if the United States immediately ceased all attacks upon the North, ended all military action in the South, and withdrew its troops and other foreign troops entirely from Vietnamese soil, allowing the Vietnamese to settle the issue by themselves. To enforce such a policy, the Japanese government should deny the United States all use of bases both in Okinawa and in Japan proper, and cease all forms of cooperation with the United States in connection with its operations in Vietnam.

On a number of other specific issues, the tone of Mainstream speeches and resolutions was similar. Adamant opposition was expressed to the Japan–Korea treaty, and demands were made for the development of friendly and expanded relations with North Korea; a struggle "to destroy the 'China containment' policies of U.S. imperialism" was urged and the Satō "anti-China" policy was condemned; the Asanuma–Peking agreement that American imperialism was the source of all threats to peace in Asia and the common enemy of all Asian peoples was reiterated; a campaign to smash the Mutual Security Treaty was pledged; and all forms of cooperation between the Japanese government and "anti-Communist" forces in Asia currently underway were denounced.

With respect to questions touching upon the Sino–Soviet dispute, however, the Socialist Party moved with extreme caution and trepidation, revealing the fact that the crisis in the international Communist world had affected them as deeply as it had affected the Japanese Com-

---

[82] *Japan Socialist Review*, No. 104, February 15, 1966, p. 13.

munists at this point. Chairman Sasaki was openly accused of issuing a statement which sounded sympathetic to the Chinese nuclear tests, and the leaders were queried as to whether any secret pledges on this matter had been made during their recent trip to China.[83] Narita countered by insisting that the basic line of opposition to *all* nuclear tests remained unaltered, but an uneasy mood prevailed on this matter. The China issue, indeed, was involved in many of the questions raised from the floor and in private conversations. For months, as we have noted, Peking had been wooing certain segments of the Socialist Party, and the Sasaki faction in particular was known to hold strong pro-China sentiments. On the other hand, the official party position was still in most respects much closer to the Soviet line, and here, too, ties had been intimate both at the official and unofficial levels, as has been indicated.

Thus, in complete contrast to the openness with which the United States was attacked, Socialist Party spokesmen were extremely careful in their references to China and the Soviet Union. Criticism was muted, and certain subjects were treated as "too delicate" to be discussed. For example, a Miyagi prefecture delegate, apparently pro-Peking, asked what the party's attitude was toward Soviet diplomacy in view of the fact that the U.S.S.R. was pursuing a policy of peaceful coexistence with the United States, giving aid to India, and supporting the "reactionary forces" of Indonesia. Secretary-General Narita responded by admitting that there were "some variations" between the two major Communist powers on the subject of people's liberation movements. They should reach agreement on this matter, he asserted, but "it will do no good to criticize one of them."[84] Narita added that when the Socialists had visited Russia in 1964, they had had a "heated debate" on this matter and that he felt that the Soviet Union should take resolute actions on behalf of the Vietnamese people. (Earlier, he had insisted that the Socialists had had a "heated debate" in Peking over the question of nuclear tests.)

Debate over the party's Action Program and the amendments proposed from the floor provided additional evidence of the substantial split that existed within the party between "pro-China" and "pro-Soviet" elements. If the official position in certain respects was closer to the Soviet line, it was not sufficiently close for some elements within the party. "Peaceful coexistence" *and* "the struggle against imperialism" were underlined as the essence of Socialist foreign policy, with

---

[83] See, for example, the exchange between a Wakayama Prefecture delegate and Narita-Sasaki, *ibid.,* No. 103, February 1, 1966, p. 14.

[84] *Ibid.,* p. 23.

five "promoters" of this position being identified in the world scene: socialist countries; labor forces in capitalist countries; national liberation movements; positive neutralist and nonaligned forces in newly developing countries; and the peace movement and international public opinion for peace. The wording and order of this list might be considered "pro-Soviet," since it did not give top billing to the non-Western world in general and to the national liberation movements specifically. Moreover, opposition to all nuclear tests by whatever nation and support to Gensuikin were continued.

Secretary-General Narita at least appeared anxious to establish the image of a party independent of both Peking and Moscow. His references to "heated debates" with both the Russians and Chinese were an obvious attempt in that direction. Independence from the Japanese Communist Party was also much at issue. Hostile questions on this matter poured in from the delegates. But the position established in 1965 was reiterated: one-day joint struggles on an *ad hoc* basis and participation in liaison committees, but no involvement in a permanent united front at this point.

If the Socialist Party "left" was torn by the Sino–Soviet cleavage, this did not begin to define adequately the full range of division within the party. Much of the tension produced during the four days of stormy debate related to the broad split between the Mainstream Sasaki faction on the one hand, and the opposition Eda, Wada, and old Kawakami factions on the other (Kawakami himself had died in December 1965). Many observers, indeed, now regarded the Socialist Party as a coalition of separate parties completely incapable of unified action. While many differences were partly a result of power rivalry and personal factionalism, the critical differences stemmed from important ideological and policy questions. The Sasaki faction favored a united front with the Communists; the anti-Mainstream factions were opposed. The Sasaki faction wanted to work toward a unification of the anti-A and H Bomb groups; the moderate factions wanted to maintain an identity separate from Gensuikyō. The Sasaki faction could be considered pro-Communist in general, and pro-China specifically; the anti-Mainstream factions either leaned toward the Soviet and East European Communists or were inclined toward "anti-Communism." Naturally, these differences affected positions on every specific issue—the intensity of attack upon the United States, the degree of identification with North Korea and North Vietnam, and attitudes toward Asian regionalism among non-Communist states versus concepts of Afro–Asian "solidarity."

The precarious balance within the party was graphically revealed by the election of officers which took place on January 22, 1966. Sasaki Kōzō was reelected Chairman over Eda Saburō by the narrow margin of 295 to 276 votes. Narita Tomomi was reelected Secretary-General over Katsumata Seiichi by 321 to 246 votes. Some other contests were even closer, and in the new Central Executive Committee, partly appointed, the anti-Mainstream factions actually obtained a majority.

The 27th Socialist Party Congress thus revealed three facts of major significance: a strong "left" position continued to dominate the party, but a moderate challenge of sizable proportions was being mounted; the party was basically, and possibly irrevocably, split on some issues of fundamental importance; and both the Soviet Union and Communist China were deeply involved in the internal affairs of this party, as they were in the affairs of the Japanese Communists. Each of these facts was well known to the JCP leaders and undoubtedly had some influence upon the critical policy decisions that now had to be made.

Less than two weeks after the conclusion of the Socialist Congress, *Akahata* ran two interesting articles only three days apart. On February 1, the JCP organ sharply denounced the Soviet Union for "beautifying" the foreign policies of the Sato government and continuing to interfere in the internal affairs of Japanese "peace and democratic movements," specifically, for rendering support to Shiga, Kamiyama, and other "anti-party renegades."[85] The attack was a savage one, and while the main charges were levelled against Radio Moscow rather than Soviet government officials, the editorial ended with a full-fledged assault upon "the revisionist, opportunist line peddled everywhere by international modern revisionism." As might have been expected, Peking quickly reprinted this piece, giving it a prominent display.

Three days later, on February 4, *Akahata* published a lengthy article entitled, "For the Strengthening of International United Actions and a United Front Against American Imperialism."[86] Despite Peking's blunt December rejection, the burning issue of a united front was reraised. The essence of the article was contained in one theme: under the present complicated international circumstances, it was essential to combine the struggle against modern revisionism with the effective establishment of a broad united front against American imperialism. There was no retraction of the old charges against the Russians; indeed, most of them were repeated. However, it was argued that in order to conceal the failure of their previous line, the current Soviet leaders

---

[85] *Akahata*, February 1, 1966, p. 1. For an English summary, see *Peking Review*, No. 8, February 18, 1966, pp. 18–20.

[86] *Akahata*, February 4, 1966, pp. 1–2.

had begun to adopt a two-faced position, seeking to appease imperialism and to support national liberation movements at the same time. Nevertheless, a strenuous effort to establish a united front was still desirable in order both to awaken the masses currently living under revisionist rule to its dangers *and* to save the international revolutionary movement. (The bombing lull against North Vietnam had ended on the final day of January.)

It was now clear that the Japanese Communist Party leaders intended to make another appeal to Peking, with the *Akahata* articles of early February setting the stage. The JCP line had now been firmly established: combine an unremitting struggle against "modern revisionism" with a struggle for Communist unity, using Vietnam as a point of departure. Now, for the first time, some of the internal radical opponents of the JCP sensed a shift in the party line. *Atarashii Rosen,* organ of the Naitō faction, asserted that the February 4th article represented an attempt of the Yoyogi faction to escape from the profound contradictions and isolation that marked their previous policy as a result of its exclusively pro-China character.[87] It further asserted that the total isolation of China throughout the non-Western world, Pekings' increasing interference in the internal affairs of other parties, and the plight of the Indonesian Communists whom the Yoyogi leaders regarded as a model had combined to force a retreat. Moreover, the journal added, the dangerous situation in Vietnam demands the unity of the "peace-loving forces." The pro-Soviet dissidents thus hailed the new line while continuing to criticize Mainstream attitudes toward the Soviet Union. As could have been expected, the Liberation Front spokesmen sharply denounced the "new betrayal," asserting that the February 4th article proved the correctness of their charge that the Miyamoto–Hakamada faction was deeply infected with revisionism.

With the background having been prepared, a high-level Japanese Communist Party delegation led by Miyamoto himself left for China, North Vietnam, and North Korea on February 10, 1966. The delegation included such Mainstream stalwarts as Oka Masayoshi, Kurahara Koreto, Yonehara Akira, Sunama Ichirō, Ueda Kōichirō, Fuha Tetsuzō, and Kudō Akira. It landed first in Shanghai where it met with Liu Ning-i; Chao An-po, P'eng Chen, and K'ang Sheng came from Peking to join the meetings on February 13. On February 17, the JCP delegation flew from Canton to Hanoi, conferring there with all of the top Vietnam Workers' Party leaders and remaining for ten days. On Febru-

---

[87] "The Tactical Shift of the JCP—A Critique of the Anonymous Article Dated February 4," *Atarashii Rosen,* No. 171, February 14, 1966, p. 1.

ary 28, the delegation returned to China, going to Peking where it was greeted by Teng Hsiao-p'ing and other prominent party leaders. A conference on March 3 involved Liu Shao-ch'i, Teng Hsiao-p'ing, P'eng Chen, K'ang Sheng, Liao Ch'eng-chih, and Liu Ning-i. On March 11, the JCP delegation left Peking for Pyongyang where it was met by all the top North Korean leaders, headed by Kim Il-sŏng. After ten days, the delegation returned for a third time to China, arriving in Peking on March 21 and remaining there until early April. Clearly, the Japanese Communist leaders regarded this mission as one of major importance and dedicated some two months to achieving their primary goals: a continuous struggle on behalf of "correct Marxism–Leninism" (unremitting pressure upon the Soviet Union to abandon all manifestations of the "soft line" and to rededicate itself to *revolutionary* leadership— without interferring with other parties) *and* the immediate creation of a united Communist front on behalf of the hard-pressed Vietnamese Communists. Confronted by the grim turn of events in Vietnam and in Indonesia, the Japanese Communists were assuming leadership in a renewed drive for Communist unity, a drive which had earlier been spearheaded by Ho Chi-minh and Aidit to no avail.

All evidence strongly indicates that JCP goals were fully supported by the Mainstream leaders of both Hanoi and Pyongyang. The joint communiqué signed in Hanoi was appropriately cautious in dealing with issues critical to the Sino–Soviet dispute, but it revealed as close an identity of views between Japanese and Vietnamese Communists as was possible under the circumstances.[88] It was not difficult, of course, to condemn American actions in Vietnam in unmeasured terms and to pledge full support for the Communist position. It was equally easy to denounce all policies of the Sato government, especially their full cooperation with "American imperialism" and the establishment of treaty relations with South Korea, that "first step toward the formation of a Northeast Asia military alliance."

The communiqué made no mention of "modern revisionism" nor of any of the problems plaguing the Communist world. However, both parties "confirmed that to form and expand a united front of the peoples of the world for world peace and national independence against American imperialism is the most important and urgent task at present." Both parties pledged themselves to make every effort to achieve this task.

As might have been expected, the joint communiqué signed in Pyongyang with the leaders of the Korean Workers' Party was far less cautious

---

[88] For the full text of the communiqué, see *Akahata,* March 1, 1966, p. 1.

in denouncing "modern revisionism." [89] That statement read: "U.S. imperialism is the No. one common enemy of the world's people. . . . Modern revisionism has been obscuring this fact by beautifying U.S. imperialism. The delegations of the two Parties unanimously consider that the anti-U.S. struggle is closely linked with the struggle against opportunism which is shunning it. . . ."

On the issue of unity, however, the Hanoi and Pyongyang communiqués were remarkably similar. Said the Pyongyang statement, "They [the two parties] are convinced that it is the first and foremost task of the socialist countries and communist and workers' parties to unite broad anti-imperialist forces and concentrate all strength on the struggle against U.S. imperialism."

And in conclusion,

Unity is the powerful weapon of the working class. The unity of the ranks of the international communist movement multiplies its strength several fold.

Hence, a struggle should be waged in defense of the purity of Marxism–Leninism, opposing modern revisionism and, at the same time, guarding against dogmatism and factionalism in the international communist movement. The delegations of the two Parties stress that all the communist and workers' parties without exception should strictly abide by the forms governing relations among fraternal parties, if the unity of the socialist camp and the solidarity of the international communist movement are to be genuinely solid. There can be no party with a privileged position within the international communist movement. All parties, big or small and whether of a socialist country or not, are equal and independent.

Unilateral will should not be forced upon fraternal parties and any acts of meddling in their internal affairs and bringing pressure to bear upon them are absolutely impermissible.

In its context, the final section seemingly pointed primarily, if not exclusively, at the Soviet Union. These same issues had been raised countless times before with Soviet "crimes" in mind. Was it possible, however, that another party was now also being warned? Did this communiqué, coming after heated and fruitless debates with the Chinese, carry forward the struggle on two fronts?

Significantly, despite the fact that the JCP delegation made three separate trips to China in the course of this mission, no joint CCP-JCP communiqué was issued. It will be remembered that a similar situation

---

[89] For an English text of the communiqué signed in Pyongyang, see *The People's Korea*, March 30, 1966, pp. 2–4.

had prevailed at the time of the disastrous March 1964 meetings in Moscow between the JCP and the CPSU: Meanwhile, rumors circulated to the effect that not only were the Chinese Communists refusing flatly to consider any rapprochement with the Soviet party under present circumstances, but they were also exerting great pressure upon the European Communists, including the Russians, to open a "second front" in the West and upon the North Koreans to open a "second front" in Korea to relieve pressure upon Vietnam and unleash a global revolution.

Grave charges against Peking were circulated to various Communist parties by the Soviet Union during this period, charges that included the assertion that Peking was obstructing Soviet aid to Vietnam, provoking numerous border incidents along the vast Sino–Soviet border, and seeking deliberately to involve the Soviet Union in war with the United States.[90]

---

[90] The complete text of a "secret" CPSU letter addressed to all fraternal Communist parties was supplied to the German periodical *Ost-Probleme* by the newspaper *Die Welt*. A mimeographed translation has been prepared by Professor Klaus H. Pringsheim, and I have been privileged to use it. (The letter was presumably sent in January or February.)

In a detailed account of relations since October 1964, the CPSU made the following basic points. In an attempt to create a favorable political climate, the CPSU discontinued open polemics and invited a Chinese delegation headed by Chou En-lai to attend the 47th anniversary of the October Revolution at Chinese request. Moreover, in February 1965, a Soviet delegation headed by Kosygin stopped in Peking enroute to Hanoi and Pyongyang to reestablish contacts. A "far-reaching program" for normalization was submitted, including concrete suggestions about trade expansion, scientific, technical, and cultural exchange, and "the coordination of foreign policy activities." All proposals were rejected and, on the contrary, Chinese party leaders in effect declared war upon the Soviet state and party. Such party leaders as Ch'en Yi even propagated the thesis that military strife between the two nations was possible, and, in fact, numerous border conflicts have been perpetrated, with the number increasing in recent months. The Chinese have suggested indeed that they may "reestablish their historical rights," despite the fact that the present Soviet–Chinese boundary has "a firm international juridical basis."

With respect to Vietnam, the attitude of the CCP has caused "tremendous damage." The CPSU takes the position that aid to "Socialist Vietnam" is "a holy international duty," and it has delivered large quantities of weapons— one-half billion rubles worth of war materials in 1965 alone. The Soviet Union is also giving extensive military and material assistance to the National Liberation Front. The Vietnamese are very satisfied, saying "We will defeat the Americans with Soviet weapons." More than once, the CPSU has suggested to the Chinese joint actions for the support of Vietnam, but these proposals were totally rejected. Indeed, the Chinese have refused to allow Soviet transport planes to fly weapons over Chinese territory and have created obstacles to rail transport of war materials as well. The Chinese want a protracted Vietnamese war "in order to maintain the international tensions and in order to portray China as a besieged fortress. . . . There is ample reason

The Chinese answered in kind, in some of the most acrimonious language yet used in the dispute. On February 20, for example, while the JCP delegation was in Hanoi, the Peking press asserted: "The Khrushchev revisionists may collaborate with the United States, India, and Japan to build a 'containment wall' around China. But the people of Asia and the whole world want revolution and the great influence of China cannot be 'contained' by any force. By perpetuating acts of betrayal, the Khrushchev revisionists only make themselves the enemy of

---

to claim that one of the goals of the policy of the Chinese leadership in the Vietnam question consists in the provocation of a military conflict between the U.S.S.R. and the U.S.A. They want a collision of the U.S.S.R. and the U.S.A. in order (as they themselves say) 'to watch the battle of the tigers while sitting on the mountain.' "

The Chinese have been willing to sacrifice the interests of the national liberation movement to their own chauvinistic big-power desires. As a result, they have suffered serious failures in Africa and Asia, whereas the Soviet Union is everywhere rendering effective assistance to peoples in their struggles for liberation and progress. The Chinese, on the contrary, are aiding American aggressors by widening the disagreement in the socialist community. In some thirty countries, the Chinese have created fractional groups, each of which directs its attacks against Marxist–Leninist parties and the general line of the world Communist movement. In this fashion, the CCP meddles in the affairs of other parties, causing grave difficulties. This is equally true in connection with international democratic organizations. But it is now clear that the Chinese ideological-theoretical platform is exclusively "to serve the nationalistic superpower policy of the Chinese leadership."

They aim at world war, as Lin Piao in his speech published in September 1965 makes clear. The CPSU has always recognized armed as well as peaceful forms of struggle for power, but the Chinese leaders have only one weapon— armed uprising. Their endeavor to force all parties of nonsocialist countries to accept the goal of immediate revolution independently of real conditions is an effort to force a putschist, conspiratorial tactic upon the Communist movement (Indonesia?—author). This tactic allows the imperialistic bourgeoisie to massacre revolutionaries and "exposes the active ranks of a number of Communist Parties to destruction." The CCP leaders completely ignore the great variety of conditions in the non-Western world, turning to all peoples with an appeal for armed insurrection. They take a casual attitude toward war, ignoring the fact that a global conflict would take millions of lives.

We are against adventurism and pushing peoples into a thermonuclear war. We favor isolating imperialist circles through joint efforts. The Chinese, while criticizing other parties for insufficient revolutionary spirit, themselves show extreme caution and pronounced patience toward imperialist powers. Their foreign policies, of course, derive in part from internal difficulties and deviations, such as the cult of personality centering around Mao. Far from correcting the errors, the CCP is restricting democracy still further, rejecting Leninist norms of party life and engaging in administrative tyranny. The Soviet party will continue to seek normalization, but it will also take measures against splittist activities on the part of the Chinese. It will not be deterred, however, from seeking the unity and solidarity of the world Communist movement.

the peoples and will end up in disgrace. They cannot be of any service to U.S. imperialism."[91]

Thus, it was no surprise when the CCP Central Committee wrote to Moscow on March 22, the day after the JCP delegation had returned to Peking, firmly declining the invitation to attend the 23rd CPSU Congress scheduled to open one week later. The Chinese lashed out at the Soviet leaders in the most violent terms:

Since coming to power, the new leaders of the CPSU have gone farther and farther down the road of revisionism, splittism and great-power chauvinism. The moment you came to power, you declared that you would resolutely carry out the Khrushchev revisionist general line of the 20th and 22nd Congresses. You told us to our faces that there was not a shade of difference between Khrushchev and yourselves on the question of the international communist movement or of relations with China. Far from publicly retracting the anti-Chinese Open Letter of July 1963 and the anti-Chinese report and resolution of February 1964, you have intensified your activities against China by more insidious tactics. Despite the tricks you have been playing to deceive people, you are pursuing U.S.–Soviet collaboration for the domination of the world with your whole heart and soul. . . .
Your clamor for "united action," especially on the Vietnam question, is nothing but a trap for the purpose of deceiving the Soviety people and the revolutionary people of the world. . . . You have worked hand in glove with the United States in a whole series of dirty deals inside and outside the United Nations. . . . Not only have you excluded yourselves from the international united front of all the peoples against U.S. imperialism and its lackeys, you have even aligned yourselves with U.S. imperialism, the main enemy of the people of the world, and the reactionaries of all countries in a vain attempt to establish a Holy Alliance against China, against the people, against the national liberation movement and against the Marxist–Leninists.[92]

In mid-February, the Soviet Union had reiterated its appeal that the leaders of Hanoi, Peking, and Moscow meet together to work out a program of coordinated aid and support for the Vietnamese Communists. There is every reason to believe that the Japanese Communist delegation, supported by Pyongyang and Hanoi, had urged the Chinese to accept this offer—and failed. We cannot know, of course, the details of the various meetings between Chinese and Japanese Communist leaders, but it can be assumed that behind the scenes tension ran high. On Marth 25th, while the Miyamoto delegation was in Peking, the JCP

---

[91] As reported over Radio Peking, February 21, 1966.
[92] For the English translation from which these quotations are taken, see *Peking Review*, No. 13, March 25, 1966, pp. 5–6.

sent a cable to Moscow also declining the invitation to attend the 23rd
CPSU Congress. The cable was brief, however, and while the language
was sharp, only one issue was stressed, namely, the support being given
"anti-Party elements" like the Shiga group. There was no mention of
Soviet policy concerning Vietnam—merely a final paragraph which asserted: "If you too really want unity of the international communist
movement and normalization of relations between the Japanese and
Soviet Parties as fraternal Parties, it stands to reason that you should
frankly examine the cause of present-day conditions and take positive
steps based on the principles of Marxism–Leninism and proletarian internationalism."[93]

The day after the above cable was dispatched, on March 26, Chinese
leaders provided a rally for the Japanese delegation in Peking. Speaking
at the rally, Miyamoto reiterated the February 4th line, balancing an
attack upon "modern revisionism" with the need for a united front
against "American imperialism." It was clear that Peking and Yoyogi
had been unable to reach a basic agreement. The Miyamoto mission
had failed.

When the Miyamoto delegation returned from its abortive mission
in early April, a thorough policy reexamination was undertaken at the
highest levels. Ratification of the new policy came in the course of the
two-day Central Committee 4th Plenum meeting, April 28–29, although
orders were initially given not to discuss the Plenum decisions even
within party ranks. Because wild rumors spread, both in and out the
party, this order was reversed, and in its May 11th editorial, *Akahata*
spelled out the new line. Even before the 4th Plenum, however, the
basic outlines of party policy for the future were signalled in an important speech delivered in Tōkyō on April 21 by Yonehara Akira on the
occasion of the 96th anniversary of Lenin's birth.[94]

Yonehara dwelt at length upon the importance of party independence.
At the outset of his speech, he asserted that Lenin in his famous work,
What Is To Be Done?, had stressed the point that it was not useful
merely to memorize indiscriminately the experience of foreign revolutionary movements, but that all such movements had to be treated criti-
cally and weighed independently so that they could be adapted to
one's own use. The minds of others cannot become our minds,
asserted Yonehara.

---

[93] For the English translation, see *Peking Review,* No. 15, April 8, 1966,
p. 21.

[94] This speech, "with some revisions," was published in *Zenei,* No. 251,
June 1966, pp. 18–31. An English translation appears in *JPRS* 36,230, pp.
54–86.

"If the Bolshevik Party had not had an independent spirit—if they had had the concept of trimming one's policy to whatever 'famous' foreign leaders had to say—the view of Shiga Yoshio—the Russian Revolution would never have succeeded." But, significantly, Yonehara quickly added that one could say the same thing in connection with the Chinese revolution. The Chinese had established a correct theory and path for revolution, the path of Comrade Mao Tse-tung. Mao's theories had triumphed over numerous errors, the mistakes of right and left opportunism. But in order to establish this correct path, Comrade Mao and others had had to fight resolutely against incorrect external influences.

Then Yonehara went on to assert, "We cannot establish a correct path and theory for revolution in our country unless we maintain an independent stand." Not only are the U.S.S.R. and China evidence of this fact, but so is Cuba. The Cuban revolution had succeeded because "the wrong influences from outside the country" had been excluded. (This extraordinary statement was made, it is to be noted, *after* the violent denunciation by Castro of the Chinese for their interference in the internal affairs of the Cuban Party, a denunciation made in early 1966.) Yonehara followed this statement quickly with the assertion, "You must have heard of China and Albania who have developed socialist construction very well by resisting the economic pressures of the major powers and modern revisionism." And then he mentioned—in a coupling that had special significance—(North) Korea and Rumania as states evidencing a capacity to achieve socialism through independence.

Indeed, Yonehara had obviously been building up to these two states, particularly North Korea. Praising Korean reconstruction, he went on to assert "the truth is that [along with aid from socialist countries] there were also pressures and interferences on the part of large countries which opposed the policies of reconstruction and the program of the Korean Workers' Party." With extraordinary frankness, Yonehara was signalling the fact that the earlier dilemma of North Korea was now the dilemma of the Japanese Communist Party. Korea too had been faced with pressures from and interference by *both* the Russians and the Chinese. And the Korean Communist Mainstream—personified by one man, Kim Il-sŏng—had faced internal dissidents who had followed blindly either the Soviet or the Chinese line. But Kim had cast off external influences and triumphed. Purging both the pro-Soviet and the pro-Chinese groups, Kim had thrown in his lot with national communism. (Yonehara veiled only this last point; all else he spelled out in graphic manner.)

In his selective recollection of JCP history, Yonehara also revealed much about the travails of the past decade. Our party was greatly weakened between 1955 and 1958, he admitted, and this was the result of mistakes in policy made before that time. (More honestly, he might have put a heavier emphasis upon the errors during the period 1950–1955, but that would have raised old ghosts within the party). The correct course, however, was charted (by the new Miyamoto–Hakamada–Nosaka Mainstream), and "we did not talk this over previously with the Soviet Communist Party or the Chinese Communist Party." When our program was finally adopted at the 8th Congress, Yonehara asserted, both the Russians and the Chinese praised it highly, but they rated it after we had completed it, he insisted. From the autumn of 1959, Yonehara stated, Khrushchevian revisionism poured into the international Communist movement. Our delegates could have contributed to unity at the time of the Bucharest meetings by firmly maintaining independent views from the very beginning, and by asserting their principles, "but we did not do so," he added in the one prominent element of self-criticism.

At this point, Yonehara's logic faltered. Having insisted vehemently that it is impossible to divide Communist parties into pro-Soviet versus pro-Chinese, and that each party is and must be completely independent, he argued that the great struggle remains between those who hold to "true Marxism–Leninism" and those who oppose it. Thus, if the JCP at that point was prepared to state that neither the Soviets nor the Chinese are infallible guides to truth ("big countries are not always right, small countries are not always wrong"), the community of the orthodox and that of the heretic still existed. In the very midst of seeking to admit and defend a pluralistic Communist world, Yonehara continued to champion a monolithic ideology. Having issued his declaration of independence, he bowed low before the old myth of *true* Marxism–Leninism which sanctioned, indeed demanded, dependence.

Despite this very basic contradiction, however, Yonehara quite consciously was setting up a meaningful, new division within the Communist world as well as a defense for national communism. The small Communist states and parties must band together to protect themselves against the big Communist states and parties. In reality, of course, that trend had been underway in Asia for several years. Consultation and interaction between the parties of Indonesia, North Korea, North Vietnam, and Japan had become increasingly important after 1963. Could such a political framework permit the Japanese Communist Party to survive, if necessary, without either Soviet or Chinese aid?

On the home front, the thrust of Yonehara's speech was unmistakably clear. The fight against right-wing revisionists now had to be coupled with a fight against left-wing dogmatists. To the pro-Soviet renegades, the Japanese Communist Party now had to add the pro-Chinese renegades.

The May 11th *Akahata* editorial established the new line officially, setting forth the basic decisions of the 4th Plenum.[95] The struggle on two fronts now took on a new meaning. The Japanese Communist Party dedicated itself to a simultaneous—and by implication, *equal*—struggle against "modern revisionism" and "dogmatism–sectarianism." Of course, the party strove valiantly to prove that this position in fact represented no change in policy, and that even before the 9th Congress, or at least with the 9th Congress, the party had dedicated itself to this course of action. It could cite the formal words to prove its case, but in fact, its claim was false, as any careful survey of the content of its past policies and pronouncements made clear.

To be sure, the two fronts were not being attacked equally—at least at this point. All of the old charges against the Soviets were repeated in the May 11th editorial, and the CPSU was cited by name as various revisionist crimes were analyzed in detail. No catalogue of explicit sins were ascribed to the CCP, nor was it ever mentioned by name. However, the JCP firmly announced that it had "taken precautions" against the tendency to react passively to the new "dual attitude" of the CPSU leaders and also against the mistake of "underestimating" the task of consolidating an international united front against American "imperialism." Moreover, the editorial showed no restraint in attacking by name the Ōsaka "anti-Party dogmatists," who had either deserted or been expelled from the party. The big damage caused by the party split following the "1950 question" and the onset of "ultra-left adventurism" had taught the party a very important lesson—the need to firmly uphold the line of self-reliance and independence.

In concluding, the May 11th editorial summoned up Japanese experiences with foreigners throughout their history, particularly experiences since the Meiji Restoration, and then demanded a rejection of "foreign worship and flunkeyism." The struggle on two fronts would advance, asserted the editorial, as flunkeyism was cast off and as the entire

---

[95] "Let the Entire Party Study the Decision of the Party Congress in Order to Make Efforts for the Consolidation of the International United Front Against U.S. Imperialism and for the Genuine Unity of the International Communist Movement," *Akahata*, May 11, 1966, p. 1. An official English translation appears in *Bulletin Information for Abroad* (a publication of the Central Committee of the Communist Party of Japan), No. 52, Tōkyō, 1966, pp. 7–17.

party membership mastered the capacity for self-reliance and independence, truly uniting patriotism and internationalism.

Never in its history had the Japanese Communist Party attempted so ardently to place itself in the mainstream of Japanese evolution, to fit itself into the pendulum-like swing toward and away from external influences that had characterized the most basic political forces operative in Japan. The new line was to be enunciated on numerous other occasions during the spring and summer of 1966, and in a variety of ways. From May 21 to June 15, an important JCP delegation led by Kasuga Shōichi visited Rumania.[96] There can be little doubt that the symbolic significance of this visit had been closely calculated, and it was even more significant in the aftermath of the fiasco suffered by Chou En-lai in Bucharest.[97]

The JCP delegation was probably very pleased with the joint JCP-Rumanian Communist Party statement which included a reaffirmation of the vital importance of the unity and solidarity of the social camp, the necessity of defending the purity of Marxism–Leninism against any type of deviation, and the need to respect the independence and equality of each Communist party, large or small.

During June and July, both *Akahata* and *Zenei* published numerous articles extolling the struggle on two fronts and denouncing both "right and left deviationists." The new line was clearly under attack within party circles. To what extent would the pro-China elements in and out of the party create major problems? Would large-scale purges be necessary? Some of the arguments that could be mustered by the pro-China faction were advanced by Niijima Junryo.[98] If the CCP were leading the fight against revisionism and on behalf of true Marxism–Leninism, how could another party remain faithful to its principles by abandoning the struggle and seeking shelter in isolation or in some type of mechanistic "centrist" position? "Independence" had become a term designed to deceive the masses, a substitution of old nationalist verbage

---

[96] For details, and the joint communiqué, see *Akahata,* June 17, 1966, p. 1.

[97] Chou arrived in Bucharest on June 16, the day after the departure of the Kasuga group, and remained in Romania for eight days. Chou's desire to openly attack Soviet revisionism and his attempt to commit the Romanians to this course resulted in a serious behind-the-scenes struggle and a stunning failure for Chinese diplomacy.

[98] Niijima's article, "The Significance of Nuclear Tests and Rectification," appeared in *Economist,* Tōkyō, May 31, 1966, pp. 22–28. An English translation appears in *JPRS* 36,230, pp. 42–53. Fuha Tetsuzō responded to Niijima with an article, "Flunkyism Which Denies Independence," *Akahata,* June 10, 1966, p. 1.

for true proletarian internationalism. One could not be neutral in the face of truth. Between Marxism–Leninism and modern revisionism there was no half-way position.

Party spokesmen for their part now took on the "anti-Party dogmatists" directly. They were charged with being sycophants who unconditionally worshipped the leadership of foreign parties. The epithets once reserved for men like Shiga and Kamiyama were now being turned against the Liberation Front worshippers of Mao. And the LF Program was attacked as an attempt to duplicate the 1951 Program, a program that had led to disaster. The Liberation Front group, argued Shimotsukasa Junkichi, had failed to grasp the nature of contemporary Japan.[99] Japan was a highly developed capitalist nation, not a backward peasant society. Their strong emphasis upon land reform, mechanically borrowed from the Chinese revolution, was misplaced, given Japanese circumstances. So was their thesis that the main blow should be delivered against the Satō government, and that the tactics of violence involving guerrilla warfare should be given primacy. These tactics had been thoroughly discredited in the 1950–1955 period. Japan was not China.

The debate continued as the time approached for the annual Gensuikyō conference, always a convenient occasion for measuring currents within the Communist movement both in Japan and in the international scene. In 1966, once again, three separate conferences were held, symbolizing the fragmented condition in which the Japanese "left" currently found itself. On July 28, the Asian People's Conference Against Atomic and Hydrogen Bombs opened, sponsored by the National Council for Peace and Against Nuclear Bombs (Kakkin Kaigi), an organization made up of Democratic Socialists and some Liberal Democrats. Matsushita Masatoshi, President of Rikkyō University, presided over the session, with some thirty-seven Asian representatives present from such nations as India, Thailand, Laos, Indonesia, Malaysia, Taiwan, the Philippines, Ceylon, Australia, and Hongkong. Premier Satō sent greetings to the conference. The resolutions included a statement of opposition to Chinese and French nuclear tests, demands for the abolition of nuclear weapons, and a plea for cooperation among Asian nations for the creation of peace in the Far East.

---

[99] Shimotsukasa Junkichi, "The Essence and the Absurdity of Anti-Party Dogmatists," *Zenei*, July 1966, pp. 56–70. An English translation appears in *JPRS* 37,008, pp. 1–23. See also, Wakabayashi Sen, "The Struggle on 'Two Fronts'—Based on the Experience of Our Party and International Lessons," *Akahata*, June 30, 1966, p. 5, translated in *JPRS* 36,716, pp. 85–91; and Yonehara Akira, "Problems and Tasks of the Japanese Communist Party," *Akahata*, July 25, 1966, pp. 3–4, translated in *JPRS* 37,126, pp. 34–45.

The meetings of the JCP-sponsored Gensuikyō opened in preliminary session on July 30, with the so-called 12th World Congress being scheduled in Hiroshima from August 5 to 7. All elements within the Communist world recognized that high stakes rode on this conference, and an enormous amount of intricate maneuvering had been taking place behind the scenes. A few days before the sessions opened, the Japanese government refused Liu Ning-i, whom the Chinese had selected to head their delegation, entry into Japan on the grounds that Liu had made politically seditious remarks in the course of his 1965 speech to the conference. Peking immediately blasted the Japanese decision, asserting that it proved how fearful the Holy Alliance—U.S. imperialism, Soviet revisionism, and Japanese militarism—had become over the prospect of the militant solidarity of the Chinese and Japanese people. The Japanese Communist Party also issued a bitter condemnation of the action. There were some, however—possibly including the Chinese—who believed that the JCP was secretly pleased.

In any case, Chou En lai's greetings to the conference reiterated the current Chinese line with a vengeance. "U.S. imperialism, modern revisionism and the Japanese militarist forces," said Chou, "are trying by hook or by crook to sabotage the militant solidarity of the Chinese and Japanese peoples, and they are trying to realize the scheme 'to contain China.' All these are vain attempts. Through their experience in struggle, the people have recognized who are their real friends, who are their false friends, and who are their enemies."[100]

Surely this last sentence was an appeal—and a warning—to comrades of the Japanese Communist Party. But it failed. The storm broke on August 1 when Gensuikyō officials accepted the registration of the World Federation of Democratic Youth, a Soviet-bloc organization. It will be recalled that Soviet-bloc delegates had walked out of the 1964 Gensuikyō Congress and had not been represented at the 1965 Congress because of the organization's ruling that participants should agree to support the 10th Congress resolutions *and* not attend any other Japanese peace conference. Had the decision to accept the World Federation of Democratic Youth in 1966 been worked out in collaboration with the JCP, or did it merely represent a strategy conceived by the Soviet bloc?[101]

---

[100] "Premier Chou En-lai Greets the 12th World Conference Against Atomic and Hydrogen Bombs," *Peking Review*, No. 32, August 5, 1966, pp. 15–16.

[101] Viktor V. Grishin, Chairman of the All-Union Central Council of Soviet Trade Unions had visited Japan on June 17–25 at the invitation of Sōhyō and Chūritsu Rōren, and on June 23, he had a one-hour talk with JCP leaders at party headquarters. Whether this meeting or other Soviet-JCP contacts dealt with the Gensuikyō Congress is not known.

Whatever its origins, the tactic succeeded in blowing the 1966 Gensuikyō "World Congress" completely apart. For forty-eight hours, Gensuikyō officials and pro-Peking foreign delegates argued over the issue, with the former insisting that they had no basis for excluding the WFDY delegate, and the latter insisting that such revisionists had to go. In the early morning of August 3, when Gensuikyō officials made it clear that they would not alter their decision, thirty-three foreign delegates proportedly representing sixteen nations withdrew from the congress, leaving only about twenty foreign representatives from seven nations counting Japan, and six international organizations.[102] Thus, the 12th Gensuikyō "World Congress" ended in a fiasco, with more than one-half of the foreign delegates departing and insisting that they would never again take part in the congress. The resolutions approved by the rump group on August 7, all JCP-line positions, were lost in the excitment over the split.

Many of the dissidents went immediately to China. On August 6, one group of delegates arrived in Peking, where they were met by such stalwarts as Kuo Mo-jo, Liao Ch'eng-chih, and Liu Ning-i. Another group arrived in Canton on August 7. They were received as conquering heroes. At an August 7 banquet in their honor, Liu Ning-i congratulated them on their "brilliant success," repeating word for word the themes Chou En-lai had stressed in his greetings of July 28.[103]

---

[102] For a detailed account, see *Yomiuri Shimbun*, August 3, 1966, p. 1.

The delegates of Japan, Korea, Romania, the United States, Guinea, Denmark, and Frace were those who upheld the position of Gensuikyō officials and remained in attendance.

In his welcoming speech of August 7, Nosaka Sanzō lashed out at the Peking position. Insisting that unity was the most urgent task for the Communists so that "an effective counterblow against the American imperialist criminals" could be launched, he went on to assert, "It is regrettable to note that today there are those who advocate, only as lip service, the ideal of establishing a general united front against imperialism. . . . Some of the socialist countries have been refusing to become part of such an international united front under the pretext that they do not accept 'revisionism.' Needless to say, such beliefs and pretensions do not favor the expectations of the Vietnamese people as revealed by the Premier Ho Chi Minh's appeal." *Akahata*, August 7, 1966, p. 1.

[103] For the full text of Liu's speech, see "We Absolutely Cannot Accept Taking 'United Action' with the Soviet Revisionist Leading Clique," *Peking Review*, No. 34, August 19, 1966, pp. 22–24.

Note particularly Liu's following challenge: "The Chinese people have full confidence in the development and consolidation of the friendly relations between the peoples of China and Japan. No force can undermine the fraternal friendship and militant unity between our two peoples. It cannot be undermined by either the U.S. imperialists or the Japanese militarists, and it absolutely cannot be undermined by the Soviet revisionist leading clique and its old and new followers of various descriptions."

There could be no question that the JCP had aligned itself with the Soviet bloc on this occasion as far as Peking was concerned, and was thus to be exposed to the full force of Chinese wrath. Peking-sponsored allegations were as nasty as could be conceived. One Laksen Mututantri of Ceylon was quoted as saying, "The majority of foreign delegations . . . refused to be corrupted or intimidated by the special agents of the U.S. Central Intelligence Agency and the police of the Satō government."[104] Evidently the CIA, whose prowess is amazing if one believes Communist stories, had finally succeeded in buying off the Japanese Communist Party! Saionji Kinkazu, so-called "Japanese peace champion" and permanent Peking house-plant, echoed a more traditional line of abuse: "A handful of the leading members of Gensuikyō, by brazenly trampling on the principles and tradition for which we have striven, are selling out the Japanese people and their comrades-in-arms the world over. I hold this handful of people in utter contempt. We cannot but condemn them, because they do not serve the people but serve the most unholy 'Holy Alliance,' that is, the U.S. militarism of Johnson, the modern revisionism headed by the Soviet leading cliques, and the Japanese reactionaries headed by the Satō government."[105]

What an extraordinary change had occurred in Gensuikyō and in Peking-JCP relations in the course of a single year! The Japanese Communists, however, were not without allies in the Communist world. On August 11, Pyongyang hailed the success of the 12th Gensuikyō Congress via *Rodong Shinmun*.[106] "All the resolutions adopted at the conference are absolutely just and right," asserted the article, "since they accord with aspirations of the world's peace-loving people fighting to smash the U.S. imperialists' policies of aggression and war and defend the peace of Asia and of the world."

According to the North Koreans, neither the machinations of the U.S.-Japanese reactionaries nor the withdrawal of the delegates "of some countries" had destroyed the success of the congress. The article concluded by saying, "The Congress was a meeting of great significance for defending and developing the . . . brilliant tradition of the movement against A-H Bombs, and was a great contribution to world peace. . . . The Korean people fully support it."

The Pyongyang-Yoyogi alliance was holding firm in the face of the withering blasts from Peking. On August 8, *Akahata* had carried a

---

[104] *Peking Review*, No. 33, August 12, 1966, p. 4.

[105] *Ibid.*, pp. 4–5.

[106] For an English translation, see *The People's Korea*, August 24, 1966, p. 6.

lengthy unsigned article championing autonomy and independence.[107] Once again, the Soviet party was accused of revisionism, but mounting pressure, according to *Akahata,* had caused it to follow a two-faced position. This made essential a policy of combining a resolute fight against revisionism with the struggle for unity. Unfortunately, the Shida group was currently echoing the doctrine of a certain foreign party, taking a dogmatic, left sectarian line, one contrary to Lenin's teachings and harmful to the interests of the Vietnamese people. Thus, the JCP had to intensify its two-front struggle against modern revisionism and against dogmatism and sectarianism, upholding true independence.

For the first time, the JCP came close to equating Chinese dogmatism as a deviation equal to Soviet revisionism, using the Shida group as a stalking horse for Peking. On August 12, *Akahata* was joined by *Rodong Shinmun.* The organ of the Korean Workers' Party carried a lengthy article entitled, "Let Us Defend Independence."[108] This article, closely paralleling the *Akahata* piece, presented an elaborate, forceful defense of national communism in which resistance to external pressures and the development of patriotism became supreme virtues.[109]

Neither of these articles, of course, resolved the central paradox noted earlier in connection with Yonehara's speech. On the one hand,

---

[107] See also Toyota Shiro, "The People's Revolutionary Tradition and the Japanese Communist Party Platform," *Akahata,* August 7, 1966, p. 5. An English translation appears in *JPRS* 37,546, pp. 19–25.

[108] For an English translation, see *The People's Korea,* August 17, 1966, pp. 1–7.

[109] Note the following passages: "The communists are making revolution with the country and the nation as a unit. The basic duty of the communists of each country is, first of all, to fulfil the revolution in their own country successfully. They can contribute to the world revolution only when they successfully carry out revolution in their own country.

"For successfully carrying out revolution and construction in one's own country, one should educate the people in patriotism. One can fight better for the prosperity of the country and happiness of the people when he loves his country and has national pride.

"Without arming the people with socialist patriotism, it is impossible to build socialism and communism. Socialist patriotism is one of the powerful factors propelling social progress under socialism.

"Such patriotic spirit is not born of itself. It can be fostered only when one knows better one's own country. One should be well acquainted with the history and fine tradition of one's own country and with the reality of today.

"If one is ignorant of the past and present of his country he cannot have patriotism, national pride or the spirit of independence, nor can he display enthusiasm and devotion in revolution and construction.

"One who has no pride in his nation will inevitably fall into national nihilism" (*ibid.,* p. 4).

Marxism–Leninism was defined as a guide to action, not a dogma—a creed to be "tested, replenished and enriched through practice."[110] But on the other hand, stern admonitions were sounded to the effect that deviations of right and left had to be scrupulously avoided and vigorously attacked when they appeared. Indeed, both articles ended on a familiar note: "Our Party will fight to safeguard the purity of Marxism–Leninism against modern revisionism, dogmatism and factionalism."

Step by step, both the Japanese Communists and the North Koreans were advancing the struggle on two fronts, the struggle against Soviet revisionism and Chinese dogmatism. In these articles, there were strong suggestions that Soviet errors of the past were now being equalled by Chinese errors of the present.[111]

Meanwhile, the third anti-A and H bomb conference, that of Gensuikin, had been successfully concluded. In contrast to the traumatic developments affecting Gensuikyō, the 1966 Sōhyō-Socialist Party-sponsored meeting which opened in Hiroshima on August 5 produced few surprises or changes from positions of the previous year. Some fifty foreign delegates were present, supposedly representing twelve nations and three international organizations, with the Soviet–East European bloc naturally having a large group in attendance.[112] The resolutions adopted were generally in line with the policies adopted at the 27th Socialist Party Congress of January, noted earlier. It was agreed at the

---

[110] *Ibid.,* p. 3.

[111] Note, for example, the following passage from the *Rodong Shinmun* article (from the English translation in *The People's Korea*): "The dogmatists [within our Party] also opposed our Party's policy on intellectuals. They criticized our Party's policy of educating and remoulding old intellectuals as 'leading the Party toward the right.' They argued that the old intellectuals must be purged since they are 'capitalist elements.'

"It is true that most of the old intellectuals are of propertied class origin and served the exploiting class in the past. But they experienced foreign imperialists' oppression and national discrimination. Therefore, they possess a certain degree of revolutionary character.

"The dogmatists saw only the negative side of the old intellectuals, failing to see their positive side" (p. 4).

Could there have been a more timely indictment of the Chinese "cultural revolution," currently reaching a new pitch?

[112] For a detailed account, see *Shakai Shimpō,* August 3, 1966, p. 2. The U.S.S.R. delegates numbered twelve; Czechoslovakia—four; Hungary—two; Yugoslavia—two; World Federation of Democratic Youth—two; the World Federation of Trade Unions—two; and the World Council of Peace—two. There were also seven delegates from the United States, including the Secretary of SANE.

subcommittee level to substitute the phrase "American intervention in Vietnam" for the term "American imperialism." Otherwise, the line on Vietnam was compatible with the Communist position.

The surface harmony evidenced at the Gensuikin conference, however, was misleading. As the fall of 1966 approached, all elements of the Japanese "left," including the Socialists continued to be in a state of division and disarray. Internal cleavages, moreoever, were exacerbated by an ever-widening stream of external pressures and influences, as both the Russians and the Chinese roamed at will over the Japanese political horizon.

Quite naturally, Peking stepped up its campaign to influence the Socialist Mainstream faction as its relations with the JCP deteriorated. The Sasaki group sent a stream of delegates to the Chinese capital, and some 600 youths, most of them having Socialist connections, were scheduled to visit China in the fall until the Japanese government refused permission. The Russians, however, had no intention of being excluded from the scene. Thus, on August 18, for example, a four-day conference "For Peace and Friendship Between the Japanese and Russian Peoples" opened in Khabarovsk, with 264 Sōhyō–JSP delegates present. At that meeting, resolutions were passed demanding the unity of all anti-imperialist forces and the end of U.S. aggression in Vietnam. These were but a few instances of the ardent Chinese and Soviet efforts to penetrate the Japanese "left," efforts bound to add to existing divisions and tensions.

Meanwhile, the broader struggle between the "left" and "moderate" forces was continuing to unfold, both within Sōhyō and within the Socialist Party. At the Sōhyō annual convention held just prior to the Gensuikin conference, Horii Toshikatsu was elected Chairman, replacing the veteran Ōta. This and other actions signalled a possible end to the most recent "left" swing within Japan's largest labor federation. At the same time, factional strife between the "left" and "moderate" groups within the Japan Socialist Party continued unabated, with each group girding itself for another showdown at the next National Congress.

Within the Communist ranks, confusion was equally great. Peking was naturally seeking to support elements like the Liberation Front group and had begun to appeal to grass-root members over the head of party leadership. As the 10th Party Congress approached, Mainstream JCP leaders had to ask themselves whether a large scale purge of pro-China elements within the party would be necessary. Since June 4, 1966, notice of Peking radio programs in Japanese had ceased to appear in

the columns of *Akahata*.[113] Moreover, JCP organs had practically ignored the much heralded "cultural revolution" in China. Translations
of Mao's collected works sponsored by the party had been quietly
suspended. The line of the JCP journal devoted to international communism, *Heiwa to Shakaishugi no mondai* (*Problems of Peace and Socialism*), long a vehicle for the dissemination of Peking views, had shifted.
On July 6, the JCP youth front, the Democratic Youth League, announced it would not participate in the youth trip to China because of
a busy schedule and "the need to combat schismatic activities." More
importantly, pro-Peking elements began to be removed from important
party posts. Thus, even before the split at the 12th Gensuikyō Congress,
the JCP had begun to move sharply away from its former pro-
China stance.

After the August crisis, this trend was accelerated. Immediately, orders went out from party headquarters to all local branches advising
them that the only pictures permissible in party offices were those of
Marx, Engles, Lenin, and Katayama—meaning that Mao had to go.
Chinese Communist Party journals disappeared from official JCP book-
stores and outlets, just as Russian literature had disappeared two years
earlier. And additional "disloyal officials" were dismissed from the party
or from their posts. The Chinese struck back with attacks upon those
who could not "distinguish between friends and enemies," and with
attempts to infiltrate such local party branches as the Tōkyō City
Committee.

This was the situation when the 10th Party Congress opened on
October 24, 1966. In the weeks preceding the Congress, the struggle
against pro-Peking elements within the party had been conducted vigorously, with some forty individuals being purged. Action against the
Yamaguchi Prefectural party organization was particularly sharp, with
a number of leaders being ousted from the party on charges of having
defied party orders, operating with "a blind trust of the line of a cer-

---

[113] For an "explanation," see Oka Masuyoshi (Chief Editor of *Akahata*)
in *Akahata*, July 10, 1966, p. 1. Said Oka, "We will introduce as many
as possible of the radio programs that seem necessary from the position
of our Party." Actually, Oka was dealing with broader issues. Some readers
had asked why *Akahata* did not treat international Communist problems when
these were given much coverage elsewhere. Oka replied that *Akahata* is a
weapon for the correct advancement of the party. "In treating international
problems, particularly the problems of foreign Communist and Workers' Parties,
we have to be especially prudent. . . . Regarding the policies of foreign
Communist and Workers' Parties, moreover, there are some of which our
Party cannot approve, and yet it is not appropriate to comment upon or
criticize these issues."

tain foreign party." Hokkaido, Tōkyō, Ehime, and several other prefectural party organizations were also affected, as well as the Japan–China Friendship Association. Among those purged was Central Committeeman Nishizawa Ryūji, son-in-law of the late Tokuda Kyūichi.

The 10th Party Congress was dominated by Miyamoto and, in many respects, represented the culmination of his rise to power.[114] The keynotes to the party position were the struggle on two fronts and the establishment of an "independent" position, themes underlined in the Central Committee Report adopted by the Congress. Marxism–Leninism was to be protected against "all opportunistic distortions and deviations," whether these were modern revisionism (Moscow) or dogmatism-sectism (Peking).

Once again, the primary enemy was seen to be "American imperialism," which now regarded Japan as the basis of its policy of "Asian aggression." Under the aegis of the United States, the Japanese monopoly capitalists and the Liberal Democratic Party, asserted the report, were attempting "to resurrect militarism and imperialism" via the maintenance of the Mutual Security Treaty and by allowing the Constitution to deteriorate, while positively cooperating with and supporting American policies.

In its quest for power, the party had the obligation not to surrender to bourgeois parliamentarism. At the same time, however, it had to smash to antiparty Shida faction doctrinaires who opposed "the revolutionary use of parliament" and favored instead "an ultra-left adventurism," which completely ignored the objective conditions of Japan, including the fact that it was an advanced capitalist society.

The correct route to power was via a "national democratic united front," one based upon the principles of genuine independence, democracy, peace, neutralism, and the improvement of the people's livelihood. Such a front had to build upon such mass organizations as the labor and peasant unions, politicizing them and orientating them against the twin enemies, American imperialism and Japanese monopoly capitalism.

With what forces in the political arena could a united front be constructed? The Central Committee took an optimistic view of trends. The Satō government, representing the Liberal Democratic mainstream, had betrayed its "ultra-right" predelictions in a gross manner. Hence, some factional struggles over Asian policies had developed even within

---

[114] All documents pertaining to the Congress are contained in *Zenei*, December 1966. The Central Committee Report as approved by the Congress was first published in *Akahata*, September 1, 1966, pp. 1–4.

the "reactionary" camp. The significance of this conflict, however, should not be overestimated, since it was being conducted within the framework of basic LDP policies.

The Democratic Socialist Party remained an "anti-Communist right-wing social democratic party," but even it was prepared to disagree with the Liberal Democrats on such an issue as the electoral reform bill. Meanwhile, the Kōmeitō, while retaining some conservative elements, displayed real promise, responding as it had to the Communist appeal for a joint struggle on the electoral system issue and departing from its hitherto anti-leftist coalition policies. Most importantly, the forces within the Japan Socialist Party favorable to united front policies had made recent gains. The right wing of the Japan Socialist Party continued their "opportunistic line," avoiding any thoroughgoing struggle, however, and the deep conflict within that party had produced vacillations and a lack of vigor. Nevertheless, the desperate attempts to isolate the JCP and split the democratic forces had failed. "On-the-spot" joint struggles had been conducted five times, and the establishment of the Three Party Liaison Conference by the JCP, JSP, and Kōmeitō on the electoral system issue could be accounted a most significant event. Unfortunately, the peace movement remained divided, continued the report, and, in analyzing this situation, the Central Committee was prepared to make no concessions. The 11th and 12th Gensuikyō World Conferences had shown the correct route, both on issues and on tactics. Neither big-power chauvinism as practiced by the modern revisionists nor splittism from the left as attempted by the dogmatists would prevail.

In this fashion, the 10th Congress Report raised and answered all of the old issues, with the answers indicating the continued "left" tendencies within the party, despite the new emphasis upon complete independence. Certainly, one of the most interesting sections of the report was that containing a brief recapitulation of major trends since 1945, primarily because it revealed so clearly the new thrust and the forces behind it.

Despite various gains, in the first five postwar years, the "correct development" of the party had been hindered by "the error of right-wing opportunism based upon the theory of peaceful revolution under the American Occupation." During the next five years, however, the "ultra-leftist adventurism adopted by a portion of the party leadership produced major losses." In this period, moreover, the weaknesses of the paternalistic, individualist leadership (Tokuda) which had been developed in the course of the party's postwar reconstruction came to the fore, blocking the correct development of such principles as democratic centralism and collective leadership, and promoting intraparty bureaucracy as well as permitting the infiltration of undesirable elements like Itō Ritsu and Shida Shigeo into party leadership ranks.

Only after 1955 (with the beginning of Miyamoto–Hakamada ascendancy) did the party start to pursue the correct line, with the 7th Party Congress in 1958 marking a milestone in the development of new programs and regulations that aimed at creating mass struggles against "all types of opportunism and sectism." Now the party program "creatively applies Marxism–Leninism to the conditions of Japan, overcoming past mistakes of both a leftist and rightist nature, presenting to the Japanese people the route of a liberation struggle, lifting high the four banners."

One of the striking aspects of this analysis, and of the report in general is the absence of any praise, or indeed, mention of Nosaka Sanzō. The party, in considerable measure, now appears to be seeking to cast off its past. It is clear, moreover, that the strictures against both Moscow and Peking remain firm, with familiar themes being advanced. The "international modern revisionists," confronted with "the failure of opportunism, splittism, and big-nation chauvinism," had been forced to make some policy changes. In particular, they had begun to stress the anti-imperialist struggle and the need to strengthen socialist solidarity instead of "their previous open subservience to American imperialism and the desire to convene an international conference to provoke an open split in the Communist movement." They continued to avoid any self-criticism, however and, of equal importance, to avoid any basic policy shift. Thus, they pursued a two-faced attitude, meanwhile continuing their interference in the internal affairs of the party and the Japanese progressive movement in general.

At the same time, doctrinaire and sectarian elements, at home and abroad, continued to follow left-adventurist policies that were totally in error, policies that actually supported the revisionists because of their mistaken character. To refuse to join in any type of joint effort to aid the Vietnamese people, for example, was narrow dogmatism that weakened the international Communist cause. To pursue splittist policies in the peace movement and elsewhere, moreover, could only serve the cause of American imperialism. Meanwhile, the Shida faction, abetted by "some foreign elements," continued its subversive activities, "adopting an attitude of flunkyism and doctrinarism when it talks about the views of a certain foreign Party."

The 10th Party Congress thus officially sanctioned the new era of "the struggle on two fronts," the climax of trends intensively underway for many months and possibly implicit in Miyamotoism for a much longer period. At the same time, it continued themes long implanted in Japanese Communist Party doctrine: treatment of the United States as the main enemy, with "Japanese monopoly capitalism" as a major but subordinate force; tactics that involved the use of parliamentarism, but a refusal to be bound by legal procedures and hence an implicit acceptance of violence as a necessary revolutionary means; and the goal of a national democratic united front centering upon "liberation," looking toward a People's Democracy.

As the Communist Party of Japan seeks to sustain and strengthen its new policy of "independence and autonomy," it is necessary to analyze the factors involved in the party's movement away from Peking. First, how shall we characterize the shift itself? Did it represent a dramatic change, or the culmination of a trend long underway, however camouflaged? There is some truth in both characterizations.

Certainly, the change was of major proportions and it produced swift repercussions. For some years, Yoyogi had stood with Peking on all substantive issues of importance, representing an ally seemingly faithful and loyal. As we have seen, Peking had reciprocated, displaying JCP polemics prominently, providing the party with substantial economic aid, and maintaining the closest personal relations with party leaders. Japanese Communist leaders, including Miyamoto, took their vacations in China, underwent medical treatment there, and were accorded every privilege. Hundreds of party members or Youth League members went to China each year. Therefore, when the cleavage developed in the spring and summer of 1966, the Japanese Communist Party was drastically affected. Financial relations between the two parties, propaganda distribution, and personal relations were all dramatically altered in a very short space of time. As in the case of the Soviet crisis earlier, moreover, the JCP (Yoyogi) suddenly had to guard against "subversive activities" within its ranks promoted directly or indirectly by Peking. Conditions of intimacy and alliance suddenly turned to those of guerrilla warfare.

It is true, however, that a "neutral" or "independence"-oriented element had long existed within the party. The debacle that followed the events of 1950, the unfolding of the Sino–Soviet dispute, and the broadest trends within the Communist world, moreover, tended to strengthen that element in certain respects. After 1955, Miyamoto was generally regarded as the "neutral" faction leader, and the internal politics of the JCP were coalition politics, a united front of "neutrals" and "pro-China" elements against the small, determined "pro-Soviet" group. At that time, alignment with China and union with the pro-Peking forces was essential given the nature of relations with Russia. Once the Soviet contingent had been purged, however, and the party was secure on its "right" flank, some readjustment was possible. That readjustment was obviously underway in 1964, with the April 17 strike issue a key catalyst and the 9th Party Congress a scene of some preliminary skirmishing. The critical period, however, came in the fall of 1965 and the spring of 1966 when the JCP, in close coordination with the Korean Workers' Party, sought to get the Chinese to accept the Soviet proposal for an international united front to aid Vietnam and were completely rebuffed.

It is enormously important to note the striking parallel between the politics of the JCP during this entire period and those of the Korean Workers' Party at an earlier point. The Korean Communists also had begun from a position of being mere appendages of Soviet power and Soviet policy. They too had swung sharply into the Chinese orbit as a result of events surrounding the Korean war and the policies of Khrushchev. Pro-Soviet elements within the party had been ruthlessly purged as Kim—long reckoned by some a Russian puppet—consolidated his power. And Kim as early as 1955 had begun to use "independence" and "autonomy" as key issues, demanding that the "love of fatherland" and "respect for things Korean" be a cardinal principle of Korean Communists. In the late 1950's, moreover, a purge of "pro-China" elements had gotten underway, together with a reorientation of Korean policies. And Kim and his followers were to complain bitterly against the attempted interference of outside *forces* (meaning both Russia and China) in the internal affairs of their party. Nevertheless, the Korean Communists had sided strongly with Peking on the substantive issues that developed between Moscow and Peking after 1958, and by 1963 party organs were savagely attacking the Soviet leaders and their policies. It was in this same period that close liaison developed among the small Asian Communist states and parties. The policies enunciated by Brezhnev and Kosygin met with some favor from this group, especially the proposal for a *modus vivendi* to aid Vietnam.

Along with comrades elsewhere, the JCP regarded an international united front as of critical importance in preventing a Communist defeat in Vietnam *and* in the general task of driving American power out of the Far East. Such a front, argued JCP leaders privately, might represent the first step in ending the Sino–Soviet cleavage, a possibility of massive importance to the party. As long as the breach continued, both the party and the broader Japanese "left" were certain to be further divided, and external interference in Japanese "left" politics was inevit-able. If a united front could not be established among Communists, moreover, the chances for a successful coalition with the Socialists, a strategy that was critical if the Communists hoped to advance on the home front, were reduced.

One can assume, therefore, that the sessions between Japanese and Chinese comrades were tense, even stormy. Personal animosities un-doubtedly developed. Major efforts must have taken place on both sides to persuade and cajole. Discussions lasted not merely for hours, but for days, and were broken off and renewed. Japanese Communist leaders had the opportunity to see Chinese dogmatism firsthand and at close range.

When the differences could not be solved, the conflict quickly got out of hand, partly because of the nature of the international Communist movement today. A "leftist" faction within the JCP, the Liberation Front, had already charged the Mainstream leaders with revisionist errors, and now the trouble with China represented their opportunity to bid for power—with Peking aid. Thus, the earlier drama involving the Voice of Japan faction had to be replayed. Just as in the case of the North Koreans some years previously, Mainstream leaders learned that major Communist powers do not take defeats or rebuffs from minor Communist states and parties lightly. Now, both Peking and Moscow were looking for new allies in the Japanese political scene, but the Jap-anese Communist Party did not have the same capacity as the Pyong-yang dictatorship had had to safeguard itself.

If the issue of the united front and trends involving internal JCP politics demanded a reappraisal of Peking policies and goals, there may well have been additional factors involved. It is clear, for example, that the fate of the PKI (the Communist Party of Indonesia) weighed very heavily upon the Japanese Communist leaders during this period. As noted earlier, the JCP had come to regard the PKI as an example of extraordinary success, and Aidit had come to have substantial in-fluence with JCP leaders. Indeed, a meaningful alliance between the two parties had been achieved. Both Japanese and North Korean leaders have recently hinted that they hold Peking responsible, directly or indi-rectly, for the abortive coup of September 30, 1965, and the subsequent destruction of the Indonesian Communist Party. Indeed, there are strong indications that Peking more or less simultaneously urged militant poli-cies upon a number of parties, arguing that the time was ripe for revo-lution and that the opening of new fronts was essential to victory in Vietnam. There have been repeated rumors, for example, that the

Korean Communists themselves were subjected to Chinese pressures to open a second front on the Korean peninsula, and that such pressures were also applied to the Russians with respect to Europe. Thus, the Japanese and Korean Communists may well have had increasing reason to doubt the wisdom of Chinese tactics either as these applied to the international scene or—as advanced by Liberation Front adherents at home—as they applied to Japan. "Left adventurism" had produced disaster for the Japanese Communists in the 1950–1955 era. It had seemingly produced disaster for the Indonesian Communists in 1965— yet Peking stubbornly persisted in demanding that militancy be the key concept and tactic, at least *for others*.

As we have noted, however, the growing estrangement from Peking has not—to date—produced a rapprochement with Moscow. If the Japanese Communist Party position is one of independence from the major Communist states today, it is also one of isolation, a point which we shall further assess in our conclusions.

VII

THE CURRENT STATUS
OF THE PARTY

As the 10th National Congress opened in October 1966, the Japanese Communist Party had a membership of 270,000 organized into some 13,170 cells, with 239 district committees and 46 prefectural committees serving as intermediate links to higher party authority (see Table I; Tables I-XXI appear at the end of this chapter). Membership had increased substantially since the 9th Party Congress when the party had claimed to have only somewhat more than 100,000 members. Subscriptions to *Akahata,* another index of party strength, were also considerably higher, with 326,000 subscribers claimed for the daily edition and 1,180,000 Sunday edition subscribers.[1]

What accounted for this substantial growth in membership over a two-year period? There is absolutely no indication that it was the result of party policies on substantive issues or a product of general conditions in Japan and the world. The gain appears to have represented essentially the formal recruitment of individuals already a part of the Communist vote, as a result of the strong emphasis upon organizational work that followed the 9th Party Congress. In sum, party cadres working at grass-roots levels, had scored meaningful successes without in any sense changing the political topography of Japan, or even the Japanese "left."

The central party organization remained unchanged. The Presidium represented the apex of power and contained nine regular and four

---

[1] In the greetings of Nosaka, the claim of nearly 300,000 party members was made. See *Zenei,* December 1966, p. 4.

alternate members.[2] Four of these thirteen members—Nosaka (Chairman), Miyamoto (Secretary-General), Hakamada, and Oka were designated Standing Members, constituting an Executive Committee. These were the men who made the basic decisions and held the real power. The Party Secretariat, whose members overlapped to some extent with the Presidium, was composed of sixteen members, supervising the special departments and publication bureaus of the central party organization.[3] Approximately 500 individuals, including those serving on party publications, were located in the headquarters.[4] The Party Central Committee consisted of 108 members, 66 of whom were regular members and 42 of whom were alternate members. There was also a Central Control and Audit Committee of nine.

This formal organizational structure, of course, does not vary in any significant degree from that of most other Communist parties. The principles of "democratic centralism" apply in Japan, meaning in fact a tight control over all party matters by the small coterie of men who occupy the summit positions. Unlike some parties, particularly those which have attained power, the Japanese Communist Party has probably not had an overwhelming preponderance of control gravitate into the hands of a single individual.[5] Certainly a man like Tokuda in his time had very considerable power, but other individuals like Nosaka played vital roles. Even when internal critics charged the leadership with "bureaucratism," Stalinism, and "dictatorship," they generally referred to the Mainstream *faction,* not exclusively to Tokuda. At present, there can be no question that Miyamoto is the single most important

---

[2] For detailed information on party organization and leaders, I am much indebted to Hirotsu Kyōsuke, Chief of the First Department of the Public Safety Investigation Bureau. As of mid-1966, prior to the 10th Party Congress, Presidium members were as follows: regular—Nosaka Sanzō, Miyamoto Kenji, Hakamada Satomi, Matsushima Harushige, Oka Masayoshi, Kurahara Koreto, Kasuga Shōichi, Yonehara Akira, and Kawada Kenji; alternate—Konno Yojirō, Nishizawa Tomio, Ōfuchi Seiki, and Fujiwara Ryūzō.

[3] Members of the Secretariat in the same period included Miyamoto, Hakamada, Oka, Konno, Nishizawa Tomio, Anzai Kuraji, Sunama Kazuyoshi, Uchino Takechiyo, Takahara Shinichi, Doki Tsuyoshi, Ii Yashirō, Iwabayashi Toranosuke, Tsukada Taigan, Okamoto Hiroyuki, Shimotsukasa Junkichi, and Ichikawa Shōichi.

[4] Party publications included *Akahata, Zenei, Sekai Seiji Shiryō, Bunka Hyoron (Cultural Review), Gikai to Jijitai (Parliament and Self-Government), Gakushū (Study),* and *Dokusho no Tomo (Friend of Reading).*

[5] For an analysis of broad trends with respect to Communist Party leadership, see my introductory chapter, "Communism in Asia: Toward a Comparative Analysis," in Robert A. Scalapino (Ed.), *The Communist Revolution in Asia —Tactics, Goals, and Achievements,* Englewood Cliffs, New Jersey, 1965.

figure in the Japanese Communist Party. It still appears, however, that critical decisions are made in the context of a somewhat broader group, with Hakamada, Nosaka, and Oka at least involved. Even in Communist politics, a basic political principle of Japan seems to apply: oligarchy, not the authority of a single man, constitutes the key to the political structure; factionalism or cliquism—the small leader-follower group—represents the nexus of Japanese politics.

The figures relating to membership set forth above naturally tell us little about the socioeconomic composition of the party. Fortunately, in 1962, when party members numbered approximately 100,000, the Japanese Communist Party published some data concerning membership in connection with the current House of Councillors campaign. These statistics, as of the end of March 1962, are presented in Tables II-V and reveal a number of interesting facts about the strength and socioeconomic composition of the Japanese Communist Party in the early 1960's. As might be expected, the great bulk of party membership comes from the metropolitan areas, with the Kantō region alone accounting for 40 percent of the total membership. It is also in these areas, notably Kantō and Kinki, that the party has the highest ratio of members to eligible voters, although the variations on this score are not great. Measured in terms of ratio of members to eligible voters, the party is weakest in Chūgoku, Shikoku, Kyūshū, and Tōhoku; strongest in Kantō, Kinki, and Hokkaidō.

Party members are predominantly young; more than 70 percent are under the age of 40. In occupational terms, "petty bourgeois" and "bourgeois" groups are strong, with the "pure proletariat" probably not numbering over one-third of the total membership. This is also reflected in the educational statistics. Nearly 15 percent of the party members are university graduates, and an additional 25 percent are higher school graduates, suggesting the relatively high percentage of "intellectuals" and "quasi-intellectuals" in the party. Based on these statistics, the average party member is a young man whose political experience lies wholly in the postwar period, a man with a high school education or better, who in occupational terms would be classified as "petty bourgeois" by the Marxists themselves.

Why do Japanese join the Communist Party of Japan? Extensive research on this subject has not yet been undertaken for the post-1945 period, but on the basis of pre-World War II surveys prepared by the Japanese police and my own relatively limited interview program, I would suggest that three basic factors have had the highest priority. First, the appeal of friends, relatives, and associates has probably been

the most significant factor, although naturally it is dangerous to isolate a single factor. There can be no doubt, however, that most members, particularly from the younger age brackets, come into the party as
a part of their sociopolitical community. Joining the party is not an
individual act so much as it is a projection of a relationship with
friends, family, or acquaintances in the classroom, factory, or shop into
the political sphere. This is, of course, a universal characteristic of
political behavior, but it is especially important in Japan, given the
political culture of that society. It lies at the root of basic organization
and political expression in all facets of Japanese life, and not even
those like the Communists who supposedly reject so much within their
culture escape it.

Since the party has been populated extensively with student-
intellectual types, it is not surprising that another major factor inducing membership is the intellectual stimulus derived from discovering
Marxism–Leninism in its various forms. To those who "get religion,"
membership may be both an emotional and intellectual experience.
Indeed, for many, the emotional release may be the primary stimulus,
and this raises the complex question of psychological motivations for
joining "extremist" groups. There can be little doubt that certain types
of people, or people with certain types of problems, achieve psychological satisfaction as well as some sense of identity from engaging in radical
politics, "right" and "left." Fragmentary evidence suggests that this is
a very important factor in the case of the Japanese Communist Party.

This is not to ignore the more prosaic and "official" factors inducing
party membership, namely, economic problems and social discrimination. Certainly, the latter factor is important to Korean radicals living
in Japan and to members of the outcast community who turn to communism. A sense of economic grievance or social injustice, moreover,
is likely to accompany rapid socioeconomic change. Progress often
breeds radicalism as much as stagnation. Hence, the phenomenal growth
of the Japanese economy in recent years has not necessarily blocked
party expansion among trade unionists, for example, although the percentage of such individuals who are Communists remains very small.

What additional data on the Japanese Communist Party can be obtained by a close scrutiny of postwar election results? Let us look first
at the national scene, beginning with the House of Representatives
elections (see Table VI). Table VII shows a breakdown by prefecture and metropolitan district of the percentage of votes obtained by
Communist Party candidates in each of the postwar House of Representatives elections (again, the 46 prefectures and districts have been

divided on a regional basis into the eight major regions). Table VIII presents the top five metropolitan districts and prefectures for the JCP in terms of percentage of votes, and Table IX presents the low five.

These statistics show that the Japanese Communist Party is essentially a weak party, although one with certain enclaves of strength. Slight overall increases have occurred in the popular vote since 1963, but the party still polls only approximately 4 to 5 percent of the total national vote in elections for the House of Representatives, vastly less than the vote polled by the Communist parties of certain other relatively advanced states, notably France and Italy. Any comparison with such states, to be sure, is hazardous. However, under present conditions, the Communist Party of Japan cannot be considered a major political force.

In regional terms, the party is strongest in central Honshū, notably the Chūbu and Kinki regions, partly as a result of the metropolitan concentrations in this part of Japan. It is weakest in such regions as Hokkaidō, Tōhoku, and (with the exception of Fukuoka Prefecture) Kyūshū, indicating that the party lacks appeal in agrarian areas. This is also indicated by the figures relating to the top and bottom districts and prefectures for the JCP. With the exception of Kōchi, the top districts are heavily metropolitan, and the low five prefectures are strongly rural.

The substantial difference in the urban and rural Communist vote is further confirmed by the data given in Table X. In overall terms, the urban vote of the JCP is more than twice as high as its rural vote. Table X also shows that the party makes its best showing in the major industrial centers, polling about 7 percent in such areas at present. It does less well in the mining regions, reflecting the fact that the major miners' unions are controlled by the Socialist Party. Its purely agrarian vote is extremely weak and through the 1960 elections was actually declining in percentage terms.

Statistics for the House of Councillors elections are given in Tables XI–XVI. These figures generally supplement and strengthen the conclusions drawn from the House of Representatives election data. Despite some recent gains, the Japanese Communist Party polled only between 4 and 7 percent of the national vote in the councillors' elections. Its greatest strength lies in the three metropolitan areas of Kyōto, Tōkyō, and Ōsaka, where the JCP vote ranges between 8 to 15 percent. The House of Councillors statistics show that the JCP had been receiving up to 1965 about 6 to 10 percent of the vote in the most heavily industrial areas of Japan, approximately 4 to 5 percent in the key mining regions, and about 1 to 2 percent in the strongly agrarian sections of the country. Its overall urban vote ranged from 3 to 6 percent, whereas its rural vote was generally 1 to 3 percent. In 1965, these figures, particularly those relating to the urban vote, rose somewhat.

The regional and prefectural patterns of Communist Party strength and weakness can be drawn from the above figures. The metropolitan districts and prefectures in which the JCP polls its highest percentage of votes are generally those of Kyōto, Ōsaka, Tōkyō, Ishikawa, Kōchi, Kanagawa, Fukuoka, and Nagano. These are mainly areas of urban concentration, with one or two exceptions. The prefectures in which the party makes the weakest showing are the heavily rural prefectures such as Kagoshima, Kumamoto, Fukui, Saga, and Miyazaki.

Since Communist gains were fairly significant in the 1965 House of Councillors election, and since this is the most recent election for the Japanese Upper House, some analysis of this contest might be appropriate. For the first time, the party ran one candidate in each of the 46 prefectures, in addition to running two candidates for the national seats. In both the national and prefectural constituencies, substantial voting gains were made. The Communist national candidates were both elected easily, placing second and fifth among all candidates (in comparison with sixteenth and seventeenth in the previous election). The party went from 1,123,946 votes in the national constituency to 1,652,-363, a gain of some 500,000 votes, raising its percentage from 3.1 to 4.4 of the total national vote. Gains in the prefectural constituencies were even greater. Two candidates were elected, with Nosaka the highest vote-getter in a local constituency. The party added some 950,000 votes to its total for the 1962 election, and garnered 6.9 percent of the total prefectural vote.

The relative position of the Communists within the "left" bloc also improved in terms of votes. In the national constituency, Communist votes increased from 9.52 percent (1962) to 12.96 percent of the total "left" vote. (The Socialist percentage declined from 73.4 percent to 68.4 percent, while the Democratic Socialists gained slightly, from 16.1 percent to 17.4 percent.) In the prefectural constituencies, the Communists went from 10.8 percent (1962) to 15.1 percent, whereas the Socialists dropped slightly (72.1 percent to 71.3 percent) and the Democratic Socialists also declined (16.0 percent to 13.3 percent).

As usual, the Communist Party did well in the metropolitan areas. Its national constituency vote in Kyōto was 12.5 percent of the total; in Tōkyō, 9.7 percent, in Ōsaka, 9.3 percent. In the prefectural constituencies, the same general pattern prevailed: Kyōto, 20.3 percent; Tōkyō, 15 percent; Nagano, 10.5 percent; Ōsaka, 9.5 percent; Kōchi, 9.1 percent.

What were the reasons for Communist gains? Three main factors would appear to be involved. First, the Liberal Democratic Party suffered from recent disclosures of massive corruption in the Tōkyō Assembly involving LDP members and from the severe recession that affected Japan from the beginning of 1965. The Socialist Party, on the other hand, was characterized by weak leadership and inadequate organization. Consequently, a larger percentage of the "protest" vote went to the Communists, who had been emphasizing organization in a major way since the 9th Party Congress, and who had concentrated unprecedented energy and funds on this election. Japanese Communist Party Membership had increased, with the party now claiming some 150,000 members. Subscriptions to *Akahata* had also risen substantially. Daily *Akahata* circulation had risen from 120,000 in 1962 to 200,000, and the Sunday *Akahata* had gone from 260,000 to 700,000 subscribers. Making use of these organizational propaganda assets, the party put hundreds of workers into the field and conducted one of the most intensive campaigns in its history. Organization and effort were certainly critical elements in the Communist electoral gains of 1965.

There was also some indication that the image of the Japanese Communist Party had changed, or was in the process of changing. A full ten years had passed since the era of "left extremism," when the party had been synonymous with Molotov cocktails, riots, and other forms of illegal action. Despite the fact that the party continued to follow the "hard line" on ideological and policy issues, its *actions* had been relatively moderate. The Miyamoto line emphasized united front policies whenever possible and an avoidance of violence *at this stage*. Using these tactics, the party had gradually moved from the status of complete outlaw toward that of acceptable, if unconventional, radical.

The effect of issues in this election, particularly foreign policy issues, is debatable. The Communist Party played heavily on the issues of "peace" and "depression." They sought to appeal to an electorate worried about the possibilities of a general Asian war. For these purposes, the Vietnam crisis, the issue of Japanese–South Korean relations, and the question of American–Japanese military relations could all be utilized, and they indeed became central Communist targets, along with recession topics. The Socialists, however, used the same issues and generally handled them in a similar fashion. One may guess that foreign policy questions in particular benefited the Communists primarily in a negative sense. They were not forced to fight any heavy adverse tide of public opinion on a burning issue. The drift was either neutral or in their general direction.

The results of certain recent elections at the prefectural and local level are shown in Tables XVII-XX. Before drawing any conclusions from these tables, let us examine briefly one recent and widely heralded local election, that for the Tōkyō City Assembly which was held on July 23, 1965. This election could not have been conducted under more disadvantageous conditions for the Liberal Democratic Party. A major scandal had erupted with many Liberal Democratic Assemblymen being accused of corruption and in some cases being forced to resign. As a result, the Liberal Democratic Party organization was badly split, lacking in enthusiasm, and at a low ebb in its public relations. The recession continued, moreover, and it had had a particularly severe effect on Japan's greatest metropolis. The situation in Vietnam was especially critical at this point, and there was a widespread conviction that the United States would probably lose the war.

The heavy defeat of the Liberal Democrats under these circumstances was perhaps not surprising. That party lost 30 seats in the Assembly, and some 750,000 votes. It received only 30.2 percent of the total vote in 1965, in comparison with 48.2 percent in the previous election, and obtained 39 seats (including 1 independent inclined to the LDP), in comparison with 69 in the previous contest. For the first time in history, the conservatives became a minority in the Tōkyō Assembly. The Socialist Party gained 13 seats, electing 45 candidates to become the leading party in the 120-man Assembly. The Socialists, however, obtained only 28 percent of the vote, the same percentage obtained in the previous Assembly election. The Kōmeitō, the Sōka Gakkai party, obtained 23 seats, electing all of its candidates, and received 13.8 percent of the vote as compared with 10.5 percent previously. The Communists won 9 seats, an increase of 7 seats, and obtained 10.1 percent (384,589 votes) of the total vote in comparison with only 4.5 percent (178,392 votes) previously. The Democratic Socialists became the fifth party, obtaining 4 seats and getting 6.8 percent of the vote, as against no seats and 5.2 percent of the vote previously. Independents obtained 11.6 percent of the total vote.

It is obvious that many of the factors applicable in the House of Councillors election three weeks earlier were also in operation here. Among them were the weaknesses of the "major" parties; the recent organizational gains of the Japanese Communist Party; the inroads made by the JCP into lower middle class and working class voters as a result of some change in the Communist image; and the effect of corruption, recession, and peace issues on a metropolitan electorate.

Many observers described this as an election based on organization, particularly in view of the low turnout: only 58.58 percent of the eligible voters, in comparison with a previous 67.85 percent. Clearly the greatest gains were scored by the two parties most tightly organized for the election: the Communists (whose Tōkyō membership had reportedly risen from 17,000 in April 1963 to 30,000) and the Kōmeitō, which claimed a national increase from 3,400,000 households to 5,400,-000 at this point. Corruption was certainly a critical issue, and practical problems such as garbage disposal, water, and high prices appear to have influenced a substantial number of voters, particularly women. The conservatives suffered from certain technical problems as well—too many conservative candidates ran, with the result that the conservative vote in some districts was badly divided.

A close examination of the voting pattern indicates that the Communists scored their gains by taking votes *both* from the Socialists and from the conservatives. A certain number of lower middle class and labor voters switched from their traditional pattern of voting for the Liberal Democratic Party candidate to voting for the Communist candidate, with the issues of city management probably playing the most important role. It is also important to note, however, that even in this situation where many factors favored them, the Communists did not gain significantly in comparison with their vote percentage in the recent House of Councillors election or in earlier House of Representatives contests. The Communist vote in Tōkyō now appears to be approximately 10 percent under generally favorable conditions.

When we look at the statistics in Tables XVII-XX, what general conclusions are in order? With a very few exceptions, as of the mid-1960's, the Japanese Communist Party is weaker in terms of prefectural and local politics than at the national level. On its own, the party has not yet been able to elect a candidate to any prefectural governorship, nor does it hold any mayorship throughout Japan. It has captured less than 1 percent of the 2,688 prefectural assembly seats in the nation, less than 3 percent of the city council seats, and about 1 percent of the town and village council seats.

Of course, if we survey only those contests in which the party competed, the statistical showing of the JCP is considerably better. In the governorship races of 1963, for example, when the JCP put up a candidate in seven races, its percentage of votes in those contests was as follows: Akita, 12.9 percent; Okayama, 12.1 percent; Nagano, 11.8

percent; Kanagawa, 7.5 percent; Tochigi, 4.9 percent; Mie, 4.0 percent; and Hokkaidō, 1.5 percent.[6] It should be noted, however, that in each of these contests, except that in Hokkaidō, the JCP candidate was the only opposition candidate against an independent (generally incumbent) candidate. Thus one could only cast an opposition vote by voting Communist, so these figures are not necessarily an accurate measure of true Communist strength. On the other hand, they indicate that even in essentially rural prefectures, 10 to 12 percent of the voters can be induced under certain circumstances to cast a ballot for a Communist.

It is reasonably clear that the Communist Party could increase its percentage of the total vote by running more candidates in local and prefectural elections. Indeed, that is its announced objective, and in 1963 it fielded a significantly larger number of candidates for the prefectural assembly elections, as well as for the city, town, and village council races. In these specific contests, consequently, its percentage of the vote rose, going from 1.1 percent to 2.1 percent in the prefectural assembly contests; from 2.4 percent to 3.3 percent in the city council races; and from 0.7 percent to 1.5 percent in the town and village council contests. Communist leaders heralded these gains, and they caused some stir in non-Communist circles. In terms of percentage increase, they did represent major advances. It is clear, however, that the JCP has a long way to go before it can be considered a formidable contender for power, whether at the local, district, or national level.

In summary, the Japanese Communist Party of today is essentially an urban party. Under optimum conditions, it can count on 8 to 15 percent of the vote in the great metropolitan centers of Japan (up to 20 percent in Kyōto), and from 5 to 10 percent of the vote in large and medium-sized towns. Much of its organizational strength continues to come from young intellectuals and quasi-intellectuals—cadres who are drawn from the urban centers and who have a high school or college education.

The number of industrial workers and white-collar employees who are party members has been growing, although it is questionable whether such groups constitute a majority of party members even at this point, and certainly they do not represent the controlling element at the top- and middle-echelon leadership levels. No doubt, these "proletarian" forces provide a more stable element in party membership than the intellectual group. A substantial portion of the "Young Officers" now

---

[6] Statistics were drawn from Jichishō senkyo kyoku (The Local Autonomy Ministry Election Bureau), *Senkyo nenkan, 1960–1963* (*Election Yearbook 1960–1963*), published March 1964, p. 295.

moving into control, however, must be considered "petty bourgeois intellectuals" in Marxian terms. Finally, very few party members come from the purely agrarian class, and despite the substantial efforts now being made in certain regions, there is no indication that this situation will change dramatically. Pure "bourgeois" types also occupy a limited position in membership roles, although they are not completely absent.

The Japanese Communist Party is thus a coalition of urban "petty bourgeois" and "proletariat" elements—more accurately, of a small number of quasi-intellectuals and skilled workers, with some white-collar employees who in reality fall into the quasi-intellectual category in most cases. Most party members are relatively young, have come to the party recently, and—if past experience is any gauge—are not likely to remain for a lifetime. The party, as we have indicated also obtains substantial support from a number of the 600,000 Koreans now living in Japan, the majority of whom are affiliated with the Communist-dominated General Federation of Korean Residents in Japan. This federation, directly under the North Korean government, is available to the Japanese Communist Party for a wide range of purposes.

The strengths and weaknesses in party membership, as we have noted, are reflected in the various election statistics. The current evidence suggests that the Japanese Communist Party, under normal conditions, can count on about 15 to 25 percent of the vote of the urban organized workers, but not more than 1 to 2 percent of the purely agrarian vote. Its support from the union workers, young intellectuals, and white-collar employees thus enables it to poll about 8 to 15 percent of the metropolitan vote, whereas in the strongly rural areas, as we have noted, the JCP vote rarely goes over 3 percent, and is generally 1 to 2 percent.

Meanwhile, what of those men—the Voice of Japan group on the one hand, and the Liberation Front faction on the other—who proclaim themselves Communists but refuse to accept the discipline of the Japanese Communist Party (Yoyogi)? Despite the substantial assistance given the Voice of Japan group by Soviet sources, it has not prospered. As we have noted, this dissident movement was formed by Shiga and Suzuki after they were ousted from the JCP in the late spring of 1964. In late August 1964, moreover, they were joined by Kamiyama Shigeo and Nakano Shigeharu, who were suspended from JCP membership at the time of the 10th Plenum meetings, completing the purge of top pro-Soviet leaders within the Japanese Communist Party.[7]

---

[7] For the official account of the removal of Kamiyama and Nakano, see *Akahata*, October 2, 1964, pp. 1–2, or the translations which appear in *TICD* 665, *JPRS* 27,224, pp. 61–78, and *TICD* 662, *JPRS* 27,148, pp. 45–52.

At a press conference on October 3, 1964, Shiga, Suzuki, Kamiyama, and Nakano refused to accept the expulsions as legal, claimed to be "genuine Communists," and suggested that they might form a new party.[8] *Pravda* gave full coverage to this press conference, thus indicating the new Russian policy of featuring the dissidents as the "true Marxist–Leninist force" in Japan. On October 30, the Soviet trade union newspaper *Trud* published a report by Vasily I. Prokhorov after his return from the Sōhyō Convention. His report referred to the Voice of Japan group as a band of "genuine Communists" who were struggling valiantly to correct the mistakes of the JCP leadership. Prokhorov sharply criticized the JCP as an "antiworker and antipeople's party." Soon after, on November 4, Shiga visited the Soviet Union as a guest of the Marxism–Leninism Institute. Despite the warnings of *Akahata* that "if some people abroad think that this handful of despicable antiparty revisionists are still useful to them, they will surely be severely condemned by history," Shiga was given a hearty welcome.[9]

Shortly after he returned, on December 2, the Shiga group announced that they planned to form a new Japanese Communist Party which would be called JCP (Voice of Japan) in contrast to the JCP (Yoyogi faction). Already, on November 26, Shiga had exchanged messages with the Mongolian People's Republic on the occasion of its 40th anniversary. Premier Tsendenbal had expressed his gratitude to Shiga for the greetings, and through him thanks "to all the Communists of Japan." The Mongolian Premier had used the title, Japanese Communist Party (Voice of Japan) in sending his response. It was widely assumed that the Soviet Union would grant official recognition to the new party at least by the time of the 26-Party Conference in Moscow which opened on March 1, 1965. No such recognition was forthcoming, at least publicly, possibly because of the reservations of certain East European Com-

According to the Central Committee, both men had engaged in "divisive anti-party activities." Kamiyama had made trips to local areas and carried on "factional operations," and had refused to cooperate with the Presidium in its investigation. He had actively opposed the party line at the 1964 New Japanese Literary Society Conference and on numerous other occasions. Nakano had upheld Kamiyama in these various acts, and both had allied themselves with such antiparty revisionists as Shiga, Suzuki, Kasuga, and Naito.

For Kamiyama's retort, see Kamiyama Shigeo, *Nikkyō shidōbu ni atau— kokusai kyōsanshugi no sōrosen o. mamotte* (*An Open Letter to the Japanese Communist Party Leaders—In Defense of the General Line of International Communism*), Vol. I, Tōkyō, August 30, 1964, pp. 107–147.

[8] For details, see *Atarashii Rosen* (*The New Line*), October 12, 1964, p. 1.

[9] Moscow Radio carried a full account of Shiga's trip, with the appropriate comments.

munist parties. The CPSU, however, continued to treat the Shiga group as the true Marxist–Leninists of Japan and to castigate the Yoyogi group as Chinese puppets.

Soviet strategy was clear. The CPSU hoped to see the Japanese Communist Party (Voice of Japan), properly supported at home and abroad, supplant the Japanese Communist Party (Yoyogi) as the leading Marxist–Leninist body in Japan and the only recognized Japanese Communist Party in the international movement. At the same time, Soviet authorities hoped to isolate Yoyogi by aiding in the development of a broad united front of the left which would join the Voice of Japan group with Sōhyō and the Japan Socialist Party. It was willing to give moral, political, and financial support to such a front.

In the fall of 1964, for example, the Soviet Union had announced the founding of a new Japanese-language magazine, *International,* which would be circulated among Japanese Communists. At the end of October, a Japanese–Soviet Book Center was opened, to rival the Peking-oriented book store controlled by the Yoyogi faction. In late November, *Akahata* claimed that this book center appeared to be the new source of subversive activities against the JCP by "antiparty revisionists" at home and abroad, and asserted that the Kasuga and Shiga factions were uniting to support the center.

Despite these and other efforts, however, the Voice of Japan group has remained small and relatively ineffective, capturing scarcely 10 percent of the hard-core Communists. Kamiyama was disastrously defeated when he ran for a House of Councillors seat in Tōkyō against Nosaka, who received the highest number of votes among the prefectural candidates. The problems of the dissidents could be summed up easily: they lacked any organizational roots—whether in labor, the student movement, or in intellectual circles.

Essentially, the JCP (Voice of Japan) represents only a small number of veteran Communists, relatively well known, but not in control of any substantial body of followers. As we have seen, the Mainstream JCP leaders have controlled fully 80 to 90 percent of the organization from the time that Miyamoto and Hakamada joined this group in the mid-1950's.

The same general problems beset the "left-deviationists," the Liberation Front faction. The strength of this faction is also quite minimal at present, numbering a few thousand at most. This group, however, probably worries the JCP Mainstream more than the Voice of Japan group, both because JCP leaders anticipate intensive Chinese involvement in Japanese internal politics and because a number of the younger, more militant members of the party have long had "pro-China" training and sentiments. It remains to be seen whether extensive purges of such individuals will be necessary or whether they can be "reeducated."

Meanwhile, official JCP organs like *Akahata* and *Zenei* have considered it necessary to devote increasing attention to answering the attacks of the dissidents and launching counterattacks of their own. Quite naturally, their central weapon has become nationalism. Strange analogies and arguments have crept into JCP writings. For the first time in its existence, the Communist Party appears anxious to link itself in some fashion with the mainstream of Japanese history. Thus, it advances the thesis that throughout the course of modernization, Japan has been confronted by the interaction of indigenous and external forces, and, consequently, it has been natural for some Japanese—even within the Communist Party—to be caught up in the "sycophantic and dogmatic trend" of unconditionally worshiping the leadership of foreign parties and regarding the documents of other fraternal parties as more important than the Marxist–Leninist classics and the documents of the JCP, using such sources as a basis for passing judgment on Japanese problems.[10]

Against each faction, of course, the party has had its separate battle. Toward the Voice of Japan group, the JCP (Yoyogi) has maintained a position of rigid opposition despite overtures from this group for "a unity among all Japanese Communists." There can be no unity, asserted one Mainstream spokesman, with the antiparty Shiga elements, who sought to destroy revolutionary discipline and are still furiously engaged in destructive activities against the party.[11] All of the charges of revisionism made against the Russians—which continue to pour forth from JCP (Yoyogi) writers—were also made against the Shiga group and its allies. Thus, they were charged with a deceitful attitude toward aiding Vietnam—one which added up to defeatism and a lack of will. By asserting that those who insist upon total support for the Vietnamese Communists are "indiscrete" and "rash," they play into the hands of "American imperialists," claimed one author.[12]

---

[10] See Shimotsukasa Junkichi, "The Essence and Absurdity of Anti-Party Dogmatists," *Zenei*, July 1966, pp. 56–70. An English translation appears in *JPRS* 37,008, pp. 1–23. See particularly p. 4.

[11] See the article by Masuda Kanichi, "The Theoretical and Ideological Bankruptcy of Dissident Japanese Communists," *Akahata*, July 14, 1966, p. 5; an English translation appears in *JPRS* 37,008, pp. 24–31 (p. 25).

[12] *Ibid.*, pp. 29–30. For an attack upon the Vietnam position of the Zengakuren anti-Mainstream "Trotskyites" by the Communists, see the *Akahata* editorial of June 22, 1966, p. 5.

Toward the Liberation Front group, the JCP (Yoyogi) attack comes from another angle. Arguing that the Front's program is a mechanical adoption of the Peking line, the JCP writers continue to insist that theories of the inevitability of violent revolution and the importance of moving into guerrilla warfare are guaranteed to isolate the party and reduce it to ruin, as happened from 1950 to 1955.[13] Only a united front operating in a political fashion can halt "American imperialism" and "Japanese militarism."

It is perhaps ironic that the Mainstream leaders, while pleading for a united front within the international Communist movement, and anxious for a united front with the Socialists and other left elements outside the party, are totally disinterested in unity with those dissident factions who advance rival claims for the title of true Marxist–Leninists. This is explained, of course, by the assertion that the united front between independent and autonomous parties is not a tactic applicable to a single Communist party, where complete discipline on behalf of majority decisions must be maintained.

As it struggles against "heretics" within the mother church, upon what front organizations can the Japanese Communist Party (Yoyogi) count? Perhaps the most dramatic gains for the party in recent years have come via the organized student movement, as suggested earlier. By the end of 1965, *Zengakuren,* involving some 320 student governments, continued to be divided into a number of factions, but the JCP-controlled Democratic Youth League held approximately 55 percent of the total organizational strength. The two factions of the Marxist Student League (the old Mainstream force within Zengakuren) held only about 10 percent; the Structural Reform group 9 percent; the Socialist Student League 5 percent; and other smaller groups accounted for the remaining strength.

Thus, the Democratic Youth League, which had first succeeded in reorganizing *Zengakuren* under its control in December 1964, appeared to have established its primacy, although the organization was not capable of acting as a unit—either on substantive policies or in tactical terms—on most issues. Communist organs continued an avalanche of attacks against the "Trotskyites" and "revisionists" within the student movement, and were answered in kind. Despite its claim to represent some 200,000 students, moreover, *Zengakuren* was far weaker and less significant by 1965–1966 than in earlier periods. Hence, if the Com-

---

[13] Shimotsukasa, "The Essence and the Absurdity of Anti-Party Dogmatists," p. 19.

munists were to count heavily upon student support, a major revitalization of this organization would be necessary.

In so far as intellectuals were concerned, Communist hopes rested strongly upon the Japan Democratic Writers' League established on August 26, 1965, after the New Japan Literary Society was abandoned because it had come under the control of anti-JCP elements. The Writers' League started with 93 members; a year later, it had perhaps double that number and a thousand supporters. Few top literati, however, joined the group, and the Chinese "cultural revolution," particularly, the abject "self-criticism" of Kuo Mo-jo, a favorite of Japanese leftist intellectuals, profoundly shocked all literary circles in Japan. Despite the increasing separation between Yoyogi and Peking, recruitment of intellectuals into the Communist camp suffered a severe setback. Whether the new nationalist line of the JCP will overcome this situation remains to be seen.

Within the labor movement, as has already been suggested, the JCP tended to fare poorly, in part perhaps because the top Socialist leadership under Ōta and Iwai had moved sharply to the left, capturing many of the issues upon which the Communists normally might have expected to stand alone. In addition, the Communist blunder in connection with the April 17th strike issue cost the JCP heavily, despite its hasty retreat. In overall terms, indeed, the rank and file of organized labor have increasingly indicated a restiveness with the intensive politicization of the Japanese labor movement, and that is one factor involved in the current shift toward moderation symbolized by the selection of Horii as the new Sōhyō Chairman. Whether the Communists will be able to increase their strength within Sōhyō under these new conditions is unclear, but they start with no more than 20 percent overall strength, despite the enclaves established earlier in some important unions.

The Communists have long sought to establish themselves in the small and medium business world. Through Zenshoren (National Federation of Commercial and Industrial Organizations), they have organized some 100,000 persons, and in their 21st annual meeting held in Hiroshima on May 12-13, 1966, with 1,100 delegates, a goal of 300,000 members within three years was announced. Indeed, Communist success among this group is much more substantial than in the rural regions. Communist-front peasant associations contain less than 40,000 members.

Once again, the evidence strongly suggests that the immediate prospects for massive Communist Party growth are not favorable. Surveying the major socioeconomic interest groups—and the chief organizations currently existing to represent them—there is no indication that the JCP can expect a substantial upswing in student-intellectual, labor, business, or farmer support. A tight organization and major emphasis upon the training of cadres and grass-roots work has paid dividends to the party during the last several years, but there is strong reason to believe that membership gains have represented essentially the more efficient enrolling of elements already within the broad influence of the party.

Perhaps one additional factor has contributed to the growth in party membership—and vote—in the last several years, namely, the possession of increased funds. As we have noted, the party has recently run an increased number of candidates, particularly at the local and prefectural levels. It has also replaced the gloomy old cavern that had served as party headquarters for so many years. A modern Central Committee headquarters building has been erected, with eight floors above ground, and two floors underground. (Should we consider this symbolic?) In addition, the party has sponsored a large number of social, athletic, and political events under the energetic leadership of the younger leaders. From whence do the funds come?

To obtain a detailed, accurate knowledge of JCP finances, of course, is not possible and we must be exceedingly careful in using such data as is available. All parties, in accordance with the Political Funds Registration Act, are required to list their revenue and expenditures. These listings, needless to say, are far from being a true measure of party finances, since all parties grossly understate income and output. They *do* indicate trends within a given party, however, and in crude terms probably provide the basis for comparisons among parties. Japanese Communist Party figures in recent years indicate a sharp upward progression.[14] In 1960, the party reported an income of 204,710,000 yen, a figure 1.7 times greater than that of the previous year; expenditures were listed as 196,930,000 yen, 1.5 times greater than those of 1959. In 1961, JCP income was listed as 378,720,000 yen, 1.8 times greater than that in 1960, with expenditures totaling 377,090,000 yen, 1.9 times greater than those of the previous year. In 1962, party revenues were listed as 490,820,000 yen, 1.3 times greater than those in 1961, with expenditures being 489,990,000 yen, also 1.3 times greater than those of 1961. For the first half of 1963 only, income was listed as 316,810,000 yen, and expenditures for the same period were tabulated at 315,630,000 yen, with the November elections of that year still to be fought.

---

[14] For an extremely interesting article on JCP finances, from which the statistics used here are drawn, see Fukuda Katsuichi, "Concerning the Financial Situation of the Japanese Communist Party," *Kōan Jōhō*, February 1964, pp. 1–17.

What would be a more realistic estimate of JCP funds? One estimate, based upon a study of party materials and various intelligence sources, places total party expenditures (local and district as well as head-quarters) in 1963 at approximately 4,000,000,000 yen, with the center and the local-prefectural units spending about the same amount.[15] Table XXI indicates the supposed sources of revenue and the broad uses to which that revenue was put.

The budget sketched there is approximately seven times larger than the figures reported to the government. If one takes the official figures alone, however, it is interesting to note that the 1962 figures for the JCP were 18 percent more than those reported by the Liberal Democratic Party, 2.35 times greater than those of the Japan Socialist Party, and 4.2 times greater than those of the Democratic Socialist Party. The figures for the first half of 1963 were 24.5 percent greater than those of the LDP, 3.25 times those of the JSP, and 11.5 times those of the DSP. It is highly unlikely that the Japanese Communist Party has been receiving and spending more money than the massive conservative party, but its revenue and expenditures are certainly much greater on a per capita vote basis. In recent elections, moreover, plentiful Communist funds have been evidenced by the profusion of posters, leaflets, and other types of propaganda dedicated to the Communist candidates.[16]

If the unofficial budget is roughly accurate, additional facts of major importance are revealed. As far as headquarters is concerned, only a very small portion of the funds in 1963 came from membership dues or the contributions of JCP officials. Approximately 40 percent of head-quarters revenue, however, allegedly came from Communist China or other foreign sources. Naturally, the party has always brushed aside all allegations of Chinese subsidization and presented the sources of its funds in a way that made them appear totally indigenous. How did Peking contribute? Foreign funds came in a variety of ways, some of them very indirect. The largest sum came from the sale of Chinese publications in Japan and in the form of "contributions" from companies trading with Mainland China. Apparently, direct contributions to individual party leaders have also been made, some of which took

---

[15] *Ibid.*, p. 3.

[16] For example, in the 1963 House of Representatives elections, the Communist Party had 231,886 posters, as compared with 215,371 for the Liberal Democratic Party, 184,393 for the Socialist Party, and 112,124 for the Democratic Socialist Party. The figures for sound trucks were: Liberal-Democratic Party—36; Socialist Party—20; Democratic Socialist Party—6; Communist Party—12. See The Local Autonomy Ministry Election Bureau, *1963 House of Representatives Elections*, p. 25.

the form of precious stones and other items that could be converted into cash. Peking has also contributed—both openly and covertly—to such front organizations as Gensuikyō, as we have previously noted.

If the figures presented in Table XXI are reasonably accurate, they indicate that the Chinese Communists until recently played a significant role in the capacity of the Japanese Communist Party to expand its activities. Certainly, this appears to have been one factor heightening the influence of Peking over the JCP in recent years, and it is entirely possible, as various sources have stated, that it was also a factor making the decision to challenge Peking a very painful one. It has been suggested that only after the JCP had doubled its membership and greatly increased the circulation of its leading organs did it feel strong enough to assert an independent position. And early indications are that this act has cost the party financially. The Chinese Communists have cancelled trading agreements with certain Japanese firms known to be close to the Communist Party of Japan. Chinese Party publications have been removed from JCP bookstalls, thereby ending one source of revenue. And the flow of JCP leaders to Peking has ended, at least so far as the Mainstream group is concerned. Since the loss of Chinese revenue is not being made up currently by Moscow, are there other alternatives? To what extent does increased indigenous support fill the gap? Are external funds being obtained from North Korea?

In the final analysis, despite recent gains, the Japanese Communist Party leaders are cognizant of the fact that it would take a miracle to bring the party close to power in the normal course of events. The prospect of a massive defeat for the non-Communists in the world scene, particularly a defeat of the United States, is a recurrent dream. Similarly, the horizon is always scanned for the oft-predicted, but never arriving, major Japanese depression. In the absence of some dramatic change in the world balance of power or a collapse of the domestic economy, any immediate influence of the Japanese Communist Party is strongly dependent upon the reestablishment of a broad united front on the left—a fact that even the most dogmatic party theorists are forced to admit.

TABLE I

JCP Membership in Mid-1966

Prefecture or Metropolitan Area	District Committees	Cells	Members
Hokkaidō	11	550	10,200
Aomori	6	130	1,900
Iwate	7	210	3,700
Miyagi	6	240	3,400
Akita	6	170	2,600
Yamagata	6	170	1,400
Fukushima	6	210	2,700
Ibaraki	6	270	2,100
Tochigi	6	90	1,000
Gumma	4	180	3,100
Saitama	4	180	3,700
Chiba	5	200	2,400
Tōkyō	6	2,160	39,500
Kanagawa	7	530	10,900
Niigata	4	320	6,200
Toyama	2	120	1,300
Ishikawa	3	160	1,600
Fukui	3	90	600
Yamanashi	4	70	900
Nagano	4	420	7,700
Gifu	5	180	2,400
Shizuoka	3	280	3,400
Aichi	7	580	10,200
Mie	6	150	2,100
Shiga	3	90	1,100
Kyōto	9	530	9,200
Ōsaka	10	1,140	17,300
Hyōgo	7	680	8,100
Nara	2	80	1,200
Wakayama	4	200	2,400
Tottori	3	80	1,200
Shimane	4	100	1,100
Okayama	4	170	2,200
Hiroshima	5	300	3,400
Yamaguchi	6	220	1,600
Tokushima	3	80	900
Kagawa	2	110	1,100
Ehime	5	220	2,300
Kōchi	6	190	2,900
Fukuoka	13	550	11,200
Saga	3	120	1,400

TABLE I (*Continued*)

Prefecture or Metropolitan Area	District Committees	Cells	Members
Nagasaki	3	150	1,400
Kumamoto	6	140	2,100
Ōita	5	140	1,800
Miyazaki	3	100	1,100
Kagoshima	6	120	1,200
Total	239	13,170	200,700

SOURCE: Kōan Chōsachō (Public Safety Investigation Bureau), Tōkyō, August 1, 1966.

TABLE II

COMPARISON OF JCP MEMBERS TO TOTAL NUMBER OF VOTERS BY REGION[a]

Region	Percent of total JCP membership	Total no. of eligible voters as of Dec. 20, 1961	Percent of total eligible voters belonging to JCP
1. Hokkaidō	4.94	2,770,369	0.16
2. Tōhoku	7.65	5,316,854	0.13
3. Kantō	40.37	17,436,780	0.21
4. Chūbu	10.70	7,715,674	0.14
5. Kinki	17.50	8,710,896	0.18
6. Chūgoku	4.96	4,219,372	0.11
7. Shikoku	3.67	2,505,605	0.13
8. Kyūshū	10.21	7,267,539	0.13
Total	100.00	55,943,089	0.16

SOURCE: Kōan Chōsachō, *Nihon Kyōsantō no genjō* (*Current Conditions of the Japanese Communist Party*), Tōkyō, July 1, 1962.

[a] Contemporary Japan is ordinarily divided into eight regions defined as follows: (1) *Hokkaidō,* the northernmost island; (2) *Tōhoku,* northeast Honshū, encompassing the prefectures of Aomori, Akita, Yamagata, Iwate, Miyagi, and Fukushima; (3) *Kantō,* east and portions of central Honshu, including Gumma, Tochigi, Ibaraki, Chiba, Tōkyō, Kanagawa, and Saitama; (4) *Chūbu,* central Honshu, including Niigata, Toyama, Ishikawa, Nagano, Yamanashi, Gifu, Shizuoka, and Aichi; (5) *Kinki,* south central and eastern Honshu, encompassing Shiga, Kyōto, Fukui, Ōsaka, Nara, Wakayama, and Mie; (6) *Chūgoku,* southern Honshū, including Shimane, Tottori, Hyōgo, Okayama, Hiroshima, and Yamaguchi; (7) *Shikoku,* including all four prefectures of that island—Kagawa, Tokushima, Kōchi, and Ehime; (8) *Kyūshū,* the entire southern island encompassing its seven prefectures—Fukuoka, Saga, Nagasaki, Ōita, Kumamoto, Miyazaki, and Kagoshima. (In the prewar era, the Ryūkyūs were considered a ninth region.)

TABLE III

Age of JCP Members

Under 20	20–29	30–39	40–49	50–59	60 and over	Unknown
0.41%	27.09%	44.09%	15.21%	7.81%	1.74%	3.74%

SOURCE: Kōan Chōsachō, *Nihon Kyōsantō no genjō.*

TABLE IV

Occupations of JCP Members

Professional party workers	2.15%
Factory workers	13.58%
General workers[a]	10.51%
Self-employed workers	5.27%
Civil servants[b]	12.75%
Teachers[c]	6.64%
Students	1.55%
Persons engaged in farming, fishing, and forestry	11.35%
Company and shop employees	9.25%
Shopkeepers	7.20%
Company managers	0.76%
Independent entrepreneurs	4.26%
Other	3.66%
Unemployed	4.55%
Unknown	6.52%

SOURCE: Kōan Chōsachō, *Nihon Kyōsantō no genjō.*

a This category includes workers in small handicraft plants, carpenters, plasterers, and other construction workers.

b This category includes those working in public enterprises.

c All teachers, including those teaching in public institutions, are included in this category rather than in the civil servant category.

TABLE V

Education of JCP Members

University graduates	Higher school[a] graduates	Middle school graduates	Primary school graduates	Unknown
14.58%	24.87%	31.85%	6.86%	21.84%

SOURCE: Kōan Chōsachō, *Nihon Kyōsantō no genjō.*

a Prewar higher school, postwar high school.

TABLE VI

THE JCP IN HOUSE OF REPRESENTATIVES ELECTIONS, 1946–1963

Election	Number of JCP candidates	Percent of total number of candidates	Male candidates	Female candidates	Total JCP vote	Percent of total vote	Number of candidates elected	Percent of total candidates elected
22d (Apr. 10, 1946)	143	5.2	136	7	2,135,757	3.8	5	1.1
23d (Apr. 25, 1947)	120	7.5	113	7	1,002,903	3.7	4	0.8
24th (Jan. 23, 1949)	115	8.4	112	3	2,984,780	9.8	35	7.5
25th (Oct. 1, 1952)	107	8.6	103	4	895,765	2.5	..	..
26th (Apr. 19, 1953)	85	8.3	82	3	655,990	1.9	1	0.2
27th (Feb. 27, 1955)	60	5.9	58	2	733,121	2.0	2	0.4
28th (May 22, 1958)	114	12.0	114	..	1,012,035	2.6	1	0.2
29th (Nov. 20, 1960)	118	12.6	118	..	1,156,723	2.9	3	0.6
30th (Nov. 21, 1963)	118	12.9	118	..	1,646,477	4.0	5	1.1

SOURCE: The statistics in this chart, with the exception of those for the 30th election, were taken from Kōan Chōsachō, *Sengo ni okeru Nihon Kyōsantō no senkyo kekka, Shūgiin giin sōsenkyo no bu (The Election Results of the Japanese Communist Party in the Postwar Era—Section Concerning the House of Representatives)*, no date or place of publication, pp. 25, 33. The 30th election statistics came from Jichishō senkyo kyoku (The Local Autonomy Ministry Election Bureau), *Shūgiin giin sōsenkyo—kekka shirabe (General Elections of the House of Representatives—Final Survey)*, November 21, 1963, pp. 10–11.

TABLE VII

PERCENTAGE OF VOTE OBTAINED BY THE JCP IN HOUSE OF REPRESENTATIVES ELECTIONS BY REGION, 1946–1963

(L = less than)

Region	22d Election (4/10/46)	23d Election (4/25/47)	24th Election (1/23/49)	25th Election (10/1/52)	26th Election (4/19/53)	27th Election (2/27/55)	28th Election (5/22/58)	29th Election (11/20/60)	30th Election (11/21/63)
1. Hokkaido	7	3	5	3	3	3	2	2	2
2. Tōhoku									
Aomori	2	3	8	3	2	2	2	1	3
Akita	2	0 (?)	7	2	2	2	2	2	3
Yamagata	2	2	6	1	L 1	0	1	1	1
Iwate	2	2	6	L 1	0	L 1	1	2	2
Miyagi	3	2	4	1	2	L 1	1	1	2
Fukushima	2	2	4	2	L 1	0	L 1	2	2
3. Kantō									
Gumma	4	3	8	2	2	0	1	2	2
Tochigi	3	2	8	2	L 1	L 1	1	L 1	L 1
Ibaraki	4	2	8	2	4	L 1	2	2	2
Chiba	3	2	13	2	2	0	2	1	2
Tōkyō	9	9	18	4	4	5	5	5	7
Kanagawa	5	5	15	4	2	4	4	5	5
Saitama	6	5	13	4	2	L 1	2	2	3
4. Chūbu									
Niigata	3	3	15	2	1	2	2	2	3
Toyama	1	2	6	3	1	0	2	1	3
Ishikawa	4	7	11	3	L 1	L 1	2	5	7
Nagano	8	8	14	5	5	4	4	5	8
Yamanashi	4	4	12	3	0	0	2	2	1
Gifu	L 1	2	5	2	2	0	2	2	2
Shizuoka	2	3	8	2	2	2	3	2	2
Aichi	4	4	10	3	3	3	2	3	4

TABLE VII (*Continued*)

Region	22d Election (4/10/46)	23d Election (4/25/47)	24th Election (1/23/49)	25th Election (10/1/52)	26th Election (4/19/53)	27th Election (2/27/55)	28th Election (5/22/58)	29th Election (11/20/60)	30th Election (11/21/63)
5. Kinki									
Shiga	2	2	10	2	3	0	2	2	3
Kyōto	5	3	13	5	3	6	6	9	14
Fukui	3	1	3	L1	L1	0	L1	1	L1
Ōsaka	6	6	20	6	6	8	10	11	13
Nara	3	4	9	4	2	2	1	1	2
Wakayama	2	2	9	2	2	0	2	4	5
Mie	2	4	8	2	1	0	L1	1	2
6. Chūgoku									
Shimane	4	6	11	3	0	3	3	2	3
Tottori	2	5	17	3	2	4	2	2	2
Hyōgo	4	3	12	3	1	L1	2	2	4
Okayama	4	2	10	3	2	2	2	2	2
Hiroshima	2	2	10	2	0	L1	1	2	3
Yamaguchi	3	5	12	2	0	0	2	1	2
7. Shikoku									
Kagawa	2	2	10	1	L1	1	L1	1	1
Tokushima	1	1	6	2	0	0	1	1	1
Kōchi	5	3	6	0	2	0	1	2	10
Ehime	3	3	6	2	L1	L1	L1	1	2
8. Kyūshū									
Fukuoka	3	4	9	2	2	2	2	5	6
Saga	2	3	7	1	1	0	2	2	1
Nagasaki	1	2	6	2	1	L1	1	1	2
Ōita	2	3	10	L1	L1	0	1	1	2
Kumamoto	1	1	5	1	L1	0	L1	1	1
Miyazaki	2	2	5	L1	L1	L1	L1	1	2
Kagoshima	L1	L1	3	L1	L1	L1	L1	L1	L1

SOURCE: This chart was prepared by the author, based on data provided in Kōan Chōsachō, *Sengo ni okeru Nihon Kyō-santō no senkyo kekka, Shūgūin gūin sosenkyo no bu*, and from Jichishō senkyo kyoku, *Senkyo nenkan, 1960–1963 (Elec-tion Yearbook 1960–1963)* March 1964.

TABLE VIII

Top Five Metropolitan Districts and Prefectures for the JCP
in Terms of Percentage of Votes in House of
Representatives Elections, 1946–1963

22d Election (4/10/46)		23d Election (4/25/47)		24th Election (1/23/49)	
Tōkyō	9.35	Tōkyō	8.55	Ōsaka	20.07
Nagano	7.94	Nagano	8.05	Tōkyō	18.01
Hokkaidō	6.64	Ishikawa	6.84	Tottori	17.02
Ōsaka	6.36	Ōsaka	6.02	Kanagawa	14.95
Saitama	5.92	Shimane	5.54	Nagano	13.64

25th Election (10/1/52)		26th Election (4/19/53)		27th Election (2/27/55)	
Ōsaka	6.09	Ōsaka	6.01	Ōsaka	8.09
Kyōto	4.97	Nagano	4.77	Kyōto	6.00
Nagano	4.77	Tōkyō	3.60	Tōkyō	5.17
Tōkyō	3.79	Kyōto	3.37	Tottori	4.27
Saitama	3.62	Aichi	2.78	Nagano	3.97

28th Election (5/22/58)		29th Election (11/20/60)		30th Election (11/21/63)	
Ōsaka	10.10	Ōsaka	10.98	Kyōto	13.50
Kyōto	5.76	Kyōto	8.93	Ōsaka	13.39
Tōkyo	4.97	Nagano	5.26	Kōchi	9.56
Kanagawa	4.47	Ishikawa	5.00	Nagano	7.81
Nagano	3.86	Kanagawa	4.86	Tōkyō	6.88

SOURCE: Kōan Chōsachō, *Sengo ni okeru Nihon Kyōsantō no senkyo kekka, Shūguiin giin sōsenkyo no bu*, pp. 48–50, and Jichishō senkyo kyoku, *Senkyo nenkan, 1960–1963*, pp. 225–229.

TABLE IX

LOW FIVE METROPOLITAN DISTRICTS AND PREFECTURES FOR THE JCP
IN TERMS OF PERCENTAGE OF VOTES IN HOUSE OF
REPRESENTATIVES ELECTIONS, 1946–1963[a]

22d Election (4/10/46)		23d Election (4/25/47)		24th Election (1/23/49)		25th Election (10/1/52)	
Nagasaki	1.29	Toyama	1.45	Gifu	4.87	Kagoshima	0.89
Tokushima	1.09	Fukui	1.45	Miyazaki	4.55	Miyazaki	0.88
Kumamoto	0.99	Tokushima	1.15	Miyagi	4.31	Ōita	0.64
Gifu	0.97	Kumamoto	1.12	Fukui	3.05	Iwate	0.94
Kagoshima	0.87	Kagoshima	0.58	Kagoshima	2.63	Kōchi	0

26th Election (4/19/53)		28th Election (5/22/58)		29th Election (11/20/60)		30th Election (11/21/63)	
Iwate	0	Fukui	0.79	Kagoshima	1.11	Kagoshima	0.77
Yamanashi	0	Mie	0.78	Nara	1.06	Tochigi	0.94
Shimane	0	Ehime	0.65	Fukui	1.03	Fukui	0.98
Yamaguchi	0	Miyazaki	0.63	Kumamoto	1.03	Yamanashi	1.03
Tokushima	0	Kagawa	0.42	Tochigi	0.80	Kumamoto	1.22

SOURCE: Kōan Chōsachō, *Sengo ni okeru Nihon Kyōsantō no senkyo kekka, Shūguiin giin sōsenkyo no bu,* pp. 48–50, and Jichishō senkyo kyoku, *Senkyo nenkan, 1960–1963,* pp. 225–229.

[a] In the 27th General Elections, the Japanese Communist Party ran no candidates in 17 prefectures: Kumamoto, Wakayama, Shiga, Mie, Gifu, Toyama, Chiba, Yamagata, Fukushima, Gumma, Yamanashi, Fukui, Yamaguchi, Kōchi, Tokushima, Saga, and Ōita.

TABLE X

PERCENTAGE OF VOTE OBTAINED BY JCP IN VARIOUS AREAS OF
JAPAN, HOUSE OF REPRESENTATIVES ELECTIONS, 1946–1960

			Area		
Election	Urban	Rural	Four large industrial	Key mining	Strongly agrarian
22d	5.72	3.08	7.82	6.65	..
23d	5.39	2.93	7.29	5.58	2.50
24th	13.27	7.68	19.05	12.48	7.74
25th	3.57	1.91	5.53	3.32	1.91
26th	2.81	1.34	6.03	2.90	1.54
27th	2.82	1.07	6.89	3.80	2.41
28th	3.33	1.47	6.30	2.60	1.41
29th	3.74	1.69	7.20	4.82	1.38

SOURCE: Kōan Chōsachō, *Sengo ni okeru Nihon Kyōsantō no senkyo kekka, Shūgiin giin sōsenkyo no bu,* pp. 50–59, 64–65, 66–67, 68–69.

TABLE XI

THE JCP IN HOUSE OF COUNCILLORS ELECTIONS, 1947–1965

Election	Number of candidates		Percent of total candidates	Number elected	Percent of total elected	Occupations of national candidates
1st (April 20, 1947	National	12	4.9	3	3.0	3 trade unionists, 1 farmer, 7 scholars, 1 housebuilder
	Prefectural	29	8.8	1	0.7	
	Total	41	7.4	4	1.6	
2d (June 4, 1950)	National	12	3.8	2	3.6	4 trade unionists, 2 farmers, 2 scholars, 2 housebuilders, 1 musician, 1 other
	Prefectural	38	15.1	..	..	
	Total	50	8.9	2	1.5	
3d (April 24, 1953)	National	3	1.3	..	..	1 trade unionist, 1 musician, 1 other
	Prefectural	9	4.2	..	..	
	Total	12	2.7	..	..	
4th (July 8, 1956)	National	3	2.0	1	1.9	1 trade unionist, 1 musician, 1 other
	Prefectural	31	16.2	1	1.3	
	Total	34	10.0	2	1.6	
5th (June 2, 1959)	National	2	1.6	1	1.9	2 trade unionists
	Prefectural	34	16.3	..	..	
	Total	36	10.9	1	0.8	
6th (July 1, 1962)	National	2	1.8	2	3.9	2 trade unionists
	Prefectural	45	20.4	1	1.3	
	Total	47	14.3	3	2.4	
7th (July 4, 1965)	National	2	0.02	2	3.9	1 trade union leader, 1 musician
	Prefectural	46	19.7	2	2.7	
	Total	48	14.5	4	3.2	

SOURCE: Kōan Chōsachō, *Sengo ni okeru Nihon Kyōsantō no senkyo kekka, Shūgiin giin sōsenkyo no bu,* p. 30. (The 1965 election results have been taken from *Kōan Jōhō* [*Report of the National Security Agency*], July 1965.)

TABLE XII

JCP Votes and Percentage of Candidates
Elected in House of Councillors
Elections, 1947–1965
(N = National; P = Prefectural)

Election		JCP votes	Percent of total national votes	Percent of candidates elected
1st	N-	610,948	2.9	25.0
(April 20, 1947)	P-	720,257	3.3	3.4
			Total	10.0
2d	N-	1,333,872	4.8	16.7
(June 4, 1950)	P-	1,637,451	5.7	..
			Total	4.0
3d	N-	293,877	1.1	..
(April 24, 1953)	P-	264,729	0.9	..
			Total	..
4th	N-	599,254	2.1	33.3
(July 8, 1956)	P-	1,149,009	3.9	3.2
			Total	5.9
5th	N-	551,915	1.9	50.0
(June 2, 1959)	P-	999,255	3.3	..
			Total	2.7
6th	N-	1,123,946	3.1	100.0
(July 1, 1962)	P-	1,760,257	4.8	2.2
			Total	6.4
7th	N-	1,652,363	4.4	100.0
(July 4, 1965)	P-	2,608,771	6.9	4.3
			Total	8.3

SOURCE: Kōan Chōsachō, *Sengo ni okeru Nihon Kyōsantō no senkyo kekka, Sūgiin giin sōsenkyo no bu,* p. 34. (The 1965 election results have been taken from *Kōan Jōhō,* July 1965.)

TABLE XIII

TOP FIVE METROPOLITAN DISTRICTS AND PREFECTURES FOR THE JCP
IN TERMS OF PERCENTAGE OF VOTES IN HOUSE OF COUNCILLORS
ELECTIONS (NATIONAL CANDIDATES ONLY), 1947–1962

1st Election (4/20/47)		2d Election (6/4/50)		3d Election (4/24/53)	
Okayama	5.06	Okayama	9.18	Tōkyō	3.48
Nagano	4.79	Ōsaka	8.82	Okayama	2.66
Tōkyō	4.47	Gumma	8.66	Miyazaki	1.84
Kanagawa	3.97	Tōkyō	8.19	Nagano	1.58
Shimane	3.95	Kanagawa	7.70	Kyōto	1.28

4th Election (7/8/56)		5th Election (6/2/59)		6th Election (7/1/62)	
Kyōto	5.47	Kyōto	6.01	Kyōto	8.76
Tōkyō	5.45	Ōsaka	4.70	Ōsaka	6.25
Ōsaka	5.38	Tōkyō	3.40	Tōkyō	6.21
Kanagawa	3.11	Kanagawa	2.89	Fukuoka	4.66
Hyōgo	2.38	Niigata	2.49	Kanagawa	4.30

SOURCE: Kōan Chōsachō, *Sengo ni okeru Nihon Kyōsantō no senkyo kekka, Sūgiin giin sōsenkyo no bu,* p. 39.

TABLE XIV

LOW FIVE METROPOLITAN DISTRICTS AND PREFECTURES FOR THE JCP
IN TERMS OF PERCENTAGE OF VOTES IN HOUSE OF COUNCILLORS
ELECTIONS (NATIONAL CANDIDATES ONLY), 1947–1962

1st Election (4/20/47)		2d Election (6/4/50)		3d Election (4/24/53)	
Miyazaki	1.66	Hokkaidō	2.35	Fukui	0.48
Gifu	1.58	Iwate	2.30	Tochigi	0.47
Shiga	1.53	Kagoshima	2.28	Kagoshima	0.40
Nara	1.29	Tokushima	2.00	Gumma	0.38
Kagoshima	1.29	Kōchi	1.09	Ibaragi	0.37

4th Election (7/8/56)		5th Election (6/2/59)		6th Election (7/1/62)	
Ōita	0.84	Saga	0.94	Kumamoto	1.40
Nagasaki	0.82	Kagawa	0.93	Ibaragi	1.35
Miyazaki	0.77	Kagoshima	0.90	Saga	1.30
Saga	0.75	Kumamoto	0.87	Fukui	1.30
Kumamoto	0.63	Miyazaki	0.81	Kagoshima	1.28

SOURCE: Kōan Chōsachō, *Sengo ni okeru Nihon Kyōsantō no senkyo kekka, Sūgiin giin sōsenkyo no bu,* p. 39.

TABLE XV

PERCENTAGE OF VOTE OBTAINED BY THE JCP IN VARIOUS AREAS OF JAPAN,
HOUSE OF COUNCILLORS ELECTIONS, 1947–1962
(N = National; P = Prefectural)

Election	Urban		Rural		Four large industrial		Key mining		Strongly agrarian	
	N	P	N	P	N	P	N	P	N	P
1st	3.33	4.34	2.64	2.78	4.61	5.66	4.12	5.73	2.43	1.97
2d	6.27	6.66	3.97	5.29	8.19	6.59	5.09	7.57	3.69	4.90
3d	1.63	1.49	0.77	0.64	2.41	2.94	1.08	1.13	0.65	..
4th	2.80	4.93	1.28	2.67	5.28	10.01	1.77	2.62	1.22	2.42
5th	2.37	3.77	1.16	2.67	4.03	5.25	1.39	2.79	1.07	2.32
6th	3.89	5.78	1.85	3.28	6.24	9.50	4.45	5.44	1.52	3.18

SOURCE: Kōan Chōsachō, *Sengo ni okeru Nihon Kyōsantō no senkyo kekka, Shūgiin giin sōsenkyo no bu,* pp. 44, 50, 51, 52.

TABLE XVI

PERCENTAGE OF VOTE OBTAINED BY THE JCP IN THE CITIES
OF KYŌTO, TŌKYŌ, AND OSAKA IN HOUSE OF
COUNCILLORS ELECTIONS, 1947–1962
(N = National; P = Prefectural)

Election	Kyōto		Tōkyō		Osaka	
	N	P	N	P	N	P
1st	2.94	4.83	4.47	6.59	3.14	4.51
2d	3.13	.....	8.19	.....	8.82	14.06
3d	1.28	.....	3.48	4.82	0.92	.....
4th	5.47	8.96	5.45	12.99	5.38	6.50
5th	6.01	8.76	3.40	3.41	4.70	6.92
6th	8.76	13.05	6.21	11.92	6.25	6.96

SOURCE: Kōan Chōsachō, *Sengo ni okeru Nihon Kyōsantō no senkyo kekka, Sūgiin giin sōsenkyo no bu*, p. 53.

TABLE XVII

PREFECTURAL GOVERNOR ELECTIONS AND THE JCP
1947–1963

Election	Number of JCP candidates	Total number of candidates	Percent of total number of candidates	JCP votes	Total votes	Percent of total votes	JCP candidates elected	Total candidates elected
April 5, 1947	9	..	..	258,044	26,740,467	0.96	0	..
April 30, 1951	8	94	8.5	204,937	27,601,911	0.74	0	34
April 23, 1955	2	48	4.2	181,685	17,538,043	1.03	0	21
April 23, 1959	7	53	13.2	485,356	20,076,626	2.42	0	20
April 23, 1963	7	58	12.0	521,074	20,215,769	2.58	0	20

SOURCE: This chart was prepared by the author from Japanese Communist Party sources, and four volumes of Jichishō senkyo kyoku, Senkyo nenkan covering the period 1953–1963.

TABLE XVIII

PREFECTURAL ASSEMBLY ELECTIONS AND THE JCP
1955–1963

Election	Number of JCP candidates	Total number of candidates	Percent of total number of candidates	JCP votes	Total votes	Percent of total votes	JCP candidates elected	Total candidates elected
April 23, 1955	119	5,556	2	318,677	36,051,299	0.88	10	2,613
April 23, 1959	122	4,860	2	437,824	38,604,785	1.1	12	2,656
April 30, 1963	176	4,657	3.8	848,305	40,122,779	2.1	22	2,688

SOURCE: Jichishō senkyo kyoku, Senkyo nenkan—1953–1957; 1958–1959; 1960–1963.

TABLE XIX

City, Town, and Village Mayoral Elections and the JCP, 1955–1963

Election	JCP candidates	Total number of candidates	JCP votes	Total votes	Percent of total vote	JCP candidates elected	Total candidates elected
April 23, 1955							
City	12	401	76,093	8,600,677	0.9	0	174
Town/Village	9	3,092	5,235	3,837,451	0.1	1	1,663
April 23, 1959							
City	19	387	179,220	9,173,871	1.8	0	177
Town/Village	14	2,332	7,523	4,736,391	0.2	0	1,227
April 23, 1963							
City	12	346	84,383	9,343,871	0.9	0	170
Town/Village	8	1,868	9,428	3,959,005	0.2	0	1,105

SOURCE: Jichishō senkyo kyoku, *Senkyo nenkan*—1953–1957; 1958–1959; 1960–1963.

TABLE XX

City, Town, and Village Council Elections
and the JCP, 1955–1963

Election	JCP candidates	Total number of candidates	Percent of total vote	JCP votes	Total votes	Percent of total vote	JCP candidates elected	Total candidates elected
April 23, 1955								
City	336	19,395	1.73	323,799	16,788,326	1.93	131	9,972
Town/Village	371	55,152	0.7	47,178	7,474,269	0.6	190	43,939
April 23, 1959								
City	384	17,910	2.1	509,069	20,837,011	2.4	218	11,827
Town/Village	295	39,085	0.8	62,050	8,216,815	0.7	168	31,252
April 23, 1963								
City	570	18,171	3.1	880,991	23,976,529	3.3	369	13,111
Town/Village	528	37,685	1.4	129,704	8,725,959	1.5	314	30,068

SOURCE: Jichishō senkyo kyoku, *Senkyo nenkan*—1953–1957; 1958–1959; 1960–1963.

TABLE XXI

ESTIMATED REVENUE AND EXPENDITURE OF THE JCP IN 1963[a]

Headquarters Revenue and Expenditures

Income

Akahata and other party publications.................1,300,000,000 yen
Aid from external sources, notably Communist China......1,000,000,000 yen
Fund-raising campaigns and special contributions........ 100,000,000 yen
Party dues... 37,000,000 yen
Total...2,437,000,000 yen

Expenditures

Publications of all types...........................1,000,000,000 yen
Subsidies to local and prefectural party organizations.... 600,000,000 yen
Maintenance expenses for headquarters................ 400,000,000 yen
Salaries and wages for party employees............... 190,000,000 yen
Total...2,190,000,000 yen

Local and Prefectural Party Revenue and Expenditures

Income

Mass campaigns for fund raising.....................1,000,000,000 yen
Subsidies from headquarters........................ 600,000,000 yen
Collections from local sources...................... 400,000,000 yen
Membership dues................................ 170,000,000 yen
Total...2,170,000,000 yen

Expenditures

Construction and maintenance of party headquarters, propaganda, and organizational funds..............2,000,000,000 yen
Salaries and expenses for 1700 local and prefectural party workers................................... 360,000,000 yen
Total...2,360,000,000 yen

SOURCE: *Kōan Jōhō*, February 1964, p. 3.

[a] An unexplained discrepancy between income and expenditures exists in this tabulation, yielding a deficit of some 550,000,000 yen. It must be kept in mind, however, that in any case these figures are essentially guesses.

VIII

PROSPECTS AND PROBLEMS

The Japanese Communist Party is now nearly half a century old. It was one of the first Communist parties to be established in Asia, and in many respects conditions in Japan seemed to augur well for its growth. Indeed, the Marxist who took his creed seriously had ample reason to believe that Japanese Communism could set the pace for communism in all other Asian societies.

By 1920, Japan could be considered an industrial state, with more of its gross national product derived from manufacturing, mining, and related fields than from agriculture. Clearly, industrialization would continue at an accelerated pace, and out of the great urban complexes would come millions of new workers—proletariat for the party. In other respects as well, Japanese society provided the sociopolitical foundations for the development of communism as envisaged by Marx. The nation-building process, for example, had been accomplished in its most critical phases by the end of the nineteenth century. Mass literacy had been achieved by the second decade of the twentieth century. Thus, a people long possessed of a highly homogeneous culture now had a modern political framework, a heightened political consciousness, and the means to articulate this consciousness.

If one examined the potentialities from the standpoint of class analysis, that favorite Marxist approach, once again, Japanese society seemed to offer multiple opportunities for Communist growth. The Japanese intellectuals were excellent candidates for party leadership pending the rise of the "true proletariat." Unlike some emerging societies, Japan had a distinguished intellectual tradition and a sizable intellectual community. The prestige of the Japanese intellectual in his society, moreover, was relatively high, especially if he adhered to his assigned function. In modern times, that function, translated politically, was to play the role of the social critic, separated from active participation in the political processes.

Marxism served as a magnificent weapon of social criticism. It was also a weapon easily acquired by the Japanese intellectual, partly because of its essential simplicity and partly because the role of German thought in general had been extensive in his training. Indeed, Japanese culture—and even the Japanese language—contained a strong element of compatibility with German thought and mode of expression. Marxism, in a certain sense, was but one branch of the modern Germanic impact upon the Japanese intellectual. And that impact was a major one in the late nineteenth and early twentieth centuries primarily because of the similar timing of modernization and the similar character of the political elites who assumed the leading roles in Germany and Japan.

We have noted briefly certain additional reasons for the appeal of Marxism to the Japanese intellectual. In part, Marxism answered his need for a new faith, one that would combine "truth" and "science" and relieve his deep sense of intellectual isolation by connecting him with the universal stream. Marxism also represented a philosophy of optimism, assuring its adherents that all societies would ultimately travel the same road and reach the same high goal, the brotherhood of man. To those disillusioned by Western-style parliamentarism (and many Japanese intellectuals experienced disillusionment at an early point), communism was the new democracy, whereby science and faith, the particular and the universal, could be united. And for these same reasons, it was a promising methodology, a mode of analysis that could claim science without discarding value. It provided a simple conceptual framework in which to fit all social phenomena.

If the Japanese intellectual, having acquired a "proletarian consciousness," was thus available to lead the Communist movement, from whence would come the masses? On the surface, this did not seem to constitute a serious barrier. Could these not be drawn from both the modern and the traditional sectors of the society, combined in artful fashion? Japan surely was an ideal environment in which to seek the capture of a raw, first-generation-peasant industrial labor class. That class was rapidly growing in numbers, and it was experiencing many of the anxieties and frustrations on which radical movements feed. Yet, for the most part, this was not a lumpen proletariat, existing in a dazed stupor. The new Japanese working class had had a rudimentary education and thus could be reached by a wide range of communications. Nor was it so desperately poor as to make the avoidance of starvation its sole concern. It could be and was interested in "progress." In these respects and in others, the working class appeared to have substantial potentialities for tutelage and organization at the hands of a vanguard elite.

The peasant was also less "backward" than in most of the Asian societies surrounding Japan. He was at least semiliterate as a result of the intensive program in mass literacy pioneered by the Meiji government. In most cases, he lived close enough to urban centers to be greatly influenced by the successive tides of economic and social change. Indeed, in increasing numbers, he participated in urban life on either a full-time or part-time basis, carrying his experiences back into the heart of rural Japan. Tenancy, that great source of revolutionary protest, was a serious problem. More than 50 percent of the arable land was cultivated by tenants, and more than two-thirds of all farm families were pure tenants or part tenants. Could not this combination of political capacity and socioeconomic grievance be exploited?

Despite these seeming advantages, however, communism did not flourish in Japan. The intriguing question is "Why?" As in the case of all complex social phenomena, many factors were involved. The timing and the methods of Japanese modernization—closely interrelated elements— were both of critical importance to any explanation of Communist weakness. The Japanese modernization experiment began in the mid-nineteenth century, and by the time of the Russian Revolution, it had reached a fairly advanced stage. This particular timing was conducive to a pace, a set of attitudes, and certain methods not generally available, certainly not easily established, in societies seeking to undertake modernization at a later time.

Only one basic model was available to the Japanese, that of the pioneer Western nation-state. What did this Western nation-state model provide? Its emphasis was on an intensive use of all myths, symbols, and institutions for the creation of a powerful nation, capable of committing its people to an infinite variety of purposes; the gradual development of representative institutions, as the primary means of legitimizing power and providing a mass base for political strength; support for economic modernization, with the state providing vital assistance to private entrepreneurs, but generally limiting its direct operational role to those segments of the economy not capable of being run adequately or efficiently by private means.

Such a model had certain points of conformity with, or adaptability to, Japanese traditions and capacities, as well as other points of major divergence. The character of Japanese modernization, in any case, is to be understood in terms of a process of snythesis involving early Western experiences and the indigenous value-institutional structure. This process, moreover, was directed by a modernizing oligarchy closely wedded in some respects to the traditional order. Clearly, the Meiji leaders were "progressives" in a certain sense. They dedicated themselves to nation-building and economic modernization with remarkable concentration. Moreover, they were not hesitant to borrow those methods and techniques appropriate to the tasks, however different they might be from prevailing practices.

At the same time, however, the Meiji political elite came largely from the traditional ruling class and partook rather deeply of its values. These men were not so estranged from their society as to desire its complete destruction. On the contrary, after some initial uncertainty and fairly radical experimentation, the Meiji leaders relied more and more heavily upon the maximization of built-in Japanese resources—both values and institutions—for the purpose of rapid modernization. In this manner, they minimized the type of waste and destruction involved in revolution, and at the same time bequeathed to their successors a socioeconomic order containing many traditional components.

It is reasonable to assert that Japanese modernization was conducted by an enlightened but increasingly conservative elite who was prepared to use the past to the fullest extent in constructing the future. Like Burke, these men did not wish to see the cultural traditions of their society swept away in some revolutionary floodtide. Modern Japan thus retained powerful links with the past, and some of these links provided impressive barriers to the Communist movement. Neo-Confucianism, made applicable to the nation-state and transmitted to the masses through a universal, compulsory education system, equipped the citizenry with an ideology and code of behavior far more pervasive and satisfying than that existing in most societies at whatever stage of development.

Nationalism was personified in the Emperor, and the imperial institution became a powerful magnet, drawing toward it mass loyalty. The traditional familial system was protected by the state and whenever possible, strengthened. No sustained assault was conducted against the fundamental hierarchical character of social relations in general. Intricate social distinctions, while no longer given full legal protection, remained a crucial part of the fabric of Japanese society, buttressed by the new as well as by the old value-institutional system. Similarly, the small group, leader-follower nuclei governing the fundamental nature of all Japanese organization—so antagonistic to pure individualism and to true mass-based politics alike—remained impervious to change.

We must be careful not to suggest that tradition *per se* constituted a great monolithic barrier to communism in Japan. The evidence available from elsewhere suggests that communism can often make effective use of tradition—more effective use perhaps than Western-style liberalism. It is undoubtedly too early to pass final judgment upon the techniques of Chinese Communism under its first-generation revolutionary leaders, but no trained observer can avoid being impressed with the extensive degree to which tradition—whether of thought, style, or policies—has pervaded Chinese Communist actions. If there is a major element that is new and revolutionary in contemporary China, there is much reflective of the past—the Confucian past, the Imperial past, and the Boxer past.

Perhaps then, it is less upon the role of tradition and more upon the nature of the political elite that we should place our emphasis in contrasting the political experiences of such societies as modern Japan and China. There can be little doubt that the Japanese political elite was centrally a product of "independent development" in a society that managed to escape colonialism. Unlike most of Asia and Africa, Japan was neither subjected to colonial rule nor did it undergo a lengthy period of weakness and disunity during which quasi-colonial conditions existed, as in the case of China.

The absence of colonialism and the relative success of modernization in its central facets—together with the particular timing of Japanese emergence into the world stream and the unique set of Japanese traditions—shaped the character of the modern political elite in that society and its capacity to legitimize itself quickly. In contrast to most societies of Asia, Africa, *and* Europe, the average Japanese citizen did not feel alienated from his government. At the same time, mass mobilization on a radical, truly egalitarian scale was precluded. All organization and decision-making, as we have emphasized, revolved around the small leader-follower group, with an intricate system of federations when necessary. If this reflected a strong premodern or early-modern element, it also symbolized the continuance of a high quotient of Japanese-style pluralism. Thus, the most critical ingredients of the modern "totalitarian" state or party remained outside the scope of Japanese sociopolitical capacity.

These were some of the critical factors inhibiting Communist success in prewar Japan. In essence, as can be seen, they relate to the experience of Japan with the Western world, an experience which in turn was affected both by accident and by capacities indigenous to Japanese society. In the final analysis, the Japanese Communists were not able to vie for the honor of initiating the modernization process; they arrived much too late. Nor were they able to find the effective issues or means of organization whereby to capture that movement in its more mature phases; whatever the mistakes and ineptitudes of the governing elite, its relative economic and political successes thwarted the Communists consistently. The primary sources of protest available to the Communists in many emerging societies—the existence of colonial or neocolonial conditions, the presence of economic stagnation, or the dominance of a blind reactionary, corrupt political elite—were not available in Japan.

Indeed, the Japanese Communists were forced to fight nationalism because its cultivation was in the hands of their opponents, and its primary symbol was the Emperor system. In fact, the essential issue became "Japanese imperialism," not the threat of subordination to a foreign power in the era before 1945. Nor was it possible to categorize the political elite of Japan as blind reactionaries or as totally corrupt. Once again, the absence of a colonial heritage was of signal importance. Colonialism very frequently destroyed or fragmented beyond repair the traditional and even the modern-moderate elites that might otherwise have been available for the initial tasks of nation-building and economic development. With a few exceptions such as the Philippines—and some of the societies where native monarchies survived—colonialism tended to guarantee first-generation revolutionary elites who were highly ideological, intensely politicized, and often charismatic in style and appeal.

The Japanese political elite, however, had to be described differently. Strongly nationalist, it was also conservative, experienced, pragmatic, and possessed of some degree of technical competence. Moreover, it had a vital *esprit de corps*, serving with some of the same efficiency and sense of obligation as characterized the elite of another conservative, hierarchical society, Great Britain. Corruption played a substantial role in Japanese politics as it did in the politics of all developing societies, but it never reached sufficient proportions to threaten the efficiency of political or economic operations.

Nor could one speak of the stagnation of the Japanese economy after the mid-nineteenth century, although there were recurrent crises and an uneven development. In this respect, Japan stood in sharp contrast to such Western societies as France and Italy, where major obstacles developed to thwart economic-political development, and peoples acculturated to progress were frustrated by long periods of nondevelopment. In sum, the Japanese industrial revolution, unlike that of France, was never frozen, and the march toward political unification and mass commitment was never halted in front of the type of seemingly insurmountable barriers that have long existed in Italy.

If the issues were missing for the Communists, the problems of organization were also formidable in two senses. As we have stressed, the Japanese Communist movement, like all political movements in modern Japan, had an enormous problem in breaking through the small-group character of Japanese organization and thereby creating a true mass movement. On the other hand, the Communists were constantly harassed by the one organization in Japan with major power—the national government. The efficiency of a well-operated police state, albeit one with a number of liberal elements, was never more clearly demonstrated than against the Communists in prewar Japan.

In the postwar era, Japanese Communism has had certain new opportunities. The traditional order suffered a profound shock as a result of military defeat and the American revolution with its thrust in the direction of egalitarianism, competition, and unfettered political freedom. For the first time since the early Meiji period, the legitimacy of the state was placed in doubt. Even the Emperor system was challenged from a variety of sources. The most fundamental popular beliefs were shaken, and the atmosphere was strongly conducive to the development of revolutionary doctrines.

Student and intellectual circles were especially affected. They were influenced partly by the fact that in their analysis of Japanese "imperialism," the Communists had been "correct," all others "wrong"; the Communists had been "pure," all others "impure." Who else had opposed Japanese militarism so vigorously and predicted its fate so accurately? Who else had dared to criticize all of the old, traditional institutions, including the Emperor system, when most liberals had been frightened into silence? Some intellectual recruits to communism came as a result of their guilt complex, others because they believed they had found truth, still others because Marxism appeared to be the political wave of the future. But more importantly, Japanese society now spawned a rootless, restless younger generation, uncertain of its values, its role, and its very identity.

In the years immediately after World War II, the Japanese intellectual shared in great measure the type of alienation commonly ascribed to the French intellectual. Frustrated by what he regarded as inadequate recognition of him by his society and possessed by deep conflicting currents of self-doubt and snobbishness, the Japanese intellectual often sought relief by assaulting his society in total terms. It was natural to use ideological instruments in conducting this attack, and to alternate between nihilistic pessimism and cosmic utopianism. This strongly anti-national bent accorded with the current Communist position, for the Communists alone of political groups had consistently operated outside the Japanese political culture. They alone had lacked a Japanese identity.

Labor represented for the Communists another potentially rich source of support. In the fundamental reordering of Japanese interest groups that followed the American Occupation, trade unionism was given special emphasis. Phoenix-like, organized labor arose from the ashes of war and defeat, pushed forward by SCAP authorities as a part of the democratization process. Lacking any legitimacy within the past traditions of its own society and emerging in a revolutionary era, the Japanese labor movement naturally took on militant political overtones. In important respects, moreover, SCAP aided this by the very speed with which they thrust labor forward and by the fairly drastic processes which they used to eliminate or restrict those labor leaders connected with the old order. It cannot be denied that the left enjoyed a certain respectability among some Americans as a result of the continuing aura of the American–Soviet wartime alliance and the overriding concern with destroying the Fascist-militarist menace.

Yet another vital question was asked by the Japanese Communists in the first months after surrender. Could the peasants be mobilized? Could the millions of farm boys, many of them from poor tenant families, who had fought so loyally for the Emperor be enlisted in a vastly different political cause? Certainly, by 1945, they had had extensive organizational experience—and in a mass organization, the army. Just as clearly, most of them were dispirited, troubled with respect to basic values, and concerned over their economic future.

It was under these conditions that the Communists became legal, emerging from the long, black night of prison, exile, or a subversive, underground existence. Quickly, top Communists acquired certain positions of importance, especially in intellectual circles and in the labor movement. At this point, Japanese Communism seemed en route to the more classical form of radical strength, a power based upon the urban classes, with the true proletariat as its mass base. The climax of this era was reached in the period 1947–1949, with the first great crisis for the Communists coming at the time of the abortive February 1 strike, and the last great victory coming with the spectacular election gains in 1949. The Communists are hopeful that the gains of the last few years presage another, more spectacular advance. Whatever the future, however, the decade and a half after the 1949 elections represented a period of frustration for the Communists. Why?

It is appropriate to start an exploration of Communist weakness by examining the broadest trends within the socioeconomic groups to which the Communists sought to appeal. Certainly, the proclivities of the Japanese student-intellectual community for Marxism, or at least for a ritualized "leftist" political response, have remained strong. In considerable measure, the Japanese intellectuals have continued to be alienated from their society—or at least from their government. Among the older elements at least, feelings of inferiority remain deeply rooted, together with a sense of estrangement from the world of the official and the political leader. Most intellectuals continue to live within their own subculture, largely separated from the other subcultures that surround them. And their subculture has habituated them to a political style as well as to a set of political affiliations—so long practiced and so necessary to psychological security that among the older generation no basic changes are likely. Any substantial changes would mean the destruction of close-knit group relations and the loss of identity insofar as the individual is concerned. It would be almost as painful and as difficult to effect as the task of converting an Islamic Filipino to the Catholic–Luzon culture.

Up to date, however, ritualized leftism has had outlets other than the Communist Party of Japan, and for the overwhelming majority of Japanese intellectuals of this inclination, the Japan Socialist Party has been more appealing. A few prominent intellectuals have been active Communists, but to most, the Japanese Communist Party in the past has been too obviously a nonindigenous force whether identified with Moscow or Peking. Marxism, anti-Americanism, militant nationalism—all could be found in the Socialist Party for those having these persuasions. Moreover, the Socialist Party did not have to bear responsibility for Tibet, Hungary, or the debasing self-criticism of Kuo Mo-jo after his many years of faithful service to Peking. Indeed, the Socialist Party did not have to bear any responsibility and did not require a single, rigid line. It permitted or at least suffered major variations of ideological and policy position. These conditions were far more in line with the proclivities and commitments of the old-line left and left-liberal intellectuals.

Moreover, a new phenomenon has recently emerged within the Japanese student-intellectual community. A sharp challenge, led generally by the younger generation, has developed to the traditional ideological and policy positions of the traditional "avant-garde" intellectual, and to his political mood and style as well. Marxism increasingly is assuming the role of an old-fashioned, outmoded ideology no longer suitable for Japan and, more importantly, no longer exciting. The academic fortresses of Marxism are now being defended primarily by tired old men who have had no new ideas in decades. Meanwhile, Japanese society has changed at an incredible rate, posing a vast array of new opportunities and problems, neither of which can be met by simplistic, antiquated formulae. Many young Japanese intellectuals, intensely aware of these facts, are searching for more modern, more complicated methods of analysis. Inevitably, they are being drawn toward some of the more sophisticated methods now being used experimentally by Western social scientists, because that which is truly *avant-garde* lies mainly here. Moreover, for an advanced society, truth lies in complexity—and precision. Some of the young Japanese intellectuals who are genuinely modern may well borrow from Marxism, but only to go beyond it. In any case, the basic thrust of their movement constitutes a major challenge to both the Communist and left Socialist positions.

At the very heart of the new intellectual movement in Japan is the quest for realism, a quest started and then abandoned by the intellectual Marxists decades ago. Marxism, claiming to be science, ceased to employ scientific techniques in Japan at a very early point and merely applied ready-made foreign formulae to indigenous problems. The testing of hypotheses through field work, the objective collection of data, and the use of various measurements were largely ignored. "Pure theory" held sway on the one hand; legalistic-institutional studies on the other. Old myths—Marxist, *Kojiki*,[1] or merely formalistic—were merely repeated in ritualistic fashion. Meanwhile, the divergence of Japanese society from all of those myths became ever more pronounced, especially after 1945. Thus, events have encouraged a younger generation of Japanese intellectuals to demand that all of the sacred scriptures of the past be submitted to reexamination, and that there be no forbidden words or ideas, that the censorship self-imposed by intellectuals for the last twenty years be lifted. The battle has just been joined, and its outcome remains uncertain, but the Communists and left Socialists can only view such trends with foreboding.

Hence, while the Japanese Communist Party has regained control of Zengakuren, that organization itself has rarely been weaker or less

---

[1] One of the Japanese mythological works much in vogue with the ultranationalists.

representative of current student sentiment in Japan. Among mature intellectuals, moreover, the Japanese Communists have lost ground in recent years in contrast to their overall membership gains. Even among the solidly left intellectual group, recent events covering the broad spectrum of world communism from Belgrade to Peking have been disconcerting. Increasingly, the Japanese intellectual has had at least some awareness of incidents involving his genre throughout the world. The arrests of Milovan Djilas and Mihajlo Mihajlov, the trials of Soviet writers Daniel and Sinyavsky, and, above all, the fantastic Chinese Communist "cultural revolution," involving the purge or demeaning of scores of well-known intellectuals, have created a suspicion of communism which, like most political moods, may pass but which is currently more profound than at any time in Japanese history. In this sense, incidentally, the JCP decision to separate itself from Peking may be viewed as an absolutely necessary act if it is to salvage any substantial intellectual support—despite the risks of alienating the militant young activists who espouse the Peking line.

Whatever the future political trends relating to the Japanese intellectual community, two current tendencies will, in all likelihood, continue. The assault upon orthodox Marxism will continue within the academic community, with new methodologies and new modes of thought gradually acquiring increased strength. And political fragmentation within that community, especially within the "left" intellectual group, will also continue. It is possible that the Japanese Communist Party can turn its new nationalist stance to advantage if world trends favor it and if the past is rapidly forgotten. It is more likely, however, that the generation of Japanese intellectuals now coming onto the stage will move away from, not toward, Marxism–Leninism—old and new. The Japanese Communist Party may well become increasingly the symbol of eccentrism— the politically absurd—as it has become in most other advanced societies. For as the Japanese intellectual travels and reads more widely—and he is already one of the most mobile intellectuals in the world—he will become aware of the fact that communism is, at most, a technique of rapid modernization. Whether it is a desirable, or even an effective technique will continue to be debated. In any case, however, we have reached a stage of global evolution where it is no longer intellectually respectable to suggest that advanced states need to retreat to conformity, coercion, and the high quotient of primitivism implicit in most current forms of communism in order to preserve themselves.

If the Communists have been unable to capture any significant portion of the student-intellectual community, their gains among the organized workers have also been deeply disappointing to them. As noted earlier, Communist strength within Sōhyō at present does not exceed 20 percent, and it may be less. The strongly anti-Communist Dōmei Kaigi, moreover, is showing remarkable vigor. Why have the Japanese Communists fallen so far short of the results attained by their French and Italian comrades in the labor movement? Many factors, of course, are involved. The Japanese labor movement, as a large-scale movement, is relatively recent, dating only from the period after 1945, and hence, the overwhelming proportion of workers lacks the traditions of radicalism and organization present in Western Europe. Many of the Japanese workers are still first-generation urbanites, drawn from a peasant culture at once conservative and paternalistic.

Once again, however, the fact that Japan has had a reasonably important Socialist Party, and that most key "left" labor leaders have belonged to this party, is of major significance. After 1947, the JCP was never allowed to capture any major portion of the labor movement. However much to the "left" they may have moved, Sōhyō leaders have consistently fought the Communists, identified themselves with the Socialist Party, and used every conceivable method to get their members to vote the Socialist ticket. The Communists have also contributed mightily to their own problems in the Japanese labor movement by exhibiting an extraordinary degree of rigidity both with respect to united front tactics and with respect to grass-roots issues. On the one hand, they had rebuked and insulted Socialist labor leaders a sufficient number of times to make even the more doctrinaire Marxist types suspicious. On the other hand, they have repeatedly demanded that the workers make economic sacrifices for abstract political issues.

The Japanese labor movement, given the timing of its development and the circumstances of its society, has naturally had a strong political orientation, particularly at the top levels. But this fact must be coupled with another, equally significant one, namely, the phenomenal development of the Japanese economy in the past fifteen years. Rapid economic growth has not only allowed the worker to move toward meeting some of his material desires. It has also structured his patterns of demand and tactics of struggle. In essence, it has rapidly increased the quotient of "economicism" in the labor movement. While the Communists are urging him to sacrifice his wages by a continuous series of demonstrations against the Japan–Korea Treaty, the visit of American nuclear-powered submarines, and myriad other causes, he himself wants to concentrate the struggle upon wages, working conditions, and other issues that will determine the extent to which he shares in the prosperity of recent years.

The initial attack of the JCP upon the April 17th strike in 1964 was but one evidence among many of the party's willingness to sacrifice the interests of the worker for those of the Communist Party. But more importantly, the broadest trends within the Japanese labor movement are away from the intense politicization demanded by the Communists. These trends, moreover, will continue if the present momentum of socio-economic change can be maintained. As I have remarked elsewhere, "barring some unsuspected disaster, organized labor in Japan is likely to take on those forms of political expression and behavior that can be classified as symbolic of the 'mature' labor movement of an 'advanced' society."

Whatever the initial promises, therefore, the Japanese Communist Party failed signally in its efforts to mobilize the type of social forces for revolution which the classical Marxists had envisaged. The urban classes, especially the "petit-bourgeois intellectuals" and the "proletariat," while they do provide the party with the bulk of such vote as it polls, are not to be counted within the Communist fold today. The signs, moreover, are mainly adverse to their being recruited in significantly larger numbers. If the Japanese Communists have failed in efforts to reach revolution and power via the front door, they have also failed to achieve success via the back door. If the urban classes have not swung behind communism in massive numbers as Japan has evolved into a highly industrialized, "advanced" nation, the rural classes have not been recruited via a play upon backwardness. Neither the "European" nor the "Asian" routes to communism have worked for the Japanese comrades.

As our knowledge of the Chinese Communist revolution gains in depth and breadth, a considerable amount of revisionism will probably be in order. It is quite possible, for example, that we have thus far exaggerated the effectiveness—and certainly the degree of perfection—achieved by party organization in China. We have scarcely begun to deal with the phenomenon of National Communism, moreover, and at present some ominous parallels with National Socialism suggest themselves. Similarly, the precise relation of the peasant to revolution in the Chinese context and elsewhere may need careful reexamination. It has long been argued—and not without substantial evidence—that the Asian peasant is backward and capable of being aroused politically only with great difficulty. Thus, the *Asian* route to communism is often regarded as akin to a miracle. That route involves the peasant centrally and makes use of both persuasion and coercion. On the one hand, the Communists parade issues such as land reform, equality of treatment, an end to official repression and corruption, and a host of local grievances. On the other hand, they employ an apparatus capable of terrorism either at the massive level or in the most precise form. But it must not be forgotten that the Asian peasant, or at least the peasant of Northeast Asia, has had a lengthy experience in protest, in organization, and in some of the basic techniques now involved in guerrilla warfare. Peasant petitions for the redress of grievances or the rebate of taxes; peasant "riots" and revolts against constituted authority; and peasant skill in evading officials, hoarding food, and conducting "underground" operations—all of these constitute a political tradition of formidable extent, and one which can often be utilized by the Communists.

The Japanese Communists' lack of success with the peasant of Japan is not due to the absence of the political traditions noted above. Undoubtedly, it is important that Japanese feudalism underwrote a strong paternalism which provided for responsibilities and rights across blood lines, thereby creating a sense of community. Nevertheless, traditional Japan, notwithstanding the hierarchical, paternalist, communal patterns of society, witnessed peasant riots and a range of other political activities involving organization. As we have seen, moreover, the peasant threatened to become a source of revolution prior to World War II when "rightist" elements undertook political mobilization in the rural areas, playing upon many of the same grievances—and same techniques— as the Communists, and, in some cases, using the label, "National Socialism."

Thus, it can be argued that the Communists were defeated less by the "conservatism" of the Japanese peasant and more by the fact that the Japanese agrarian revolution after 1945 was conducted by other hands and via other means. That revolution, moreover, was given extended meaning because it took place in the context of a broader socioeconomic change encompassing urban as well as rural Japan. The peasant, indeed, became quasi-urban as he or members of his family worked part-time in factories and in a variety of ways found the city or the town changing the patterns of his life. As in so many other respects, the Japanese Communists were never able to make contact with reality in terms of the Japanese farmer.

If the weakness of Japanese Communism can be partly explained by a careful examination of its relation to the major socioeconomic groups of Japanese society, there are other, equally significant factors that have been apparent in this study. One is the fact that despite the major defeat suffered in World War II, the Japanese state survived with sufficient authority to lay claim to the loyalty of its citizens. It is easy to emphasize the misgivings of the articulate, the alienation of the intellectuals, and the confusion of the masses in the years after 1945. But the Japanese state had been in the process of socializing its citizens for some three-quarters of a century. The legitimacy of the state had not been established overnight, and its foundations—including the imperial institution—were not lightly laid. No doubt, in comparison with the militarist era, the legitimacy of the national government is more precarious today. In comparison with the attitudes of the French or Italians, however, not to mention the peoples of most of the rest of Asia and of Africa, the Japanese citizen accepts the authority of that government.

In turn, the power of the state after the war was maintained. As in the prewar era, the Japanese government, abetted by SCAP, once again played an important role in curtailing Communist Party development. A series of heavy blows were struck at Communist organizations—both party and extra-party, as we have seen. Unquestionably, the capacity of the state to play such a role related partly to its legitimacy in the eyes of the overwhelming majority of citizens, partly to the traditions of state action and the training of state officials, and partly to the topography of Japan, a topography making the Yenan approach virtually impossible.

Finally, major emphasis must be given to the dependent status of the Japanese Communist Party itself, and the massive errors made as a result of this status, together with the party image that was conveyed to the Japanese people. In the years immediately after 1945, the rise or fall of the Japanese Communist Party was intimately connected with the prestige of the international Communist movement and, more particularly, of the Soviet Union. Russian prestige, unfortuately for their Japanese comrades, was low and became lower in the course of the initial postwar years. The actions of Russia in declaring war upon Japan in the final Wagnerian days of holocaust and, even more, the studied callousness with which the Russians handled the prisoner-of-war issue in contrast to American policies made a deep impression upon almost all Japanese during this period. And however much the Japanese Communist Party now sought to camouflage the fact, its existence as a branch of an international movement, the headquarters of which were in Moscow, could not be hidden.

Nosaka's policies, so strongly influenced by his experience in Yenan, and reflective also of his own personality, did have an impact. In making the party "lovable," he made it more popular. These policies, however, were blown to pieces by the Cominform blast of 1950. That attack, prophetically symbolizing the intervention of both Moscow and Peking in the internal affairs of the Japanese Communist Party, proved conclusively how little independence the party had during this era. At the end of five years of arduous labor and important gains, the Japanese Communist Party was once again deeply and bitterly divided, rendered an agent of foreign interests in the public eyes, and once more forcefully set on a course of political action that bore no relationship to the realities of its own society.

In the era that lay ahead, it was a further liability for the Communists that a competitive party existed concerning whose independence there could be no question. As we have already emphasized, the presence of a significant and militant Socialist Party was undoubtedly a factor complicating the problem of Communist Party growth at all stages, and never more so than in a period when the latter party had been revealed as totally subordinate to foreign sources.

The descent into ultra-leftism, which began in 1950 and lasted for the duration of the Korean War and beyond, was a powerful additional factor in abetting a decline which would undoubtedly have occurred in some degree in any case. Economic growth was beginning to affect all elements of the society. The intellectual, as we have noted, was being shaken by Communist aggression in Korea. The Socialists were rebuilding their ranks. However, it was the foolish attempt of the Communists to recreate a Yenan in Japan under totally different conditions that cost them so heavily, even among those whom they counted as loyal supporters.

A low point was reached by the Communists in these years. Beginning in 1955, the present era opened—the slow, painful retreat from "left-adventurism"; the gradual rise of a new Mainstream leadership—the Miyamoto–Hakamada–Nosaka triumvirate; and the tempestuous storms within the international Communist movement that pushed the party first toward "neutralism," then toward Peking and into a violently anti-Soviet position, and finally toward "autonomy and independence," variously translated as isolation, "a plague on both your houses," or National Communism.

The gains scored by the Japanese Communists since the "left adventurist" period have not been spectacular. As we have noted, even in the metropolitan regions where their strength is greatest, the Communists generally poll less than 15 percent of the vote. Only in a handful of city wards—chiefly in Ōsaka, Tōkyō, and Kyōto—can the JCP count on regular majorities. Nevertheless, the gains of recent years and particularly the factors that underlie them should not be ignored. Perhaps three major developments are involved, developments we have traced in this study.

First, a generational change has occurred, or is occurring, in Japanese Communist leadership, and a new premium upon organization, especially grass-roots organization, now exists. The younger generation of Japanese Communists, powerfully influenced in a number of cases by Chinese methods, are concentrating less on abstract ideology and the endless theoretical debates that historically occupied the JCP, and more on the techniques of creating an effective organization and the tactics of successful revolution. The age of the ideologue is ending; the era of the activist is beginning in Japanese Communism. If this trend continues to prevail, it may have far-reaching significance. The Chinese impact upon Japanese Communism has been far more important in defining pragmatically the nature of power and in directing the attention of a militant younger group of leaders toward power than in any other respect. And that impact is likely to survive the current break with Peking.

Moreover, a set of Japanese radicals has appeared who really seem to want to hold power rather than merely to talk about it. Thus, increased organizational work at the cell and district levels has taken place, together with intensive efforts at strengthening Communist propaganda and all mass-media activities. And with varying degrees of success, the Japanese Communists continue ceaselessly to establish new front organizations while seeking to bolster old ones.

A second essential element in Communist gains has been the united front successes of recent years. Events have convinced the Communists that mass mobilization on behalf of revolution in Japanese society is possible, and that the truly critical issues are those of "national independence" and "peace." There can be little doubt that some individuals have come into the Communist fold because the party has been able to identify itself with these issues, and many individuals, non-Communist themselves, have been willing to work with the party on such issues.

United front activities have not necessarily been to the advantage of the Communists. A united front experience, even repeated experiences, may be essential to the education of certain non-Communists who otherwise remain unconvinced of the true nature of Communist tactics and policies. Many left Socialists in Japan have become enlightened on these matters the hard way, and despite the continuing ambivalence of a large number of Socialists regarding the desirability of a front with the Communists, the strong skepticism in moderate circles is directly related to experiences of the recent past as well as to profound differences of basic ideology. Communist involvement in united front operations has also necessitated Communist commitments and a sharing of responsibility for the results. This in turn has created problems within the party as well as outside, arguments over tactics, even the awakening of some Communists to new values and political affiliations.

Nevertheless, the united front remains the only promising technique whereby the Japanese Communist Party can build itself into a vital political force. The Communists, their conservative opponents, and the Socialists of all varieties, in addition to the Komeitō, are aware of that fact. Every party in Japan also knows well that the issues upon which such a movement might be built are the broad issues of nationalism and "peace." Social reform issues are good subordinate causes, as are some matters of domestic politics like the single-member district proposal. Such issues, however, can never be the foundation for a broadly-gauged united front endeavor. The Communist goal of a "Democratic Coalition Government" dedicated to "independence" and "neutralism" hinges upon an agreement to fight together on issues of foreign policy and cooperate in the revitalization of such fronts as the Anti-Mutual Security Treaty Council.

Will the Socialists cooperate on a significant scale? Despite the bitter experiences of the past, such a possibility cannot be ruled out. Tolerance for Marxism within left Socialist circles in Japan remains high, as we have seen. Hence, there is a certain capacity to "understand" the Communist position, an automatic tilt toward the "progressive" camp. Equally important, perhaps, is the fact that the issues involved are ones about which many Socialists feel deeply—so deeply that they may decide to accept support from all quarters offering assistance. Thus, the one-day joint struggles and the liaison councils have come into existence, and one powerful wing within the Socialist Party would currently accept more permanent united front relations with the Communists.

The key to any future united front probably lies with the intensity and cycle of development ultimately characterizing such issues as Vietnam, American control of Okinawa, the use of Japanese facilities for American atomic-powered craft or nuclear weapon carriers, the pace and nature of Japanese rearmament, and the renewal of the Mutual Security Treaty. These are the concrete issues upon which future unity between Socialists and Communists most logically depends. The measure in which such unity is achieved may well be contingent upon how the United States and the Japanese government handle these problems.

In any case, however, a Socialist–Communist united front is likely to be incomplete. As we have noted, the Japan Socialist Party at present is in reality two parties, and it is inconceivable that the moderate factions would accept a full-fledged united front under present conditions. In broad terms, the Japanese political situation regarding the "left" resembles that of Italy, although the ideological formulations of the Communist Party differ markedly. The Japanese socialist movement extends from such moderate elements as the Democratic Socialist Party, the position of which approximates that of the British Labor Party, to centrists like the moderate factions of the Socialist Party and—for some purposes, the Kōmeitō—to militants like the Sasaki faction of the Socialists, a group currently taking a position similar to that of the Nenni Socialists in the period when the Nenni faction was working wholeheartedly with the Italian Communists.

As is the case in France and Italy, it seems unlikely that the entire Japanese "left" can achieve close working relations in the foreseeable future, not to mention organic unity. A united front that would encompass the moderates and center remains at least as logical and as possible as one involving the "hard left." The prospects that Japan will move toward coalition politics within the next decade are reasonably good. A projection of current electoral returns certainly points in that direction. Note, for example, the figures in Table XXII.

TABLE XXII

CONSERVATIVE AND "PROGRESSIVE" VOTE IN
HOUSE OF REPRESENTATIVES ELECTIONS

Election	Conservative vote	Percent of total vote	"Progressive"[a] vote	Percent of total vote	Percent of the JCP vote within "progressive"
April 1946	25,656,040	46.3	11,994,161	21.6	17.8
April 1947	16,111,914	58.9	8,178,842	29.9	12.3
Jan. 1949	19,260,500	63.0	7,721,414	25.2	38.7
Oct. 1952	23,367,671	66.1	8,664,826	24.5	10.3
April 1953	22,717,348	65.7	10,209,311	29.5	6.4
Feb. 1955	23,385,502	63.2	11,903,638	32.2	6.2
May 1958	22,976,846	57.8	14,106,028	35.5	7.2
Nov. 1960	22,740,271	57.6	15,508,004	39.3	7.5
Nov. 1963	22,423,915	54.7	16,576,545	40.4	9.9

SOURCE: Kōan Chōsachō, *Sengo ni okeru Nihon Kyōsantō no senkyo kekka, Shūgiin giin sōsenkyo no bu,* p. 95 (with exception of 1963 data).
[a] Progressive refers to the Socialist Party and all other "left" parties.

That the dominant coalition will be strongly leftist and involve the Communist Party, however, seems most unlikely. Rather, one might assume that the Communists will be able to work closely only with a portion of the left Socialists unless—as suggested earlier—some internal or international catastrophe develops. The central point, however, is that Japanese politics, particularly the politics of the "left," are reflective of a complex socioeconomic-political evolution, and, for this reason, are more comparable with the politics of Western Europe than with those of the truly "backward" nations.

If there are useful parallels to be found between Japanese and West European politics currently, they do not extend to all aspects of the Japanese Communist Party. As we shall note in a moment, the current position of the JCP within the international Communist movement does have a relationship, although not a precise identity, with that of various European Communist Parties. In its basic ideological-policy stance, however, the Communist Party of Japan must be placed on the left wing of the international Communist movement, a position it shares with almost all of the Asian Communist parties. This can be clearly seen by following carefully, as we have attempted, the evolution of official party policies on two or three critical issues.

At present, the JCP position on "peaceful coexistence" and its policy toward "American imperialism" can only be described as hard-left. The primary enemy, according to the Japanese Communists, is the United States, since Japan is a semicolonial nation under the political and economic control of American imperialism and its subordinate ally, Japanese "monopoly capitalism." While Japanese capitalism has admittedly grown more powerful in recent years, it is still a secondary force, taking orders from its American superiors. Since the United States is also the chief opponent of world peace, focusing the attack on America serves the causes of Japanese independence and global peace. Thus, in company with other elements of the international Communist "left wing," the JCP insists upon taking a very hard line against the United States, emphasizing the prime importance of national liberation movements in the global struggle for Communist victory, and insisting that "peaceful coexistence" can never be advanced as an excuse for avoiding confrontation with "world imperialism headed by the United States." Thus, the Party makes one of its central charges against "modern revisionism" the allegation that Soviet leaders continue to appease "American imperialism" and render less than full and enthusiastic service to liberation-revolutionary movements. Coupled with this accusation, however, has now been added one against Peking: blinded by their dogmatism and narrow nationalist concerns, the Chinese Communists are blocking the type of united front which alone can thwart the United States in Vietnam.

Outlining the nature of the Japanese revolution, the Japanese Communist Party once again places itself on the "left" end of the international Communist spectrum. In modified form, the Communists have retained the concept of a two-stage revolution, with the first stage dependent upon a broad united front of all "progressive" and "patriotic" forces which would at some critical juncture come under Communist control. Under these conditions, Japan like China would move in uninterrupted fashion from a "people's government" to a "socialist government," with the proletariat class (JCP) assuming complete hegemony. Thus, the united front becomes an indispensable tactic at home as it does abroad, and, indeed, a close interrelation between domestic and international tactics is currently regarded by the party as of critical importance.

The Japanese Communists have currently rejected the theories of structural reform as Kautskyist doctrines, "petty bourgeois-inspired revisionist concepts totally out of harmony with true Marxism–Leninism." It has insisted that to bind the revolution to parliamentary tactics alone is to weaken, and possibly to eliminate, the chances of victory. The ruling class will not abandon power without a struggle, and "American imperialism" will not give up its position in Japan—or the world—without the most massive pressures being exerted on it. In essence, therefore, force and violence must remain an indispensable, although not exclusive, aspect of Communist revolutionary tactics. Any accommodation to American–Japanese ruling circles, any appeasement of American imperialism, is to join the camp of revisionism and defeatism.

In ideological terms, as can be seen, the Japanese Communist Party generally upholds at all critical points the "left line" of world communism today against opposition both from the domestic left and from the mainstream of Western Communists. As we have noted, developments—and particularly the recent move away from Peking—have spawned a "left opposition" to Mainstream JCP leadership, and on the important issue of united front tactics, the party does indeed separate itself from the "left" as represented by Peking. In broader terms, however, the JCP has not yet been powerfully affected by the currents that have swept into Italian Communism and even into some of the parties of Eastern Europe. More in company with the French Communist Party, the Japanese Communists seem for the present to be frozen ideologically in a Stalinist position, although as we have noted, their foreign policy at the moment is strongly based upon nonalignment within the Communist world, at least insofar as Moscow and Peking are concerned.

This ideological position may change, but one may well ask why old-fashioned *left* Marxism should still dominate the JCP, and, indeed, retain considerable power throughout the Japanese socialist movement as a whole. Clearly, as we have emphasized, Japanese society in its economic and political development has grown away from the simplistic premises of Marxism–Leninism in much the same manner as other advanced societies. Why then has the Japanese left not moved away from orthodox Marxism at the same rate as the left of Western Europe, possibly even portions of the left in Eastern Europe?

In part, the answer lies in the unique role that the United States has played in postwar Japan, including the fact that Japan has entered into an economic, political, and military alliance with America that is more intimate than any alliance in her long history. Thus "the American issue" has had continuing potency. The Japanese, it must not be forgotten, are a people long accustomed to making foreign policy decisions for and by themselves, and they have been by no means immune to strong xenophobic tendencies. Marxism–Leninism has thus been able to gain certain advantages from the character and circumstances of recent American–Japanese relations, especially since these could be projected into the complex panorama of Asia as a whole. Leninism in particular provides one of the more dynamic methods of exploiting currents of antiforeignism and nationalism.

Of equal importance is the fact that Japanese economic development has been more recent, more rapid, and in certain respects, more uneven than that of the advanced Western world, and it has also taken place against a very different cultural background. The strains of individualism so powerfully interwoven into the cultural traditions of the West were largely absent in Japan. The types of liberal challenges both to social and economic injustice and to political authoritarianism characteristic of the West have been fewer and weaker in Japan. Many more doubts have existed concerning the viability of parliamentary democracy, even by those who wish it well, and hence, the nondemocratic left have had fertile soil in which to work.

Nor can one ignore the impact of the Chinese Communist victory, whatever the future may hold. As we have noted throughout this study, the Japanese Communist movement was powerfully affected by this event from 1950 onward. Party programs were strongly influenced, party leaders were closely associated, and party members were deeply indoctrinated with the Chinese experience. A generation of Japanese Communists, whatever private reservations they may have held, were accustomed to defend Chinese Communist policies and leaders unstintingly. And for the critical decade between 1955 and 1965, the Japanese Communist Party was reconstructed with extensive reliance upon the Chinese model.

As we have seen, the current trend—in very broad terms—is away from Marxism in Japan. If we take the Socialist Party as an example, "pure Marxism" has been slowly losing ground to various revisionist theories, although the battle has been fierce and is far from concluded. Gradually, and with infinite difficulty, the Mainstream of the Japanese left is moving in the direction of social democracy. As a result, the Japanese Communist Party is threatened with increasing isolation if it stubbornly retains its old orthodox-left position. Given the nature of Japanese society, moreover, it seems clear that Italian Communism would constitute an infinitely more appropriate model than Chinese Communism for the Communist Party of Japan. Indeed, it is possible that concurrently with the party's effort to establish a position of independence from Peking as well as from Moscow, some type of "opening to the right" will take place. If this occurs, however, it is likely to be modest in dimensions and fiercely resisted. Given the nature of conditions in Asia and the existence of an embryonic but potentially meaningful "left opposition," the JCP will have to proceed with the utmost caution.

The Chinese revolutionary model, it should be stressed, has had a deep emotional appeal to Japanese radicals. It represents yet another *Asian* thrust against Western power in Asia, and thus it touches some of the deepest wellsprings of Japanese nationalism. Moreover, it proposes techniques whereby a revolution can be successfully mounted and the old order totally destroyed, and it is to this end that the Japanese Communists are dedicated. Communist success in China, in addition, gave to the Japanese Communists an enormous psychological boost, suggesting as it did the validity of Marxist claims that theirs was the wave of the future. Finally, the Chinese Communist emphasis upon both theory *and* action has had a deep impact upon the younger element within the Japanese Communist movement, as witness the recent strides in organization and mass-media utilization.

For the moment, the Mainstream JCP leaders must concentrate their energies primarily upon the firm establishment of their new international position, a position which must at present be considered precarious. As we have noted, the Communist Party of Japan has gone through a number of phases in its relations with the international Communist movement since 1945. In the immediate postwar years, the party occupied its traditional position of being a branch of the internationale, then operating as the Cominform, with policy subject to the complete domination of the Soviet Union. Russia, however, had neither the time nor the facilities to coordinate policy closely, and, even in these years, the revolutionary experiences of the Chinese were not without their impact in Japanese Communist circles.

The 1950 crisis ended one era and began another. Confronted with massive interference in their internal affairs both by the Soviet Union and by the newly established People's Republic of China, the Mainstream JCP leaders capitulated and saved their positions. This event, however, produced deep splits within the party, splits that have not been healed down to the present. It also forced the party to turn sharply to the left in accordance with current Stalinist–Maoist policies. A disastrous period followed, one in which the party went from failure to failure and dropped into insignificance on the Japanese domestic political front.

By 1955, when the current Mainstream leaders emerged on the scene, the party began to rebuild both its organization and its policies, leaning heavily upon Peking. Given its internal weaknesses and divisions, and also the tendency of the Soviet Union during this period to withdraw from Asia, this trend was perhaps inevitable. In addition, contemporary Chinese policies coincided with many of the main goals of the Japanese Communists, despite the enormous differences in the nature of the two societies, and many Communist leaders, including important elements of the younger group, were intimately connected with Chinese comrades.

The ties with Peking were ultimately to be greatly strengthened as a result of the Sino–Soviet dispute. Initially, the JCP in company with certain other Asian Communist parties strove desperately to maintain a neutralist position. Neither the Soviet Union nor Communist China was publicly criticized, and both were praised with paragraphs, phrases, and even words carefully measured to provide absolute equality. Sensitive subjects were omitted from public discussion or were raised in the most circumspect fashion. Meanwhile, "the little Communists," with men like Ho Chi Minh and Aidit taking the lead, made every effort to serve as mediators between Moscow and Peking.

Neutralism failed because at best it could be sustained only for a temporary period in the hope that the Sino–Soviet breach would be mended. To be "neutral" on the various issues confronting the Communist world was manifestly impossible. Such a position, long held, would have laid the Japanese Communists—and all Communists—open to charges of hypocrisy and artificiality. Moreover, neither the Russians nor the Chinese were prepared to accept the validity of a neutralist position.

Beginning in 1961, at the time of the 22nd CPSU Congress, the JCP was forced to take stands on substantive issues that placed it closer to the current Peking line than to that of Moscow. Soviet pressure on the party notably increased at this point, and the situation became increasingly uncomfortable. The alignment of the JCP with Peking on all major issues increased during the fall of 1962 and reached its climax in the 1963–1964 period. By this time, Mainstream JCP leaders stood strongly on the Peking line and belligerently accused Khrushchev and the CPSU of a series of major crimes and errors, both against the Japanese Communist Party and against the world Communist movement. After the March 1964 Moscow meeting between the two parties, an almost total breach existed, with the Soviet Party giving aid, moral and material, to those denoted by the JCP as "anti-Party traitors."

Two years later, the position of the Japanese Communist Party had evolved to a new point. Without retracting any of its charges against the Soviet party—on the contrary, supplementing them in some cases—the Mainstream leaders began to strike out against "dogmatism" and "sectarianism," clearly aiming their shots at the Chinese Communists because of their refusal to consider an international united front on behalf of the Vietnamese Communists. Aligned with North Korea openly—and North Vietnam privately?—the JCP(Yoyogi) proclaimed itself a totally independent, autonomous party, beholdened neither to Moscow nor Peking.

In considerable measure, this development was in line with broad trends discernible in the international Communist movement. At this point, the evolution of polycentric communism has produced a series of new phenomena, including the emergence of National Communism on an ever expanding scale; the creation of alliances within the Communist world based upon balance-of-power principles and national (party) interest concepts; and the diminution of both Soviet and Chinese influence upon foreign parties. In certain respects, the Japanese Communist Party has gone further than others in giving expression to the new age. Its vocabulary, like that of Pyongyang and Hanoi, is filled with nationalist and patriotic appeals; and accompanying these appeals is a militancy, a justification of violence, that lies uneasily beside its theses of peaceful coexistence. One of truly critical questions of the future, rendered urgent by the current developments in China, is the extent to which National Communism will challenge and overturn many of the principles as well as the tactics of International Communism. If this issue was first raised long ago, when Stalin committed himself and the party to building "socialism" in one nation, it has now reached infinitely more meaningful proportions since not one national Communist state but many have been projected onto the scene stimulating the patterns of competition, conflict, and alliance reflective of Western nationalism in its mature phases. Much that develops under the rubric of contemporary National Communism may radically alter previous estimates of Communist ideology and practice.

What kind of balance sheet can the Japanese Communist Party draw up at this stage in its evolution and that of the Communist world? On the one hand, it appears to be in the process of achieving "independence" after a lengthy period of subordination to foreign forces. Some JCP critics, as we have noted, refer to the party's current position as one of unprecedented isolation, since it is separated at the moment both from Moscow and Peking. They doubt that an alliance of small Communist states and parties against large ones can be sustained, particularly in periods of grave crisis. They believe that the JCP will once again have to align itself with either the Soviets or the Chinese.

Whatever the validity of this estimate, the Japanese Communist Party today stands with Pyongyang—but not with Moscow or Peking. It faces two groups of dissidents, moreover, each claiming to represent "true" Marxism–Leninism and illustrating the fact that the great divisions within the Communist world have enhanced factionalism at the same time as they have enabled the independence of Communist parties prepared to exert themselves in this direction. There is no likelihood that the Japanese Communists can be effectively reunited in the foreseeable future, and while Yoyogi commands the overwhelming majority of members—as well as the advantages of a "centrist" position on tactics and policies—the prospect of continuous Soviet and Chinese involvement in the internal affairs of the fragmented Japanese "left" is an ominous fact of life, likely to color both the JCP and its various "leftist" rivals.

In the broadest sense, the Japanese Communists are children of their times. Their current international stance of independence, their acceptance of a balance-of-power approach, their reliance upon concepts like sovereignty, national interest, and patriotism all reveal how far the world Communist movement has shifted from its original premises. Any forthright Communist would have to say, "We are all revisionists now," which makes the burning issue of "modern revisionism" so ironic in the final analysis. And because they are Asian—*and* Japanese—the Communists of Japan have long been unable to escape one major paradox. On the one hand, they have been attracted to the hard line exemplified by the Communists of backward, emerging societies—the lean, harsh, puritanical, militant doctrines that flow from parties like the Chinese and, on the surface at least, seem so unpromising in terms of compromise, coexistence, evolution, and peace. The sense of being backward, inferior, and humbled by Western power dies hard. Yet on the other hand, the Japanese Communists cannot escape entirely from the fact that they are members of an advanced society, indeed, one of the most powerful nations in the present world. Thus at least some Japanese Communists, and a larger number of self-proclaimed Marxists, have seen value in facing up realistically to the changed nature of their society. They have scanned the new theories of such comrades as the Italians, and they have begun to study closely the experiences and views of the more "advanced" East European Communists. Concepts such as those of "structural reform" have made an impact as attempted Marxian adjustments to the late twentieth century. To date, what we might call loosely the Asian component within Japanese Marxism–Leninism has continued to maintain its supremacy insofar as the Mainstream leadership is concerned. The line is still "left" and the elements of primitivism abound in contemporary Japanese Communist Party doctrine. Indeed, this same situation affects portions of the left Socialists, as we have seen. Ultimately, changes are likely to occur. Only the timing is in doubt.

The chances for Communist success in Japan, however, do not appear promising barring external interference. In the most fundamental sense, Japan is a post-Marxist society. Marxist doctrines, whether of economics or of revolution, have less and less validity for this society as it joins the ranks of the advanced nations of the world. Japanese Communists, whatever the doctrinal changes they can effect, will never be able to use the Communist appeal that has had the greatest impact in our times, namely, the appeal that only they can eradicate the deep-seated obstacles to change in stagnant or fragmented societies, and that only they can fully mobilize the people for a drive toward modernization within one generation. The Japanese, having attained modernity, can afford freedom.

SOURCES

1. PERSONAL INTERVIEWS

Aidit, Dipa Nusantara. December 1961.
Andō Jimbei. November 1963.
Arahata Kanson. August 23, 1957.
Fukumoto Kazuo. September and October 1957.
Kasuga Shōjirō. November 26, 1963.
Nabeyama Sadachika. August 21, 1957.
Naitō Tomochika. November 27, 1963.
Nosaka Sanzō. January 16, 1962.
Ōta Kaoru. November 28, 1963.
Satō Noboru. November 1963.
Taniguchi Zentarō. October 1957.
Yamabe Kentarō. November 1963.
Yamakawa Hitoshi. October 12, 1957.

2. DOCUMENTS AND MONOGRAPHS

Arahata Kanson. *Kanson jiden (Autobiography of Kanson)*, Tōkyō, 1960.
——. *Roshiya ni hairu (Entering Russia)*, Tōkyō, 1924.
Communist Party of China, Central Committee, Text of the 14 June 1963 Letter of the Central Committee of the Communist Party of China in Reply to the Letter of the Central Committee of the Communist Party of the Soviet Union of 30 March 1963 ("A Proposal Concerning the General Line of the International Communist Movement," republished in pamphlet form by the Foreign Languages Press, Peking, 1963).
Communist Party of Japan. *Nihon Kyōsantō gojūnen modai shiryō shū (A Collection of Documents Concerning the Japanese Communist Party Incident of 1950)*, 3 vols., Shin-Nihon Shuppan-sha, Tōkyō, 1957.

————. Central Committee, Report of the Japanese Communist Party Central Committee to the 9th Party Congress, November 25, 1964, *TICD* 691, *JPRS* 28,456, pp. 1–298.

————. Central Committee, Text of the 15 July 1964 Letter of the Central Committee of the Japanese Communist Party to the Central Committee of the Communist Party of the Soviet Union, *Peking Review,* July 31, 1964.

————. Central Committee, Text of the 26 August 1964 Letter of the Central Committee of the Japanese Communist Party in Reply to the Letter of the Central Committee of the Communist Party of the Soviet Union of 18 April 1964, *TICD* 653, *JPRS* 26,892.

Communist Party of the Soviet Union. Central Committee, Text of the 18 April 1964 Letter of the CPSU Central Committee to the Central Committee of the Japanese Communist Party, *TICD* 636, *JPRS* 26,058.

————. Central Committee, Text of the 11 July 1964 Letter of the CPSU Central Committee to the JCP Central Committee, *TICD* 636, *JPRS* 26,058.

Doolin, Dennis J. *Communist China—The Politics of Student Opposition,* Hoover Institution Studies, Stanford, 1964.

Dore, R. P. *Land Reform in Japan,* London, 1959.

The First Congress of the Toilers of the Far East, Communist International, Petrograd, 1922.

Griffith, William E. *The Sino–Soviet Rift,* Cambridge, Massachusetts, 1964.

Hudson, G. F., R. Lowenthal, and R. MacFarquhar. *The Sino–Soviet Dispute,* London and New York, 1961.

Japanese Government. Home Ministry, *Shakai ūndō no jōkyō (Conditions of the Social Movement),* issued annually.

————. Jichishō senkyo kyoku (The Local Autonomy Ministry Election Bureau), *Senkyo nenkan (Election Yearbook),* various years.

————. Jichishō senkyo kyoku (The Local Autonomy Ministry Election Bureau), *Shugiin giin sosenkyo—kekka shirabe (General Elections of the House of Representatives—Final Survey),* November 21, 1963.

————. Kōan Chōsachō (Public Safety Investigation Bureau), *Nihon Kyōsantō gaikaku dantai ichiran (A Survey of Organizations Around the Communist Party),* Tōkyō, July 1, 1962.

————. Kōan Chōsachō (Public Safety Investigation Bureau), *Nihon Kyōsantō no genjō (Current Conditions of the Japanese Communist Party),* Tōkyō, July 1, 1962.

————. Kōan Chōsachō (Public Safety Investigation Bureau), *Sengo ni okeru Nihon Kyōsantō no senkyo kekka, Shugiin giin sosenkyo no bu (The Election Results of the Japanese Communist Party in the Postwar Era— Section Concerning the House of Representatives),* no date or place of publication.

————. Labor Ministry, *Rōdō undō shi shiryō—1949 (Documents on the History of the Labor Movement—1949).*

Kamiyama Shigeo. *Nikkyō shidōbu ni atau—kokusai kyōsanshugi no sōrosen o mamotte (An Open Letter to the Japanese Communist Party Leaders— In Defense of the General Line of International Communism)*, Vol. I, Tōkyō, August 30, 1964, pp. 107–147.

Kautsky, John H. *Moscow and the Communist Party of India*, New York, 1956.

Kazama Jōkichi. *Mosko kyōsandaigaku no omoide (Memories of the Moscow Communist University)*, Tōkyō, 1949.

Kondō Eizō. *Comintern no misshi (Secret Messenger of the Comintern)*, Tōkyō, 1949.

Koyama Hirotake. *Sengo Nihon Kyōsantō shi (A History of the Postwar Japanese Communist Party)*, Tōkyō, 1958.

———. *Sengo no Nihon Kyōsantō (The Postwar Japanese Communist Party)*, Tōkyō, 1962.

Kublin, Hyman. *Asian Revolutionary: The Life of Sen Katayama*, Princeton, 1964.

Levine, Solomon B. *Industrial Relations in Postwar Japan*, Urbana, Illinois, 1958.

Lowenthal, Richard. *World Communism—The Disintegration of a Secular Faith*, New York, 1964.

MacFarquhar, Roderick. *The Hundred Flowers Campaign and the Chinese Intellectuals*, New York, 1960.

Mao Tse-tung. *On the Correct Handling of Contradictions Among the People*, New Century Publishers, New York, July 1957.

Mehnert, Klaus. *Peking and Moscow*, New York, 1963.

Murakami Kanji. *Nihon Kyōsantō (The Japanese Communist Party)*, Tōkyō, 1956.

Nihon Kyōsantō daiyon-kai daigo-kai zenkoku kyōgikai kettei shū (The Collected Resolutions of the 4th and 5th National Conferences of the Japanese Communist Party), Shinyō-sa, 1952.

Nihon rōdō nenkan (Japan Labor Yearbook), various years.

Nikkan Rōdō Tsūshinsha (ed). *Sengo Nihon Kyōsanshugi undō shi (A History of the Communist Movement in Postwar Japan)*, Tōkyō, 1955.

Noda Ritsuta. *Hyōgikai tōsō shi (A History of the Hyōgikai Struggle)*, Tōkyō, 1931.

Nosaka Sanzō no ayunda michi (The Road That Nosaka Sanzō Walked), The Committee for the Publication of Materials on Nosaka Sanzō, Tōkyō, 1964.

Ōi Hirosuke. *Sayoku Tennōsei (The Left Wing Emperor System)*, Tōkyō, 1956.

The Origin and Development of the Differences Between the Leadership of the CPSU and Ourselves, Comment on the Open Letter of the Central Committee of the CPSU by the editorial departments of *Jen-min Jih-pao* and *Hong-ch'i*, September 6, 1963. English pamphlet edition.

Ōsugi Sakae. *Nihon dasshutsu ki (Memoirs of Escape from Japan)*, Tōkyō, 1923.

Packard, George R., III. *Protest in Tokyo, The Security Crisis of 1960*, Princeton, 1966.

Sakai Toshihiko. *Nihon shakaishugi undō shi (History of the Japanese Socialist Movement)*, Tōkyō, 1954.

Sakei gakusei seito no shuki (The Notes of Leftist Students), 3 vols., the Student Section of the Ministry of Education, Tōkyō, 1934-1935.

Sakisaka Itsurō (ed.). *Kōzō kaikaku ron (Theories of Structural Reform)*, Tōkyō, 1961.

Sakisaka Itsurō. *Shakaishugi kakumei ron (Theories of Socialist Revolution)*, Tōkyō, 1961.

Scalapino, Robert A., and Junnosuke Masumi. *Parties and Politics in Contemporary Japan*, Berkeley, California, 1962.

Shinoda Tatsuji. *Nihon Kyōsantō Senryaku senjutsu shi (The History of the Tactics and Strategy of the Japanese Communist Party)*, Tōkyō, 1952.

Suzuki Bunji. *Rōdō undō ni-jū nen (Twenty Years in the Labor Movement)*, Tōkyō, 1931.

Suzuki Mosaburō. *Aru shakaishugisha no hansei (Half the Life of a Certain Socialist)*, Tōkyō, 1958.

Swearingen, A. Rodger. *Communist Strategy in Japan, 1945–1960*, The RAND Corporation, RM–4348–PR (AD 462101), April 1965.

Swearingen, A. Rodger, and Paul F. Langer. *Red Flag in Japan: International Communism in Action, 1919–1951*, Cambridge, Massachusetts, 1952.

Tagawa Kazuo. *Nihon Kyōsantō shi (A History of the Japanese Communist Party)*, Tōkyō, 1960.

Taniguchi Zentarō. *Nihon Rōdō Kumiai Hyōgikai shi (A History of the Labor Union Council of Japan)*, 2 vols., Tōkyō, 1948.

Tokuda Kyūichi. "Report to the 18th Enlarged Central Committee Plenum," in Communist Party of Japan, *Nihon Kyōsantō gojūnen mondai shiryō shū (A Collection of Documents Concerning the Japanese Communist Party Incident of 1950)*, Tōkyō, 1957, pp. 11–16.

Tokuda Kyūichi den (The Biography of Tokuda Kyūichi), Tōkyō, 1952.

Tsukahira, Toshio G. *The Postwar Evolution of Communist Strategy in Japan*, Center for International Studies, M. I. T., Cambridge, Massachusetts, September 1954.

U.S. Department of Commerce. Office of Technical Services, Joint Publications Research Service, *Translations on International Communist Developments (TICD)*, Washington, D.C., various numbers.

Watanabe Haruo. *Katayama Sen to tomo ni (Together with Katayama Sen)*, Tōkyō, 1955.

———. *Nihon Marxshugi undō no reimei (The Dawn of the Japanese Marxist Movement)*, Tōkyō, 1957.

Yaginuma Masaji. *Nihon Kyōsantō undō shi (A History of the Japanese Communist Party Movement)*, Tōkyō, 1953.

Yamamoto Katsunosuke and Arita Mitsuho. *Nihon kyōsanshugi undō shi (A History of the Japanese Communist Movement)*, Tōkyō, 1950.

Yamazaki Gorō. *Nihon rōdō undo shi (A History of the Japanese Labor Movement*, Tōkyō, 1957.

Zagoria, Donald S. *The Sino–Soviet Conflict*, Princeton, 1962.

3. ARTICLES

"The Aggressive Action of U.S. Imperialism Against Cuba Is Still Continuing," *Akahata*, November 3, 1962, p. 1.

"Appeal for International Common Action," English text of the 9th World Conference Resolution, *Peking Review*, No. 33, August 16, 1963, pp. 32–33.

"Appeal to the People," *Akahata*, No. 1, October 20, 1945, p. 1.

Arahata Kanson. "The Profintern's Criticism of the Japanese Labor Movement," *Rōnō*, Vol. IV, No. 9, November 1930, pp. 2–12.

"Concerning the Situation in Japan," *For a Lasting Peace, For a People's Democracy!*, January 6, 1950, p. 3.

"Declaration Concerning the Withdrawal from the Labor–Farmer Party," *Rōdō Shimbun*, No. 186, November 1926.

"Emergency Action Against the War Provocation Policy of American Imperialism," *Akahata*, October 25, 1962, p. 1.

"For the Strengthening of International United Actions and a United Front Against American Imperialism," *Akahata*, February 4, 1966, pp. 1–2.

"For the Unity and Advance of the International Communist Movement" (*Akahata* editorial, November 10, 1963), *TICD* 539, *JPRS* 22,197, pp. 80–86.

"For the Unity of the International Communist Movement and for the Struggle Against Two Enemies," *Akahata*, December 29, 1961, p. 1.

Fuha Tetsuzō. "Flunkyism Which Denies Independence," *Akahata*, June 10, 1966, p. 1.

Fukuda Katsuichi. "Concerning the Financial Situation of the Japanese Communist Party," *Kōan Jōhō*, February 1964, pp. 1–17.

———. "The Trend of the Japanese Communist Party with Respect to the Sino–Soviet Dispute," *Kōan Jōhō*, July 1964.

Hirotsu Kyōsuke. "The Japanese Communist Party at a Turning Point," *Toki no Kadai (Topics of the Time)*, August 1966, pp. 6–12.

"How Does the Japanese Communist Party Think of the So-called 'International Ideological Conflict'?" (*Akahata*, November 10, 1963), *TICD* 538, *JPRS* 22,194, pp. 20–31.

"Immediate Demands of Communist Party of Japan—New Programme," *For a Lasting Peace, For a People's Democracy!*, November 23, 1951, p. 3.

Inomata Tsunao. "The General Strategy of the Japanese Proletarian Class," *Rōnō*, Vol. I, No. 1, December 1927, pp. 118–125.

"Japan Today," a 42-page supplement to *The New Leader*, November 28, 1960.

"Japanese Intellectuals Discuss American–Japanese Relations," *Far Eastern Survey*, Vol. 29, No. 10, October 1960.

Kasuga Shōjirō. "On Behalf of the Japanese Road Toward Socialism," *Atarashii Jidai*, No. 1, November 1961, pp. 76–80.

――――. "Organizational Problems of the Socialist Renovation Movement," *Atarashii Jidai*, February 1962.

Katayama Sen. "A Japanese Victory," *International Socialist Review*, Vol. XII, No. 9, March 1912.

――――. "Letter from a Japanese Comrade," *International Socialist Review*, Vol. XIII, No. 8, February 1913.

"Kennedy and U.S. Imperialism," *Akahata*, March 10, 1964 (reprinted in pamphlet form by the Foreign Languages Press, Peking, 1964).

Kōtoku Denjirō. "Changes in My Ideas," *Heimin Shimbun*, February 5, 1907, p. 1.

"The Leaders of the CPSU Are Betrayers of the Declaration and the Statement," *Jen-min Jih-pao (People's Daily)*, December 30, 1965, p. 1. For an English translation, see *Peking Review*, No. 1, January 1, 1966, pp. 9–12.

"Let the Entire Party Study the Decision of the Party Congress in Order to Make Efforts for the Consolidation of the International United Front Against U.S. Imperialism and for the Genuine Unity of the International Communist Movement," *Akahata*, May 11, 1966, p. 1. For an English translation, see *Bulletin Information for Abroad*, No. 52, Tokyo, 1966, pp. 7–17. (This is a publication of the Central Committee of the Communist Party of Japan.)

"Let Us Defend Independence," *Rodong Shinmun*, August 12, 1966. For an English translation, see *The People's Korea*, August 17, 1966, pp. 1–7.

"Let Us Defend the Unity of the Socialist Camp and Strengthen the Solidarity of the International Communist Movement," *Rodong Shinmun*, January 30, 1963.

"Let Us Fight Against Modern Revisionism and Strengthen the International Struggle Against American Imperialism," *Akahata*, December 7, 1965, p. 1.

"Let Us Maintain the Revolutionary Position of Marxism–Leninism on the Second Anniversary of the Moscow Manifesto," *Akahata*, December 4, 1962, p. 1.

Liu Ning-yi. "We Absolutely Cannot Accept Taking 'United Action' with the Soviet Revisionist Leading Clique," *Peking Review*, No. 34, August 19, 1966, pp. 22–24.

Liu Shao-ch'i. "Speech by Liu Shao-ch'i at the Conference on Trade Unions of Asia and Oceania," *For a Lasting Peace, For a People's Democracy!*, December 30, 1949, p. 2.

"Long Live Leninism!," *Hong-ch'i,* April 1960.

"The Manoeuvres of the Reactionary Forces and Anti-Party Revisionists around the International Communist Movement," *Akahata,* January 24, 1963, p. 1.

Masuda Kanichi. "The Theoretical and Ideological Bankruptcy of Dissident Japanese Communists," *Akahata,* July 14, 1966, p. 5. For an English translation, see *JPRS* 37,008, pp. 24–31.

Miyamoto Kenji. "On the Amendment of the Action Program," *Zenei,* April 1, 1948, pp. 21–22.

"More on the Philosophy of Nehru," *Jen-min Jin-pao,* October 27, 1962; also summarized in *Akahata,* October 31, 1962.

"Mourning for the Third Year of Ōsugi's Death," *Rōdō Undō,* September 1, 1925.

"The Nature of the Criticism of the 'Draft Report' by the Voice of Japan," *Akahata,* November 18, 1964, p. 5 (*TICD* 679, *JPRS* 27,830, pp. 27–52).

"The New Task of Communists and Patriots—Struggle Against Power with Power," *Naigai Hyōron,* No. 4, October 12, 1950.

Nezu Yūjirō. "The Essence of Reactionary Antagonism and Its Direction— A Refutation of Mr. Abe's Theory," *Rōnō,* Vol. I, No. 1, December 1927, pp. 49–59.

Niijima Junryo. "The Significance of Nuclear Tests and Rectification," *Economist,* Tōkyō, May 31, 1966, pp. 22–28. For an English translation, see *JPRS* 36,230, pp. 42–53.

Nosaka Sanzō. "Labor Aristocracy," *Shakai Kairyō,* Vol. I, No. 2, June 1917.

———. "Love, Knowledge, and Power," *Rōdō Oyobi Sangyō,* No. 53, January 1916.

———. "The Mazda Lamp Factory," *Rōdō Oyobi Sangyō,* No. 82, June 1918.

———. "No One Is Bad—If One Says 'Bad,' Then All Are Bad," *Rōdō Oyobi Sangyō,* No. 86, October 1918.

———. "The Path We Should Pursue," *Shakai Kairyō,* Vol. I, No. 4, August 1917.

Oka Shigeki. "Katayama Sen and America," *Kaizō,* July 1951.

"On the Intervention and the Subversive Activities of the CPSU Leadership and Organization in the Democratic Movement of Our Nation and People," *Akahata,* June 22, 1965, p. 1 (reprinted in *Zenei,* August 1965, pp. 15–31).

"On the New Line of Struggle—What the New Situation Demands of Us," *Akahata,* No. 1, October 20, 1945.

"On the Occasion of the 45th Anniversary of the October Socialist Revolution," *Akahata,* November 7, 1962, p. 1.

"On the Partial Nuclear Test Ban Treaty," *Akahata,* July 29, 1963, p. 1.

"On Premier Ikeda's Letter to Premier Nehru," *Akahata,* November 8, 1962, p. 1.

"Open the Struggle in the Large Factories and Mines Based upon Action Principles," *Rōdō Shimbun-Zenkyō*, No. 3, January 30, 1929, p. 1.

"Party Unity and Solidarity with All Democratic Forces," *Akahata,* January 1, 1955.

Passin, Herbert. "The Sources of Protest in Japan," *The American Political Science Review,* Vol. LVI, June 1962, pp. 391–403.

"Premier Chou En-lai Greets the 12th World Conference Against Atomic and Hydrogen Bombs," *Peking Review,* No. 32, August 5, 1966, pp. 15–16.

Reischauer, Edwin O. "The Broken Dialogue with Japan," *Foreign Affairs,* Vol. 39, No. 1, October 1960, p. 11.

"A Reply to Zhukov's Open Charges," *Akahata,* July 15, 1964, p. 2.

"A Report on the Anti-Bomb World Conferences and Their Characteristics," *Kōan Jōhō,* No. 143, August 1965.

"Resolution for Defence of Peace, Independence, Democracy of Japan in the Tense National and International Situation," dated March 4, 1965, *Sōhyō News,* No. 244, March 10, 1965, pp. 8–10.

Scalapino, Robert A. "Japan," in Walter Galenson (ed.), *Labor and Economic Development,* New York, 1959.

———. "The Left Wing in Japan," *Survey,* No. 43, August 1962, pp. 102–111.

———. "Moscow, Peking, and the Communist Parties of Asia," *Foreign Affairs,* Vol. 41, January 1963, pp. 323–343.

———. "The Sino-Soviet Conflict in Perspective," *The Annals of the American Academy of Political and Social Science,* Vol. 351, January 1964, pp. 1–14.

Shiga Yoshio. "Speech of December 1945 before the People's Assembly for the Prosecution of War Criminals," *Akahata,* December 19, 1945, p. 1.

Shimotsukasa Junkichi. "The Essence and the Absurdity of Anti-Party Dogmatists," *Zenei,* July 1966, pp. 56–70. For an English translation, see *JPRS* 37,008, pp. 1–23.

"The Sino–Indian Border Problem Must Be Settled by Means of Negotiation," *Akahata,* October 31, 1962, p. 1.

"The Tactical Shift of the JCP—A Critique of the Anonymous Article Dated February 4," *Atarashii Rosen,* No. 171, February 14, 1966, p. 1.

Takabatake Motoyuki. "The Political Movement and the Economic Movement," *Shin Shakai,* February 1918.

Takahara Shinichi. "Concerning the Party Literati Who Signed Anti-Party Statements Last Year," *Akahata,* November 23, 1962 (*TICD* 341, *JPRS* 17,111, pp. 1–16).

Tanaka Seigen. "The Era of the Armed Communist Party," *Bungei Shunjū,* Vol. 28, No. 7, June 1950, pp. 188–203.

Tokuda Kyūichi. "On the 30th Anniversary of Founding the JCP," *For a Lasting Peace, For a People's Democracy!,* July 4, 1952.

Toyota Shiro. "The People's Revolutionary Tradition and the Japanese Communist Party Platform," *Akahata*, August 7, 1966, p. 5. For an English translation, see *JPRS* 37,546, pp. 19–25.

Uchino Takechiyo. "Attending the 'World Congress for Peace and Disarmament,'" *Akahata*, July 27 and 28, 1962.

"Under No Circumstances Can Burglar Actions Be Justified," *Akahata*, November 1, 1962, p. 1.

"Unite All Revolutionary Forces and Wage a More Powerful Anti-Imperialist Struggle!," *Rodong Shinmun*, December 6, 1965. For an English translation, See *The People's Korea*, No. 249, December 15, 1965, pp. 1–2.

Wakabayashi Sen. "The Struggle on 'Two Fronts'—Based on the Experience of Our Party and International Lessons," *Akahata*, June 30, 1966, p. 5. For an English translation, see *JPRS* 36,716, pp. 85–91.

Watanabe Mitsuru. "Meeting the Year 1955," *Zenei*, January 1955.

"We Will See How the Modern Revisionists Have Degenerated," *Akahata*, September 20, 1962.

"Why Has Armed Revolution Not Become the Issue of Our Party?," *Naigai Hyōron*, No. 5, January 25, 1951.

"Why Kamiyama and Nakano Were Expelled from the Japanese CP," *Akahata*, October 1964, p. 2 (*TICD* 665, *JPRS* 27,224, pp. 61–78).

Wurfel, David. "The Violent and the Voiceless in Japanese Politics," *Contemporary Japan*, Vol. 29, November 1960, pp. 663-694.

Yamakawa Hitoshi. "A Change of Direction for the Proletarian Movement," *Zenei*, July-August 1922.

———. "Toward a United Political Front!" *Rōnō*, Vol. I, No. 1, December 1927, pp. 3–48.

Yonehara Akira. "Let Us Widely Propagate the Significance of Victory in the 11th Gensuikyō World Conference," *Akahata*, August 21, 1965 (reprinted in *Zenei*, October 1965).

———. "Problems and Tasks of the Japanese Communist Party," *Akahata*, July 25, 1966, pp. 3–4. For an English translation, see *JPRS* 37,126, pp. 34–45.

Zhdanov, Andrei A. "The International Situation," *For a Lasting Peace, For a People's Democracy!*, November 10, 1947, pp. 2–4.

Zhukov, G. A. "Voice of Hiroshima," *Pravda*, August 25, 1963.

4. FOREIGN PERIODICALS CITED OR MENTIONED

Akahata (Red Flag)
Asahi Shimbun (Asahi News)
Atarashii Jidai (The New Age)
Atarashii Rosen (The New Line)
Bulletin Information for Abroad
Bungei Sensen (Culture Front)

Bunka Hyōron (Cultural Review)
China Quarterly
The Class Struggle
Dokusho no Tomo (Friend of Reading)
For a Lasting Peace, For a People's Democracy!
For Peace
Gakushū (Study)
Gikai to Jijitai (Parliament and Self-Government)
Hechima no Hana (Flower of the Gourd Squash)
Heimin Shimbun (The Commoner News)
Heiwa to Dokuritsu (Peace and Independence)
Heiwa to Shakaishugi no mondai (Problems of Peace and Socialism)
Hong-ch'i (Red Flag)
International
Izvestiia
Japan Socialist Review
Jen-min Jih-pao (People's Daily)
Kaihō (Emancipation)
Kindai Shisō (Modern Thought)
Kōan Jōho (Report of the Public Safety Investigation Bureau)
Kōzō Kaikaku (Structural Reform)
Leninshugi (Leninism)
Marxshugi (Marxism)
Marxshugi-Leninshugi (Marxism-Leninism)
Marxshugi no hata no moto ni (Under the Banner of Marxism)
Musansha Shimbun (Proletarian News)
Naigai Hyōron (Internal-External Review)
Nihon no koe (Voice of Japan)
Peking Review
The People's Korea
Pravda
The Revolutionary Age
Rikugō Zasshi (The Universe Magazine)
Rōdō Oyobi Sangyō (Labor and Industry)
Rōdō Sekai (Labor World)
Rōdō Shimbun (Labor News)
Rōdō Shimbun-Zenkyō (Labor News, National Council of Labor Unions)
Rōdō Undō (The Labor Movement)
Rodong Shinmun (Labor News [North Korean Workers' Party Organ])
Rōnō (Labor-Farmer)
Rōdō Shimbun (Labor-Farmer News)
Sekai Seiji Shiryō (Documents on World Politics)
Shakai Kairyō (Social Reform)
Shakai Mondai Kenkyū (Study of Social Problems)

Shakai Shimpō (Socialist News)
Shakai Shisō (Social Thought)
Shakaishugi (Socialism)
Shakaishugi Kenkyū (Studies of Socialism)
Shin Shakai (The New Society)
Shin Shakai Hyōron (New Society Review)
Sōhyō News
Toki no Kadai (Topics of the Time)
Tokushin Geppō (The Monthly Report of the Special Security Agency)
Trud
Zenei (Vanguard)

5. JAPANESE PARTIES, FACTIONS, AND GOVERNMENT AGENCIES

Bunka Dōmei (Cultural League)
Chūritsu Rōren (Federation of Independent Unions)
Dōmei Kaigi (Japanese Confederation of Labor)
Gakusei Shakai Kagaku Rengōkai (Student Social Science Federation)
Gensuikin (Japan Congress Against A and H Bombs)
Gensuikyō (The Japanese Council Against Atomic and Hydrogen Bombs)
Gyōminkai (Men of the Dawn Society)
Gyōmin Kyōsantō (Men of the Dawn Communist Party)
Heimin Gakuren (Student Federation Against the Security Treaty and for the Defense of Peace and Democracy)
Heiwa Dōshikai (Comrades for Peace)
Hyōgikai (see Nihon Rōdō Hyōgikai)
Jichishō senkyokyoku (The Local Autonomy Election Bureau)
Jiyūtō (Liberal [Liberty] Party)
Kakkin Kaigi (Congress for the Prohibition of Nuclear Weapons)
Kensetsusha Dōmei (League of Builders)
Kōan Chosachō (Public Safety Investigation Bureau)
Komeitō (Party for Justice and Fairness)
Kōtō Gakkō Remmei (Higher School Alliance)
Marxshugi Gakusei Dōmei (Marxist Student League)
Minseitō (Democratic Party)
Musan Taishūtō (Proletarian Mass Party)
Nihon Kyōsantō (Japanese Communist Party)
Nihon Minshu Seinen Dōmei (Japan Democratic Youth League)
Nihon Nōmintō (Japan Farmers' Party)
Nihon Rōdō Hyōgikai (Labor Union Council of Japan)
Nihon Rōdō Kumiai Zenkoku Kyōgikai (see *Zenkyō*)
Nihon Rōnōtō (Japan Labor-Farmer Party)
Nihon Shakaitō (Japan Socialist Party)

Rikken Minseitō (Constitutional Democratic Party)
Rikken Seiyūkai (Friends of Constitutional Government Association)
Rodō Nōmintō (Labor-Farmer Party)
Rōnō (Labor-Farmer)
Rōnōtō (Labor-Farmer Party)
Sanbetsu (Congress of Industrial Unions)
Seiyūkai (Friends of Constitutional Government Party)
Shakai Minshutō (Social Democratic Party)
Shakai Minshūtō (Social Mass Party)
Shakaishugi Kenkyūkai (The Association for the Study of Socialism)
Shakaishugi Kyōkai (Socialist Society)
Shinjinkai (New Men's Association)
Sōdōmei (General Federation of Labor)
Sōhyō (General Council of Trade Unions)
Sōka Gakkai (Value Creation Society)
Suiheisha (Levellers' Association)
Yūaikai (The Friendly Society)
Zengakuren (National Federation of Student Self-Government Associations)
Zenkoku Gakusei Rengōkai (see *Zengakuren*)
Zenkyō (National Council of Japanese Labor Unions)
Zenrō (General Federation of Japanese Trade Unions)

INDEX

Abe, Isoo: attacked as social reformer at Comintern 4th Congress, 22; role in Shakai Minshutō, 24

Agriculture. *See* Farmers

Aidit, D. N.: criticism of Khrushchev's action on Albania, 140 n 7; influence on JCP, 225–226; ties with JCP leaders, 290

Akahata (Red Flag): reissued in 1928, 35; first issue after World War II, 48; 4th Congress Report, 52 n 4; Shiga's speech on Emperor system, 52 n 5; translation of *Pravda* editorial on independence of each national Communist Party, 57 n 9; JCP's initial reaction to Cominform's criticism, 62 n 17; Shiga's article attacking Tokuda-Nosaka group over Cominform issue, 63; personnel purged, 85; documents of 6th National Conference, 88 n 11; attacked International faction as "Trotskyites," 91; purge of Itō Ritsu, 93 n 13; defended Soviet nuclear tests before 8th Gensuikyō conference, 123 n 37; views of Uchino, United Front Bureau head, on JSP's position regarding Soviet and American nuclear tests, 124 n 39; approved Soviet nuclear tests, 122 n 34; editorial signaling 1955 change of policy, 99; published new program drafted by Miyamoto

Kenji at 7th Party Congress, 100 n 7, 101 n 8; JCP's attack on Sōhyō, 132; Nosaka's Nov. 1961 speech regarding Sino-Soviet dispute, 138, 138 n 5; Moscow correspondent propositioned by Soviet Party leaders, 137 n 3; congratulatory telegram sent to CPSU, 140; denied seriousness of Sino-Soviet dispute in 1962, 147; article on "primary enemy" issue at 1962 Moscow Congress for General Disarmament and Peace, 148; defense of Chinese against Indians over border incident, 150, 151, 151 n 26; Khrushchev's concession to American demands over Cuban incident, 151; shift of JCP's position on CPSU's foreign and ideological stances, 152; new tactical line over Sino-Soviet dispute, 153; plea for settlement of Sino-Soviet dispute, 154; account of 4th plenary meeting and resolutions, 149, 149 n 22; attack upon Titoism, 149, 149 n 21; approval of Moscow treaty, 161; documents leading to escalation of conflict with CPSU, 167; attack upon Soviet policy during "showdown" conference, 169; Central Committee announcement on nuclear test ban treaty, 170; views of American imperialism, 192 n 76; accused by CPSU of distorting Russian views, 174; denounced Shiga's "Voice of Japan Comrades Society," 171; subscribers in 1964, 226; recanted April 17 Strike opposition, 230; support for united front in 1965, 243; attack upon USSR for internal interference, 245; attack on CPSU for intervention in Japanese politics, June 1965, 253–256; circulation curtailed in Russia, 255; major editorial of Dec. 1965 attacking revisionism and supporting an international united front, 259–260; articles of February 1966 attacking CPSU and supporting united front, 265–266; editorial of May 11, 1966 outlining new JCP policy, 275–276; extoled struggle on two fronts, 276; upheld "autonomy and independence" theme, August 1966, 280–281; number of subscriptions, 292; official account of removal of Kamigama and Nakano, 302 n 7; attacked opening of Japanese-Soviet Book Center, 304; counterattacked Voice of Japan, 305, 305 n 11, 12

Akamatsu, Katsumaro: attacked as social reformer by Comintern 4th Congress, 22

Albania: Workers Party praised by Miyamoto Kenji, 108, 108 n 18; as issue in Sino-Soviet dispute, 136, 138, 139; not considered enemy by Nosaka, 161 n 12; and JCP, 147, 148; used to symbolize China in third stage of Sino-Soviet dispute, 208; defended in JCP 9th Congress Report, 223; 1966 JCP evaluation, 273

Alexandrov, G.: headed Soviet delegation to Gensuikin 1965 Conference, 249

All-Japan Federation of Peasants' Co-operatives: under Communist influence, 134 n 54

All-Japan Free Labor Unions: under direct Communist control, close ties with WFTU, 129 n 48; 130, 131

All-Japan Harbor and Bay Construc-

tion Workers: under Communist (anti-Mainstream Sōhyō) influence 131, 131 n 50

All-Japan Local Government Workers: under Communist control, 131, 131 n 51, 132 n 51

All-Soviet Trade Unions Central Council: Sōhyō protest against Soviet nuclear testing, directed to, 122 n 34

American Communist Party: Asian section of, 9; Katayama Sen joined, 11

American Federation of Labor: Congress of Industrial Organization delegation to Japan and contacts with Sōhyō, 238–242

Anarchism. See Anarcho-syndicalists

Anarcho-syndicalists: struggle with social democrats after Russo-Japanese War, 2, 3; involved in Great Treason Case, 3; influence on socialist movement during World War I, 4; delegation solicited for First Congress of Comintern, 9; quarrel with Communists, 9, 12, 13 passim, 14; importance in labor and socialist movements from Bolshevik Revolution up to 1923, 6, 14; optimistic view of Russian revolution, 11; influence on Yamakawa Hitoshi, 12; reasons for failure in Japan summarized, 13; decline in Japanese labor movement, 14; murder of Ōsugi, 14; influence upon labor and intellectual movements, 15; Ōsugi Sakae introduced French syndicalism, 16; tactics questioned by Takabatake Motoyuki, 16; attacked by Yamakawa Hitoshi in Zenei, 20

Anarcho-syndicalism: Zengakuren Mainstream's position after 1958, 133

Andō, Jimbei: Zengakuren founder and leader of Structural Reform group, 133 n 53; led Socialist Student Front, 145

Anti-Ampō Movement: participants in, 114

Anzai, Kuraji: chief of personal section of JCP, 146; JCP Secretariat member, 293 n 3

Aono, Suekichi: translated Lenin's *What Is To Be Done,* mentioned by Fukumoto, 30 n

April 17th Strike: JCP admits error in 9th Party Congress Report, 217–218; JCP opposition and Sōhyō reaction, 229–231; cost JCP heavily, 307

Arahata, Kanson: involvement in socialist movement during World War I, 3; edited *Kindai Shiso,* 3 n 5; left for Moscow to report to Comintern Executive Committee, 18; returned to Japan from Vladivostok meeting to create united workers' party, 21; went to Shanghai with Sano and Tokuda, 22; given responsibility for organizing Kansai area in re-establishing JCP in 1925, 25; called Bolshevist Communist, not Marxist Communist, by Fukumoto Kazuo, 27 n 37; only old leader who took active role in establishing 2nd JCP, 28; appointed as leader of 2nd JCP, 31; wrote article critical of Profintern in *Rōnō,* 33 n 44

Asahi Shimbun: results of 1960 polls on political parties' popularity, 115

Asanuma Inejirō: signed joint anti-American declaration with Peking, 252 n 73

Asō, Hisashi: entered Yuaikai, 5; and Nihon Rōnōtō, 24

Association of Japanese Socialists in America: established by Katayama Sen, 7; drew key members from "Katayama's boys," 8; provided radical groups in Japan with socialist materials, 11

Atarashii Jidai (The New Age): Kasuga's statement of defection appeared in, 110 n 21; Kasuga's objection to Socialist Renovation program in, 145 n 16

Atarashii Rōsen (The New Line):

edited by Naito Tomochika, 81 n 3; outline of Socialist Renovation group's position on JCP, 144 n 15; circulation, 145; carried account of anti-Soviet activities of Mainstream JCP leaders, 149 n 20; noted JCP policy shift, 266; reactions of Voice of Japan group to JCP expulsions, 303 n 8

Australia: representatives at Kakkin Kaigi Conference, 277

Bakunin, Mikhail Aleksandrovich: influence upon Japanese radicals, 5

Bandung: diplomatic offensive by CCP, 88

Bellamy, Edward: influence on Nosaka Sanzō, 4

Beria, Lavrenti: impact of his purge, 88

Bikini Day: designated by peace leaders, 231

Blanc, Jean Joseph Charles Louis: influence on Shakaishugi Kenkyūkai, 1

Bolshevism. *See* Communism

Bonin Islands: JCP 9th Congress position on, 221

Brezhnev, Leonid: visit to Yugoslavia and Sino-Soviet dispute, 149

British Communist Party: Manifesto and programs used as a model by early Japanese Communists, 5; joined by Nosaka, 5

Browder, Earl: purge, 77

Bucharest: exchange of attacks between CPSU and CCP, 105

Bukharin, Nikolai Ivanovich: contacts with Katayama Sen, 7; major contribution to 1927 thesis, 29; criticized Fukumotoism, 29; purged, 42

Bulganin, N.: impact of his removal, 88

Bulgaria: participated in Hiroshima International Conference of 1964, 235; in Gensuikin 1965 Conference, 249

Bungei Sensen (Culture Front): 1927 thesis published in, 31

Bunka Domei (Cultural League): founded by students of Waseda University, 11, 26

Bunka Hyōron (Cultural Review): 293 n 4

Bureaucracy: elimination of old forces advocated by Nosaka in 6th Congress, 59; and present Soviet rulers, 206; JCP leadership, 293

Buraku Liberation League: under Communist influence, 134 n 54

Burke, Edmund: Meiji elite, compared with, 331

Burma: liberation war by Liu Shao-ch'i noted, 65

Cadres: expansion of system advocated at JCP 9th Congress, 227–228

Capitalism: Japan's shift from agrarian society to industrialist, 3; anti-liberal, antidemocratic elements in Japanese capitalism, 20; Communist debate over possibilities of bourgeois liberalism, 21; U.S. representing a stronghold of capitalism in 5th JCP Congress report, 54; "Japanese monopoly capitalism" regarded as primary enemy by anti-Mainstream faction at 7th Party Congress, 101, 110–111; defined by structural reformists, 102; position of "Japanese monopoly capitalism" as analyzed in JCP 9th Congress Report, 216 n 3; "Japanese monopoly capitalism" regarded by JCP as subordinate ally to "American imperialism," 347

Castro, Fidel: five demands endorsed by JCP, 152, 152 n 31; Russian foreign policy attacked by JCP for its surrender to U.S. demands and for not defending Castro government, 189

Central Committee: Shiga documents attacking Mainstream faction presented to enlarged Central Committee plenum, 91; Tokuda report about Cominform attack, 91. *See also* JCP

Central Federated Council of Rural Labor Unions: official JCP organ, 134 n 54

Ceylon: representatives at Kakkin Kaigi Conference, 277

Chao An-po: met Miyamoto mission, 266

Chao, Pu-cha: head of Chinese delegation to 9th Gensuikyō Conference, 159

Chang, T'ai-lei: requested Yamakawa and Sakai to send delegates to First Congress of Comintern, 9; attempts to convert Japanese anarchists to Bolsheviks failed, 9

Ch'en, Tu-hsiu: met Ōsugi Sakae, 12; equated with Yamakawa by Comintern, 39

Chiang Kai-shek: under attack at 6th JCP national conference, 88 n 11

Chinese Communist Party: Fukumoto analysis, 30 n 42; comparison with JCP, 38f.; alliance with Kuomintang, 38; influence upon JCP on issue of nationalism, 53; struggle with Kuomintang, 57; views on Asian revolution identical with CPSU in 1949–50, 66; intervention in JCP over Cominform issue, 63, 64f.; independence from Soviet Union, 77; intervention in support of Cominform criticism of JCP, 78; regarded as a model in 1951 thesis, 82, 84; diplomatic offensive at Bandung, 88; influence at 6th JCP Conference, 95–96; influence through Japanese exiles, 93; power struggle within JCP determined by, 91; reactions to attack on Stalin at 20th Party Congress, 99; growing influence within JCP, 146–147; reactions to Soviet-Yugoslav rapprochement, 149; influence at 4th plenum meeting of JCP Central Committee, 149; JCP's stronger affinity for Chinese position in Sino-Soviet dispute, 153; influence on JCP's intraparty struggle, 162; dissemination of materials in Japan,

164; attempts to cultivate Japanese against USSR, 165; its position on war and peaceful co-existence defended by JCP, 191; fight for leadership of world Communist movement, 197–198; advocated equality and autonomy, 197; use of Confucian concept of revolution to challenge Soviet domination, 198; reactions to Soviet aid, 199–200; positions on war, peace and revolution versus those of CPSU, 203f.; and JCP's position on Sino-Soviet dispute, 209–210; influence on JCP, 211–213; use of CCP conceptual model by JCP in 9th Congress Report, 216; 218–220; influence upon 9th Congress, 228–229; first Chinese nuclear test and Japanese reaction, 237; role in 11th Gensuikyō World Congress, 248–249; walkout from 1965 Sōhyō convention, 249–250 n 69; relations with Japanese Socialist Party, 1964–1965, 251–252; rejected "united front" proposals of JCP and KWP, 260–261; treatment by Socialist Party in 1966, 262–263; meetings with Miyamoto mission, February-April 1966, 266–272; violent attacks upon CPSU in connection with Vietnam, 270–271; declined invitation to 23rd CPSU Congress, 271; attack upon new "Holy Alliance," 278; Chou visit to Bucharest, 276 n 97; struggle at Gensuikyō 12th World Congress, 278–280; anger at JCP over Gensuikyō crisis, 280; overtures to Sasaki faction of Socialists, summer 1966, 283; criticized in 10th JCP Congress, 287; evaluation of CCP Asian policies by Korean, Japanese Communists, 290–201; financal aid to JCP, 309–310; deteriorating relations with JCP, 310; criticized by JCP for blocking united front, 347; impact of CCP's victory on JCP, 349–350; appeal of Chinese model to Japanese radicals, 350

Chinese nuclear testing: JCP 9th Party Congress position on, 215

Chou, En-lai: retort to Khrushchev's attack on Albania at 22nd CPSU Congress, 136; greetings to 10th Gensuikyō World Conference, 233 n 34, 234

Christian socialism: founders of Shakaishugi Kenyūkai, 1; dominant theme of Shakai Minshūtō, 2; major element in Shakaishugi Kyōkai, 2; influence upon old Japanese radicals, 15

Chu, Tsu-chi: activities at 9th Gensuikyō conference, 160

Ch'ü, Ch'iu-pai: compared to Fukumoto by Comintern, 39

Chūō faction: replaced Fuchū faction after Occupation, 90

Chūritsu Rōren: participated in invitation to Soviet labor leader, Grishin, 278 n 101

Class Struggle: and Katayama Sen, 8

Cole, G.D.H.: influence on Fukumoto Kazuo, 27

Colonialism: as interpreted by Liu Shao-ch'i, 65; issue at 7th Gensuikyō Conference, 119; its absence shaped modern Japanese political elite, 332

COMECON. See Council for Mutual Economic Aid

Cominform: and Zhdanov's "two camps" speech in 1947, 57, 57 n 9; attack on Nosaka's position, 61 ff.; Nosaka criticism supported by CCP, 64; influence in 1951 thesis, 80; impact of its Nosaka criticism on JCP factional struggle, 91; end of, 195; attack of 1950 on JCP blamed upon Stalin in CPSU letter to JCP, 175 n 73

Comintern: "First Congress of Toilers of Far East," 9; themes of First Congress, 15; Shanghai Bureau, 12, 16; Third Congress of, 12, 16, 20; involvement with Asian anarcho-syndicalists, 15; decision to drop support of Ōsugi and shift to new group, 16; and founding of JCP, 18; fourth Congress of, 18, 22; disapproved JCP's decision to disolve party, 22; theses and preliminary movement toward re-establishment of JCP in 1925, 25; special committee on Japan problem, 29; 1927 Thesis, 29, 29 n 41; against Rōnō-ha's positions on revolution, 32; 6th Congress, 34; Far Eastern Bureau in Shanghai, 34; policies on Japan led JCP to "left-extremism," 37; "united front from below" theme and Zenkyō, 41; 10th Congress of 1929, 42; technique of using indigenous scapegoats in correcting errors and redefining policies, 38, 39; analysis of Far Eastern policies, 39, 40; Shanghai Bureau activities, 40, 41 *passim;* referred to in connection with debate on "revolution" at 7th JCP Congress, 101 n 8; end of, 195

Communes: attacked by CPSU as being ultra-radical, 201

Communism: origins in Asia, 6–9 *passim;* influence of Marxism-Leninism on students, intellectuals and labor, 10; Leninism introduced into Japan by Takabatake Motoyuki, 10; Bolshevik theories of elitism and proletarian dictatorship under attack by anarchists, 12; quarrel with anarcho-syndicalists, 9, 12, 13 *passim,* 14; as science of successful revolution, 13; rise in Japanese labor and intellectual movements, 16; and nationalism, 195; shift from monolithism to polycentrism, 195; instrument for completing nation-building process, 206; as technique of rapid modernization, 338; comparison of national communism with national socialism, 340; evolution from monolithism to polycentrism to national communism, 352. *See also* Marxism, Japanese Communist Party

Communist Committee: established in 1921, 15–16

Communist Manifesto: introduced by Koizumi Shinzō, 5

Communist Party of China. *See* Chinese Communist Party

Communist Party of Indonesia. *See* PKI

Communist Party of Japan. *See* Japanese Communist Party

Communist Party of the Soviet Union: Cominform's attack on Nosaka's theory published, 62 n 18; views on Asian revolution identical with CCP in 1949–50, 66; and power struggle within JCP, 91; 20th Party Congress, 96; impact of 20th Party Congress on JCP, 99 ff.; 22nd Party Congress and Sino-Soviet dispute, 136; received JCP's congratulatory telegram, 140; attacked *Akahata* article for giving support to China, 148 n; JCP's dissatisfaction with Khrushchev's policies, 152; JCP's attempt to avoid direct attack on, 153; sent letter to JCP in effort to mend relations, 155; attempts to isolate Mainstream JCP, 162–163; showdown conference with JCP, 168–169; ties with Shiga faction, 169; attack on JCP Mainstream policies, 169; open break with JCP, 171ff.; made public letters sent to JCP, 171–172; charges against JCP over interparty relations, 172 ff.; accused JCP of preventing Soviet literature distribution, 174; charged JCP with echoing Chinese line, 175; accused by JCP of interfering in internal affairs, 177; relations with JCP, 167–168; confrontation with JCP over Communist tactics and strategy, 179–195; defended its role in supporting national liberation movements, 179–180; attacked JCP's opposition to nuclear test ban treaty, 180 ff.; defended policies of peaceful coexistence, 183 ff.; Soviet economism criticized by JCP, 186–188; Europo-centrism attacked by JCP, 187–188; Soviet attempt to rehabilitate Yugoslavia criticized by JCP, 189; attacked by JCP for Soviet policies in Cuban crisis, 189; accused by JCP of revisionism, 195; domination of world Communist movement challenged by CCP, 198; positions on peaceful coexistence vs. those of CCP, 202 f.; attacked by JCP for uncomradely attitude, revisionism, and other "crimes," 209–210; as analyzed by JCP 9th Party Congress, 222–225; relations with Japanese Socialists in connection with peace movement, 1963–1964, 232–233; tactics regarding 1964 Gensuikyō Conference, 233; absent from 11th Gensuikyō Conference, 1965, 248; participated in Gensuikin 1965 Conference, 249–250; involvement in Japanese politics, 252–255; attacked by *Akahata*, 255–256; attacked by Korean Communists, 258–259; attacked by *Akahata*, Dec. 1965, 259–260; attacked by CCP on Vietnam, 260–261; treatment by Socialist Party in 1966, 262–263; "secret" letter to all fraternal parties, 1966, 269–270 n 90; evaluation under JCP "struggle on two fronts" thesis, 275–277; relations with Japanese Socialists, summer 1966, 283; criticized in 10th JCP Congress, 287; castigated Yoyogi group as Chinese puppets, 304; supported Voice of Japan group, 303–304. *See also* Soviet Union

Communist Youth League: and Zenkyō leaders, 37; recruitment urged in 4th Congress of JCP, 51

Confucianism: legacy in CCP, 198; impact of Neo-Confucianism, 331

Congo: Soviet policy attacked by CCP, 205

Constitution: JCP 9th Congress position on, 221

Council for Mutual Economic Aid: CCP accused by CPSU of undermining, 202

Cuba: tribute paid by Nosaka, 138–139; impact of its crisis on Sino-Soviet dispute, 147; JCP's views on U.S. and Soviet Union policy in Cuban crisis, 151–152; failure of Soviet policy attacked by JCP, 189; Chinese accusations of Soviet capitulation, 204; 1966 JCP evaluation, **273**

Czechoslovakia: at 9th Gensuikyō conference, 159; at Hiroshima International Conference of 1964, 235; at 3rd Gensuikin Conference, 282 n **112**

Daniel, Yuli: impact of trial on Japanese intellectuals, 338

Democracy: "people's democracy" to be established, 48, 50; lack of intraparty democracy denounced, 110; as slogan in anti-Ampō movement, 115 n 24, 116; Communism as "new democracy," 329

Democratic Centralism: advanced by Comintern, 22; lack in Zenkyō criticized, 41; as JCP tactic in peace movement, 116; used by JCP to control Gensuikyō, 127 n 43; used by JCP to control labor unions, 130 n 49; advocated at Moscow conference, 196–197; practice in JCP, 293

Democratic Socialist Party: left Gensuikyō to form Kakkin Kaigi, 118; as analyzed by JCP in 9th Party Congress report, 216–217; participated in Kakkin Kaigi Conference, 1966, 277; analysis by JCP 10th Party Congress, 286; in 1965 House of Councillors election, 297–298; in 1965 Tōkyō City assembly, 299

Democratic Youth League: front organization of JCP, 123 n 36; fight with JSP's Youth League, 126; influence on Zengakuren, 133 n 53; membership increased, 137 n 2; dominated 9th Gensuikyō Conference, 158 n 44; gains, 220; as JCP front organization, 226; canceled China visit, 284; control of Zengakuren, 306

Denmark: delegate upheld Gensuikyō, 279 n 102

De-Stalinization: and its impact, 97 ff.

Diet: JCP candidates elected, 72; tactics of Kishi government, 114–115 n 24; voted on nuclear test ban treaty, 169–170

Djilas, Milovan: impact of his arrest on Japanese intellectuals, 338

Doki, Tsuyoshi: chief editor of *Akahata*, 146; denounced Shiga's "Voice of Japan Comrades Society," 171; as JCP Secretariat member, 293 n 3

Dokusho no Tomo (Friend of Reading): JCP publication, 293 n 4

Domei Kaigi (Japanese Confederation of Labor): as analyzed by JCP in 9th Party Congress report, 217; showing vigor, 339

Eda, Saburō: headed JSP delegation to 8th Gensuikyō Conference, 128; attitude toward united front with JCP, 1965, 247; defeated in JSP January 1966 election, 265

Eda faction: position in January 1966 Socialist Congress, 264–265

Eighth Congress of JCP: reevalued by JCP, 274

Eisenhower, Dwight: administration compared with that of Kennedy in JCP's criticism of American imperialism, 192

Elections: universal suffrage demanded by anarcho-syndicalists, 14; under universal manhood suffrage, 33 f.; JCP record, 1946–1949, 72–73; Nov. 1960 results, 115; JCP increases in local elections, 156; JCP gains at local levels after 1960, 226; 1965 Tōkyō City Assembly election, 299–300; JCP's foreign policy issues in 1965 House of Councillors election, 298–299; JCP in House of Representatives—strength and weakness, 295–296; JCP votes in urban and rural areas, 296; regional votes for JCP House of Representatives, 296; JCP in House of Councillors, 296–297; JCP 1965 House

of Councillors—results and analysis, 297–298

Emperor System: viewed by 1931 and 1932 Theses, 42–43; overthrow advocated in *Akahata* and 4th Congress report, 48–50; positions of JCP on, 52, 53 *passim;* Nosaka's analysis in 6th Party Congress, 59; mass loyalty drawn to it against Communist mobilization, 331

England: Nosaka Sanzō in, 5; influence on moderates through Fabian Society, 24; British imperialism considered as important as American in CPSU's letter to JCP, 184–185; JCP rebuttal on British imperialism, 194

Eta. See Outcast Community

Fabian Society: and Japanese moderates, 24

Factionalism: as reason for failure of JCP's united front with Nihon Shakaitō, 74; survey of JCP's factional divisions, 90 ff.; role of personal rivalries, 90; Chūō and Kansai factions in JCP, 90; policy division between Mainstream and International factions after Cominform criticism, 92–93 n 12; and 1950 Cominform criticism, 94; split formally mended at 6th Party Conference, 94; and 1951 Draft Thesis, 94; beginning of fundamental Party realignment at 1955 conference, 99–100; debate over draft program at 7th Party Congress, 101; summary of points of difference between two JCP factions, 103 n 10; at 16th plenary session of JCP Central Committee and 8th Party Congress, 109; struggle within JCP related to Sino-Soviet dispute, 111; in Liberal Democratic Party with reference to Mutual Security Treaty, 114; in Zengakuren, 133–134 n 53; in Communist controlled intellectual organizations, 134–135 n 54; Mainstream faction vs. Kasuga-Naitō forces over Sino-Soviet dispute, 137, 139; Yoyogi vs. Socialist Renovation group, 144; within JCP in early 1962, 145–146; within JCP over Sino-Soviet dispute, 153; intraparty struggle at 4th plenum meeting of JCP's Central Committee, 149, 149 n 22; within JCP, 168 n 65; split of JCP over vote on nuclear test ban treaty, 169 ff.; basic organizational principles of Japan apply to JCP, 294; Yoyogi, Voice of Japan and Liberation Front, 302, 305–306

Far Eastern Workers' Communist University: and Japanese students, 35

Farmers: as raw recruits for industrialization, 3; little attention paid to by JCP, 21; role in revolution, as defined by Rōnō-ha, 32; JCP's failure to develop mass base in rural areas due to land reform, 71; enjoy prosperity, 84; and JCP organizations, 134 n 54; JCP 9th Party Congress position on, 219–220, 227; Communist-front peasant associations, 307; postwar potential for Communist growth, 330, 335; failure of JCP in rural areas, 340, 341

February 1 Strike: prepared by Sanbetsu, 69

Federation of Japanese Women's Organizations: under JCP influence, 135 n

For a Lasting Peace, For a People's Democracy!: Andrew Zhdanov's report, 57 n 9; Liu Shao-ch'i's speech at Conference on Trade Unions of Asia and Oceania, 64 n 23; criticism of Nosaka, 61; 1951 report of JCP, 81–82; English translation of 4th Conference resolution, 86 n 8

Foster, William Z.: article translated in *Shakaishugi*, 11 n 16; introduced to Fukumoto Kazuo, 30 n

Fourier, Francois Marie Charles: influence on Shakaishugi Kenkyūkai, 1

France: influence of revolutionary ideas on Shakai Minshutō, 2; JCP compared with French CP, 75; French imperialism considered important in CPSU's letter to JCP, 184, 185; French imperialism unimportant in JCP's rebuttal of Soviet letter, 194; delegate upheld Gensuikyō, 279 n 102

Fuchū faction: members imprisoned for many years, 90

Fuha Tetsuzō (alias of Ueda Tetsuzō): member of spring 1966 Miyamoto mission, 266

Fujii, Keiji: chief of Finance Section of JCP, 146

Fujiwara, Ryūzō: JCP presidium member (alternate), 293 n 2

Fukumoto, Kazuo: path to Marxism, 26 ff., 27 n 37; attended Comintern meeting on Japan in Moscow, 29; later recollections and appraisal of his purge in Moscow, 29–30, n 42; relations with Jonson, 30 n 42; relations with Bukharin, 30 n 42; relations with W. Z. Foster, 30 n 42; removed from Central Committee of JCP, 31

Fukumotoism: survey of, 26 ff.; criticized by 1927 Thesis, 29, 30, 31 *passim;* emphasis on importance of theory, 27–28; theory of "separation and unity" borrowed from Lenin, 28; control of Communist movement in 1926–27, 28; struggle with Yamakawaism, 26, 29, 32 *passim;* and Zenkyō leaders, 37; compared to Ch'ü Ch'iu-pai and Li Li-san theories by Comintern, 39

Furuichi, Haruhiko: entered Yuaikai, 5

Gakusei Shakai Kagaku Rengōkai (Student Social Science Federation): successor to Zenkoku Gakusei Rengōkai, 26

Gakushu (Study): JCP publication, 293 n 4

Garst, Charles: in early Japanese socialist movement, 1 n 1

General Federation of Korean Residents in Japan: status, 72; North Korean influence, and ties with JCP, 302

Gensuikin (Japan Congress Against A and H Bombs): inauguration, 245–246; criticism of Gensuikyō, 246; program, 246–247; 2nd Conference in 1965, 249–250; aid from Soviet sources, 253–254; 3rd Conference, 282–283

Gensuikyō (The Japanese Council Against Atomic and Hydrogen Bombs): JCP target, 116–117; background, 117–118 n 27, n 28; Chinese donation for relief fund at 6th Gensuikyō meeting, 118 n 28; 6th Conference, 118; constitution and "democratic centralism," 110, 7th Conference, 119–120; split, 122 f.; Chinese influence at 8th Conference, 123–124, 124 n 38, 124 n 40; 8th Conference, 123, 125; 9th Conference, 158–160; reorganization, 156–157; Sōhyō-Socialist attitude in 1964, 232; 10th World Congress, 233–234; 11th World Congress, 1965, 247–249; 12th World Congress, 1966, 278–280

George, Henry: influence on Shakai-shugi Kenkyūkai, 1 n 1

Germany: influence of social democracy on Shakai Minshūtō, 2; Marxism introduced by Takabatake Motoyuki, 16; "German imperialism" considered as important in CPSU's letter to JCP, 184–185; "German imperialism" unimportant in JCP rebuttal of Soviet letter, 194; influence on Japanese intellectuals, 329

Gikai to Jijitai (Parliament and Self-government): JCP publication, 293 n 4

Goda Hideichi: role in Liberation Front, 256

Gompers, Samuel: discussed by Takabatake Motoyuki in Shin Shakai, 10 n 13

Gomulka, Wladyslaw: reemerged as leader, 97

Government: suppression of anarchists, 13; secret police murder of Ōsugi Sakae, 14; mass arrest of Communists in 1928, 34; suppression of JCP, 39, 40–41, 43 passim; pressures against Communist labor leadership in post-February 1 Strike era, 69; role in curtailing postwar JCP development, 342

Great Treason Case: 3

Grey, B.: Communist background, 17 n 24

Grishin, Viktor: visited Japan, 278 n 101

Gubanov: ordered Japanese firm to reform Japan-Soviet Society or withdraw, 254

Guerrilla warfare: physical conditions prevented JCP from developing, 39; reported in progress in Malaya and the Philippines by Liu Shao-ch'i, 65

Guinea: delegate upheld Gensuikyō, 279 n 102

Gyōmin Kyōsantō (Men of the Dawn Communist Party): founded by Waseda University radicals and Kōndō Eizō, 17; distributed anti-military handbills, 17; dissolution, 17; formed the nucleus of the first proto-Communist party, 11

Hagerty, James: Zengakuren demonstrates against, 115 n 25

Hakamada, Satomi: succeeded Miyamoto Kenji as chairman of JCP and arrested in 1935, 43; spoke at 5th Party Congress, 54; factional position, 90; played significant role in drafting new program at 7th Party Congress, 100–101 n 7; close contacts with Chinese Communists, 101 n 7; trips to Peking and Moscow, 107; a leader of Mainstream group after 7th Party Congress, 109; sent letter to Eda Saburo, protesting JSP role at 8th Gensuikyō

Conference, 128; one of leaders dominating JCP, 136; proletarian background; regarded as top leader of "pro-China" faction, 146; ties with Nosaka, 146; conflict with Kamiyama at 4th plenum JCP Central Committee, 149 n 22; mission to Moscow for showdown conference, 169; consolidated power in JCP, 228; political ascendancy, 287; positions in Party, 293, 293 n 2, 3

Hasegawa, Hiroshi: retained in Politburo after struggle over Nosaka's theory, 67; factional position, 90; removed from Central Committee, 103

Hatoyama, Ichirō: his government attacked as being supporter of American forces at 6th JCP Party Conference, 89 n; message to first Gensuikyō meeting (as Premier), 118 n 28

Hayashi, Inoue: editor of *Sekai Seiji Shiryō*, China-lobby leader, 147

Haywood, B.: discussed by Takabatake Motoyuki in *Shin Shakai*, 10 n 13

Hechima no Hana (*Flower of the Gourd Squash*): published by Sakai Toshihiko, 3 n 5

Heimin Gakuren (Student Federation Against the Security Treaty and for the Defense of Peace and Democracy): JCP organized to take over Zengakuren, 133 n 53

Heimin shimbun (*The Commoner News*): Kotoku Denjirō's article appeared in, 2 n 3

Heiwa Dōshikai (Comrades for Peace): far left wing of JSP and Sōhyō, 129

Higashikuni, Naruhiko: message to first Gensuikyō meeting, 118 n 28

Hirano, Yoshitarō: Director of Institute of Chinese Studies, head of Japan Peace Committee, 117 n 27; presided over 9th Gensuikyō Conference, 159

Hiroshima Appeal: passed at Hiroshima Conference, 236

Hiroshima Conference Against Atomic and Hydrogen Bombs: 127, 127 n 44

Hiroshima-Nagasaki Conference of 1964: 234–236. See also Gensuikin

Hisatome, Kōzō: entered Yuaikai, 5

Ho Chi Minh: role of compromiser at Moscow Conference of 81 parties, 108 n 19; position of public silence over Sino-Soviet dispute, 140 n 7

Hong-ch'i (Red Flag): comment on open letter of Central Committee of CPSU, 98 n 1; article challenging Khrushchev's views, 104

Hong Kong: representatives at Kakkin Kaigi Conference, 277

Honjō, Sumio: Chairman of Ministry of Construction Workers, member of WFTU Executive Committee, 129 n 48

Hook, Sidney: attacked by Soviet delegate, Mitin, at 8th Gensuikyō Conference, 126

Horie, Kiichi: influence on Nosaka Sanzō, 4; and Shakai Minshūtō, 24

Horie, Muraichi: Director of Japan-Soviet Union Society, 171

Horie, Yūichi; factional position, 90

Horii, Toshikatsu: elected Sōhyō Chairman, 283, 307

Hoshiro, Tsutomu: removed from position in *Akahata* for pro-Soviet views, 171

Hososako, Kanemitsu: joined Ōyama and Kawakami in attempts to establish Rōnōtō, 35–36

Hosokawa, Karoku: factional alignment, 90

Hosoya, Matsuta: worker-leader in Zenkyō, 37

Hoxha, Enver: praised by Miyamoto Kenji, 108, 108 n 8; praised JCP on Nosaka's 70th birthday, 147; Soviet attack on Chinese transfer of aid to Hoxha regime, 201–202

Hungarian Revolution: impact on Japanese intellectual Communists, 134 n 54; attitude of Sōhyō, 241

Hungary: Chinese advice in favor of Soviet intervention against Nagy regime in, 98; at 9th Gensuikyō Conference, 159; at 3rd Gensuikin Conference, 282 n 112

Hyogikai. See Nihon Rōdō Hyōgikai

Hyōgo: anti-Mainstream group drew strength from Hyōgo prefecture party organization, 109

Ichikawa, Shōichi: wrote draft program for 2nd JCP, 28; appointed as leader of 2nd JCP, 31; helped reorganize JCP after mass arrests of 1928; representative to 6th Comintern Congress, 34; leader in establishing Communist Bureau in 1928, 35

Ii, Yashirō: JCP Secretariat member, 293 n 3

Ikeda, Hayato: attack on Ikeda government by Nosaka appears in Pravda, 148; his support of Nehru on border issue attacked by JCP, 151; Ikeda government "forced" to sign nuclear test ban treaty, according to CPSU, 182

Imperialism: and Rōnō-ha position, 32; Liu Shao-ch'i's views, 15; Stalin quoted in 1951 Thesis, 82; "American imperialism" opposed at 7th Party Congress of JCP, 103; Japan considered imperialist nation by Kasuga Shōichi, 110; views of Kasuga Shōjirō, 110–111; as issue at 7th Gensuikyō conference, 119; position of Chinese delegate to 8th Gensuikyō Conference, 125; American imperialism regarded as primary enemy, 148; Nehru attacked by Chinese as being a tool of "American imperialism," 150; CPSU attacked JCP with reference to nuclear test ban treaty, 161; CPSU claimed "American imperialism" being contained by

U.S.S.R., 184; Soviet advocacy of struggle against not only "American imperialism" but also imperialism of other nations, 184–185; polarization theory rebuked by JCP, 192, 192 n 96, 193 n 98, 194; disintegration of Soviet empire, 195–196; Russian imperialism charge by CCP, 200; JCP's position of subordinating peaceful coexistence to struggle against "American imperialism," 210; JCP's current position on "American imperialism," 347

India: as example of "national liberation war" mentioned by Liu Shao-ch'i, 65; JCP's attack on Indian government over Sino-Indian border incident, 150; at 9th Gensuikyō Conference, 159; JCP attitude as expressed in 9th Party Congress, 215, 223; discussed in Socialist 1966 Congress, 263; representatives at Kakkin Kaigi Conference, 277

Indonesia: liberation war in progress according to Liu Shao-ch'i, 65; discussed in Socialist 1966 Congress, 263; Soviet references to abortive revolt, 270 n 90; representatives at Kakkin Kaigi Conference, 277; Korean and Japanese Communists' analysis of abortive coup, 290. See also PKI

Inomata, Tsunao: leader of Rōnō-ha, 8; visited Katayama Sen in New York, 8; his article setting forth Rōnō thesis, 32 n 43

Intellectuals: founded Shakaishugi Kenkyūkai, 1; new group created by Western impact, 3; and Taishō radicalism, 5; moved into labor movement, 5; shifted to left, 9; increasing Communist influence, 14; introduction of Leninism, 16; influence of Russian revolution, 17; found stimulus in Marxism; major role in establishing JCP, 19; in Shakai Minshūtō, 24; in Nihon

Rōnōtō, 24; leadership in a 1925 JCP, 25; as Zenkyō leaders, 36–37; role of "quasi-intellectual" in JCP, 45–46; Communist influence in postwar literary and cultural associations, 72; organizations under Communist influence, 134–135 n 54; sympathetic to JCP's anti-Mainstream faction, 136; pro-Soviet tradition, 146; analysis of in 9th JCP Congress Report, 220, 227; postwar potential for Communist growth, 334; challenge to old fashioned Marxism, 337

International: new Japanese-language journal, founded by CPSU, 304

International Conference of Communist Parties: convened in 1957 to commemorate 60th anniversary of Russian Revolution, 98

International Education League: Kōndō Eizō's project, 14, 15 *passim.*

International faction: rise, 84, 90; outsted from Party posts over Cominform attack, 92; seek Soviet support, 91; control 10 percent of party, 94; gradual disintegration of, 100; control $\frac{1}{3}$ of Congress votes at 7th Party Congress, 101; gains at 7th Party Congress, 103; and Sino-Soviet dispute, 106–107

International Socialist Review: Katayama Sen's account of Tōkyō streetcar strike, 6 n 10

International Student League: Zengakuren affiliated with, 132–133

International Workers of World (IWW): Kotoku Denjirō's contacts with, 3; Nosaka Sanzō influenced by, 7

Ishida, Seiichi: assistant editor of *Akahata,* 146; denied seriousness of Sino-Soviet dispute, 147

Ishimoto, Baron: contacts with Katayama Sen, 8

Ishimoto, Shizue. *See* Kato Shizue

Italian Communist Party: Togliatti's structural reform and its impact on JCP, 109

Italian Federation of Labor: "structural reform" and JCP, 87

Italy: anarchist failure, 13; JCP compared with Italian CP, 75; influence on JCP through Italian Federation of Labor and its "structural reform," 87; influence on JCP through Togliatti's theory of structural reform, 102, 109

Itō, Ritsu: spoke at 5th Party Congress, 54 n 7; Mainstream Politburo member after Nosaka crisis, 67; factional background, 90; close ties with Tokada, 92; rival of Shida Shigeo in struggle for power after Tokuda's death, 93; ousted from Party for being a spy, 93; compared to Lavrenti Beria, 93 n 13; criticized in JCP 10th Party Congress, 287

Ivanov, E. V.: ordered Sōhyō leader to oppose pro-JCP Japan-Soviet Society, 254

Iwabayashi, Toranosuke: JCP Secretariat member, 293 n 3

Iwai, Akira: Secretary General of Sōhyō, 129; called for reorganization of Gensuikyō, 156; attacked JCP for April 17 Strike opposition, 230; reelected Sōhyō Secretary General, 1964, 231; reacted to first Chinese nuclear test, 237; met Meany delegation in Tōkyō, 239

Iwasa, Sakutarō: Ōsugi's follower, 14; attempts to uphold anarchist influence in labor and intellectual movements, 16

Iwata, Yoshimichi: arrested in 1932, 43

Izvestiia: Chekonin, correspondent in Japan, and information on JCP, 164

Japan Coal Miners Union: Sōhyō Mainstream federation under Communist control, 131, 131 n 51

Japan Congress Against A and H Bombs. *See* Gensuikin

Japanese Council of Youth Organizations: made protest at 7th Gensui-kyō Conference, 119

Japan Democratic Culture League: founded under JCP auspices, 134 n 54

Japan Democratic Writers' League: establishment and membership, 307

Japan Marxist Student Alliance: revolutionary Marxist faction controlling Zengakuren in 1958, 133

Japan Newspaper Workers Union: under Communist influence, 131, 131 n 50

Japan Peace Committee: successor to Society for Defense of Peace, headed by Hirano Yoshitarō, 117 n 27; JCP front organization, 123 n 36

Japan-Soviet Friendship Society: tool of Soviet influence in Japan, 163–164; under assault by JCP, 164; CPSU's accusations against JCP, 174; Soviet purge attempts attacked by *Akahata*, 253–254, internal problems, 254–255

Japan-Soviet Liaison Society: founded, 254–255

Japan Teachers Union (Nikkyōso): Sōhyō's Mainstream federation, Communist-Socialist background, 131

JCP (Japanese Communist Party): origins, 14, 18; major role played by intellectuals and students in first phase of JCP, 19; as a branch of international movement directed from Moscow, 19; first ideology, 20 f.; reorganization and "natural development" faction, 21; influence in Nihon Rōdō Hyōgikai, 23; struggle with social democrats over control of labor movement, 23; control of Rōdō Nōminto, 24; moving to left in 1925–26, 25; publications, 25; division within movement—"Yamakawaism" and "Fukumotoism," 26; infiltration of labor unions by members of Gakusei Shakai Kagaku Rengōkai, 26; battle over legalism vs. illegalism, 35, 36 *passim;* attack on Ōyama group for deserting party, 36; compared with Chinese Communist Party, 38 f.; technique of attack on "right wing" and "left wing," monopolizing center, 38; summary of prewar legacy, 44 ff.; and nationalism, 44–45; and factionalism, 46; small leader-follower group, 46; new line and initial postwar programs, 48 ff.; positions and policies toward allied powers, 48–49, 54 f.; 4th Congress Report, 51–52; 5th Congress, 53–55; 6th Party Congress and policy adjustments to initial postwar policy, 57; 6th Congress program, 58 ff.; struggle between Mainstream and anti-Mainstream, 60, 63, 67; reactions to Cominform's attack on Nosaka's theory, 61, 62; leadership in united front, 66; attitude toward Sino-Soviet criticism, 67; assessment of results attained by "lovable" tactics, 67, 68 ff.; membership, 67–68, 72 *passim;* influence in labor movement in 1945–49, 68 ff.; mass organization, 68; failure to capture labor movement, 69–70; success in penetrating student-intellectual groups, 71; and "peace movement," 72; failure to form united front with Nihon Shakaitō, 73–74; united front with Rōnōtō, 76; compared with French and Italian Communist Parties, 75; foreign control and intervention, 76 ff.; compared with Yugoslav Communism, 78; JCP's Central Directorate established to take place of Central Committee and Politboro, 85; 4th Party Conference, 86; 6th National Conference, 92–94; 6th Party Conference, 99; shift in policy from extremism to legalism following 20th Party Congress in Soviet Union, 99 ff.; Central Committee of, 100; plenum resolution of 1956, praising 20th Party Congress of Soviet Union, 100; Central Committee of, 100 n

6; 7th Party Congress, 100, 100 n 6; 101 ff.; 1957 programs and Chinese influence, 101; basic issues at 7th Party Congress, 101 ff.; agrarian programs at 7th Party Congress, 103; Central Committee of, 103; presidium of, 104, 104 n 11; Central Committee, power and role limited by presidium, 104 n 11; 8th Party Congress and Sino-Soviet rift, 104; effects of Sino-Soviet cleavage on, 106 ff.; Mainstream group claims support from both CPSU and CCP, 106, 106 n 14; JCP's position on Sino-Soviet dispute at Central Committee of 1960, 107; position on Sino-Soviet dispute at Moscow conference of 81 parties, 108; 4th Plenum of, 108 n 18; 5th Plenum of, 108 n 18; 7th Party Congress of, 109; 8th Party Congress, 109; Central Committee of, 109; Politburo of, 110; 8th Party Congress attacked for being unrepresentative gathering by Kasuga, 110; shift of position over Sino-Soviet dispute, 111 ff.; 8th Party Congress of, 112–113; initially led anti-Ampō movement, 114; did not play commanding role in organization of anti-Ampō movement, 115; in Zengakuren and Hagerty Incident, 115 n 25; effect of anti-Ampō movement upon, 115, 115 n 26; strategy and tactics in peace movement, 116 ff.; control of Gensuikyō, 117; United Front Breau of, 117 n 27; Front Organization—Japan Peace Committee, 117 n 27; delivers protest to CPSU against resumption of nuclear tests, 120 n 32; its "neutralism" compared with that of JSP, 121; and Democratic Youth League, 126; organizations and tactics at Gensuikyō Conferences, 127 n 43; influence in labor unions, 129 ff.; strength in Sōhyō, 129 ff., 129 n 47; organization and tactics in controlling labor unions, 130 n

49; and Zengakuren, 132 ff.; Central Committee, 132 n 52; and peasant organizations, 134 n 54; and intellectuals, 134, 134 n 54, 135 n 54; leadership after 8th Party Congress, 136; neutral stance at 22nd CPSU Congress, 137; Mainstream faction defends itself against Kasuga group's attack, 139; congratulatory telegram sent to CPSU on 44th Bolshevik Revolution, 140; neutralist position on Sino-Soviet dispute, compared with that of North Korea and North Vietnam 140 n 8, 141 ff.; question of Albania, 162; silence on issues involving Sino-Soviet dispute, 143; emphasis on independence and equality in connection with Sino-Soviet dispute, 143, 143 n; leadership in 1962, 146; organization of, 146–148; new power center—China returnees, 146–147; 4th Plenum meeting of CC, 149; Propaganda, Education and Culture section, 149; and Soviet-Yugoslav rapproachement, 149; on Indian border dispute, 150–151; on Cuba, 151–152 *passim;* dissatisfaction with Khrushchev's foreign policies and ideological positions, 152; 5th Plenum meeting of CC, 154; last effort to hold neutralist position in Sino-Soviet dispute, 154–155; deteriorating relations with CPSU, 155; 6th Plenum meeting of CC, 158; shift from neutralist position over Sino-Soviet dispute, 161–171; views on nuclear test ban treaty, 161; positions for 9th Gensuikyō Conference, 162; Kasuga-Naitō group and CPSU, 162–163; trouble in Japan-Soviet Union Society, 164; 7th Plenum meeting of CC, 165–166; shift toward Chinese line, 166–167; CPSU charged with revisionism, 167; showdown conference with CPSU, 168–169; attack from CPSU, 169; action on Shiga's anti-party positions at JCP Presidium, 170; Central Committee announcement on Shiga, 170; power of Mainstream faction, 170; open break with CPSU, 171 ff.; spreading conflict with CPSU over interparty relations, 172 ff.; attempts to root out Soviet literature from Japan, 174; accused by CPSU of following Chinese line, 175; proclaimed independence from CPSU, 176–177; CPSU's interference in JCP's internal affairs, 177; counterattacked Soviet charges of JCP's subservience to CCP, 178–179; confrontation with CPSU over communist tactics and strategy, 179–195; rebuttal of CPSU's accusations, 186 ff.; attacked Soviet "economism," 186–188; criticized Soviet Europocentrism, 187–188; criticism of Soviet attempt to rehabilitate Yugoslavia, 189; attacked Cuba policies, 189; supported CCP against Soviet charges, 191; charges of modern revisionism against the CPSU, 195; position on minority rights within international Communist movement, 209; attacks upon CPSU, 209–210; following Chinese line, 210; influence of CCP—basic reasons analyzed, 211 ff.; paradox—nationalism vs. subservience to foreign power, 213; Maoism vs. structural reform, 213; 9th Party Congress, 214–229; basic policies and tactics as set forth by 9th Congress, 220–221; relations with other Asian Communist Parties, 225–226; membership and organization in 1964, 226–227; organizational tactics as outlined in 9th Congress Report, 226–228; Party security measures outlined in 9th Congress, 228; Mainstream leaders consolidated power via 9th Congress, 228; "independence and autonomy" stance sought, 228–229; position on united front with Socialists, 1965,

243; platform for House of Councillor elections, 1965, 243 n 58; attitude toward Socialist Party in 1965, 243–244 n 58; attitude toward Liberal Democratic Party in 1965, 243–244 n 58; attitude toward Democratic Socialist Party in 1965, 243–244 n 58; attitude toward Komeitō in 1965, 243–244 n 58; participation in 11th Gensuikyō World Conference, 248; 1965 soft line toward Socialist Party, 250–251, 251 n 72; emergence of Liberation Front "left" opposition, 256–258; major factions, 258; collaboration with Korean Workers Party, 258–260; new line of Dec. 1965 as revealed in Akahata, 259–260; relations with CCP shift, 260–261; renewed attacks on CPSU but support for Vietnam united front, 265–266; major mission to China, North Vietnam, North Korea—Spring 1966, 266–272; declined invitation to 23rd CPSU Congress, 271–272; important CC 4th Plenum meeting, April 1966, 272; new policy outlined, 272–277; alliance with other Asian Communist Parties, 274; Kasuga delegation visited Rumania, 276; talk with Grishin, Soviet labor leader, 278 n 101; growing alliance with KWP, 280–282; purge of pro-China elements and shift from Peking, 283–285; 10th Party Congress, 284–288; basic causes for shift from pro-Peking line, 288–291; parallels with Korean Communists, 289; membership of, 292; central organization, 292–293; leadership of, 293–294; socio-economic composition of, 294, 301–302; factors involved in joining Party, 294–295; gains in 1965 House of Councillors election, 298; foreign policy issues in 1965 House of Councillors election, 298–299; 1965 Tōkyō City Assembly election, 299–300; votes in prefectural and local elections, 300–301;

Shiga's group plans to form a new JCP against Yoyogi faction, 303; attacked Voice of Japan group, 303; castigated by CPSU as Chinese puppets, 304; Yoyogi faction attacked Liberation Front, 306; and intellectuals, 307; influence in small and medium business, 307; finances, 308 ff.; budget compared with that of JSP, DSP and LDP, 309; sources of funds, 309–310; influence of CCP through financial aid, 310; deteriorating relations with CCP, 310; opportunities for Communist growth, 328 ff.; reasons for failure of Japanese Communism, 330 ff.; postwar potentials for Communist growth, 334 ff.; and intellectuals, 338; failure in labor movement, 338–339; 1950 foreign interference in internal affairs analyzed, 342–343; shift of position in Sino-Soviet dispute summarized, 343; change in leadership and organizational techniques, 343–344; prospect for united front, 344 ff.; current position on "peaceful coexistence" and "American imperialism," 347; criticized CCP for blocking united front on Vietnam, 347; current ideological positions, 348–349; influence of CCP on, 349–350; shift of position in Sino-Soviet dispute, 351; aligned with North Korea, 352–353; use of nationalist appeal and militancy, compared to Pyongyang and Hanoi, 352; balance sheet, 353 f.

Japanese Communist Party (Leninist Faction): founded, 257

Japanese Communist Party (Liberation Front). See Liberation Front, Shida Shigeo

Japanese Communist Party Reconstruction Committee: organized in Ehime, 257

Japanese Communist Party (Voice of Japan). See Voice of Japan, Shiga Yoshio

Jen-min Jih-pao (People's Daily): attacked Nosaka and supported Cominform criticism, 64; urged unity within JCP, 95; Mao's speech on liberalization, 98 n 1; comment on open letter of Central Committee of CPSU, 98 n 1; hailed 7th Gensuikyō Conference, 120 n 31; attacked Yugoslavia, 149 n 21; editorial on Nehru, 150–151

Jichishō Senkyokyoku (The Local Autonomy Ministry Election Bureau): election statistics, 301 n 6

Jiyūminken undō (civil rights movement): as background for Japanese socialism, 15

Jiyū Minshutō. *See* Democratic Liberal Party

Jiyūtō (Liberal Party: pre-1945): left-wing elements in *Shakai Minshutō*, 2

Jiyūtō (Liberal Party: post-1945): JCP's assault in *Akahata*, 49; membership compared with JCP, 66

Johnson, Lyndon: JCP analysis, 192 n 96

Jonson: Latvian revolutionary, commercial attaché in Tōkyō Russian Embassy, hostile to Fukumotoism, 29

Kaganovich, L. M.: his purge as a reflection of Soviet instability, 88; ousted from Politburo and Central Committee of CPSU, 98

Kaihō (Emancipation): as outlet for radical socialists, 11

Kaizō: article on Katayama Sen, 6 n 11

Kakkin Kaigi (National Council for Peace and Against Nuclear Bombs): 1966 Conference, 277

Kakudō (Revolutionary Comrades Association): as JCP faction in National Railway Workers Union, 131

Kamiyama, Shigeo: factional background, 90; assessment of JCP 6th Party Conference, 100 n 4; attributed failure of united front to JCP Mainstream mistakes, 133 n

52; leader of anti-Mainstream faction after 8th Party Congress, 136; led pro-Soviet faction, 146; and CPSU, 154 n 37; account of his illness and intraparty affairs at 4th Plenum Central Committee meeting, 149 n 22; abstained from vote in JCP Central Committee's action on Shiga and Suzuki, 170; supported by Russians, 255; defeated by Nosaka in contest for House of Councillors seat in Tōkyō, 304; suspended from JCP membership and joined Shiga's Voice of Japan group, 302

Kanda, Asano: removed from head position in Women's Bureau of JCP, 171

K'ang Sheng: met Miyamoto mission, 200–207

Kansai faction: anti-Mainstream, international faction led by Shiga and Miyamoto, 63; attacked Mainstream leaders, 67; replaced Kuramae faction after Occupation, 90

Kasuga, Shōichi: apologized at Sōhyō 1964 convention for JCP policies, 230; JCP presidium member, 293 n 2

Kasuga, Shōjirō: his view on 1951 Thesis, 81 n 3; his view on JCP's interest in "structural reform", 87 n 10; his view on Chinese interference in JCP, 96; factional position, 90; as leader of structural reform group, urged discussion on Sino-Soviet dispute, 106–107; as structural reform advocate, 109; withdrew from JCP, 109 ff.; statement of defection, 110 ff.; his position compared with Soviet line, 111; leader in forming preparatory commission for a Socialist Reform Movement, 144; left Socialist Renovation group to form Unified Socialist League, 145; and Sino-Soviet dispute, 148–149

Katayama, Sen: lectured on British landlord system and European socialism at Shakaishugi Kenkyūkai ism at Shakaishugi Kenkyūkai meetings, 1 n 1; early ideological position, 6; supported Tōkyō streetcar strike, 6, 6 n 10; life in United States, 6 ff.; activities in 1914–1921, 6 ff.; contacts with S. J. Rutgers, 6; joined American Communist Party in 1919, 7; became a Marxist-Leninist, 7; helped to bring about a unification of American Communist Party, 7; Comintern mission to Mexico, 7; personality of, 8; contacts with Japanese radicals in New York, 11–12; and Palmer raids, 11; served as chairman of Far Eastern People's Congress, 7–9 passim; played a minor role in Moscow Comintern meeting on Japan, 29; gave Comintern instructions to Japanese students returning home from Moscow, 35

Katayama, Tetsu: headed Socialist-Democratic coalition government, 58

Katō, Kanjū: married Baron Ishimoto's wife, Shizue, 8; and Nihon Rōnōtō, 24

Katō, Shizue: contacts with Katayama Sen, 8

Katsube, Gen: Kasuga-Naitō faction member, approached by CPSU, 162, 163 n 51

Katsumata, Seiichi: defeated in SP elections, January 1966, 265

Kautsky K. J.: precursor to modern revisionists, according to JCP, 194, 194 n 99

Kawada, Kenji: JCP Presidium member, 292 n 2

Kawai, Etsuzō: attended Moscow meeting of Comintern on Japan, 29; blamed by Fukumoto for worsening relations with Bukharin, 30 n 42

Kawakami, Hajime: edited *Shakai Mondai Kenkyu,* 11; influence on Fukumoto Kazuo, 27; criticized by Fukumoto Kazuo, 27; joined Ōyama and Hososako in efforts to reactivate Nihon Rōnōtō, 35–36

Kawakami, Jōtarō: and Nihon Rōnōtō, 24; his faction within JSP and Sōhyō, 129; death, 264

Kawakami (Jōtarō) faction: position in 1966 Socialist Congress, 264–265

Kazama, Jōkichi: and 1931 Draft Thesis to build Party, 42; arrested in 1932, 43; recanted, together with Sano and Nabeyama, 43

Keio University: graduates entered Yuaikai, 5; Nosaka Sanzō attended, 4

Kennedy, John F.: impact of his announcement of resumption of nuclear tests on Gensuikyō, 122; naval blockade of Cuba, 150; position on Cuba blockade attacked by Akahata, 151 n 28; position on nuclear testing assaulted by Akahata, 161; statement on test ban treaty used by JCP to criticize USSR, 188; revisionists' "praise" of Kennedy administration attacked by JCP, 194 n 99

Kensetsu Dōmei (League of Builders): founded by students of Waseda University, 11

Khrushchev, Nikita: his secret speech denouncing Stalin at 20th CPSU Congress, 97; moved against domestic opponents, 98; lectured Chinese Communists on revolution, relations with U.S. in Peking, 104; attacked Chinese Communists, 105; his message to 8th Gensuikyō Conference, 125; public attack on Albania at 22nd CPSU Congress, 136; Nosaka's private views on, 142, 142 n 13; visit to U.S. and CCP's attack, 150 n 23; concession to American demands for evacuation of missiles reported in Akahata, 151 151 n 28; policies attacked by JCP over Cuban blockade, 152; credited for striking blows at American imperialism, in CPSU's letter to JCP, 184; his "capitulation" to American demands over Cuban crisis criticized by JCP, 189; attacked by JCP for his attempt to prevent China from acquiring nuclear weapons, 190; his views on obligations of advanced Communist society to emerging ones, 198–199; accused by CCP for capitulating to American thrusts over Cuban crisis, 205; as symbol of Soviet authoritarian attitude toward Communist world, 212; attacked by JCP in 9th Congress Report, 222–225. See also Khrushchevism

Khrushchevism: attacked by Akahata, 1965, 253, 255–256

Kiangsi: and Mao Tse-tung, 39

Kikunami Katsumi: JCP delegate to Warsaw World Peace Council, criticized by CPSU for opposing Soviet policy of peaceful coexistence, 185–186

Kim, Il-sŏng: neutral stance on Sino-Soviet dispute compared with Nosaka position, 140 n 7; absolute control over Korean Workers' Party, 153 n 33; met with Miyamoto mission, 267; praised by JCP, 273; foreign policies, 289

Kindai Shisō (Modern Thought): and Arahata Kanson, 3 n 5

Kishi, Nobusuke: became main target in anti-Ampō movement, 114 n 23; 115 n 24; resignation of Kishi government, 115

Kōan Jōhō (Report of the National Security Agency): article on JCP finances, 308, 308 n 14

Koizumi, Shinzō: introduced Communist Manifesto, 5

Kollontai, Alexandra: contacts with Katayama Sen, 7

Komatsu, Yūichirō: succeeded Shiino Etsuo as chairman of Directorate, 93

Komeitō: as analyzed by JCP in 9th Party Congress Report, 217; analyzed by JCP 10th Party Congress, 286; in 1965 Tōkyō City Assembly election, 299–300

Kondō, Eizō: contacts with Katayama Sen, 8; returned to Japan in 1919, 9; on staff of Ōsugi Sakae's

Rōdō Undō, 12; and Japanese-American cultural ties, 14; close ties with Yamakawa Hitoshi, 15; role in founding Japanese Communist Party, 16; and Gyōmin Kyōsantō, 17; end of Communist activities, 17, 18 *passim*

Konno, Yojirō: arrested in 1932, 43; Mainstream member in Politburo after Nosaka issue, 67; reemerged into open, prepared to assume leadership, 94; removed from Central Committee, 103; JCP Presidium (alternate) member, 293 n 2, 3

Korean War: 1951 Thesis and CPSU, 81 n 2; its end and JCP's tactics against U.S. forces in Japan, 88; Chinese claim that only Soviet Union profited, 260

Korean Workers' Party: *Rodong Shinmun* editorial of December 1965 outlining basic KWP policies, 258–259; meetings with Miyamoto mission, 267–268; and JCP, 274; upheld Gensuikyō, 280; championed "independence," 281–282 nn 109, 110, 111; parallels with JCP, 289

Koreans: Korean minority in Japan under Communist influence, 72; as JCP members, 295, 302. *See also* Korean War, Korean Workers' Party, North Korea, and Republic of Korea

Kōtō Gakkō Remmei (Higher School Alliance): organized as a result of Shinjiakai efforts, 26

Kotoku, Denjirō (Shūsui): advocated direct action of workers, 2; symbolized leftward trend of socialist movement, 2; contacts with IWW, 2; in United States, 2; involvement in Great Treason Case of 1910, 4; resolution for direct action defeated at Nihon Shakaitō convention, 3

Kozlov, F.: defense of democratic centralism quoted by Nosaka to counter Kasuga's attack, 139

Kōzō Kaikaku (Structural Reform):

monthly organ published by Unified Socialist League, 145

Kropotkin, Peter: influence on radical intellectuals, 5; discussed at Shinjinkai meeting, 11

Kuboyama, Aiichi: ceremonies on anniversary of death, 231

Kudō, Akira: member of Spring 1966 Miyamoto mission, 266

Kuo, Mo-jo: attack on test ban treaty at 9th Gensuikyō Conference, 159; received Gensuikyō dissidents, 279; "self-criticism" and its impact on Japanese left intellectuals, 307

Kuomintang: alliance with Chinese Communist Party, 38

Kun, Béla: played role in writing 1927 Thesis, 29

Kurahara, Koreto: JCP Presidium member, 293 n 2; member of Spring 1966 Miyamoto mission, 266

Kuramae faction: origins and significance: 90

Kyōsantō: *see* Japanese Communist Party

Labor movement: Kōtoku's proposal for organized workers, 2; first-generation worker class created, 3; anarcho-syndicalist influence after Russian revolution, 6; shift to left, 9; journals, 11; decline, 13; origins of Sōdōmei, 14; failure of anarcho-syndicalism, 13; increase of Communist influence, 14; influence of Russian revolution, 17; impact of Yamakawa's article on labor movement, 21; discussed at Profintern, 1925, 23; split of Sōdōmei, 23; leaders in Nihon Rōnōtō, 24; Communist influence through students, 26; role in revolution, as defined by Rōnō-ha, 32; attempts to establish underground successor to Nihon Rōdō Hyōgikai, 36 f.; *Rōdō Shimbun—Zenkyō* advocated need to learn from Russian labor unions, 37; Communist influence in, 68–69; democratization movement, 69; toward economic unionism after February 1 Strike, 70; role of working class in "structural reform" theory, 102; Togliatti's structural reform and its impact on JCP, 109; Sōhyō —its background, 128 ff.; government unions and Communist influence, 129 f.; nongovernmental unions, 130 f.; under non-communist control after 1960, 132; analysis of JCP 9th Party Congress, 219, 227; JCP influence in 1965, 307; postwar potential for Communist support, 335; character of Japanese working class, 329–330; failure of JCP to gain in unions analyzed, 338–339. *See also* Domei Kaigi, Hyōgikai, Sōhyō, Sōdōmei

Labor Unions. *See* Domei Kaigi, Hyōgikai, Labor movement, Sōdōmei, Sōhyō

Landlords; target of assault at 4th JCP Congress, 50, 51 *passim. See also* Farmers

Laos: representatives at Kakkin Kaigi Conference, 277

Lassalle, Ferdinand: influence on Shakaishugi Kenkyūkai, 1

Leadership: Japanese conservative elite in modernization, 332 f.

Lenin, Nikolai: served as basis for Katayama's discussion group in New York, 8; discussed at Shinjinkai meeting, 11; second-generation Japanese radicals' road to socialism through, 15; Fukumoto borrowed theory of "separation and unity" from, 28; quoted to defend CPSU's position on peaceful coexistence, 186; used by JCP to criticize Soviet's short-range gain in signing nuclear test ban treaty, 191; quoted in JCP's attack on Soviet rapprochement with "American imperialism," 193 n 98; used by JCP to identify modern revisionists, including CPSU, with Kautskyism, 194, 194 n 99; theories on peasants utilized in 9th JCP Congress Report, 219–220

Lenin Peace Prize; awarded to Yasui Kaoru, 117 n 27; awarded to Ōta Kaoru, 249, 249 n 69

Leninism: as publication of Liberation Front, 256

Leningrad International Youth League Congress: attended by Zengakuren, 128

Liaison Committee of the Three Atomic-Victim Prefectures: origin and purpose, 231

Liao Ch'eng-chih: received Gensuikyō dissidents, 279; met with Miyamoto mission, 267

Li, Li-san: compared to Fukumoto for being leftist by Comintern, 39

Liberal Democratic Party: factional rivalries at time of anti-Ampō movement, 116; as analyzed by JCP in 9th Party Congress Report, 216; participated in Kakkin Kaigi Conference, 277; assaulted by JCP 10th Party Congress, 285–286; in 1965 House of Councillors election, 298; 299–300

Liberation Front: established, 256; organization and program, 256–258; denounced JCP policy shift, 266

Liberation Front faction: attacked by JCP (Yoyogi), 275, 277; criticized for upholding Peking line by *Akahata*, 281; attacked by JCP 10th Party Congress, 285; "left-deviationists" worry JCP Mainstream, 304–305; criticized by Yoyogi faction, 306

Liebknecht, Karl: discussed at Shinjinkai meeting, 11

Liu Ning-i: speech to 10th Gensuikyō World Conference, 233 n 34, 234; participated in 11th Gensuikyō World Conference, 248–249; met Miyamoto mission, 266–267; refused entry into Japan, 278; received Gensuikyō dissidents and delivered speech, 279, 279 n 103

Liu, Shao-ch'i: speech at Conference on Trade Unions of Asia and Oceania in 1949, 64, 65 f.; gave account

of Sino-Soviet dispute to Hakamada and Mainstream leaders, 106
n 15; met with Miyamoto mission,
267
Lin, Piao: Soviet reference to Lin's
1965 speech, 270 n 90
Lovestone, Jay: met Sōhyō leaders in
Tōkyō, 239; letter to Iwai, 239–240
Luxemburg, Rosa: discussed at Shinjinkai meeting, 11

Maeno, Ryō: approached by CPSU,
as charged by JCP, 162, 163 n 51
Malaya: referred by Liu Shao-ch'i as
place for guerrilla warfare, 65
Malaysia: representatives at Kakkin
Kaigi Conference, 277
Malatesta, Errico: influence on radical
intellectuals, 5, 6
Malenkov, Georgii M.: his ouster reflective of Soviet instability in world
Communist movement, 88; purged
from Politburo and Central Committee of CPSU, 98
Maniwa, Suekichi: contacts with
Katayama Sen, 7; delegate to First
Congress of Comintern, 8, 9; leader
in establishing Communist Bureau
in 1928, 35; arrested in 1929, 40
Mao, Tse-tung: and Nosaka Sanzō,
84; delivered "Let One Hundred
Flowers Bloom" speech, 98; rumors
of apology for his Party's role in
1950–1951 events, 108 n 18; sent
message to Nosaka on his 70th
birthday, 147; JCP acceptance of
Mao's theories on use of peasants,
219–220; greetings to the Gensuikyō
10th World Conference, 234; role
assessed by JCP, 273. See also
Maoism
Maoism: influence on 1951 Thesis, 81,
84; Soviet definition of, 205
Marx, Karl: influence on Shakaishugi
Kenkyūkai, 1; influence of Communist Manifesto on Nosaka Sanzō,
7; served as basis for Katayama's
discussion group in New York, 8;
discussed at Shinjinkai meeting, 11;

second-generation Japanese radicals
started with, 15. See also Marxism
Marxism: first introduced into Japan,
1, 10; and late Meiji socialist movement, 1; German influence, 16; as
overseas movement, 6; Japanese
intellectuals found emotional and
intellectual stimulus in, 19; JCP
sought to apply 19th century Marxism to advanced society, 21; division of Japanese proletarian parties,
1925–1926, 24–25; impact on
Socialists, 74; influence on JSP regarding its position on "neutralism," 121; analysis of JCP 9th Party
Congress, 224–225; as publication of
Ehime left Communists, 257; appeal to Japanese intellectuals, 329;
challenged by young Japanese intellectuals, 337; persistent influence
of left Marxism on JSP's ideological position, 348–349; shift from
orthodoxy to revisionism in JSP,
349–350. See also Communism
Marxism-Leninism Institute: Shiga
visited Soviet Union as guest of,
303
Marxist Student League: old Mainstream force within Zengakuren,
306
Marx-Lenin Institute, Peking: young
cadres received training at, 93
Marxshugi (Marxism): a theoretical
journal of new JCP, 25; dominated
by student Marxists, 26; carried
Fukumoto article in every issue
since 1924, 27; 1927 Thesis appeared in, 31; run by Fukumotoists, 32
Marxishugi no Hata no Moto ni
(Under the Banner of Marxism):
Fukumoto Kazuo set forth his views
in, 27
Mass line: JCP use of in 9th Party
Congress Report, 219
Mass media: on Soviet atmospheric
nuclear test in Siberia, 125. See
also Press
Matsumoto, Noboru: with Kazama

Jōkichi sought to rebuilt JCP in 1931, 42

Matsumoto, Shichirō: attempted to "reform" Japan-Soviet Society, 254–255

Matsumoto, Saneki: removed from Central Committee, 103

Matsushima, Harushige: JCP Presidium member, 293 n 2

Matsushita, Masatoshi: presided over Kakkin Kaigi Conference, 277

Meany, George: led U.S. labor delegation to Japan, 238–239

Mexico: Katayama undertakes Comintern mission to, 7

Mihajlov, Mihajlo: impact of his arrest on Japanese intellectuals, 338

Mikoyan, Anastas I.: sat in Japanese Diet gallery on occasion of voting on nuclear test ban treaty, 170

Militarism: JCP's record with respect to, 73

Ministry of Commerce and Industry Workers: under Communist influence, 130, 130 n 49

Ministry of Construction Workers: under Communist influence, 129

Ministry of Labor Workers: under Communist influence, 130, 130 n 49

Ministry of Transportation Workers: under Communist influence, 130, 130 n 49

Minrōren (Democratic Labor League): formed in 1948, 69

Minseitō (Democratic Party): in 1928 election, 34

Mitamura, Shirō: defected from Communism, 43

Mitin, M. B.: Soviet delegate to 8th Gensuikyō Conference, 125; speech at 8th Gensuikyō Conference transmitted through mass media, 126

Miyahara, Toshio: ousted from JCP over Cominform's criticism of Nosaka, 63

Miyamoto, Kenji: served as Chairman of Party Central Committee after arrest of Noro Eitarō, 43; spoke at 5th Party Congress, 54 n 7; led

Anti-Mainstream international faction over issue of Cominform's criticism, 63; JCP's veiled attack on SCAP in Zenei, 58 n 10; retained in Politburo after struggle over "Nosaka's theory," 67; attacked Mainstream leaders at Central Committee meeting of 1950, 67; factional background, 90; attacked by Mainstream as "Trotskyite," 91; assumed compromiser role, 94; shifted position by deserting international faction and becoming a leader in new Mainstream faction, 96; Chinese plan to make him Secretary-General of JCP rumored, 96; star on rise, 100; drafted new JCP program for 7th Party Congress, 100; close contacts with Chinese Communists, 101 n 7; assumed post of Secretary General, 104; went to Peking and Moscow to attend celebrations, 107; praised Hoxha and Albanian Workers Party, 107–108, 108 n 18; reported on trip to Soviet Union, China, and North Korea at 5th plenum of JCP, 108 n 18; responded to Suslov's inquiries, showing resentment against "big power chauvinism," 109; led Mainstream group after 7th Party Congress, 109; led faction dominating JCP after 8th Congress, 136; championed "neutral" line, 140 n 8; Secretary General, heading "neutral" faction, 146; neutralist policy of JCP attributed to, 155 n 38; conflict with Kamiyama at 4th Plenum Central Committee of JCP, 149 n 22; returned to Japan to convene Central Committee meeting on expulsion of Shiga, 170; denounced Shiga's "Voice of Japan Comrades Society," 171; consolidated power in JCP, 228; expressed support for Sasaki Kōzō position, 247; stated frustrations over united front difficulties, 251 n 72; attacked by Liberation Front Group, 257–

258; mission to Asian Communist states, Spring 1966, 266–272; 10th Party Congress climaxed rise to power, 285; role in JCP after 1955, 288–289; standing member of Executive Committee of JCP presidium, Secretary General of JCP, 293, 293 n 2

Mizunuma, Kūma: attempted to maintain anarchist influence in labor and intellectual movements, 14

Molotov, Vyacheslav M.: his post-Stalin purge, 88; ousted from Politburo and Central Committee of CPSU, 98; CPSU's accusations of Chinese support of anti-party faction headed by, 201

Mongolia: an issue in the Sino-Soviet dispute, 205; participated in Hiroshima International Conference of 1964, 235; in Gensuikin 1965 Conference, 249; Shiga exchanged messages with, 303

Morigasaki Conference: decision to dissolve JCP, 22

Moritaki, Ichirō: made keynote report to Hiroshima-Nagasaki Conference of 1964, 234–235; sponsored Gensuikin, 245–246

Moscow Conference of Eighty-one Parties: JCP position for unity, 105, 108

Moscow Conference of March 1964: analysis by JCP in 9th Congress Report, 225

Moscow Congress for General Disarmament and Peace: in 1962, 148

Moscow Declaration of 1957: issued at International Conference of Communist Parties, 98; JCP's support at 7th Party Congress, 103; sought by JCP as basis for Sino-Soviet agreement, 137–139; issued as unanimous decision of parties assembled, 196

Moscow Statement of 1960: 105–106; sought by JCP as basis for Sino-Soviet agreement, 137–139; supported by *Akahata,* 152; used by

JCP to criticize Yugoslavian "revisionists," 189 n 93

Moscow Treaty. *See* Nuclear test ban treaty

Murai, Tomoyoshi: on Marx at Shakaishugi Kenkyūkai meeting, 1 n 1

Murphy, J. T.: played role in writing 1927 Thesis on JCP, 29

Musan Taishūtō (Proletarian Mass Party): formed by Rōnō-ha with Suzuki Mosaburō as Secretary General, 35

Musansha Shimbun - (*Proletarian News*): began publication in 1925, 25; dominated by student Marxists, 26; 1927 Thesis published in, 31

Mutual Security Treaty: struggle over, 114 ff.; 5th Gensuikyō meeting issue, 117–118 n 28; JCP 9th Congress position on, 221; Sōhyō opposition in 1965, 244–245; JCP demand for united front in 1965, 245

Mututantrie, Laksen: assaulted pro-JCP delegations to Gensuikyō 12th World Congress, 280

Nabeyama, Sadachika: formed a liaison with Fukumoto Kazuo, 29; informed Bukharin of problems with Fukumotoism, 29; became leader of 2nd JCP, 31; recanted Communism, 43

Nagasaki Conference Against Atomic and Hydrogen Bombs: 127, 127 n 44. *See also* Gensuikyō, Gensuikin, Kakkin Kaigi

Naigai Hyōron (*Internal-External Review*): illegal JCP journal, 85

Naitō, Tomochika: views on 1951 Thesis, 81 n 3; elected to Central Committee, 103; noticed Sino-Soviet disagreement in *Jen-min Jih-pao,* 106 n 13; leader in forming Preparatory Commission for a Socialist Reform Movement, 144

Nakanishi, Atsushi: ousted from JCP over Cominform's criticism of Nosaka, 63

Nakanishi, Kō: his position on revolution attacked by Nosaka, 59; ousted because of his support of Cominform's criticism of Nosaka, 63; factional affiliations, 90

Nakano, Shigeharu: forced JCP to pay homage to CPSU, 154 n 37; voted against JCP decision to expel Shiga and Suzuki, 170; suspended from JCP membership, 302

Nakao, Katsuō: attended Moscow meeting of Comintern on Japan, 29; ideological leader of Hyōgikai, attended Yoshiki meeting for reestablishing second JCP, 28

Namba, Hideo: helped reorganize JCP after mass arrests of 1928, 34

Narita, Tomomi: headed Socialist delegation to Russia, 1964, 232; explained Socialist foreign policy, 1966, 263–264; reelected SP Secretary, January 1966, 265

National Committee for Buraku Liberation: founded in 1926, inherited prewar Suiheisha (Levellers' Association), 134 n 54

National Council for Peace and Against Nuclear Bombs. See Kakkin Kaigi

National Council in Opposition to Military Bases: Socialist influence and Communist influence at local level, 123 n 36

National Council in Opposition to the Security Treaty and for the Safeguarding of Peace and Democracy: offspring of united front organization during anti-treaty movement, used by JCP to strengthen united front, 122, 122 n 35, 123 n 36

National Customs Workers: under Communist influence, 130, 130 n 49

National Electric and Communications Workers: Sōhyō Mainstream federation under Communist influence, 131, 132 n 51

National Electric Workers: under Communist control: 130, 130 n 49

National Federation of Auto Transport Workers: representative of WFTU in Japan, 129 n 48; under Communist influence, 131, 131 n 50

National Federation of Printers and Publication Workers: under Communist influence, 131

National Federation of Regional Women's Organizations: protests at 7th Gensuikyō Conference, 119

National liberation movements: Soviet role in supporting defended in CPSU's letter to JCP, 179–180; CPSU attacked by JCP for neglecting, 194; JCP's support for, 210; JCP 9th Congress pronouncement, 215–216; 220–221, 224; JCP's support of, 347

National Metal Workers Labor Unions: under Communist influence, 131

National Ministry of Justice Workers: under Communist influence, 130, 130 n 49

National Movement for the Return of Okinawa: influence of JCP on, 123 n 36

National People's Council for the Settlement of the Okinawan Problem: activated to reinforce United Front by JCP, 122, 123, 123 n 36

National Pulp Industry Workers: under Communist influence, 131, 131 n 50

National Railway Workers Union: Communist factors in, 131

National socialism: and Sano-Nabeyama recantations, 43

National Tax Commission Workers: under Communist influence, split, 130, 130 n 49

Nationalism: traditional thought in Shakaishugi Kyōkai, 2; and pre-1945 JCP, 21; prewar JCP unable to capture, 44; and new posture of JCP, 53; national liberation wars in southeast Asia emphasized by Liu Shao-ch'i, 65; in anti-Ampō movement, 114–116; principles of JCP used to attack CPSU, 168; CPSU charged JCP catering to nationalist and chauvinist sentiments under Chinese influence, 173; use of Communism for nation building, 195; Soviet domination and control of international Communist movement challenged, 196; triumph over Communism, 206; and new 1966 JCP policy, 273–276; as expressed in 10th JCP Congress, 287–288; JCP's new weapon for counterattacking dissident groups, 305; personified in Emperor, 331; comparison of national Communism and national socialism suggested, 340; appeal of Chinese revolutionary model to Japanese nationalism, 350–351

Nearing, Scott: influence on Fukumoto Kazuo, 27

Nehru, Jawaharlal: Chinese attack upon him supported by JCP, 150, 150 n 23, 151; attacked as tool of "American imperialism," 150; compared to Chiang Kai-shek and Kuomintang, 151

Nemoto, Hiroshi: reported on his Soviet trip, 128 n 45; headed Central Executive Committee of Zengakuren, 133 n 53

Neutralism: advocated by structural reformists, 103; represented by JSP at 7th Gensuikyō Conference, 119; as practiced by JCP, 141–153 passim; JCP's position over Sino-Soviet dispute in disarray, 153–155 passim; policy failure of JCP in Sino-Soviet dispute, 161 ff.; collapse of JCP position in Sino-Soviet dispute, 351–352

New Japan Literary Society: abandoned by JCP, 307

New Japan Women's Society: JCP connections, 123 n 36; founded in 1962 under JCP aegis, 135 n 53; as JCP front organization, 226

Nihon Kyōsantō; See Japanese Communist Party

Nihon Minshu Seinen Dōmei (Japan Democratic Youth League); most significant JCP youth organization, 134 n 53

Nihon Nōmintō (Japan Farmers' Party): moderate to conservative in politics, 24; and 1928 election, 33–34

Nihon Rōdō Hyōgikai (Labor Union Council of Japan): split from Sōdōmei and established, 23; served as vehicle for JCP between 1925 and 1928, 23; dissolved by government, 23; student Marxists' influence in, 26; dissolution of, 34

Nihon Rōdō Kumiai Zenkoku Kyōgikai (National Council of Japanese Labor Unions): leadership and program, 36–37; established in 1928, 36; 1929 arrests, 1930 election, 41; took radical action in accordance with Comintern instructions, 41; views of its own function—extremism, 38

Nihon Rōnōtō (Japan Labor-Farmer Party): represented center position, 24; control by student Marxists, 26; and 1928 election, 33; dissolved by government order, 34

Nihon Shakaitō (Japan Socialist Party): general convention (1907) of, 2; compromise resolution passed in 1907, 3; split of socialist movement, 3; influence of Rōnō ideology on, 33. For post-1945 era, see Socialist Party

Niijima Junryo: supported pro-China cause, 276–277

1927 Thesis: criticized Yamakawaism and Fukumotoism, 29 ff.; approved at Central Committee of JCP in Ibaraki in 1927, 31

1931 Draft Thesis: and Kazama Jōkichi, 42; Comintern displeased with, 42

1932 Thesis: upheld by postwar JCP, 56; stood as basic document for JCP until 1946, 42

1951 Thesis: fundamental changes mark 1951 Thesis, 80–81; amalgam of Stalinism and mature Maoism, 81; drafted by Tokuda under influence from CPSU and CCP, 80–82; compared with 1946 program, 81–82; JCP's land programs modeled after CCP, 84; declared not fitting for changed situation at 7th plenary meeting of Central Committee, 100; replaced at 8th Party Congress, 112; adopted by Liberation Front Group, 257–258

1951 Draft Program: Stalin blamed by CPSU for participation in, 175

Nishi, Masao: helped Yamakawa and his wife with publication, 20 n 27

Nishikawa, Yoshihiko: elected to Central Committee, 103

Nishizawa, Ryūji: removed from Central Committee, 103; purged by JCP as pro-Peking, 285

Nishizawa, Tomio: JCP Presidium member (alternate), 293 n 2

Noro, Eitarō: arrest of, 43

North Korea: its existence saved by Communist China, 88; second front advocated by international faction to aid North Korean army, 92 n 12; position on Sino-Soviet dispute at Moscow Conference of 81 Parties, 108; support from Socialists, 251; praise and evaluation from JCP, 273; delegates upheld Gensuikyō, 270 n 102; JCP aligned with, 352–353. See also Korean Workers' Party, Rodong Shinmun

North Vietnam: Sōhyō support after bombing, 242–243; support from Socialists, 251. See also Vietnamese Workers' Party

Northeast Asia Military Alliance: JCP opposed creation of, 116; JCP 9th Congress position on, 221

Nosaka, Sanzō: boyhood and youth, 4 f; influenced by IWW publications, 4; influenced by Edward Bellamy's Looking Backward, 4; appearance and traits of early life described by Suzuki Bunji, 4 n 7; as social reformer, 4–5; shifted to Marxism, 4–5; read Communist Manifesto, 5; attended Far Eastern People's Conference, 5 n 9; activities in England and Russia, 7, 7 n 9; joined British Communist Party in 1920, 5, 5 n 9; gave Japanese students in Moscow Comintern instructions, 35; released from prison, reached Moscow in 1931, 42; played role in preparing 1932 Thesis in Moscow, 42, 56; his report on Party Declaration at 5th Party Congress, 54, 54 n 7; took leading role in JCP policy formation, 53; influence from Yenan, 53; speech at 6th Party Congress, 57 n 8; reported to 6th Congress on "revolution," 59 f.; defended by JCP over Cominform's attack, 63, 67; relations with Mao Tse-tung, 64; issued self-criticism, 67; called for "Japanization" of Marxism-Leninism, 77; his "lovable" position compared with Chou En-lai's peace offensive at Bandung, 88; factional background, 90; attacked by international faction, 91; 1951 Thesis compiled after consultations in Moscow and Peking, 95; reemerged victorious, 94; mentioned substantial Chinese influence, according to Kasuga Shōjirō, 96; returned to public after long exile, 99; delivered political report to Central Committee at 7th Party Congress, 100; as Mainstream leader after 7th Party Congress, 109; called for unity of international Communist movement at 22nd CPSU Congress, 136–137; cautious stand on Sino-Soviet dispute, 138–139; views of Albania and Yugoslavia, 141 n 12; position on de-Stalinization, 162 n 13; views on Khrushchev and his actions, 142, 142 n 13; on breakdown of monolithic Soviet domination, 143 n 14; ties with Hakamada, 146; referred to as Emperor, 146; 70th birthday and messages from Communist world, 147; attacked American culture and "imperialism," 148; talks with Zhukov, 163; denounced Shiga's "Voice of Japan Comrades Society," 171; attacked Peking in Gensuikyō welcome speech, 279 n 102; role minimized in JCP 10th Party Congress, 287; Party posts, 293, 293 nn 2, 3; defeated Kamiyama in contest for House of Councillors seat in Tōkyō, 304

Nuclear test ban treaty: Moscow treaty discussed by *Akahata*, 161; JCP's attack on CPSU-sponsored treaty, 164; JCP's non-support at 7th plenum Central Committee meeting, 166; role in Japanese Diet, 169; supported by Shiga, 170–171; signed, 158; CPSU's criticism of JCP's opposition to nuclear test ban treaty, 180 ff.; JCP's attack on USSR's role in nuclear test ban treaty, 189 ff.; JCP criticized Soviet arguments for, 190; first step in U.S.-USSR rapprochement, JCP claimed, 192–193; Chinese accusations of Soviet "betrayal," 205; attitude of JCP 9th Congress toward, 223; supported by Gensuikin Conference, 236

Nuclear testing: Soviet test defended by Nosaka, 139; Bikini incident and Gensuikyō Conference, 156; Sōhyō reaction to first Chinese atomic test, 1964, 237. *See also* Nuclear Test Ban Treaty

Nuclear war: attitude of JCP at 9th Congress, 223

Nuclear weapons: JCP's support for Communist camp to develop its own nuclear capacity, 210

Ōfuchi, Seiki: JCP Presidium member (alternate), 293 n 2

Ogasawara: U.S. control opposed by JCP at 7th Party Congress, 103; described in 1961 program at 8th Party Congress, 112

Oka, Masayoshi: member of Spring 1966 Miyamoto mission, 266; "ex-

plained" JCP new policies toward Peking, 284 n 113; Party posts, 293, 293 nn 2, 3

Okamoto, Hiroyuki: JCP Secretariat member, 293 n 3

Okinawa: U.S. control, opposed by JCP at 7th Party Congress, 103; described in 1961 program at 8th Party Congress, 112; one of "peace" issues developed by JCP, 116; issue at 2nd and 4th Gensuikyō meetings, 118 n 28; issue raised in JCP's attack on U.S. over Cuban blockade, 151; American control attacked by JCP, 156; JCP 9th Congress position on, 221; attitude of Sōhyō toward, 240

Ōsaka: anti-Mainstream group draws strength from, 109

Ōsugi, Sakae: and socialist movement during World War I, 3, 3 n 5; introduced French syndicalism, 10; attacked Lenin government, 12; contacts with Koreans, 19; reissued *Rōdō undō*, 20; ties with Comintern, 12

Ōta, Kaoru: protested Soviet nuclear tests, 122 n 34; regularly reelected President of Sōhyō, 128; reelected Sōhyō Chairman, 1964, 231; met Meany delegation in Tokyo, 239; letter to Meany, 240–242; cable to Hanoi after bombing, 242–243; shared platform with JCP in 1965, 245; received Lenin Peace Prize, 249, 249 n 69

Ōta-Iwai line: dominated Sōhyō, 128–129

Outcast community: analysis of in JCP 9th Party Congress Report, 220; and CCP, 295

Outer Mongolia: *see* Mongolia

Ōyama, Ikuo: attempted to reactivate Labor-Farmer Party, 35–36

Pa Chin: Chinese delegate to 8th Gensuikyō Conference, 125

Paris: 1949 First Conference for Defense of Peace held in, 72

Parliamentarism: marked (late) Meiji

socialist movement, 1; programs of Shakai Minshutō, 2; use by Communists, 13; criticized by Yamakawa in *Zenei*, 20; supported by moderates, and by center partially, 24; Nosaka on "peaceful revolution," 56; role redefined by structural reformists, 102–103; "tyranny of majority" became prominent aspect of anti-Ampō movement, 115 n 24; attitude of JCP at 9th Party Congress, 224; Japanese intellectuals disillusioned with, 329

Palmer Raids: Katayama Sen went into hiding in New Jersey, 7

Peace: as a tactic in 1951 Thesis, 83; struggle for world peace and peaceful coexistence adocated at 7th Party Congress of JCP, 103; JCP's utilization as tactic for united front after 8th Party Congress, 114; issue in JCP's strategy, 116 ff.; JCP and 9th Gensuikyō Conference, 156–163; JCP's position on "peaceful coexistence" criticized by CPSU, 183 ff.; JCP's position on peaceful coexistence summarized, 191 ff; Soviet position on peaceful coexistence vs. Chinese one, 202 ff.; JCP's position of subordinating peaceful coexistence to struggle against American imperialism, 210; JCP 9th Congress position on, 221, 224; JCP's position on "peaceful coexistence" and its policy toward "American imperialism," 347. *See also* Gensuiken, Gensuikyō, Kakkin Kaig˙

Peace and Independence: as organ of Liberation Front group, 258

Peace Preservation Law: amendments to, 40

Peasant. *See* Farmers

Peking: conference of Trade Unions of Asia and Oceania held at, 64; JCP leaders flee into exile in Peking after Cominform attack, 93; visited by Khrushchev, 104

Peking Radio: endorsed 1951 Thesis, 95

People's Republic of China: Mutual defense pact with Soviet Union in 1950, 64; Chinese revolution as a model for Asia, advocated by Liu Shao-ch'i, 65; diplomatic offensive at Bandung in 1955, 88; growing influence in Asia, 88; represented world "peace force" against U.S. at 6th Party Conference, 89 n 11; involvement in East European troubles, 98; dispute with Soviet Union reflected in debate at JCP's 7th Party Congress, 101; Japanese recognition demanded at 6th Gensuikyō meeting, 118 n 28; position on 9th Gensuikyō Conference, 159–160; governed by first-generation revolutionaries, compared to Soviet Union, 206; "cultural revolution" shocked Japanese literary circles, 307. *See also* Chinese Communist Party

People's Republic of Mongolia. *See* Mongolia

P'eng Chen: met Miyamoto mission, 266–267

Philippines: listed by Liu Shao-ch'i as place for guerrilla warfare, 65; representatives at Kakkin Kaigi Conference, 277

PKI: JCP contacts with, 225–226; and JCP, 274; its fate affecting JCP, 290. *See also* Aidit, Indonesia

Police: police suppression of JCP described by CPSU, 172; control of Communists, 334

Politburo: attacked by Shiga for lack of self-criticism over Cominform assaults, 91

Political Funds Registration Act: 308

Port Construction Workers: under Communist influence, 130, 130 n 49

Potsdam Treaty: Nosaka's insistence on enforcing treaty, 59

Poznan: workers' riots occurred in, 97

Prague: First World Conference for Defense of Peace, 1949, held in, 72

Pravda: speech by Liu Shao-ch'i at Conference on Trade Unions of Asia and Oceania appeared in, 64

n 23; endorsed 1951 Thesis, 95; published Nosaka's article devoted to attacks on Ikeda and Kasuga, 148; Zhukov's attack on JCP over test ban treaty, 163; supported Shiga faction and attacked Mainstream JCP leaders, 171; supported Shiga's Voice of Japan group, 303

Preparatory Commission for Socialist Reform Movement: formed with Kasuga and Naito as leaders, 144

Press: role in anti-Ampō movement, 114 n 24. See also Mass Media

Problems of Peace and Socialism: shift away from Peking line, 284

Profintern: discussed Japanese labor movement and passed resolution on unity of labor, 23; policies on Japan led JCP to "left extremism," 37; critical of Zenkyō policy, 41

Prokhorov, Vasily I.: defense of Voice of Japan group and attack on JCP, 303

Proletarian Youth League: to be brought under JCP, 22; dissolution of, 34

Public opinion: Asahi Shimbun poll on political parties, 115

Public Safety Investigation Bureau (Kōan Chōsachō): survey of Communist strength in Sōhyō, 129 n 47

Radio Moscow: supported Shiga faction and criticized JCP Mainstream leaders, 171; carried account of Shiga's trip to Soviet Union, 303 n 9

Red International of Trade-Unions. See Profintern

Republic of Korea: relations with Japan developed by JCP as issue, 116; diplomatic negotiation with Japan raised by JCP, 151; talks with Japan under attack by JCP, 156; JCP 9th Congress position on, 221; Sōhyō opposition to Korean treaty, 244

Revisionism: JCP 9th Congress atti-

tude toward, 222–225; attacked by Akahata, 255–256; position of the Korean Communists in December 1965, 258–259; renewed JCP attacks in 1966, 265–266, 268; denunciations in the Pyongyang Communique of March 1966, 268

Revolution: JCP's arguments about one-stage and two-stage process of, 21; one-stage revolution advocated by Rōnō-ha, 32; "peaceful" revolution espoused at 5th Party Congress, 56; JCP's basic position during Occupation: two-stage, 55 ff.; "peaceful" revolution defined and defended by Nosaka at 6th Party Congress, 60; "peaceful revolution" evaluated by JCP, 75–76; from "bourgeois-democratic revolution" to "national-liberation democratic government" in 1951 Thesis, 82; peaceful parliamentary program discussed at 7th plenary meeting of Central Committee, 100; Mainstream's "people's democratic revolution" vs. anti-Mainstream's "democratic bourgeois revolution" at 7th Party Congress, 101; different interpretations at 7th Party Congress, 101 n 8; Japan compared with Chinese model, 113; JCP and CCP positions on revolution attacked by CPSU, 183; CCP uses Confucian heritage to challenge Soviet domination, 198; attitude of JCP at 9th Party Congress, 224; JCP's position on, 347–348

Revolutionary Age: and Katayama Sen, 8

Rhee, Syngman: Japanese rearmament, along with Rhee, attacked by 6th National Conference, 88 n 11

Rice riots of 1918: reported to Japanese radicals in New York, 8

Rikken Seiyūkai (Friends of Constitutional Government Party): in 1928 election, 34

Rikugo Zasshi (The Universe Magazine): details on Shakaishugi Kenkyūkai, 1 n 1

Rōdō Nōmintō (Labor-Farmer Party): under Communist control, 24

Rōdō Oyobi Sangyō (Labor and Industry): edited by Nosaka Sanzō, 4; articles by Nosaka Sanzō, 4 n 8, 5 n 9

Rōdō Sekai (Labor World): manifesto of Shakai Minshutō, 2 n 2

Rōdō Shimbun (Labor News): 24 n 33; Hyōgikai organ and daily newspaper, 25

Rōdō Shimbun-Zenkyō (Labor News): Zenkyō organ, 37, 37 n 48; goal not to capture Diet, but to destroy Diet, 41

Rōdō Undō (The Labor Movement): reissued by Ōsugi Sakae, 12; anarchist movement in 1921–1923, 14 n 18; article on Ōsugi's death, 14 n 20

Rodong Shinmun (Labor News): support of Chinese line in, 153 n 34; major editorial of December 1965 supporting international united front, 258–259; upheld Gensuikyō, 280; championed "independence," 281–282, 282 n 111. See also Kim Il-sŏng, Korean Workers Party, North Korea

Rokossovski, Marshal Kostantin: Polish Central Committee refused to reelect, 97

Rōnō (Labor-Farmer): published by Yamakawa faction: Rōnō-ha, 32; Yamakawa's and Inomoto's articles setting forth Rōnō thesis appeared in, 32 n 43; Arahata's article on independent Communist faction appeared in, 33 n 44

Rōnō-ha (Labor-Farmer Faction): led by Inomata Tsunao, 8; leaders of Nihon Rōnōtō affiliated with, 24; influence of its national Communism on postwar Japanese Socialist Party, 33; thesis on revolution, 31; relations with Comintern, 32–33; formed Musan Taishūtō with

Suzuki Mosaburō as Secretary General, 35; and 1931 Draft Thesis, 42; referred to in connection with debate on "revolution" at 7th Party Congress, 101 n 8

Rōnō Shimbun (Labor-Farmer News): dominated by student Marxists, 26

Rōnōtō (Labor-Farmer Party): united front achieved with JCP, 74

Roy, M. N.: played role in writing 1927 Thesis, 29

Rumania: delegate upheld Gensuikyō, 279 n 102; praise from JCP, 273; Kasuga delegation visit, 276

Russell, Bertrand: influence on Fukumoto Kazuo, 27

Rutgers, S. J.: contacts with Katayama Sen, 6

Safarov: played leading role in First Congress of Comintern, 9

Saionji, Kinkazu: upheld Peking line after Gensuikyō 12th World Congress, 280

Sakai, Kamesaku: entered Yūaikai, 5

Sakai, Toshihiko: active in socialist movement during World War I, 3; leaned toward Marxian socialism, 3 n 5; edited Hechima no Hana, 3 n 5; received radical books and magazines from Katayama Sen, 8; edited Shin Shakai, 10; served as vanguard in introducing "advanced socialism" to intellectuals, 11; formed Friday Society, 11 n 15; request from Chang T'ai-lei for Japanese delegates to First Congress of Comintern, 16; publishing plant reestablished by financial support from Comintern, 17; treated as heretic by Comintern after Shanghai Thesis, 22; called Bolshevist Communist, not Marxist Communist, by Fukumoto Kazuo, 27 n 37

Sanbetsu (Congress of Industrial Unions): dominance of civil service and government enterprise unions in, 68; organized in 1946 under

Communist control, 68; planed February 1 Strike, 69; poststrike decline, 69

SANE: sent greetings to Gensuikin, 246; delegates attended 3rd Gensuikin Conference, 282 n 112

Sano, Fumio: wrote draft program for 2nd JCP, 28; attended Moscow meeting of Comintern on Japan, 29; removed from Central Committee of JCP, 31

Sano, Hiroshi: reestablished Communist Party Bureau in 1929, 40

Sano, Manabu: roster of JCP members discovered in quarters of, 18, 19 passim; went to Shanghai with Arahata and Tokuda, 22; made Chief of Political Bureau of Preliminary Committee for JCP, 25; translated Engels' work, 30 n 42; appointed as leader of 2nd JCP, 31; helped reorganize JCP after mass arrests of 1928—representative to 6th Comintern Congress, 34; arrested in Shanghai in 1929, 40; denounced Communism, 43

Sasaki, Kōzō: attitude toward united front with JCP, 1965, 246–247; willingness to condemn United States as global enemy, 252 n 73; analyzed Vietnam War, 262; pro-China sentiments, 263; reelected Chairman of Socialist Party, January, 1966, 265; taking position similar to that of early Nenni Socialists, 346

Sasaki (Kōzō) faction: pro-China proclivities, 251–252

Sato Eisaku: sent greetings to Kakkin Kaigi Conference, 277

Satō, Noboru: ousted from JCP over "Nosaka" criticism, 63

SCAP: see Supreme Commander of the Allied Powers

Scheidemann, ... : discussed by Takabatake Motoyuki in Shin Shakai, 10 n 13

Sekai Seiji Shiryō (Documents on World Politics): JCP journal entrusted with publishing foreign Communist documents for guidance of Party members, 147; special issue devoted to Albanian question, 148; attacked by CPSU as tool to distort Soviet views, 174

Seligman, Edwin: influence on Fukumoto Kazuo, 27

Shakai Kairyō (Social Reform): article by Nosaka Sanzō, 4 n 8

Shakai Minshutō (Social Democratic Party): first socialist party, 1; dissolution of, 2; programs, 2, 2 n 2; moderate-political vehicle of Sōdōmei, 24; and 1928 elections, 33–34

Shakai Mondai Kenkyū (Study of Social Problems): edited by Kawakami Hajime, 11

Shakai Shimpō (Socialist News): took position against Soviet nuclear tests, 122 n 34

Shakai Shisō (Social Thought): 1927 Thesis published in, 37

Shakaishugi (Socialism): and Sakai Toshihiko, 11 n 15

Shakaishugi Kenkyū (Studies of Socialism): edited by Yamakawa Hitoshi, 11

Shakaishugi Kenkyūkai (The Association for the Study of Socialism): first meeting of, 1; second meeting of, 1 n 1

Shakaishugi Kyōkai (Socialist Society): organized, 2; four main currents in, 2

Shanghai Thesis: criticized JCP, 22

Shida, Shigeo: Mainstream Politburo member after Nosaka issue, 67; attacked by Kansai faction over Cominform criticism, 67; factional background, 90; won power struggle against Itō Ritsu after Tokuda's death, 93; symbol for "leftist" policies at 6th Party Conference, 96; reemerged victorious to assume leadership, 94; came forth in public after long exile, 99; disappeared, symbolizing end of era of "left adventurism," 100; led Liberation

Front, 256; criticized in JCP 10th Party Congress, 285, 287

Shiga, Yoshio: leading role after release from prison in 1945—"appeal to people" in *Akahata*, 48; referred to Emperor as top war criminal, 52; spoke at 5th Party Congress, 54 n 7; leader of anti-Mainstream international faction on issue of Cominform criticism, 53; attacked Mainstream leaders at Central Committee meeting of 1950, 67; retained in politics after Cominform crisis, 67; factional background, 90; leader of Kansai faction, 90; presented Central Executive Committee with attack on Mainstream faction over Cominform criticism, 91; attacked Mainstream as "Trotskyite," 91; remained in party as anti-Mainstream leader at 8th Party Congress, 112; led anti-Mainstream faction after 8th Party Congress, 136; head of pro-Soviet faction in JCP, 146; voted for nuclear test ban treaty in Diet, 170–171; expelled from JCP, 170; formed "Voice of Japan Comrades Society," 171; attacked in JCP 9th Party Congress Report, 222, 225, 228; Soviet support attacked by *Akahata*, 253, 255-256; charged with "flunkyism" by JCP leaders, 273; visited Soviet Union as guest, 303; his groups plan to form a new JCP against Yoyogi faction, 303; exchanged messages with Mongolian People's Republic, 303

Shigeda, Yōichi: sent to Shanghai Bureau of Comintern by Kondō Eizō, 17, 17 n 24

Shiino, Etsuō: took chairmanship of Central Directorate, 85, 92; purged by government in 1951, 93; thanked CCP for advice on unity, 95; role in Liberation Front, 256

Shimotsukasa, Junkichi: attacked Liberation Front faction, 277; JCP Secretariat member, 292 n 3

Shin Shakai (New Society): Article introducing Leninist themes by Takabatake Motoyuki, 10 n 13; continued to carry Marxist banner initiated by Takabatake Motoyuki, 10

Shin Shakai Hyōron (New Society Review): and Sakai Toshihiko, 11 n 15

Shinjinkai (New Men's Association): founded by Tōkyō University students, 10; program, 10; and Kōtō Gakkō Remmei, 26

Sino-Indian border dispute: impact of Sino-Soviet dispute on JCP, 147; and JCP's views, 150–151. *See also* India

Sino-Soviet dispute: opening stages, 98 ff.; impact on JCP's 7th Party Congress and its new program, 101–102; and Russo-American rapprochement, 104; and Sino-Indian border controversy, 104; impact on JCP, 106 ff.; lull in, 120 n 31; Chinese bogus representatives at 8th Gensuikyō Conference challenged by Soviet Union, 124 n 40; at 8th Gensuikyō Conference, 126–127, 127 n 42; at 22nd CPSU Congress, 136; JCP's "neutral" position after 22nd CPSU Congress, 137 ff.; JCP's view on Indian border dispute, 150–151; JCP's views on Cuban incident, 151–152; Soviet-Yugoslav rapprochement, 149; failure of Moscow talks, 158; JCP shift from neutralism, 161–171; CPSU-JCP relations in, 161 n 68; waged in Japan, 163–165; failure of CPSU-JCP talks, 169; border issues not mentioned in JCP's rebuttal to CPSU, 188 n 93; nuclear test ban treaty and U.S.-Soviet rapprochement designed to contain China, 192, 193 n 97; the three basic issues, 195–198; Soviet aid and Chinese dissatisfaction, 199–200; Soviet refusal to provide China with aid in nuclear program, 200; charges of

Soviet interference with internal affairs of CCP, 200; "Soviet alliance with American imperialism through nuclear test ban treaty" attacked by CCP, 200–201; Soviet accusations concerning Chinese support for anti-party group headed by Molotov, 201; over tactics and strategy for Communist victory against "imperialism" and "capitalism," 202 ff.; Cuba-Soviet "capitulation" to American thrusts, in Chinese view, 204; Chinese attack on nuclear test ban treaty, 205; over minority peoples near Sino-Soviet borders, 205; over ideology —restoration of capitalism vs. Maoism, 205; clash of national interests, 205–206; timing of two revolutions, 206, developmental conditions— power and status quo, 206; escalation in 5 stages, 206 ff.; nation-to-nation competition vs. world revolution, 207; produced splits and factionalism within foreign Communist parties, 208–209; effects on Soviet domination over external parties, 209; and JCP's position and problem, 209 ff.; JCP's position similar to that of CCP, 209; JCP 9th Congress analysis of, 222–223; struggle over 10th Gensuikyō World Congress, 233–235; impact upon Japanese Socialist Party, 1966, 262–264; CPSU "secret" letter of 1966, 269–270 n 90; Chou visit to Bucharest, 276 n 97; general effect upon JCP, 288–290

Sinyavsky, Andrei: impact of trial on Japanese intellectuals, 338

6th Party Conference: held in 1955 to end party strife, 88–89

Social democrats: against anarcho-syndicalism, 3–4; struggle with Communists over control of labor movement, 23; weak in publications, 25

Socialist Party: under attack by JCP in *Akahata* and 4th Congress Report, 49, 52; coalition government with Minshutō, 58; right-left split, 73; JCP's failure to form united front with, 73–76; attacked by Tokuda in 1951 report, 80; initially led anti-Ampō movement, 114; role in anti-Ampō movement, compared with that of JCP, 115; and Gensuikyō, 117; and 7th Gensuikyō Conference, 119; neutralism compared with that of JCP, 121; protest against Soviet nuclear tests at 8th Gensuikyō Conference, 123 n 37; withdrew in protest at 8th Gensuikyō Conference, 125–126; and "peace" movement prior to 9th Gensuikyō Conference, 156; JSP's support solicited from USSR, 162; as analyzed by JCP in 9th Party Congress Report, 217, 217 n 6; 218; relations with the JCP during 1964–65, 229–253; relations with Soviet representatives in connection with peace movement, 1963–1964, 232–233; attitude toward united front with JCP, 1965, 246–247; relations with CCP, 1964–65, 251–252; relations with Soviets, 1964–65, 252–253; swing to the left and internal factionalism in 1965, 247, 251–252; 27th Party Congress of 1966, 261–265; rising anti-Americanism, 262–263; 1966 foreign policy, 263–264; relations with JCP discussed in 1966 Congress, 264; internal factionalism, 264–265; January 1966 elections, 264–265; relations with Peking, Summer 1966, 283; relations with Soviet Union, Summer 1966, 283; analyzed by JCP 10th Party Congress, 286; votes in 1965 House of Councillors election, 297, 298; in 1965 Tōkyō City Assembly election, 299–300; competing outlet for Japanese intellectuals against JCP, 336; stood in JCP's way in labor movement, 339; shift of ideological position from orthodox Marxism to revisionism, 349–350

Socialist Renovation Group: Kasuga-

Naito faction attacks Yoyogi group, 144

Socialist Student Front: unit of Unified Socialist League, led by Andō Jimbei, 145

Socialist Student League: strength within Zengakuren in 1965, 306

Society for the Defense of Peace: organized in 1949 in conjunction with First World Conference for Defense of Peace, 72; predecessor to Japan Peace Committee, 117 n 27

Society of Comrades for the Voice of Japan: attacked by JCP at 9th Congress, 222. *See also* Voice of Japan

Society to Protect Life and Health: as JCP front organization, 226

Sōdōmei (Japanese Federation of Labor): and end of anarchist power in labor movement, 14; convention of 1922, 14; represented politically by Shakai Minshūtō, 24; splits with Nihon Rōdō Hyōgikai and Communists, 23; the prewar roots of Socialism, 68

Sōhyō (General Council of Trade Unions): initially led anti-Ampō movement, 114; role in anti-Ampō movement compared to that of JCP, 115; and Gensuikyō, 117; and 7th Gensuikyō Conference, 119; protested to USSR against resuming nuclear tests, 122 n 34; protested against Soviet nuclear tests at 8th Gensuikyō Conference, 123 n 37; background from mid-fifties, 128 ff.; JCP's strength in, 129 ff., 129 n 47; 19th National Convention, 132; and peace movement prior to 9th Gensuikyō Conference, 156; as analyzed by JCP in 9th Party Congress Report, 217, 217 n 6; 219; relations with JCP during 1964–65, 229–253; events of 26th convention of 1964, 231; relations with Soviet representatives in peace movement, 1963–64, 232–233; joint declaration of friendship with Soviet Union delegation, 238; support for USSR,

242 n 54; 1964 contacts with AFL-CIO delegation in Tōkyō, 238–239; subsequent exchanges with AFL-CIO leaders, 239–242; attitude toward JCP in 1964, 240; general political philosophy in 1964 as expressed by Ōta, 241; 1964 attitude toward the Vietnam War, 241, 242–243; 1964 attitude toward ICFTU, 242; 27th Special Convention of 1965, 244; attitude toward U.S. Asian policies, 242, 244–245; opposition to Sato government, 244; opposition to Korean treaty, 244; swing to the left in 1965, 247; 28th National Convention, 1965, 249–250 n 69; 29th Special Convention, 1965, 251 n 71; talks with Soviet labor leader, Grishin, 278 n 101; delegates attended Khabarovsk Conference, 283; new chairman elected, 283; JCP influence in 1965, 307; current Communist strength in, 339

Sōhyō News: 119 n 29; Iwai's speech on Gensuikyō in, 156 n 41; Sōhyō's position on 9th Gensuikyō Conference in, 158 n 44

Soka Gakkai: analyzed in JCP 9th Party Congress Report, 217, 220. *See also* Komeitō

Soviet All-Union Central Council of Trade Unions: Leaders' 1964 visit to Japan, 238

Soviet Peace Committee: sent greetings to Gensuikin, 246; absent from 11th Gensuikyō Conference, 1965, 248, 248 n 67; collaboration with Gensuikin charged by *Akahata*, 253–254; supported Japanese dissident Communists, 255

Soviet Union. *See* Union of Soviet Socialist Republics, Communist Party of the Soviet Union

Stalin, Joseph: his insistence on subordination of foreign Communists to Comintern mentioned by Fukumoto, 30 n 42; sought explanation for Chinese fiasco, 38; his death and its impact, 87–88; denounced by Khrushchev at 20th Party Congress, 97; blamed by CPSU for Cominform attack and for participation in 1951 Draft, 175 n 73. *See also* Stalinism

Stalinism: challenged by Rōnō-ha, 32; and JCP, 76–77; influence on 1951 Thesis, 81

Stockholm Peace Petition: 6,000,000 Japanese signatures, in Tokuda's report, 83

Structural reform: JCP interest in, 87; basic elements summarized, 102–103; under attack by Mainstream faction, 109; Zengakuren faction, 133, 133n 53; supported by dissident Socialist Renovation group, 144; rejected by JCP as Kautskyist doctrines, 348

Students: and Fukumotoism, 28–29 *passim;* JCP's most successful influence on, 71. *See also* Democratic Youth League, Zengakuren

Student organizations: 132 ff.; gains for JCP in student organizations, 306. *See also* Democratic Youth League, Zengakuren

Suez attack: attitude of Sōhyō, 241

Sugiura, Keiichi: Hyōgikai candidate of Nihon Rōnōto for 1928 election, 33

Suiheisha (Levellers' Association): brought under JCP, 22; dedicated to emancipating outcasts, 134 n 54

Sun Yat-sen: his death and the united front, 38

Sunama, Ichirō: member of Spring 1966 Miyamoto mission, 266; JCP Secretariat member, 293 n 3

Supreme Commander of the Allied Powers: and release of political prisoners, including JCP members, 48; regarded by 5th Party Congress as completing bourgeois-democratic revolution, 54–55; political orientation—shift from reform to reconstruction, 57–58; intervened in February 1 Strike, 69; labor policy—its shift, 70; land reform and JCP,

70–71; pro-Communist elements within, 73; role in curtailing Communist development, 341, 342 *passim*

Suslov, M.: showed anger at Miyamoto Kenji over Sino-Soviet dispute, 109

Suzuki, Bunji: headed Yūaikai, 6; and Nosaka Sanzō, 5 n 9

Suzuki, Ichizō: leader of anti-Mainstream faction after 8th Party Congress, 136; leader of pro-Soviet faction, 146; expelled from JCP (House of Councillors member), 170; attacked in JCP 9th Party Congress Report, 222, 228; feted in Soviet Union, 255

Suzuki, Mosaburō: and Katayama Sen, 8, 14; delegate to First Congress of Comintern, 19; and Nihon Rōnōto, 24; became Secretary General of Musan Taishūtō when formed by Rōnō-ha in 1928, 35; supported Asanuma statement, 252 n 73

Suzuki, Seiichi: wrote letter to Lovestone, 240

Tadokoro, Teruaki: helped Yamakawa and his wife with *Zenei,* 20 n 27

Taguchi, Unzō: attended Third Congress of Comintern, 7; and Katayama Sen, 7; delegate to First Congress of Comintern, 18

Taigyaku Jiken. *See* Great Treason Case

Taiwan: representatives at Kakkin Kaigi Conference, 277

Takahara, Shinichi: JCP Secretariat member, 293 n 3

Takabatake, Motoyuki: introduced German Marxism, 10; organized state socialist group in 1919, 10; questioned about anarcho-syndicalist faction, 10; wrote first Japanese article introducing Leninist ideas in *Shin Shakai,* 10 n 13

Takagi, Masayoshi: discussed readings

on socialist movement at Shakaishu-gi Kenkyūkai meeting, 1 n 1

Takahashi, Kamekichi: and Kataya-ma Sen, 7

Takahashi, Teiji: aided Nabeyama in his anti-Fukumoto position, 29

Takase, Kiyoshi: Sakai Toshihiko's son-in-law, delegate to First Congress of Comintern, 9

Takatsu, Seidō: on staff of Ōsugi's *Rōdō Undō*, 12

Takayama, Yoshizō: entered Yūaikai, 5

Takenaka, Tsunesaburō: belonged to Kansai faction, 90; removed from Central Committee, 103

Tanabashi, Kotora: entered Yūaikai, 5

Tanaka, Seigen: reestablished Communist Party Bureau in 1929 and became Chairman, 40; recanted Communism, 43

Tang, Tseung: walked out of 1965 Sōhyō convention, 249–250 n 69

Tass: Soviet statement on Sino-Indian border controversy released by, 104; on Sino-Indian border incident, 150 n 23

Teller, Edward: attacked by Mitin at 8th Gensuikyō Conference, 126

Teng, Hsiao-p'ing: met with Miya-moto mission, 267

Thailand: representatives at Kakkin Kaigi Conference, 277

Third International. *See* Comintern

Tibet: rebellion viewed by JCP in favor of Chinese Communists, 150

Titoism: used by Mainstream faction of JCP during Cominform crisis, 63; Stalin's break with Tito, 77; JCP compared with Tito, 78; term used by Shiga against Mainstream faction, 91; used by Chinese for attack on Khrushchev, 104–105; Kasuga faction charged with being Titoists, 112; Tito's vacation in Soviet Union and Sino-Soviet dispute, 149; considered by JCP as arch-revisionist, contrary to Russian claims, 189

Togliatti, P.: his structural reform theories espoused by international faction at 7th Party Congress, 102; his structural reform theories advanced by Kasuga group, 109

Tokuda, Kyūichi: delegate to First Congress of Comintern, 9; went to Shanghai with Arahata and Sano, 22 n 30; took lead in reporting Comintern desires when founding JCP, 18; became chairman of preliminary committee for reestablishing illegal JCP, 25; attended Moscow meeting of Comintern on Japan, 29; leading role after release from prison in 1945 "Appeal to People" in *Akahata,* 48; speech at welcome rally in 1945, 50; his general report at 5th Party Congress, 54–55, 54 n 7; speeches at 6th Party Congress, 57 n 8; report to 6th Party Congress reinforcing Nosaka themes, 60 n 11; denied JCP controlled by Soviet Union, 76; attacked by anti-Mainstream faction for not joining Nosaka's self-criticism, 67; Mainstream Politburo member after Nosaka issue, 67; his report to 18th Central Committee, 79 ff.; died in Peking in 1953, 87; factional background, 90; impact of his death on JCP, 93; Shiga Yoshio attacked in attempts to overthrow, 91; and cult of personality, 100; criticized as paternalistic and dogmatic before 20th CPSU Party Congress and afterward, 111; criticized in JCP 10th Party Congress, 286–287

Tōkyō: anti-Mainstream group drew strength from Tōkyō party organizations, 109

Tōkyō earthquake: murder of Ōsugi, 14

Tōkyō streetcar strike: supported by Katayama Sen, 6, 6 n 10

Tōkyō Transport Workers' strike: and Zenkyō, 38

Tōkyō Unitarian Church: first meeting of Shakaishugi Kenkyūkai held at, 1

Tōkyō University: graduates entered Yūaikai, 5; students founded Shinjinkai, 10; Shinjinkai and Kōtō Gakkō Remmei, 26

Tolstoi, Leo Nikolaevich: influence on radical intellectuals, 5, 6

Tōsō Dzeho: organ of Tōkyō City Committee of JCP, alleged Japan-Soviet Union Society as being tool of anti-JCP elements, 174

Tradition: used by Meiji elite for modernization, erecting barrier to Communist movement, 331; Chinese Communists' use of, 332

Trotsky, Leon: influence on Katayama Sen, 7; his position supported by Rōnō-ha, 32

Trotskyite: used by factions of JCP at time of Cominform criticism, 63; used by Mainstream faction against international faction, 92; Mainstream Zengakuren, erroneously denoted, 133

Trud: published Prokhorov's report on Voice of Japan group and JCP, 303

Tsendenbal Y.: Premier of Mongolian People's Republic, expressed thanks for Shiga's greetings, 303

Tsukada, Taigan: JCP Secretariat member 293 n 3

U Thant: proposal on Cuba and Khrushchev's agreement reported in Akahata, 151 n 28

Uchino, Takechiyo: Chief of United Front Bureau of JCP and Director of Board of Japan Peace Committee, 117 n 27; Central Committee member and Chief of United Front Department, wrote article in Akahata about 1962 Moscow Congress for General Disarmament and Peace, 148; removed from position of United Front Bureau for his pro-Soviet views, 171; JCP Secretariat member, 293 n 3

Ueda, Kōichirō: member of Spring 1966 Miyamoto mission, 266

Ueda, Shigeki: helped Yamakawa and his wife with publication, 20 n

Ueda Tetsuzō. See Fuha Tetsuzō

Underground activities: preparations for, 85

Unified Socialist League: upheld Soviet position in Sino-Soviet dispute, 145

Union of Soviet Socialist Republics: impact of Bolshevik Revolution on Japanese left, 3 n 5; Nosaka Sanzō in, 7 n 9; revolutionaries in New York influence Katayama Sen, 7; success of Bolshevism, 13; anarchosyndicalists' actions on behalf of, 14; First Congress of Comintern opened in Moscow in 1922, 14; tactics of Comintern in Asia, 15; influence of Bolshevik Revolution on students, intellectuals and labor, 17; mistreatment of anarchists in, 20; JCP members gathered in Vladivostok to discuss plans for developing Unified Workers' Party, 21; students returning from Moscow took leadership of JCP in 1924–28, 34–35; role of Far Eastern Workers' Communist University in Moscow, 35; occupation of Japan and JCP, 54–55; mutual defense pact with China in 1950, 64; represented "world peace voice" against U.S., as reported at 6th Party Conference, 89 n 11; dispute with China reflected in debate at JCP's 7th Party Congress with particular reference to U.S., 101; Miyamoto Kenji cited Suslov's statement as example of "big power chauvinism," 109; resumption of nuclear tests and Gensuikyō, 120; nuclear tests and 8th Gensuikyō Conference, 123; and 8th Gensuikyō Conference, 125; defended by JCP over Cuban incident, 151; tried to solicit support from Sōhyō, 162–163; activities at Tōkyō Embassy, 164; its mission to oppose "imperialists' nuclear might," according to CPSU's letter to JCP, 184; disintegration of Soviet empire, 195–196; faced with postwar tasks of military and economic growth and aid to neutral societies as well as "fraternal countries," 199; aid to People's Republic of China, as claimed by CPSU, 199; governed by functionaries, 206; JCP attitude toward in 9th Party Congress, 215, 222–225; delegates attended 3rd Gensuikin Conference, 282 n 112; advantages with Japanese Socialists, 252; impact of postwar actions upon JCP's development, 342. *See also* Communist Party of the Soviet Union

United front: various proletarian parties' position on, 24–25; urged by 1931 Draft Thesis, 42; with Nihon Shakaitō in 4th Congress Report, 52; in 5th Party Congress, 53, 57; JCP's failure to achieve with SCAP and Nihon Shakaitō, 73–74; advocated by Mainstream for encompassing bourgeois, workers and peasants at 7th Party Congress, 101; Mutual Security Treaty as most significant opportunity in Japanese history, 114; JCP's tactics in peace movement, 116; failure in peace movement, 122–123; Socialist-Communist split at 8th Gensuikyō Conference, 128; disrupted after 8th Gensuikyō Conference, 132; prior to 9th Gensuikyō Conference, 156–157; between JCP and JSP through reorganization of Gensuikyō, 157; Chinese attempt to build in competition to Soviet-dominated movement, 198; position of JCP in 9th Party Congress Report, 216–219, 224, 228; joint Sōhyō-Socialist-JCP "peace" activities in 1964–65, 231–253; position of JCP 10th Party Congress, 285–286; promising technique for JCP in future, 344 ff.;

CCP criticized by JCP for blocking united front for Vietnam, 347

United Socialist League: established by Kasuga group, 145

United States: Occupation of Japan and JCP, 48, 53, 54 ff.; attack on its role in Japan in 1951 Thesis, 83; condemned in 1951 Thesis, 81; all-out war with U.S. avoided by Communist China, 88; military bases in Japan attacked at 6th National Conference, 88 n 11; represented "international war forces," as reported at 6th Party Conference, 89 n 11; regarded as primary enemy by Mainstream faction in new program of 7th Party Congress, 101; military bases in Japan attacked at 7th Party Congress, 103; control of Okinawa and Ogasawara opposed at 7th Party Congress, 103; military bases in Japan analyzed in 1961 program at 8th Party Congress, 113; anti-Americanism lacking in anti-Ampō movement, 115 n 25; military involvement with Japan developed by JCP as issue, 116; military bases as issue at 2nd Gensuikyō Conference, 118 n 28; regarded as enemy by JCP, 148; JCP's attack on Cuban blockade, 151, 152 *passim;* atomic submarines and military bases attacked by JCP, 156; attacked as enemy of peace by Chinese delegate at 7th Gensuikyō Conference, 160; as analyzed by JCP in 9th Party Congress, 214–216; 221–222; Sōhyō-Socialist opposition to nuclear powered submarine visits, 237; rising anti-American sentiment of Socialists, 237–238; policies of 10th Gensuikyō World Conference, 1964, 234; policies of Hiroshima Conference, 1964, 236; reaction of Sōhyō to bombing of North Vietnam, 242–243; attacked by Korean Communists, 258–259; "American imperialism" attacked by Korean and Japanese Communists, 258–260; denunciation of U.S. by Asian Communists in joint communiques, 267–272; attitude of JCP in 10th Party Congress, 285; role in JCP's "left" ideological position, 349

U.S. National Committee for a Sane Nuclear Policy. *See* SANE

USSR. *See* Soviet Union, CPSU

Vietnam: Liu Shao-ch'i reports progress of national liberation, in, 85

Vietnam War: Soviet policy attacked by CCP, 205; JCP attitude as expressed in 9th Party Congress, 215, 221; joint Socialist-Communist protest rally in 1965, 245; position of Korean Communists in Dec. 1965, 258–259; 1966 Socialist position, 262; JCP efforts on behalf of a united front, 265–272; Moscow and Peking exchange charges, 269–271 n 90; and Chinese Communist Asian policies, 290–291; Shiga group's support for Vietnam Communists attacked by Yoyogi faction, 305, 305 n 12

Vietnam Workers' Party: position of public silence over Sino-Soviet dispute compared with that of JCP, 140 n 7; meetings with Miyamoto mission in Hanoi, 266–267; and JCP, 274. *See also* North Vietnam

Violence: tactic of anarcho-syndicalism, 13; and Zenkyō, 38; urged and used by JCP in late 1920's and early 1930's, 41, 63; Liu Shao Ch'i's advocacy of armed struggle against imperialism, 66; JCP's support for armed struggle at 4th Party Conference, 86; JCP's failure in using terrorism compared with success of CCP in 1935–1949, 86–87; JCP 10th Party Congress line, 288; JCP's advocacy of force as indispensable tactic, 348

Voice of Japan: circulated in Russia, 255

Voice of Japan Comrades Society: formed by Shiga Yoshio, 171; attacked by JCP (Yoyogi), 275; fail-

ure to prosper, 302, 304; Shiga group's plan to form a new JCP against JCP (Yoyogi faction), 303

Voitinsky, Gregory: met Ōsugi Sakae, 12; headed Far Eastern Bureau of Comintern, 12; ordered reestablishment of JCP, 22, 22 n 30; and Shanghai Thesis, 22; as evidence of Soviet role in Asian Communism, 46, 47 *passim*

Wada, Hiroo: attitude toward united front with JCP, 1965, 247

Wada (Hiroo) faction: position in 1966 Socialist Congress, 264–265

Wada, Kiichiro: his death, 14

Waseda University: graduates entered Yūaikai, 5; Bunka Dōmei founded by students of, 11; Gyōminkai founded by students of, 11; Kensetsusha Dōmei founded by students of, 11; Takahashi Kamekichi graduated from, 7; and Inamata Tsunao, 12; radicals formed Gyōmin Kyōsantō, 17; student clashes over issue of military training in 1923, 18

Watanabe, Haruo: delegate to First Congress of Comintern, 8–9; and Katayama Sen, 7

Watanabe, Masanosuke: made Chief of Organization Bureau of preliminary committee for JCP, 25; attended Moscow meeting of Comintern on Japan, 29; wrote draft program for 2nd JCP; a leader of 2nd JCP, 31; helped reorganize JCP after mass arrests of 1928—representative to 6th Comintern Congress, 34

Watanabe, Mitsuru: article calling for shift of policy appeared in *Zenei*, 99

What Is To Be Done: Japanese translation by Aono Suekichi mentioned by Fukumoto, 30 n 42

Workers Party of Korea: *see* Korean Workers' Party

Workers Party of Vietnam: *see* Vietnam Workers' Party

Women's International Democratic

Federation: JCP accused by CPSU of splitting Federation, in line with CCP, 175

Women's organizations: under JCP influence, 135 n 54

Workers' Education Association: to be brought under JCP, 22

World Conference for the Defense of Peace: first held in Paris and Prague, 72

World Congress for General Disarmament and Peace: criticized by Chinese delegation at 8th Gensuikyō Conference, 124 n 38; 8th Gensuikyō Conference resolutions in line with view of, 126

World Council of Peace: blasted by Liu Ning-i at 10th Gensuikyō World Conference, 234; sent greetings to Gensuikin, 246; absent from 11th Gensuikyō Conference, 1965, 248, 248 n 67; Japanese representatives ousted, 254; delegates attended 3rd Gensuikin Conference, 282 n 112

World Federation of Democratic Youth: source of Gensuikyō crisis, 278–280; delegates attended 3rd Gensuikin Conference, 282 n 112

World Federation of Trade Unions (WFTU): Ministry of Construction Workers affiliated with, 129, 129 n 48; JCP attacked by CPSU for supporting CCP in actions to split, 175; delegates attended 3rd Gensuikin Conference, 282 n 112

World Peace Conference: held in Paris and Prague, 117 n 27

World Peace Council: influence on 7th Gensuikyō Conference, 120; JCP attacked by CPSU for supporting CCP in "splittist" actions, 175; JCP delegate, Kikunami, attended, 185

Yamada, Rokuzaemon: elected to Central Committee, 103

Yamaguchi Commercial Higher School: teaching position for Fukumoto Kazuo, 27

Yamakawa, Hitoshi: activities during World War I, 3; formed Wednesday Society, 11 n 15; served as vanguard in introducing "advanced socialism" to intellectuals, 11; Chang T'ai-lei visited and asked for Japanese delegates to First Congress Comintern, 14; close relations with Kondō Eizō, 15; and Shakaishugi Kenkyū, 18; attacked vulnerability of anarcho-syndicalism in Zenei, 20; treated as heretic by Comintern after Shanghai thesis, 22; criticized by Fukumoto Kazuo, 27, 27 n 37; criticized by 1927 Thesis, 29; compared with Ch'en Tu-hsiu as being rightist by Comintern, 39

"Yamakawaism": against "Fukumotoism," 26, 29, 32 passim

Yamamoto, Kenzō: Hyōgikai candidate of Nihon Rōnōto for 1928 election, 33; helped reorganize JCP after mass arrests of 1928—representative to 6th Comintern Congress, 34; gave Comintern instructions to Japanese students in Moscow, 35; heard arrests and dissolution of JCP in Moscow, 42; remained in exile, 40

Yamamoto, Masami: Moscow-trained student, arrested in 1932, 43

Yamamoto, Senji: elected to Diet as Nihon Rōnōtō candidate, 34

Yasui, Kaoru: Gensuikyō Chairman, Lenin Peace Prize winner, served as adviser to Japan Peace Committee, 117 n 27; took position against Soviet nuclear tests at 8th Gensuikyō Conference, 123 n 37; opposed JSP at 8th Gensuikyō Conference, 125

Yasutsune, Ryōichi: toured Soviet Union for Sōhyō-Socialist peace movement, 232

Yenan: as model for JCP, 86–87; pattern impossible to practice in Japan, 342–343 passim

Yi, Ch'un-suk: contacted Ōsugi on

behalf of Shanghai Bureau of Comintern, 12

Yonehara, Akira: headed JCP delegation to 11th Gensuikyō World Conference, 248; analyzed Conference, 247-248, n 66, 67; delivered JCP greetings to 29th Sōhyō Convention, 1965, 251 n 71; member of Spring 1966 Miyamoto mission, 266; outlined new 1966 JCP policy, 272-275; JCP Presidium member, 293 n 2

Yoshida, Shigeru: his government compared with Kuomintang, 80; his regime attacked as "running dog" of "American imperialism" in 1951 Thesis, 81-82; "reasons" for the defeat and overthrow of his government given at 6th Party Congress, 89 n 11

Yoshihara, Tarō: attended Third Congress of Comintern, 7; and Katayama Sen, 7; ties with Comintern's Shanghai Bureau, 17; suspected as agent for Japanese government, 17

Yoshikawa, Yūichi: contact with Russians, 253-254

Yoshino, Sakuzō: and Shakai Minshūtō, 24; Fukumoto Kazuo as a disciple, 27

Yoyogi: as nickname for postwar JCP, 60, 60 n 12; denounced by international faction, 92; JCP labeled by Socialist Renovation group, 144; Shiga group planned to form a new JCP (Voice of Japan) against, 303; CPSU's attempts to undermine JCP (Yoyogi faction), 304

Yūaikai (The Friendly Society): headed by Suzuki Bunji, 4; graduates of Waseda, Keiō, and Tōkyō Universities became student cadres in, 5; and Nosaka Sanzō, 4

Yugoslavia: JCP compared with Yugoslav Communist Party, 28; following revisionist path, said Aidit, 140 n 7; treated as enemy by Nosaka, 161 n 12; rapprochement with Russia and its impact on Sino-Soviet dispute, 147; criticized as modern revisionism by JCP, 154; at 9th Gensuikyō Conference, 159; used to symbolize Russia in Sino-Soviet dispute, 208; Soviet attempt to rehabilitate Yugoslavia attacked by JCP, 189; JCP attitude as expressed in 9th Party Congress, 215; in Gensuikin 1965 Conference, 249; delegates attended 3rd Gensuikin Conference, 282 n 112

Zaibatsu: target in JCP's new programs, 50-51 passim

Zenei (Vanguard): began publication under Yamakawa, 20; Party leaders' speeches and reports at 5th Party Congress, 54 n 7; and 6th Party Congress, 57 n 8; JCP's cautious attitude toward SCAP, 58 n 10; documents of 6th National Conference in, 88 n 11; formal declaration on purge of Itō Ritsu, 93 n 13; Watanabe Mitsuru's article dealing with shift of policy, 99; documents and reports of 7th Party Congress, 100 n 6; reports, resolutions and speeches of 8th Party Congress, 112 n 22; extolled struggle on two fronts, 276; counterattacked dissident groups such as Voice of Japan and Liberation Front, 305, 305 n 10

Zengakuren (National Federation of Student Self-Government Associations): organized in 1948 by Communist leaders, 71; anti-Mainstream group gained strength from student leaders of, 109; initially led anti-Ampō movement, 114; Mainstream faction played more important role in anti-Ampō movement than JCP, 115; its JCP faction demonstrated against James Hagerty, 115 n 25; Mainstream disrupted Gensuikyō in 1962 by anti-Russian slogans, 122; expelled from Gensuikyō, 124; leaders arrested in Moscow by Soviet government, 128, 128 n 45; leadership and factions, 133, 133 n

53; structural reform group in, 145; gravitating back to JCP, 220; anti-Mainstream's position on Vietnam attacked by JCP, 305 n 12; composition in 1965 (factions), 306

Zenkoku Gakusei Rengōkai (National Students' Federation): merger of Shinjinkai, Cultural League, and Kōtō Gakkō Remmei, 26

Zenkyō. *See* Nihon Rōdō Kumiai Zenkoku Kyōgikai (National Council of Japanese Labor Unions)

Zen Nihon Rōdō Kumiai Kaigi (Zenrō) (General Federation of Japanese Trade Unions): left Gensuikyō to form Kakkin Kaigi, 118

Zenno, Zenshirō: leader in Zenkyō, 37; reestablished Communist Party Bureau in 1929, 40

Zenrō. *See* Nihon Rōdō Kumiai Zenkoku Kyōgikai

Zenshōren (National Federation of Commercial and Industrial Organizations): JCP influence in, 307

Zhdanov, Andrei: "two camps" speech in 1947, 57

Zhukov, E. M.: Soviet delegate to 7th Gensuikyō Conference, 120, 120 n 32

Zhukov, George A.: role in 9th Gensuikyō Conference, 158–160; talked with JSP, 162–163; headed Soviet delegation to 1964 "peace conferences," 233; secret contacts with Gensuikin leaders charged by *Akahata,* 253–254; demanded reform of Japan-Soviet Society in 1964, 254

Zhukov, Marshal: ousted as Minister of Defense and Commander of Army, 98

Zinoviev, Grigorii: played leading role in First Congress of Comintern, 9

OTHER RAND BOOKS IN THE
SOCIAL SCIENCES

Brodie, Bernard. *Strategy in the Missile Age.* Princeton University Press, Princeton, New Jersey. September 1959.

Davison, W. Phillips. *The Berlin Blockade: A Study in Cold War Politics.* Princeton University Press, Princeton, New Jersey. April 1958.

Dinerstein, H. S., and Leon Gouré. *Two Studies in Soviet Controls: Communism and the Russian Peasant; Moscow in Crisis.* The Free Press, Glencoe, Illinois. February 1955.

Dinerstein, H. S. *War and the Soviet Union: Nuclear Weapons and the Revolution in Soviet Military and Political Thinking.* Frederick A. Praeger, Inc., New York. April 1959.

Fainsod, Merle. *Smolensk Under Soviet Rule.* Harvard University Press, Cambridge, Massachusetts. September 1958.

Garthoff, Raymond L. *Soviet Military Doctrine.* The Free Press, Glencoe, Illinois. May 1953.

George, Alexander L. *Propaganda Analysis: A Study of Inferences Made from Nazi Propaganda in World War II.* Row, Peterson and Company, Evanston, Illinois. February 1959.

Goldhamer, Herbert, and Andrew W. Marshall. *Psychosis and Civilization.* The Free Press, Glencoe, Illinois. June 1953.

Gouré, Leon. *Civil Defense in the Soviet Union.* University of California Press, Berkeley, California. January 1962.

Gouré, Leon. *The Siege of Leningrad.* Stanford University Press, Stanford, California. June 1962.

Halpern, Manfred. *The Politics of Social Change in the Middle East and North Africa.* Princeton University Press, Princeton, New Jersey. October 1963.

Horelick, Arnold L., and Myron Rush. *Strategic Power and Soviet Foreign Policy.* University of Chicago Press, Chicago, Illinois. April 1966.

Hsieh, Alice Langley. *Communist China's Strategy in the Nuclear Era.* Prentice-Hall, Inc., Englewood Cliffs, New Jersey. March 1962.

Janis, Irving L. *Air War and Emotional Stress: Psychological Studies of Bombing and Civilian Defense.* McGraw-Hill Book Company, Inc., New York. June 1951.

Johnson, John J. (ed.). *The Role of the Military in Underdeveloped Countries.* Princeton University Press, Princeton, New Jersey. May 1962.

Johnstone, William C. *Burma's Foreign Policy: A Study in Neutralism.* Harvard University Press, Cambridge, Massachusetts. March 1963.

Kecskemeti, Paul. *Strategic Surrender: The Politics of Victory and Defeat.* Stanford University Press, Stanford, California. April 1958.

Kecskemeti, Paul. *The Unexpected Revolution*. Stanford University Press, Stanford, California. October 1961.

Leites, Nathan. *The Operational Code of the Politburo*. McGraw-Hill Book Company, Inc., New York. February 1951.

Leites, Nathan. *A Study of Bolshevism*. The Free Press, Glencoe, Illinois. December 1953.

Leites, Nathan, and Elsa Bernaut. *Ritual of Liquidation: The Case of the Moscow Trials*. The Free Press, Glencoe, Illinois. October 1954.

Leites, Nathan. *On The Game of Politics in France*. Stanford University Press, Stanford, California. April 1959.

Mead, Margaret. *Soviet Attitudes Toward Authority: An Interdisciplinary Approach to Problems of Soviet Character*. McGraw-Hill Book Company, Inc., New York. October 1951.

Melnik, Constantin, and Nathan Leites. *The House Without Windows: France Selects a President*. Row, Peterson and Company, Evanston, Illinois. June 1958.

Rush, Myron. *The Rise of Khrushchev*. Public Affairs Press, Washington, D.C. January 1958.

Rush, Myron. *Political Succession in the USSR*. Columbia University Press, New York. February 1965.

Selznick, Philip. *The Organizational Weapon: A Study of Bolshevik Strategy and Tactics*. McGraw-Hill Book Company, Inc., New York. February 1952.

Smith, Bruce Lannes, and Chitra M. Smith. *International Communication and Political Opinion: A Guide to the Literature*. Princeton University Press, Princeton, New Jersey. December 1956.

Sokolovskii, V. D. (ed.). *Soviet Military Strategy*. Prentice-Hall, Inc., Englewood Cliffs, New Jersey. April 1963.

Speier, Hans. *German Rearmament and Atomic War: The Views of German Military and Political Leaders*. Row, Peterson and Company, Evanston, Illinois. July 1957.

Speier, Hans, and W. Phillips Davison (eds.). *West German Leadership and Foreign Policy*. Row, Peterson and Company, Evanston, Illinois. October 1957.

Speier, Hans. *Divided Berlin: The Anatomy of Soviet Political Blackmail*. Frederick A. Praeger, Inc., New York. October 1961.

Tanham, G. K. *Communist Revolutionary Warfare: The Vietminh in Indochina*. Frederick A. Praeger, Inc., New York. November 1961.

Trager, Frank N. (ed.). *Marxism in Southeast Asia: A Study of Four Countries*. Stanford University Press, Stanford, California. December 1959.

Whiting, Allen S. *China Crosses the Yalu: The Decision to Enter the Korean War*. The Macmillan Company, New York. November 1960.

Wolfe, Thomas W. *Soviet Strategy at the Crossroads*. Harvard University Press, Cambridge, Massachusetts. November 1964.